Annual Report of the American Institute of the City of New York

by American Institute of the City of New York

TRANSACTIONS

OF THE

AMERICAN INSTITUTE,

OF THE

CITY OF NEW YORK,

FOR THE YEAR

1858.

ALBANY:

C. VAN BENTHUYSEN, PRINTER.

1859.

AMERICAN INSTITUTE.

Trustees and Committees.

STATE OF NEW YORK.

No. 188.

IN ASSEMBLY, APRIL 15, 1859.

TRANSACTIONS OF THE AMERICAN INSTITUTE.

To the Hon. D. W. C. LITTLEJOHN,
Speaker of the Assembly:

I herewith transmit the Annual Report of the American Institute of the city of New York, for the year 1858.

Very respectfully,
Your obedient servant,
W. B. LEONARD,
Corresponding Sec'y.

SEVENTEENTH ANNUAL REPORT

OF THE TRUSTEES OF THE AMERICAN INSTITUTE.

The undersigned Trustees, in conformity with the Law of May 5, 1841, beg leave to present a report of the acts of the Institute for the year 1858:

The American Institute, encouraged by the success which had attended the fairs held in the Crystal Palace during the three preceding years, and stimulated by the very liberal act of the corporation of the city of New York in putting it in possession of the Crystal Palace, considered it due to the public and the municipal authorities, that an exhibition of unprecedented interest should be provided for the year 1858. With this view, and to fulfill, as far as possible, the objects for which a charter had been granted by the Legislature of the State, an expenditure far beyond the usual limit was ventured upon. A large sum was expended upon machinery and engines, and upon other fixtures, in order that all exhibited inventions in Mechanics, or in the Chemical and Physical sciences, might be presented to the public in actual operation, or fully tested by experiment. It cannot be doubted that this unusual completeness of preparation would have been followed, had fate permitted, with consequences beneficial to every section of our country.

With such full and complete preparation, the Thirtieth Annual Fair was opened on the 15th of September, 1858. The prospects of success appeared more favorable than those of any preceding exhibition, for the attractions which it presented to the visitor were unparalleled. The motive power provided for driving machinery was great, the machines intended to be driven by it, numerous, and worthy of admiration; the preparations for conveniently exhibiting the products of agriculture and manufactures, and the inventions of mechanical skill, were ample, and were fully occupied; the implements of husbandry were more numerous than had ever before been collected in any one place; in fine, every branch of American industry, and every natural product of our country, were fully represented.

The managers of the fair had the gratification to find that their efforts were appreciated. The receipts from visitors equalled their most sanguine expectations, and warranted the conclusion that the heavy preliminary expenses would not only be fully repaid, but that a large surplus would remain to be devoted to the encouragement of the meritorious exhibiters.

On the 5th of October, a melancholy end was put to these agreeable, but not over sanguine expectations. By the act, in all probability, of an incendiary, a few minutes sufficed to sweep away all hopes of success. The building, intended by its planners to be proof of fire, presenting to outward view no other materials but iron and glass, the artistic pride of our city, was brought to the ground in a shapeless heap of ruins, in a time so short the officers and servants of the Institution had barely time to escape with their lives. The great preliminary outlay made by the Institute was thus, in a great measure, lost; property to a great amount, belonging to exhibiters from sixteen States of the Union, was totally destroyed; and what was even more to be deplored, many valuable inventions were obliterated under circumstances which may ·prevent the inventors from attempting to revive them.

It is not surprising that many of the exhibiters should have desired that a new place should have been provided in which the duplicates of the articles they had lost might be brought to the notice of the public. The subject was investigated by the managers; after mature deliberation it was found impracticable to hold such a fair, that would be satisfactory to the public, and promote the interest of the exhibiters.

The wisdom of the course of the managers is now rendered palpable by the result of the exhibition which was attempted as a substitute. The lamentable failure of this attempt is not referred to in any spirit of exultation, but as affording the most complete evidence that had the Institute yielded to the instances of parties desirous of a re-opened exhibition, it would have wasted its remaining resources in a hopeless enterprize.

One providential circumstance attended the catastrophe at the Crystal Palace. The conflagration took place at an hour at which visitors are rarely numerous. An hour earlier would have found numerous loungers, while two or three hours later would have seen the halls crowded with women and children. The scene of horror that would have ensued in the last contingency, exceeds all imagination.

The exhibition of fat beeves, sheep, swine, and poultry, intended to have been held in the Crystal Palace in the month of December, was necessarily transferred to a place of less convenience, known as "The New York Tattersalls." The exhibition was, notwithstanding, fine and interesting, although it did not entirely fulfill the anticipations of the board of managers and the committee of agriculture.

Severe as has been the double loss inflicted upon the Institute, in the funds expended in preparation, and in a place of exhibition, it is not destitute of resources. By an economic use of these it hopes to be able to resume its regular exhibitions. In the meantime, it continues its labors in other directions. A Committee on Manufactures, Science and Arts, and a Committee of Agriculture, are ready at all times to investigate and report upon all discoveries and improvements which may be presented to them.

The Farmers' Club of the Institute, continues its useful labors, and the Polytechnic Association discusses the processes of the mechanical and chemical arts.

A library, now consisting of 9,000 volumes, is open to the members of the Institute, and to strangers, while the admission to membership is so easy, that no resident of the city can be said to be excluded from its privileges. The right of taking out volumes for more careful study is not denied; and the daily, weekly and monthly publications, lie upon the tables.

The American Institute has, in its previous annual reports, confined itself to a simple exposition of its acts. It has left to the public the task of developing, from its simple and unpretending statements, the amount of benefit it has conferred upon the city and upon the State.

Crippled in its resources, by an unavoidable misfortune, it may not be improper that it should urge its desires to public aid.

Leaving out of view all general subjects, it is believed that the Institute may, with confidence, claim that through its fairs it has been the chief instrument by which the great wholesale trade in domestic manufactures has been centered in New York; that, by the hundreds of thousands of strangers it has attracted to its exhibitions, it has increased the value of real estate, promoted many branches of industry, and increased the receipts upon all converging lines of internal communication.

Trusting in such services, the American Institute has ventured to approach the corporation with a petition to allow it to occupy the space on which the Crystal Palace formerly stood, on the condition of rendering it an ornament to the neighboring part of the city.   Should the petition be favorably received, it may require Legislative provision to carry it into effect, and the Institute trusts that when such application shall come to be considered by your honorable bodies, it may meet with a favorable reception.

Respectfully submitted,

JAS. RENWICK,
WM. HALL,
JOHN A. BUNTING,
BENJAMIN AYCRIGG,
HENRY MEIGS,
W. B. LEONARD,
JOHN GRAY, *Trustees*,

NEW YORK, *April 1st*, 1859.

FINANCES.

The following is the financial condition of the American Institute, on the first day of February, 1859 :

Balance in the treasury February 1, 1858,.........		$3,019 08
The RECEIPTS of the past year have been—		
From rent of store 351 Broadway, Nov. 1, 1857, to Nov. 1, 1858,.........................	$3,500 00	
From Treasurer of the State of New York, ...	950 00	
From excess of receipts over expenditures at the Crystal Palace, ...	581 89	
From Hunter Woodis Benevolent Society, use of Crystal Palace,........	1,000 00	
From R. C. Orphan Asylum, use of Crystal Palace, ...	500 00	
From sales of old iron,...............	93 25	
From sale of straw, ...	5 87	
From sale of Transactions,............	1 00	
From admission fees, and dues from members,..............................	1,584 00	
From note discounted by Butcher's and Drover's Bank, 3 mo's, $3,000.00, less discount $52.93, ...	2,947 07	
		11,163 08
Am't to be accounted for, includ'g last years balance,		$14,182 16

Brought forward, - $14,182 16

EXPENDITURES.

Real Estate.

Interest on mortgage. Nov. 1, 1857, to Nov. 1, 1858,	$845 00	
Taxes, 1858,	928 06	
Water tax,	19 00	
Insurance,	135 50	
Repairs,	4 65	
		$1,932 21

Library.

Books,	$95 44	
Periodicals,	111 88	
Binding books,	55 86	
" catalogues of library,	16 20	
Subscriptions to newspapers,	93 84	
		373 22

Crystal Palace.

Rent, 4 mo's to May 1, 1858,	$2,200 00	
New line of shafting,	400 00	
Judgment, O'Dea v. Am. Inst.,	115 42	
Passing lease,	25 00	
		2,740 42

Account of 28th Annual Fair, 1856.

Silverware for premiums,	$174 09	
Engraving,	18 50	
Paper for diplomas,	10 50	
Expenses of plowing match,	19 50	
		222 59

Account of 29th Annual Fair.

Gold and silver medals,	$173 77	
Cups and silverware,	151 48	
Engraving,	212 92	
Medal cases,	41 00	
Filling diplomas,	106 60	
Books,	10 00	
Advertising,	80 38	
Printing list of premiums, &c.,	123 77	
Paint, oil, &c.,	63 65	
Oil for machinery,	89 00	
Iron pipes,	75 48	
Sounding board,	27 82	
Poles for Fat Cattle Show,	3 50	
		1,159 37

Account of 30th Fair, 1858.

Appropriation, per vote of the Ins., Dec. 2, 1858, $3,000, less am't repaid $514.40,	$2,485 56	

Carried forward,	$2,485 56	$6,427 81	$14,182 16

Brought forward, ...	$2,485 56	$6,427 81	$14,182 16
Use of boiler, ...	$100 00		
Cartage, ...	76 62		
Traveling expenses of Agent,	67 63		
		2,729 81	

Miscellaneous Bills.

Insurance on library, ...	$38 25		
Printing blanks, &c., ...	18 40		
Advertising, ...	25 00		
Blank books, stationery, &c.,	32 80		
Fuel, ...	52 75		
Light, ...	70 98		
Ice, ...	19 56		
Directories, ...	7 50		
Freight and boxes, Transact'ns from Albany, ...	64 89		
Agent's expenses at Albany, ..	10 00		
Delivering notices, ...	8 26		
Filling certificates, ...	1 80		
Repairing clock and settee, ...	3 50		
Fees, suit Am. Ins. v. Commissioners of Emigration, ...	9 50		
Petty cash, advertising meet'gs Farmer's and Mech's Club, subscript'n to small pap'rs, cleaning, postage, &c., ...	224 45		
		587 64	

Salaries.

Coresp'ding sec'y and agent, ..	$1,308 52		
Recording secretary, ...	833 33		
Clerk, ...	1,325 00		
Librarian, ...	700 00		
Messenger, ...	152 00		
		4,318 85	

Total expenditures, ...		14,064 11
Leaving a balance in the treasury, Jan. 30, 1859, ..		$118 05

AMOUNT OF PROPERTY HELD BY THE INSTITUTE
JANUARY 31, 1859.

Real estate 351 Broadway, cost	$45,000 00	
Building, 89½ Leonard street, ...	800 00	
	$45,800 00	
Less mortgage, ...	13,000 00	
		$32,800 00
Carried forward, ...		$32,800 00

Brought forward,_____ $32,800 00

Library and fixtures, per last report,
    January 30, 1858, _____ $12,387 85
Added by purchase of books and bind-
    ing, during the year,_____ 263 18

                                       12,651 03

Office furniture, safes, &c., _____ 350 00

Property at Crystal Palace, per last re-
    port, January 30, 1858,_____ $4,005 00
Added this year, by purchase of new
    shafting, _____ 400 00

                          $4,405 00

Damaged by fire at the Crystal Palace,
    Oct. 5, 1858, estimated at_____ 3,405 00

Present value,_____ 1,000 00

Gold and silver medals and cups, per last
    report, Jan. 30, 1858, on hand from
    Twenty-ninth Fair,_____ $784 00
Less destroyed at Crystal Palace, _____ 71 50

                                     712 50

                                    $47,513 53

Cash in treasury January 31, 1859, _____ 115 05

      Total,_____ $47,628 58

BENEDICT LEWIS, Jr.,
N. G. BRADFORD,
JOHN M. REED,
JOHN GRAY,
S. R. COMSTOCK.
          Finance Committee.

REPORT

OF THE BOARD OF MANAGERS OF THE THIRTEENTH ANNUAL FAIR OF
THE AMERICAN INSTITUTE.

The Board of Managers commenced their labor in preparing for
the holding of the Thirtieth Annual Fair, on the 26th of February
last. On that day their organization was completed, by the elec-
tion of Frederick W. Geissenhainer, jr., as chairman, Bailey J.
Hathaway, as vice-chairman, and John W. Chambers, as secretary;
also, the appointment of the usual standing and floor committees.

The active operations of the Board were, however, retarded
until the 29th day of June, in consequence of the difficulties presented in the securing of a suitable location. All the buildings
approximating to the wants of the Institute, were duly canvassed
and found inadequate, except that heretofore occupied by us, the
Crystal Palace. This building, having been in a transition from
the receiver of the exhibition of the industry of all nations, to
the mayor, aldermen and commonalty of the city of New York,
previous to which the receiver and bondholders of the palace
refused to let the building to the Institute under any circumstance, although offered the same sum as was subsequently paid
the mayor, aldermen and commonalty of the city, viz., $5,000 per
annum, and all repairs.

The delay thus met with cannot in justice be attributed to any
want of energy on the part of the Board of Managers, or to the
Trustees, to whom they are indebted for their persevering efforts
in finally securing the palace for the exhibition. So short, indeed,
was the time for its preparation (less than sixty working days),
that success, to many, was problematical; and hence unusual zeal
and energy were requisite, and never did a Board of Managers
exert themselves more manfully, or devote their time more profitably, to the interests of the Institute, as the large and compre-
hensive exhibition which they opened to the public will well
attest.

In this short time, over three thousand exhibiters were secured from the various States of our Union, and we may safely say that over three times that number were personally approached in reference to making exhibitions at the fair.

We may here remark, that not only have the number of our exhibiters increased, but in each article exhibited we find an increase of genius and skill. Few, yes, very few, of the exhibiters were contented to exhibit an article previously exhibited; and unless presenting some intrinsic merit, the board were as reluctant to give them space.

The exhibition of agricultural implements, for novelty and utility, we say without hesitation, has never been equalled.

The pomological display, containing the contributions of several pomological societies of other States, (considering the general dearth of fruit during the last fall,) was well worthy the commendation it constantly received from those capable of forming a judgment as to its merits.

And the agricutural and horticultural departments far surpassed any previous exhibition of the Institute.

We were pleased to find the great interest taken in naval architecture; over 150 specimens were exhibited, and an examination would satisfy the most skeptical that we still have the genius, though not the counsel, of a STEERS.

The display of domestic manufactures was not equal to the previous year, owing to the general depression of trade in that branch of industry. Yet small, nevertheless we secured a very choice exhibition.

The exhibition of mechanical manufactures far exceeded any previous exhibition.

Three steam engines, varying from thirty to eighty horse power, were the motive power provided, with the additional engine erected last year, from the manufactory of Messrs. Corliss & Nightingale. Auxilliary engines were erected on the north and south sides of the palace, of five and eight horse power, to furnish motion for the competing bread-mixing and baking machines.

The display of machinery was so varied and large as to occupy almost half of the main floor.

And we cannot pass without noticing the great perfection displayed in the arrangement and construction of the fire engines built for the fire department of this and adjoining cities.

The photographic art, wonderful as it is, creates new wonders by the improvements made from year to year. The display this year may well be called the perfection of the art.

But to do more than generalize the different classes, would require a report as extensive as the merits and numbers of the articles exhibited. We therefore pass to that unpleasant duty which we are loth to assume—to inform the Institute, officially, that the magnificent exhibition, whose value reaches far beyond dollars and cents, was, on the afternoon of the 3d of October, in forty minutes, almost totally consumed by fire, together with the world-renowned building in which it was located.

At about fifteen minutes to five o'clock, while about thirteen of the Board of Managers were standing in the south nave, discussing some matters relative to the fair, a flood of light was seen at the east corner of the north nave, in the department where the patterns of the building were compactly stored away—where no person could obtain access except by climbing over the patterns, a height of at least ten feet. Several of the managers at once ran to the fire, let on the water from the two hydrants under the stairs on the sides of the north nave, rather over fifty feet from the fire. But owing to repairs on the Croton pipes, the head of water in the reservoir was so low that it would not rise over seven feet from the floor; and so rapid was the progress of the flames, that in less than five minutes they had reached the roof, and then ran along as fast as a person could walk, melting the glass on the top sashes, which in its fall fired the floors below.

The smoke was so dense, and the fire made such rapid headway, that it was impossible, except at the risk of the lives of those in the passage ways, to have saved any large article of the exhibition. From the first, the efforts of the employees were directed to secure the safety of those distributed around the building, and we may congratulate ourselves that not a life was lost in a fire where more than a thousand persons were scattered over acres of buildings.

The questions have been asked us frequently, What was the origin of the fire? Did it not originate from the gas? Why did you not have means at hand to put out the fire? As these same questions may be re-asked us by the members of the Institute, we shall answer them at once, and declare it to be our firm and sincere belief, that the building was willfully set fire to, and that combustible liquids were used to accelerate its progress.

That it did not originate from the gas, as it had not yet been turned on for lighting. That those who allege that the building was lighted by pipes made of gutta percha, only exhibit their ignorance of the history and value of that article. We solemnly assert that there were no gutta percha pipes laid or used to light the late Crystal Palace, in any part of the building.

As to the means provided in case of fire! Before the opening of the fair, the chairman, as has been customary heretofore, (a custom as old as the Institute,) sent a written request to the chief engineer to designate six engines, four hook and ladder and six hose carriages for exhibition, the use of which we could have at hand in case of fire. The chief engineer, in accordance with the request, designated four engines, four hose carriages, with two hook and ladder trucks, which were distributed around the building. Sixteen hydrants, one under each flight of stairs, with two lengths of hose, one hundred feet each, made fast to the hydrants. Seven large steam pumps. These we did consider a sufficient protection, and would have been had the fire been such from its first inception as to have been within human control with the aid of water. We have the assurances of old members of the fire department, who were eye witnesses, that no human power could have stayed the flames.

The building, with its noble exhibition, has gone; but we have a more glorious building—a building whose great architect has given to it a mind of illimitable capacity to improve, advance, and encourage it onward, has ever been our aim. While republics of old have looked to ease and luxury, as the perfection of the social system, ours has looked upon activity and industry as duties required of man by his nature. Ease and luxury as the positive prohibition of that God who is ever working in his own great palace—the advancement of the human family.

We sincerely condole with the exhibiters, whose losses have been severe. Those who, through our exhibition, hoped to secure the reward for years of labor, and those kind feelings expressed under circumstances of so much affliction, we appreciate, and thank them for convincing us, as they do, that we have met with but a short revulsion. And to the one hundred and fifty exhibiters who desired us to continue the exhibition, we say we regretted the conclusion forced upon us that it was inexpedient for us to do so, no less than they did. Our experience, endorsed by the largest exhibiters, convinced us that no exhibiter could duplicate any large article in time for another, and as desired, immediate exhibition.

How much, indeed, are we fortified in this determination by the unanimous voice of the exhibiters, when they declare "their losses to be the result of years of labor and toil."

The finances show a degree of prosperity financially hitherto unattained, and show that the Institute would have realized a large surplus over and above all expenses. Retrenchments in expense had become the desire of each member, and never had it been so practically carried out. To it we are indebted for the fact that we are not compelled to ask of the Institute more than $3,000 to pay our deficiency. Almost all our heavy bills of printing, labor, repairs, carpenter's work, &c., had been balanced by our receipts,—a thing unprecedented so early after the opening of a fair.

After mature deliberation, we found it to be utterly impossible to award the premiums with any degree of certainty and satisfaction.

The exhibition of fat cattle, sheep, swine and poultry, advertized to be held in the Crystal Palace, was held December 15, 16, and 17, in the Tattersalls stables, corner of Sixth avenue and Thirty-ninth street,—the best place the Institute could secure. The exhibition, though small in numbers, compared favorably with the best productions of the land in point of quality.

We have had discouragements to overcome such as have never fallen to the lot of a board of managers; but we feel that the storm is but the forerunner of the calm and sunshine. That when its dark clouds disappear we shall witness a renewed sunshine at the hands of those who are still our firm friends, and who, though in the shipwreck have lost all, are still ready to embark with us in a future undertaking, as we devote ourselves to the protection and advancement of industry in the various vocations of life.

The unity of the Board has been broken. Those twenty-four joyous minds that on the 26th of February met in deliberation, will meet no more on earth. The fiat has gone forth, and our beloved brother, Cornelius V. Anderson, in accordance with its demand, has been summoned beyond the region of things earthly. His wise counsels, his amiable manner, his tender affection, will ever be remembered by the members of this board, and above all that unfaltering faith, which having guided him through life, was to him a strong and sure defence in the hour of death. How strongly doth circumstances of the past year remind us of the uncertainty of human things. That our lot is but for a season. That in comprehending the depths of the science of the world around us, we are but comprehending the designs of the eternal one, and as we work according to those designs, we are working in harmony with the laws of Nature's God.

The following is a condensed statement of the receipts and expenditures of the Thirtieth Annual Fair:

RECEIPTS.

Sales of tickets at Crystal Palace,	$5,975	50
" fifteen cent tickets do	22	45
" tickets at Fat Cattle Show,	71	50
" damaged coal,	75	00
" locks,	1	25
	$6,145	70
From American Institute, (appropriation,)	3,000	00
	$9,145	70
Less discount on uncurrent money,	3	93
	$9,141	77

EXPENDITURES.

Labor, before the fire, pay rolls,	$1,534	32
" after the fire, do	752	25
Printing and publication committee, printing, advertising, &c.,	1,422	06
Light committee,	1,230	86
Machine committee,	990	97
Committee on the reception of goods,	168	14
Flag committee,	262	34
Carpenter's work,	122	44
Finance committee, ticket sellers,	93	00
Ticket committee, ticket receivers,	110	55
Music committee, music,	610	00
Horticultural Committee, expenses,	228	12
Premium committee, silver cups,	396	00
Miscellaneous bills,	216	23
Cattle show,	415	05
Anniversary address, use of Lecture Room Cooper's Institute,	75	00
	$8,627	33
Balance on hand,	$514	44

The following premiums were awarded in the Horticultural department, part of two series having been adjudged:

Five $15 silver cups, seven $10 silver cups, six large silver medals, thirty-two small silver medals, nine diplomas, and fifty-six volumes of books. Valued at $380.

At the Fat Cattle Show:

One $30 silver cup, one $20 silver cup, two $15 silver cups, four $10 silver cups, one $8 silver cup, three silver medals, one bronze medal, three diplomas, and one book.   Valued at $146.

Making the total value of premiums $526.

Respectfully submitted,

F. W. GEISSENHAINER, Jr.,   THOMAS W. FIELD,
BAILEY J. HATHAWAY,   GEORGE TIMPSON,
W. H. DIKEMAN,   CORN'S V. ANDERSON,
B. LEWIS, Jr.,   JOHN JOHNSON,
JOHN GRAY,   SAM'L D. BACKUS,
GEORGE F. NESBITT,   D. R. JAQUES,
JOHN F. CONREY,   CHARLES TURNER,
JOHN A. BUNTING,   WM. H. BUTLER,
CHARLES A. WHITNEY,   WM. H. ADEE,
WM. EBBITT,   JAMES C. BALDWIN,
JOHN V. BROWER,   WM. SEWELL,
THOS. F. DE VOE,   WM. B. LEONARD.

NEW YORK, *January* 6, 1859.   *Managers.*

BURNING
OF THE CRYSTAL PALACE.

The following address, on the occasion of the late disastrous conflagration of the Crystal Palace, was prepared by a special committee, appointed at a meeting of the American Institute on the 15th of October, consisting of Messrs. D. M. Reese, Benjamin Aycrigg, Joseph P. Simpson, Robert Lovett, and James Bogardus, which address was presented to the Institute on the 5th of November, adopted, and four thousand copies ordered to be printed for distribution.

The American Institute of the city of New York has recently been visited by a grievous calamity in the destruction of the Crystal Palace by fire. Our Thirtieth Annual Fair and exhibition was in the full tide of successful progress at the time, and that spacious building was overflowing with the evidences and products of American industry, in the various departments of "Agriculture, Commerce, Manufactures and the Arts." This valuable property of inventors and exhibiters, together with the property of the Institute, to a large amount, was suddenly consumed in the overwhelming conflagration, thus, within a single hour, reducing all to a heap of ruins.

Under such circumstances, one consolation is left us, in the assurance we are able to give our members, friends and patrons, at home and abroad, that this calamitous visitation could neither be foreseen nor averted by any human ingenuity; our Board of Managers, and their employees, having used all the vigilance in their power in providing for the prevention of such a disaster, which can only be ascribed to the torch of an incendiary, against which no possible sagacity could have availed. We find, however, an additional source of congratulation in the fact that we have no loss of human life to deplore, which would have been a deeper source of regret to us all had it occurred; but, although a multitude of men, women and children were within the building at the time of the fire, we rejoice to say that all escaped without damage to limb or life, which must be regarded as a Providential interposition in our behalf.

It is not within our power to ascertain the aggregate amount of property consumed. The loss to the Institute itself cannot easily be estimated, for our fair had but for a few days been fully opened, and although the heaviest expenses of the exhibition had been incurred, yet the receipts had only commenced, and at the date of the fire had not met the outlay of our Board of Managers, falling short of the expenditures not less than $2,000. But we were looking forward to a successful and remunerative exhibition, which indeed was foreshadowed by its early success, and the intrinsic attractions of the fair, which has heretofore never failed to command patronage. Hence the impracticability of stating fully our own loss by the abrupt close of the exhibition; although to replace the actual property of the Institute destroyed, will probably involve the expenditure of $10,000.

But how insignificant are our own losses, compared with the vast accumulation of property belonging to inventors and exhibitors, which shared the same fate; for comparatively nothing was saved from the common ruin. To estimate the intrinsic price in the market of very many of the inventions and discoveries, the specimens and models of which were burned, would very inadequately set forth the loss sustained by their owners. Many of these were new and useful in a high degree, and some of them the toilsome product of years of mental labor, and constituting, perhaps, the only earthly possession of the inventors and exhibiters, to whom they were of priceless value. They looked to the termination of the fair, and the rewards of the Institute, as the beginning of their fortunes. Surely our own severe losses as a corporate body are inconsiderable, compared with the losses of our inventors and exhibiters, to whom our heartfelt sympathies are extended, and for whom we hope for a brighter day in the future.

The Institute would gladly have responded to the loud call made upon them, to renew and continue their exhibition for the present year, had the project been at all feasible. But we were constrained to concur with our Board of Managers in the judgment that it was wholly inexpedient. Our practical experience for more than a quarter of a century, it must be supposed, has familiarized us with the great difficulties and heavy expenses connected with the getting up and conducting these fairs. Thus instructed, it is our matured opinion that any attempt to re-open and continue the exhibition for the present year would have proved a failure, and have involved an expenditure beyond any of our available means; and subjected the Institute to the incubus of a debt, which would have crippled us for our future annual duties and responsibilities. Hence we have been anxious to satisfy all those who share with us in the common disappointment and sacrifices which this calamity has inflicted, that a renewal of the fair, at present, would have been unwise and unsuccessful. Our Board of Managers, on whom the renewed toils would have devolved, did not shrink because of the time and labor and sacrifices involved, but only yielded to the conviction forced upon them, that no suitable place could be obtained, and prepared for the exhibition in time for success, without an expense which the Institute could not sustain.

This interruption took place so early in the exhibition, that the judges had not yet decided upon the merits of any of the articles for competition, except in the case of a part of the horticultural specimens, so that, except to these, no premiums could possibly be awarded. This will be a sufficient answer to those who have complained that the prizes offered, all of which were ready, were not distributed. It could only be done indiscriminately, if done at all, since merit was not yet adjudicated; nor could the managers make the awards in the absence of any report from the judges, who for the most part, had not even entered upon their labors, or seen the articles to be submitted to their scrutiny.

Thus much, by way of explanation, it has been deemed proper to say, as due to the numerous inventors and exhibiters who suffer with us in this dire calamity. Although the American Institute might proudly appeal to the public for their sympathy and co-operation in this hour of trial, in view of its past history; by referring to the fidelity with which they have annually fulfilled their obligations and engagements, even on the occurrence of untoward events, which have rendered the fair and distribution of premiums a task involving us in heavy sacrifices and expenses.

Need we refer to the memorable year 1853, when the postponement of the opening of the World's Fair from the 1st of May, as appointed, till later in the season, rendered the opening of our exhibition necessarily a bill of expense? Our loss of nearly $6,000 by that fair was anticipated, and yet we felt it our sacred duty to see that American industry, thus called to compete with the handicraft of the oldest nations of Europe, should not be overshadowed; and that our American artisans called into competition with the workmen of all other countries should have a fair field, and all the encouragement our countenance and patronage could afford.

Hence, under these inauspicious circumstances, we opened our exhibition at Castle Garden as aforetime, and though our expenses were nearly $11,000, our gross receipts failed to reach $5,000, yet we did not regret the sacrifice, but distributed our premiums as usual, in fulfillment of the duty we owed to American industry, to which all our means and available resources have ever been consecrated.

It will also be recollected that in the following year, 1854, for the first and only time in our history we held no exhibition. The State Agricultural Society, a kindred institution of great merit and usefulness, had honored our city by selecting it for their annual fair, not in competition with us, but in co-operation with us. Hence, we cheerfully resigned the field to them, and paid over to them as in duty bound the annual donation of the State for our cattle show, which was held by the State Society, aided by the officers and managers of the Institute.

For the satisfaction of all concerned, and to remove misapprehensions known to exist to some extent, we here subjoin a tabular statement of the receipts and expenditures of all our fairs during the last eighteen years, viz : from 1839 to 1857 inclusive. It will here be apparent that our revenues from this source yield but an inconsiderable result, even when our exhibitions have been most successful. Hence, though in last year's fair our receipts were nearly $29,000, yet our net proceeds barely exceeded $1,700! And this, when the services of our Board of Managers by day and night for nearly two months continuously, were wholly gratuitous, with the exception only of their meals when on actual duty. Had we been obliged to hire the labor they rendered, the expense would have consumed the whole proceeds, and our expenses exceeded our receipts.

		Receipts.	Expenditures.	Surplus.
12th Annual Fair, 1839,.....	$8,831 41	$7,631 41	$1,200 00
13th " " 1840,.....	6,581 25	5,128 30	1,452 95
14th " " 1841,.....	7,050 00	5,571 31	1,478 69
15th " " 1842,.....	6,741 75	5,825 75	916 00
16th " " 1843,.....	8,808 80	6,283 52	2,525 28
17th " " 1844,.....	10,249 71	7,484 63	2,765 05
18th " " 1845,.....	12,600 43	8,683 49	3,916 94

				Receipts.		Expenditures.		Surplus.	
19th Annual Fair,	1846,____	$14,312	00	$10,225	25	$4,086	75
20th	"	"	1847,____	15,275	27	9,619	06	5,656	21
21st	"	"	1848,____	17,546	00	12,031	91	5,514	09
22d	"	"	1849,____	18,770	23	11,384	05	7,432	18
23d	"	"	1850,____	22,419	14	16,289	13	6,130	01
24th	"	"	1851,____	20,763	50	14,141	27	6,622	23
25th	"	"	1852,____	25,429	49	16,181	17	5,248	32
26th	"	"	1853,____	4,950	56	10,909	84	*
27th	"	"	1855,____	27,705	19	21,821	30	5,883	89
28th	"	"	1856,____	27,861	26	23,145	05	4,616	21
29th	"	"	1857,____	28,666	83	†26,947	98	1,718	85

The grand object of our fairs and exhibitions has never been to make money, save so far as our profits might enlarge and extend our usefulness to the cause. Had it been otherwise, our managers might have restricted the admission, by placing all their tickets on sale, and thus, by possibility, enhanced the aggregate of the receipts. Instead of which, they have adopted the wiser and more liberal policy of extending complimentary invitations to those whose patronage to science and art it is desirable to secure, as well as to public men in every profession, to enlist their favor. By including the families of the members in their tickets, extending to exhibiters, military corps, and others, free admission at all times, and scattering ladies' tickets among their friends, they have thus crowded their exhibition with visitors, and increased the attractions of the fair to citizens and strangers, who were ready to purchase tickets at the door. And though the thousands who nightly thronged our fairs without pay, may have led to the exaggerated estimates made of our receipts; yet we are persuaded that they contributed to bring other thousands in sufficient numbers who did pay, so that our large expenses have all been met, and a sufficient margin to sustain the Institute.

We claim for the Institute, that in this, and in every other department, our financial transactions will bear the closest scrutiny, and that our resources have been husbanded with the strictest regard to economy. Nor are we able to discover any reduction of expenses in conducting the general affairs of the Institute, which can now be made without sacrificing its efficiency and diminishing its usefulness. We have no sinecure offices, nor do we pay any salaries, except for the indispensable clerical helpers in our business office, none of whose places could be adequately filled at less rates. By the ownership of our premises on Broadway, eligible and spacious halls are secured for our ex-

* Deficiency $5,959 28.
† The rent of the Palace is not included in this amount.

tensive library, repository, our Farmers' and Mechanics' clubs, our committees, secretaries and clerks, and for all our business operations, at a mere nominal rent; while the revenues of our rental of the unoccupied portion of the building, are adequate to meet the interest upon our small indebtedness, the taxes, insurance and other incidentals. May we not then claim, on behalf of the American Institute, that by its thrifty and prudential management of its fiscal concerns, its officiary is entitled to the confidence of all its members and friends at home and abroad.

We now submit a statement of the amount annually expended for premiums, during the last nineteen years, which will exhibit one item of the outlay attendant upon each fair. It will serve to show that we are steadfastly pursuing the great and good objects for which the Institute was incorporated by the Legislature of our State, viz: "bestowing rewards and other benefits upon all who make improvements in any of the arts, or excel in any department of American industry." To these objects, all our means, resources and availabilities have ever been, and still will be, sacredly devoted.

Cost of Premiums Awarded by the American Institute from 1835 to 1857.

8th Annual Fair,	1835,	...	$779	00
9th " "	1836,	...	1,034	50
10th " "	1837,	...	1,093	50
11th " "	1838,	...	1,259	50
12th " "	1839,	...	1,155	44
13th " "	1840,	...	842	50
14th " "	1841,	...	1,183	03
15th " "	1842,	...	1,155	96
16th " "	1843,	...	1,191	55
17th " "	1844,	...	1,192	44
18th " "	1845,	...	1,848	17
19th " "	1846,	...	3,225	10
20th " "	1847,	...	2,592	78
21st " "	1848,	...	3,089	83
22d " "	1849,	...	2,482	61
23d " "	1850,	...	4,303	72
24th " "	1851,	...	4,091	76
25th " "	1852,	...	4,917	43
26th " "	1853,	...	3,366	77
27th " "	1855,	...	3,269	97
28th " "	1856,	...	5,593	49
29th " "	1857,	...	3,160	34

For further and ampler details of all the proceedings of the Institute, we refer to the annual reports made to the State Legislature according to law, and which are printed by that body annually.

We need scarcely allude to the influence and effects of these annual fairs and exhibitions of the American Institute upon the interests of this great city. When it is recollected that more than four hundred thousand visitors have been ascertained to have been present during the few weeks that our fairs have been held, and that a vast proportion of these were strangers brought hither for the purpose in large parties by steamboat and railroad excursions from the numerous cities and towns within hundreds of miles of New York, the importance and advantage thus conferred upon the merchants, tradesmen, hotels, restaurants, etc., of New York, can scarcely be over-estimated. Indeed our whole country derives benefit from these annual gatherings, for here the gifted sons of toil from the north and the south, the east and the west, are wont to greet each other, while in healthful rivalry they compete for the prizes distributed among those who excel from every section of our common country. They thus lose their sectional spirit, or it becomes merged in the grand purposes of the American Institute—the advancement of American science and art, the reward of our national genius and industry.

Finally, we assure our patrons and friends everywhere, that though we are "cast down" by the recent unforeseen calamity, yet we are not "destroyed." We can still survive the catastrophe with that modicum of public patronage heretofore awarded to the Institute and the continued favor of the inventors and exhibiters of the country, who, having proved in all the past with what zeal and fidelity we have served their interests, will confide in our continued efforts in their behalf in the future. Arousing ourselves, therefore, from the depression into which our recent disappointment and grievous loss have thrown us all, and enlisting with renewed energy and perseverance in the service of American industry in all its departments, whether of genius or labor, let us nerve ourselves anew in the good work of fostering and encouraging our native artisans, and thus continue to confer benefits upon our common country.

LIST OF PREMIUMS

AWARDED BY THE MANAGERS OF THE THIRTIETH ANNUAL FAIR OF THE AMERICAN INSTITUTE.

FAT CATTLE EXHIBITION.
Fat Cattle.

Judges—Thos. White, Wm. Lalor, David B. Reed.

Theodore Wheeler, Dover, Dutchess county, N. Y., for the best pair of Durham grade cattle, (fed over six months by the exhibiter.) Silver cup, $30.

Obed Wheeler, Dover, Dutchess county, N. Y., for the second best pair of white Durham grade cattle, (fed over six months by the exhibiter.) Silver cup, $20.

James A. Hamilton, Lima, Livingston county, N. Y., special premium, for the best fat ox, "Livingston Chief." Silver cup, $10.

James Van Alstyne, Ghent, Columbia county, Y. N., special premium for sixteen head of Hereford steers. Silver cup, $15.

Robt. D. Cornell, Clinton, Dutchess county, N. Y., special premium, for a pair of Durham steers, fed from calves by the exhibiter. Silver cup, $10.

Fat Sheep.

Judges—Thos. White, Wm. Lalor, David B. Reed.

Wm. S. Holmes, Marathon, Cortland county, N. Y., special premium, for the best fat wether, (Leicestershire breed.) Silver cup, $10.

Robt. D. Cornell, Clinton, Dutchess county, N. Y., special premium, for Southdown ewes. Silver medal.

Fat Hogs.

Judges—F. Rollwagen, Stephen H. Cornell.

James A. Hamilton, Lima, Livingston county, N. Y., for the best fat hog. Silver cup, $8.

James A. Hamilton, Lima, Livingston county, N. Y., for the second best fat hog. Silver medal.

James A. Hamilton, Lima, Livingston county, N. Y., for a fine lot of thirty-five fat hogs, average weight 480 pounds, special premium. Dip.

Fancy Poultry.

Judges—D. Fowler, Edwd. M. Hedden, John Tilton.

Wm. Simpson, jr., West Farms, N. Y., for the best and greatest variety of poultry. Silver cup, $15.

Joshua Weaver, Fordham, N. Y., for superior English (colored) dorkings, special premium. Silver medal.

James Cauthers, No. 22, Sixth street, for silver pheasant fowls, special premium. Bronze medal.

M. R. Beam, No. 154, Twentieth street, for the best and largest variety of pigeons. Silver cup, $10.

Joshua Weaver, Fordham, N. Y., for superior English pouters. Dip.

E. W. Hammond, No. 88, Clinton street, for an exhibition of pigeons and African bantams. Diploma.

W. L. Clemens, No. 89, West Fortieth street, for a cage of doves. Brown's book on poultry.

HORTICULTURAL EXHIBITION.
Fruit—First Series.

Judges—Wm. S. Carpenter, Wm. J. Davidson, Thos. Hogg.

John W. Bailey, Plattsburgh, N. Y., for the best collection of named varieties of apples. Silver cup, $15.

Thos. H. Fentrees, Greensboro, N. C., for the second best collection of named varieties of apples. Large silver medal.

Westbrook & Mendenhall, Greensboro, N. C., for the best twelve named varieties of table apples. Large silver medal.

Ellwanger & Barry, Rochester, N. Y., for the best collection of fifty named varieties of pears. Silver cup, $15.

Hovey & Co., Boston, Mass., for the second best collection of fifty named varieties of pears. Large silver medal.

H. E. Hooker & Co., Rochester, N. Y., for the best twelve named varieties of pears. Large silver medal.

P. T. Quinn, gardener to Jas. J. Mapes, Newark, N. J., for the second best twelve varieties of pears. Village and Farm Cottages.

Mrs. F. B. Durfee, Fall River, Mass., for the best collection of foreign grapes. Silver cup, $10.

James Wiggins, gardener to Jas. Brown, Wehawken, N. J., for a collection of foreign grapes. Silver medal.

James Scanlan, gardener to Mr. G. Colt, Paterson, N. J., for sixteen varieties of foreign grapes. Silver cup, $10.

C. W. Grant, Iona, N. Y., for the best twelve bunches of Catawba grapes. Silver medal.

Wm. A. Underhill, Croton Point, N. Y., for the best twelve bunches of Isabella grapes. Silver medal.

C. W. Grant, Iona, N. Y., for the second best twelve bunches of Isabella grapes. Diploma.

J. W. Clark, Sandusky, Ohio, for the best twelve free stone peaches. Thomas' Fruit Book.

Ellwanger & Barry, Rochester, N. Y., for a collection of named varieties of plums. Silver medal.

Alexander McCullum, gardener to Mrs. Jas. Hooker, Poughkeepsie, N. Y., for fine peaches. Transactions Am. Institute.

Flowers and Plants.

Wm. H. Mitchell, Harlem, N. Y., for the best display of cut flowers. Silver cup, $10.

David Clark, Seventy-seventh street and Broadway, for the second best display of cut flowers. Silver medal.

A. G. Burgess, East New York, L. I., for the best one hundred blooms of named dahlias. Silver cup, $10.

Chas. S. Pell, New York Orphan Asylum, New York, for the second best one hundred blooms of named dahlias. Silver medal.

A. G. Burgess, East New York, for the best twenty-four blooms of named dahlias. Silver medal.

Chas. S. Pell, New York Orphan Asylum, for the second best twenty four blooms of named dahlias. Parson's Rose Manual.

David Clark, Seventy-seventh street and Broadway, for the best twelve named roses. Gray's Text Book of Botany.

Wm. Fitzpatrick, Twenty-ninth street and Broadway, for the best floral design. Silver cup, $15.

Parsons & Co., Flushing, L. I., for the best collection of evergreens. Silver medal.

Amateur's List.

Chas. S. Pell, New York Orphan Asylum, New York, for the best display of cut flowers. Silver medal.

T. Wilder, gardener to G. H. Striker, West Fifty-second street, for the best twenty blooms of named dahlias. Silver medal.

Chas. S. Pell, New York Orphan Asylum, New York, for the second best twenty blooms of named dahlias. Buist's Flower Garden Directory.

Chas. S. Pell, New York Orphan Asylum, for the best twelve blooms of named dahlias. Downing's Cottage Residences.

Vegetables.

Judges—John Burgess, P. Cavinah, Geo. Lovecraft.

Henry Zeh, Blackwell's Island, for the best assortment of culinary vegetables. Silver cup, $10.

S. Ruth, gardener to J. Fitch, Blackwell's Island, for the second best assortment of culinary vegetables. Silver medal.

S. Ruth, gardener to J. Fitch, Blackwell's Island, for the best collection of vegetables for cattle. Silver medal.

Garret Mead, Workhouse, Blackwell's Island, for the best twelve long blood beets. Vol. Horticulturist.

S. Ruth, gardener to J. Fitch, Blackwell's Island, for the second best twelve long blood beets. Munn's Land Drainer.

Samuel Love, Fifty-third street, between Sixth and Seventh avenues, for the best twelve turnip-rooted beets. Vol. Saxton's Rural Hand Book.

D. W. C. Morris, Cedar Park, Bergen Point, N. J., for the second best twelve turnip rooted beets. Vol. Cultivator.

Henry Zeh, Blackwell's Island, for the best twelve carrots for the table. Hovey's Magazine.

Samuel Love, Fifty-third street, between Sixth and Seventh avenues, for the second best twelve carrots for the table. Munn's Land Drainer.

Garret Mead, Workhouse, Blackwell's Island, for the best four drumhead cabbages. Bridgeman's Gardeners' Assistant.

S. Ruth, gardener to J. Fitch, Blackwell's Island, for the best three purple egg plants. Vol. Rural New Yorker.

Garret Mead, Workhouse, Blackwell's Island, for the second best purple egg plants. Vol. Cultivator.

D. W. C. Morris, Cedar Park, Bergen Point, N. J., for a variety of long egg plants. Transactions.

Henry Zeh, Blackwell's Island, for the best peck of yellow onions. Vol. Working Farmer.

W. S. Carpenter, Harrison, Westchester county, N. Y., for the best assortment of tomatoes. Neill's Gardeners' Companion.

Samuel White, North Shore, L. I., for the best peck of red onions. Vol. Am. Agriculturist.

W. S. Carpenter, Harrison, Westchester county, N. Y., for the best collection of named varieties of potatoes. Silver medal.

Robert Marshall, One Hundred and Third street, and Ninth avenue, New York, for the best bushel of potatoes for the table. Silver medal.

W. S. Carpenter, Harrison, Westchester county, N. Y., for the second best bushel of potatoes. Diploma.

Henry Zeh, Blackwell's Island, for the best three Boston marrow squashes. Neill's Gardeners' Companion.

Henry Zeh, Blackwell's Island, for the best three crookneck squashes. Dana's Muck Manual.

S. Ruth, gardener to J. Fitch, Blackwell's Island, for the best three green or striped crookneck squashes. Vol. Am. Agriculturist.

Wm. S. Carpenter, Harrison, Westchester county, N. Y., for the best three squashes of any other other variety. Vol. Working Farmer.

D. W. C. Morris, Cedar Park, Bergen Point, N. J., for the best three pumpkins for table use. Bridgeman's Gardeners' Assistant.

D. W. C. Morris, Cedar Park, Bergen Point, N. J., for the best twenty ears of new sweet corn. Silver Medal.

W. S. Carpenter, Harrison, Westchester county, N. Y., for the best twenty ears of new sweet corn. Leibigs' Ag. Chemistry.

Garret Mead, Workhouse, Blackwell's Island, for a bushel of Mercer potatoes. Transactions.

D. W. C. Morris, Cedar Park, Bergen Point, N. J., for the second best peck of tomatoes. Vol. Cultivator.

Fruit—Second Series.

Judges—A. S. Fuller, Matco Donadi, Wm. H. Mitchell.

John W. Bailey, Plattsburgh, N. Y., for the best collection of apples. Silver cup, $15.

Hovey & Co., Boston, Mass., for the best fifty varieties of pears. Silver cup, $15.

J. H. Sanborn, Plattsburgh, N. Y., for the best twelve varieties of pears. Large silver medal.

P. T. Quinn, gardener to Jas. J. Mapes, Newark, N. J., for the best six varieties of pears. Silver medal.

James Scanlon, gardener to M. G. Colt, Paterson, for the best four varieties of foreign grapes. Silver cup, $10.

James Scanlon, gardener to M. G. Colt, Paterson, N. J., for the best two bunches of Black Hamburgh grapes. Silver medal.

James Scanlon, gardener to M. G. Colt, Paterson, N. J., for the best two bunches of Verdilho grapes. Silver medal.

C. W. Grant, Iona, N. Y., for the best four varieties of Native grapes. Large silver medal.

R. T. Underhill, Croton Point, N. Y., for the second best four varieties of Native grapes. Diploma.

Joseph Bartlett, Huntsville, Dutchess county, N. Y., for the best twelve bunches of Isabella grapes. Silver medal.

R. T. Underhill, Croton Point, N. Y., for the second best twelve bunches of Isabella grapes. Diploma.

R. T. Underhill, Croton Point, N. Y., for the best twelve bunches of Catawba grapes. Silver medal.

C. W. Grant, Iona, N. Y., for the second best twelve bunches of Catawba grapes. Diploma.

E. M. Peake, Hudson, N. Y., for the best twelve bunches of Rebecca grapes. Silver medal.

J. McBride, Westchester county, N. Y.. for very fine oranges and lemons. Transactions.

A. P. Cumings, Westchester, N. Y., for very fine guava. Transactions.

Abraham Brower, 257 Henry street, for ripe figs. Transactions.

Amateur's List.

H. Tanner, gardener to J. S. T. Stranahan, Brooklyn, for the best five varieties of pears. Silver medal.

Henry Payson, Brooklyn, L. I., for the best twelve table pears. Trans.

John Ryan, gardener to Mrs. Parish, Union Square, for the best two bunches of Black Hamburgh grapes, grown in the open air. Trans.

H. Tanner, gardener to J. S. T. Stranahan, Brooklyn, for the best six bunches of Isabella grapes. Silver medal.

Thos. R. Lees, Brooklyn, L. I., for the second best six bunches of Isabella grapes. Diploma.

Edward Richards, Mott Haven, N. Y., for the best six bunches of Catawba grapes. Silver medal.

H. Tanner, gardener to J. S. T. Stranahan, Brooklyn, for the second best six bunches of Catawba grapes. Diploma.

J. Couzens, Dobb's Ferry, N. Y., for four bunches of Fontainbleau grapes. Transactions.

Vegetables—Second Series.

Judges—T. J. Leaming, C. Zeller, Samuel C. Barnes.

S. Ruth, gardener to J. Fitch, Blackwell's Island, for the best assortment of culinary vegetables. Silver cup, $10.

Henry Zeh, Blackwell's Island, for the second best assortment of culinary vegetables. Silver medal.

S. Ruth, gardener to J. Fitch, Blackwell's Island, for the best vegetable roots for cattle. Silver medal.

Henry Zeh, Blackwell's Island, for the best twelve long blood beets. Vol. Horticulturist.

S. Ruth, gardener to J. Fitch, Blackwell's Island, for the second best long blood beets. Munn's Land Drainer.

Samuel Love, Fifty-third street, New York, for the best twelve turnip rooted beets. Vol. Saxton's Rural Hand Book.

Henry Zeh, Blackwell's Island, for the best twelve carrots for the table. Vol. Hovey's Magazine.

Samuel Love, Fifty-third street, New York, for the second best twelve carrots for the table. Munn's Land Drainer.

Chas. S. Pell, New York Orphan Asylum, for the best twelve roots of salsify. Vol. Saxton's Rural Hand Book.

James Amm, Elizabeth, N. J., for the second best twelve roots of salsify. Vol. Saxton's Rural Hand Book.

Henry Zeh, Blackwell's Island, for the best twelve parsnips. Vol. Agriculturist.

D. W. C. Morris, Cedar Park, Bergen Point, N. J., for the second best twelve parsnips. Munn's Land Drainer.

S. Ruth, Blackwell's Island, for the best four heads of cauliflower. Silver medal.

James Amm, Elizabeth, N. J., for the second best four heads of cauliflower. Diploma.

H. Cammann, Fordham, N. Y., for the best drumhead cabbage. Bridgeman's Gardeners' Assistant.

Henry Zeh, Blackwell's Island, for the best Savoy cabbage. Vol. Am. Agriculturist.

S. Ruth, gardener to J. Fitch, Blackwell's Island, for the best purple egg plants. Vol. Rural New Yorker.

S. Ruth, gardener to J. Fitch, Blackwell's Island, for the best twelve roots of celery. Silver medal.

Henry Zeh, Blackwell's Island, for the best peck of white onions. Vol. Hovey's Magazine.

Henry Zeh, Blackwell's Island, for the best peck of yellow onions. Vol. Working Farmer.

S. Ruth, gardener to J. Fitch, Blackwell's Island, for the best peck of tomatoes. Neill's Gardeners' Companion.

Henry Zeh, Blackwell's Island, for the best half bushel of white turnips. Allen's Farm Book.

Wm. S. Carpenter, 468 Pearl street, N. Y., for the best collection of potatoes.   Silver medal.

Wm. S. Carpenter, 468 Pearl street, N. Y., for the best bushel of potatoes for the table.   Silver medal.

J. Van Wickel, Newtown, L. I., for the second best bushel of potatoes for the table.   Diploma.

D. W. C. Morris, Cedar Park, Bergen Point, N. Y., for the best bushel of potatoes for cattle.   Vol. Working Farmer.

E. C. Bramhall, Bergen, N. J., for the best three Boston marrow squashes.   Neill's Gardeners' Companion.

Henry Zeh, Blackwell's Island, for the best three yellow crook neck squashes.   Dana's Muck Manual.

Henry Zeh, Blackwell's Island, for the best three green striped neck squashes.   Vol. Am. Agriculturist.

P. Koerber, Tremont, N. Y., for the best three squashes of other varieties.   Vol. Working Farmer.

P. Koerber, Tremont, N. Y., for the best three pumpkins for table use. Bridgeman's Gardeners' Assistant.

Henry Zeh, Blackwell's Island, for the best twenty ears of sweet corn. Silver medal.

George Leeds, White Plains, N. Y., for the best twenty ears of yellow flint corn.   Saxtou's Rural Hand Book.

Robert Marshall, One Hundred and Third street and Ninth avenue, N. Y., for twenty ears of Virginia white corn.   Transactions American Institute.

REPORTS OF COMMITTEES.

Report of the Committee on Manufactures, Science and Arts, on Miller's Safety Steam Boiler Alarm.

The committee on Manufactures, Science and Arts, to whom was referred "Miller's Safety Steam Boiler Alarm," having examined the apparatus presented by the inventor, and heard his explanations in relation to the same, beg leave to

REPORT:

That, in the opinion of the committee, the arrangements of its parts and manner of applying it to steam boilers for the purpose of giving notice to the attendants of a deficiency of water, when that condition of things occurs, is well adapted to accomplish the intended purpose; and that its application to steam boilers used in mills and manufactories, will tend much to prevent the danger which results from such deficiency.

The apparatus is simple in its construction and mode of operation, and will, probably, prove durable and effective.

Respectfully submitted,

JOHN D. WARD,
JOSEPH DIXON,
T. B. STILLMAN,
Committee.

NEW YORK, *October 20th*, 1858.

Report of a Select Committee appointed to examine the Paying Out Machinery on board of the United States Steam Frigate Niagara, used in laying the Atlantic Telegraph cable, and to furnish a report thereon concerning the design and construction thereof.

The committee appointed under a resolution of the Institute of the 2d September last, in reference to the paying out machinery used to lay the Atlantic cable from the steamers Niagara and Agamemnon, understand that the object of their appointment was to hear and ascertain from authentic sources the part which Mr. Wm. E. Everett, an American engineer, has performed in connection with so interesting an event as the successful laying of a telegraph cable between the two continents.

The American Institute may well be excused for desiring to have placed on record the fact, if such has been the case, that to the mechanical ingenuity and ability of an American engineer is due the creation of the machinery through which the Atlantic cable was successfully laid; but it is in every wise incumbent on the committee to whom has been assigned the ascertainment of the truth in this particular, to be cautious to make no claim on behalf of a fellow-countryman which, with those who know the history of the proceedings, will not, in any particular, be sanctioned. In this view of the duty which they have undertaken, your committee have availed themselves of such sources of information as have been accessible to them, and submit the following

REPORT.

The points that presented themselves to their consideration were:

1*st*. Was the instrument then on board of the Niagara, like that used in the first essay to lay the Atlantic Telegraph Cable, and if not, was it novel, and if so, by whom was it designed?

2*d*. If novel, who were the authors of its essential features?

3*d*. By whose authority was it constructed, and to whom was its design and construction confided?

4*th*. If the instrument had proved inadequate in design, or insufficient in the proportion of its parts, who would have been held professionally responsible for its failure by those who authorized its construction?

In the investigations necessary to determine these points, the following elements were arrived at, viz.:

That the instrument employed in the first essay to lay the cable, designated by being described as having four sheaves, was held to have been inadequate for its purpose without essential modifications in several of its operations.

That the essential features of this instrument were: that the cable in its course was alternately carried in opposite directions, at every sheave; that as the sheaves had a common diameter and were geared to a common speed, that the cable leaving the last sheave, being submitted to its own tensile strain in suspension, the delivery of it was less than the supply of it to the first sheave, an operation producing either a slip, or an accumulation of slack, involving a surge or a slip in the cable, and that the cable was parted twice from the effect of these operations in the first essay to lay it.

That the brake used, in connection with this instrument, by its want of adaptation to the varying and sudden requirements of relaxation, was unsuited to the safe control of an alternating resistance, one-third of which was initially expended in the weight of the cable in suspension, and that the *inertia* of such brake was superior to the impulse consequent upon a demand for cable, unless with the ready and never-failing coöperation of an operator stationed at the instrument.

That the direction of the first essay was wholly confided to officers in the employ of the Atlantic Telegraph Company, and that upon the return of the squadron after the first essay, the several officers commanding the vessels, the engineers of the company, and Chief Engineer, Wm. E. Everett, U. S. N., were invited to meet the Directors of the Company in London, to advise regarding some course to be adopted, by which the causes of the late failure might be obviated.

That at this meeting Mr. Everett, counselled the Directors of the Company to seek the advice of two or three Engineers, and to be guided by them in regard to the design and construction of the paying out machinery, which course being adopted, he was asked to select such persons as he thought proper; that he called upon Mr. John Penn, and by him was introduced to Mr. Joshua Field and Mr. John Lloyd, Engineers-in-Chief, R. N.; that these gentlemen having been requested by the Directors to act as a Committee and to report their views regarding a paying out instrument, consented to act, and accompanied him to Plymouth, to inspect the paying out instrument then on board of the Niagara, and to obtain an explanation of the cause of the failure; and returned to London and agreed that after consideration they would prepare a report embodying their views; that during the interval between their return to London and the completion of the report, Mr. Everett designed a paying out instrument having but two sheaves, a tracing of the design of which is annexed and lettered A.

That these gentlemen completed their report, which being submitted to Mr. Everett, he dissented from it in consequence of its recommending the paying out instrument of four sheaves instead of two, that he was asked to make a minority report, to which he objected, and assigned the following reasons:

"I did not feel authorized to do so: first, because it would have appeared absurd to recommend counsellors to the Directors, and when their advice was rendered, to pronounce it erroneous; second, I appreciated their superior experience and knowledge, and for these reasons, finding I could not persuade them to my opinion, I signed their report, as in duty bound, for the interest of the Company."

The joint report was then delivered, and is as follows:

B.

LONDON, *September*, 1857.

GENTLEMEN:—Having examined, agreeable to your request, the apparatus and arrangements on board of the Niagara, for paying out the Atlantic Telegraph Cable, and given the whole subject our careful consideration, we beg to lay before you the conclusions at which we have arrived.

We consider the paying out sheaves require no alterations except those suggested by Mr. Bright, in a memorandum, which he was good enough to place in our hands, a copy of which we append, namely, "To have one groove only in each of the sheaves, to make the groove deeper and wider at the periphery, and fit them with guards to prevent the cable coming off, to apply scrapers for removing the tar from the grooves; and to make the circumference of each successive sheave which the cable passes over as much larger than the preceding, as the cable is found to stretch by the application of the increasing strain which it has to bear in passing around the several sheaves when it is being payed out, with the maximum strain, and thus greatly diminish or perhaps entirely obviate the slipping of the cable on all the sheaves.''

We may add that we see no reason why this apparatus should not also be used for hauling in the cable when necessary, if sufficient engine power be provided for that purpose.

The most important consideration, however, to which we have directed our attention is, how to guard against the strain being brought on the cable while paying out, greater than it is considered capable of bearing without a risk of damage; that is, having determined the maximum strain, how to counteract the numerous causes which have a tendency to increase it, and which, especially when brought into operation simultaneously, would otherwise endanger or destroy the cable.

The means which we recommend for this purpose are, the substitution for the present brakes of the others, moving with the same regular velocity, but of twice the diameter, and having their rubbing surface of gun metal about 12 inches wide, each brake being capable of doing the whole work, but both may be in operation together, if found convenient. They should be constructed on the plan patented some years ago by Mr. Appold. Their rims should be lined with strips of lignum vitæ, about three inches broad, and half an inch apart, and immersed about one-third of their diameter in cisterns of salt water, it being found by experience that brass and lignum vitæ work together under great pressure with no appreciable wear. Mr. Appold's brake has the advantage of insuring a uniform holding power, so long as the pressure on the lever remains unaltered, capable of being increased or diminished to any required degree with certainty.

A slight movable sheave of the same size as those on the paying out apparatus should be introduced, and be arranged to move horizontally on the deck, through a space of about 20 feet, by the action of strong springs of vulcanized India rubber. The cable, by passing over that on the stern of the ship, would be relieved from the great irregularities of strain to which it would otherwise be subject, and the position of this sheave would at all times be the surest indication of the maximum strain on the cable, a matter of the utmost importance to be known, as upon it should depend the adjustment of the brakes and other operations for insuring the safety of the cable itself.

The importance of carrying these principles into operation is enhanced in our minds by our conviction that any injury sustained by the cable in deep water would probably be irreparable, it being exceedingly doubtful whether the cable could by any contrivance be safely arrested, if broken while running out, or raised from the bottom of the sea.

As an additional means of obviating the danger of breaking the cable, we recommend the adoption of some kind of compensating arrangement to allow for the rise and fall of the stern of the ship in a sea-way, which may be controlled either by springs or weights. We have seen at Mr. Hodges, of Southampton Row, vulcanized springs which we feel satisfied would answer perfectly. We think, with these additions and alterations, the apparatus would be greatly improved, and might be confidently expected to answer its intended purpose.

We now beg to offer some observations on matters which, although of comparatively minor importance, ought, in our opinion, to be attended to, in order to insure as far as may be practicable the success of an undertaking so novel, great and difficult.

Correct instruments should be provided for indicating the speed of the ship and the distance run, as well as the rate at which the cable may be running out, and the whole quantity expended. By means of these instruments and the adjustment of the paying out apparatus, the rate of the cable above that part of the ship may, we think, be regulated with considerable exactness, and the excess, we venture to suggest, should not be less than one-third. This appears to be the only means of allowing the cable to sink into the hollows at the bottom of the sea, instead of hanging as it might otherwise do in some places in long loops, supported only at their ends, and consequently having to bear strains, which, if not at first, might ultimately produce fracture, when the strength of the iron wire became impaired by oxidation. All the machinery should be covered by a kind of house on deck, to protect the attendants from the weather; it should be well lighted at night, and proper accommodation be provided for the men when off duty. An adequate number of efficient attendants should be hired to superintend the machinery, who should relieve each other at short intervals, and the greatest care should be taken to keep all the indicators and other instruments in good working order.

In conclusion, we beg to say that we think no practical difficulty would be found in carrying out all the mechanical arrangements we have suggested, and we also think that they should be carried out under the special superintendence of the officer intrusted by the Company with the important duty of laying the cable, assisted by the most able practical machinist who may be willing to undertake the execution of the work, who should make an experiment on shore on the proposed brake, as soon as one can be finished, and such other experiments as he may deem necessary to enable him to arrange the details in the most effectual manner.

We are, gentlemen, your very humble servants,

T. LLOYD,
JOSHUA FIELD,
JOHN PENN,
WM. E. EVERET.

Soon after this, Mr. Everett's services were applied for to the Navy Department, at Washington, by the Atlantic Telegraph company, by the following letter:

ATLANTIC TELEGRAPH Co., 22 Old Broad St., }
LONDON, *October* 30, 1857. }

SIR :—The directors of this undertaking having had the advantage, subsequent to the failure of the cable, of the scientific aid and advice of Mr. Everett, the chief engineer of the United States steam frigate Niagara, and having conceived a very high opinion, both of his personal qualities, and of his mechanical knowledge and ability, are now desirous of availing themselves of his valuable services in the re-adjustment and alteration of the machinery and appliances, upon which so much will depend when the next attempt is made to lay the cable.

I am, therefore, instructed to inquire if the regulations of the American service would permit Mr. Everett's return to this country, for such purpose, soon after the arrival of the Niagara at New York, and if so, to state that the directors would be very greatly indebted to you, if leave of absence, and the requisite permission to act in behalf of the enterprize in this particular, could be extended to him,

I have the honor to be, sir,
Your most obedient servant,
GEORGE SAWARD, *Secretary.*

To the Hon. ISAAC TOUCEY,
  Secretary of the Navy, Washington, D. C.

Mr. Everett was then in England, and, in anticipation of an affirmative reply from the Department, he, before leaving England, arranged to have the paying out instrument set up, in order that he might compare its results with the new one (having but two sheaves), which he designed to adopt, and upon his return there, (January, 1858,) learned that, in consequence of the first reply of the Navy Department having been in the negative, no steps had been taken towards the construction of the required machinery.

On the 21st of that month, however, he received the following instruction :

THE ATLANTIC TELEGRAPH Co., 22 Old Broad St., }
LONDON, E. C., 21*st January*, 1858. }

Messrs. EASTON & AMES :
  Gentlemen—Mr. William E. Everett, United States Navy, having been authorized to superintend the construction of machinery at your establishment, any work which he may desire to have done for the company, in connection with the machinery for paying out the cable, will be authorized.

Yours truly,
GEORGE SAWARD, *Secretary.*

That from this time to the first of March, was employed by him in procuring and setting up the required machinery, and that the entire month of March was consumed in experimenting upon Appold's brake, before anything satisfactory was obtained in its results, the chief difficulty being, as assigned by him, " that when loaded, say at 2,000 lbs. when running, if the machine was stopped, the clinging, or griping, of the brake blocks to the drum, would require nearly one hundred per cent more to place it in motion. This would have proved fatal to the adoption of the brake, and all the labor and time expended would have been lost. Fortunately, the difficulty was obviated, at the last moment, by cutting the surface of the blocks into small sections of about one and a half inch.

"It should be understood that the brake was a patent, and not an original one with me; but the expense and time required to adapt it to the desired purpose, was two-fold more than all the other experiments combined. As before contemplated, I had, in connection with the brake experiments, made comparisons with the two and four sheave machine, and the results were to me conclusive in favor of the former, and I took a frame of a machine placed on board of the Niagara, formerly for hauling in, but never used, and upon this I constructed the first machine, completing the same during the last week of April, and which machine was used on board the Agamemnon, in laying the cable.

"Immediately after completion, most of the prominent engineers in London were specially invited to inspect its operation, and to inform the directors of their opinion of its fitness for the required purpose (as per letter below), and the public at large were also admitted. So far as I am informed, not one suggestion was received for its modification at that time."

ATLANTIC TELEGRAPH Co., 22 Old Broad St., }
LONDON, 19*th April*, 1858. }

Dear Sir—The first set of the completed machinery which has been constructed for paying out the Atlantic Telegraph Cable, will be erected and running at the works of Messrs. Easton and Ames, 28 Gravel Lane, Southwark, on Thursday next, the 22d instant, and I have been instructed by the Directors to ask the favor of your presence in London on that day soon after 10 o'clock, A. M., as convenient, for the purpose of examining its capabilities and witnessing its operations, and I am instructed to ask of you the further favor, that after such examination of the same shall have been completed, that you will kindly favor me with a letter, for the information of the Board, stating whether, in your opinion, it is well adapted to the intended purpose, and also containing any suggestions that may strike you as to any modifications therein that would, in your opinion, render it more perfect.

Should you kindly consent to be present, your expenses will be defrayed by the Company.

I am, dear sir, yours faithfully,

GEORGE SAWARD, *Secretary*.

That the instrument designed by Mr. Everett and constructed under his supervision not only differed from that proposed by the Commission (as given in report B.), but so much so that it elicited the following letter :

LONDON, *30th April*, 1858.

Dear Sir—With reference to your request of the 28th inst., we beg to state, for the information of the Directors of the Atlantic Telegraph Co., that the machinery for paying out the cable is, in our opinion, well calculated to answer the intended purpose, and that we have no alterations to suggest.

The apparatus for showing the speed of the ship and for recording the total distance run, should of course be completed and fixed on board the Agamemnon and Niagara before the preliminary trials are commenced on board those ships, and the apparatus for showing the rate at which the cable is being paid out and for registering the total quantity, should also be fixed on board.

There will be ample time for this purpose, and no difficulty need be anticipated.

We are, dear sir, yours very truly,

T. LLOYD,
JOHN PENN,
JOSHUA FIELD.

CYRUS W. FIELD. Esq., etc., etc., etc.

That in this instrument, the direction of the curvature of the cable over the sheaves was the same ; that the occurrence of slack or nipping of the cable in running out was avoided by the two sheaves revolving independently of each other; that the brake used in connection with this instrument was self-acting, and that varying strains upon it were readily and safely encountered ; that the inertia in the delivery of the whole apparatus was reduced to a minimum and that the cable entered the paying out instrument under an initial strain, whereby the injurious effect of a slack was set aside ; that in a second letter from the Telegraph Company (G.) Mr. Everett's connection with the design and construction of the instrument is again referred to, and so fully conceded that he was directed to have a complete instrument forthwith constructed for the Niagara (the one completed having been appropriated for the Agamemnon), as will be seen by the following letter :

G.

ATLANTIC TELEGRAPH Co., 22 Old Broad St., }
LONDON, *April 24th*, 1858. }

Dear Sir—As you have now reported to the Managing Committee, that the paying out machinery for H. M. S. Agamemnon is completed, and that it has been working satisfactorily during the last three days, and that you do not consider any alteration necessary to increase its efficiency, and as another set is required for the U. S. Frigate Niagara, the Managing Committee have authorized and instructed me to request that you will immediately give directions to Messrs. Easton and Ames to put another set in hand for that ship, and I am further to request that you will continue your supervision over the construction of the machinery, and also undertake to superintend and direct its being properly fixed and fitted on board the Niagara.

I am further instructed to request that you will take charge of the operation of experimenting upon and subsequently paying out of the cable from the ship, in doing which you will have the coöperation of Messrs. Woodhouse, Follansbee, and of such Assistant Engineers as you may consider it requisite to appropriate to such service.

You are also authorized to make such preparations and arrangements as are necessary to enable you to carry out the foregoing instructions.

I remain yours truly,

GEO. SAWARD, *Secretary.*

Wm. E. Everett, Esq., etc., etc.

That the paying out instrument constructed from the drawings of Mr. Everett and made under his immediate direction were fitted on board of the steam frigates Niagara and Agamemnon, from which vessels and with these instruments the Atlantic Telegraph Cable was successfully laid.

Reviewing, then, the elements submitted, we have arrived at the following conclusions:

1st. That the apparatus used in the first attempt to lay the Atlantic Telegraph Cable, composed of the paying out instrument of four geared sheaves, and the brake used, failed, and that the use of them was wholly abandoned in the second attempt.

2d. That although Appold's brake was attached to the apparatus used in the second essay and made an integral and essential portion of it, yet it was very materially modified before it could be adapted to the peculiar purpose for which it was resorted to.

3d. That the paying out instrument by which this cable was laid, had but two sheaves, running independent of each other, and that in this essential feature it was wholly novel.

4th. That this instrument and the modification of Appold's brake was constructed from the designs of and under the direction of Chief Engineer Wm. E. Everett, U. S. N.

5th. That the entire apparatus was constructed by the authority of the Directors of the Atlantic Telegraph Company, and that its design and construction was confided to Mr. Everett alone.

Finally, that if the apparatus had proved inadequate to the required purpose, that Mr. Everett could alone have been held professionally responsible, as the paying out instrument of his design was essentially different from that recommended by the commission of engineers.

In conclusion, your committee have to add, that although without proper paying out machinery in the vessels of transportation, it would not have been practicable to lay the cable, yet that the mere possession of such machinery did not constitute all that was requisite to attain this end, as the proper stowage of the cable and the manner of its delivery to the paying out machine was equally necessary to success.

The important duty of superintending both the stowing and the delivery on board of the Niagara and Agamemnon was delegated to Messrs. W. H. Woodhouse and Samuel Canning, civil engineers of London, to whose skill, ingenuity and unremitting attention is to be ascribed in a large degree the successful issue of the laying of the Atlantic telegraph cable.

Respectfully submitted, by

CHAS. H. HASWELL,
HORATIO ALLEN,
GEO. W. QUINTARD,
JOHN A. BUNTING,
JOSEPH P. PIRSSON,
CHAS. W. COPELAND.

NEW YORK, *March* 3, 1859.

Report of the Library Committee.

The Library Committee of the American Institute, respectfully submit the following report upon the affairs of the library for the year ending February 10, 1859.

At the date of our last report the library contained eight thousand and thirty (8,030) volumes, and there have been since added one hundred and eighty-six (186) volumes, making the total number of volumes now in the library, eight thousand two hundred and sixteen, (8,216.)

The additions made to the library during the year, have been obtained as follows, viz:

By purchases, ...	43	volumes.
presentation, ...	78	do
subscription, ...	88	do
exchange, ...	10	do
pamphlets, ...	27	do
	186	do

Those obtained by subscription consist of journals, magazines and reviews, which have been received and bound up during the year; those obtained by exchange were received in exchange for works of which the library contained duplicates, and the twenty-seven (27) volumes of pamphlets are those pamphlets which have been received from time to time, and have been assorted, arranged and bound during the year.

The library now contains a collection of two hundred and forty-nine (249) volumes of rare and valuable pamphlets; fifty-nine (59) volumes of these were collected by the late Dr. Samuel L. Mitchill, and were presented to the Institute by the late Dr. Samuel Akerly—the remaining one hundred and ninety (190) volumes have been obtained from various sources, and arranged, bound, and suitably indexed by the librarian.

During the past year there has been expended for books and binding, as follows:

For purchases,... $96 46
    binding,.. 72 06

                                                                  $168 52

It will be perceived that the committee have steadily adhered to the plan pursued for several years past, of purchasing such works only as come within the scope and sphere of the Institute. A library containing a good collection of works relating to the industrial pursuits has been much needed by the farmer, mechanic, inventor and manufacturer, and to supply this desideratum would add much to the character and usefulness of the Institute. The library has already made great progress in this direction, and it is hoped that in the course of a few years it will be worthy of ranking as the Technological Library of the country. Among the works purchased during the past year will be found the following, viz :

Rogers' on Iron Manufacture or Metallurgy. 8 vo. London, 1857.

Muspratt's Chemistry applied to the Arts and Manufactures. 5 vols. 4 to. London, 1859.

Grantham's Iron Ship Building. 2 vols. 4 to. London, 1858.

Herbert's Horse and Horsemanship of the United States. 2 vols. 4 to. New York, 1858.

The amount expended for books during the past year has been less than it has been for several years previous, and this is explained by the pecuniary condition of the Institute. The library committee, in view of the temporary embarrassment of the Institute, consequent upon the destruction of the late Crystal Palace, have felt warranted in making such expenditure only as has been immediately necessary, and could not well be deferred. The number of books purchased, therefore, has been necessarily limited.

Among the works which have been presented, are many of great value. Important contributions have been received from the Imperial Agricultural Society of Vienna, through the Honorable Charles F. Loosey, Consul General of Austria ; from the Regents of the University of the State ; from the Smithsonian Institution ; from Captain L. A. Huguet Latour, of Montreal, and others, as will be seen by reference to the annexed list of contributions. Measures have been taken by which the number of volumes obtained in this manner, gratuitously, will be largely increased. It is hoped that many of the works and documents published by the governments of this country and Great Britain, will be thus acquired.

The library committee have recently issued a circular to the publishers of all periodicals of an agricultural and mechanical nature, published in the United States, soliciting the contribution of a copy of each of their publications, to be placed in the library of the Institute. The committee are happy to announce that this circular has been cordially responded to, the following named periodicals having been already received, viz :

American Stock Journal, New York; Ohio Cultivator, Columbus, Ohio; North Western Farmer, Dubuque, Iowa; Wisconsin Farmer, Madison, Wisconsin; Southern Rural Magazine, Montgomery, Alabama; Southern Planter, Richmond, Virginia; South Countryman, Marietta, Georgia; Planter and Mechanic, Jackson, Mississippi; Ohio Valley Farmer, Cincinnati, Ohio; Pioneer Farmer, Des Moines, Iowa; Rural American, Utica, New York; Prairie Farmer, Chicago, Illinois; North Western Prairie Farmer, Chicago, Illinois; Working Farmer, New York; Genesee Farmer, Rochester, New York; American Farmers' Magazine, New York; North Carolina Planter, Releigh, North Carolina; Michigan Farmer, Detroit, Michigan; Scientific Artisan, Cincinnati, Ohio.

Circulars have been also recently transmitted to the agricultural societies of every State in the Union, soliciting copies of their published journals and reports, and a number of societies have already responded, and requested the Transactions of the Institute in return.

There are upwards of five hundred (500) volumes of duplicates of works in the library, which are still undisposed of. The committee have endeavored to sell or exchange them, but they have succeeded in disposing of but few. Owing to the unusually low prices at which books have been selling at public sale, the committee have not felt warranted in disposing of them in that manner. It is proposed, however, to have them sold at auction as soon as they would be likely to bring fair prices.

In 1851, the Institute provided for the increase of the library by making an annual appropriation of five hundred dollars ($500) for five years, for the purchase of books. Of this appropriation, amounting to $2,500, there has been expended as follows:

In 1851–52,	$498 68
1852–53,	350 00
1853–54,	304 16
1854–55,	225 57
1855–56,	106 78
1856–57,	91 61
1857–58,	307 79
1858–59,	96 46
	$1,982 05

There still remains therefore, unexpended, the sum of five hundred and seventeen dollars and ninety-five cents ($517.95) at the disposal of the committee for additional purchases.

In 1850, the total number of volumes then in the library was four thousand five hundred and eighty (4,580.) There have since been added three thousand four hundred and sixty-eight (3,468) volumes.

The library, therefore, has been nearly doubled in number of volumes during the past nine years, and from the character of the works which have been added, the committee can safely say that it has been quadrupled in value and usefulness.

The committee cannot close their report without renewing the testimony they have frequently had occasion to bear, to the sustained zeal, energy and matured experience with which the library has been conducted during the past year by the librarian, Mr. Ezekiel A. Harris ; to his uniform courtesy to visitors and members, and his activity in having our very valuable collection of pamphlets arranged and suitably bound and indexed ; in conducting a correspondence with agricultural societies in all the States, and procuring exchanges ; and in caring for the preservation and good order of our large and growing collection.

WILLIAM HIBBARD,
D. MEREDITH REESE,
WILLIAM LAWTON,
DAVID R. JAQUES,
WILLIAM H. BROWNE,
WILLIAM B. LEONARD,
Library Committee.

NEW YORK, *Feb.* 3, 1859.

OPENING ADDRESS

AT THE THIRTIETH ANNUAL FAIR OF THE AMERICAN INSTITUTE,
SEPTEMBER 21, 1858.

By the Hon. HENRY MEIGS, *Recording Secretary.*

LADIES AND GENTLEMEN—I am performing a duty more agreeable to me than all others of the whole year; I have the honor to open to you our halls and dome, containing a feast of reason—one which gratifies every good taste, satisfies every sound judgment, pleases our patriotism, strengthens and enlightens it, gives *solids* to our use and enjoyment, and adds the finished *graces* of fine arts. When another does a great or a good deed every one admires it, when our own beloved child does it the admiration is thrice exalted, and the joy is felt at the heart.

Here, then, are some of us, old American fathers—I the oldest of all—showing you, in a real palace, equal to one of Aladdin's, our bright progeny, the children of our new nation—lovely and civilized—the first ever seen on the Americas since the deluge, all (nearly) born and grown in my time! No ancient genius here before us like that of the old world, from century to century slowly adding invention to discovery in every line of knowledge of art, no Egyptian, or Greek, or Roman to lead the way! Here, where the tameless fierce Indian had left the ground untilled and forest untouched for ages, here behold the magic change, and on it the smiles of our Creator, of whom our forefather (our pious Æneas) said "*Qui transtulit sustinet*"—" He who transplanted us will sustain us." And let us never forget that for the mighty land He has saved for us that we should " till it and keep it," we are bound by immortal bonds to bow down before Him, thank Him every hour and exert every nerve and every thought to His glory, and thus keep ourselves before him worthy of his infinite maintaining power and blessing.

In the beginning of our labors here we suffered all the pioneer difficulties; all was rough, and must be hewn and made smooth, all was to feel for the first time the wonderful operations of labor and of art. A vast natural world was to be converted, by its only master, civilized man, into one adapted to his unlimited artificial works. All the powers of earth, air and sea have been enslaved to do his work, and he has yet but begun. He, like Rarey among wild horses, will tame steam 'til it shall fly with him more than a hundred miles an hour on land, and never hurt a hair of his head, and over all oceans and never scald a finger, and never let him sink. He will talk through tens of thousands of wires at Behring's straights with all mankind; he will, if he thinks best, clothe the world in silk; he will go through all the deserts of Africa and elsewhere with ice and cool cars; he will bring the spring waters by artesian wells from under the desert, irrigate with them the burning sands, and make them a garment of grain and fruit trees, and to "*blossom like the rose*." He will, in his crystal palaces of the frigid north, grow the fruits of the sunny south; he will make earth a garden, render climate itself an average of beauty, and use, and health to himself; he will unlearn all the savage that is in him, and supply its place with all the loveliness of Christian life, illustrated by all human art and knowledge. We feel assured of this, for history has taught us that the progress of christianity is constant from the day of Christ, and always in close chained connection with all civilization, all knowledge, all that is good in this world. Every pagan system must fall to pieces, being made as tools of clay, but our salvation here and forever is through Him.

Ladies and Gentlemen, we earnestly invite you to look carefully, thoroughly, into all the things displayed before you; if you will do that you will often find occasion to admire an article which at the first look seemed unworthy of a place in a palace; but that is a frequent mistake, and you will often say: "Well, indeed I did not see that, how curious it is." Each exhibitor here supposes (at least) that his article is worthy and is new. All that are admitted by the managers are new in some particular, and many in highly important points. All deserve attention. They are the annual harvest of the work and genius of our republic. That harvest which, of wheat only, has ever been the joy of the year to every human being, is here extended to all the good things of nature and of art. God has pleased to create every other living being with limits to the operation of its body and instinct, but man, born utterly helpless in body, has a mind, like the wonderful plates of the photographer, excessively suscepti-ble of impression, but so wonderfully superior to even that physical miracle, that millions of vivid images impressed upon it remain forever visible at pleasure, coming before him like the scenes in the stereoscope by a touch of the will. To him alone then of all living creatures progress belongs—everlasting progress to the right minded—for whom religion exists and immortality. Placed by his Maker upon the most lovely orb of our part of the heavens, an orb whose glorious appearance at a distance is enchant-ing, a globe smooth as a polished ball of ivery, colored by its green fields and its parti-colored oceans, some pale green, some dark green, some pale blue, others splendid ultramarine, some almost purple, some yellow and some white; with each of its poles clothed with pure white snow, it looks like the ivory globe painted in richest coloring, having white silver tips at either end, the inequalities of its surface being small as dust on a thirteen-inch globe, and its oceans no deeper than the thin coat of water which would remain for a minute upon the surface of the thirteen-inch globe after dipping it in water, and, as a whole, its gravity so overpowers its cohesion, that if its whole mass was granite it would be as plastic, under the immense forces which act upon it, as air itself, so that the figure it maintains is an oblate spheroid, with its polar and equatorial diameters differing about thirty miles, to which form its atmosphere and its oceans all maintain as perfectly as its granite, for actual experiment long ago settled the fact that our atmosphere has the same density all over the globe, and the great tidal wave influences the land as well as the oceans to some extent. Such a globe is ours, and a knowledge of that fact must prompt every right soul to obey the first law given to him at the creation of him, to till it, adorn it, "and have dominion over the fish of the sea, and over the fowl of the air, and over the cattle, and *over all the earth.*" Mark the power here conferred upon the creature whom the Creator made "after his image and after his likeness."

I love to recall often the duties and powers of man, and the first steps he took here, and his unquestionable destinies. The fact was revealed by Deity—he has thus far led us onward! and we become day by day more and more deeply indebted for the magnificent privileges he extends to us, and will more and more, if we can conduct ourselves so as to deserve it! And in one way, we here try, by combining the genius and labor of thousands, to increase all works of utility and beauty—so that ultimately an admired article, so precious that none but the rich can have it, may in the end, become common to all. *Such is the aim and end of the American Institute!* and in truth of many modern institutions for the restoration and increase of knowledge, (or as the celebrated Lord Bacon called it,) the instauration of knowledge.

The ancient fairs, some of which were maintained for several months, and were visited by several millions of people, were places of sale and exchange as well as view. The managers of this fair have restored that good old practice, so that buyers and sellers can add profit to pleasure in the palace.

We have learned, and practically, the power of union—for as the united strength of a thousand men lifts vast weights, so that of a thousand minds roll away the great stones which close the portals of the intellectual world. Some such openings made disclose an apparent miracle! From what small beginnings we have now witnessed the most wonderful fact which man ever had anything to do with! We have seen a giant's work in the deep fathomed line of lightening laid on the bed of the stormy Atlantic! What a grand line compared with Franklin's first *kite line, so timidly let up to a thunder cloud!* And both lines were the results of the working of American brains! Such is the will of God! to whom be all the glory.

Early in 1857, the project of this Ocean telegram was considered by the Mechanics' Club of the American Institute, and for practical purposes it was believed that *thousands of cables required for the use of the world,* would be laid in Behring's Straits, latitude 65° to 66°, where Asia and America have bold promontories, only fifty miles apart, with the Diomedes islands Ratmanoff, Kruzensten, and a rock about midway, from which islands at a moderate elevation, both continents are visible ; where the water is not more than two hundred feet deep ! with muddy bottom, and where an eternal current runs from south to north and no ice islands from the Northern sea can ever come. That we believe will be the great Telegram avenue of the world ! The Emperor of Russia is now examining it ; and any school boy can tell you, by the *rule of three*, how many more wires the world must have than we have along the avenues near this palace. Such was the judgment of the Mechanics' Club of the American Institute sixteen months ago, as you will see in the volume of our Transactions for 1857.

But the grand object of the Institute has been obtained—that object was to establish all the manufactures of importance at home—to begin with things of the first necessity and then go on to the last degree of excellence in them, and finally, to every work of art. We began to make nails, not those hob nails which England sneeringly said we could not and should not make—but cut nails, for driving and holding fast, ten times better and five times cheaper—the *cut nails of America !* And we began to make cotton goods ! and we have made more *useful cloths of cotton* than were ever made before, and at almost one-fourth the cost of the slazy stuffs we paid so dear for 60 years ago. We have commenced work in iron and steel, and we defy all the earth in the approaching iron and steel crops, soon to appear from the hands of our cyclops ! We have more ore, and more coal land than Britain has land ! We have copper in bars ready made in our mines—of hundreds of tons weight—our great trouble is to cut it up so that we can handle it ! When mankind have all worked up their coal and iron, we will supply them ! and as our folks often say, no mistake. And is all this idle boasting and selfishness ? No, my fellow citizens, the work is for universal good ! the better and cheaper the goods, so much the better for all men ! We can make a good shirt now for every human being ! Let our continent speak for herself—she can grow cotton ! India is trying, but can't do it—she has too much heat and drought together ! Africa is trying ! North America can grow it and will grow it, *and cover them all over with cotton,* of all the best kinds and at the least cost.

We can supply the world with machinery !—our forests as well as our mines back us for that ! We have been called, in my early days, a *wooden world !* and if any body has a notion to build a wooden Leviathan, we have American trees on our west coast which will make a keel which will square ten to twenty feet, and will make masts large enough for a ship ten times longer than the great ship. And we can copper her if she was too long to turn round in the British Channel ! Call this Yankee boasting ? My good friends, neither I nor you can boast loud enough of our position and our means ! for they are mighty.

We are of late years making great efforts to repair the desolation of millions of good acres caused by bad farming, and to increase the quantity, quality and variety of our crops. Hundreds of agricultural clubs and societies have come into existence very recently. Our farmers are learning agricultural wisdom by meeting and interchanging their opinions and their facts. They are unlearning many poor practices and learning good ones ! The power of co-operation is at work to revolutionize an impoverished tillage. It is no longer a disgrace to till the soil—no more clodhoppers or villeins ! but honorable farmers and gardeners, saluted by all the great and good with hearty sincere greetings, in city and in country. The proper station of the farmer is being established between the rich and the poor !—the grand medium from which all power emanates—the happy conservatory of all our real blessings—health of body and of mind, all new, useful and beautiful productions,—and with them lessons of wisdom in the great art of tilling and keeping the earth—and always that pureness of religion which unites with the purity of the air the farmer breathes ! and that content which towns and cities know but little of.

Intelligent farming, unlike any other work of man, never tires and can never wholly fail. If he is on a poor soil he enriches it and keeps it rich, whereas every other business destroys that on which it lives. The workers in wood kill forests, miners dig out the last bushel of ore, never again to grow, while just farming finds a world poor, and after thousands of years leaves it far richer than he found it. Such is the remunerating power of the grand art of cultivation, man's true occupation and enjoyment; to which the heart of every true man turns from every other employment and pursuit—from royalty, from trade, from all manner of manufactures, from every species of business, to the farm and garden at last—and I repeat the remark of Theophrastus, of Athens, who lived 100 years, 2,200 years ago, '' *That a man tires of everything but a garden and farm.*''

And while the great body of our people thus enjoy the fruits of industry in the fields, another large mass of people whose labor there is not needed, turn all their energies of soul and body to the arts, constantly striving to excel all that ever has been done before. And what a theme for congratulation the improvements are ? Hardly anything made by hands is without some improvement, not even iron and steel, which have employed the genius, the good fortune and the never ceasing work of men, and at this moment more the subjects of study and experiment than they ever were before. How to make pure tough iron perfectly homogeneous, so that every square inch of boiler plates (for example) shall be of equal strength, thus insuring safety under a known pressure of steam ; or chain cables, every link of which shall be perfect in texture and in welding, so that the great ship may depend upon its holding her firmly through the tempest; these are great objects of human science and care. Can anything interest us all, more than safety on railroads and oceans ? There are human diseases which have defied all the powers of medicine, until they are called the *opprobriums of medicine*, like consumption and some others. There are also *opprobriums of mechanics*, of which the iron and management of steam is the greatest. The blood of thousands of innocents, old and young, cries for amendment. Let us not rest until we have so amended all this terribly disgraceful fault, that the world will come to America because her ships never burn, blow up or sink, and none but accidents such as all men and all law call " *Actus Dei*," acts of God, can occur. And while driven by an irresistible impulse to *go ahead*, let us for God's sake and his human beings, *look ahead!*

And, in the hurry of our multitudinous works, let us remember to do nothing to impair the health of our bodies and souls. Whatever wealth we make, whatever wonderful means we invest for bodily ease, flight or rest ; if we could travel by telegram and rest on summer clouds, we must, as men, have strong bodies, rendered so by due labor and temperance, religious strength, and, with all, long and happy lives. And whatever we print with lightning speed, no matter what it be, of science or of pleasure, let every one that can read a newspaper read his *Bible first, not as he does the newspaper, but as he does the book of his money and estate,* so that when he mixes in the maelstrom of human affairs he can no more forget his *Bible* than his *bank book, deeds and bonds.* I say this as an old man of some reading, especially in quest of religious truth. The world may grow dim with age, but that book is eternal light, and may it be yours forever.

Ladies and Gentlemen, you will join us in the wish that our people may, by their genius and power, always execute works worthy of palaces, and always have palaces to put them in.

PROCEEDINGS OF THE FARMERS' CLUB.

[ORGANIZED JUNE 22, 1843.]

The Farmers' Club of the American Institute is under the direction and control of the committee of agriculture.

The meetings are held on the first and third Mondays of each month, at 12 o'clock M., at the rooms of the Institute, in the Peter Cooper Institute, Eighth-street and Fourth avenue.

In consequence of the interest manifested in these meetings, they have been held weekly during the past winter and spring.

The meetings are free to the members of the Institute, and all other persons connected with the pursuit of agriculture, or who may desire through this medium to diffuse information on the subject of cultivation.

The Club will be happy to receive written communications at its meetings on the subject of agriculture, horticulture, the raising and improvement of stock, and chemistry applied to agriculture.

Rules and Regulations of the Farmers' Club, adopted by the Committee of Agriculture of the American Institute, April 4, 1859.

1. Any person may become a member of this Club, and take part in the debate by simply conforming to its rules.

2. Any member for disorderly conduct may be expelled by a vote of the majority.

3. The minutes of the Club, notices of meetings, &c., shall, as formerly, be under the control of the recording secretary.

4. The Club shall be called together from 12 M. to 2 P. M.

5. A chairman pro tem. shall be chosen at each meeting.

6. The first hour of the meeting may be devoted to miscellaneous subjects, as follows: papers or communications by the recording secretary, communications in writing, reports from special committees, subjects for subsequent debate proposed, desultory or incidental subjects considered.

7. The principal subject of debate shall be taken up at 1 o'clock (but may be introduced earlier by vote of the meeting), and continue until 2 o'clock unless a vote to adjourn prevail.

8. No person shall speak more than fifteen minutes on the principal subject unless by consent of the meeting.

9. All controversy or personalities must be avoided, and the subject before the meeting be strictly adhered to.

10. Questions pertinent to the subject of debate may be asked of each through the chairman, but answers must be brief, and not lead to debate.

11. The chairman may at any time call a person to order, and require him to discontinue his remarks.

May 8, 1858.

Present—Hon. R. S. Livingston, Solon Robinson, Hon. John D. Ward, of Jersey city; Adrian Bergen and Hon. John G. Bergen, of Gowanus, Long Island; the venerable Benjamin Pike, of Jersey; Wm. Silliman, of West Chester; Judge Doughty, of Jersey; Mr. Chilson, Mr. Stacey, Thos. W. Field, of Brooklyn; Mr. Fuller, of Williamsburgh; Prof. James J. Mapes, of Jersey; Mr. Paine, of Brooklyn; Mr. Baker, Mr. Hite, of Morrisania; Mr. Bruce, Wm. Lawton, of New Rochelle; R. G. Pardee and others—between 50 and 60 members.

Hon. Robert S. Livingston in the chair.   Henry Meigs, Secretary.

Mr. Pell read the following extracts:

VALUE OF OPIUM.

Opium is the production of a well-known plant called *Papaver somniferum*, or poppy, a native of Persia, but now found in every part of the known world. In India one hundred thousand acres of land is appropriated to its growth, giving constant employment to thousands of people. The seed is sown in November, and the juice collected in February. When the flower drops off an incision is made around the capsules in the evening, from which a milky sap exudes, and is hardened into a dark mass by the following day's sun; this constitutes crude opium. There are two localities for the cultivation of this drug in Bengal, subject to the East India Company. Another in the province of Malera is beyond their control, but passes through their territories to the market at Bombay, upon which they levy a tax of five millions of dollars. The income from this tax, together with the revenue received at Calcutta in 1846, amounted to the enormous sum of fifteen millions of dollars. In 1848 19,111 chests were sent from Bombay into China, and from Calcutta 36,000 chests, worth $550 per chest, or thirty-two millions of dollars; on this sum the Chinese pay an advance of many millions more in pure silver. It is well known that the British government in India have derived a revenue for the last six years of over eighty millions of dollars, and without this drug they could not sustain themselves. Four hundred millions of dollars have been paid by the Chinese within fifty years for opium alone.

VALUE OF TOBACCO.

Tobacco, next to salt, is now the product generally most consumed by man. It is grown in every climate, and all nations have adopted its use. The annual production is now not less than two millions one hundred thousand tons. It may strike you more forcibly when I state that all the flour consumed by the inhabitants of England, Scotland, Ireland and Wales only weighs five millions of tons, so that the annual crop of tobacco weighs as much as the wheat consumed by ten millions one hundred thousand Englishmen.

VALUE OF INSECTS—(COMMERCIALLY SPEAKING).

This is a matter we never think of, still it is one of immense importance. England pays a million of dollars annually for the dried bodies of the cochineal insect, and the same sum for lac, produced by an insect of India that punctures certain trees. The silkworm causes an annual circulation of two hundred and twenty millions of dollars ; the honey bee a million ; gall nuts, produced by an insect, a million ; cantharides, or Spanish fly, two hundred thousand dollars. The eggs of silk worms are a commercial commodity of considerable value ; twenty-three thousand five hundred eggs weigh precisely a quarter of an ounce ; the worm produced by one of these eggs lives fifty two days, and increases in weight ten thousand fold in thirty-one days, and during the last twenty-five days of its existence cannot be induced to eat anything. Seven hundred and forty pounds of leaves I found would yield seventy-one pounds of cocoons, producing, if they all yielded as the one measured, a thread thirty-seven millions four hundred and eighty-eight thousand feet long, or seven thousand one hundred miles. As there are one hundred thousand species of insects, and time will not permit us to discuss them all, we may as well stop here.

COMPARISON OF THE SEASON.

Wm. Lawton, New Rochelle : I have a daily record of the flowering and fruiting of the principal trees for 30 years past—the following is a memorandum for a few years past. It is remarkable to see how regularly and even the seasons come forth, and that the temperature is nearly the same ; the variation in seasons comes principally from the moisture of different years. The Mayduke cherry has one peculiarity—it brings forward a partially second crop, it ripening some two weeks after the first set. This cherry and the Black Eagle bloom at the same time, yet the Mayduke ripens two weeks the earliest, and it is a most valuable fruit. The tree is not so ornamental as some other kinds—the Black Tartarian and Black Eagle in particular are valuable for ornamental trees, independent of fruit. In regard to the seasons, as indicated by my cherry trees, the following is from my memorandum of the time of blooming : 1850, May 9 ; '51, May 8 ; '52, May 11 ; '55, 12 ; '56, 8 ; '58, 1. In 1854, May 7, the trees were in bloom when the weather came on so cold that asparagus froze solid. There was a great deal of rain in the last weeks of April. The variation in wet and dry seasons has more effect upon early spring vegetation than variations of heat and cold. Whether land is underdrained or not makes a great difference in the season of flowers and fruit—the soil that is well underdrained producing not only the most and best fruit, but it matures earlier.

NATURAL LAWS FOR FLOWERS AND FRUIT.

Thos. W. Field, Horticulturist, Brooklyn, gave the following points upon the subject under this head as follows : Some of the laws which govern the blossoming of fruit trees, are : 1. That flowers are fertile in proportion to the size of the fruit. Nearly all the flowers of plants producing small fruit of their kind are fertile or perfect in their sexual organs. Few of the flowers of plants producing large fruit of their kind are fertile or contain both sexual organs perfectly developed. The Duchesse d'Angouleme pear and Hovey's strawberries are examples. . 2. The flowers of highly developed fruits or those fruits which are nearly perfect in their kind, are the most imperfect in their blooms, and exhibit fewest fertile blooms. The rationale of these laws exhibit their infinite wisdom. If every blossom of a tree were fertile, there could be no large fruit, as the nutriment would be distributed to too large a number of fruits.

THE POTATO QUESTION.

Solon Robinson read a letter from Ghent, N. Y., which states that the writer, Cornelius J. Hogeboom, had twice tried the experiment of planting large and medium potatoes, with a result very decidedly in favor of the large tubers. He also tried very small ones. The yield of the crop from the large seed was one-eighth better than the medium size, and the medium one-fifth better than from the small ones, the product of the latter being like the seed in size, and few in the hill. He thinks with more care in selecting seed there would be less potato rot.

Thos. W. Field.—It is my opinion that much of the disease of potatoes comes from the unripe condition of the tubers when affected by sudden change in the weather. The great error in the discussion of the potatoe rot is the assumption of the position that rot is a specific disease; while rot is but the decomposition of the tuber after its death, and may be the result of many diseases. Thus, rot of the potato was in 1857, produced after eight or ten days of hot, rainy weather, during which a succulent growth was produced, which was so immature as to loose their leaves under the heat of the unclouded sun, and the unripened tubers rotted.

Mr. Lawton.—I cannot find from all accounts that I have read that there is any theory to account for the potato disease. It is an inscrutable disease, the course of which has not been discovered, and hence no remedy is applicable, and discussion of the question nearly useless. Who can tell what has blighted the sycamore all over the country? Perhaps it is owing to the winter, as was at first thought, but no one knows.

Mr. Meigs said that in every country where potatoes are grown, the rot has destroyed more or less of them in a field—*seldom the whole*—seldom all in the *same row*—but some everywhere, on every land, high or low, wet or dry. There being always *some excepted*, we must search out the cause of this. As in Asiatic cholera, like exceptions are by millions—so even in small pox some persons cannot be infected. Now God has given to man a powerful reason with which he investigates every question. After men were destroyed by millions by the *venereal disease*, it was suddenly cured by Paracelsus, about 300 years ago, to the amazement of all the learned faculty of that day. *He used mercury*, for the first time since creation.

Again, after centuries of terrible devastation of human life by *small pox*, and no cure or prevention, so from Constantinople Lady Mary Wortley Montague, wife of the British ambassador, became satisfied of the comparative safety of inoculation. She inoculated her son of six years old, who had but six pustules of it and soon recovered. It was then tried on criminals successfully. This was the *first step* since creation to destroy one of the most frightful of human maladies ! The *second step*, about sixty years ago, was by Jenner, who, from the milk maids of northern Italy, caught the knowledge that the light disease about the udder of the cow was a preventive, and gave it out to mankind. So that at this moment there are fifty millions of people living who would have died of small pox.

Therefore, I say, it is permitted to us to search out causes and cures, "Felix qui potuit exquirire causas rerum." Happy he who can search out the causes of things.

Solon Robinson.——The subject is one of such vast importance to the world that we may discuss it at every meeting, and may be laughed at for our pains; yet if our discussion should be the means of discovering a cause, or a cure for the disease, we could well afford to lay down at last, satisfied that we had at least done one good thing in our lives for the benefit of our race.

A. Bergen.——I do approve discussion upon all questions relating to agriculture, as it may develope something beneficial, not only relating to potatoes but fruits. Our old stock of Long Island cherry trees has failed, and we have not found out the cause, or a good substitute. A few years ago we could raise barley; now that has passed away, and we are obliged to substitute other crops. By talking with one another we may learn the cause.

Prof. Nash.——After all the discussion we know nothing about the potato disease, yet we may discover something. I am sure that if we plant early we are more likely, or at least, so far have been, to get good crops. Yet this may fail. Another point of a practical nature is this : that if we prepare our ground well, and feed it such ingredients as the crop needs, we are more sure to get a good crop than by the opposite course.

Mr. Field.——I am sure that I know that on wet soils, or on recently manured soil, potatoes do rot more than upon dry, manured land. So, if we have learned this fact, we may learn others by continual discussion of the question.

Mr. Lawton.——This theory will not held good, since I have failed upon dry soil, while in the same field, on very wet soil, my potatoes were entirely sound.

Prof. Nash.——The fact that the writer of that letter did plant large potatoes and get a greater yield, is unimportant, and it corresponds with the experience of most farmers. As to potatoes on wet or dry soil, I have known a crop good on swamp land and bad on the adjoining hills, the same year.

Mr. Field.——Lime on carbonaceous soil has the effect to make the vines less succulent and more hardy, and that may account for its prevention of rot on such soil.

RENOVATING WORN-OUT SOILS.

The hour for miscellaneous business having expired, the chairman called up the regular question of the day, and asked Solon Robinson to give his views upon the subject.

Solon Robinson.—The southern planters, particularly of cotton and tobacco, are the greatest destroyers of one of earth's best gifts to man, the power of reproduction and tenfold multiplication of all food-producing seeds that man may plant. They have rendered millions of acres, once fertile, so utterly unproductive that they have been abandoned as worthless and forsaken by the owners, and afterward, in changing owners, have been counted at a mere nominal value. Within ten years, the lands of some of the old Virginia plantations, within two days' easy water carriage of New York, have been, as it were, begging purchasers like a hawker's wares, at one to four dollars an acre ; lands, too, that were once considered garden-spots of America, the surroundings of palatial residences of princely owners. Rich acres of light sandy loam, worn down to such utter barren-ness that a whole acre, aye, a whole field, would not produce, as an old negro truly said to me once, "poverty grass enough to make dis chile's ole hen a nest." Yet that very field, so utterly barren, so cropped when newly cleared of its oak forest with tobacco, that it would no longer pay for crop-ping; then planted with Indian corn till Indian corn would not produce enough to pay the labor ; then sowed with rye until its largest crop of three bushels an acre often failed, and then given up to grow old field pines and poverty grass, the last effort of exhausted fertility to produce vegeta-tion. Yet such lands as these have been reclaimed. It was upon just such a field as this that the old negro stretched his hand over when he illustrated its former barrenness by the fact that he had tried in vain to gather grass enough to make a hen's nest. ·

"Now look at him !" said he, proudly. "See de clover and de wheat. Seventeen bushel to de acre, first time trying ; and de clover—oh, you see him ! A'nt he big? But I did tink my massa done gone crazy, sure, when he tell dis nigga dat he goin' sow wheat on dat field. I never 'spec to see the end again in dis world."

Faithless at the first, the old fellow was now exultantly jubilant to see the waving crop upon this abandoned old field—to see its remembered fer-tility, almost a hundred years before, again restored.

This pleasant scene was at the home of the Hon. Willoughby Newton, Westmoreland county, Virginia, one of the pioneers in the renovation of worn-out lands. Now, what Willoughby Newton and his compeers have done there may be done here, and there again, and everywhere where old fields abound that have been exhausted of their productiveness.

There has been no miracle wrought, no magic wand waved over the land ; no costly application, and there is no mystery in the process ; it is simply this : Sow 200 pounds of guano per acre, lightly plowed in, or well har-rowed in with the seed, one bushel of wheat and six to eight quarts of clover seed per acre. Thresh the wheat and return the straw to the soil, evenly spread on the surface, and let the clover grow until ripe the second year and then turn it under, having dressed it in the spring with a bushel of plaster per acre, and in the fall with thirty to fifty bushels per acre with powdered lime. This is a sure and cheap mode of restoring old barren fields to fertility.

Other lands equally barren have been made profitably productive by the use of green sand marl, and in both cases without cost, because every year the increased crops have paid the expense; and I now contend that all the worn out fields of all the old States—and their number is legion—may be all renovated and made productive at only the cost of interest of money upon the investment in fertilizers. No matter what the fertilizer may be, whether lime, plaster, ashes, potash, guano, marl, phosphates, muck or animal manures, so that the first application be used mainly for the purpose of growing a manurial crop on the land—something to be buried in the soil—something that will make it rich in a cheaper manner than can be possibly done with any substance that is to be brought upon the land either by an expense of money or labor.

We are apt to look upon the whole system of Southern agriculture, here at the North, as very much behind our own. But let me tell you that there are very many Southern planters from whom very many Northern farmers might learn some very profitable lessons. The system of renovating worn-out lands, as described, and the system of rotation practiced by some corn and wheat growers, where grass, hay and cattle were secondary objects, might be studied to advantage by some of us who are wise in our own opinion.

We might learn some lessons too in swamp-draining, since one of the most extensive drainers that I know of in the United States is to be found in South Carolina.

There is another subject of vital importance to all cultivators of hilly lands, and it is one that this club might discuss advantageously, upon which we can learn some valuable lessons from cotton planters in Georgia, Florida, Alabama and Mississippi, in each of which States I have seen large plantations, located upon extremely uneven surfaces, where every furrow was plowed level, and every row planted level, no matter where it begun and ended, so that the ends were on the same level, or how far the ends might be apart. By this plan the absurd folly of planting up and down the hill side is got rid of, and the washing away of the soil prevented. This would be an important adjunct to any plan adopted to renovate some worn-out fields once fertile, and now worthless, upon our hill-sides.

Prof. Nash.—The process of side-hill ditching is borrowed from the Belgians, and is one of great importance upon all light soils, but in New England there are millions of acres of land valuable for grass that are worthless for the plow, owing to the number of stones. The excellent remarks read are only applicable to arable lands. Now much of this New England pasture land is run out, as it is said, and no longer productive in grass. What can be done to renovate that? I hope at the next meeting some one will be ready to answer this question.

STRAWBERRIES.

R. G. Pardee.—The necessarily very brief notes of the sayings of the Farmers' Club, hardly convey a sufficient answer to the very proper inquiry, how strawberries can be cultivated for fifty cents a bushel. I have said this does not include the cost of gathering and selling, and in Western New York, where experiments have been largely tried, good land can be bought for $50 per acre, the interest of which is $3.50. I never purchased, but raised my own plants. I once stimulated a single plant of Burr's New Pine so as to produce me 1,400 good plants for sitting out in less than six-teen months. So, of course, no economical market raiser will expend large sums of money for plants, but raise them from a few pure plants. Again, I would select good land in suitable condition, and rich enough for corn and potatoes. I am opposed to all stimulating animal manures for the strawberry, or land over-enriched, as some portions of the gardens are, but I have always preferred land in the best possible condition for a crop. Then apply a moderate coating of unleached ashes, lime and salt, say three bushels of ashes, one of lime, and four or six quarts of salt, and, if need be, prepared muck or leaf mould or turf. See that the land selected is neither too wet nor too dry, neither too sandy nor too heavy, too high nor too low. Then plow, sub-soil and harrow thoroughly, and in favorable weather set out the plants twelve to sixteen inches apart in rows three feet, so as to let a horse cultivator pass between them. Keep them clean in the usual way, and of course they can be cultivated in this manner very nearly as cheap as corn and potatoes. Care must be taken to select a suitable location, and soil in the right condition, well prepared; then set out the plants in such condition and weather as not to be seriously checked in their growth from the transplanting; select the best varieties, and keep each one separated from all other runners; permit no plant nor runner to remain nearer than a foot to every other plant; always keep them clean, and not only uniform large crops may be expected, but superior fruit, and all at a cost of less than fifty cents per bushel for the mere cultivation, as my own and others' observation and experience abundantly attests. The difficulty is, so many do something as directed and neglect others, which prove equally fatal, while many are clogged with old ideas, habits and customs on this subject, from which they only break away one thing at a time. This will not do. If you mulch your bed with tan, the mulch will keep down the growth of weeds near the plant. I would let runners grow, and in the fall take a fine rake and pull up the weak plants of the runners. This is cheaper than any plan of cutting off the runners, and does not injure the plants. In setting plants, I would use the plants from the first end of the runners, because the roots are stronger than those at the little end of the vine. The Wilson strawberry has been so well tested for four years past that I should be willing to adopt it into field culture. The universal market berry here is the Crimson cone, which is in favor on account of its ability to bear transportation. The Wilson will, I think, bear transportation equally well.

Mr. Fuller, (horticulturist.)—I want everybody to try to raise seedling strawberries, currants and gooseberries. There is a chance at least to get one new sort. Last fall I put the seeds of all the pears I tasted at the fair into my pocket. What is the result? Why 500 seedlings from some of the best known sorts of pears. What if I get one new sort? So I have planted many other seeds; and I shall be perfectly satisfied if in all my experiments I obtain one new and good fruit, to leave as a bequest to the world, like this Wilson strawberry.

The fruit and flower question will be discussed next week; also, Indian corn, in all that relates to its cultivation and use.

The Club, by unanimous vote, desired the weekly meeting to continue as long as so many citizens attend them. Two of the board of agriculture, viz., Messrs. Mapes and Lawton, assented to it.

The club then adjourned to Monday, May 10th, at noon.

H. MEIGS, *Secretary.*

_____

May 10, 1858.

Present—Messrs. President Pell, Solon Robinson, Thomas W. Field, of Brooklyn; Hon. John G. Bergen and Adrian Bergen, of Gowanus; Paine, of Brooklyn; Fuller, of Williamsburgh; Rev. Mr. White, of Staten Island; Wm. Lawton, of New Rochelle; Provoost, of Williamsburgh; Treadwell, Bruce, W. Silliman, of Westchester; Geo. Rapelye, Mr. Brett, of Brooklyn; Mr. Carman, Mr. Doughty, of Jersey; Mr. Chilson, Mr. Hite, of Morrisania; Mr. Van Wyck, Civil Engineer, Mr. Stacey and others—56 members in all.

President Pell in the chair. Henry Meigs, Secretary.

Benjamin Aycrigg, of New Jersey, one of our vice-presidents, submitted the following paper:

I understand that an opinion prevails to some extent that plants taken from the salt meadows will not do well on the dry ground.

Such was my own supposition when I saw them transferred from the Newark nursery to a light, dry, sandy soil in my own neighborhood. But finding them succeed better than those from other sources, I, last spring, procured 540 hedge plants and small trees from the same nursery. Out of the entire 540 set out, I have lost but four, or less than one per cent.

This result, that I suppose unusual, I attribute to several causes, viz: the plants have unusual masses of fibrous roots; these are all secured uninjured from the soft ground, that may almost be called mud. The plants were all in their places the same day that they were taken up. I put them down according to directions received at the nursery, and did not kill them with kindness.

Any one desiring to see these plants can do so in one hour from this place, and you know the direction.

Yours respectfully,

B. AYCRIGG.

The Secretary stated that it having been suggested by the Club, some months ago, that although the grape vines transferred from western Europe to the United States have not become acclimated, yet perhaps those from other grape countries might. The Hon. Charles F. Loosey, Consul-General of Austria, has imported for United States from Hungary eleven kinds o their best wine and table grape *vines*, well assorted and in growing order, to the number of 200. *Resolved*, That the thanks of this Club be given to him for this valuable contribution to the vineyards of our country.

Passed unanimously.

The vines were distributed to the members, to be forthwith planted.

Hon. John G. Bergen remarked on wheat crop, that some time ago there was read at this Club, by the Secretary, a translation made by him from French works, an account of better and larger crops of wheat being obtained by sowing several kinds of it together—better crop than from any one sort alone. Mr. Bergen suggested that such might be the result in planting various kinds of corn together. Accidentally this has occurred and with successful results.

Mr. Pell.—Corn cobs will show the mixture by the parti-colored grains on it. Still mixed corn gains on an acre some twelve bushels, and wheat ten.

The patent *Buckeye mower* of Aultman & Miller, manufactured by John P. Adriance of Worcester, Massachusetts, was exhibited to the Club.

Mr. Bancroft, of 43 McDougal street, presented for trial some bottles of his champagne cider, which pleased members by its fine quality, and because, unlike *our wines*, this was pure *American juice*.

The chairman then called up the subject of the day, viz.:

INDIAN CORN.

Solon Robinson—Farmers, are you ready ?—are you ready to plant the seed of this most important of all American crops, grass only excepted ?

If you are not ready, you have no time to lose. Now, to-day, is the time to think, and to get ready. In this latitude, the 20th of May has long been established as the right time for planting Indian corn, and it is generally thought that the less deviation from that period the better it will be for the product.

There is another period, and one of no little importance, homely as it may seem, for fixing the proper time for putting the seed in the ground. It is a day in the calendar of the aborigenes, which our pilgrim fathers found established among those original corn planters. In answer to the question, "What time in the spring do you plant corn ?" the answer was "When the leaves upon the oak trees are as large as the ears of the squirrels that sun themselves on the branches, then our squaws plant the seed that has been so carefully preserved in the smoke of our wigwams."

There is much truth in the old Indian rule, both in preserving the seed which was hung up in clusters of ears, by the braided husks, to the poles of the wigwam, and in the time of planting it—the time pointed out by nature, not the almanac, when the ground had become sufficiently warm to insure rapid vegetation.

We have known many New England farmers who rigidly adhered to the Indian rule, and watched the general appearance of the oak trees for the time to plant corn.

Experience has proved that the 20th of May, as a general rule, corresponds very well with the time of putting forth oak leaves " as large as a squirrel's ear," and then it is the fittest time for planting. That day is close at hand.

Now, farmers, are you ready? for upon this depends this great, this most valuable and important crop—a crop that Americans would need a long training to learn how to do without. A crop that would be less easily dispensed with than any other one known, because there are millions of human beings in these United States, who rely upon it as the staple of their existence. It is the source, too, of a very large proportion of our fat beef, mutton, pork, lard, and our fat roast turkeys, geese, ducks and other birds, and it enters very largely into the clothing of our bodies, heads and feet, since wool and hides come from corn ; and without that as food for the laborers, we do not see how a cotton crop would be grown, since the toiling slave thinks himself so poorly fed upon other food than corn bread and bacon, that he could not do his hard and hot field-work, if fed upon lean meat and wheat flour.

Indian corn then is the great American staple—the grand necessity of all American agriculture. The grand success in its production is, first of all, in the preparation of the seed, and the soil in which it is to be planted.

The great, the immense importance to all the people of this country of this crop warrants us in appealing most earnestly to every individual who will or can attempt to grow it, to make an effort this year to increase the product per acre, and in so doing lessen the expense of production.

It is our candid opinion that an annual increase of ten per cent. on the expense of growing Indian corn would add fifty per cent. on the average to the product of all the acres planted. Can farmers increase their profits so easily in any other way ?

There is no crop grown that varies so much in its general yield as this of Indian corn. We think that in all the southern States, excluding the alluvions, the average per acre will not equal ten bushels, while a crop of forty bushels upon some of the richest river bottom is considered a first rate one. It is not very surprising that the yield is so light. Look how it is planted—that is, in many, if not in most instances.

A negro man or woman, with a small mule and a shovel plow—three sticks of wood and a piece of iron—goes to the field and scratches two or three marks about two inches deep in the loose earth, in the place where the rows are to be, leaving the " middles " to be " broke out " after the corn is planted and has come up. This is a part of the cultivation or " tending the crop," and this, as well as all subsequent plowings, is done with the same implement—the shovel plow.

We have seen many fields that had been planted every year to corn since the forest was destroyed, that never had been planted four inches deep, and never had a shovel full of manure, and yet, with such slight scratching of the surface as we have alluded to, were expected still to produce a crop of grain that requires a deeply-worked, rich soil. It is no wonder that such fields do not produce ten bushels to the acre, and it is not a subject for question that they might be made to yield fifty. Not, however, by planting, as their owners frequentry do, one stalk in a place, three to five feet apart.

That there is no necessity for such miserable crops, even upon the light, pine-wood lands of the south, has been fully proved over and often. Even last season, Charles A. Peabody, of Columbus, Ga., raised upon the light land on the opposite side of the river, in Alabama, an average of over 120 bushels per acre, on a field of some twenty acres; and it is stated in the southern papers as a fact, that over 200 bushels were grown last year upon one acre in South Carolina. We hope the statement is authentic, and if so it will set off against a great many other acres in that State that do not yield three bushels per acre.

At the west, upon all the boasted corn lands of the great corn-growing States of Ohio, Michigan, Indiana, Illinois, Wisconsin, Iowa, Missouri, and Kentucky, we do not believe the average yield of all the acres planted is thirty bushels, although well authenticated crops of ten acres each in the last named State have averaged over one hundred and fifty bushels per acre, and crops of one hundred bushels are not unusual in all those States. Still, it is a fact well known to us, that a crop grown upon the richest prairie soil, that yields from forty to sixty bushels per acre, is accounted first rate and fully satisfactory to the producer. We also know that in many instances these crops could have been doubled, without any other expense than plowing the ground four inches deeper. This has been proved, and can be again.

"What fools not to use a better plow and stronger team! I wish I could double my crop; I guess I would, in short order."

This expression comes from nearer home. It is, in spirit, the cry of all New England, New York and New Jersey corn growers—victims of blind prejudice and false education in farming. Scarcely one of them but could, if he would, get as well as wish, double his production, as easily as his brother of the south or west.

"How can we do it?" The question comes to us upon every breeze, and so to the winds we give the answer. Perchance it will be wafted back to the eye or ear of the questioner.

You must abandon the absurd notions of your ancestors, who plowed shallow and hoed deep. The system is not much better than the one so common at the south, of scratching where the rows are to be planted, and plowing the "middles" afterward, if such work is worthy of the name of plowing.

It is no bare assertion that most of the corn fields of all the eastern States might be made to double their yield by the use of a plow that would reverse the surface ten inches, bringing the lower five to the top, and leaving them loose and friable, and then following in the same furrows with a subsoil lifter that would loosen the compact earth eight or ten inches deeper, to say nothing of the advantage of turning under a strong grass or clover sod to decay and furnish food for the grain at the very time when it was most needed. All this is independent of manures, either from the farmyard, or sea side, or muck beds, or city streets, or from Peru, or any of the manufactories of artificial fertilizers, and is within the reach of all corn planters who may be unable to procure the other means of fertility and increase of the crop, without some of which it is now useless to attempt to grow Indian corn in all the eastern States.

We lay it down as the first rule for all corn growers, whether manure is to be used or not, that, at least in all the old States, no crop of Indian corn can be profitably grown upon land that has not been underdrained or subsoil plowed, and that is not plowed at least eight inches deep for each crop, and most thoroughly pulverized before the seed is put in the ground. This is of much more importance than the after working, particularly where the after labor of culture is, according to time-honored notions in New England, devoted to hilling the earth with a hoe up around the growing stalks. The same practice has been carried by emigrants to the west, but is there fast giving way as it is slowly at the east, to cultivation by the plow, cultivator, or horsehoe.

No specific directions can be given for planting that will fit all localities where we hope these hints will be read ; but, as a general rule, half the labor of after culture will be saved by proper preparation of the ground before planting. One of the best implements ever used for marking out the rows is a subsoil lifter. We have seen an ordinary plow coulter, eighteen inches long, fastened to a beam with handles, and used for marking the rows with decided benefit, as it made a temporary drain for the young plants, which every farmer knows cannot bear any excess of water, even for a few hours, in a hot sun, without serious injury to all the aftergrowth of stalk and production of grain.

It would greatly surprise some of the old corn planters of the eastern States, to see what crops are sometimes grown at the west, in fields where a hoe never was used.

It would be equally surprising to know how small a price per bushel it costs to grow corn in some rich virgin soils. The Hon. Henry L. Ellsworth, of Lafayette, Indiana, has had three thousand acres of corn in a season, grown for five cents a bushel. That is, he contracted with parties to plow, plant, till and grow the crop ready for harvesting for three dollars an acre, and the yield gave sixty bushels per acre.

" Five cents a bushel !" exclaims one of a host of corn growers. "If I believed that story I never would plant another acre of corn in this State, where every bushel costs fifty cents, and sometimes a dollar, if we count our labor at anything like what it is worth."

True, and yet we really believe that corn growing can be made as profitable here as there, even should it cost fifty cents a bushel, which it need not. Numerous experiments have fully proved that it can be grown for less. We have now before us an article printed in *The Homestead* (Hartford, Conn.), which give us detailed accounts of the cost and profit of growing Indian corn in that State, which is sometimes said to be so worn out that it will not grow corn with any profit to the planter, and hence it is pining to emigrate to the rich corn lands of Indiana, Illinois, Iowa, or Kansas.

Here is an extract from that article, which we commend to the attention of all our corn-planting readers:

"Before we put in our corn for this season, let us look at the methods used to secure some of the premium crops of last season. Nathan Hart, Jr., of West Cornwall, raised the largest corn crop reported to the State Agricultural Society last year. The soil was a rich friable loam, which had been in grass for the last forty years, and had received no manure except the droppings of the cattle. It had probably been pretty well manured in this way; hay had probably been foddered upon it. Twenty-four ox cart loads of manure from the barn cellar were applied to this crop (half cord we presume). The land was plowed seven inches deep on the 9th and 11th of May. The seed was of the Dutton variety. It was soaked for thirty-six hours in a warm solution of saltpetre, and rolled in plaster and planted May 23, four kernels in a hill, the hills from two to two and a half feet apart in the rows, and the rows three feet apart. It was hoed three times by hand, after the horse-hoe, at intervals of eight days, commencing June 13.

"The crop was cut up by the roots during the week commencing September 17, and husked the first week in November. The yield was ninety-eight bushels, one peck, six quarts; estimated value of crop, including stalks and pumpkins, ... $103 43
Cost of raising, ... 37 50

Balance profit of the crop, ... $65 90

"Wm. H. Putnam, of Brooklyn, stands next on the list of competitors. The soil was a wet, black loam, with a heavy, compact subsoil, which had been three years previous in grass, with no manure. Sixteen full loads of stable manure from under cover were plowed in, and ten loads of compost, made from fermented stable and hog manure, well mixed with rather poor summer-made yard manure, was put in the hill. His land is plowed eight inches deep; and if it is cold and wet, suitable manure is applied in the hill and the corn dropped upon it. The land is furrowed three feet, and the corn dropped two and one-half feet apart in the furrow. Plaster is dropped upon the corn. It undergoes no preparation. At least six quarts of seed are used to the acre—variety, the Rhode Island premium, planted May 27. The corn is cultivated and hoed twice, and thinned to four spears in the hill. The corn is cut up by the roots, and stacked. The yield was

95¼ bushels to the acre, and the value of the crop put at........ $96 40
Cost of cultivation 26 50

Balance of profit...................................... $69 90

"James A. Bill, of Lyme, took the third premium. His soil is a gravelly loam, cultivated the two previous years in corn, and the third year previous in grass. Forty loads of barn-yard manure were plowed in deep for each crop of corn, and a dressing of 150 bushels of ashes the first year for corn. No manure was applied to the land when in grass. Forty loads of manure were used the present year. The land was plowed June 1st, and planted June 5th, with Dutton corn three and one-half feet apart each way. Six quarts of seed were used, after soaking until nearly ready to sprout, and planted June 5th. Ten days after planting, it was hoed; again the last of June; and the third time about the middle of July. The land is perfectly flat, no hills being made. The crop was cut Sept. 30, and the yield was eighty-nine bushels.

Whole value of crop... $95 50
Cost of cultivation 9 50

Balance of profit, ... $85 00

The value of the manure is not estimated, which would take off at least $20 from the profit, leaving it about the same as the other premium crops. It will be noticed that Mr. Bill plants very late, June 5th. This is his practice every year. He plants, also, six inches further apart one way, and a foot further apart the other. With a smaller variety of corn, and closer planting, we think this acre would have taken the first premium."

Now, these crops were grown in as unfavorable a season as we have had in many years, in a State not marked upon our country's map as one of the corn-growing States, and not, so far as we can see, with a very extraordinary amount of labor, and yet with a very handsome profit upon that labor, and leaving the soil in better condition than it was before.

In conclusion, we adopt for all the Eastern States, and make them our own, the concluding words of *The Homestead*, because they are truth, and that is immutable, and as such we earnestly commend them, and all that we have said; because now is the time to lay your plans for the crop of this year to get a good one.

The hints that we gain from these premium crops, that ought to affect our practice this season, are briefly these: For selection of land, where this is practicable, take a rich, strong loam, with a heavy turf, the older the better. Plow not less than eight inches deep, and deeper, if it does not bring up more than an inch of the subsoil. Put on at least forty loads of manure to the acre, and more if you have it, reserving a part for the hill, unless you use some other concentrated fertilizer. Make the surface soil as loose and mellow as possible before you plant. Use the smaller varieties of corn, like the Rhode Island Premium, or the Canada Bush or yellow, and plant three feet by two and a half apart, four stalks in a hill. Plant as late as the last week in May or the first week in June, and hoe four times—making the cultivator or horse-hoe do as much of the work as possible. With straight rows, and a practiced hand to hold the cultivator, it leaves a precious little work for the hoes. Cut the corn about the middle of September by the roots, and shock it. There is more corn, and the fodder is better. This process will give us corn at 50 cents a bushel or less.

Upon the virgin soil of the prairies, or upon the bottom lands of some of the western rivers, men will not, of course, follow these directions, because they can get a large acreable yield with less labor, and some of them have been so long in the practice of raising corn in the slovenly, careless manner they do, that it is as useless to ask them to improve as it is to ask a New England farmer who never grew 40 bushels of corn upon an acre, to believe that his neighbor has grown it. Both east and west, and north and south, the process will still work on in the old way, notwithstanding all the facts spread before them; yet we will hope that one or two may be induced to resolve upon improvement.

Mr. Treadwell exhibited 120 dark leaden colored worms of a little over one inch long, which he took from ten hills of corn destroyed by them in his garden. He asked for a remedy.

President Pell put on a reasonable dose of salt and lime.

Mr. Treadwell procured some, which being sprinkled well over the worms being in mass in a small glass tumbler, all died in about 12 to 15 minutes.

Mr. Pell desired to say that after all the signs given for the time of corn planting, he had long practised the planting on the first day of June, and always found his crop the better for it.

Mr. Fuller said that the best way was to plant *by the weather* rather than the day of the month.

J. G. Bergen.—The most certain method of all is to plow deep and well, manure well, cultivate thoroughly, and you shall have a good crop in any summer you may find. But when the land is merely skimmed, as a great many farmers do it, let them *as they do*, always lay the blame on the season. I get sixty bushels on an acre and some profit, but I can make more by other crops. Land is too dear with us to leave profit.

Mr. Meigs.—But sir, you must not count the land, for if that where we are—which is worth a great price—bore corn, the corn might be 100 bushels per acre, and really a highly profitable crop, and leave the land just as valuable as before.

T. W. Field said that his friend Mr. Bergen raised crops more profitable than most men.

Adrian Bergen.—The corn fodder is fed to horses who have got the heaves by eating hay, and the fodder cures them. My observation about soaking corn is that early planted corn if soaked, is apt to rot. The strife of neighbors trying to beat each other in planting corn, has been injurious to the production. As a general rule, the earliest planted is not the best, and I am not quite satisfied about soaking corn before planting.

Mr. Fuller, horticulturist, Brooklyn.—I find that all well prepared soil is much earlier than soil that lies compact and hard. Manuring warms it and brings forward the crop.

A. Bergen, a Long Island farmer.—Prepare your land well, and you can depend upon a corn crop in all seasons. Farmers fail because they do not plow, dress and prepare the soil well.

John G. Bergen.—I can grow sixty bushels per acre, but I can grow other crops to greater profit, because I grow market garden vegetables.

T. W. Field.—I believe that upon an average the Indian corn crop is the most profitable of any—even more so than carrots. Every one cannot grow carrots, but every one can grow corn. After all, it is adaptation of crops to location. I believe that everywhere Indian corn growing may be made profitable. Here the stalks are very valuable, while at the west nearly worthless.

A. Bergen.—I find corn-stalks valuable for feeding horses; they cured mine of heaves.

Mr. Ambler of Harlem.—I came here to learn how to plant corn, as I have a little farm in Connecticut, where we think the fodder of an acre of corn worth as much as an acre of grass. By deep plowing I reclaimed a very badly cultivated piece of land that had been for many years planted in buckwheat or rye, without manure, and with but little rest and but little product. I planted a portion to corn, after plowing seven inches deep, which was considered very deep plowing in that locality. I applied no manure, and at first the corn looked miserable, until about the first of July, when it began to grow, and it proved to be the best crop in the town of Bethel. Next year I sowed oats and got a good crop, and sowed clover and had an excellent crop of clover—the whole attributable to deep plowing—that is, deeper than it had ever been plowed before. I am satisfied that we can make corn growing in Connecticut more profitable than in Illinois, simply by increasing the depth of the soil with the plow.

Mr. White, of Staten Island.—I plowed an acre of land never before cultivated to corn, and used very little manure, but plowed deeper than it had been before, and got the best crop in the neighborhood.

T. W. Field.—Some of the Long Island farmers say that they have grown 128 to 130 bushels of corn per acre, planted 4 feet 8 inches apart.

Mr. Fuller.—I have traveled Illinois pretty well, and I have never seen 100 bushels per acre. I have been told that a corn crop near St. Louis was worth only fifteen cents a bushel, and fifty bushels per acre there is a full yield.

T. W. Field.—The largest corn crops have generally been grown in districts of poor soil. In Central New York, 70 bushels is a full crop. In Connecticut, on the Thames river, I saw a crop of 14 acres that measured over 1,400 bushels. It had formerly been manured with bones very largely, some twenty years previous.

John G. Bergen.—In regard to large corn crops, I have heard much of them at the west, but I never saw better crops in Ohio than upon Long Island. I grew one acre that gave a little over 100 bushels per acre. I try to plow as deep as I can, but deep plowing is not best for all lands, under all circumstances. In one place in Pennsylvania I noticed that the land for corn was plowed shallow, and that deep plowing did not produce the best crops.

The President.—Lands differ, and sometimes deep plowing may reach gravel and injure the soil. Although I have injured some soil by too deep plowing, say twenty-two inches deep, yet I have improved a hundred acres where I ever injured one acre. Roots penetrate just as deep as the soil is aerated. All cereals require phosphate of lime, potash and soda. If these be removed by long cropping, the soil will not produce good crops. By deep plowing a new supply is obtained, just as it was upon ground described by Mr. Ambler, that only grew five finger vines. Do not consider a soil worn out until you have proved it so, not only that the surface is exhausted, but all below that within reach of the plow.

HOW TO KILL WORMS.

A gentleman showed about half a wine glass full of worms, of a reddish brown color, as large as the coarsest knitting-kneedle, and about three-quarters of an inch long, and very hard, with many legs and a voracious disposition to eat vegetables. They are so prevalent in some gardens in Brooklyn that a dozen or twenty are often found under one hill of corn. He said, "What shall I do?"

Solon Robinson.—Salt them with a mixture of salt and lime.

Upon this hint the secretary sprinkled a little upon those exhibited, and in two minutes every one was dead.

HUNGARIAN GRAPE VINES.

A lot of grape vines from Hungary, imported and presented to the Institute by Mr. Chas. F. Loosey, Consul-General of Austria, was distributed; and a parcel of Kansas melon seed, presented by Thaddeus Hyatt, on account of the very superior quality of the melon, were given to such persons as chose to try to grow them.

Several subjects before the club to-day were not reached for want of time, will be discussed next Monday.

Subjects for the next meeting—By Solon Robinson, "Indian Corn;" by R. G. Pardee, "Flowers" and "Small Fruits;" by Solon Robinson, "The most economical method of renovating worn-out land."

The club then adjourned to Monday next at noon.

H. MEIGS, *Secretary.*

May 17, 1858.

Present—Messrs. Robert L. Pell, Leonard Wray, of London; Solon Robinson, Provoost, Vine Dresser, of Williamsburgh; Fuller, Treadwell and Wm. Lawton, of New Rochelle; Paine, of Brooklyn; Doughty, of Jersey; Stacey, Chilson, Davoll, Butler, Van Vleck, Pardee, Leonard, Chambers and others—58 members.

President Pell in the chair. Henry Meigs, Secretary.

The Secretary read the following translations, made by him, from the latest Paris works received by the American Institute.

[Bulletin Mensuel, &c., Paris, February, 1858.]

OPENING ADDRESS OF VICE-PRESIDENT M. DROUYN DE L'HUYS.

" Buffon said, in 1764, 'We hardly make use of all the riches which Nature offers us; she gave us the horse, the ox, the sheep, and all other domestic animals, to serve, to feed and to clothe us, and still there are many other animals *in reserve* which can supply the want of them, which we have but to subject and make them supply our wants. Man does not know sufficiently what Nature has done and can do, but he rather loves to abuse what he does know.' Buffon appealed to the Directors of the Jardin des Plantes, in 1739, for the culture of useful plants, other than those medicinal plants to which it then was wholly confined. A hundred years ago nobody ever dreamed of any other use for that garden! Without abusing the garden, however, which was then called *le Jardin Royal des Plantes Medicinales*, for that was then the name of the Museum of Natural History, he desired that it should be consecrated to the theoretical and practical study of *all the vegetable* productions of nature.

" Without going back beyond historical times, the grape vine, which, next to the cereals, holds the greatest and most beautiful rank in our culture, came to France from Asia Minor with the *first Phocean emigrants*. After 700 years it was so little cultivated by the Gauls that Domitian flattered himself that he could destroy the whole of the vines! and 200 years since that the Emperor Probus was unable to acclimate more vines. But the net profit of the Roman conquests was the importation of new trees and plants, which, for 2,000 years, have given so much satisfaction to the wants and enjoyment of the western world. The last and happiest importation for us was the mulberry and silk worm from India, by the Emperor Justinian. Soon after the dark ages invaded the Roman world—profound night extended all over Europe.

" If (said Buffon) you want examples of the power of man over vegetable nature, you have only to compare our garden vegetables, flowers and fruits of the same species with those of fifty years ago. You can do it by means of the colored drawings of them commenced in the time of Gaston d'Orleans, and continued to this day. We then had two sorts of chicory and two of lettuce, both bad enough! now we have fifty sorts! excellent. Our nut and seed fruits are totally different from and superior to the old ones, which they resemble only in name!"

[Societe Imperiale et Centrale D'Horticulture. Paris, Mars, 1858. Napoleon III., Protecteur.]

NYMPHÆA GIGANTEA,

So named by Hooker, is a native of New Holland, was first discovered by Bidwell, in the northeast part of that immense island, in the district of Wide Bay.

In 1852 many English gardeners had obtained it, by the name of *Victoria Fitzroyana*, from seeds.

Van Houtte got it, and in 1854 it went into many gardens. It first flowered in Van Houtte's aquarium in 1854, yielding in succession a great number of its beautiful flowers. The native flower is a foot in diameter, and some have seen it eighteen inches in diameter. It belongs to the section established by Planchon, by the name of *Cyanea*, in which are arranged all the *blue* flowers known to this day.

ON WATERING TREES, &c.

Several members expressed their opinion that watering the roots of trees was not so good for them as sprinkling the leaves.

Mons. Janin said that the effect of the latter was better than watering deeply the soil at the bottom of a tree.

Instances of the injurious effect of the latter were given by members.

New works on agriculture and horticulture, and the Transactions of their societies, to the number of *seventy-six*, were announced as added to the library.

A SEED ASSORTING MACHINE.

By adequate revolution and current of air, seeds are readily assorted into three distinct lots. The good heavy seeds, next in density, and the third, the lightest seed.

The velocity of this machine is *necessarily uniform during the operation*. The best results are obtained by *thirty revolutions per minute*. The most weighty and dense seeds produce more and of *better quality*. Such seeds alone, being planted a few successive years, we shall have much better crops.

GRAPES OF ALGERIA.

At the last exhibition in the Crystal Palace, in 1856, wine from Algerian grapes was exhibited. It is there an entirely new culture. Our vines have been introduced there ; many varieties were exhibited. White and red wines, dessert liquors, dry wines, like the sherry, (Xeres) and Paxarete; some generous wines, rich in quality and perfume ; a most agreeable *Bouquet !* The Algerians want experience, but they will soon have the best wines. The judges preferred those from M. Michaud of La Senia, and M. Castelli of Birkadem. A still more recent article has been introduced into Algeria, viz : The Sorgho Sucre, of which they use the fodder for stock ; make excellent alcohol, next to that from grapes. Tobacco and mulberry, promise largely for the future. Opium of excellent quality is raised. The madder is rich in color. Orange trees are the richest fruit bearers of Algeria, and will soon produce great profits. The citrons and lemons are very fine.

SANDY HILL, GEORGIA, *April* 28, 1858.

To the Members of the American Institute and Farmers' Club:

I take some interest in your discussions, and would like very much to know what your opinions are in relation to peas and clover being injurious to fruit trees, and perhaps you will confer a favor to more than one by discussing the subject. My experience is that peas are rank poison to fruit trees, especially the pear, when grown amongst them; and an old farmer of four score or more, informs me that he has known more than one valuable orchard injured past recovery, by having a crop of red clover grown in it; and I think I have sustained some injury from the same cause.

The question in point with me is this: Which is it, what those crops draw from the earth or air that injures the trees; if from the earth, will cultivating about the trees remedy the evil; if from the air, what is the remedy?

A FARMER.

CLOVER AS A MANURE.

Instead of plowing your clover under for manure, burn it on the ground and plow the ashes under, and your crop will be increased ten or more percent. Who will try a piece and report result? A friend informed me that he plowed in a crop in the spring for corn, a part of which had been burned over, and the result was one-third more on the burned portion.

A FARMER.

PRESIDENT PELL ON THE PRODUCTION, HABITS, &c. OF FISH.

The President read a paper upon fish culture. He states that he is trying to grow the moss bunker for manure, and hopes for success in growing them, but thinks the use of this fish the cause of disease in the districts where used. As many as 6,000 moss bunkers have been taken in a seine at one haul upon our coast. Mr. Pell also has in his ponds the black bass of the Lakes—a fish that grows as large as shad. Another fish from the Lakes very much resembles the black bass, and flourishes in artificial water. Both do well, and are easily caught with a hook. The dace is a good fish for ponds, as he prefers still water. The rock bass is a common fish in Lake Champlain, and is much esteemed, and can be cultivated without difficulty. The muscalonge, from the Lakes, is an excellent fish, and appears well calculated for artificial water if pure. This fish grows large, and somewhat resembles the pickerel or pike of the lakes. Mr. Pell has the stickleback, the curious little fish that builds a nest something like a bird. Haddock he has tried, but failed of success, notwithstanding he salted the pond. The haddock is much inferior to the codfish, although frequently salted and sold as cod. He also gave accounts of experiments with several other varieties, and how to transport fish alive safely. Mr. Pell thinks it is possible to stock all the streams in the country with fish, and thereby increase the food of the people to a very great extent without any expense.

STRAWBERRIES.

Solon Robinson.—I have a letter from B. Bristol, Wallingford, Conn. He says:

"We have just finished setting a field of strawberries in drills thirty inches apart. I propose to cultivate them with a horse hoe the fore part of the season; the latter part, when the runners push out, with the hand hoe, and let them cover the ground. The cost of setting this plantation has been $15 an acre, exclusive of the manuring. Now, can this bed be made to produce more than one crop profitably—if so, what course is to be taken next season with it, when the crop is taken off? I should like to know what is the best mulching where tan bark is not to be had. We have used spoke shavings, but found them injurious to the soil?"

Mr. Pardee.—I think he may have three crops or more from his bed. Saw-dust is a good mulch, so is straw, and so is new cut fine grass, if not put on too thick. I should be afraid of salt hay. Plaster, I know, is injurious. Lime and ashes are valuable. In the fall, pull up the weak runners and cover the ground with straw. The second crop will be best. When the old vines get too thick, run a plow right through the old row, and leave the new plants that come from the runners, by which a strawberry bed may be kept in bearing many years.

Wm. Lawton, New Rochelle.—I have used salt hay freely, with great success. It makes a very nice, clean mulch, and I find the vines very productive when I have used salt marsh hay. It prevents runners from taking root, and where it is required to get new roots, the salt mulch must be removed.

POTATOES.

Solon Robinson read a letter from Joel Hitchcock, of Lawrence, St. Lawrence county, N. Y., declaring his belief that he had discovered a method by which he could avoid the disease producing the potato rot, and that in experiments continued six years he had greatly augmented the product, and raised the quality of the potatoes to a high standard of excellence, and made the vines so healthy that they bear seed-balls abundantly, while upon ground treated in the ordinary way, the potatoes were unripe and watery, the vines without seed-balls, the tubers affected with the disease, and only half the quantity from the other part of the field. In conclusion, he offered to send a bushel of the potatoes, which he believes are restored to healthiness, to be planted by members of the club, to see if they will produce healthy crops, and, if so, he will tell how to do it.

On motion of Mr. Robinson, it was

Resolved, That the secretary request Mr. Hitchcock to forward the potatoes by express, and that he distribute them as soon as received.

Solon Robinson also read from a letter, written by George H. Gale, of Exeter, N. H., the following remedy against the potato disease:

"You must select the soundest tubers and sprout them in due time by laying them on a sunny side of a bank, and cover them slightly with horse manure to sprout, and then put them carefully into sand or gravelly loam (new ground is the best) as soon as the ground will allow from the frost, to get them as far matured as possible before the critical period arrives; when that time comes and the leaves show much rust, cut the tops close to the ground to prevent any communication to the tuber."

From another letter, written by Dr. Hosea Fountain, of Yorktown, (no State named,) upon the subject of potato disease, Mr. Robinson made some extracts, showing the Doctor's opinion, that other vegetables are affected by the same cause that produces the rot in potatoes, as he had observed when the potato tops turned black, that cabbage, onions, rutabagas and carrots have been killed, and grapes and cherries affected by the same atmospheric influence. Potatoes raised from seed balls rotted just as bad as older sorts; and he thinks the disease always commences in the tops, and comes all of a sudden, and if severe enough to kill them at once, so as to stop the circulation, the tubers may escape, as they do when the diseased tops are mowed off. Unfermented manure produces late growth of vines, and this as well as wet ground and late planting, leaves the vines green and liable to the influence that kills the tops and rots the roots. As preventives, the Doctor recommends seed of hardy varieties, planted early on dry ground, hilling-up to shed rain, and sowing lime, sulphur and chlorine on the tops. Swamp muck used as manure has proved advantageous. After the top is struck with disease the only safe easy remedy appears to be in mowing the tops. The Doctor urges experiments based upon the theory that the disease is, like the cholera, an atmospheric one, and may be prevented by similar means—disinfecting the air, and plants when attacked, and guarding against disease producing causes.

The President.—There is no difficulty, at least I have found none, in raising potatoes free of disease, when the ground is properly prepared. I contend that to grow good potatoes, all land requires under-draining and plowing 20 inches deep, and then planted with cut seed, and the land limed, the potatoes will not rot. I am planting 500 bushels this year, and I shall be surprised to find ten rotten potatoes. I always rub off sprouts, but I plant those sprouts and got good tubers, and I believe if any man has the disease upon his farm it is his own fault.

INDIAN CORN.

Mr. Lawton read a letter from Mr. A. Granger, of this city, who says he reads the reports of the meetings with great pleasure, and writes some facts that he has learned about late planting corn. He said that a field cut off by worms was planted in Michigan, June 23, which produced the best crop in the neighborhood. Mr. Lawton said that intimately connected with this subject is the temperature of the weather. Here is a table extracted from records kept by Delatour in this city, which gives the aggregate average temperature of the first fifteen days of May, since 1849, which, being divided by fifteen, gives the average of the temperature of the same period in each year, which shows at a glance how one year compares with another:

TABLE *of average temperature of the first fifteen days in May.*

	1849.	1850.	1851.	1852.	1853.
Aggregate averages,	718	775	786	782	768
Average of fifteen days,	48	$51\frac{2}{3}$	$52\frac{1}{3}$	52	51

	1854.	1855.	1856.	1857.	1858.
Aggregate averages,	754	739	708	752	840
Average of fifteen days,	$50\frac{3}{3}$	$49\frac{3}{3}$	47	50	54

This shows an average of temperature for the first half of this May 2° above the average. This gives promise of great crops of fruit. The cherry trees are promising remarkable crops, and so are apple trees. Although we have had considerable wet weather, the rain has not fallen sufficient to injure anything.

SMALL FRUITS.

Mr. Lawton named the following cherry trees as valuable : May Duke, Black Eagle, Frazer's Black Tartarian, Plum-stone Morello, English Morello, the Napoleon Bigarreau. The Ox-heart is a good cherry, but not certain to produce. Bloodgood's Honey cherry is a good sort, and the tree very ornamental and grows very large. A cherry presented to me under the name of Musgrave is a good cherry. I have another, the Ellerslie cherry, that is very curious, as all the limbs grow in serpentine form. He denounced the old Morellos and Black Mazards as nuisances on any place. I advise every one to select such trees as they know succeed well in their neighborhood.

Mr. Pardee said that the " Early Purple Guigne" is the earliest known variety of cherries.

CRANBERRIES.

Solon Robinson.—I hold in my hand an interesting letter upon the subject of cranberries, which I will read ; it is as follows :

" BARNEGAT, OCEAN CO., N. J., *May* 8, 1858.

"*Dear Sir*—I notice in *The Tribune* at a late meeting of the Farmers' Club, that the subject of transplanting cranberries was brought up. Could you put me in a way to find out what the New England cranberry growers consider a good crop, natural growth and transplanted ?

" There are scores of acres in this vicinity that yield often over 100 bushels per acre from natural growth. Transplanting is here a new thing, and not been carried on long enough to know how successful it will prove. The heaviest yielding cranberry bog in this section is one in the woods some twenty miles from any habitation (except cabins), which is said to have yielded 300 bushels to the acre one season. In the vicinity of this bog are hundreds of acres of land which appears to be naturally such as at your meeting was described as the best adapted for transplanting. As this land is held at only a nominal price (from $1 to $3 per acre) it would doubtless pay to try transplanting there. At any rate it will be tried. It ought to pay better than New England land, for which, in addition to the higher price of land, heavy expenses sometimes have to be incurred to make it precisely like this is naturally. Our shore people here are nearly all seafaring men, but of late some few of them are turning their attention to the soil. Their experiments thus far prove that though our land may not be as good as in other sections, yet it will prove as profitable to till, especially as we are but a day's journey from both New York and Philadelphia markets.

" Have any of the members of your club ever experimented with the mud from salt water rivers, bays, &c. ?   A thorough going farmer, the most scientific one in this section, and who has farmed most of his life in the western States, after three or four years' fair trial with the mud from the bay, asserts that a load of it, after laying in the barn yard over winter, is superior to the same quantity of marl.   I have seen enough of it tried, prepared thus, to know that it is equal to marl.

" Do the Long Island members of your club make much use of shells (oysters, &c.) ?   Is it not their experience that burning shells is a waste ? The 'Indian shell fields' in this section are our best fields.   In former times the Indians from the Delaware would come here, and after catching and opening clams and oysters would string them around their necks to carry back with them ; the shells which they strewed around gradually crumbled, and the fields where they are are always far ahead of any lands around.   Shells crushed quite fine will last a lifetime, but if well burned they last only a season or two.

" Being anxious to obtain some facts in regard to transplanting cranberries, how they yield, &c., in other places, I ventured to trouble you with this letter.   EDWIN SALTER."

Mr. Robinson continued.—Now what a chance is here for any one disposed to make money out of labor upon land.   Let him go and buy a tract of this marshy ground and plant it with cranberry vines.   As to the yield of transplanted vines, Mr. Pardee states that one piece produced 30 bushels the first year of bearing, 100 bushels the second year, 200 bushels the third year ; and another gentleman reported here a short time since a crop of 400 bushels.   In regard to the use of mud and pulverized shells, I propose that we take that up as a question for discussion at the next meeting.

Mr. Pardee.—I want to have the Club continue to discuss the subject of small fruits and flowers.   Now there is the Cherry currant ; it is a large showy fruit, but is it any better than the Red grape or White grape currant? Except for making jelly, is this new variety an improvement?   It is very acid, and perhaps no better than the old sorts.   About raspberries, I have no doubt that all will yield double if protected in winter.   I think the Orange and Fastolffe are the best sorts.   The Allen raspberry appears to be hardy.   Houghton's seedling gooseberry never mildews, and therefore it is preferable to the imported sorts.   The country is flooded with seedlings of all sorts of fruits, that, however good, are rarely as good as old sorts, and frequently worse.   If I had but one cherry, I would choose the Old Black Tartarian.   The Mayduke is a good cherry, and ripens early, but as it is red a long time before ripe, it is apt to be eaten when very acid and really unfit to eat.   When it is fully ripe it remains but a very short time.   I should like to have the club devote one day particularly to flowers.

It was agreed that this question should take the lead at the next meeting in preference to the other subjects on hand.

The meeting was full to-day, as it has been every Monday of late, including the sex that loves flowers, and it is hoped they will be present, and find something interesting, at the next meeting.   It is an excellent place for people from the country to drop in and rest an hour or two in the middle of the day.   The hour is noon on Monday—the place 351 Broadway, up stairs.

Subjects for the meeting of May 24, proposed by Mr. Pardee, "Flowers." By Solon Robinson, "Sea mud and shells of salt water rivers, bays, &c., as fertilizers."   By Mr. Pardee, "Small fruits."

H. MEIGS, *Secretary.*

May 24, 1858.

Present—Messrs. President Pell, Paine, of Brooklyn; Dr. Edgar F. Peck, of Brooklyn; Thos. W. Field, Treadwell, A. S. Fuller, R. G. Pardee, Van Vleck, of Newark; Meeks, Prosser, James I. Mapes, Newark; Solon Robinson, Stacey, Capt. Geo. F. Barnard, Mr. Bruce, Mr. Chilton, Mr Leonard, Mr. Chambers, and many strangers; Wm. Lawton, of New Rochelle, Horticulturist—fifty-eight in all.

President Pell in the chair for a short time—who asks William Lawton to the chair.   Henry Meigs, Secretary.

The Secretary read the following transactions and extracts from works received by the American Institute, since the last meeting:

[Journal of the Society of Arts, London, with nearly 400 affiliated societies—published once a week.]

RELATIVE FOOD VALUE OF THE GRAIN OF INDIA.
(By J. Forbes Watson, M. D., of the Bombay Army.)

A question of vital interest to nations, and pre-eminently so to one like India, containing 176 million of people.   The *slightest enlargement of size of a grain, greatly increases their amount of food.*

It is a common and a great mistake to suppose that *rice feeds India*—as a general rule, it is the food of the richer classes.   Eggs, fish and meat are permitted to various classes, although contrary to the Brahminical vegetable doctrine.   The poor eat much cajanus (a bean), and other pulse.

Wheat is *par excellence* best, containing as it does almost the precise requisite balance between the nitrogenous or flesh-forming constituents, and the non-nitrogenous or heat-yielding and fat forming elements, and indeed wheat-flour may be taken as the standard by which to compare the relations between the nutritive components of other grain.   Wheat bread will support the system for a longer period than any other compound.   (Corn bread excepted.   H. Meigs.)

Liebig has taken wheat bread as a proper standard to guide us in the due admixture of ingredients constituting a suitable diet.

Agriculture has made more progress in India, than is supposed.   Rotation has been practiced there for ages, and their agricultural implements, although *rude looking*, are well adapted for tillage.

Wheat crops are prominent in Central India and to the north, and almost to the sea side in Guzerat.   The Indian wheat contains less water and more nutriment than the European wheat.   The Indian wheat is very hard, so as to prove detrimental to mill stones !   Barley is much used in Northern India, and is the chief food of many districts. That from Nepaul is very fine. It is richer than European barley. The millet feed great numbers of our population, more than all other cereals together. They are more nutritious than rice. At the head of them stands the *Bagra*, the great Indian millet. Their horses are fed chiefly on the Cicer-Arietinam, *a pea* called *Gram*, with hay. The bean called " *Soja-hispida*," is singular in having forty-six per cent of nitrogenous matter—nearly 12½ lbs. of oil or fat, 13 ounces of phosphorus, 1¼ ounce of sulphur, and nearly *half an ounce of iron !* It is the source of the well known "*Soy sauce.*" Another bean " Catjang tahoo," a Dolichos resembles the *Soja*. This is probably the one which being pressed for oil, leaves the Tanping, an oil cake, which is brought as a sort of *dry paste* to Shanghai, to the value, annually, of 2½ million pounds sterling, or $12,500,000. It is fed to pigs and buffaloes, and is also used for manure.

Journal De La Societe Imperiale et Centrale D'Horticulture. Paris, March, 1858. Napoleon 3d, Protecteur.]

MAGNOLIA-GRANDIFLORA, NORTH AMERICA—HOW TO RAISE THEM.

Have a young plant placed in very well prepared light soil. As it puts out branches near the surface in autumn, layer these for new trees, and the old root will produce new branches next season. This layering will succeed if done in February. As soon as the layers take root, cut them from the old tree and set them out. It is good to cover these young ones with straw in severe cold weather.

EFFECT OF CHANGE OF CLIMATE ON VEGETABLES, VIZ:

We have introduced (France) the cabbage from England, cauliflower from Cypress and from Egypt, horse-radish from China, skirret (water parsnip) from China, scorzonera from Spain, potato from America, eschalot from Palestine, a bean from India, melon from Bucharia, squash from Egypt and Arabia, not to mention a crowd of trees, shrubs and plants, annual or otherwise, which vegetate very well here. However, although they produce fruit here as large, or even larger than in their native lands, yet their fruits rarely possess the rich taste and aroma they have at home. Sometimes when taken from a cool climate to a much warmer one, they improve. For instance, the grape vines carried by the Dutch from Holland to the Cape of Good Hope, gained immense amelioration of quality, In Surinam, the greater part of our garden vegetables transferred there, vis: pears, beans, asparagus, are better than they are in Europe. Fruit not so at all.

EXHIBITION—CRYSTAL PALACE—CHAMP ELYSEES.

Calceolaria.—Duval, the younger, gardener of Prince Napoleon at Bellevue, has there a lot of *half woody* calceolarias in good growth. They are strong and full of flowers, red being the predominant color. He has golden yellow flowers.

Pelargonium.—Rousseau, gardener at Paris, has a fine collection. Rene Lottia, at Port Marly, has from the seed some with pure white, very regular form, and spotted with remarkable purple brown spots. The Pelargonium, Glory of Paris, is of abundant flowers, of a cherry red hot color, and the flowers large. Duval has raised some that have fine spots only, and are called *fine spot.*

New and beautiful petunias, vervains, of various and rich colors, splendid varieties of pensées, stock gillies, pæonies, rhododendrons, azaleas, kalmias—Mr. Briot has some from the seed, now 30 years old—Irises, roses, yellow and moss roses, new, very fine. Tulips again figure—double ones, the callinsia, viscaria, schizanthium, linus, grandiflorum and many others. The pyrethrum roseum, from Caucasus, and Indicum. One of them, Tom-pouce, (Tomb-Thumb,) a very small plant only 16 centimeters (7 inches and a fraction) high, flowers of a lively purple rose color. Orchids of great variety and beauty. Tree-fern arborescent, from New Holland, much admired. Bromelias, from Brazil, in fine condition. Gloxinias in many varieties, with fine lively colors, of soft effect, so that they *caress* the eye ! " Nuances adoucies caressent agréablement l'organ de la vision." Begonia magnifica, from New Granada, introduced in 1855. Bochmeria argentea, from Chicopas, in '57. Colea speciora, from Tabasco, '57, with many others. Fine Cinerarias, whose flowers resemble those painted on paper. The blues are from the deepest indigo to azure.

Rhodoleia Championi.—Hooker called it from Captain Champion, who first discovered it at Hong-Kong. In some points it resembles and rivals the Camellia ; soon flowers, each branch bearing six to eight rose colored flowers a little over three inches in diameter. Leaves evergreen and bright.

Begonia laciniata.—An ornamental plant in every acceptation of the word, by the rich spots on its leaves, and by the ample size and double coloring of its flowers.—Bengal.

Tithonia tagetiflora.—A very vigorous annual, growing over six feet high ; its flowers, of a very bright orange color, are beautiful, and it has a fine and ample foliage. It came originally (seed of it) from the vicinity of La Vera Crus, Mexico, by Thiery, a French traveler, in 1778. In 1821 it went to the London Horticultural Society.

Daniel Hutchings, of Redfield, presents a small model of a plan for holding cattle in their stalls by the neck, so that they stand or lie down easily without being troubled with halters or ropes.

Mr. Van Vleck, of Newark, presents gooseberry pickles, having spices with them, and thus yielding a catsup of high excellence, hardly surpassed by any of our sauces.

Miss Miller, of his family, presented the seed vessels of the common *buckhorn*, readily fashioned so as to resemble four-footed animals.

Another lady knew them better by their country title, *beau-catchers*, by reason of their triangular incurvated horns.

Mr. Paine, of Brooklyn, exhibited a fine cut section of the great seed vessel of a nelumbium, from China. It contains twenty-eight seeds, resembling in size and figure acorns without their cups, each seed in a cell, very hard. Mr. Paine observed that it was not easy to break one of them with a hammer. The great leaves of this water lilly fold up at night, and unfold at sunrise. The seed contains the leaves of a new plant, perfect, and of a beautiful green. Some fanciful myths are attached by the Orientalists to this noble lotus.

R. G. Pardee distributed among the members some seeds of the highly improved hollyhocks.

H. Meigs said that he had obtained some from London several years ago, which were of all tints from white to black (as called), many petaled,— out-rivalled dahlias, which were alternated with them. The varied splendor of the colors attracted great numbers of butterflies. It was their *third year* from seed.

R. G. Pardee, an amateur culturist of flowers and fruits, said : The first requisite in raising flowers is drainage. Every little garden needs an under-drain. The soil must be deeply tilled, and at least 25 per cent of the earth should be pulverized as fine as flour. For manure, never use anything but compost. In the city, families may get an excellent compost from the street. Such as the street sweepers usually gather is about half sand or loam and the balance droppings of live stock and other good fertilizing substances, containing woody fiber and some lime and free potash. People should strive to grow a few good plants rather than a variety, and there are many of the old sorts that are quite as good for ordinary cultivation as the newer ones. If a family have but a single plant, and that is well cultivated, and the selection good, it will always be very attractive, and generally give better satisfaction than a great variety. It would be hardly worth while for any private family to grow one-half of the two hundred sorts of Dahlias. Of roses, I have named a small variety with which I would be contented, out of the very large list given by florists ; and what we want of Dahlias is, one or more that is good, rather than a great assortment, for many of them are not worth cultivating in our common gardens. Chrysanthemums are a most excellent plant ; they are so hardy and easily propagated. Verbenas should have a place in all gardens, great or small, and you can get new varieties from seed of your own plants. Perhaps no plant in England at the present time is attracting more attention than the Hollyhock. The fine double ones are very beautiful. I hold in my hand a catalogue of over 900 flowers, yet I would not care to cultivate more than a dozen sorts. It is a little hard to keep sorts perfect. German Asters are very apt to produce single flowers from the seed. The only course is to watch the flowering, and pull up every one that shows a single flower. The same fact is applicable to many other sorts. None but the best Pinks and Carnations should be allowed to grow. Some of the Carnations have been dwarfed to get rid of the long stem. One of the best climbers is the Cobea Scandens. It grows rapid and the flowers are very fine. In planting flower seed, you will find great advantage in scalding some of them.

The rose seeds, for instance, need scalding very much. So the Globe Amaranth, though it does well soaked in milk; in fact milk is the best thing that I ever tried. The Canary-bird flower is a fast growing climber, and will festoon an arbor in a few weeks. The Morning Glory as a climber, must not be neglected. There are several new varieties, with beautiful variegated flowers. All the things that I have named in my little list will give satisfaction, and it will be a pretty fair guide to persons who desire to make up a selection, and really do not know what to order. Most of those who would be amateur florists in this city and vicinity, are limited in space, and consequently can select only a limited number. Many farmers could, and their wives and daughters generally would increase their stock, if they knew what to get. It is such that I hope to benefit by naming a few hardy varieties, that I know, by my own experience, will give satisfaction.

CHOICE LIST OF FLOWERS—By R. G. Pardee.

1. Roses—Souvenir de Malmaison, Giant de Battalles, Baron Provost, La Reine, Madam Lafay; Crested Moss, for its peculiarity; Adelaide Moss, Aimée Vibert, Madam Bosanquet, Solfatare, Augusta, and Queen of the Prairies. 2. Dahlias—such as Belle de Paris, Duchess of Wellington, Miss Vyse, Yellow Superb. 3. Tree-Peony? 4. Chrysanthemums, Dwarfs, and in variety. 5. Scarlet Geraneums—such as Defiance, &c., and Princess Alice Pink. 6. Salvia Splendens, Major, and other kinds. 7. Fuchsias, Verbenas, Petunias, Heliotropes, Lantanas, Veronicas, Tulips, Hyacinths, and other things in that class. 8. Holyhocks. 9. Annual and Hardy Phloxes. 10. Of the annuals select the best German Asters, Ten Weeks Stock Gillias, Double Balsams, Pansies, Verbenas, Petunias, Pinks and Carnations, Portulaccas, &c. 11. For climbing annuals—Cobea Scandens, Scarlet Cypress Vine, Canary-bird Flowers, and the best Iponicas, or greatly improved variety of the Morning Glory. 12. Early Hardy Plants—Wigelia Rosea and Amabilis, Forsythia Vivi déssima, Dielytra Spectabilis, and Spirea Prunifolia.

Mr. Fuller, Horticulturist, of Brooklyn, read an interesting paper upon the flowers and flowering shrubs generally cultivated in this country. He says: I propose to name only the class of hardy plants. The most of those named by Mr. Pardee, are of the semi-tender kind, but the list is a good one. I name the following, and first the roses, that I should recommend, although some of them are very old sorts. Many of the roses called perpetual are not perpetual blossoms. They may bloom twice a year. I put the Queen of the Prairie at the head of the list of hardy roses. Of the many flowering shrubs, if I could have but a dozen, I would take those I have named in my list. I know of no new plant superior to the Judas tree, from Japan. The Magnolia Grandiflora does not succeed at New York; in the most sheltered situations the tree loses its leaves in winter.

So far as I have named the same flowers that Mr. Pardee has, it will only go to corroborate the value of those he has selected as an amateur, for I have been working among them as a gardener nearly all my life, and so far as I can facilitate the cultivation of flowering plants and shrubs by naming a good selection, I will gladly do so, as follows:

LIST OF HARDY SHRUBS AND PLANTS—By Mr. Fuller.

June Roses, blooming once, five varieties: Madame Plantier, pure white; La Belle African, very dark; General Foy, violet, spotted; Persian Yellow, deep yellow; Coupe de Hebe, pink.

Moss Roses, blooming once, five varieties: Alice Leroy, red or pink; Cristata, crested, very large, roseate; Laneii, bright red; Unique de Provence, white; Etna, flame color.

Perpetual Moss Roses, five varieties; General Drouet, violet red; Madam Edward Ory, carmine; Salet, bright rose; Herman Kegel, red, slightly striped.

Hybrid Perpetual Roses, ten varieties: Caroline de Sansal, pale incarnadine; Blanche Vibert, white; Giant of Battles, bright crimson; Prince Noir, very dark; Madam Trudeaux, bright carmine; Pius IX., large crimson; Crystal Palace, shaded, incarnadine; Baron Prevost, roseate; Sydonie, light pink; La Reine, very large, rosy lilac.

Climbing Roses, five varieties: Queen of the Prairies, deep pink; Baltimore Belle; Mountjoy, white border, pink center; Mrs. Hovey, pale blush; Perpetual pink, deep pink.

Shrubs, twelve sorts: Spiræa prunifolia, pleno, dbl. white; Spiræa Reversii, pleno dbl. white; Fortuni, red; Pyrus Japonica, red; Wiegela amablis, pink; Wiegela rosea, pink; Ribes Sanguinea, red flowering currant; Dentzia Grasselas, dwarf, white; Calycanthus lævigatus, sweet scented shrub; Curcis Japonica, Japan Judas tree; Philadelphius coronarius, mock orange; Magnolia gracilis, purple.

Herbaceous plants: Achillea Pleeno, double white; Champanula, double white; Campanula, double blue; Dielytra spectabilis; Dictamnus, white; Dictamnus, red.

Digitalis of varieties; Lupinus polypyllus, of varieties; Lychnis, double scarlet and white; Spiræa, double white and double red; Yucca filamentosa, flower white; Phlox, Roi Leopold striped.

Climbing plants for Arbors: Aristolochia sipha; Bignonia grandiflora; Bignonia sanguinea; Wistaria sinensis, blue; do do, white; Ampelopsis, tricolor; Lonicera, scarlet trumpet honeysuckle; do, chives, evergreen, blush; do, yellow monthly; Clematis flamula.

Peonies, Lilies, &c.: Pæonia Whitleyi, double white; Pæonia Pottsii, double crimson; Lilies—Lancifolium album, white crested; do punctatum, pink crested; do longiflorum, Chinese long white.

Wm. Lawton, of New Rochelle, said: Although the lists given might be largely extended, people may be very much benefited by selections from the plants named. He mentioned the althea, and also the Japan flower, as good additions to the list of hardy plants. Its golden yellow flowers come so early in the spring they are much admired, and if the shoots are

cut back the plants will bloom again late in the fall. Plants that can be
raised with the least care are the kinds that will be generally most admired
by that class who have not much time to devote to flower cultivation.

Mr. Fuller.—The best list of flowers and plants that I have seen in any
book, is one in a work upon the garden, lately published by Fowler &
Wells. It is highly important that persons, in sending for plants, should
give the botanical name.

USE OF LIME FOR TREES.

Solon Robinson read a letter from Wm. P. Gates, Windham, Conn.,
which, alluding to a former discussion before the club, inquires: "Why
use lime with ashes, since the analysis of ashes gives lime as one of the
component parts, and as minerals having progressed through plants are
considered more efficient and better adapted to the want of plants ?   Is
not the lime in ashes sufficiently large for the use of plants ?   One question further—Cannot apple trees in want of lime be supplied in sufficient
quantities by the application of unleached ashes ?   If they can, it would
seem to be the best application, inasmuch as you get other necessary ingredients at the same time."

Thos. W. Field.—The analysis of ashes given is one from pear wood ashes,
which a farmer can never get in the ashes he buys for manure, and hence
the advantage of adding lime.   There is a much larger amount of lime
needed on trees and their fruit than of potash, when used as a fertilizer.

Solon Robinson.—Of the use of lime for trees, I would say that the very
best application I ever saw for peach trees, both to give them vigor and
stop the borers, is half a bushel of lime placed around the crown of the
roots.

Prof. Mapes.—In New Jersey we get a good many ashes that are not
leached, and these contain lime that is far more valuable than that from
limestone.   The principal value of leached ashes is the phosphate of lime,
and that can be obtained from other sources much cheaper.   The potash of
ashes from a burnt haystack is more valuable than potash found in any
mineral that contains potash.   So are the ashes of any tree containing potash worth more than potash, lime or soda in a mineral condition.   The
higher the organism from which we derive plant food, the more valuable it is.   The blood of a man is of far more value than the blood of a
lower order of animals.   Now the top of Bunker Hill monument is composed of the ingredients that in a decomposed state would grow cabbage,
yet who would think of trying to grow a crop on the top of that monument ?
You must look at plants as the crystallization of the ingredients of which
they are composed.   Millions of dollars are wasted every year by pursuing
false theories.   Now, it is a fact that the ashes of a rose bush are worth a
hundred times more than the ashes of an oak tree to grow roses.   They
are all ready to assimilate into a new growth of rosewood.   Leaves and
grape-vine pieces laid about the roots of a grape-vine form its best fertilizer.
The potash of ashes from a fire that has been much burned, in an air-tight

stove, for instance, are far more valuable than the ashes of a log heap. The lime of shells is more valuable than that from rocks, for immediate effect, for the simple reason that it comes from organized life, and previous to that it had existed perhaps thousands of years in plants and other animal life.

Prof. Mapes continued his original and interesting theory by many other illustrations. The delicious perfume of flowers are due to the condition of their constituent parts; by crushing the flower it vanishes! The learned professor has long conceived this beautiful and just theory of the power of animal and vegetable life to receive their original constitutents and to render them progressively more and more perfect, until it is now proved by him to be true that *one pound weight* of the same (apparent substance— the same by the most profound chemical analysis) material which has existed in animal or vegetable for ages, and which has been a million times used by them, is worth more to the animal and vegetable than one thousand pounds weight of the original material! And this is due to forms which are assumed, and establish what I call the condition of the animal or plant.

The members manifested their gratification with the learned gentleman's explanation of his theory.

LUNAR INFLUENCE.

Solon Robinson.—I have a letter from Charles S. Weld, of Penobscot county, Me., who appeals to this club against the opinion of his neighbors, upon the subject of lunar influence. He says that he has thoroughly prepared his ground for sowing peas, May 15, but his neighbors declare that if he puts his seed in the ground before the moon changes he will grow nothing but vines and blossoms. They have tried it and know it, and that is the end of the argument.

The reading of this letter and the comments upon it created a great deal of merriment. Solon Robinson said he knew one man who would not, upon any account, lay the worm of a rail fence in the old of the moon, because he " had tried it and knew it," that it would rot down in half the time.

Thomas W. Field said that he could prove that planting near the sea shore in a certain time of the moon would produce a very serious effect upon the crop, because at the planting it would be the time of low water, and when the tide turned the seed would be submerged. He could not conceive of any other possible effect that the moon could have upon seed, and, in short, that all the belief in lunar influence was a sort of lunacy that the world had been afflicted with quite long enough.

In this opinion all present appeared to concur, and treated this belief in the moon's influence as more laughable than serious.

Subject for the next meeting, proposed by Solon Robinson, " The most economical method of renovating worn out lands."

By R. G. Pardee, " The small fruits."

By Solon Robinson, " The mud and shells of our salt water rivers and bays as manure."

The Club then adjourned to May 31.   H. MEIGS, *Secretary.*

May 31st, 1858.

Present—Messrs. Solon Robinson, Adrian Bergen, of Gowanus ; Hon. John G. Bergen, Wm. Silliman, of Westchester ; Hon. Hugh Maxwell, Prof. Nash, Mr. Hite, of Morrisania ; R. G. Pardee, T. W. Field, of Brooklyn ; Fuller, of Williamsburgh ; Treadwell, Stacey, Rev. Mr. White, of Staten Island ; Wm. Lawton, of New Rochelle ; Dr. Turnipseed, Charles Truell, J. W. Chambers, Mr. Disturnell, Judge Scoville, Mr. Bruce, Prof. Mapes, and others—63 members in all.

————, in the chair. Henry Meigs, Secretary.

The secretary read the following translations, &c., made by him from the works last received by the Institute, viz :

Revue Horticole. Paris, April, 1858.

THE TREES OF PARIS.

All innovation finds opponents, no matter what improvement may be offered, men differ so much in taste and mode of examination. If fifty persons are consulted, fifty different opinions will be obtained. But, however, there is a general judgment in a people which overrules those of individuals. We have no sort of difficulty in selecting a case. We refer to the decortication (barking) of trees of our public squares and promenades. Is it useful ? Does it remedy any evil ? After serious reflection, and in spite of the opinions of very distinguished men, we have no hesitation in pronouncing for the negative. If decortication is done at all, it must be very skillfully—to do good by it is an exception. It seldom helps a sickly tree, but on the contrary hastens its death. An examination of the two kingdoms, vegetable and animal, will explain this result. Vitality in animals is at the centre. In vegetables that centre rots and the outside lives. Willows show this fact in a remarkable manner All rotten within, all alive without. The seat of life therefore in the latter is the *periphery*, in animals, *central*.

Many wonder why elms do not flourish in Paris. The reason is that the city air is constantly vicious, producing effects in a way unknown to us. They suffer a sort of double aphyxia, one by the air, the other at the roots, from infiltrated street gas, &c., &c.

RUBUS NUTOMS.

This very pretty raspberry grows on the Himalaya Mountains, near Sikkins, at the heighth of about 1,300 feet above the level of the sea.

[Journal De La Societe Imperiale Zoologique D'Acclimatation, and La Societe Protectrice des Animaux, 1857.

These societies take charge of the safety of birds, &c., favorable to our crops.

We translate from a memoir on this subject, just received by the Institute from Paris. The Institute some years ago addressed a memorial to the Legislature of New Jersey, recommending protection to certain birds. New Jersey passed a law to that effect.

NEW OBSERVATIONS ON THE UTILITY OF PRESERVING BIRDS INTERESTING TO AGRICULTURE.

"In my July pamphlet, I spoke of the disease of plants, as caused by certain insects, and I uttered the wish that government would take suitable measures for the destruction of such as were injurious, and protection of the useful birds, by providing for the security of their eggs and nests, and themselves, also. Large numbers and sorts of birds, not only kill our enemy insects, but also efficaciously hinder the reproduction of plants hurtful to agriculture and horticulture. Among some others of our native birds, our larks eat up the seeds of tares, thistles, corn poppy, blue bottle, wild mustard, and others. It is true, that after those are gone, the birds eat a little of our grain, but generally such grain as was not covered with the harrow when planted, and which when it grows is rather hurtful than good to the growing crop, being incomplete, and in a measure stopping the circulation of air among the good plants, as well as consuming the fertility of the land. These tithes (dime) which they take of our grain, they earn for clearing the field. This lark not only eats some seeds, but insects also, especially worms and caterpillars, chrysalides, ant's eggs, crickets, grasshoppers, and with which they also feed their young. They eat the innumerable larvæ of the cecidomia so destructive of grain. Linnets, which we often see in flocks, render like service. The goldfinch is another able friend. The chaffinch, (or finch,) the green grosbeak, the wagtail—these are sometimes shut up in the barn with the threshed grain, to destroy the caterpillars, butterfly moths, weavils, and the larvæ. As to the sparrows, they destroy immense numbers of caterpillars and beetles. Rats and mice are destructive of our grain in barns. Let the night birds live about us. The owl and others. They make perpetual war on rats and mice, and we have, say 4,326,000 heads of families in the country. Let the night birds be preserved by each master, and the saving of our food would be not less than nearly thirteen millions of hectolitres, or *thirty-four millions of English bushels of grain*, and more.

H. Meigs.—The destructive insects have always been famous. Sacred and profane history speak much of them. Among the advances society has recently made, this one has not received that attention its vast importance demands. There is a necessity for determining with the utmost precision the habits and exact time that we may apply our energies thus, and not waste them as we have done. We must extinguish the sparks and not wait until there is a flame.

In 1850, the Farmers' Club requested the New Jersey government to protect that class of small birds which destroys insects hurtful to our crops, and in March, 1850, that State passed the following act and had enforced its provisions, viz:

Substance.—Not lawful for any man to kill, (except on his own premises,) the night or musquito hawk, chimney swallow, barn swallow, martin or swift, whipporwill, cuckoo, king-bird or bee martin, woodpecker, olaip or high hole, cat bird, wren, blue bird, meadow lark, brown thrusher, dove, fire bird or summer red bird, hanging bird, ground robin or chewink, bobolink or rice bird, robin, snow or chipping bird, sparrow, carolina lit, warbler, bat, black bird, blue jay and the small owl.   Penalty five dollars. Same for destroying eggs and nest.

[London Quarterly Review, April, 1858.]

PROGRESS OF ENGLISH AGRICULTURE.

There is rarely a great invention received by the world of which the germ is not to be found in some preceding age.   This is the case with the system of artificial manures, which has recently worked such wonders in agriculture, and which is touched upon as follows, in " The new and admirable Arte of Setting Corne, (wheat) by H. Platte, Esq., published in 1601, by Peter Shorte, dwelling at ye signe of ye Starne, on Bred Street Hill.   Shavoings (shavings) of horne upon mine owne experience, I must of necessity commende, by means whereof I obtayned a more flourishing garden at Bishopshall, in a most barren and unfruitful plot of grounde which none of my predecessors could ever grace or beautifie either with knots or flowers.   I have had good experience with singular good success by strewing the waste sope ashes upon a border of summer barley.   Malte duste may here also challenge his place, for foure or five quarters thereof are sufficient for an acre of ground.   And Sal-Armoniake being a volatile salt, first incorporated and rotted in common earth is thought to be a rich mould to plant or set in.   Dogges and cattes and other beasts, and generally all carrion, buried under the rootes of trees, in due time will make them flourish and bring forth in great abundance."

Also great inventions in Agricultural implements were made and forgotten.   The reaping machine, by the Gauls ; horse-hoe-drill, water and wind threshing machines, in a few obscure places.   Fresh meat six months per year was a luxury of the richest only.   An old cow salted down in Autumn, with some flitches of fat bacon, supplied whole families until Spring. Ichaboe, on the coast of Africa, had a bed of guano 1,100 feet long, 400 broad, and average depth of thirty-five feet ; all of which was carried off before the close of 1844.

He who lives within the diameter of a little circle, has ideas as narrow as his horizon, but when he views a single great agricultural exhibition he goes home a wiser and better farmer.

[Journal of the Society of Arts—London, August, 1857.]

TRUFFLES.

Mr. Martin Ravel, of France, (a truffle merchant,) has just published a very original and curious theory on the growth of Truffles.

That is formed by the Truffigene fly, that in winter flies about the oak trees, which produce the truffle—penetrate the ground, pricks the extremities of the fibrous roots, and then deposit their eggs in the spot.   A milky fluid issues in drops which form the truffles.   The wounded root dies, and the truffle is left isolated.   The process resembles that of the gall nut on

the oak, which is produced by an insect. Only some species of oaks produce truffles, difficult to say which. One sign is, that the ground all about
the truffle oak, is entirely free of all vegetation ; and when the truffles begin to be produced, every trace of grass disappears.

A. Bergen.—I wish the members of the club would talk more about
birds—for instance what can be said about crows, and whether we should
make war upon all birds. I try to preserve them on my farm, for I am
particularly fond of their sweet singing—the little wren for instance—but
I don't like crows ; they pull our corn, and do other mischief.

Prof. Nash.—I believe we should make friends with all birds. I will
not except even crows. We have made war upon birds until we have
fewer than any of the European countries. Even the robin has been
attacked as a noxious bird because it eats a few cherries, and yet the robin
lives upon curculio.

The chairman stated that the supervisors of counties in this State have
the right to enact laws to prevent the killing of birds. I like birds, but
I fail to see the value of the crow. As to his eating carrion, that I don't
think much in his favor. Tarring the seed will prevent the crows from
pulling corn. I have known small birds to do a good deal of harm, but I
would not exterminate them.

Mr. Meigs.—Jersey not merely makes law, but in all important cases
executes it, and does so with this bird law.

THE NUISANCE OF DOGS.

Wm. Lawton.—The crow is a very timid bird, and is easily kept out of
mischief by scarecrows or by feeding them with sowed corn. We have
another nuisance much greater than all the birds. I allude to dogs, the
most worthless of all animals, and most noxious, too, to our best interests.
They entirely prevent the raising of sheep in Westchester county, and
give nothing in return ; and I don't see how a Christian man can intrude
a great uncouth dog into a neighbor's house. I have no objection to a
shepherd having a dog if it is useful to him, or a pet bear or tiger ; but of
what use are the ordinary curs? I estimate that it costs the State of
New York three millions of dollars to maintain the dogs, besides the life
that is lost from the bites of rabid ones.

Prof. Nash.—I must approve all that is said in favor of birds and
against the worthless, mischievous dogs. I have just heard of a loss of
$200 worth of sheep in Amherst, Mass.; but I must say there is one
greater nuisance than dogs—it is the men with guns, who infest the whole
country, destroying all the birds. I doubt whether man can ever destroy the
insects that effect destruction of crops. There is a law of nature that
provides a balance in all natural things, and if we would not be eaten up
by insects, we must protect the birds ; and if we would raise sheep and
furnish cheaper food for the poor, we must make war upon the dogs to
the point of extermination. Not the tenth part of the sheep are kept in
Berkshire county, that would be kept but for dogs, as I was informed

while there upon a visit only a few days ago, and that, too, where much of the land cannot be profitably used for anything else but sheep-walks.

Mr. Silliman, a farmer of Westchester county, stated that he had just lost $40 worth of sheep by dogs.

Mr. Weaver, of Maryland, corroborated the opinion that dogs prevented the keeping of sheep—they certainly did in that State.

T. W. Field.—I don't know of any use of dogs except to make sausages, and as for crows, they are in the same category. I have had a dozen fowls destroyed of a night by dogs. They are the greatest nuisance in our county. I have seen the dogs hunt in packs upon Long Island and New Jersey. The poorest class of community are the class that own most dogs, for which they have no possible use.

The discussion was further continued with great animation, and an almost unanimous opinion that dogs are a great nuisance generally, and that the people of this country are generally mistaken in their views about birds, and that they should be protected and encouraged to dwell side by side with man.

Solon Robinson stated that crows always follow instead of preceding settlements of men in a new country; and that he had kept a good many sheep on the western prairies, and always had more sheep destroyed by dogs than by wolves, where the former are supposed to be more sparse, and the latter numerous and ravenous. He could poison the wolves or trap them, but he must not touch a neighbor's dog.

REAPING MACHINE.

By Mr. Meigs.

An article upon their history says that the first reaping machine was made by the Gauls, before the time of Julius Cæsar. By the description, it was something like the Illinois header, being pushed before the team, and gathering the heads, leaving the straw standing in the field. This was given to the club by the secretary long ago. They adapted the height of the wagon body to that of the grain—to reap the heads only. They had a clipping apparatus for that purpose, moved by the action of the wheels. The wagon was pushed forward by the team, so that the straw was trod into the soil as it always ought to be, to preserve its fertility, *for no straw should be taken off* except for beds for the farmer and for his stock. *So the Gauls understood it nearly two thousand years ago.*

SMALL FRUIT.

This regular question was now called up, and elicited remarks from several persons, of which the following is a brief synopsis.

T. W. Field.—With regard to the raspberry business, I have yet to learn that it is entitled to precedence over any other crop as a profitable one. The plant requires such an amount of labor, and almost as much care as plants in a green-house. It is very difficult with me to grow perfect berries. As to strawberries, I do not see why as many bushels of strawberries cannot be grown upon one acre, as of potatoes, with the same amount of manure; but care must be taken not to use manure that produces fermentation.

Wm. Lawton.—I have used wood mold to the best advantage, for fertilizing strawberries.

The chairman stated that his raspberry field was no longer profitable, that is, not as profitable as strawberries. The old stock raspberries of Long Island were hardy, and needed no covering.

Dr. Ward.—I am amazed at what has been said about raspberries. It is contrary to my experience of eight years. If the fruit of others is not perfect, the soil is not adapted to this plant I have grown all the sorts most common, and never find imperfect berries. I also find the business profitable; they cost less than strawberries. I cover mine for winter; a man and boy can cover three-fourths of an acre a day. The lifting out of the vines in spring takes but little time, as the plants would have to be attended to beside. The after-work is small, compared to the value of the crop. I have been equally surprised at seeing in a late article in the Horticulturist, that pears cannot be grown in this country to any advantage.

Solon Robinson.—Have you seen the reason why the writer of that article did not succeed? A practical gardener gives it in the last number of Moore's Rural New Yorker. He says the ground is a stiff clay, undrained, and so wet it produces sedge grass and moss, and of course, cannot produce good pears, particularly upon the cold, bleak eastern shore of Grand Island, Niagara river.

T. W. Field.—I have no doubt of the success of Dr. Ward, but he is an exception in the raspberry business.

As to the failure of L. F. Allen in growing pears, it is not to be wondered at, when we know how and where he grows them.

Mr. Freeman, of Ravenswood, said: I covered two acres with raspberries at an expense of $15, and I believe that I can make the business profitable.

Prof. Nash.—1 have always noticed that wild strawberries grew best upon light, dry, new land, without manure, and I want the error corrected that amoniacal manure is necessary.

R. G. Pardee.—My first experiments were with barn-yard manures, and I made my bed very rich, and failed to get a gill of fruit. I grew great vines but no berries; yet the idea prevails that a large quantity of manure must be used upon the strawerry bed, and people are hard to convince of the bad effects of high manuring for a crop of strawberries. Lime is a valuable application, particularly lime slaked with water saturated with salt. About raspberries, I have to repeat that raspberry-growing in Milton, upon the Hudson, is profitable. If the vines produce imperfect berries, the canes are imperfect. Spurious kinds are very common all over the country.

Dr. Ward stated that he had the greatest difficulty in eradicating spurious canes among his best raspberries. He believes that they hybridize, or that the plant sprouts and produces canes that are worthless for fruit. I have noticed, said he, that the stools that produce the greatest number of canes are the most worthless; and yet these are the very ones that are usually sold for propagation. Such canes I have to pull up and burn every year. I suppose I have burned a thousand this spring. I hope this discussion of small fruits will be continued.

The Chairman.—We will continue that and the other questions before the club.

The Secretary.—As to the destruction of the seeds of weeds by birds— reminded the club that when snow covers the earth, the birds which remain, are seen shaking the seeds from weeds standing above the snow and eating them, and in that way myriads of weed seeds are destroyed by birds. And when spring brings the flocks from the South, they all feed for some time on the seeds lying upon the ground, before any seeds have grown, of either weeds or of our useful crops, *and it is not until midsummer that any of our valuable grains are fit for their food.*

Mr. Edgar, of Hudson city, Jersey, complains of the poor condition of his pea crop, and asks for information how to remedy it.

Subjects adopted for next meeting, proposed by Prof. Mapes, " The most economical method of renovating worn out land."

By Rev. Mr. White, " The small fruits, continued."

By Mr. Solon Robinson, " The mud and shells of our salt water rivers and bays, as manure."

The club adjourned to Monday next, at noon.

H. MEIGS, *Secretary.*

———

June 7, 1858.

Present—Messrs. Dewey, Dr. Peck, Thos. W. Field, Paine, Stacey, Bixby, Lawton, of New Rochelle; Mr. Bruce, Rev. W. White, of Staten Island; Solon Robinson, Hon. Horace Greeley, Prof. Mapes, Prof. Nash, Goodwin, Chambers, Leonard, Fuller and Treadwell, Mr. Bell, Mr. Geissenhainer, Mr. Vanderveer, Mr. Chilson, R. G. Pardee, Adrian Bergen, of Gowanus, and others—55 members in all.

Prof. Nash, in the chair. Henry Meigs, Secretary.

GRAFTING.

By Mr. Meigs.—This highly valuable art is of very ancient origin.

Aristotle's (about 2200 years ago,) graft is considered to be the most ingenious ever invented for escutcheon grafting.

Place the bud on the bark of the subject—trace its outline with the sharp point of a pen-knife—the moment this bark is lifted from the sap wood set in the bud and cover it with the bark, showing only the eye out, then fix it as we do buds, as to ligatures, &c.

Pliny graft (nearly 1800 years,) remains unaltered. One nurseryman in Normandy and Brittany used it exactly as Pliny did, and he says that it had been used from time immemorial! He did not invent it. The subject being cut off horizontally, the grafts are put into it in as many places as you please, between the bark and sap wood, and all are then covered by the same material, now called *Onguent de Saint Fiacre, or Hackney coach grease*—that is cow dung, fresh, mixed well with some of the soil, (not clay, for that cracks in drying) and over that, ligatures to keep all steady.

The Tschudy graft recently successfully employed by Baron Tschudy, with herbaceous plants, such as melon or pumpkin, tomato or potato, consists in uniting quickly the two surfaces of stalks of like size, cut with a knife as keen as the sharpest razor, and then very careful ligatures and nursing. Good crops of tomatoes and potatoes have been raised this way. (The tomato and potato are both Solanums, and the *seed ball* of potato is the *tomato* of it! *Meigs*.)

The *Magon graft*, by the Phenicians, of the earliest age, was by *approach*. They had noticed branches of trees rubbing off their barks in hard gales, and then when quiet *growing together at the bruised spot !* and they applied it to their fruit trees successfully.

Terence describes a graft done by boring a hole in the subject with a sort of augur or gimlet, and inserting the graft in that.

The *Crown graft* of Pliny, is mentioned by Theophrastus, nearly 400 years before Pliny.

The *Graft of Atticus*.—The subject is cut off horizontally and split in the middle, and the graft shaped wedge form to fit the split, each graft to have three eyes at least—the subject may be larger than the graft, and in that case, it is fitted with one edge next the bark of the subject—*all closed up with dung.*

Atticus recommended grafting good grape vines on the stalks of *wild grape vines !*

Trees (pear,) which have become exhausted of their strength by old age, are (in Western France,) cut off and crown grafted with young and fruitful pear grafts.

Apples and pears hate one another, and grafting does not answer between them.

TOMATO.

Is hard to ripen in open air, in France, being originally from Mexico. (I always thought it an indigenous plant here in latitude 40° and upwards, under its old name of *Love-apple*—considered dangerous to eat when I was young—some 70 years ago. H. Meigs.)

EGG PLANT.

Melongena or Aubergine, came originally from Africa. It is rather indigestible, and few stomachs can manage it well. The white one, which grows about as large as a large hen's egg, is a little poisonous, and is rather cultivated for ornament than for use. (I used to grow them as large as turkey eggs, and eat them when sliced and fried like apples. H. Meigs.'

[Journal De La Societe Imperiale Et Centrale D'Horticulture—Napoleon 3d, Protecteur, Paris, April, 1858.]

STRAWBERRIES.

In the middle of last century, the celebrated English gardener and botanist, Philip Miller, in his Gardeners' Dictionary, gave excellent instructions on the culture of strawberries. He distinguished four kinds, viz: Fragaria vesca, eatable; F. Virginiana, F. Muricata, prickly, and Chiloensis, and a few other varieties.

Twenty years ago Mons. De Longhe, occupied a great deal of time with strawberries, and raised a great number of varieties. The best kind he calls *The Constant*, on account of its permanent character, its hardihood and ready adaptation to various soils, its strong fruit stalks and its abundant yield. It has a fine conical figure and a delicious taste. The Gardiner's Chronicle, has said that France has never eaten a good strawberry; it says that England, is par excellence, the land for strawberries, owing to its *humid*, mild climate! American strawberries are very productive, but lack sugar and aroma. These have been improved by crossing with our black strawberry, which is poor in quantity of fruit, but delicious in quality.

OLD GARDENS

Are hard to cultivate. The soil has been regularly dunged every year; it is black with richness, doubtless, but it does not suit either our common vegetables or our fruit trees. Many plants do not flourish in it, and fruit trees make nothing but wood; peach gets gummy, pears sterile, apples sickly; gooseberry and strawberry give us leaves and little fruit. Most gardeners are convinced that garden soil cannot be too rich, as they see asparagus, rheubarb, and a few other plants, accommodate themselves to it, they suppose that other plants can do so too—but they add more dung and the trees die of plethora. There is no remedy for this but removing the soil and replacing it with new fresh earth. Turf soil is best. Keep some of the old garden for the plants that love it, such as asparagus, rhubarb, &c. Drainage is always good. Salt and lime, in some measure, help the over rich land.

KEEPING FRUIT IN WINTER.

This is a question of high interest and difficult to settle. Mr. Thieme has succeeded for many years by a cheap and simple plan. In the beginning of winter he puts his fruit up in boxes or casks, putting together every variety of fruit, especially *not placing in contact such as ripen at the same time*, and separating the layers by fine dry sand, *neither very dry nor moist*. He does this in the spot where they are to remain, out of the reach of frost—say a good cellar or cave. When taken out for use, wash them. Chopped straw has answered in place of sand. His preserved fruits never wrinkle, and they keep their flavor.

The Secretary stated that he had some further pages of President Pell's valuable essays on fish, and desired to read it.

T. W. Field.—The larger the quantity of fruit together, the better it ripens, and nothing but pure sand should be used to pack fruit in. A few pears will not ripen alone, but in contact with other fruit will ripen perfectly, and still retain their aroma.

Wm. Lawton thought them excellent food, and he also advocated the use of cucumbers as one of the most digestible of vegetables, and quite nutritive.

T. W. Field.—The nutritive part of a cucumber cannot exceed half of one per cent, according to the most careful analysis.

Mr. White, of Staten Island, corroborated the indigestibility of egg-plants, and notwithstanding the encomiums of Mr. Lawton upon cucumbers, he thought the less we eat the better.

Dr. Peck adverted to the great profit which can be derived from gardening near this city. He read the following statement:

A FIFTY ACRE GARDEN.

MESSRS. EDITORS:—Thinking that a few facts and figures relative to Garden Farming on Long Island would not be uninteresting to the readers of your *Rural*, I took the trouble to question a "Long Island Farmer," who is working just fifty acres of land, as to the amount of "truck" he manages to take from his land, and the money he receives for it. He kindly obliged me with the necessary figures, which enable me to make an exhibit of his operations; and as he required from me no bond of secrecy, I take the liberty to expose him to the farming community, that all may see what can be done on a small farm.

The person referred to is J. Remsen Bennett, (a subscriber to the *Rural*,) of Bay Bridge, Long Island, six miles from New York city. His land fronts on New York Bay about 400 feet, and extends back to the 3d Avenue, running from Brooklyn to Fort Hamilton. Upon the water front he has lately erected a mansion, which for completeness, beauty and convenience, will compare favorably with any farm-house in the country, having all the modern appliances of water, furnace and gas. The gas is made in a house erected for the purpose, a few rods from the dwelling, and is used not only for house purposes, but is also conducted to his barns, carriage-houses, work-shop, store-rooms, &c., &c., which are all brilliantly lighted as occasion requires. His barns and out-houses are all on a scale ample and roomy, and constructed upon the most approved plans.

His land is divided into lots of about equal size, lying each side of a wagon-road running through the centre of the whole, and terminating upon the Avenue. The lands are divided by hedge and fence, and are all equally accessible to the wagon-road. The hedge is used as a protection to the young plants from the spring winds, and answers an excellent purpose. Besides being a practical man, Mr. Bennett is an experimental farmer, and no expense is spared and no labor considered too great in testing different manures, and trying the different methods of promoting early growth and prime quality of vegetables. His manure bills are probably larger than any other man's working the same number of acres. His hot-bed sash, when in use, covers a space of 3,600 square feet. He employs three men the year through; eight men in the spring, and ten men in summer, in addition to eight or ten women and girls for pickers, as the season advances and the crops mature. He also gives full employment to 1,000 bushel baskets and 150 barrels in getting his stuff to market, which, in summer, is done by boats of his own, which he keeps constantly plying backwards and forwards from New York, one of these being a boat of thirty-one tons and the other twelve tons. Six horses are constantly kept at work, and the array of plows, harrows, rakes, hoes, drills, &c., &c., together with numerous wagons and carts is ample, and all of the latest and most approved make.

Mr. Bennett is decidedly a working man, and by the united effort of his head and hands, accomplishes, each and every year, results such as you find noted below, and which I took from his books, (a regular set of which he keeps when others sleep,) and which, if not unusual and astonishing to most of your readers, I must confess they are to me. In order to bring the figures into a condensed form, I have put them in shape, as below shown. It will be borne in mind that a second crop from land is not an unusual thing on Long Island.

Acres.	Description.	Crop.	Yield.	Amount sold for.	Remarks.
¾	Turnips, ...	only	106 bu.	$45 24	
5	Cauliflower, ...	2d,	8,070 heads,	621 21	Partial failure.
10	Cucumbers, ...	only	370,300	2,997 38	
12	Tomatoes, ...	1st&2d	5,695 bu.	4,069 64	
2	Egg plant, ...	only	8,507	946 20	
2	White squash, ..	only	956 bu.	408 98	
3	Beans, ...	1st	611 bu.	653 00	
3	Peas,..........	1st	542 bu.	587 86	
6	Corn, ...	2d	63,532 ears	614 84	
—	Apples, ...		166 bar.	608 30	Sent to Europe.
8	Potatoes, ...	1st	1,146 bu.	1,509 55	
1¼	Striped squash,..	only	524 bu.	261 25	
	Grapes, pears and quinces,..........			65 09	
				$13,388 54	
	Deduct expenses, ...			4,022 30	
				$9,366 24	

EXPENSES.

Wages, ...	$2,318 73
Manures,..	1,389 44
Horses feed, (bought,)................................	314 13
	*$4,022 30

Mr. Meigs said: Long Island is well known to those who understand its true character, to be capable of such gardening as this, from end to end, and will *end* in becoming the *greatest garden* the world ever saw, attached to the *greatest city ever built.*

A. Bergen said, that Mr. Bennett, the first farmer mentioned, was one of the most careful managers, and where he might succeed another might fail.

* A complete work-shop and a pair of hands accustomed to the use of tools, brings the amount of money paid out for repairs and fixings to so small a figure that Mr. B. did not take it into consideration in giving me amounts from his books.

IMPROVING EXCESSIVELY RICH GARDEN SOIL.

T. W. Field.—I wish to call attention to the subject of excessive rich garden soil, becoming barren. I believe a continuance of any one kind of manure to excess will render a soil unfit for crops in general.

R. G. Pardee.—I have experienced the same difficulty of over rich soils, and have found the best remedy an application of lime and salt mixture. I found some soils so rich that strawberries could not be produced until the lime and salt had been used. The true proportion is one bushel of salt dissolved and used to slack three bushels of lime.

ABOUT STRAWBERRIES.

I can say that English strawberries and English apples are not grown here, but we have strawberries in this country superior to any of the English in flavor, though not generally so in size.

The Chairman.—I fully agree with Dr. Peck, that cucumbers, properly treated, are not unhealthy. The fault is generally a want of sufficient mastication. As to the quality of English strawberries, I am satisfied, from experience, that our strawberries, although generally smaller than the English, are superior in flavor.

Dr. Peck.—I have never seen any cultivated strawberries equal to the wild ones that I used to gather in youth in Dutchess county.

Mr. White bore testimony to the value of the salt and lime mixture for strawberry ground; also that the soil must not be made too rich, and that his best prospect of a crop at this time is from vines set on the poorest ground he has.

THE RASPBERRY QUESTION.

Solon Robinson read a letter from a resident of Brooklyn, who states his good success in growing all the raspberries that he wishes for family use from a small bed of the Fastolf variety, manured with rotten chips, and layered in winter. He thinks the statement made that good sorts will hybridize and run to barren stalks that must be pulled up and burned, all humbug. In fact, he commences his letter by saying:

"I have yet to learn of one valuable idea suggested by your so-called 'Farmers' Club.' It seems to me the few who are not unmitigated old fogies, are unmitigated humbugs."

Mr. Meigs remarked, that almost every man who came to this club for the first time, imagined he knew almost as much about farming and gardening—and commonly more—*as he knew less.* Now here are members from 91 years old down to 27, half of them farmers. Let the writer attend next time, and he shall *go to the head*, as school boys say, as the greatest fogy and humbug of the whole. Yes, Mr. Chairman, we often come here to teach as *masters*, and sneak away as *bad scholars.*

Here we have the old endless war of opinion about the wholesomeness of cucumbers. I have a great mind to reiterate the good old story of the celebrated Prince Metternich—prince in diplomatics and prince in gastronomics—about the dressing of cucumbers. I may as well. "He directs the choicest unfaded cucumbers to be sliced thin into very cold water, to remain long enough to extract the dangerous element from the cucumber, then suit yourself as to salt, pepper, vinegar, &c., &c.; lastly, to open the window and throw the whole into the street."

Tiberius, the tyrant,, while he was cutting off Roman heads by dozens, was raising cucumbers on his little rock, by having hotbeds on wheels so that he could wheel them into the sun to ripen them in winter. Let us avoid rulers who live on cucumbers.

CORN SOWED FOR FODDER AND FOR PLOWING UNDER.

Solon Robinson read a letter from Warren Hutchins, dated Bethel, Vt., which says:

" I plow evenly, sowing the seed in every third furrow, and roll the ground and harrow lightly in the direction of the furrows. I run a cultivator once or twice between the rows. If the crop is to be plowed in for manure, I commence about September 1st, with a plank fastened on the beam to break down the stalks, so that they will turn under well, making my furrow across the rows. I find this a cheap way to enrich land that lies far from the stables.

" This day, June 1st, I have sowed an acre for fodder, with the assistance of a boy half a day. Last year, a half acre left to ripen had 25 bushels of ears, besides a great yield of fodder."

Solon Robinson said: I have sowed corn as late as July 1st, in Indiana, and got a great crop of good fodder. I sowed broadcast, and would always do so unless I had a large drilling machine to put it in rows, ten inches apart. I certainly would not plow it in, unless the land had been previously deeply plowed, as it would cover the seed too deep.

COST OF A WISCONSIN WHEAT CROP.

A correspondent of the Tribune has given us the following estimation of the cost of raising a wheat crop in Wisconsin, which is very fair on paper, and very good in fact, every time it don't fail.

I take 120 acres, and fence 80 with rails $10\frac{1}{2}$ feet long, got from the land. I used mortised posts, 10 feet apart, making a fence with three rails, the lowest $2\frac{1}{2}$ feet from the ground, making a strong fence against large stock ; stone handily got from a ravine and bluff near, to underpin at leisure.

The estimate is for debt and credit as follows:

Wheat Crop to Sundries, Dr., viz :

To 120 acres of raw land at $5,.....................		$600 00
two months of man breaking, at $14 ; board $10,	$38 00	
use of team, plow, &c., for same,..............	75 00	
		113 00
two months of man making and hauling rails, at $12,......................................	24 00	
board, $10 ; use of team, $10, ...	20 00	
		44 00

To two months making fence, at $12, $24 ; board, $10, ... $34 00
120 bushels seed wheat at $8 (present value of such wheat
    for St. Louis market),................................ 96 00
harrowing and sowing 80 acres, at $6, (large estimate,) .. 48 00
harvesting and shocking 40 acres at $1, ... $40 00
harvesting and shocking 40 acres at $1.50,...... 60 00
stacking 80 acres at 40 cents,................. 32 00
board of harvest hands,....................... 20 00
                                                 152 00
threshing-shed and farming mill,...................... 50 00
four months' threshing at $12 ; board $2,.............. 68 00
(Use of team, &c., largely paid for by straw thrown daily
    to stock.)
one month man marketing, $12 ; board, $5 ; team,
    $40, ... $57 00
                                                57 00
miscellaneous and personal services,.................. 100 00
    Total,.. $1,362 00

Contra, Cr.

By 120 acres improved farm at $10,............. $1,200 00
To farming mills, &c., on hand,................ 50 00
                                           $1,250 00
To 2,000 bush. wheat, Dr., (52 cents per bush.,).. $1,120 00

The wheat used and parceled out would much more than meet the item for personal services, &c. Again, raw land in the neighborhood will not readily sell at $5, while improved would readily bring over $10. My object has been to figure so as to make the wheat cost something. The real profits of the operation were fully $1,600.

THE POTATO DISEASE.

A letter from T. Sheldon, of Gouverneur, N. Y., read by Solon Robinson, states the opinion of the writer to be that the potato rot is caused by the puncture of an insect to deposit its eggs—in fair weather in the vines, and in foul weather in the tubers ; and that it is the virus injected that produces decay. He thinks an application of some bug-dispelling substance might keep them off, and suggests whale-oil soap.

Mr. R. thought sulphur a better application, and that it could be had in the cheapest form in sulphate of lime—ground plaster.

Another letter, from A. Turner, Port Washington, (without any State,) expresses the same opinion of the bug theory of the disease. He says :

"A little black bug, not much larger than the head of a pin, leaves an almost undiscoverable substance on the potato leaves, which turns black and kills the vines, and the rot of tubers follows. He thinks some bug deposits a poisonous substance upon other vegetables, injuring them very much for food.''

Another letter states that a person has planted the big end of potatoes without an eye, and raised good crops. Has anybody else ever tried this experiment, and also what portion of all the eyes planted produce vines? Do all? and is a multitude any better than one sprout?

HOW TO MAKE COWS GIVE DOWN.

A letter writer wants to know if there is any way to make a cow give down her milk? To which Mr. Solon Robinson replied: I have often heard that one man could lead a horse to water, but two could not make him drink. The great mistake of most people in the management of horses, cows, and in fact men, is trying to make them do things by force, instead of milder means. Now the best way to make a cow give down that I have ever tried, is to coax her. Patience and perseverance will generally overcome the difficulty and effect a cure. I have seen cows that had been trained to being fed when milked, until they would only give down when bribed to do so. Strapping up the fore leg of a cow with a strap slipped over the bent knee so that she cannot walk, until milked, will sometimes cause her refractory disposition to dry up.

Prof. Nash.—If a cow will give down by gentleness, it is no use to try to make her do it.

Mr. Greeley called up Prof. Mapes.

RENOVATING OLD LAND.

Prof. Mapes.—I believe all lands that ever have been fertile, are capable of being made productive again. They are only exhausted of some one of the constituents of plants. Water always contains carbonic acid, and this is a solvent of inorganic substances. The green sand particles of the green sand marl, have a very strong decomposing power, and that is one of the reasons why it is beneficial—it dissolves other substances that plants feed upon. If you abstract all the parts of a soil that produce plants, it could not be restored, but that can hardly be the case, while the earth down to the center is a store-house of the primaries of all plants and animals. Now what is necessary to fit these constituents for the use of plants, for that is what is wanted to restore what is called worn-out soil to fertility again. When a plant decays and goes back into the soil, that soil is prepared to produce a new order of plants, and so they go on toward perfection. Originally the land produced only mosses and lichens. The best means to render worn-out land fertile, is by underdraining, not alone to drain but to aerate the soil, and allow just water enough to decompose the constituents for the use of growing plants. In England there is not a field that has been under-drained that has not been doubled in value, and so it can be here. So that no one can say he cannot afford to under-drain. A soil to be renovated must be mechanically prepared before anything added can be fully beneficial. Land will improve more while growing a crop than in a naked follow, if that crop is supplied with the proper pabulum of the crop. The very things added to the soil to benefit one crop, cause that to add to the fertility of the soil for another. Whatever is true in England of under-draining and sub-soiled land, is true here, and I state it as a fact, that one-half the usual quantity of manure upon drained land will be of more benefit than the whole quantity upon land in its natural, wet condition. No under-drained or subsoiled field ever suffers with drouth, or runs out of grass. The air as it passes through the drains and soil is divested of all its ammoniacal gasses, and thus adds fertility to the soil. All mineral substances, whether carbonate of lime, phosphate of lime, sulphate of lime, potash, soda, salt, or other constituents of plants, are valuable in proportion to the source from whence they are derived. The higher the organization of animal or plant, the more valuable the mineral obtained. The mineral phosphatic rock, which gives by analysis the same results as calcined bones, is worthless for manure, and a quantity of carbonate of lime from the pure limestone given to a field equal to two per cent of the soil, would render it barren, while forty per cent of the same mineral exactly, according to analysis, is extremely fertile. The cause is, one has never undergone any change since its deposit, and the other has passed through a long course of organized life.

Mr. Bell, the patentee of a very ingenious mode of making tight, strong, cheap boxes, by machinery, exhibited some which hold an even quart. These just filled with small fruit, pack well, and save in space about 20 to 30 per cent. They cost $5 per 100 boxes.

Mr. Robinson observed that as we had now reached June, perhaps the old meetings of once in a fortnight might be now resumed.

The large majority of members objected. They wished the club to be held every Monday.

The subjects adopted for the next meeting, same, with another proposed by Mr. Robinson, viz: "The best time to cut grass, and the best manner of making hay."

The club then adjourned to Monday, June 14th, at noon.

H. MEIGS, *Secretary.*

June 14, 1858.

Present—Messrs. Prof. Nash, Andrew S. Fuller, of Williamsburgh; T. W. Field, of Brooklyn; Treadwell, of Brooklyn; Lawton, of New Rochelle; Stacy, Pardee, Dr. Poole, of New Jersey; Mr. Bruce, Mr. Davoll, Mr. Silliman, Mr. Paine, Solon Robinson, Mr. Leonard, John W. Chambers, and others—nearly sixty in all.

Wm. Lawton, of New Rochelle, in the chair. H. Meigs, Secretary.

The Secretary read the following extracts and translations made by him from works received by the American Institute, from Europe and elsewhere, since the last meeting, viz:

[Revue Horticole—Paris, May, 1858.   Journal D'Horticulture Pratique.]

BEGONIACEÆ—BEGONIAS.

This family of flowers attracts much attention.

About the middle of the 17th century, there was discovered in the Island of St. Domingo, a plant which the Botanist, Plunier, dedicated to Governor Begon, the great Protector of Botanists.   It was afterwards found in Brazil, in Mexico, in Peru, in India, and even in China.   They have all received, naturally, the generic name *Begon* or *Begoniaceæ*.

This genus may be distinguished by thick stalks, fleshy, articulated, knotty.   Leaves alternate, petiolate, rounded, oval or lanceolate, entire or denticulate, or lobed, sometimes cordiform, (heart shape.)   Almost always with their sides unequal, &c., &c.   They are generally treated as hothouse plants.   The fleshy and tuber rooted ones, keep from October to February. They grow best in a soil made one-third heath soil, one-third rotten wood, one-sixth of garden mould, and one-sixth of fine sand.   The pots being well drained, water them for a few days after they are potted.   You must not let drops of water touch their leaves, *for it will spot them!*

Here follows a catalogue of about 40 *varieties : Begonia Fuchsicides,* (like the Fuchsia,) grows and spreads on a trellis, ten to twelve feet, and its numerous vermillion red flowers, pendent like the Fuchsia.   Some have bunches of white flowers veined with red, some have perfume, some resemble roses, some are yellow, some have leaves red below, &c.

INSECTS, WITH DRAWINGS, GREATLY MAGNIFIED.

Plant Louse, proboscis for sap (four inches long.)—All the varieties of this louse render the plants and trees sickly by exhausting their sap.   The Wood louse, or Aphis produces 100 young at a time, and that ten times a year, and one egg which is deposited in the ground, to hatch next spring. By calculation, one Wood louse produces in one year, five millions of descendants, besides the egg for next year.   There are about sixty species of the Plant louse.

Curculio has very numerous species—as Larva, (worms,) they devour vegetable roots, leaves, &c.   One of them, the *Bruchus Pisi*, gets into peas and beans, one pierces bowers, one cuts off young shoots of fruit trees, the last three cut the leaves of the Pansies, (Pensees,) Polianthus, Beans, Clover, Ranunculus.   They hide at the roots of the plants in day time.

[English Scientific Societies—Chemical Society, January 21, 1858.]

SPONGIOLES OF PLANTS—THEIR ACTION.

Dr. Daubeny read a communication he had received from Baron Liebig, relative to the absorbent powers of soils.   Baron Liebig maintains that the spongioles of the plants, in obtaining their supply of saline matter do not act by simple absorption, but exert a real chemical decomposing action upon certain ill defined compounds which the saline matter formed with the insoluble constituents of the soil.   Dr. Daubeny also referred to the ammoniacal emanations from volcanoes, and suggested that they might arise from the aqueous decomposition of certain nitrides, such as the Nitride of Boron and the Nitride of Titanium.

The Secretary read the following on Curculio, viz:

[Hancock county, Illinois, June 5, 1858.]

THE PLUM—THE CURCULIO.

Assuming that the *Curculio* is the greatest enemy to this most delicious fruit, as it is, indeed, to all the smooth-skinned fruits—the writer proceeds to give a number of remedies from Thomas' Fruit Culturist, and other sources, most of which have been efficacious in some instances, but all of which have failed in others, and cannot be relied on as infallible.

But it is the design of this article to call attention to another remedy, which it is hoped and believed will prove a safeguard against the ravages of this destructive insect, and supersede all others. We allude to the *dry lime* remedy, as discovered and applied by James B. Mathews, of Warsaw, Illinois. The experiment of Mr. Mathews was a thorough one, and proved eminently successful.

In the spring of 1856, Mr. Mathews had on his lot about a dozen thrifty young wild Chickasaw plum trees, which fruited finely. They were growing in an irregular cluster, and were well situated for the experiment he was about to make.

Commencing before the curculio made his appearance, he divided the cluster of trees into three portions; on one of these he sifted fine lime about once a week, through the summer, and until the fruit was beyond the reach of the destroyer; on another portion he put none whatever; and on the third he put none, until after the curculio had commenced operations upon its fruit, and had made serious havoc, when he applied the lime about as on the first.

The result was: The fruit of No. 1 was *entirely protected;* on No. 2 the fruit was *totally destroyed;* while on No. 3, the insects which had commenced their depredations were driven away, and all the fruit which was yet uninjured at the time was saved.

His mode of applying the lime was by means of a sieve attached to a pole, long enough to reach over the trees and sift the lime down upon them. This was done either in the morning while the dew was on, or after a rain; and thus the lime was made to remain a long time upon the tree, adhering to the leaves, branches and fruit.

The expense and trouble attending this mode of prevention are but slight—much less than in most other cases.

Mr. Mathews is of the opinion that this is the most effectual remedy against the curculio ever yet discovered.

[London Athenæum, September, 1857.]

BIRDS' SONG AT CERTAIN HOURS.

A German woodsman has marked time by birds: The chaffinah sings before the dawn; sylvia atracapilla or black cap, sings about one hour later; quail begins about half an hour after that; hedge sparrow about half an hour after the quail ; blackbird nearly an hour later than the quail, is the mocking bird of Europe, imitates tunes so well that Mons. Dureau de La Mealle made all the blackbirds of a French canton sing the Marseillaise hymn by letting loose among them a blackbird which had learned it. The lark sings two and one-half hours after the chaffinch ; black-headed titmouse, one-half hour later than the lark ; sparrow one-half an hour after titmouse.

We lay this before our club that the times of song of our birds may be noted—*especially by the ladies !*

H. MEIGS, *Secretary.*

DOUGLAS STRAWBERRY.

Douglas, of Washington city, has one *highly praised.* He has lately sent to the market, from his beds, *six hundred quarts* gathered the day before !

Messrs. Fowler & Wells, presented a copy of the Manual of Horticulture published by them. It is a small duodecimo volume. The instructions, well condensed, will be found very useful by ladies as well as men, in managing their gardens.

Mrs. Fowler presented a splendid bouquet from her garden, containing *fifteen* varieties of roses and *Mrs. Fowler* asks the secretary to "insist that every farmer who plants *Indian corn* shall set out at least one perpetual hardy rose bush by his *kitchen .loor.* Should he do so (she affirms) that on the principle of ' reflex influence ' his butter will catch the *aroma of the flowers!* be much sweeter and command a higher price in the market."

When the above was read the members applauded by clapping their hands.

Solon Robinson suggested that his honey might also partake of the sweetness of this flower, if grown abundantly near the bee-house.

Mr. Kedzie presented pamphlets descriptive of " The Rain Water Filter," manufactured by James Terry & Co., of Rochester, New York. It is intended for the benefit of the people of our extensive lime-stone regions.

William Lawton presented several sorts of rhubarb petioles, grown from seed he received from the American Institute, three years ago.

Prof. Nash.—Dr. McMunn, of this city, formerly of Port Jervis, N. Y., a microscopic investigator, says the curculio does no harm to the plum of healthy trees ; that they never attack a tree to the injury of the fruit until the tree is diseased ; that the appearance of the curculio is a symptom of disease in the tree. Prof. Nash said that the doctor challenges the world to show where the curculio produces any injury where the tree is not previously diseased.

Andrew S. Fuller.—Now, I take the direct opposite of this doctor ; and I know that his theory is wrong, or else why does the curculio sting pears and cherries upon strong, healthy trees ?

THE PLANT-LOUSE.

All sorts of plant-lice render plants sickly, and some of them are so prolific that one pair will produce in one year five millions of progeny, and there are sixty different varieties. Whatever will destroy this insect will be of great benefit to mankind.

SPONGIOLES.

A paper of Dr. Doubenrey, of London, on the spongioles of plants, shows their offices, one of which is to furnish moisture to soften the earth where the roots are about to enter, as well as to furnish a decomposing liquid to solve many compounds needed for the sustenance of plants.

Judge Meigs remarked that he had often noticed the brace roots of Indian corn dropping water upon the earth just where they are about to penetrate, and where they could not while the earth was baked hard.

R. G. Pardee.—Mr. Crossman, of Rochester, produced in his garden, seedlings of great size at eighteen months old, which he made so by careful selection of the largest plants for producing seeds, and then selecting the best of the plants for cultivation. We may all, by the same course, increase the size and value of our rhubarb, as well as by buying. In fact I had rather have plants from seeds of Crossman's growing than plants from most gardens.

Andrew S. Fuller.—In my garden at Brooklyn, I grew and exhibited at the fair last year, a stalk of rhubarb from Caboon's seedling. that weighed eight lbs., free of the leaf, which was twenty-two feet around. The proper soil for rhubarb is moist, rich land, underdrained; just such land as we have on Long Island by the thousands of acres, lying almost worthless.

HOW TO GROW SEEDLING PLANTS.

Strawberries.—Andrew S. Fuller.—We want strawberries of an earlier and better variety. To obtain such, we must sow seeds of the earliest and latest sorts, and persevere until we get improved sorts to suit our wants. It is not difficult to grow seedling strawberries. Select the largest and best berries, fully ripe, and put them in dry fine sand, and crush and rub them thoroughly until the seeds are distributed evenly through the mass. Prepare a bed in a shady place, in light, sandy loam, thoroughly pulverized. Sow the sand containing the seeds evenly, and sift soil an eighth of an inch deep over them; and, if the weather continues dry, water gently every evening. The plants will begin to come up in two weeks, and so on till winter, when the bed shall be covered two or three inches deep with straw or leaves, which must be raked off in the Spring, and the plants transplanted eighteen inches apart, in suitable beds.

Gooseberries.—We want a better gooseberry, if it can be had, one that will not mildew, and will produce abundantly and regularly. Let us plant seed of the best we have, and try. The seed should be washed clean from the pulp, and put in dry sand, in a cool place, to keep till spring. It must be cool, because these, and currant seeds, start at a low temperature, and they cannot be safely planted in the fall. Keep the seeds till late in the spring, and plant the seed in beds, as directed for strawberries, cover them an eighth of an inch deep, litter the beds next winter, and transplant when a year old.

Currants.—We want better currants—one twice the size of the noted cherry currant, sweet enough to eat without sugar. We may get it from a seedling. Let us try seeds from the largest and sweetest we have, and not be content till we make an improvement. The currant seed should be treated just like the seed of gooseberries.

Raspberries.—We want a raspberry that is really hardy, of good flavor, and that will continue bearing through the autumn. We have nearly succeeded by seedlings, but not quite. We must keep trying. It is easy to produce new raspberries from seed, and by perseverance we may be successful.

Blackberries.—We want better, earlier blackberries, and so we do later ones. The way to get them is to sow seeds, grow plants, and prove them, and when we get a better variety, reject the old ones. Horticulturists have done much in the last twenty years, but we should never rest, so long as there is room for improvement. Now, let every person try to get ahead of his neighbor in growing seedlings, and not wait for some one to send to Europe for new varieties, which we might have produced ourselves. We have paid millions to foreign countries for fruit trees, which we might have produced ourselves, and at less cost. It is not for fruit trees only that we are sending away our money, but for ornamental trees and plants, very many of them natives of our country. I have seen, within the last few weeks, hundreds of plants imported from France, at a great cost, that can be found growing wild, within one mile of the importer's residence. Importers either think plants better if imported, or in their ignorance they do not know that they are indigenous. I have even known that most common tree, the sweet gum (liquid amber), imported, and several of the most common spiræas.

R. S. Pardee.—I am much interested in these remarks of Mr. Fuller, who is known as a practical gardener, about seedling plants, and I hope the idea may be acted upon. Why should not the female portion of the community devote attention to the production of seedlings? Three of our first grapes originated with ladies. I wish they would make it a matter of interest and amusement, producing seedling roses. Many very valuable seedling plants have been produced at almost no cost. The first new seedling tree pœony, Mr. Fuller states, brought the producer $1,700. Let us, then, select the best seeds of the best plants, of all kinds, and grow them in the best soil, and see what you can produce. I wish to suggest that every lady who attends here, or who reads with interest the report of these proceedings, should suggest a question that she wishes answered, and that such questions be read at each meeting. If we discuss the question of seedlings, we shall elicit many interesting facts, and it should be generally known that all our choicest plants, fruits, and flowers, have come from seedlings.

Solon Robinson.—The Mr. Caboon, spoken of in connection with rhubarb plants, has made more out of a seedling than any farmer in Wisconsin. Mr. Fuller said, "Yes—for I knew him when he was poor; and he sold half of his garden for $10,000, beside all else that he has made out of a seedling rhubarb plant,"

THE BEST TIME TO CUT GRASS FOR HAY.

This question having been proposed by Solon Robinson, the chairman called upon him to give his views. He replied, that instead of that, he would read a letter from L. W. Saunders, of Milan, Ohio, which is not far from Sandusky, upon this question. It was written to the "Tribune," and reads as follows:

In your paper of the 22d, you say that the best time to cut hay should be authoritively settled, and not left to mere assertion. Now, every farmer will have his own opinion, and most of them will follow that opinion, regardless of what others may write or say. I have had some experience, having cut from 60 to 125 tons of hay, every year, for the past ten years. My experience has been, that timothy grass, for hay, should be cut as soon as it is out of blossom; then, if well cured and salted, horses or cattle will eat it up clean, and such hay appears to have more heart in it than that cut at any other time. I always save such for my heavy spring work, and my horses will do the same work, with less grain, and keep in equally good, if not better, condition than if cut later. If cut earlier, i. e., while the blossom is on, hay will be dusty, and horses will not do the same amount of work on it. My rule is, as soon as the last blossom is off, to commence cutting, and, as far as circumstances will admit, to take up in the afternoon what is cut in the forenoon. (If you wish to have good hay, never leave it exposed to the dew while spread out.) When put in the barn, or stack, I put about four to five quarts of salt to the ton on it, sprinkled as even as may be. And, another thing—I never cock up hay and leave it till Friday or Saturday to haul in; but whenever a load of hay is cured, it is hauled to the barn, or stacked. By following this course, I have very rarely lost any hay by getting wet, and I never yet learned that I lost time, though I know I saved hay by it. After I commence, I follow up my haying as fast as possible; in a good season, having it all safe in about ten days; in a bad one, part of it may get ripe, though such hay is always inferior.

Where hay is cut with a scythe, it is usually spread, as it is termed, but that is not the best way. If any farmer who is in that habit, will let the grass be in the swath till it is cured on top, and then turn it over by running the handle of a pitchfork or rake full length under one edge and then raising, he will find he can do it full as fast, and make a great deal better hay.

In regard to stacking, I think three or four ton stacks the best size, but would rather build a two-ton stack than have a load of hay stand out over night, if it was cured. By building larger stacks, persons frequently have to wait two or three days to get hay enough to build it; in the mean time a rain comes up and wets it, and I have found in my experience that large stacks are more liable to waste or damage while feeding out or selling.

In regard to red-top grass, I do not think it should be cut so early, but *that* should not get ripe. Where clover and timothy are mixed, I always follow the same plan as regards timothy alone; by that means the clover cures easy and the hay does not become mouldy, smoky or dusty.

Solon Robinson.—Now, I fully concur in this opinion of Mr. Saunders in all respects, and think it very safe doctrine for any one to follow who is in doubt upon the subject. This question of the best time to cut grass is one of very great importance, upon which farmers should think more, and prove by experiment that their course is right.

Prof. Nash.—That Mr. Saunders is a wise farmer. None but a wise one would have written such a sensible letter. I would suggest a strong approbation of that letter. Its teachings are good. I only vary in opinion from him very little. I would cut timothy a trifle earlier than the writer recommends. You may pitch upon the time when grass should be cut, but, practically, it cannot always be carried out. Sometimes hoeing interferes, and sometimes it is more profitable to let grass stand, so as to save the grain crop at the right time.

Mr. Lawton.—Cattle will not eat early-cut grass with more avidity than late-cut hay, but I cannot say that it is equally beneficial.

Prof. Nash.—A farmer always should take into account what his hay is for. Milk cows should have hay made from grass cut earlier than for working animals.

Subjects for next meeting.—Mr. Meigs moves the subject of " The mud and shells of our salt water rivers and bays," first proposed by Solon Robinson; Mr. Lawton, " The management of small farms;" Prof. Nash, " The most economical method of renovating worn out land," first proposed by Prof. Mapes ; Mr. Pardee, " The small fruits," continued.

The club then adjourned.

H. MEIGS, *Secretary.*

June 21, 1858.

Present—Messrs. Dewey, of Brooklyn ; Dr. Ward, of Newark ; Fuller, of Williamsburgh ; Field, of Brooklyn ; Wm. R. Prince, of Flushing : Adrian Bergen, of Gowanus ; Wyckoff, of Williamsburgh ; Stacey, Pardee, Dr. Turnipseed, Solon Robinson, Mr. Baker, Mr. Davoll, Mr. Paine, Mr. Leonard, John W. Chambers, Benjamin Pike, of New Jersey ; Mr. Bruce, Mr. Boyd, of Illinois ; Treadwell, Col. Devoe, Miller, and others—between sixty and seventy members.

Adrian Bergen, farmer, of Gowanus, in the chair. Henry Meigs, Secretary.

The Secretary said, that one of the intelligent ladies, who visit our club by special invitation, has done us the honor to write verse suitable to us, which he would now read—reminding the club that without them no civilization, no happiness, and no existence—that they keep the sacred fire which would have been extinguished at the *fall* if Eve had not come out of Paradise with Adam!—that here we celebrate the powers and glories of ladies—*Flora, Pomona and Ceres.* Welcome then to the ladies.

THE POEM.

DEDICATED TO THE FARMERS' CLUB, WITH THE COMPLIMENTS OF THE AUTHORESS, FANNY W. BRUCE, OF WILLIAMSBURGH, L. I.

Behold the roseate June is here,
  With flowery vines and dewy gems,
While clustering buds and berries bright,
  Hang pendent from their fragrant stems:
The tulip in her brilliant garb
  So proudly rears her crimson vest,
While daisy, in her modest bloom,
  Peeps timid from her grassy nest.

The varied roses droop their heads,
  Like blushing maids in coyful pride,
While orange-wreaths and lilies white
  Deck summer as a lovely bride;
And lo! the violet so meek,
  The peony and mignonnette,
The jasmine, larkspur, daffodil,
  And she that bids us not forget.

The myrtle, telling of true love,
  And snow-drops all so fair and frail,
Narcissus, iris, and sweet-pea,
  And pink so delicately pale,
Carnation, grove-love and harebell,
  Magnolia and rich woodbine,
The passion-flower, verbena pure,
  And golden-gemmed loasa-vine.

Like fairies met in riv'ling throngs
  Along the banks of every stream
Sweet Flora's flowry jewels now,
  In varied beauty, glorious gleam,
Mocking the rainbow's heavenly dyes,
  With many a dazzling radiant hue;
And emblems, too, of mortals, each —
  Of pride, of worth and virtue true.

The cherries twinkle through each bough,
  So brilliant in the morning light,
While strawberries, like coral gems,
  Glow temptingly upon the sight;
The raspberries, like rubies, gleam
  Amid their downy emerald leaves,
And clustering currants, thickly hang
  Where sunlight glittering fret-work weaves.

And birds their rapturous notes pour forth
  In strains of gladness on the air,
E'en as in Paradise of old,
  Ere earth had known of sin and care:
The Oriole's mellifluous songs
  Now rouse the drowsy early morn,
The whip-poor-will in carols soft
  Proclaims the twilight's hazy dawn.

The rills adown the mountains glide,
With joyous songs of glad delight,
And fountains leaping in the air,
Gleam like transparent shafts of light;
While sleepy cows with lagging steps
Amid the fruitful pastures rove,
The sportive lambs in frolic wild,
With graceful antics, playful move.

The busy ants in armies march
To labor where the sunbeams glow;
The merry bees, like changeful friends,
From flower to flower haste to and fro;
The butterfly, so languid, soars
And flaps her gaudy wings, so vain!
And locust, darting swiftly by,
In whirring hums its drowsy strain.

The healthful trees extend their arms,
In their green robes of summer drest;
The sloping hill, in verdant pride,
Bears high its grassy velvet crest.
The trees, the plants, each drop of dew,
Proclaim the great Creator's power,
Who made each star a rolling world,
And shaped the modest daisy flower.

Iris her maxy pennon hangs
Athwart the dreamy azure sky;
While in the west the piling clouds,
Like mimic mountains quaintly lie.
Pomona laboring with the sun,
A store of luscious fruit will heap;
While Ceres soon the ripening grain
With thrifty care will plenteous reap.

Oh, woman! turn from fashion's halls,
Where pomp and folly warp the heart;
Learn from the flowers this lesson true,
That nature needs no gauds of art:
Let these sweet gifts our time employ,
That now to vanity is given,
Then we, though clothed in mortal form,
May show the attributes of heaven.

All hail the farmers! men, indeed!
The hardy tillers of the earth;
Nature's true noblemen are they,
Of sturdy, sure and matchless worth.
Long may the members of this club
In wisdom meet, as they do now,
Imparting knowledge to the world—
The heroes of the soil and plough!

PESTS OF THE FARM.

Judge Meigs.—The club will notice the drawings on the walls, of magnified plans of insect life, which have been prepared by Dr. Waterbury for his proposed common-school lectures, upon which he will make some remarks.

AGRICULTURAL EDUCATION.

Dr. Waterbury made some pertinent remarks upon this subject, and showed its advantages by a series of drawings, exhibiting the structure of several destructive insects, pests of the farm. He showed the great lack of the right kind of education in our common schools to teach the most practical things of life. He stated that not only students but teachers are frequently ignorant of the distinction between an insect and a worm, a butterfly and a bird. What, said he, is the education of girls ? Are they ever informed of a single fact regarding the animal or vegetable world ? What is an agricultural college ? One that will do a good work. It is simply brains, not fine buildings and endowed professors. The great work must be done in our common schools. The real theory of discussions in this club is the theory of the structure of the animal and plant kingdom. The doctor proposed at the next meeting to discuss the peculiarity of the several insects illustrated by the diagrams on the wall, and show how the lower orders of living things, which are sometimes very destructive, are sustained, how multiplied, and, incidentally, how their ravages may be prevented. The whole tenor of his remarks was to give instruction of the most useful kind, such as would be useful to every child and to most adults, and he was unanimously invited to continue the subject next Monday.

Solon Robinson—I hope the club will now dispense with other business, and hear Dr. Ward upon a question of deep interest, not only to every citizen of New York, but to a vast number of the owners of land in the vicinity who do or might grow fruit for market.

VARIETIES OF STRAWBERRIES.

Dr. Ward, of Newark, N. J., exhibited some twenty sorts of strawberries, to show what can be done in ordinary fruit culture with improved varieties. In his remarks upon the subject Dr. Ward said, the first and most important thing about fruit culture, that he would speak of, was a spring box for carrying the berries to market, without the least injury to the most tender fruit. It is the invention of Osgood, Worcester, Mass. It is a box suspended in a frame by elastic straps, so as to take off all hard jars from every direction.

In relation to the strawberries exhibited, Dr. Ward said the main object was to show what great improvements could be made by cultivation ; and for this purpose he exhibited the original type and the several most approved seedlings. He did not intend to exhibit the largest, but the average, and those shown were a fair sample of what could be done in field culture.

As profitable for cultivation as market berries, Mr. Pardee has named six kinds, one of which—the extra red—is too acid for market purposes ; but of thirty varieties that I have cultivated, twenty-three of which are here represented, I will only speak briefly of some of the most prominent. The one much cultivated at Cincinnati, called the Iowa berry, is only good because very early. The Genesee seedling is without an equal for its beauty, and is of a pleasant flavor.

The McEvoy's Superior is too soft for marketing and apt to rot, though fine looking.

Longworth's Prolific, which can be grown thirty-two to the pound, is a remarkable fine berry.

The Wilson Seedling has one objection for field culture—its heavy berries beat down to the earth and injure, without the land is well mulched. It is a vigorous grower, and very prolific—the most so of all.

The Virginia Scarlet is the earliest of all varieties, but it is good only for a very early crop.

The Monroe Scarlet grows in clusters and is easily separated from the stalk, and good on that account.

The Wyllie is much like the Monroe, but not easily separated.

The Walker is an excellent berry, but too soft for market. Yet it is very rich when picked and eaten in the garden, and well worthy the attention of private families. It is an honest berry.

The Crimson Cone is a great market berry, but too soft for transportation without injury.

Burr's New Pine is the richest berry that we have. It bears rather shyly. It is not productive enough for a market-gardener's fruit, but should be in every garden.

The Wilson Berry is a very good berry for transportation, as well as very prolific.

The Hovey Seedling is one that I cannot dispense with, it is always satisfactory. The average is not very large, but very good, and bears carriage pretty well.

The Boston Pine should always be grown by the side of the Hovey, both for a fertilizer and for its fruit.

The Moyamensing Pine is a good late berry; valuable for preserving as sweetmeats.

Young's Seedling from Philadelphia is nothing but a Hovey seedling.

A nameless berry that originated on my place has many good points; but I must not say too much about it. The excellence of the berry is, that in itself it is all that we want; it don't need sugar, has a fine aroma, is of good size, and is very hardy; the foot-stalk stands up well, so that the fruit don't get dirty.

The Peabody Seedling on the table was raised by Wm. Lawton, at New Rochelle.

Mr. Charles A. Peabody, of Columbus, Ga., originated this variety by crossing the Ross Phenix with a wild strawberry of Alabama. It is hermaphrodite in its character, producing fruit without the aid of another plant, and it is in itself an excellent impregnator for pistillate varieties. It is a vigorous grower, and sufficiently hardy to withstand a considerable degree of heat or cold. The plants attain an extraordinary size, sometimes so large that one can not be covered by a half bushel measure. The fruit is borne upon tall runners, on stems from three to four inches long, attached to the calyx by a coval-like neck, without seeds, there being very few seeds in the berry.

"It is of singular form, somewhat irregular, and frequently measures seven inches in circumference. The flesh is firm, melting and juicy, having the most exquisite pine flavor, and requiring, when eaten, little or no sugar. This strawberry is a prolific bearer, opening its blossoms at the south during the mild days of winter, and perfecting its fruits in the spring, as the weather will permit. When ripe, their color is a rich, dark crimson; through its firmness and lack of acidity it will bear transportation better than any other strawberry."

Having confidence in the statements of Mr. Peabody, I ventured to enter pretty largely into the cultivation, and obtained from him ten dozen plants, and planted them on the 25th of April, 1857, one dozen on the rich ground of an old hot-bed, after removing a large portion of the manure. Here I obtained a fine stock of plants and a specimen of fruit the first season. The residue were planted in another compartment of common garden soil, *without manure*, and suffered to throw out runners in every direction; these also gave a specimen of fruit the first season, besides supplying a very large number of well-rooted plants, and with these I have extended my plantation to half an acre or more, and I am now preparing an additional acre for the exclusive cultivation of this magnificent variety.

The plants on the hot-bed ground are full of fine fruit, which is growing very large, but not one ripe berry. The specimens accompanying this were gathered this morning from the larger compartment, which was not more than half cleaned out from the runners this spring, and the vines are almost matted together. I have no hesitation in believing that if the plants had had room, and been properly cultivated for the fruit only, that Mr. Peabody's statement as to the *size of the plant and fruit* would have been fully confirmed. As it is, I am satisfied we have now a *perfect plant*, which can be cultivated with as little care as any plant ever introduced into the garden, without the slightest hazard of obtaining a beautiful display of flowers and a bed of barren plants. I design, however, of testing the qualities of eight or ten of the most approved varieties, and shall not be so prejudiced as to omit to give them a fair trial in competition with this variety.

Wm. R. Prince exhibited 17 varieties, 16 of them of his own seedlings, the other a new variety, a Canada strawberry called the Lady's Pine. Mr. P. said: A staminate plant produces a great many unproductive blossoms. The only exception is in Wilson's seedlings; all other sorts are less productive than pistillates.

Dr. Ward.—The most productive strawberries that I grow, are staminates or hermaphrodites, and I think that is the opinion of others.

T. W. Field.—The Virginia scarlet, or as it is called, the Scotch runner, is one of the most productive of all varieties, and yet this is a stamanate.

or hermaphrodite plant, and this is entirely contrary to Mr. Prince's theory. In my experience everywhere large numbers of blossoms give large numbers of small fruits; and on the contrary those of few blossoms, like Hovey's seedlings, produce large fruits. Mr. Longworth once said here that Hovey seedlings were not known at Cincinnati, that is, of the same kind that is known here.

Mr. Prince.—My father published the whole matter about the sexes of strawberries twenty-five years ago. The European heart hay produces staminate and pistillate flowers. I have strawberry beds that were white with blossoms that have not a single berry—all barren. The strawberries that come from England with the highest sounding names are worthless here, because they have no female plants.

R. G. Pardee.—All this matter is the old battle of horticulturists, and it is not wonderful that some of them are opinionated.

Dr. Waterbury.—I call attention that Dr. Ward stated that his little boy could tell in a moment the different kinds of blossoms, and which would prove prolific of fruit and which barren. This is just the sort of information that I contend for giving children in common schools, that is, agricultural education.

Dr. Ward, in answer to a question of T. W. Field, named the following four varieties in their order as likely to prove most profitable to the market gardener: Wilson's Seedling, Iowa strawberry, Early Scarlet, Virginia Scarlet or Scotch Runner, and Longworth's Prolific. These are what are called hermaphrodite, or staminates, and they are all great producers, and more so than any pistillates, or any others that I ever grew.

Mr. Prince.—With me the Iowa does not bear one half a fair crop. Here is one of my seedlings that is an exception to all rules. Every blossom produces a berry, and all ripen at once. I call it the Eclipse. The Ladies' Pine, originated in Canada, is a very delicate and peculiar flavored berry.

T. W. Field said that upon two beds of strawberries, growing side by side on his place in Brooklyn, he picked as many quarts of Hovey's Seedlings as three hired women picked of the common early Scarlet, and while the latter sold at twenty cents a quart, hulls off, the Hovey's sold at fifty cents, hulls on, and that was about the usual difference in this market between common and superior fruit.

Andrew S. Fuller, of Brooklyn, exhibited two very promising seedlings, selected from a great number that he has grown. We think one of them promises well as a market berry.

The strawberries of Mr. Lawton were admired for their great size and for their taste, for he gave them all to the Club.

Mr. Hite, of Morrisania, an amateur horticulturist, much and justly praised for his skill, industry and joyous culture of a garden, exhibited Peabody & Longworth's Prolific, of size superior to all. He sells them at *one dollar a quart*, while good berries are now here in market at *three cents a basket*.

Mr. Boyd, from Fond du Lac, presented wine made by him from the petioles of rhubarb, which was pronounced very pleasant—no alcohol in it.

Mr. Fuller's berries were from seedlings of August, 1856—one of them (the berry,) almost an inch in diameter. His practice in raising seedlings generally is remarkably successful.

Mr. Prince has raised fifty-five seedling strawberries, of which he has exhibited the berries of sixteen, some of them very fine, viz: No. 12, Cordova; No. 26, Eclipse, ripens all at once; No. 35, Imperial crimson; No. 36, Imperial scarlet; No. 60, Prince's globose; No. 61, Prince's climax; No. 69, Prince's scarlet magnate; No. 77, Supreme staminate; No. 79, Sylvania; No. 81, Transcendant scarlet; No. 93, Triumphant scarlet; No. 107, Prince's blush pine; No. 42, Ladies' pine, the most exquisite of all strawberries; No. 1301, New seedling; No. 41, Le Baron, very high flavor.

Subject—Dr. Waterbury's Physiology, and the others continued.

The club adjourned.

H. MEIGS, *Secretary.*

June 28, 1858.

Present—Messrs. Bruce, Doughty, Dr. Peck, Prof. Mapes, Prof. Nash, Dr. Waterbury, G. P. Pell, Don Fermier Feirer, late President of Nicaragua; Messrs. Turell, John W. Chambers, Wm. B. Leonard, Adrian Bergen and Hon. John G. Bergen, of Gowanus; Davoll, Pardee, Dr. Ward, H. P. Byram, of the Valley Farmer; T. W. Field, F. W. Geissenhainer, Jr., Paine, Hite, Solon Robinson—fifty members in all.

Prof. Nash in the chair. Henry Meigs, Secretary.

INSECTS AND THEIR STRUCTURE.

Dr. Waterbury explained the structure and natural formation of animals and insects, of great value, but of which we can give only an imperfect synopsis. He stated in regard to the caterpillar, that as simple as it appears, it is made up of a complete system of nerves, extremely sensitive, by which it is able to distinguish the kind of food suited to its taste, and to avoid every thing offensive. Advantage can be taken of this truth by the farmer, as it often is, and obstructions placed in the way of their ascent of fruit trees. He said that it was only by the study of the simple structure of insects that we can counteract the injuries to vegetation. He also illustrated the structure of the lobster, and how they breathe and take sustenance, and showed how little men knew of these animals who have handled them all their lives. By a dissected lobster he showed several interesting facts connected with the structure of animals of a low order, and how those useful may be propagated, and how the noxious ones may be exterminated. He illustrated by words and diagrams the difference between vertibræ and articulate animals and insects, and the metamorphoses of insects, and how they propagate their species, and said that to exterminate any one of a noxious class of insects, we must encourage the increase of an innocent race. For instance, it would be impossible to destroy the larva of the insects that prey upon our city shade trees by human hands, but we could encourage birds that prey upon them, so as to get rid of all their ill effects. And so of a great many other noxious things; if we knew more of them, we could easily find an antidote for their depredations, by means of some harmless insect, bird or animal, the natural food of which are the things which we wish to get rid of.

Dr. Waterbury dissected a lobster showing that it contained teeth for further mastication of its food. He showed its heart, situated under and near to its back—and the circulation of its blood—having *forty pulsations a minute, &c.* The most learned persons present were much pleased with these phenomena and with Dr. Waterbury's very intelligent easy manner of demonstration, and by his large drawings, and on the blackboard.

Mr. Solon Robinson offered the following resolution, which was seconded by Prof. Mapes, and carried unanimously, viz:

Resolved, That the lectures of Dr. Waterbury upon the structure and functions of insects and animals and plants, are well worthy of repetition before all the schools of this country, as they contain matter that should be learned by every child in America, and can be learned by the lucid manner of teaching by Dr. Waterbury more rapidly than by any other mode in common use; and therefore it is the opinion of this club, that we may benefit others by recommending such a course of lectures as the doctor is capable of giving, before schools and agricultural societies.

A CURIOUS CASE IN HOG CHOLERA.

Solon Robinson.—I have a letter detailing a curious case connected with the disease of hogs, called cholera, that I beg to call attention to now, and perhaps Dr. Waterbury may suggest a remedy. At any rate it is a subject for thought. E. C. Wright, of Gallatin county, Illinois, states, on the authority of the Rev. John Crawford, of Crawford, in that county, that the bones of swine dying with what is called hog cholera, decay as rapidly as the flesh, and that portions of the skin outlast the bones. He wants scientific men to give attention to this strange consumption of the solids, and thinks that it may be the means of suggesting a remedy for the disease so fatal and so pecuniarily distressing to a vast number of farmers in the west. Now, as we know that feeding bone meal to animals and phosphate of lime to plants that need it, has proved beneficial. is it impossible or improbable that feeding it to swine suffering from a disease that produces the effect described, may not be the means of curing or preventing the disease?

Dr. Waterbury.—There are some new theories in relation to feeding phosphates to animals. It is possible that this may have some effect.

There is an idea prevailing that feeding material that makes bones will increase their size. It is a subject well worthy of more attention.

Prof. Mapes.—When a calf is deficient in bone, that is too weak to stand, feeding bone meal to the cow that suckles the calf will furnish it with the necessary material. This fact is well known to many farmers, and that cows eat old bones with great avidity. We also know that physicians are using a solution of phosphate of lime in their practice, and there is no doubt it may be administered to domestic animals with equally good effect ; and whether, in the case named, it worked a cure or not, it is well worth trying. Many things much more simple have produced wonderful results.

Dr. Waterbury adverted to the practice of our President Pell in giving to calves, having weak limbs, phosphate of lime.

RUST ON WHEAT—A PREVENTIVE.

Solon Robinson.—I have another letter that describes an easy preventive of rust on wheat. James Laurie, of White county, Indiana, writes that rust can be prevented by taking a long cord between two men and sweeping it over the field soon after the fog, which he thinks causes rust, has settled upon it, as the rope agitates the grain and makes the water run to the ground, just as it does by agitation of wind, which he has noticed always prevents any bad effect from fogs or what are called scalding showers, whenever they are followed by a breeze sufficient to shake off the water.

SOWING CORN FOR FODDER.

Warren Hutchins wishes me to say to the club that he does not sow corn and plow it in, but scatters it in every third furrow, just where the two furrows come together, which only takes half a bushel of seed per acre. If desired to have the rows only ten inches apart, scatter seed in every furrow.

CORN OR CLOVER TO PLOW UNDER.

He says : " I feel much interest in the club discussions, and I should like to know why a corn crop is not cheaper and better than clover for manure, as it comes to maturity the first year. Please tell us the best method of managing clover that is plowed under, so as to have the seed come up and stock the land again. I plowed under a piece of clover a year ago last fall ; the next spring I plowed the ground, and sowed to rye, expecting a fine clover stock, but was disappointed. This spring I have planted the field to corn, and the clover has come up very thick and fine."

LEATHER SCRAPS FOR MANURE.

Two years ago I obtained a wagon load of scraps of leather, put it in a hole in the ground, and applied lime and ashes to the heap. I have taken out some this spring, and put in some corn-hills ; it was about half of it rotted, and the rest very tender. I should like to know the value of rotten leather for manure, and the best method to rot it.

Prof. Mapes.—I propose that we discuss the several subjects mentioned in these letters read by Mr. Robinson, at our next meeting.

RENOVATING WORN OUT LANDS CALLED BARREN.

This subject was called up, and the hour devoted to the regular questions, of which it was one, was mainly devoted to showing that Long Island lands are not naturally barren.

Prof. Nash.—I have a few words to say upon the Long Island lands. It has been stated and denied that the land is loam, and not sand or gravel. I have lately spent some days in examination of this soil, and find that statement correct, and that it is beautifully adapted to garden culture, and capable of producing various crops most profitable to the cultivator. This loam has produced and is able to produce $400 to the acre in strawberries. I wish the slanders that have been spoken against the lands of Long Island could be counteracted and their value better known and made useful to the world. Although not as rich as prairie soil, it is well worthy of the attention of small farmers and men in search of lands for homes. Such homes can be made upon the wild lands of Long Island as well, to say the least, as in the west.

Dr. Peck.—The lands lying upon Long Island do not need renovating—they only need cultivation. The whole center of the island is a natural clover field. There is scarely an acre that will not produce strawberries as well as the patch spoken of by Mr. Nash.

S. Williams, of Seneca county, said he wished barely to corroborate all that Professor Nash and Dr. Peck have said about those lands, which he had seen for the first time within a few days. I find it a natural clover region, and one of the best natural grass regions I know of; not excepting my native place, Newport, Rhode Island.

In answer to R. G. Pardee, Mr. Williams said : The best means of renovating our land in Seneca county, are draining and plowing in clover. There is no danger of manure leaching away in drains. If you can keep manure from going up, you may let it go down as much as it will. The water will always run clear from the tile drains. So says John Jonhson, of our county.

T. W. Field.—The land of Long Island is very variable in its character. A striking geological feature is that the valleys running north and south are measurably barren ; the hills are the richest. Large tracts can be obtained all over the island, at low rates, containing all the good land desired. The land needs more capital to begin with, but will prove more productive than some of the black lands. It can all be manured within itself by clover, the best method of renovating all soil. One man who scattered the gravel from a railroad cut over his farm to get rid of it, found his farm improved by it.

Dr. Peck.—Upon just such land as has been called barren, fifty-four bushels of wheat per acre has been grown, taking the State Society premium. Mr. Wilson, who died last week, left a fifty acre field of clover, right in the midst of the scrub-oak barrens, just as fine clover as ever grew ; and the whole of the soil called barren, can be renovated by clover, even upon worn out farms, and made equally productive as Mr. Wilson's.

Prof. Mapes.—The first cultivators of the Hempstead plains, I know. James Pool was the first man who cultivated this land, at a time when it was considered so poor and valueless that he was permitted to fence in just as much as he pleased ; and that land is still in use, and very productive.

Dr. Peck.—There are now some of the finest grass farms in the State, near where Wm. Cobbett lived, in North Hempstead, upon the tract still known as the Plains, and which belongs to the old town of Hempstead, and which the people will not allow to be sold, because it makes a common cow pasture, and those who use it for that, insist that it is good for nothing else.

The discussion was continued at considerable length, with a general agreement, that not only the barren land of Long Island, but all similar land, can be renovated, and made to produce any other crop, by clover, and that that is the cheapest and easiest means in the world, to renovate worn out lands.

LONG ISLAND CHERRIES.

Mr. Bartlett showed a branch, handsomely loaded with cherries, from a tree growing in the " worn out soil of Long Island," just to show how that land can be renovated, and made to produce choice fruits.

STRAWBERRIES.

H. S. Finley, in a letter from Davenport, Iowa, says : " I have not succeeded well with strawberries, and I want to ascertain the quantity each of lime, salt, and water, to apply to an acre, as I saw the matter referred to in the report in the ' Tribune,' of the proceedings of the club, which I read with great satisfaction."

R. G. Pardee gives the desired information, as follows: For a plot of ground 20 by 20 feet, I would use one bushel of unleached ashes, to give it the needed potash, and one peck of salt, dissolved in water to a point of saturation, with which slack one bushel of lime.

VISITORS OF THE CLUB.

Don Fermin Ferreir, of Nicaraugua, was present at the meeting to-day ; and a friend of his stated that he has sometimes as many as 10,000 head of cattle on his hacienda. There were also several ladies present, notwithstanding the excessive heat, and it is intended, by and by, to get up discussions in which they can take part, as in the cultivation of flowers, and household matters of great interest to the female portion of society.

Prof. Nash.—As to the true character of Long Island lands for cultivation, he has lately examined them carefully, and expresses much surprise that they should have been so long misunderstood, for he finds the soils excellent.

Subjects for next meeting, proposed by Prof. Mapes—" Use of green crops, plowed in ;" " Leather, preparation of, for manure."

The club adjourned to Monday, July 19th, at noon.

H. MEIGS, *Secretary.*

July 19th, 1858.

Present—Messrs. Lawton, of New Rochelle ; Andrew S. Fuller, of Williamsburgh ; John Bruce, Solon Robinson, Thomas W. Field, of Brooklyn ; Mr. Witt, of Williamsburgh ; Mr. Paine, of Brooklyn ; John W. Chambers, Charles Z. Erhardt, of Astoria, and others—41 members.

Richard G. Pardee in the chair ; Henry Meigs, Secretary.

The secretary read the following translations and extracts made by him from the last works received by the Institute from Europe, &c., viz :

London Farmers' Magazine, June, 1858.

SULPHUR TO PREVENT POTATO ROT.

It has been found that clay used in the purification of gas, absorbs ammonia as a sulphate. *" Five million pounds weight of sulphur* are estimated to be in our annual crop of wool—chiefly derived from the grass eaten by the sheep. This must return to the soil, or that will deteriorate. Of three acres of prime Regent potatoes, two and one half of them were dressed with coal gas clay, and all free from rot, while the half acre without clay, more than half rotted. A great discovery seems here to be close at hand.

Note by Meigs.—France has saved her grapes from the oidium by using sulphur on the leaves, fruit and vines. Let sulphur be sprinkled in our potato hills at planting.

TOBACCO GROWN IN FRANCE.

At Lille they raise 24 cwt. per acre. Government buys it all at prices fixed by itself. An ancient convent at Lille is occupied in curing it for market. 350 men and 400 women are employed at it. This tobacco is never used alone. All sorts of other tobacco are mixed with it. The cigars are made by the women. Snuff after undergoing various processes for six months, remains for one year in immense heaps of forty or fifty tons each to *acquire a scent.*

THE SORGHUM.

One field yielded *sixty tons weight of stalks per acre*, at three cuttings, for fodder. Another field *thirty tons at one cutting.*

In the South of France it yields 15 per cent of sugar. It is cut and cured in June, when three feet high. Let grow it attains eight or nine feet. No insect touches it. Hogs eat the roots boiled.

Societe Imperiale Zoologique D'Acclimatation.

Report made in the name of the council on the subject of the formation of a Garden of Acclimation in the Bois de Boulogne.   Paris, 1858.

Extracts translated by H. Meigs.

"Four years ago, this society was founded by the powerful impulse of an illustrious naturalist,' (the Secretary General, Count d'Epremesnil.)

There are already nearly 1,700 members of it, among whom we count eleven sovereigns, seventeen princes of sovereign houses of Europe, Africa, Asia and America, and above all, His Majesty, the Emperor of the French, who has honored the society with his protection, and the Imperial Princes have given their aid.

A great many of the members are out of France, in various parts of the world, acting as the most enlightened and devoted agents of the society.

In 1854, our brother member, Mr. Montigny, aided by our generous government, put us in possession of the only herd of Yaks that ever came to Europe, and they prosper and readily acclimate.   To him, also, and to our missionaries, we are indebted for three of the most precious vegetables from China.

The Igname (dioscorea batatas) distributed in 1855, by this society— its bulbilles by hundreds of thousands through all Europe, and this tuber which is so important a part of the nourishment of the Chinese, ought, on account of its merits, to be placed by the side of the potato, for it is now completely acclimated and cultivated on a great scale.   The mode of perfecting it is being studied, and one Mr. Hardy, the able and zealous director of our Algerian Nursery, is growing it of a better figure—not so long as we have it.

The sugar sorgho, also, an excellent forage and yielding very pure sugar ; the oak silk worm thrives ; the Palma Christi thrives and feels well on thistle ; the Loza for its chlorophyll, valuable ; geese of Egypt ; American patridge ; the parrot ; ducks of China and Carolina ; the black swan ; the Gambra partridge, introduced and propagated in France by the care of the Emperor Napoleon ; modern pisciculture, stocking rivers and ponds ; oysters cultivated ; lobsters, also ; leeches ; cray-fish ; the hemi-one, or wild horse of the Himmalayas, lama, &c.

It is only since 1825 that France has introduced and acclimated the beef and mutton of England, and her pigs from Middlesex, New Leicester, Berkshire, &c.

Societe Imperiale Zoologique D'Acclimatation.   Paris, April, 1858.

YELLOW LUPIN FOR MANURE.

Mons. Sacc gives to the society ten quarts of Yellow Lupin, to be tried as a fertilizer.   He says that if plowed into sandy land, while green, it changes the land to fertile soil completely, and secures a vigorous crop of other plants.   Rye or wheat thrive on it the first season.

Solon Robinson mentioned the great value of a similar plant, sometimes called the maggotty pea, that springs up after every crop on the eastern shore of Virginia, and is a natural fertilizer of the light soil of that region.

FISH RAISING.

Mons. Jules Cloquet sent a communication on this subject, *empoissonnement*, (stocking water with fish. Careful spelling is here essential, for *empoisonnement* means poisoning.) He sends trouts of various sizes alive. He uses a wheel moving in a trough to agitate and ærate the aquarium in which he keeps the trouts. The Emperor and Empress recently visited Mons. Coste's fish nursery at the laboratory of the College of France.

JAPAN RICE—TEN VARIETIES.

Mons. Von Siebold sends to the president ten sorts of rice of Japan, for trial in Southern France, or Algeria, &c. Some of these flourish in rather dry lands, and are of early growth.

Oryza Montana.—The mountain rice of China is of long grains with reddish epidermis, seems to me to be a distinct species.

Von Siebold & Co., of Leyden, (Holland,) supply their catalogues of Japanese plants, cultivated by them. The wax tree, (Rhussucccanea,) the varnish tree, (Rhus vernicifera of Japan,) are growing in their gardens. The wax tree furnishes Japan with tapers, and the latter with the varnish so celebrated. We ought to introduce to our forests their *cephalataxus pedunculata* and *ulmus keaki*, the wood very precious for cabinet work.

N. B.—We give 24 wax trees for 250 francs and 6 varnish trees for 100 francs. These trees are from 6 to 10 decimetres high (about 24 to 42 inches).

AUSTRALIAN POTATOES

were distributed for experiment. It is said that they require hilling up very early.

CHINESE YAM.   (*Dioscorea.*)

The Chinese plant the *slender upper end of this root* and eat the rest.

SEA ISLAND—LONG STAPLE COTTON.

The Algerian cotton planters have tried to grow it, and now complain, after six years trial, that if the government aid ceases they cannot sell it in competition with the Americans who have grown it the last *seventy or eighty years!* That this cotton plant requires abundant manure and irrigation, and it is apprehended *that its quality will change to short staple.*

Tallow tree seeds were received from China and some candles made of the tallow.

Bogota potatoes were received.

The olive tree from the Crimea is commended.

Fish are to be sent from France to stock Algerian rivers, &c.

No. 4 of the bulletin of the *Agricultural Society of Algiers* contains a note on the Angora goat.

CHINESE YAM. (*Dioscorea Batata.*)

This valuable tuber is now found to be remarkably easy to cultivate. It remains in the ground during the winter and multiplies in summer. It may be left in the ground like our Jerusalem artichoke which takes care of itself entirely. The large tubers may be taken for use and the small ones left to grow large in time. The vines and leaves of this yam will cover the ground sufficiently, with some help, to keep down weeds. If it is as a table vegetable, not equal to good potatoes, it will add much to the vege- table courses both in its natural condition, plain boiled, or in a sort of custard which is readily made of it, very pleasing to the palate and very wholesome. So that its hardihood, resisting frost, and keeping perfectly in its field, render it greatly superior to those vegetables which we are compelled to house every winter. It is also less exacting of manures than most plants. The Chinese say it hates manure, especially that which is valued above all others, that is *night soil* !

[Revue Horticole, Journal D'Horticulture Pratique, Paris, May, 1858.]

J. Grænland, on the peculiar functions of leaves, by careful experiments, has decided the fact that dew on the leaves of plants does not enter them at all. That the benefit is of the dew on the ground. The leaves breathe, transpiring carbonic acid and inspiring oxygen by night, and absorbing carbonic acid and transpiring oxygen by day. The common opinion that leaves absorb dew is an error ! The functions of the leaves are limited to the breathing and the transpiration of the fluids they contain in themselves, and not to absorption of water from atmosphere.

PLANTS SUITED TO AN AQUARIUM.

The thirty plants enumerated all flourish either in water or on the mar- gins of water. Those who wish to ornament their aquarium should seek for such as they may like. This rather new taste is merely an extension of the gold fish apparatus and may ultimately lead to the breeding of fish in parlors, as some now breed Canary birds and others. The nursery of valuable fishes will form an immensely useful as well as a very agreeable amusement. For breeding trout the water in the aquarium should be kept in agitation by a wheel of suitable size working in a trough, to create and maintain current and agitation. From extensive practice we may derive the knowledge of the best modes of raising all kinds for our waters, that they may teem with abundance and come to our markets from our waters, fattened, as poultry comes from the land.

THE OAK SILK WORM

occupies much attention among the silk growers of France. Mons. Jacquemart reminded the imperial society, that from its foundation, efforts have been made by it, to obtain for France, the *wild silk worm* which lives in China upon oak trees. That a committee consisting of Messrs. Guérin-Méneville, Tastet and himself had prepared a list of questions in detail relative to it, which by the care of the superior of the foreign missions, has been sent to all the French missionaries in China, who lend us powerful aid in these matters, for which we cannot be too gateful. The Abbe Bertrand, our apostolic missionary in Sutchuen, has returned very precise answers to our circular of questions. Mons. Jacquemart read it.

Mons. Guérin-Méneville stated that the facts given to us by the Abbe Bertrand coincide with those we had obtained from the director of the Russian colony established in Pekin, *who is now in Paris.* He remarks that we have some leaves of the two kinds of oak spoken of by the Abbe Bertrand, and the acorns of which were received through the Bishop Verolles and Mons. Montigny, and we now have those two kinds of oak growing here, and one of them, the *chesnut leaved one* is cultivated in the museum of natural history gardens. We can readily multiply these oaks when we shall possess the silk worm.

NOTE BY H. MEIGS.—Michaux, in his admirable North American Sylva, describes three oaks as " Chesnut White Oak," " Rock Chesnut Oak," and "Small Chesnut Oak," *whose leaves resemble those of the chesnut "Castanea vesca,"* the one said to be preferred by this new silk worm.

Charles F. Erhard, of Astoria, exhibited branches and bunches of his cherry currants, which are very large, and so closely clustered on the branches as to hide them from view.

Solon Robinson asked the privilege of making a little statement about the value of improvements made upon our common fruits, as most particularly shown in the cherry currant. Some of the members of the club, said Mr. R., will remember with what pleasure we looked upon a specimen of the fruit of the cherry currant, exhibited here last year, by Charles F. Erhard, a German gardener, at Ravenswood, that beautiful little village on the bank of the East river, opposite Blackwell's Island. It was doubted by some whether such currants could be grown, as a general thing, to such perfection. I don't doubt it—I have visited Mr. Erhard, and seen how they will grow, and how they will compare with the crimson sort growing in the same soil, and I am satisfied that all gardeners, and all farmers, should get rid of the old style currant bushes, and replace them with those of the new variety, as soon as possible ; and it is possible very soon, for even now, great as the demand is, the sets can be bought for about $70 a thousand. As some persons may inquire, " What is the cherry currant?" I have requested Mr. Erhard to allow me to read a paper prepared by him, giving that information. It reads as follows :

Description of the Cherry Currant.—It is not a distinct species of the genus *Ribes*—only a new variety of *Ribes Rubrum*, of which the red and white Dutch, and many others, are also varieties. It is, therefore, just as hardy as the common currant. The distinguishing properties of the cherry currant are : Strong, robust growth of the bush—the shoots being stouter, the leaves larger, and of a darker green, than the common sort. The blossom of the cherry currant is easily distinguished from the greenish yellow blossom of the red and white Dutch, by its darker brownish color. But the greatest and most valuable distinction of the cherry currant, consists in the uniformly great size of the berries. They measure from half an inch to five-eighths of an inch in diameter, all the berries of a bunch being generally of nearly one size, while the bunches of the common currant taper down to a very small berry at the end. Besides this, the berries are also distinguishable by their dark red color. Another and very striking feature of the cherry currant, consists in the manner the bunches are distributed over the branches. While, with the common currant, the fruit is rather thinly—at least, by comparison—scattered over the branches, the cherry currants hang in massive clusters, so tight that the stems of the fruit-strings can scarcely be seen. Branches of the bush, from one to three feet in length, are often unbroken clusters of luscious fruit, which gives the bushes a charming rich appearance.

How to grow them.—Many farmers and market gardeners seem to think these good qualities can only be brought out by very high culture, such as the amateur gardener can only bestow on a few pet bushes. This is an error. I would say: Manure, plow, and hoe them as you do your Indian corn, and you will have them in as great perfection as the nurseryman.

As the bushes grow very strong, they should be planted not less than 4x4 feet, or, perhaps, 4x5 feet apart, which will give 2,178 plants per acre. I prefer the latter method, and would plow only one way between them, allowing the branches to spread in the direction of the rows, so as to form something like a hedge. These rows should run north and south, to shield the bushes from the hottest mid-day sun. Shade to the fruit is indispensable to bring it to perfection ; if too much exposed to the hot rays of the sun, the berries ripen prematurely before they attain their full size. Now, all the shade necessary to protect the fruit is furnished by the bush itself, if you do not disable it to do so by pruning and cutting away what was evidently intended for that purpose ; and this brings me to the shape in which currant bushes should be pruned. I am aware that there exists a great difference of opinion among cultivators as to this point. Many believe that the tree shape is decidedly the best ; others think the bush form, with several branches springing directly from the root, the better and most natural shape. I have tried both ways, but prefer the latter method greatly. The great advantage of the bush form, it seems to me, consists in the system of renewal which should be combined with it.

Suppose you plant young bushes with two prongs, or branches. Plant them deep, and allow, the first year, two shoots to grow up from under the ground. These shoots will, at the same time, send out their own roots, and grow luxuriantly. If you allow, then, every year two more shoots to spring up from the root, you will, in the summer of the fourth year, have two branches each, of five, four, three, two and one years' growth. Six of these branches, that is, the five, four, and three year old ones, will be loaded with fruit; the two years' growth may have some berries, and those of this year's growth will be only straight shoots. The bushes will now be as large as they should be, and the two five year old branches may be cut out as soon as the fruit is picked; and henceforth, by allowing still two new shoots to come up every year, and by cutting out the two oldest branches after the gathering of the fruit, the bushes will be kept young, and bear fine fruit for many years more. Of course, this is only meant to elucidate the general principle. The practical cultivator will know how to modify the above rule for every individual bush.

Productiveness.—In calculating the profits of a crop great caution must be used, and casualties must not be forgotten. Although I have seen four-year old bushes that bore nine pounds of berries to each bush, I would not think it safe to put down the average yield of a full grown, five-year old bush, trimmed as above, at more than six pounds. This would amount to 13,068 pounds to an acre. The price of common currants in the New York market, generally very small sour little things, varies from four to seven cents per pound at wholesale, which certainly justifies the anticipation of six cents per pound for cherry currants for many years to come, and this would make the value of the crop per acre equal to $784.

Expenses of cultivating and gathering.—Half a day of plowing and three days of hoeing, by one man, will clean and stir the ground of one acre most effectually, which, at ordinary wages of man and horse, will cost $3.50, which makes four plowings and hoeings cost $14. Picking 13,068 pounds, at one-third cent per pound, (about 15 cents per bushel), will be $43. If we allow $27 for manure every year, the whole expense per acre would sum up to $84, leaving $700 clear, of which only the cost of bringing them to market would have to be deducted.

Mr. Robinson continued.—Now, Sir, suppose you take this as the statement of an interested nurseryman—a man who is just beginning to make it his business to propagate this new, (that is, new in this country, it originated in France a few years ago)—this new variety of currants. What then? Why simply this; truth is immutable, and no matter by who uttered, it is truth still. And so far as what I can say will encourage the propagation of this fruit I will do it by endorsing every word in that paper. Nay, I will do more, and here say that the statement is not exaggerated; it is below the fair estimate that would be made by any sensible man who has seen, as I have seen, the bushes in full bearing. There is one more thing that I will say: there are at this moment tens of thousands of acres of land upon Long Island covered with scrub oaks, worthless to the owners, every acre of which could be made to yield the product and profit set forth in that paper, if some man of means would set the idle men and women of this city to work at the business of growing thousands of acres, and tens of thousands of tons of this improved variety of currants. "Glut the market." Fudge! The fruit can be grown for two cents a pound, and that every family can eat it as a condiment with their bread and meat every day in the year, and can afford to drink a delicious, wholesome wine—currant wine—instead of getting drunk and dying as they do now from poisoned stuff called beverages. Whilst this then bears the name of American Institute, let us by every argument we can use encourage the increased production of American fruits. We have no need of sending to Zante for currants, Madeira for grapes, or France for wine; or should the folly be any longer tolerated, except by a nation of ninneys, of importing currant jelly.

The Chairman expressed his gratification in hearing Mr. Erhard's account of this superior currant.

GOOSEBERRIES.

Andrew S. Fuller, of Brooklyn, exhibited some gooseberries that would not discredit an English gardener. He said they grew upon the bush at the rate of eighteen to each foot in length, the berries being about one and a half inches in length, and just acquiring a claret color on their skins.

Mr. Lawton exhibited white gooseberries of great size, pure from all mildew and abundant on their branches. They averaged full three inches in circumference. He also exhibited branches of our old fashioned small red currant, some crystal beautiful white currants, some full sized black, and some champagne currants, the latter distinguished by a tinge of lake color very beautifully. Some persons seem to think that the club wastes time on the small fruit. Those persons may eat their roasted mutton and venison *without any currant jelly.*

Mr. Fuller.—We occasionally hear from distant fields, that what the club found fine in a fruit, does not prove so there. Certainly not. It is necessary for us to know that place and circumstances not only exercise deep influences on plants, but on animals too. Each must raise that which his place best suits. No wise farmer will plant his corn in the swamp, nor his water cress on dry land.

Joseph C. Canning, agent of the National Fertilizing Company, at 87 Fulton street, New York, presented boxes of their *new fertilizer* for distribution among the members, with the request to try it effectually. It is manufactured by a pupil of the celebrated Liebig.

Thomas W. Field, of Brooklyn, stated that he had received a box of fruit—beautiful ripe peaches, apricots, Bartlett pears, &c., from Col. Richard Peters, who grows fruit at Atalanta, in Georgia, where they ripen two months earlier than here. He exhibited the pears, which were larger than the same generally grown here.

J. A. Wagener.—The inventor of an approved harvesting machine, sends from the township of Homer, in Champagne county, in the State of Illinois, samples of Hungarian grass and clover. The grass resembles timothy, is nearly five feet high. The clover five and a half feet high. The grass is of six weeks growth. *There is one farm here with two thousand acres of it* in clover and timothy.

Mr. Field presented his volume on the pear, for which the club gave him a unanimous vote of thanks.

Questions for next meeting—by Mr. Robinson : "Mud, fresh or salt, and Muck and Peat for manure ;" "Fruits on farms."

Solon Robinson.—I have several letters from correspondents, asking and giving information.   Here is one that tells

HOW TO CULTIVATE PEAS WITHOUT THE WEEVIL.

Plant them five inches deep or more, as early in the spring as the ground will allow.   They will not blight nor mildew, nor weevil.   I plant the June pea, strawberry pea and marrowfat, and have green peas from the middle of June till green corn, here in Michigan.   I plant in rows five or six feet apart, mark the ground about two inches deep, sow a row of beets between each row of peas, cultivate same as potatoes.   Beets will stand frost as well as peas.   When the pea straw is out of the way, plow all the ground toward the beets.   This is the way to raise premium beets and clear the ground from weeds.   •

E. B. COCHRAN, Sandstone, Jackson county.

And here is another writer who wants to know the opinion of the club about plowing in clover.   He asks :

" In cases where clover grows heavy, so as to effectually shade the land, how much, if anything, is lost by not plowing under while green.   I have always supposed that the shade, together with the mold of the clover on top of the ground, would improve the land as much as plowing under. The inference I draw from reading the debates of the Farmers' Club, as published in *The Tribune*, is, that unless clover is plowed under while green the benefits are pretty much lost."

The Chairman thought this an important question, and that although the shade and decay on the ground would be valuable, it would be enough more so under the soil to pay for plowing under.

Thos. W. Field.—In regard to the question about clover—it appropriates a great deal from the atmosphere, and a greater benefit will be obtained by plowing in the crop.

Solon Robinson.—As one, I want to know if there is a man engaged in the business that can tell me the true value of an acre of clover, and whether it is worth more to plow in than it is to rot upon the ground, or cut and cure and pass through animals before it is given back to the earth as manure.   And I want to know if there is any man that can tell the value of a ton of manure, that is, as a smelter of ore can tell the value of a ton of it, which he puts into the furnace.   Does not the farmer put the manure into the earth for a similar purpose ?   One draws out refined metal, and if that is worth more than the ore and fuel and labor, then he makes a profit.

The other has for an object to change the mass of dirt into corn, wheat and fine flour, which, after all, is nothing but refined dirt, and upon the process depends the profit, and I think one should be just as well able to tell the value of the crude article as the other.   But is he ?

TURNIP SEED.

Here is another correspondent that wants to know if turnip seed, harvested from roots that were left out over winter, will produce good turnips if sown for a crop. "My neighbors," says the writer, "told me it will not produce turnips, but charlock."

"Now," said Mr. Robinson, "here is a case where we want positive knowledge. Who has it? I have not, only believe as those neighbors did, that it is not good seed."

Andrew S. Fuller.—I know of one instance where such seed was sown, and it produced turnip tops and seed, but few bulbs of any value.

THE HOG DISEASE.

Solon Robinson.—Well, here is another letter that confirms the statement of one I read at a former meeting, that the bones of hogs dying with the prevailing epidemic are so diseased that they decay in the carcass before the softer tissues. As this is the case, my remedy or preventive would be feeding bone meal liberally with plenty of sulphur.

SUBJECT FOR THE NEXT MEETING.

Wm. Lawton.—I hope members will not flag in bringing forward subjects and discussing them with energy, for we may elicit some facts of importance to ourselves and others. The oldest man here feels that he lives again while talking of fruit and trees and flowers. There is an enjoyment in such labor, and there is excitement in producing new things, and so there is in coming together in these social gatherings to discuss them.

Adjourned to first Monday in August, and to meet every first and third Monday of each month till further notice.

H. MEIGS, *Secretary.*

——

August 2, 1858.

Present—Messrs. Adrian Bergen, of Gowanus; Andrew S. Fuller, of Williamsburgh; Solon Robinson, Paine, and Dr. Peck, and T. W. Field, of Brooklyn; Chilson, of Jersey; Rev. Mr. Adamson, Secretary of the Geographical and Statistical Society; Hon. Hugh Maxwell, Mr. Stacey, Bruce and Witt, of Williamsburgh; John W. Chambers, Robert L. Waterbury, M. D., Sotham, of Oswego, Lowe—47 in all.

Dr. Waterbury in the chair; Henry Meigs, Secretary.

The secretary read the following translations and extracts made by him from works received by the Institute since the last meeting of the club, viz:

Revue Horticole, Paris, June, 1858.

THE CRYSTAL PALACE AND THE GARDENERS.

The exhibition of fruits, flowers, plants, &c., at the palace continued from the 12th to the 27th of May, and as our horticulturists had last year proved the excellence of the palace in the preservation of their articles, they came forward this year with great zeal with their numerous lots of hothouse plants and others. They were beautifully displayed, were well watered from an artificial rivulet made with hydraulic mortar, with bridges over it, kiosks near, elegant shells in it, and its banks full of flowers. Magnificent flowers of many new sorts filled the palace. Cherry, fig, raspberry, prune, and strawberry, loaded with their *hothouse* fruit; beautiful turf plats, with noble rhododendrums of bright red, attracted admiration; apple and prune trees grown in palm shape; iron garden vases, baskets, seats, settees, fountains playing, &c., &o.; an immense catalogue of plants; a palace full, and of admiring people.

The California Culturist, San Francisco, June 15th, 1858, speaks of a Chili strawberry growing there 7 inches in circumference, cherries 3 inches do; native blackberries ripe on the 15th of May, not larger or better than those east of the rocky mountains, and not comparable with " the Lawton blackberry, which, (says the Californian,) should be possessed by every owner of a garden. It is a berry of extraordinary size, an abundant bearer, and of peculiar excellence.

Thos. W. Field.—It must be very extraordinary if it is. Mr. Burgess, at East New York, has a simple plant that has now 1,840 berries upon it. I have counted the berries in a quart several times, and found from 120 to 140 berries. This would make about fifteen quarts of fruit upon a single bush.

We have fine watermelons from the Sandwich Islands, and at a fine price too, $1.50 and $2.00 a piece. Raspberries in market on the 24th of May, and plump green corn, also. A new variety of barley, Adrian's, on the river Yuba. The head of this barley is like an 'ear of corn in figure, its centre when shelled *resembling the corn cob.* There are on it six rows of large kernels, each protected by a long outstanding beard, giving the head a most beautiful appearance. It grows uniform in height and size. One root had 32 heads, containing 2,200 kernels. From these Adrian planted and has now of that sort 80 acres, presenting a most interesting appearance.

The Culturist advises showering strawberry beds. Turnips of 20 pounds were exhibited. Ten millions of acres of California excellent for grapes, among them the *gold placers.* They are producing apples, Gloria Mundi, 26 ounce, Esopus Spitzenberg, Northern Spy, Swaar, Pippin, Scarlet Siberian, Crab, Maiden's Blush, Rhode Island Greening, and others, all large fruit tempared with their originals.

[The Journal of Agriculture and the Transactions of the Highland and Agricultural Society of Scotland. Edinburgh, July, 1858.]

Extracts by H. Meigs.

THE TURNIP.

Late observations on the diseases affecting this important tuber, led to apprehension that it may fail like our potato. All the fertilizers applied to this crop have been considered as to their possible influence on its health, still the opinion gains ground that the turnip is tending to degeneracy. Such a state of things will be extremely injurious to Great

Britain, at least for a time, until she finds some plant to take its important office in the feed of the British animals. The necessity of a succedaneum for the turnip, is foreseen by this learned society.

Experiments with special manures have been tried on a large scale, and the results are here stated:

On Oats.—Guano gave greatest weight, 43 lbs. per bushel; dissolved bone about the same. On oats, 17 special manures gave no more than the common barn yard manure, viz, 39 lbs.

On wheat, the 17, one of which, sulphate of Ammonia, gave 49 bushels, and common barn yard, 37 bushels.

On hay, sulphate of ammonia gave 256 stone weight; common barn yard manure, 140 stone weight.

[Society of Arts, London.]

COFFEE IMITATIONS.

Prof. Graham, Dr. Stenhouse and Mr. Dugald Campbell, report their investigation to the Board of Inland Revenue. They examined the roasted articles because they are only given roasted to the public—and new properties are given, especially to beans by the roasting. The woody tissue of the fresh bean is horny and differs from ordinary woody fibre in its composition, and is also said not to yield sugar when treated with sulphuric acid. By the roasting, this fibre undergoes partial decomposition, and becomes friable, and the difficulty of pulverizing the seed and exhausting it by water, is removed. There is produced at the same time, a soluble brown bitter matter,—and there is the aroma, produced by the roasting, which arises from a brown oil called caffeone, so powerful that a quantity of it, almost insensible, will aromatize two or three pints of water. A great many seeds have been tried in France, as substitutes for coffee—but there does not appear to be any one truly equivalent to coffee, either physiologically or chemically. Indian corn, barley, oats, grain of all sorts, seeds of the yellow flag, grey pea, milk betch, hibisons, holly, Spanish broom, acorns, chesnuts, the small lupin, haricots, horse beans, sunflower seed, gooseberry pips, grape do, eglantine do, capsules of box. Of the seeds enumerated, the *yellow flag*, a common March plant in England, appears to have the only similarity to coffee. The roots most used are chicory, carrot, beet, rush nut, ground nut, scratch weed, fern, butchers' broom—all these have some sugar, and the flavor of burnt sugar is a general favorite in our beverages. Chicory contains *thirty per cent* of sugar. It was first introduced in Holland, in 1801, and is now largely used on the Continent and in England; six millions of killograms are annually used in France. The ashes of the plants were examined as well as of coffee. The ash of coffee is remarkably distinguished from roots and grains by the small quantity of silica it contains—not over the half of one per cent—while in ashes of chicory we found 10.69, 13.13, 30.71, and 35.85 per cent. The sesqui oxide of iron, under one per cent in coffee, and from 3.13 to 5.32 in chicory.

[Journal De L'Instruction Publique—Montreal, (Bas Canada,) Avril, 1858.]

We are indebted to our learned corresponding member, Mons. L. A. Huguet Latour, for all the publications of Canada which interest in science and arts. We translate a few extracts:

A school of Agriculture is established at the Luxemburg, at Paris, in which are already assembled every form of bee-hive in the world, from the simplest one of straw to the miniature Crystal Palace, in which the habits of the bee can be studied—and a very interesting study it is.

Agriculture is making great progress in France, and is extensively used by instructors of youth. It has become very profitable.

THE POTATO DISEASE.

Adrian Bergen exhibited some potatoes struck with the rot. They were from land manured by spreading broadcast and plowing in, with some in the hill. The disease first showed itself in the tops a few days ago. We do not intend to dig any after we discover the disease until after cold weather comes. If we dig them we are liable to lose all. By leaving them we save a part. That is our practice on Long Island.

A discussion of the old subject ensued.

Mr. Meigs remarked that all the theories failed, and it was time for us to drop it as if it was a hot potato.

Solon Robinson.—I have several things suggested by correspondents to lay before the club.

DO WORMS RAIN DOWN?

A person at Angola, Indiana, who notices that we talk about all sorts of miscellaneous matters here, wants us, in the absence of more important questions, to talk about this: "Do fish, worms, and small toads, such as are often seen after a shower, in places where it appears they must have fallen with the rain, actually come from the clouds?"

Dr. Waterbury replied.—They do not; it is one of the popular errors which are so hard to eradicate.

Mr. Robinson continued:

HOW TO WINTER YOUNG APPLE TREES.

A new beginner in the nursery business in Wisconsin, wants information of the Farmers' club upon this point. He says: "I planted last fall about three acres of ground to apple seeds, and have now some fifty thousand fine looking plants. Now, will it be the best way to take them up and house them in a cellar the first winter, or leave them standing, and shall I cover them or not? If taken up, could I graft them successfully during the winter? Which is best—to graft them in the root or stock?"

Andrew S. Fuller, a nurseryman of Brooklyn, replied.—It is the safest plan to take them up and store them in a dry cellar, or else heel them down in furrows in the nursery grounds where they grew. They may be grafted, when of the size of one-fourth to one-half inch diameter, inserting the graft in the stalk close down to the crown of the root. On account of grafting, it is better to put all that are large enough in the cellar, where they can be got at to work upon in winter. If left standing and covered, the trees are sometimes half cut off by mice.

CHERRY CURRANTS ON SANDY SOIL.

Solon Robinson.—I hold in my hand a letter from S. F. Covington, Indianapolis, which although addressed to me personally for information, I choose to answer here, because it refers to matter discussed here, and both the questions and answers are interesting to others, as well as the writer. Members, too, will notice that the number of persons interested in matters talked of here, are not merely the fifty or sixty in the way of attending these meetings. The letter reads as follows :

"I have just read your remarks upon the cherry currant at the American Institute Farmers' Club, published in *The Tribune*, July 20. You recommend the cultivation of this currant upon the waste lands of Long Island, from which I infer that it might be cultivated to advantage on the sandy lands in this State, lying near to Lake Michigan. I own some of this sand land, which is now unproductive—indeed, it is a barren waste. I am anxious to find something—and I doubt not but there is something—adapted to such lands, and in this is my apology for intruding this note upon you. I believe you know the character of the land to which I refer. Do you think the cherry currant can be made to grow upon it ? I should be very glad to have your advice, though it may be brief, upon this matter."

To be brief, then, this writer, like a host of others, supposes, because thousands of acres of land right by the threshold of this city has been permitted to remain unused and worthless, because its semi-savage occupants choose to keep it for a deer park, grouse preserve and charcoal-burners' paradise, that it is a sandy barren. I wish he could have been of the party that spent a day lately on Long Island, and wrote an account of the trip in *The Tribune.* He would have learned that it is not a barren, although treated in a barren manner by some of its owners. It is true that portions of Long Island are like the lands spoken of near the head of Lake Michigan, a sand drift. The writer is right in this. I do know the character of those lands around the head of Lake Michigan. They lie in circular ridges around from Chicago to Michigan city, extending back several miles, alternating with sand-hills, low ridges and flats, thinly covered with pine, cedar, oak, and some little other timber, and marshes, creeks, bayous, lagoons, springs, ponds, and one navigable river. Some of the ridges have been cultivated and proved productive in various crops. The greatest difficulty appears to be a tendency of water, by capillary conduction, to the surface, where the land is flat and richest, at the foot of the ridges. Such land must be underdrained, and at present, rich prairie in close proximity is too cheap and too easily cultivated to make draining and expensive preparation of land an object. No doubt the dryer ridges may be planted and successfully cultivated in these fine currants, but it must be by adding muck from the adjoining marshes, or manure from Chicago, which can be easily brought to the ground by water, or by two railroads.   The question is, will it pay ?   Perhaps it would pay to grow currants on the dry land, and cranberries on the wet, for they are natural to the whole region, and so are whortleberries.   I think the currant will grow in such land, but not without artificial fertilizers, and it might not pay.

Here is another man who has been attracted by what has been said here to try his land in the business.   He writes from Pendleton, Indiana, and says :

" I am very much interested in the proceedings of the Farmers' Club, and have been induced to make an effort to grow some of the fine fruits you talk so much about."

So he sends me a couple of dollars, and asks me to send a few Lawton blackberry and a few cherry currant plants by express.   Not being in the business, I will hand over the money to Mr. Fuller, who will aid this new convert to the religion of spreading abroad the cultivation of good fruits. So send on your money, all ye who are disposed to propagate such a religion as this.   For I contend, that if religion consists in doing good to our fellow-creatures, it is a religious duty to encourage the cultivation, the improvement and propagation of the good fruits that a good Power has made the earth produce for man's sustenance and alleviation of natural diseases.

Rev. W. Adamson, Secretary of the Geographical and Statistical Society, was requested to speak of southern Africa, where he had resided twenty-six years.   He placed on the table the horns of the ox of that country, measuring thirty-three inches from tip to tip, beautifully curving upwards from their roots where they are nearly fourteen inches in circumference.

Mr. Adamson said : The native ox of southern Africa is easily recognized as a well characterized variety.   The line of the face declines more from the vertical, and, with the general outward sweep and direction of the horns, gives the countenance an appearance of greater flatness and slope than is seen in those of Europe, or of this country, or of the mixed breeds, which by importations from Holland or Great Britain, have become common in the Cape territory.   There is nothing of the artificial evenness of back and shortness of limb, which are seen in our improved breeds.   There is a good natural undulation in the spinal ridge.   The hump above the shoulder conforms to the fashion of the zebu, or Brahmin cattle of India, and at the killing of the beast is used in the same way as the noted Bengal humps, being cut off, salted and smoked, like a ham.   The creature rises to a large size, has great bones, and long powerful legs.   The natives, before the advent of Europeans, used him for riding ; having, as a substitute for a bridle, a stick passing through the cartiledge between the nostrils, with a cord or thong from each end, carried back to the rider's hand.   They are, from injudicious treatment, far more stubborn than the steers of this country, but are not vicious in temper.

You can see from the specimen on the the table, that the horns are largely developed.   I have had a pair measuring, with the interposed frontal bone, five feet eight inches from tip to tip.   They are said sometimes to reach to six feet. In these instances, however, the bend or curve is very slight. The internal capacity of a horn is of course considerable, and, as Bruce the Abyssinian traveler mentions, they seem to have been, before the introduction of better utensils, used along the eastern coast of Africa, as vessels for holding liquids, grains, &c. They are still so used among many tribes, and give us to understand that the Greek emblem of "the horn of plenty" arose from a real practice in ancient times in using horns for the same purpose.

The traffic or transport of produce is carried on mainly by means of these oxen. On the road they get on cleverly, and at a fair pace as to speed. But the roads, generally, are shockingly bad; for the cultivable regions, though not offering mountains of great height, are marvelously ruggid and precipitous. In the mountain passes, pieces of the road may be found, up which it is not easy to conceive how an ox could creep even without a load, still less how any thing could get down, except by rolling tail over head. In some such instances the practice was to pull the load and the wagon to pieces, pack the fragments on the backs of the oxen, and, when in this way the difficulty was got over, then build all up again. Some of the plains and valleys are deep sand. From these causes a great deal of power, acting, or in reserve, must accompany a wagon. The weight dragged in it does not amount to more than about a ton and a quarter, yet the common team or span generally consists of fourteen oxen. Sometimes more are seen in yoke. But the main lines of transport have of late been greatly improved, and these long teams are disappearing.

On account of this need of great dragging force, and of the general barrenness of the territory, a farmer requires a large extent of land. He does not feel satisfied with less than 5,000 or 6,000 acres, most of which is kept in a state of rude bushy pasture, to sustain his oxen. He cultivates some thirty or forty acres, cropping it until it will yield no more, and then betaking himself to another piece. In fact the number of farms may be considered as limited by the number of springs, or of supplies of water from streams. Between such points there may be great tracts of land which are almost worthless. Hence, subdivision of farms is, as a general practice, almost impossible.

The following statistic details will serve to illustrate this point. Taking certain districts of the province of Worcester as approaching to an average of the region, we find in three of its districts that the average size of the farms is respectively, twenty-six square miles, forty-eight square miles, and twenty-one square miles. The districts differ in extent and fertility, but the average of the whole is about thirty square miles, or about 20,000 acres each. These estimates include great spaces of waste land between the farms, which, as being of no other use, the government has been subdividing among the neighboring proprietors. On any of these allotments of territory, where water is not scanty, a respectable hamlet of colored laborers may maintain themselves. The abolition of slavery is gradually leading to the subdivision of these farms among the families of the farmers to the small extent which circumstances justify it.

The average number of horned cattle on each of these farms is fifty, and of the horses twelve. The former are left, at all times, to hunt up their own food among the bushes. Horses, during the summer, when the country is parched, require to be provided with hay, which is procured from barley or oats sown for the purpose, and reaped before being fully ripe. In traveling, the horse requires provinder of the same sort, and therefore is not so convenient for long journeys as the ox; for him there are provided reserves of public lands along the roads, where he may pasture gratis. These constitute the hotels of the country, the traveler's sleeping room being his own wagon.

Wool is becoming the staple product of the country. The average number of sheep on each of the farms above mentioned is about 200; consisting partly of the big tailed variety, the fat of which, when melted and strained, serves for butter, or lard, or lamp oil.

There are vast tracts of soil very fertile, occupying a great interior region of the country, which, on account of the scantiness and irregularity of the rains, cannot be put to use, though when rains do occur in abundance, they are covered for a short time with a brilliant vegetation; the plants consisting of species having succulent stems, or tuberous roots, or bulbs covered with chaffy scales. They remain alive under the hard brown surface, until the rain refreshes and expands them into a glow of short-lived beauty. These rains, in that interior region, come from the northwest in the summer, with thunder storms. Along the coast the rains come from the sea, in the winter, as it is termed, and are tolerably abundant and regular. Nowhere except on high mountains does the temperature fall so low as to produce snow or ice. The summer temperature is less excessive than it is in this State or in Pennsylvania.

Wheat is cultivated extensively, producing a fine hard, starchy grain, the flour of which is, for some purposes, superior to that of America. Indian corn is generally raised in small patches, as a sort of garden crop. The use of it is more extensive to the eastward, where it seems to be supplanting the native millet. The sweet millet or impfee, has been immemorially cultivated among the Kaffir tribes, to be chewed as a luxury. It has not been raised for the purpose of producing sugar. About twenty-five years ago I got an experiment to this effect made successfully; but it did not seem that its culture for that purpose would there be remunerative. The crystalization was perfect, though the mode of manufacture was very rude.

Wine has long been a staple article of cultivation and export. The varieties of the grape which are in use, have been brought partly from the countries round the Indian ocean, and partly from Madeira and from Europe. The wines exported have not generally ranked high in character. This is mainly due to the high temperature of the fermenting season, and to the means which are in consequence employed to check the formation of acetic acid. We may except the sweet wines, especially the Constantia. In producing, the grape is allowed to remain long on the vine, which is pruned very low, and receives a strong radiation of heat from the soil. The berry therefore becomes desiccated, and affords a comparatively small quantity of highly saccharine juice. Hence the manufacture of sweet wines is more expensive. The climatic exposure of the Constantia vineyards affords a cooler fermenting season, and some care is employed in picking and sorting the grapes. To these circumstances chiefly may the high character of the wine be ascribed, though something may be due to the soil, which is the debris of porphyritic granite, probably abounding in alkalies. The varieties of the grape there used are European. It is the Muscadel of France, which bears the name of the Constantia grape. The wines raised on these farms are chiefly of three sorts, viz.: Frontignac, Muscadel, and Pontac. The best sells in the colony for about $5.50 per gallon, or nearly thirty times the price of the ordinary colonial Hock or Madeira wine. But other vineyards besides those of Constantia, produce sweet wines not very much inferior, selling at not more than one-fifth of the price.

Besides satisfying an enlightened curiosity, the analysis of the practice and experience of such a country illustrates what is likely to occur in such lands as north-western Texas or New Mexico.

[See Chinese Empire, Illustrated, page 23.]

" Shing-moo," " Holy Mother," is a Buddhist idol in China, consisting of a female, usually, with an infant in her arms. The legend says, that a virgin having gone to bathe in the river, left her garments on the bank, and on her return found a beautiful lotus flower lying upon them. Having eaten the flower, she bore a son, whom a poor fisherman educated, and the miracles which he performed established the divine origin of his birth. It is unnecessary to state the real source of this fable. In paintings, the Shing-moo is often represented standing upon the leaves of the nelumbium in the midst of a lake. Egyptians and Hindoos have also attributed an influence or charm to this remarkable species of water-lily, considering it emblematic of creative power. " The leaves of each succeeding plant are found evolved in the middle of the seed, perfect and of a beautiful green. When the sun goes down, the large leaves that spread themselves over the surface of the water, close up, and the returning sun unfolds them. These nations considered water as the primary element, and this beautiful and singular plant was regarded by them as a proper symbol for representing the creative power, and was consecrated by the Egyptians to Osiris and Isis, emblems of the sun and moon; and by the Hindoos to the goddess Ganyee and to the Sun."

All sects in the Celestial Empire, reverence the lotus, and believe that it is from the flower of this lily that the bodies of their saints are to be reproduced. The roots of the lotus (nelumbium,) are also used for food.

The Secretary stated that Mr. Lawton, of New Rochelle, had requested him to say that he will be happy to see any member of the club at his place, and wished to show them, especially, a field of blackberries which, because of his endeavors to extend the cultivation, has been kindly called the Lawton, by this club. And that at the next meeting of it, he would bring some of them for the members to try.

The Secretary exhibited the seed pods of the beautiful Macrophylla (long leaf) Paulownia-Imperialis, (so named after a daughter of the Emperor Nicholas, of Russia.) The pods are full of downy fibre with seeds hardly as large as mustard seed.

He presented also a pod of the white Lupin, with its bean nearly fully grown. He said that this plant had been greatly used anciently for plowing in as a fertilizer ; that it possessed the power of growing in the poorest soil, where hardly any other plant could—soil impossible for clover, buckwheat, or any of the so styled green manures. Lupin is a stout fleshy plant, can grow close, and one can have wheat upon the field where it is plowed in the first year. I urged it before the club a dozen years ago for trial. No one has ever tried it yet. Portugal could scarcely raise her bread without first fertilizing her poor lands with Lupins. Nature, you all know, first grows some moss or some small plant fit for nothing but to make a soil out of. We should always mend our land by using the most quick and suitable growths for burying in the soil. I have no doubt that those very plants which we see alone living on poor land, are those we ought to sow the seeds of on it and bury the grown plants with the plow.

Dr. Edgar F. Peck, of Brooklyn, presented stalks of timothy grass pulled on the side of the railroad of Long Island, on the barrens, (so called) forty-three miles from here. It seemed to have grown from some seed fallen from a load of hay passing by. This stalk measured five and a half feet in length. Not far from this, on a regular sown field, the timothy gave at two mowings, two and a half tons an acre for five successive years, after having been manured with barn yard manure five years before—twenty loads an acre—has had no top dressing or anything else. The hay crop was worth this year $17.50 per acre.

The regular subjects : " Mud and peat of salt and fresh water as manure," and " Fruit on farms."

Mr. Fuller spoke of the club foot in cabbage, his application of salt and lime in vain.

Mr. Meigs remarked that the doctors of the club fail in some cases as well as other doctors do.

Mr. Field never had the club foot on his place.

Mr. Fuller.—The mud and peat of our salt and fresh water, are worth more than the gold of California. The salt mud and peat was applied on a naked knoll of pebbles, on Long Island sound, and it formed a soil which bears fine trees. The mud is full of shell and small animals, enriching it.

T. W. Field.—I have examined the salt mud and found it almost half full of small shells, worms, &c., rendering it very rich in the elements of manure.

As to the Lawton blackberry, one word. A single root has grown stalks on which were fifteen quarts of the berries.

The same subject to be continued.

The club adjourned to the 3d Monday of August.

H. MEIGS, *Secretary.*

———

Aug. 16, 1858.

Present—Messrs. Doughty, Van Vleek, Brower, of Jersey; Cavanagh, Burgess, Fuller, Field, Paine, of Long Island; Capt. Porter, of the U. S. Navy; Witt, Bruce, Wm. B. Leonard, John W. Chambers, Chilson, Dick, Lawton, of New Rochelle; Solon Robinson, Dr. Waterbury, Isachar Cozzens, Walter M. Oddie, of Bedford; James Barbour, Meade, Prof. W. O. Morris, Martin E. Thompson, Prof. Nash, Steele, of Jersey city; Moore, Godwin, Rev. Mr. Adamson, late from South Africa; Mr. Lowe, and others—sixty-five members in all.

William Lawton, of New Rochelle, in the chair. Henry Meigs, Secretary.

The Secretary read the following extracts, translations, &c., made by him from the works received by the Institute since the last meeting of the club, viz:

[Journal De La Societe Imperiale et Centrale D'Horticulture, Napoleon 3d, Protecteur, June, 1858.]

CABINET MAKERS' WOOD OF ALGERIA.

The most remarkable wood exhibited at the World's Fair of 1855, in Paris, was the *Callitris quadrivalvis*, commonly known as the Thrica. (This is a Conifer-Pinacea, grows on Mount Atlas. H. Meigs.)

The first specimens of the knobs were those of Mons. Marechal who took the medal of silver gilt. These knobs (Coupes) constitute the most beautiful cabinet work known. The only one to be compared with it is Amboyna wood, of very high price. The entangled fibres of the Thrica knobs twisted and wound in every direction, they are magnificent. The fibres seem to be felted in such a way and so intimately that which ever way you cut it, it is never broken nor disjointed. The wood is very compact and marvellously adapted to cabinet work.

COTTON IN ALGERIA.

The great efforts of our government to grow cotton in Algeria, have already succeeded so far as to prove incontestibly the fact that we can produce cotton here equal to the first qualities of the cottons of the United States, as appeared at the exhibition of 1858, by the important house of Dollfus, Miez & Co., of Dornach.

The Central Nursery of Algiers sent to National Exhibition twenty varieties of cotton, from the shortest staples to the long stapled Georgia, and from a very fine prolific cotton.

WINE AND ALCOHOL OF ALGERIA.

The wines were many of them poor. Out of 32 white wines 13 were rejected, being completely acid ; 10 also on account of having some foreign material added to the native wines; nine of them were made with care, and were in good keeping. Thirty-one red wines of the vintages of '50, '51, '55, '56 and '57, were tasted, and 27 of them rejected for acidity.

SILK OF ALGERIA.

Sericulture does not answer expectation here. Mulberry trees scarce, and fears that this important crop will be lost here.

COCHINEAL.

It is feared that this product, of which Algeria has been much vaunted, will not meet our hopes, on account of the considerable cost of hand labor and the great care required. The specimens of it from our nursery are remarkable for the richness of the coloring matter.

Fine crops of Madder, *of highest quality known.*

MINERAL WEALTH OF THE OLD REGENCY OF ALGIERS.

A mountain of iron ore, yielding iron equal to the best Swedish ; Argentiferous lead—a magnificent mine now very profitably worked. Many other precious minerals. Gypsum in various localities, valuable to agriculture, &c. It has various conditions, from amorphous to perfect crystalline.— Beautiful breccias—quarries of it near Medeah, &c. Onyx alabaster, semi-transparent, very hard and beautiful, were exhibited as *transparent marble.* They are veined—come from Oran.

The day is near when Algeria will pay for the immense expenses of this conquest made by France.

By Dr. Loirean.—*Herbaceous grafts* on *woody stocks* succeed in the climate of Paris, if done after the middle of May.

THE LAWTON BLACKBERRIES.

Mr. Lawton stated his method of pruning his plants. It consists in carefully heading back all the branches to the fully ripened wood. In some cases half of the length of the plant is cut away ; generally about one-third of the length is cut away. Then all the fruit comes to perfection. Commence to head back with the plants the first year of bearing, when 200 to 250 berries may be expected from each plant, as it branches out very full of bearing limbs. Care is requisite in picking, as the berries are not ripe when they first turn black.

Mr. Burgess, a gardener of East New York, stated that he had a Lawton blackberry plant that had been set out two years, that bore this year 1,853 berries by actual count. He is saving all for seed, finding that they produce true to their kind.

Solon Robinson.—I have a few words to say upon this subject. I accepted an invitation the other day from Drew & French, fruit dealers in Barclay street, to go up with a few friends and see where and how the Lawton blackberries grow.

We visited Geo. Seymour's place, at Norwalk, Conn., and found some five acres of ground covered with this variety of blackberry, which I have no hesitancy about pronouncing a distinct variety, and altogether superior to any other ever cultivated or found growing wild. In fact, this was found growing wild in a field at New Rochelle, some fifteen years ago, and transplanted to the garden of a Mr. Secor, where it was found, after several years' experience, to bear cultivation, much better than any other wild variety ever tried. Its superior fruit soon attracted attention, and Mr. Seymour, seeing the advantage to be derived from propagation and sale of the plants, set himself at work to produce them by all the arts known to a practical and experienced nurserymen. One of the results was a sale of 85,000 plants last year, and his sales this year will be much larger if he has plants enough to fill his orders. It has been more an object to sell plants than grow fruit for market, but the production has been very large and price very remunerating.

Product per acre.—I made a careful examination of the first half acre planted, and found ten rows, of thirty-two bunches each, making 320 roots, as originally set upon the half acre. The lowest estimate of any of the gentlemen present was five quarts of berries to a bunch of roots. That would make five bushels to the row, and fifty bushels on the half acre. Knowing that it takes only an average of 120 berries to a quart, and from rough calculation of numbers, I am satisfied the average will be eight quarts to the bunch. In conversation with Mr. Lawton on Saturday last, while in his blackberry garden, he confirms my opinion of the yield, which would give eighty bushels to the half acre. But let us take the lowest estimate, one hundred bushels per acre, and we have a crop worth eight hundred dollars, at the present wholesale price of twenty-five cents a quart. And even at only one-fourth the present price, we have $200 per acre.

"Ah! but what if everybody goes to raising blackberries? then the market will be glutted, and we cannot sell them at all."

Heaven hasten that day—the day when the poor as well as the rich can enjoy an abundance of this delicious, health-preserving fruit—the day when the cultivators of it will find the market glutted, and the fruit unsaleable at sixpence a quart. When that time comes we shall have cheap *blackberry wine.* The juice of eighty quarts of these berries, mixed with water, and ninety pounds of refined sugar, will make a barrel of wine, such as I tasted at Mr. Seymour's, and such as does and will sell readily at $2 a gallon. But at a wholesale price of $1 it will still pay $200 for an acre of the berries, and for the sugar and for making, and afford a large profit upon the wine-making business.

Items of cost of wine.

2½ bushels (80 quarts) of berries, for a barrel, at 6¼c.,	$5 00
90 pounds of sugar, at 11½c.,	10 35
Crushing and mixing,	65
Cost per barrel,	$16 00

The product of wine per acre yielding 100 bushels of berries would be forty barrels, costing, exclusive of berries, $11 a barrel, and selling, at $1 a gallon, for $1,200.

Upon this calculation, will the market ever be glutted, or will the cultivation of the crop, which costs no more than a crop of corn, exclusive of the picking, ever cease to be remunerating?

There is another thing in this connection. We have, we do, we shall send Ohio whiskey to France, to be run through the stills upon the lees of the wine press, which we buy back at a high price under the name of brandy. From blackberry wine we can make a very superior brandy at less cost, and far more fit for medicinal purposes. We can also make blackberry syrup, if we have the fruit in abundance, that will cure all the summer complaints in the community, and save the lives of an army of children every year.

Every one present had an opportunity, after the adjournment of the Club, to test the quality of this fruit, Mr. Lawton and Messrs. Drew and French having each furnished a liberal supply. There was not a dissenting voice from one of the large number of men and women present, as to the excellence of the quality. The berries are sweet and rich.

RASPBERRIES.

Mr. Fuller exhibited some fine specimens of raspberries in full bearing, which were produced by a continual liberal use of liquid manure.

FLOWERS.

Mr. Burgess exhibited several beautiful seedling dahlias, seedling roses, and a valuable hardy flowering shrub, the *Wiglia Amabilis*, which he recommended to general use.

DWARF BANANAS.

Solon Robinson exhibited a specimen of bananas, grown by Parsons, Flushing, L. I., upon plants so dwarfed that they can be produced in any ordinary conservatory, comparing somewhat with the common plant as dwarf pears do to full-sized trees.

The Secretary.—I want Dr. Waterbury to say a few words upon a subject that we have had some time before us, as I understand he has been making some researches.

Dr. Waterbury.—Long Island is composed entirely of what geologists term *drift*; the bed rock lying below the level of low tide. Boulders are scattered over the northern slope and are found also on making excavations below the surface, but the southern slope is throughout composed of a loose sandy loam. The soil of the whole island is uniformly of this description, having few or no stratified beds of clay underlying it.

On this soil annually falls some 35 to 40 inches of rain, and yet there are no brooks or rivulets of much size, and consequently no gullies on the island torn by running water. The whole formation, from its porous nature, must be pervious to the ocean, so as to be underlaid by a perfectly level stratum of salt water. The rain water in the soil percolates directly downward, and accumulates in the earth and underlies the surface at variable depths as is proved by the level of the different wells. In making excavations on reaching this level further progress in the downward direction is prevented by quicksand, which is nothing but the material of which the island is composed, partially floated by the water in which it lies.

Baisley's Pond is a natural excavation into this bed of water some ten miles back of Brooklyn. When my friend Mr. T. W. Fields suggested the plan of providing water for Brooklyn by sinking wells and pumping by steam, the project was looked upon in certain quarters as little better than lunacy, but the excavation now made a mile or two back of Brooklyn, has confirmed in a remarkable manner the practicability of his suggestion. In fact the surface of Baisley's pond has been already reached at a point almost in the suburbs of the city, and it has become necessary to pump out and conduct away from the excavation more water than Brooklyn requires in order to carry on the works, and there is no doubt that by making the excavation deeper, any quantity of water could be obtained.

In clearing Baisley's pond of muck, some very interesting scientific matter comes to light concerning the origin of peat, and probably also that of coal. The peat has been formed of a floating sod or turf resting on the surface of the water and going to the bottom at certain periods—the fibre of wood, lignine being specifically heavier than water, and floating in this fluid only by virtue of the air mechanically contained in its structure. Immersed in water the woody matter seems to undergo a partial combustion, like that of wood in a charcoal pit, consuming the hydro carburets and leaving the carbon in a comparatively isolated form.

There is a range of fresh water ponds in the north-western edge of Delaware county, in this State, where the red sandstone formation of the Catskill mountains merges into the Chemung group, in which the same process of making a lake into a swamp is now going on. A kind of sedge growing on the surface of the water forms a floating sod which extends from the shore out over the surface of the pool. This floating meadow will bear the weight of a man almost to the margin, though he sinks at every step, and near the edge is obliged to make his way by means of two pieces of board, alternately standing on one and moving the other. A small shrub takes root in the floating sod a few rods back from the open water and still further towards what was originally the shore. This is succeeded by trees. Through this "fly" as it is called, a pole may be readily thrust down into the water beneath, and one can hardly venture on it anywhere without reflections on his probable fate if he were to break through. There are very good reasons for believing that the forests which formed the coal beds, grew where they are deposited, and I will venture to suggest the theory that they grew like the trees I have described, rooted in a floating mass on the surface of fresh water ponds, and that when the superincumbent vegetation became sufficiently heavy, it sunk so far as to kill the trees, which became water logged and went to the bottom to be made into coal, and that the rock which intervenes between the coal beds is the mud brought into the lake by the river between the periods of forest subsidence.

I shall not stop now to dilate on the evidence in support of this theory —to show how these ponds occur on the edge of the same formation in which the Pennsylvania coal was found ; how the coal was formed mostly out of vegetation allied to these aquatic plants ; how the hemlock trees which surround these ponds are the remains of a former flora ; how the direction of fallen trees in the coal beds is nearly uniform ; how " coal pipes " are trees which remained standing when the forest went down ; how the microscope has revealed the presence of coniferous trees during the coal era ; how a climate no warmer than the present may have been adequate to the existence of large floating aquatic plants of different species from those now known ; how marshes and bogs all indicate that the process of filling in has been carried on from above downwards ; how peat, lignite, bituminous coal, anthracite and plumbago, are manifestly allied to each other ; how leaves of the ferns remain longer in water undecomposed, than other foliage ; how stigmaria have proved to be roots instead of leaves, and how the large swamps of the present time are inhabited by allied species of evergreens.

As to the economic value of Baisley's pond, muck or peat, I may say in the absence of any knowledge derived from actual experiment, we may presume *a priori*, that it will prove analogous to charcoal in its effect on soils.

The Doctor's remarks were accompanied by diagrams illustrating his ideal section of Long Island, and as a step towards ascertaining the value of salt water mud, he made some explanation of the structure and habits of marine molusks, illustrated by a diagram of the common oyster, (ostrea edulis,) together with a dissection and demonstration of the heart, branchial mouth, intestine veins, liver, abductor muscle, &c., of this shell-fish. The heart may be seen to pulsate, in a living oyster, about thirty or forty times to the minute. It consists of a single auricle and single ventricle, devoted to the systematic circulation.

T. W. Field.—I have used swamp muck as manure several years. I always mix it with other materials, and I find this the grand necessity of this as well as other manure. We do not divide it sufficiently. Used alone, peat is of little value. The reason is, it does not decompose readily, and it is not sufficiently divided, and it contains tartaric and other acids. I can grow more potatoes with peat mixed with animal manure, than with the whole bulk in stable manure. A large number of farmers on Long Island are troubled with clump-footed cabbage, particularly where hog manure is used, or high manuring of other animal manures. I escaped this disease this year, while all my neighbors are very much troubled. I grew my plants upon loamy soil, trenched two and a half feet, and manured thoroughly with peat muck, treated with lime.

HOOKER'S SEEDLING STRAWBERRY.

Joseph H. Coggswell, writing from Poughkeepsie, under date of August 5, wishes to record his opinion that the Hooker seedling strawberry is the very best variety now in cultivation. It was originated in 1850, by H. E. Hooker, of Rochester, and grows to a size of five inches in circumference, is of deep red color, handsome form, and delicious flavor. Mr. Coggswell says: " I wait with impatience the report of the next discussion of the club, as the topic announced is one of very great importance."

T. W. Field and Andrew S. Fuller, both replied that Hooker's seedling was not a deep red here, but a scarlet, and too soft, when ripe, for a market berry. Wilson's seedling is better.

TURNIP SEED.

A letter from John R. Stork, of Coventryville, says that seed produced from "premium turnips," left out over winter, well protected, will be as good as though they were taken up and transplanted; but seed from "pin-feather turnips" will produce its like.

WHEAT WITH WEAK STRAW.

Now here is a letter upon a very important subject, which I hope, if not fully answered to-day, will be hereafter:

"FULTON, *Lancaster Co., Pa.,* 8 *mo.* 9, 1858.

"I have, for several years past, been troubled with my wheat falling before maturity. I have been induced to believe there is something wanting in the soil to impart strength to the stalks. The system that I have pursued for several years, is to manure the corn ground in the spring with clover chaff (having a clover mill), which almost invariably produces good corn; the next spring I sow the stalk ground with oats and clover seed; the oats frequently fall before ripe; the clover is let stand the next season, and either mowed or pastured; if the latter the ground is manured from the barnyard, and after harvest is plowed and sowed with wheat; the wheat stubble is again slightly manured from the barnyard, plowed and sowed again with wheat and timothy seed, with the view of setting it with grass. My fields have all been limed over twice, and some of them three times, within twenty years. I have not sufficient scientific skill in such matters as to state the quality or component parts of the soil, which might, perhaps, enable the members of the club to arrive at a correct judgment in the premises. I have been an interested reader of the proceedings of the club from time to time, and have thought that with the large experience of its members, something might be suggested that would be beneficial in imparting strength or stiffness to the wheat plant. I should be much gratified to see that the subject has been brought to the notice of the Farmers' Club; and if a practical remedy for the evil referred to can be suggested, a very important benefit will be conferred on a large portion of the farmers of this section of country, who have suffered in a similar way with myself.

"Respecfully yours, &c.,

"JOEL SNEEDLEY."

Prof. Nash.—This is a matter of immense importance to wheat-growers. Although he has limed his land, I should say not sufficiently. It must be very destitute of silicates, if lime or potash, which I recommend, would not cure the evil.

Solon Robinson.—I would recommend him to try a good dressing of salt; say five bushels per acre.

Mr. Ambler suggested that thinner seeding will have a beneficial effect in strengthening the straw.

Mr. Burgess suggessed the use of the roller upon wheat. One crop produced sixteen bushels per acre upon a portion of a field rolled more than that unrolled. It should be done as soon as the frost leaves the ground. In England, wheat that is not rolled is apt to fall down. It is first dragged by a large bush, and then rolled.

FRUIT INQUIRIES.

"STONERVILLE, Pa., *Aug.* 11, 1858.

"I have been a close reader of the reports of the A. I. Farmers' Club, and have been awaiting some hints on setting out, managing, &c., of blackberries and raspberries. Would this be the proper time to set out the raspberry and blackberry canes, or would it be advisable to leave till spring? [Early in spring.] The ground is well adapted to potatoes, so would you recommend the same application as R. G. Pardee does for strawberries, viz: ashes, lime and salt? [Yes.] Do raspberries not require more stimulating manure of animal nature than strawberries? [Yes.] Strawberries, I presume, may be put in any time through the month? [Yes.] The Lawton blackberry, I suppose, is the best? [Yes.] What kind of strawberry? [Wilson's.] What nursery would you recommend? [No one.] Or would you be willing to transmit a few plants by express, if I send the money? [No.]

"ISAAC F. CHRISMAN."

FRUIT FOR THE FARM.

Thos. W. Field.—There are some fruits better adapted to farm culture than to garden culture, and the distinction should be made by planters. There are some locations that will grow one fruit and not another. There is nowhere a Garden of Paradise, that will grow every kind of fruit. What is best adapted to any locality has to be proved by experience. Some localities will grow pears, and will not grow apples; and it will not do to plant Spitzenberg or Newtown pippins because the Baldwin apple had done well in the same localities. It is true that one sort of pears will grow in one locality and will not in another. A man may grow a specific crop, but not a general one. So, in growing fruit, a farmer should confine his fruit growing to a few standard varieties, and not attempt too great a variety.

A question for the club at the next meeting being called for, it was decided to continue "Farm Fruits."

Solon Robinson said he had a letter proposing "Market Garden Vegetables." F. K. Phœnix, of Bloomington, Ill., asks this club to discuss this question: "What are the very best varieties of vegetables for a market garden, and how and when planted and tended, and in what rotation, so as to make a complete list."

He says such a list has never been published.

The club selected the following questions for the next meeting: "The best variety of Market Vegetables," and "Fruits for Farms."

Adjourned.

H. MEIGS, *Secretary.*

August 30, 1858.

Present—Messrs. Fuller and Bruce, of Williamsburgh; Lawton, of New Rochelle; Erhard, of Astoria; Davoll and Stacey, of Brooklyn; Prof. Mapes, Prof. Morris, Dr. Tuthill, of the Times, Pardee, Solon Robinson, Dr. Turnipseed, and others—forty-one members.

William Lawton, of New Rochelle, in the chair. Henry Meigs, Secretary.

The Secretary read the following translations, &c., made by him, from works received by the Institute since the last meeting, viz.:

[Revue Horticule, Journal d'Horticulture Pratique, Paris, July, 1858.]

GARDEN COMPETITORS AT VERSAILLES,

From the 16th to the 20th of May last, under an immense tent, 116 feet in diameter.

The prize of the Empress Eugenie was given to Truffant, Jr., for his azaleas. He possesses a secret method of raising them, and their colors, brilliancy and extraordinary vividness, are admired by all beholders and amateurs. He has fifteen varieties which he has raised from the seed. He has also new and splendid rhododendrons from seed.

A beautiful new rose called the George Vibert, striped absolutely like a pink. The stachytarpheta whose flowers change their colors, was admired; it is also called verbena mutabilis, the *changeable verbenum*, grows forty inches high, very branchy (*très-ramifié*) flowers in the main, scarlet. It is readily propagated by its seeds or its cuttings.

[Revue Horticole, Journal d'Horticulture Pratique, Paris, July 16, 1858.]

GREEN TEA. (*Thea viridis.*)

The culture of it is not difficult. It is exactly the same as that of the camellia. It is multiplied from its seed sown immediately as it ripens, or by slips, or by marcotting, viz.: laying a branch under the soil or by shoots, and it may be grafted on the camellia. It flowers in September.

Many authors, De Candolle among them, regarded bohea tea and green teas as varieties of the same plant, but it appears, however, that the differences between the two plants is sufficiently striking. The leaves of the green tea are distinguished from the bohea by their greater size and bent edges, as well as solitary flowers, and less numerous, but especially in the period of flowering, which is about a month sooner than bohea. However this may be, it appears to be certain that these two plants furnish all the kinds of the tea of commerce, and that the mode of preparing the leaves, or their age, make all the difference between the black and the green. The tea which comes to us from China by way of Russia, known by the name of *caravan tea*, has the reputation of being very superior to that which comes by sea. In the European trade we know only a very limited number of kinds, but it appears that the Chinese count above thirty-six kinds of tea.

The use of tea in China goes back to the remotest antiquity, even to mythic times. Tradition says that a holy man, by prayer, night and day, and by example, improved the morals of the Chinese, that on one night, overcome by fatigue, he vainly tried to keep awake, and being unable to keep his eyes open, he cut off their eye-lids, and where they fell on the ground the *tea plant came, whose infusion keeps the eyes open!* The Dutch first brought tea to Europe in the seventeenth century.

SELF-PROPAGATION OF TURNIPS.

Solon Robinson read a letter from John Willet, Niles, Mich., which states that he sowed a piece of land with turnips and timothy in 1840. He mowed the land seven years and pastured it three more, and plowed and sowed it to wheat, small turnips having grown and seeded among the grass every year, and larger ones with the wheat. The ground, which was a black loam, heavily timbered when cleared in 1840, was planted with corn in 1853, among which many turnips grew, mostly hot, peppery and tough, but some good, and six inches in diameter. Since that year, corn and wheat alternately have been grown, and every year turnips from the original seeding in 1840. No turnips have been grown within eighty rods of the ground, so that the fact of self-propagation is well proved. The land is at present in pasture, but Mr. Willet thinks it would produce turnips again next year if planted to corn.

PERPETUAL RASPBERRIES.

Chas. F. Erhard, of Ravenswood, exhibited some branches of Raspberries with flowers, half-grown berries and ripe fruit. The only thing to be said in favor of these ever-bearing raspberries is, that they produce fruit a long time. It is not excellent.

Andrew S. Fuller, horticulturist, Brooklyn, said he had the Brinkley orange raspberry, still in bearing. He ascribes their ever-bearing to liquid manure, fresh from the cow stable.

CHESS.

R. G. Pardee.—I have a letter from a farmer friend of mine, Ebenezer Manson, of Seneca county, who says :

"I always read with deep interest and profit the proceedings of the Farmers' Club. I have a question, viz : Is there any connection between

Canada thistles and chess? Last year, on one of my low ground meadows, on which I raised oats three years ago, there was an enormous crop of Canada thistles, and there had been more or less thistles for some years. All that was done to them was to run my mower through them when I cut the grass. This year, on that part of the meadow where the thistles were largest last year, we find an overgrown crop of chess, but not a single thistle is to be seen with them. No wheat has ever been grown on the field. By what law or process has this transmutation been effected?"

Mr. Pardee continued.—We can explain why the thistles have disappeared, because we know that cutting them at the right season will kill them. But who can explain why the chess should start up there and no where else, since no one will suppose chess and thistles have any connection, whatever may be thought of wheat and chess?

Mr. Fuller related a fact of a field of oats in Wisconsin that grew no chess, but the scattered oats vegetated next spring, and grew all chess. This was in 1846, and his faith that grain could not turn to chess was shaken.

Solon Robinson.—I hope the chess question will not be revived here, since scientific men have settled the question that wheat never did, never can, never will turn to chess. But I can relate home facts that are very hard to get over, if wheat and oats both do not produce chess. I don't pretend to believe or disbelieve anything. Mr. R. then related several very strong cases of wheat and chess growing on the prairies.

RUSTY OATS.

Prof. Morris mentioned the fact of horses having died from eating rusty oats, and suggested that rust in this case was animalcula.

He said that peaches are grown in Russia by cutting back the stock of the first year to two buds, and afterwards laying it on the ground one year, and then training it on the north side of a wall.

R. G. Pardee.—The best flavored peaches I have ever eaten, as well as largest size of the variety, were grown in Canada. Greenhouse peaches are insipid and almost worthless. By the plan of layering we may be able to produce fine, healthy peaches, even if it is upon dwarf trees. We know that we cannot grow raspberries without layering.

Prof. Mapes.—We can't train a peach tree with limbs below a horizontal line, without injuring the growth of the trees. It may do to layer down the young limbs in winter, but they must be lifted early in spring.

BLIGHT IN CORN.

Mr. Ambler.—I have a farm in Bethel, Conn., and find part of my corn blighted as though touched with frost. But it cannot be, for nothing else has been touched by frost near it. I do not think I shall have two-thirds as much corn as the stalks indicate. The first symptom is spots on the leaves.

VEGETABLES FOR MARKET GARDENS.

Prof. Mapes.—It is difficult to give any general rule. Land in this vicinity filled with pulverized shells, as at Communipaw, will grow cabbage year after year. I cannot do that. I cannot grow cabbage after rutaba-gas. None of the brassica tribe will grow after using hog-pen manure, or other highly nitrogenous manure. On Long Island, cabbage is often set in the potato field to grow as the tops die down. With the cabbage, lettuce is sown. I have raised 12,000 cabbages per acre. As to the most profitable crop near New York, I can only say we can't afford to raise grain. I have raised over 100 bushels of corn to the acre, but I can't afford it, because I can raise 1,200 bushels of beets per acre, and 1,500 bushels of parsnips. I recommend beets grown in large quantity, because the market will bear a great many, and is seldom overstocked. The kind most generally grown is the long red beet, which is inferior to almost any other. It is woody. The turnip blood-beet is much better. The Bassano beet is the best for the table, but not as salable as the long red in our market. I can only raise parsnips profitably on drained land, where they grow with very little manuring. I dig them by running a lifting subsoil plow along the row, 18 inches deep, which loosens the roots so they can be pulled out by hand.

Tomatoes, I find, grow much better by cutting away the entire top, with the little fruit, the lower ones ripening ten days earlier, and are much better fruit, and being earlier sell higher.

Lima beans must be treated in the same way, by pinching off the buds when five and a half feet high. No manure suits this crop so well as Peruvian guano. To get them early plant them in sods two inches square, with the small end down, and place them in the cellar, and moisten to vegetate, and plant four sods around a pole.

Carrots will average $37\frac{1}{2}$ cents a bushel in New York, and are always salable and are easily grown. Mix the seed with one-tenth its weight of radish seed, which grows before the carrots and marks the rows, so that they can be cultivated by a horse or mule, to keep the weeds down and save hand weeding. It is good for the carrot crop to pull out the radishes for market purposes, or crush them with a roller as they stand. A mule can be trained to walk between narrow rows. A subsoil lifter is a good thing to run between the rows when the plants are small. A large lifter run by the side of the row will loosen the roots for harvest.

Melons require a peculiar trimming. Pinch off the first runner bud when the third rough leaf appears, and so on with the branches. This will make short vines in a round hill. There is nothing like deep tilth for melons. It is a good plan to bore a hole with a post auger three or four feet deep under each hill. I would pinch back the whole tribe of plants of this kind, melons, cucumbers, squashes, all in the same way.

Potatoes I cannot grow without rotting upon ordinarily plowed land. On underdrained and subsoiled land my potatoes never rot.

The vines of melons should never extend to the vines of another hill. Highly fertilized land may be planted with melon hills four feet apart, and produce a good crop.

I will say, in answer to that question about

UNDERDRAINING.

An opinion about underdraining at this day is of no account. The English government have loaned to its people $55,000,000 at 5 per cent, to enable them to underdrain their farms, and no case has been found of underdraining that land was not benefited by it. No underdrained land ever suffers from drouth. In all the loans for underdraining no loss has occurred in all England. If it was not for these improvements England could not sustain its inhabitants. The whole capacity of the land is increased to double what it was before. It is a settled question that all drains should be open at both ends.

It is settled also that the water enters the drains from below, and never runs as flush during a shower as it does the next day.

PRUNING BLACKBERRIES.

Wm. Lawton.—A lady, Mrs. A. Houghton, of St. Albans, Vermont, asks when should the pruning be done. Before the buds put forth in spring. I cut back the wood of last year's growth one-fourth or one-third. If the stalk is three feet long, cut off one foot, and so of lesser or greater growth. I would cut away all but two or three shoots in a hill, each stalk will then produce two or three hundred full sized berries.

The next meeting of the Club will be next Monday noon, when, among other things, the subject of flowers, now in session, will be treated of, and members are invited to bring specimens, which will be presented to the lady visitors. A large number of these were present to-day.

After the next meeting of the Club it is probable it will adjourn until the close of the Institute Fair at the Crystal Palace, which will be in operation during the last of September and all of October.

BUTTER MAKING.

The whole system of a premium butter maker.

Solon Robinson.—I hold in my hand a communication of great value to the dairy interest of this country. It is a letter from H. E. Lowman, of Chemung county, N. Y., giving a detailed statement of the whole system of Jesse Carpenter of that county, who is one of the most successful premium butter makers who has ever exhibited at the New York State Agricultural Fair.

I wish that other butter makers might be equally successful, and to preserve this valuable paper in a more permanent form, I produce it here that it way be printed in the volume of Transactions.

Mr Carpenter has long been known in the butter-making region and in the market as one of the most intelligent and successful dairymen and farmers in the country; and the writer of this being a neighbor of his, and interested in the pursuit of the same branches of productive industry, and feeling, he trusts, a due sense of obligation for valuable hints in their prosecution, can speak of his system and practice with positive knowledge and confidence. And believing that there is much in them both interesting and valuable, as addition to the mass of excellent information and knowledge which the club is gathering upon the subject alluded to, as well as upon all others which interest the agriculturist, the horticulturist, and the fruit-grower, and which it is, with a truly commendable earnestness and thoroughness of criticism, sending forth again, through its legitimate channels to the thousands who compose its interested auditory, he has taken some pains to get from him a particular history of the same, the substance of which, touching the main points, is as follows :

The basis for a good and profitable butter dairy is, a stock fulfilling as nearly as practicable, all those constitutional and structural conditions which combine in the animal high milking qualities, with good size, robust health and longevity. The next step is a prompt and thorough practice of the best method of treatment of the same by which the largest yield of the best quality of milk is secured. The next and best step in the achievement of a first-class dairy of butter is the application to its manufacture of an intimate and critical knowledge of the true process from the expressing of the milk to the final touch the butter receives preparatory to the transit of the package to market.

How to take the first step ? i. e., lay in the stock, or near it, Mr. Carpenter thinks can be known much more satisfactorily by reference to and study of popular authorities on the subject—writers who have made the rearing of stock with that view a speciality, and yet it is practical common sense and close and accurate observation which must be the main dependence at last. The next branch inquiry, which is none the less important, is not so easily pursued to satisfactory results by an appeal to the same sources of information. Long and close experience has confirmed Mr. Carpenter in the accuracy of the following system or mode of treatment : The best summer food for the dairy stock, that which yields the largest quantity and best quality of milk, is a mixture of the finer grasses, such as red and white clover, timothy and blue grass, all of which thrive well in desirable combination in the pasture fields of the Chemung valley. All coarse, rank and strongly-flavored weeds of whatever description, must be banished from the feeding range of the dairy stock, otherwise butter of the finest quality cannot be made. Neither should they be fed, during the milking season on any description of roots or coarse pungent vegetables, such as cabbage, if the butter is to be packed in firkins or any other vessel with the purpose of keeping.

Even pumpkins are not desirable, though they may be used without material detriment. In the spring the roots are most commonly used, and advised. A small allowance of grain is much more beneficial. It accomplishes just what is needed, without contributing to undesirable results. It gives additional strength of muscle—the main thing desired—

while if judiciously given it does not materially increase the deposit of fat. It also increases the quantity, and improves the quality of the milk, while roots and vegetables increase the quantity but rather deteriorate the quality.

During the milking season the cows must be moved from the pasture-field with great caution, to prevent over-heat of the system. That cannot take place in any degree without the milk being unfavorably affected in a corresponding ratio. And when they are in the heat of the sexual or copulating fever, the milk should not be used in the dairy, or with that from which butter for packing is to be made. For at such periods nature has provided for a medical interruption of the secretion of the animal, and the milk is greatly reduced in quantity, and in like measure improved in quality. Indeed the abnormal heat produced in the udder is of itself sufficient cause for rejecting the milk for butter making. In the fall where the grass begins to fail, and loses its nutritive or milk producing elements, there is nothing that can equal corn stalks as a substitute. The corn should be sown for the purpose.

During the winter months the stock should be stabled or otherwise sheltered from the severities of the weather for the night, and while they feed. And the care and amount and kind of food must be so appointed that they rather improve in condition and vigor than otherwise; at least, they must not be allowed to run down to poor flesh and weakness—for then, no amount of attention and good nursing through the summer will restore them to full milking capacities. The loss is irreparable for the season.

A thorough and practical understanding of the next and last branches, *i. e.*, the treatment of the milk and the process of butter making, is much much more difficult to obtain, because the knowledge is much more difficult to obtain, because the knowledge is much more difficult to impart. With all the rules that may be given, there must be superadded as conditions for their successful application, the necessity for close and critical observation. For there are constantly arising circumstances to modify the most of such which may be laid down in a general system.

For depositing the milk when strained, the tin pail of the capacity of about twelve quarts is preferable to any other kind of vessel. It is sufficiently large to fulfill all the requirements in that particular; while its superiority over the shallow pan—which is considerably used—is too palpable to admit of doubt. The following propositions in point, are sustained by facts, the application or pertinency of which all who have ever made butter, or who have been in a dairy with their eyes open to the every-day phenomena therein, will readily apprehend, viz: that milk, in order to realize from it the largest quantity and best quality of butter, must stand in an atmosphere of a given temperature a specific length of time, in all cases, in order to perfect it for the churn; that natural or artificial causes, either accelerating or retarding the processes of change in its elements from that fixed standard, have their like certain results of deterioration, both in the quality and the quantity of the butter produced; that a given quantity of milk, with the greatest surface exposure to the action of the atmosphere, in a given temperature, will change more rapidly than a like quantity in a like temperature, with a less surface exposure. The facts in proof, it need scarcely be intimated, condemn the use of the shallow pan.

Every dairy-woman has observed the effects of a close, muggy and humid atmosphere—such as often precedes rain storms in the summer—upon the milk; also of a thunder storm; also of only partly filling a vessel. In all cases named the change in the milk is much more rapid than when the temperature of the atmosphere is even, and the equilibrium of its vital elements more perfectly sustained; and then in pails filled to their capacity. In all these instances too, the milk must be churned sooner. But there is no method that will prevent a loss of product in quantity and quality.

It is difficult to reach fully the truth of the first proposition. But we can approximate to it, and then adapt our practice as nearly to such standard or rule as it is possible to do. The temperature of the room where the milk is set must never exceed 65° F., and must be as steady and even as possible. The atmosphere of the same must be kept perfectly pure; for any odor peculiar to the decomposition of vegetable or organic substances mingling therewith, will inevitably leave its taint upon the milk and its product.

When the casein is precipitated or the milk coagulated, it is ready to churn. It must not stand until the second change takes place in the lacteal or the sugar of milk; that is, until the lactic acid becomes butyric acid, the latter stage of which may be known from the discolored spots of mould gathered on the surface of the cream. The thick milk should always be emptied with the cream into the churn. There are two important reasons in support of this method. First, the cream never all rises to the surface, and there must always remain with the coagulated part quite a fraction of the fatty matter, which is lost if not churned. Second, there is a virtue in the casein and lactic acid which is essential in the process of churning to impart to the product the element of preservation. It is a fact which should be known by all dairymen and dealers, that the product of cream exclusively, however skillfully manipulated, will not, if packed for keeping, preserve for any length of time the finer qualities of good butter.

The milk in the churn, when fit for churning, should indicate 64° Fah., and should be agitated with a movement of the dash at not less than fifty strokes to the minute. Less motion will fail to divide properly the butter from the milk. When done, the butter should be taken from the churn and thrown into a tub or a small churn partly filled with water 42° to 44° Fah., and the buttermilk forced out with a small dash. It should then be put into trays and washed until the water used ceases to be the least discolored with buttermilk. It is then ready for salting, which should be done, and the trays immediately carried to the cellar. The proper amount is 1¼ oz. to the pound of butter after working—i. e., the butter should retain that amount when ready for packing. When it has stood three or four hours after the first salting, it should be stirred with a ladle and left in the form of a honey-comb, in order to give it the greatest possible surface exposure to the air, which gives color and fixes the high flavor.

Butter, when well manufactured, while standing preparatory to packing, is composed of granulated particles, between which are myriads of infinitesimal cells filled with brine, which is its life. At this period it should be touched with a light hand, as too much and too careless working will destroy its granular and cellular character, and reduce the whole to a compact and lifeless mass, with an immediate loss of flavor, and a certain and reliable prospect, if packed, of a rapid change of its character from indifferently good to miserably poor butter. It should never be worked in the tray while in a dry state, or all the ill results just alluded to will be realized. As a general rule, after the butter has stood in the trays twenty-four hours, and has been worked three or four times as directed, it is ready for packing. After the firkin is filled, it should stand a short time, and then should be covered with a clean piece of muslin, and the whole covered with brine.

It will not be out of place for the writer to state from his own knowledge, and upon his own responsibility, a few facts in connection with the above, referring solely to Mr. Carpenter's success as a dairyman. For the last twenty years, beside fattening the calves to the customary age of four weeks, he has averaged a fraction over two firkins to the cow per year. He has had butter stand in packages in his cellar for one year and a half, and open them with a flavor so fresh and sweet that the very best and most critical judges and buyers were deceived one year in its age—none even suspecting it to be the product of a former year. He never has, during that period, failed to reach in New York market the highest figure representing the maximum market for Orange county butter; and latterly, he has very often overreached the very highest market from $\frac{1}{2}$ to $2\frac{1}{2}$ cents per pound.

Messrs, W. R. Prince & Co., of Flushing, presented fine Japan lilies.

Mr. Field.—We often hear complaints by farmers and gardeners of the failure of crops, from plants, which nevertheless give large crops in other places. The Lord has given us a vast variety of plants, and all have places peculiarly fitted for their perfect success.

The club selected as subjects for consideration at the next meeting: "Summer flowers," and "Fruit for farms."

The club adjourned to Monday, September 6, 1858.

H. MEIGS, *Secretary*.

———

September 6, 1858.

Present, Messrs. Field, Paine, Euller, Burgess, Tracy, Tredwell, Hon. John G. Bergen, Adrian Bergen, of Long Island; Hon. John D. Ward, of Jersey City; Dr. Poole and Doughty, and others, of Jersey; Disturnell, Chilson, John M. Bixby, Johnson, Pardee, Solon Robinson, and others—sixty-three members.

Hon. John G. Bergen in the chair.   H. Meigs, Secretary.

The secretary read the following translations and extracts, made by him since the last meeting, viz :

Bulletin Mensuel de la Societe Imperiale Zoologique d'Acclimatation.   Paris, July 1858.

ON THE ARABIAN HORSE.

By General-Senator Daumas, to the President :

Sir—People and their governments have at all times considered the horse as one of the most powerful elements of their strength and of their prosperity.   At this time no question of rural economy and of the military art, is more dicussed than the amelioration of the horse.   Statesmen, learned societies, agriculturists, the army—every body, is occupied with this matter.   As for myself, I have never ceased to study that precious animal, as a matter of taste, and of love of my country.   I have studied everything relating to it, and I avow that the opinions of the Arabs are best.   I have written often to the Emir Abd-el-Kader, one of the most learned of Arabs, about it.   His last letter to me is as follows :

Praise be to the only God !   To him who remains ever the same, in the midst of the revolutions of this world.   My friend, Monsieur le General Daumas, safety be with you, with the mercy and blessing of God, prays the writer of this letter, in behalf of his mother, his children, their mother, and all the members of his family and of their companions !   You ask of me what is the origin of our Arabian horses ?   You resemble a sun-crack in a parched land !   no shower, however abundant, can fill it up.   However, to staunch your thirst, (if possible,) I will go to the fountain head, the water of which is always most pure and abundant.

Know then ! that with us, it is admitted that God created the horse out of the wind, and Adam out of the mud, of the earth ; and this doctrine cannot be discussed !   Many prophets (safety to them) have proclaimed that when God contemplated the creation of the horse, he said to the south wind : " I am about to make a creature of you ; *condense thyself !* "   And the wind *became condensed !*   Then came the angel Gabriel, and took a handful of that condensed wind, and presented it to God, who formed a brown bay or brown chestnut (Koummite red mixed with black), saying : " I have called thee Horse !   (Frass.)   I have created thee Arab !   I have given thee the *Koummite color !*   I have attached happiness to the hair which falls between thy eyes !   Thou shalt be lord (Sid.) of all animals.   Man shall follow you wherever you go !   Good for pursuit as for flight, you shall fly without wings !   Wealth shall rest upon your back, and good ever wait upon you !"   God then marked him with the sign of glory and hapiness—the *ghora a pelote*, or blase, on the head, and a star in the middle of the forehead !

You wish to know, now, whether God created the horse before the man, or man before the horse.   Listen.   God created the horse before the man, and this is proved by man being the superior creature ; therefore God created all that man could want, before he created him ! For the wisdom of God indicates that everything on the earth was created for Adam and his posterity. And when he had created him, he called him Adam, and said to him, " Choose between the horse and the *borak*," (the creature on which Mohammed rode across the heavens, an animal, neither male nor female, and something like a mule.)

Adam answered and said, " The most beautiful of the two is the horse." God said, " It is well. You have chosen that which is a glory to you, and will be to your children. As long as they exist my blessing shall be upon them, for I have created nothing more dear to me than man and the horse." God also created the horse before the mare. The male is more noble than the female.

Many historians say that after Adam, the horse, as well as all other animals lived in a wild state, the gazelle, the ostrich, the buffalo, and the ass. The first man, after Adam, that mounted the horse, was Ismail, the Father of the Arabs, who was the son of our Lord Abraham, the cherished of God, who taught him to call the horses, and they all ran to him. He took then the most beautiful and spirited among them, and tamed them. Afterwards a great many of them lost their purity, and only one single race was gathered, in all their original nobility, by Solomon, the son of David ; he called them the *Zad-el-Rakeb*, the Gift of Horsemen (cavaliers). To this all the Arabian horses owe their origin. It is said that Arabs of the tribe of Azed went to Jerusalem the Noble, to compliment Solomon on his marriage with the Queen of Sheba. Solomon ordered out of his stable a magnificent stallion, of the issue of the race of Ismail, and gave it to them, saying, " Behold the provisions I give you for your journey home ! When hunger seizes you, take some wood, light a fire, put your best horseman (cavalier) on this horse, armed with a good lance, and you will hardly have your wood gathered and burning before you will see your cavalier return with abundance of game from the chase. Go, and may God cover you with his protection." The men of Azed took to the road, and at their first halt, did as Solomon had directed ; and neither zebra, nor gazelle, nor ostrich, could escape from him. In gratitude they called that race of horses *Zad-el-Rakeb*. It has spread to the east and to the west. We divide into four epochs, the history of this horse. 1st. From Adam to Ismail. 2d. From Ismail to Solomon. 3d. From Solomon to Mohammed. 4th. From Mohammed to us. It is, however, thought that the Solomon race, having been forcibly divided, into many branches, has, like races of men, became varied in the color of its robe, &c. It is admitted, now, that in stony districts, his robe becomes grey, and also where the lands have a light complexion. I have often seen evidences of this fact. You ask me how Arabs know the noble horse, the *Drinker of Air ?* I answer, by the firmness of his lips, and cartilage of the lower part of the nose ; by the dilation of his nostrils ; by the leanness of the flesh about the veins of his head ; by the elegance of the neck and shoulders ; by the softness of his hair, mane and skin ; by the fullness of his breast ; by the large size of his *joints*, and by the *dryness* of his extremities. But by tradition, we learn from our ancestors, that we must discover his nobility more by moral indications than by his physical properties.

The horse has no malice in him. He loves his master, and usually will not suffer another to mount him. He will not do the prompted necessaries while his master is on his back ; he will not eat the food left by another horse. He loves to splash limpid water whenever he meets it. By his smell, sight and hearing, and by his intelligence and address, he preserves his master from a thousand accidents in the chase or in battle. He will fight for his master, and make common cause with him in everything.— *Ikatelma-Rakebhon.*

You will now comprehend the immense love which an Arab has for his horse. It is said that when Mohammed went out of his tent to received the noble horses sent to him, he caressed them with his hands and said, " May you be blessed, oh daughters of the wind." Now I pray God to grant to you happiness which can never pass away ; keep your friendship for me, for the wise Arabs have said, " Riches can be lost, honors dissipate like shadows, but a true friend is a treasure which ever remains." He who has written these lines, with a hand which death must one day dry up, is your friend, though poor before God.

Sid-el-Hadj, ABD-EL-KADER, *Ben-Mahhyeddin.*
End of Deul-Kada, 1274. *End of August,* 1857.

PLANTING WHEAT IN DRILLS.

Messrs. Fowler & Wells, of New York, in their " Life Illustrated," of September 4, 1858, recommend it by showing very superior crops raised by Mr. Brackett, of Rochester. He planted in rows two feet wide, and hills two feet apart. He planted four grains of wheat in each ; these produced thirty stalks on each square foot ; the yield nearly 116 bushels on one acre. *Five pounds weight of wheat* seeds an acre of hills.

Agricultural addresses have teemed with lessons for breeding and taking care of all our stock except the most precious—that of our children and selves. The Atlantic cable sinks to insignificance compared with the " Science of the developement of men."

We exhibit beautiful animal stock, and deformed, erisypelatory, rickety, narrow-chested, dyspeptic, teeth-rotten, flabby-muscle, scrofulous, diseased-liver, kidneys, bad nerves, crooked-backed, bad-jointed, &c., &c., girls and boys. Let all our agricultural orators open their mouths against these terrible evils of the land.

The Secretary said he took very great pleasure in reading to the Club the following deeply interesting paper on a probable remedy for the terrible enemy of our bread. It is from the Hon. Samuel Cheever, late President of our State Agricultural Society.

THE WHEAT MIDGE.

Editors Country Gentleman—From reading an essay upon the wheat midge, written by Prof. Hinds, of Trinity College, Toronto, to which was awarded the first prize by the Bureau of Agriculture and Statistics of Canada West in 1857, and from consulting the authorities by him referred to, conspicuous among which are the essays and papers of Dr. Fitch of this State, as well as from conversations had with entomologists who have studied the habits of this insect, I have come to the conclusion that it is in the power of the farmers to rid themselves mainly if not entirely of this terrible enemy.

It seems to be well ascertained, that the larvæ of this insect, after hatching from the egg deposited by the fly in the head of the wheat, and feeding upon the milky substance that forms the berry until it acquires the power of locomotion, leaves the wheat-head and descends by the stalk, or falls to the ground, when it works itself down to the depth of an inch or more, and there remains in a torpid state, unaffected by any severity of frost, through the winter. Mr. Almy, an entomologist, of Farmersville, Seneca county, who has studied the habits of this insect with great care and thoroughness, says they sometimes bury themselves where the earth is mellow, to the depth of two inches, seldom more.

Being so nigh the surface of the ground, the same solar heat which brings up the wheat in the spring, reanimates the larvæ, and they "wriggle" themselves to the surface just in time to cast their skins and take wing as the wheat comes to head, and the female, after meeting the male, commences her work of destruction, which she in a few days terminates simultaneously with her life.

Prof. Hinds, at paragraph 163, suggests their destruction as follows: "If, therefore, at any time between August and May of the following year, the ground be plowed the depth of six inches, and in such way that the furrow slices lie as compactly as possible, there can be no doubt that a vast majority of the pupæ will perish from inability to escape from their imprisonment." I have not seen it stated whether the larvæ turn themselves in the ground and come up the same end foremost as they go down, or whether they ascend by a reversed motion. If by the latter, as the plow inverts their cells, their reversed motion would carry them downward instead of upward. But if from instinct or otherwise they should move directly towards the surface, having five or six inches of compact earth to penetrate instead of one or two inches, they would arrive at the top of the ground, if they arrived at all, after the wheat had gone to the barn, and they would perish from want of accommodations for reproduction. In addition to this obstacle to their getting to the surface in time to find the wheat coming into head, the effect of the sun's rays would be many days, and perhaps weeks, longer in reaching them to produce reanimation, if they were hid to the depth of five or six inches from the surface, than it would if they were within one or two inches of it.

How to treat the Field.—There should be no clover or grass seed sowed upon any wheat or barley field where the insect will be likely to appear. It might form an objection with the farmer to plow in his stubble.

[Am. Inst.] 11

The plowing should be from the 15th of October to the 20th November, when the earth is so cold as to bring the larvæ to an active state. The furrow should not be less than seven inches deep, and nine or ten would be better.

If the ground is so wet as to be adhesive, so much the better, the furrow slice should be broken as little as possible, and laid within the last track of the plow so as to lap as little as may be.

A roller should be passed over the ground in the same direction with the plow, to force down such furrow slices as were not laid flat by the plow. In case any of the furrows should lap, a light scraper, such as used to fill the ruts in the highways, should be drawn over it, the blade oblique so as to move the dirt to the right and fill up the trenches. Following this with a roller would be useful.

If this work is thoroughly done, the field may be sowed broadcast the following spring, with spring wheat or oats, harrowing or cultivating not more than 2¼ or 3 inches deep, and then rolling.

As it is uncertain how long the larvæ can lie in the ground in a torpid state, at the depth of five or six inches, and then be reanimated on being brought to the surface, it would be safest not to plow again until it had laid through two winters, and whenever plowed it should be as late as July, so that if the larvæ should be reanimated and get upon the wing, they would find no wheat fields suited to their wants.*

To accomplish this work, there must be perfect concert of action with the farmers over a considerable extent of territory. Should they not with alacrity unite in any numbers necessary to defend themselves against an enemy that is taking the bread from our mouths, and the money by millions from our pockets ?

It would be convenient to make the experiment in some locality where a district is bounded on one or more sides by water or an extensive forest. The county of Seneca, lying between two lakes, is well adapted to the purpose. But the attempt should be made in every county and every town in the State, where the insect exists. The object is of much importance, and the cost trifling. The stubble of no wheat or barley field where the insect has shown itself this year, should pass the winter without the deep and thorough plowing and other treatment above given.

* Dr. Fitch, in the Rural New Yorker, Jan'y, 1856, says some of these maggots remain in the heads of the wheat, and are carried in great quantities to the barn, and are separated from the grain with the straw and chaff.

If the straw and chaff are housed and kept dry, the insect will probably dry up and never get upon the wing. If the chaff holding them is carefully preserved and fed to cattle or sheep, the process of mastication or digestion would probably destroy them. But a certain and probably the safest course, would be to remove all the straw or chaff holding them to a safe place and burn it. Great care in all cases should be taken to sweep the floor and scrape the ground where they fall, that none should escape. Should these precautions be omitted and the maggots get into the manure in the barn-yard, they may easily be destroyed by heaping up the manure early in the spring with sufficient wet straw to bring on a rapid fermentation, when heat enough will be produced to destroy the vitality of the maggot, or force it on to the wing before nature has provided any "green thing" for it to lay the eggs upon.

Let some of the intelligent and public spirited farmers in every county give notice that a meeting will be held at their next county fair, to discuss the subject and to appoint committees of the most efficient and reliable men in every town, and then for every school district, to see that this experiment be faithfully and thoroughly made. If it be necessary to plow up a few new seeded fields it is a matter of little moment compared to the end to be attained. No one should hesitate to make the sacrifice. But certainly none should be seeded hereafter so as to prevent this plowing, until the effort is fully made to get rid of this dreadful scourge.

If this plowing is thoroughly done, a crop of wheat may be put in, and a crop taken from the upper side of the furrow, whilst the enemy is sleeping by millions beneath it. This experiment, well tried in any county, is of more importance than many county fairs, valuable as they are.

It is not to be expected that this insect can be entirely destroyed in a single year, but it is confidently believed that if this treatment is thoroughly pursued for from three to five years, our wheat crop will be brought back to us, and that too without the suspension of wheat culture in the meantime, and at a comparatively trifling cost. Is there an intelligent farmer in the State, if he knew that the insects which are destroying him were exclusively produced on his own farm, and would not come from elsewhere, who would not make this experiment before winter upon every field on his farm where the insect has appeared this year, seeded or not seeded? Then why not all do it, as far as the mischief extends?

S. CHEEVER, *Waterford, N. Y.*

PLANTING A MARKET GARDEN.

Now, to show the influence of the discussions here upon others elsewhere, I will read a letter from Trenton, N. J., that pretty clearly shows that the writer has been influenced to plant four acres in small fruits, by reading the reports of the Farmers' Club that gathers occasionally in this room. The letter also shows how necessary it is to give line upon line, oft repeated, of the information so much needed and desired. The writer wants to know the proportions of the sort of strawberries recommended by Mr. Pardee for a market-garden plantation.

R. G. Pardee.—The writer is slightly mistaken in the sorts I did recommend. To each 100 plants I would give the following proportions :

Wilson's Albany, 60 ; Hovey's Seedling, 20 ; Longworth's Seedling, 10 ; Hooker's Seedling, 10.

I would not plant red Antwerp raspberries. For market the Franconia is better, except in peculiar locations, like Milton, on the Hudson, where Mr. Field says an acre and a quarter of land gave a crop worth $800. I would plant Fastolf raspberries for a private family.

Andrew S. Fuller.—I certainly would add Brinkley's orange, for private use or market.

Solon Robinson.—The writer wants to know where to get the plants he wants and the price. That I would not answer if I could. I will hand over the letter to Mr. Fuller.

MILK-WEED.

Now here is another letter, asking for what some very wise men might think very trifling information. Is it so? Listen. The writer has settled upon the rich land of Wisconsin, and he finds that the common milkweed (Asclepias Syriaca) is becoming a great farm pest, driving out useful plants, and he wants to know if any one here can tell him how to get rid of, or even partially suppress the nuisance.

The Chairman.—I know of nothing but much plowing and hoeing to kill that pest.

Mr. Ambler.—In Connecticut it only grows along fences and rich roadsides.

Solon Robinson.—At the west all the land is rich enough to produce it all over the field.

PEACH BLIGHT.

Now, here is a letter that given useful information. George Forshew, of Hudson, New York, says that a handful of fine salt, scattered on the ground around a peach-tree in June, has both prevented and cured the peach-tree blight.

Chairman.—I put several handfuls to a tree about mine, and it killed it.

Solon Robinson.—That is the error, you put too much. This letter says one handful. Here is another letter of inquiry about

CONVERTING STRAW INTO MANURE.

I will read an extract from a letter from Lee county, Illinois, as follows:

"Thrashing our grain soon after harvest, we have made it our practice to burn the straw each year. But now we wish to reform; we wish to convert it into manure. Thrown into great stacks, it is a long time in rotting. What shall we do to expedite the process? Will some one who knows give us information?"

For one, I would answer that I would spread the straw upon the surface as a mulch, and let time rot it. But if to be rotted in a pile, the process can be greatly expedited by simply adding a sprinkling of common salt, which will increase the moisture, and consequent decay. So would mixing in with the pile a few loads of prairie soil, particularly that from a slough; and so would any coarse, succulent green herbage. Above all, add all the waste animal matter possible to obtain, and frequently, that is not a hard matter to get around a prairie farm, where cattle die from exposure, and perhaps from want of the straw that has been burned.

DEEP PLOWING AND WEAK STRAW.

Here is a letter from Providence, Luzerne county, Pennsylvania, written by James Anderson, who says he is a man of great age and much experience. We will see directly what it has profited him. First, he says overseeding is the cause of weak straw. I say, not always. He says king birds are destroyers of bees, and proves it to his satisfaction by killing the king birds, since which the bees have prospered. I say one swallow don't make it summer. The last half of his letter contains proof in itself how sadly a man may be mistaken, notwithstanding his age and experience. It reads as follows:

"Notwithstanding all the acquirements of Prof. Mapes, from nature, experience and learning, I must beg leave to make some exceptions to his plan of deep plowing. I know that about the neighborhood of New York, the sandy and gravelly sands will bear plowing deep, particularly in Jersey. But here in Pennsylvania, there are many parts of such clay land that, if they plow below the soil into the yellow earth, their crops will be proportionately less according to depth; this is marked by the head furrows and the dead furrows; the first produces a full growth, and the second small, and in vain may you deepen that dead furrow to make it produce more. If the deep earth is always productive, then let the banks of railroad earth testify to the same."

Now, instead of Prof. Mapes's land being sandy, it is naturally one of the most compact soils I know of, breaking up in lumps like stone. In fact, it was a solid rock not many long ages since. It is clay instead of sand land, that needs deep plowing, and it is very poor evidence against deep plowing to show that "dead furrows" are not productive. Nobody in this club ever advocated such nonsense.

MOLES.

Here is another letter that criticises a statement made here about moles being insect worms, instead of grain worms. He says:

"This I *know* from every day observation to be very erroneous. I do not know but moles eat insects; be that as it may, I have no doubt their principal living is seeds and roots and other vegetables. In the winter time when the snow is deep and the ground not frozen, I have known them to destroy whole nurseries of apple trees, and even young orchards that have arrived to bearing."

Now this man is mistaken. He is talking about mice, and not moles.

The Chairman.—We will now take up one of the regular subjects.

CULTIVATION OF FLOWERS.

Andrew S. Fuller, Horticulturist, Brooklyn, exhibited a basketfull of flowers, which were distributed among the females present, and much admired by them, particularly some seedlings, of various sorts.

Mr. Fuller gave an interesting statement of the great labor of producing seedlings worth saving. He said: "I have 200 seedling phloxes, and not one worth saving. Yet all improvements come from seedlings. But the handsomest and best of all summer flowers are roses, the best of which are seedlings. The Souvenir de Malmaison is one of the best roses known.

The Hibiscus is a native, and all are single and coarse, and some day from seedlings we shall get a double flower, equal to double hollyhocks.

As yet, I have not been able to get a double one out of a vast number tried.

To get double balsam flowers, keep your seed for years, and the flowers will be more likely to come double.

Here is a hybrid trumpet creeper that I have made that I like.

A neighbor of mine has 3,000 seedling Japan lilies, and only one worth saving.

Mr. Fuller held up a branch full of green and ripe Brinkley orange raspberries—a seedling—and said that he held in his hands the handsomest flower that he knew of; it was far handsomer than bachelor's buttons, and had been an ornament to his garden all summer.

In preparing a seed bed for flowers, make the soil fine; if it were sifted it would be all the better. Don't plant too deep. The true rule is to cover seeds with earth to the thickness of a seed, and then cover the ground with a white cotton cloth. The best manure that I have ever used is liquid manure, made by water and cow droppings.

SEEDLING DAHLIAS.

Mr. Burgess exhibited a variety of new and beautiful seedling dahlias. He said—I give a dahlia plant six superficial feet. To propagate roots, lay them down in beds in spring in a warm situation, and when they have sprouted two inches above the surface, take up the root and divide it with one sprout to each cut, and plant them in holes dug two feet deep and two feet wide, and manured with a peck of compost, first setting a stake in the hole to support the stalk when it grows. I planted and grew one year 11,775 seedling dahlias, and only got six worth saving. A seedling will flower the first year, if it grows well. Seed should be planted in boxes, covered until the seed vegetates. A dahlia needs watering extensively; it cannot well be watered too much. In potting all kinds of plants in the fall, fill about half an inch of the bottom of the pot with clean sand. In keeping dahlia roots, the great thing is to dry them well before putting them away. They must then be stored in dry cellars.

A natural dahlia, the flower from which all our beautiful ones originated, has six petals. I counted the petals of one of my seedlings, the Suffolk Hero, and found 307 petals.

T. W. Field.—I wish that we could call things by their right names. The same difficulty occurs in talking about curculio. I have heard talk about catching them in bottles. A man might as well undertake to catch foxes in bottles. I think we may get rid of many insects by the plan recommended by Judge Cheever, that is burying them under the surface. I think the larvæ of rose-bugs may be served in the same way to great advantage. In relation to planting wheat, it is true that we have often seen how much better nature plants than men. Volunteer seeds of all kinds produce wonderful crops. I have now a volunteer cucumber that is a prolific bearer, and I once had a volunteer pumpkin vine that gave me I don't know how many fine pumpkins.

Solon Robinson.—I had a volunteer pumpkin vine once, that I looked upon as a sort of special interposition for my good, the first summer I lived on the prairie. It grew so wonderfully luxuriant, and blossomed so full, and bore—well now I will you just what this volunteer vine did bear to meet all my great expectations, and repay all my care and culture. It bore not the least sign of fruit—nothing beyond a blossom.

Andrew S. Fuller.—This corroborates my own experience of volunteer seeds. I root them up and plant my own seed, though we may learn something from nature.

Solon Robinson.—I have a lot of letters from the country, all expressing satisfaction with what the writers have read of what is said and done at these meetings—all going to show that, notwithstanding the sneers of some very self-conceited people about " city lot farmers" giving their experience to the country, there are some people willing to ask and receive as well as give information that may be useful to others through the medium of this club, which is not entirely composed of experimenters and theorists, but men of past and present practical experience.

The Secretary remarked—That during the holding of its annual fairs, the Institute has always suspended the meetings of its Farmers' Club, and its Mechanics' Club. Therefore, when we adjourn, it will be to a day after the close of the approaching fair.

The club adopted for next meeting, the subjects of " General harvesting," and " The best methods of preserving fruit," and then adjourned until further notice.

H. MEIGS, *Secretary.*

Tuesday, Nov. 2, 1858.

Present—Messrs. Chambers, Leonard, Pardee, Slite, of Morrisania; Chilson, Disturnell, R. L. Pell, Richard Chute, of St. Anthony, Minnesota; John Campbell, Witt and Fuller, of Williamsburgh, L. I., and others.

Mr. Pell, President of the Institute, in the chair.

Henry Meigs, *Secretary.*

The Secretary read the following translations and extracts, made by him, from the foreign and domestic works on agriculture, &c., received by the American Institute since last meeting of the Club, viz:

[Societe Imperiale Zoologique D'Acclimatation. Paris, September, 1858,]

A NEW TROUT.

By Mons. Auguste Duméril, Administrature, Professor in the Museum of Natural History.

It is well known that this fish abounds in the fresh waters of Algeria, but are not deemed very good eating. Marshal Vaillant desired that we should send some better trout and other fishes to the Algerian waters. We offered premiums, and fortunate transfers have already been made.

Dr. Guyon, one of our members, has been taking fish in the oasis of the circle of Biscara, and also further south at Tuggurth, on the northern slope of Mount Atlas, 400 meters above the sea. Those he took are interesting. A species of trout not before known to be in Algeria is found in the rapid and limpid torrents of Oned-el-Abaich, in Kybalia, near the city of Collo. This *salmonoide* (like a salmon) has a double row of teeth in the lower jaw, and is named by Mons. Valenciennes *salar*, a name borrowed from the ancient poet Ansonius, and made a generic name. It is a peculiar kind, has large, roundish black spots on its sides in regular order, and therefore is called *salar macrostigma*, or big-spotted trout. It also differs from other trout—the lateral fins are nearer together, the back one higher than it is long, the tail more forked.

SILKWORMS.

In Lombardy the disease continues; pulverized charcoal and sulphur have been fully tried as remedies but without the hoped success. I regret that the prize of 12,000 francs for a remedy is not yet won. The disease seems at present to be indomitable.

SOUTH AMERICAN LAMAS.

Mons. Vauvert De Mean writes to the President of the Society that thirty-nine lamas have arrived at Glasgow in May, 1858, on board the steamship New York from New York. They are imported by Mr. Benjamin Whitehead Gee, who comes in the ship with them.

This herd is from Peru. They came from thence by land to Guyaquil, thence by water to Panama, thence across the Isthmus to Aspinwall, thence on board a small vessel to Baltimore, thence to New York, and lastly thence to Glasgow, thus traveling by land and sea 4,000 miles.

The greatest mortality among them was on the Isthmus, when twenty of them died for want of suitable feed, by scorpions, serpents, heat and other causes. On the voyage to Baltimore two lambs perished, but on the voyage to Glasgow one lamb was born, and many of the females became pregnant. Thirteen males and twenty-six females arrived at Glasgow. This herd has cost ten thousand dollars. They are now in the best health.

In consequence of the prohibition of their export by the Peruvian government, it is feared that this heard is the first and the last which will be imported into this country. This herd ought not to be divided. I do not know to what country it will be sent.

P. S.—I have just learned that it was originally bought in Peru by a Frenchman, who intended it for France, but for reasons not clearly explained, sent it to New York to Mr. Gee. Mr. Mitchell, a delegate of the Imperial Society in London, states to the council that it has been bought for Australia, where it will soon be sent, where nothing will be neglected to acclimate it.

Note by H. Meigs.—This herd was exhibited in the Crystal Palace, at the twenty-ninth Fair of the American Institute, October, 1857.

THE PHYSICAL PROPERTIES OF SOILS AS AFFECTING FERTILITY.

By Samuel W. Johnson, Professor of Analytical and Agricultural Chemistry in Yale College, and Chemist to the State Agricultural Society of Connecticut. Presented to the American Institute, Oct. 23, 1858, by Prof. Johnson.

From this valuable essay we extract enough to show that is one which should be in the library of every farmer in America.

1st. The fertility of soil depends upon no cause or class of causes. It involes the whole range of the Physical Sciences—geology, chemistry, botany, physiology, meteorology, mechanics, hydrodynamics, heat, light, and electricity, are all intimately related to it ; it is not strange, therefore, that all the labors to illustrate such a topic should have only recently met with any degree of success.

The learned professor begins with the mechanical structure of soils. A few lichens, only, grow on a solid rock. Crush that rock to a coarse powder, and a more abundant vegetation is maintained by it. If it is reduced to a very fine dust, and duly watered, cereals will grow, and perfect their grain. There are sandy soils in the Eastern States, which, without manure, yield only the most meagre crops of rye, or buckwheat ; and there are sandy soils in Ohio, which, *without manure*, yield on an average, eighty bushels of Indian corn per acre, and have yielded this for *twenty to fifty years in unbroken succession*—the inorganic ingredients being, by chemical analysis, the *same*. There is at present known no difference, except the different fineness of the particles ; the first being, in great part, of *coarse* grains, while the Ohio soil is an exceedingly *fine* powder.

2d. The power of soil to absorb, or condense, gases or vapors. The best observations we possess are forty years old. They were made by Schubler, a teacher in Fellenberg's school at Hofwyl, Switzerland. The solid bodies condense gases. Schubler gives the absorption of water and of oxygen daily, for thirty days, by moist soil, viz :

	Oxygen.	Moisture.
Quartz sand,..................................	1.1000	0.1000
Gypsum, ...	1.7	1
Lime sand,............................	4	3
Plough land, ...	10.5	23
Clay soil (60 per cent clay), ...	6	28
Slaty marl,..................................	7	33
Loam,..	7	35
Fine carbonate of lime, ...	7	35
Heavy clay soil (80 per cent clay),.............	9	41
Garden mould (7 per cent humus), ...	11.5	52
Pure clay, ...	10	49
Carbonate of magnesia (fine powder),..........	11	82
Humus,......................................	13	120

3d. Permeability—percolation—capillarity. In coarse sands and soils, water *percolates*—runs rapidly. In fine, minute particles, water is held with great *capillary* power. Flame draws oil up the wick—so the air heats and draws up the water to the surface.

Hales and Saussure determined by experiment, that an acre of sunflowers, each plant occupying four square feet of ground, delivered by evaporation, during four months' growth, four and a half millions of pounds of water. (Equal to 75,000 cubic feet.) This water carried into the plants all the mineral matters and some organic.

[Revue Horticole, September, 1858. Paris.]

Translated by H. Meigs.

HOT BED GLASSES.

We translate the following little article with much pleasure, because it will be found highly useful to those who are obliged to be economical in their gardening and farming:

The glazing of frames usually depends upon the putty. Mine is secured by inserting the panes in groves, made so that the panes slide in and out easily. The panes must, of course, be cut parallel, so as not to bind. The great advantage of my plan is in the ready removal of a broken pane, and insertion of a new one, for I have broken much glass in trying to clear off the old putty of broken frames. I take out a broken pane, slide up those below, and put the new one in at the bottom. No more external air enters my frames, than the puttied ones. My method takes far less time and work to make it than the other.

FAVRE BELLANGER, *Gardener at Nantes.*

CULTIVATING PINE TREES.

Great credit is due to Major Phinney, of Barnstable, Massachusetts, for his noble enterprize in this great work. Eleven years ago he planted the seeds of white pine on about ten acres of worn out and otherwise useless land, which hardly produced anything but lichens! He now has, from those seeds, a forest of pine trees of average twenty feet height, and from three inches to *six inches in diameter!*

LIVE HEDGES.

Thomas Affleck, of Texas, advertises in their papers that he will plant and dress for three years, hedges of the *Cherokee Rose* for $100 *a mile.* He says that double white Mycrophylla* Rose is better. For rich bottom land, I prefer the *Chickasaw* Rose. It resembles the Cherokee, is less rampant (creeping) and has a squatty figure, and is equally well armed with thorns. Thousands of miles of Cherokee Rose hedge exists already in Texas. For the sea coast, the *Guisachee* or *Weesachee* Rose is best. For their upland soil, Osage Orange, or what is better, *Cock's Spur Hawthorn*—but that an Aphis eats the leaves this year. In Western Texas,

* Microphylla, small leaved.—MEIGS.

the Yucca or Spanish Bayonet, and the Opuntia, Prickly Pear, *alone or together, make an impassable hedge.* Here is a *Rhameus* (Rhamnus) or Buckthorn, called India rubber tree, which will make good hedges.

THE STEAM PLOW.

The Invention of Mr. Fawkes, of Lancaster, (Pa.,) at the late State Fair in Illinois.

This plow is described as a cross between a locomotive and a tender. It is mounted on two guiding-wheels and a huge propelling wheel in the shape of a drum, which overcomes the difficulties of miring on soft soil and slipping on hard smooth ground. It is said to be easily managed, and to require but a moderate amount of fuel. It draws six plows, so regulated by spiral springs as to yield to any extraordinary obstruction. The machine was tried on the most difficult soil, the unbroken prairie, and its performance is thus described in the Chicago Tribune:

" The prairie was baked so hard by drouth that the prairie-breaking plows would not run in it, and the trial of sod plows was abandoned in consequence. Notwithstanding this fact, the inventor was so confident of success that he gave the order to put the plows to work in this almost impervious soil. After a little delay in regulating to this brick-like surface, the engine moved forward, when six furrows were turned side by side in the most workmanlike manner. The excitement of the crowd was beyond control, and their shouts and wild huzzas echoed far over the prairie, as there, beneath the smiling autumn sun, lay the first furrow turned by steam on the broad prairies of the mighty west. The goal was won. Steam had conquered the face of nature, and the steam plow had become a fact; it was working over the rich rolling prairies of "Egypt," and turning up its wealth of nutritious elements for the growth of the cereal and pomonal products—self-moving, and containing a power unequalled to turn up the lower strata of soil, so rich in potash, in phosphates, in silicia, and other essential elements of vegetable growth. The long line of matchless furrows parted the crowd, and lay between the moving masses like a line of silver wove in the gray setting of the prairie. Amid the excitement, the inventor remained calm; it was enough for him to hear the glad shouts of victory which rent the air. For this he had toiled; for this his hands had become hardened and his face made swarthy over the glowing iron out of which he forged the muscles of the iron steed of the prairies.

" Mr. Fawkes and others were called out by the crowd, and made brief speeches. Mr. Coleman, a member of the board, spoke of the success of the steam plow now witnessed as marking a new era in the world's progress, and declared that the great enterprise of Fawkes may be placed side by side with the steam-engine, the steamboat, the locomotive, the cotton gin, and the telegraph. After the speaking the engine again moved forward, when the plows turned up the *loose mud drift* of Egypt, laying six furrows side by side with the most perfect ease and in the most workmanlike manner.

The consumption of fuel and water was very moderate. That the engine is a complete success there can be no doubt, and all that is now wanting is to demonstrate that, taking the whole expense into consideration, it is cheaper than horse power. If this is answered in the affirmative, it will produce the greatest revolution in agricultural progress that we have yet seen; it will take another wrinkle from the brow of labor, and give to the toiling millions lighter tasks to perform."

A NATIVE GRAPE FROM NEW JERSEY.

Rev. W. Schenck presented to the club a basket of grapes from a wild vine, discovered by his father, in the woods, who transplanted it about eighteen years ago. It is a round, thin skinned, sweet grape; bunches of moderate size; berries close together. Those who tasted them considered them the best native grape yet found.

CRANBERRIES ON DRY SOIL.

Mr. J. C. Young, of Lakeland, on Long Island, about fifty miles from New York, presented a box of cranberry plants, with their berries on them, abundant, grown by him there, last season. The plants were taken from marshy land, northerly of the Lake Ronkonkoma, in the summer of 1856, and transplanted into his land, near the lake, the land being entirely destitute of all moisture, except that from dews and rains. The plants, nevertheless, thrived, and the only trouble he had with the crop, was to get out sorrel, which grew too plentifully among the cranberries. He believes it is easily made a profitable crop on such lands.

Mr. Adrian Bergen presented ears of corn from his farm in Gowanus, Long Island Large grain; very heavy; a profitable corn.

Mr. Disturnell wished to direct attention to the remarkable agricultural capabilities of Minnesota, and introduced his friend, Mr. Chute, recently from there.

Mr Richard Chute, of St. Anthony, was requested to speak of the agriculture of that mid-region of our continent. He said that he was fearful of meeting unbelief if he should state the facts within his own knowledge, of the remarkable capabilities of the soils of Minnesota. He would say that in many vegetables it equalled those hitherto unparalleled vegetables of California—but, on his return, he would send some specimens to the club, which would testify more effectually than man can. The potatoes are very fine, so that in the markets of the west, St. Louis, and others, they have sold for two dollars a bushel, while those of that region sold for fifty cents. Snow falls in all about one foot, occasionally a little more; it lies on the ground from 90 to 120 days; travel is easy over it; the air very clear and healthy; fever and ague, and bilious fever, not known there. The Rocky Mountains take the heavy wet, and send the air pure and wholesome to Minnesota. Our lands are about half prairie; subsoil, clay, and in some places, gravelly. Forests of white pines and Norways, northerly —trees one to three feet diameter; oaks, southerly; sugar maples make, perhaps, 40 per cent of the forest. The waters abound in fish; soft-shelled turtles, plenty. Cranberries so plenty that we have shipped fifty thousand barrels of them to all parts of the river Mississippi; they are of large size. Corn is raised to sixty, and sometimes one hundred, bushels an acre. He saw tobacco there six and a half feet high. Corn, a yellow flint, ripened in sixty-seven days after planting. Soil generally a fine sandy loam. Rain, when it falls—occasionally, does so at night chiefly. About half of the land is prairie. Raspberries, wild, are so plenty, said Mr. Disturnell, that in Michigan upper peninsula, a house there had made, in the season, eleven tons of raspberry jam.

Mr. Chute.—The white pine trees often from two to two and a half feet in diameter. There are some *seven million acres of forest there.*

Mr. Disturnell read from the report of a select committee of the House of Representatives of Minnesota, 1858, " on the overland emigration route from Minnesota to British Oregon," some passages as to the Red river, in latitude 50°. " Its west side lined continuously, for thirty miles, with farms, &c. These farms have each a front of twenty-four rods on the river, and extend back a mile or two. The dwellings and barns, &c., are near the river; have lawns and shrubbery, and trees and vines. There are large churches; clean, whitewashed school-houses; mansions of pretentious dimensions, for gentlemen; elaborate fencing; the seats of retired officers of the Hudson Bay Company; an English Bishop's parsonage, with a boarding, or high school, near by; a Catholic Bishop's massive cathedral, with a convent of sisters of charity attached; windmills on the points of land on the river—twenty of them, with their large sails, are seen at work when there is a good breeze. The whole of the upper plains on both branches of the River Saskatchewan, have an agricultural value superior, naturally, to the fields of our New England, when in their primitive condition. Away up the Peace river, on the northern slope of the Rocky Mountains—around the Hudson Bay posts—General Colville states that as fine barley as any in the world, is raised, in 60° north latitude, a thousand miles nearer the north pole than Minnesota is."

The club ordered for next subjects, " Farm Fruits, and Preservation of Fruits," and " Late Fall Flowers."

The club adjourned.

H. MEIGS, *Secretary.*

November 16, 1858.

Present—Messrs. Doughty, of Jersey; Adrian Bergen, of Gowanus, Long Island; Chilson, Dr. Adamson, Fuller, Burgess, Provost and De Witt, of Long Island; John M. Bixby, Pardee, Lawton, of New Rochelle; Landis, of Hammonton, New Jersey; Prof. James J. Mapes, and others—27 members.

William Lawton in the chair. Henry Meigs, Secretary.

The Secretary read the following translations and extracts from the foreign and domestic works received by the Institute since the last meeting, viz :

[Journal de la Societe Imperiale et Centrale d'Horticulture—Napoleon 3d, Protecteur, Paris, September, 1858.]

HYBRID RHODODENDRONS.

We owe to John Standish, of England, many fine varieties, and his Perfection, Minnie and Mrs. Standish. His first hybrids were obtained from the least flower bearers, the Maximum and the Arboreum. They stand hot weather better than others. Their flowers are very compact and of the most beautiful shades of color. That able English Horticulturist says: I have always found that a hybrid produced from *two other hybrids* are much more flower bearing than one from *two different species.* To produce vigorous hybrids, it is *indispensible* to use two species or on two hybrids which have *great affinity* to each other. He says that he has hybridized the Sikkim and the Bhotan Rhododendrons, and expects flowers not only very beautiful, but also possessing odour.

TREES FROM SEED.

The celebrated Belgian, Van Mons, says that the fruit of all seedling trees is degenerate, and after the second and third generations, &c., the fruit improves. He recommends planting seeds of the *worst fruits*, which will continue to ameliorate for several generations.

SETTING OUT YOUNG PEACH AND PEAR TREES.

[Monatschrift fur Pomologie, March and April, 1858.]

Mr. Fischer, of Kaaden, transplanted many thousands of pear trees, of one year's growth, from seed sown in an asparagus bed. He pruned one-half of them at transplanting, the other half not. The latter succeeded far better than the former. He thought the cause of this was clear, (viz :) because at this first stage of growth, the growth of the roots predominates, and the terminal root (tap-root,) always best and most perfect of the roots ; the others being feeble in comparison.

WASHINGTONIA GIGANTEA.

This great tree, of California, has been grown from the seed very successfully by Mr. Fuller, of Williamsburgh, Long Island, who has exhibited them at our Farmers' Club, last summer. We are glad to see that Philadelphia has planted some in Independence square, a few days ago. Also some of the Franklinias—the fine tree of our forest, so called by the celebrated John Bartram, long ago. Also, Magnolia Conspicua, Dog-wood, and the *Silver Bell tree.* This new planting was done by William Saunders, of Germantown, well known as an able landscape gardener, under the direction of the committee on public lands, of which Mr. Cuyler is chairman.

The Washingtonia has, in California, attained the height of upwards of three hundred feet, with a diameter of about thirty feet, at an age judged to be some three thousand years. This great American tree has been named Sequoia by some, Wellingtonia by others; but we determine to call it by a greater name than any of 3,000 years—the name of our George Washington.

We wish to preserve a record of the few remaining in California—fearing that they may by some misfortune be lost; and they cannot again grow in less than probably 2,000 or 3,000 years.

The grove in Mariposa, contains 427 trees in a space three-fourths of a mile long, and one and a half mile wide. Their sizes now, are as follows:

One 34 feet diameter; two 33 feet diameter; thirteen 25 to 30 feet diameter; thirty-six 20 to 25 feet diameter; eighty-two 15 to 20 feet diameter. One tree has fallen, which measures nearly 40 feet in diameter, and 400 feet in length.

There are but five groves of these trees known, containing altogether but less than 800 trees—all growing between latitude 27 deg. 40 min. and 38 deg. 15 min. north. The Toulumne grove contains only ten trees, one or two of which are, it is said, 35 feet in diameter.

[Royal Agricultural Society of England—Journal, Vol. 19, Part 1, No. 41, 1858.]

We take great pleasure in extracting from the works of this great society.

OBSERVATIONS ON THE RECENTLY INTRODUCED MANU-FACTURED FOODS FOR AGRICULTURAL STOCK.

By J. B. Lawes, F. R. S.

I have, as others have, employed the manufactured foods on my farm. The average prices of the following stock foods for the six weeks ending July 17, 1858, were as follows:

1 cwt. of	Barley,	8.6
do	Oats,	9.2
do	Beans,	9.4
do	Peas,	9.6
do	Lentils,	10.0
do	Oilcake,	10.0
do	Linseed cake,	16.6
do	Hay,	4.0

Thus the manufactured foods cost, weight for weight, four or five times as much as the nutritive of the ordinary stock foods on our farms. Very undeniable evidence of their superiority should therefore be required to induce the farmer extensively to employ them. But it is strange that among the numerous testimonials, in general terms, no evidence based upon exact comparative experiment, showing actual weights of food consumed, and the increase in live weights obtained, has been brought forward in favor of these costly foods; nor a reference to the circulars give much insight into their composition. One professor of chemistry reports, however, that on analysis, he found besides nitrogenous and mineral matters, upwards of 50 per cent of *respiratory* matter.

[Societe Imperial Zoologique d'Acclimatation. Paris, September, 1858.]

This powerful body was organized on the 10th of February, 1854, under the protectorship of Napoleon III.

The members are several emperors, a dozen kings and eighteen princes, and 1,650 individuals and societies.

The purpose is to naturalize in France every animal of use or beauty.

Mr. Bataille has recently sent from Guiana seven red ibis, four penelope yacon, one jabirn, one heron honoré, one savacon huppee (top knot).

The red ibis is one of the most beautiful ornamental birds. They are easily bred; they are fed as poultry are; we believe they are easily domesticated. The penelopes are still more beautiful than the ibes.

FOWLS.

The greatly increasing interest in the breeds is a phenomenon as curious as it is new. Long ago England, Belgium and Holland opened a new way which we did not seem willing to go. We overlooked it with a superb indifference, as if fowls were unworthy of notice and care. But 1850 revealed some private efforts and successful competition at our agricultural fairs, and now we and all Europe are busy with fowl raising.[*]

Classification is advised, and the best breeds to be carefully separated and improved.

PRIZE ESSAY ON MANURING GRASS LANDS.

By J. Dixon.

Experience of the last twenty years, extensively, has enabled me to say, without hesitation, that bones are pre-eminent above all other manures, when permanency and cost are considered. Some farmers boil them to have more immediate effect, thinking also that they last as long. Raw bone is best. For immediate effect, grind them fine and throw them over the grass in early spring and in showery weather.

Of the permanency of raw bone.—After sixteen years the land (which had been well manured with bone broken with a heavy hammer) was the most fertile of any in the district. It is now seventy years since the bone was put on, and the land is still markedly luxuriant beyond any grass land in the district. It is said that bones do not materially help land that is *limed*, for the lime neutralizes the fertilizing properties of the bone. I tried this in 1848 on half an acre of heavily limed land, and that is *this day* superior to the rest. Bone sawings of button, comb and knife-handle makers is always effective on grass land.

[*] Five years before that the American Institute gave premiums on poultry on my motion.—H. Meigs, *Secretary of the Farmers' Club.*

ERGOT

Is found not only on grain but on many grasses, on rye grass especially at the period of its going to seed. Almost all grasses are affected by the ergot, which produces abortion in female stock. Grazed land is most subject to ergot.

NEW LAND BROUGHT INTO CULTIVATION BETWEEN NEW YORK AND PHILADELPHIA.

Mr. Landis, who is engaged in this new settlement, was requested to speak of it. He presented the first evidence of a new American settlement, that is, *a newspaper, The Hammonton Farmer*, in Atlantic county, New Jersey, volume 1, No. 15.

It appears that within a very short time this county, which had never before been settled, has already in the town a thousand people, a hundred and fifty houses, two churches nearly finished, school houses and a newspaper. As to its soil, climate and health, a highly favorable report has been made by the distinguished Dr. Jackson, of Boston. The grape flourishes there, the sweet potato and the peach, which is especially fine. A three mile fresh water lake, handsomely girt by trees, full of fish ; water some thirty feet depth. Lands easily made fertile, and kept so by the natural means there, such as muck, marl, &c. Cheap and ready access to the greatest markets in America—New York and Philadelphia. Climate much milder than the more northerly parts of Jersey. Those who desire to know more about this desirable spot for farms and gardens, will learn at the office of the parties, 87 Bleecker street, New York.

Mr. Provost, of Williamsburgh, presented for examination samples of the wine and brandy made by him on his vineyard there. He covers the ground with grape vines, and fertilizes them liberally with poudrette. His crop of wine last season was about fifteen hundred gallons from one acre. He makes one gallon of brandy from five gallons of wine. He sells the brandy at eight dollars a gallon for medicinal purposes. He can therefore make three hundred gallons of brandy from one acre, which, at $8 per gallon, is *two thousand four hundred dollars an acre.* The wine was pronounced very good, and the brandy pure and excellent.

The subject of farm fruit and preservation of fruit was taken up.

Prof. Mapes being known to be well acquainted with the processes of preservation, was requested to speak of them. He said that the ordinary method of boiling the juices of fruits with sugar, almost destroyed the peculiar flavor of them. That the true plan is to simmer the juices, taking away scum and all impurities, and then add the sugar, so that a fine jelly, having the genuine flavor of the fruit, is produced. The juice of the Catawba grape treated thus, forms a fine jelly. Mr. Lawton in trying to make jelly of citron melon, succeeded in making it very good. The professor is now engaged in a series of experiments upon keeping his finest pears, and will report how, if he is as successful as he believes he will be, by what he has already done.

He adverted to a fallacious theory on soils recently put forth imposingly, viz :   That as solid rock bears lichens, it will if coarsely granulated, produce a higher class of plants, wheat, corn, &c. ; that when finely granulated, as it is in the Miami Valley, Ohio, it produces fine crops of corn and grain annually, and has done so for a great many years.   The error which here exists I wish to correct.   The fertility of that or any other sandy soil is not owing at all to the fineness of the particles, for whether fine or coarse, *mere sand* being destitute of organic remains, has no fertility, but in fact the particles of organic matter, which have been for ages in vegetable and animal life, are in that sandy soil, giving it its fertility, and those minute organics cannot be imitated by any chemical means in our power—like the well known phosphate of lime which has progressed for ages, through animal and vegetable bodies, has gained an adaptability to the plants in such a degree that it is not too much to say that one ounce of it is worth more to plants than a ton of the rock of phosphate which has never gone through that wonderful process of progression through vegetable and animal bodies, which shows its powerful effects and defies all investigation as to its true character.   This doctrine of progression is original with Prof. Mapes, and gains by closer examination.

Mr. Disturnell placed on the table a very handsome white turnip, from New Jersey, weighing *eight pounds three ounces*—one of many from the same field.

Mr. R. G. Pardee placed on the table a number of varieties of beautiful artemisias.

Prof. Mapes adverted to the homœpathic manure—the tobacco ashes, leaves, &c., to the tobacco plant—the cuttings, leaves, &c., of grape vines to the grape vines.   No question, a scientific process, using as manures the organism in the closest affinity to the new growing plant—as the tartrate and lees of wine, &c., to the vine—one ounce of which tartrate is more beneficial to the plant than tons of the same tartrate raw, that is, not having been used by plants.

Mr. Provoost.—I apply all the refuse of my vineyard as manure to the vines.

Subjects for next meeting, Dec. 7th—" Root feed for stock ;" " Winter treatment of manure ;" " Effect of winter on clay and sandy soils ridged ;" " Sorghum and corn stalks compared as winter fodder."

The club then adjourned.

H. MEIGS, *Secretary*

December 7th, 1858.

Present—Robert L. Pell, President of the Institute, Prof. Mapes, Messrs. Benson, Benson, Jr., Hon. Frank Tuthill, Doughty and Pike, of Jersey ; Treadwell and Bruce, of Williamsburgh ; Burgess of Brooklyn ; Gardener, Dr. Gallagher, of North Carolina ; Provoost, of Williamsburgh ; Lawton, of New Rochelle ; Selleck, of Connecticut ; Davoll, of

Brooklyn ; Leonard, Chambers, Chilson, Daniel C. Robinson, and others—27 members.

President Pell in the chair ; Henry Meigs, Secretary.

Alfred G. Benson was invited to speak of the guano of Jarvis' and Baker's Islands. He said that his son was present, who had as agent of the Guano Company, visited and examined the islands, and confirmed the statements now made.

Mr. Benson here spoke for his son, (who had been introduced to the club as one who had visited the American Guano Islands,) recapitulating the history of guano enterprises in the United States. In June, 1855, the Farmers' Club had urged by resolution the government to take possession of certain guano islands to which no other nations had claim. The American Guano Company was formed, trusting solely in the representations of Captain Michael Baker, who had accidently discovered an immense deposit of this fertilizer upon islands in the Pacific. The President of the United States ordered a national ship to visit Baker's and Jarvis' Islands and report upon their promise. Commodore Mervine visited the designated vicinity and returned without landing upon them, saying that the alleged guano was worthless, that the coast was inaccessible from rocks, and that there was no anchorage for vessels. Secretary Dobbin ordered the Commodore to send another vessel to explore the islands, and the *St. Mary's* was sent. Her report confirmed the Commodore's, though, privately, the gentleman who was in command of her admitted that there was anchorage about the islands. Notwithstanding this, another expedition was sent out, the bonds of $100,000 required by the United States government having been given, buoys were laid, and two cargoes brought home. Mr Benson's son rafted the timber on shore to build houses on the islands, and boated the cargo off. In the late panic the company lost all its funds. But then, when no underwriter in the Union would take the risk of sending a vessel, Wm. H. Webb, the ship-builder, furnished a ship for the company, and in it sent out a man in whom he could implicitly trust, to report how much guano there was, and how accessible it might be. Sixty days since this agent reported that the guano on Jarvis' Island was boundless in amount and entirely accessible. Mr. Webb then bought up $18,000 worth of the shares, which had been hawked about the streets for $5 to $10 a share—or one-fifth of the whole stock. A cargo of this guano had just arrived at Brooklyn, under care of the son of D. G. P. Judd, who, selling it at $38 a ton, was realizing a profit of $18,000 off his cargo. Mr. Benson estimated the amount of guano on Jarvis' Island at 5,000,000 tons, and on Baker's Island at no less. He instanced experiments to show that it was in no way inferior to the best Peruvian article. Another company had lately been formed to bring guano from still other islands lately discovered.

The following resolutions were adopted unanimously :

Whereas, On the 22d of June, 1855, this body passed the following resolutions :

Resolved, That it is the duty of the American government to assert its sovereignty over any and all barren and uninhabitable guano islands of the ocean, which have been, or hereafter may be, discovered by citizens of the United States, and which are situated so far from any continent that, according to the law which governs nations, no other power can rightfully exercise jurisdiction over them, and to guarantee the right of property therein to the discoverer, his successor or assigns.

Resolved, That the agricultural societies of the several States be invited to concur in the foregoing, and to unite in calling upon our government at Washington, and the distinguished public men now before the country, for their views on this important question.

Resolved, That the foregoing resolutions be printed in the form of a circular, signed by the President and Secretary, and transmitted to the county and State agricultural societies of the several States, to the President of the United States, and heads of departments at Washington.

ROBERT S. LIVINGSTON, *Chairman.*
HENRY MEIGS, *Secretary.*

And *Whereas,* On the 18th August, 1856, Congress enacted a law affording the protection embodied in said resolutions, and

Whereas, One company called the American Guano Company, acting under authority and sanction of the aforesaid law, is now in successful operation, and another company, called the United States Guano Company, has just been organized, upon very large deposits found upon other islands, therefore,

Resolved, That we congratulate the farmers of our country upon the acquisition of such treasures, and that their vast value is measurably appreciated by the government of the United States.

[Journal of the Society of Arts, and of the Institutions in Union. London, Aug., 1858.]

SILK FROM NEW ZEALAND.

We extract from the *Australian and New Zealand Gazette :* " Hopes are entertained of a new branch of export of a novel character. A native variety of the silk worm is found in the bush here, clinging in countless swarms to the shrub which forms its food. The worm is enclosed in a dark colored cocoon, the exterior of which is of extraordinary toughness, and encloses a quantity of yellowish silk. The staple of which, both as to fineness and length, has been pronounced by the manufacturing houses in Glasgow, by whom it was tested, superior to that of the best European worms. Reliable authority states that there is no assignable limit to the quantity to be procured. A box as large as a small tea-chest was filled with them in in about ten minutes; two hours' gathering will give two pounds' weight of raw silk."

JARDIN DES PLANTS, PARIS.

There are growing here : the Chinese nettle, said to furnish a stronger and more glossy fibre than flax or hemp. It has also the oil pea, the wax tree, and the varnish tree, with the insects which inhabit them. They are growing potatoes from those gathered on the Cordillera Mountains. They have two new kinds of oak trees from China. France is now largely cultivating the Sorghum—excellent for cattle.

BISCUIT FODDER FOR STOCK.

Mons. Naudin, a veterinary surgeon of the Imperial Guard, has been successful in composing it of all the feed usually given to horses and cattle —straw, hay, clover, oats, barley, peas, refuse of the wine-press, pulp of roots, stalks of millet, corn, leaves of grape vine, beets, of some trees. All these are bruised and chopped together, a mucilage of barley flour and a little salt are added, and all well mixed and left for a few hours, when a slight fermentation sets in; when it is put into square moulds, made into cakes, and left to dry in a current of warm air. In this state it may be preserved for a great length of time. When wanted for use, it is moistened with about one-fifth of its weight in water, the cake is then broken into seven or eight pieces, and put into the nose-bag, or manger. The cakes should weigh about one pound each. Twenty of them are enough for the daily ration of a horse. Mastication and digestion are easier, and the general health of the animal secured. Enough can be prepared for winter. All waste of food is obviated.

Charles K. Gallagher, of Washington, North Carolina, speaks of wine: Still wine from Scuppernong, and still wine from the native Pamlico grape, dark colored—and perhaps, called *Mish*, from the German who first brought it into notice. Longworth thinks it the best, for wine, of any of our natives.

Dr. Gallagher exhibited some wine from the native grape of the vicinity of Washington, N. C., and some also from the Mish grape, supposed to be a Scuppernong stock, grafted with the Butters grape. Though there was a great deal of saccharine matter in the grape, sugar had been added in the manufacture. Prof. Mapes remarked that the fermentation of the sugar of grape, made brandy, while the fermentation of the cane sugar makes rum. Brandy decomposes animal matter, rum preserves it. The older a wine becomes to which sugar has been added, the worse it is; the older that wine which has no sugar added, the better its flavor. Old rum has higher flavor than new; brandy loses flavor with age. Hence the French, when they put up fine wines of fleeting flavor, add brandy, not sugar, after it has passed the period of fermentation. He had been making what they called "wines" from fruit, from rhubarb, &c., to which he added sugar. They certainly were very pleasant, but the trouble was, that they would stay what he made them; as fast the fusil oil separates, they become rummy. It was easy to increase and change the flavor of fruits, especially of grapes. The experiment of mixing a drop of fusil oil with a drop of different acids, was familiar, and the production thereby of the flavors of different fruits. Now, when he saw that the union of tannic acid and fusil oil gave the strawberry's flavor, it was easy to believe that dressing the strawberry bed with tan-bark would improve the flavor of strawberries—

especially when it was remembered that the wild wood strawberry, where the fallen leaves, and decaying bark of trees, furnished an abundant supply of tannic acid, had a finer flavor than any cultivated berry. But the finest flavored grapes did not produce the finest flavored wines, for the reason that they contained too much fusil oil. This topic was one of immense interest to fruit growers, and experiments were already being freely tried. There were 800 kinds of pears now in existence which were unknown when he came on the stand, and he felt sure that the palate was only just beginning to enjoy the pleasures in store for it, and which chemistry and the horticulturists were fast developing.

SEWERAGE OF PARIS.

While London poisons her Thames with the filth of almost three millions of people, and our London cannot clean her ways and by-ways, Paris has subterranean galleries in communication with the dwellings, to convey all refuse to wagons running on railways, to carry all off without being either seen or smelled!

Mr. Fuller, botanist gardener, of Williamsburg, grows successfully and readily our Washingtonia Gigantea, of California, and others. The Oregon hemlock or spruce; the Oregon pine; the Oregon Picea Fraseri, or Balsam fir; the Oregon Thuya Gigantea, Biota Orientalis. This noble tree grows rapidly and fast from grafts, &c. It hates conservatories and cities.

Our Washingtonia Gigantea, was first introduced into England in 1853, by Mr. Loob, and in 1854 into France, by Mr. Boursier de La Riviere. Mr. Loob called it the Monarch of California, of *terrible beauty !* as lofty as the dome of the Hospital of Invalids, Paris, and more than thirty feet in diameter. It grows rapidly from seed and cuttings—the latter succeeds wonderfully. I hope next spring to have hundreds of them. We ought to grow this tree by all the means in our power.

I repeat it, Mr. Cuyler, the chairman of the committee having charge of the public grounds of Philadelphia, has set them out already. The intelligent chief of our Central Park, will do his best to raise this grand vegetable monument to Washington, in the great Central Park of New York, in which city he took his first oath of the Presidential office.

Mr. Pell left the chair to Mr. Lawton.

The regular topic of the day was

THE FALL PLOWING OF CLAY LANDS.

Prof. Mapes said that twenty-five years ago he reported to the club experiments to show that the two constituents of the soil, to wit: alumina and carbon, were particularly active in receiving and retaining ammonia in the soil. That their presence enables the soil to retain the results of decomposition, else they would be washed down with the water into the wells and springs. Liebig afterward claimed this power for carbon, but overlooked it in alumina, but now all agree that it has scarcely less valuable properties of this sort than carbon. Everybody knew long ago that clayey soils held manures well, but it was commonly and erroneously supposed that it was so only by making a tight bottom to the land. Through a pound of powdered charcoal a million gallons of water would percolate, but not one particle of decayed animal matter—and alumina in which clay lands abound, was like carbon in this peculiarity. But clayey land would be puddled by dews and rains if not treated rightly, and this valuable property be of no use to the crop. Break up the clay into a fine powder, and then the rain which holds in solution the exudations of all kinds of animal substances, surrenders to it a rich burden of fertilizers; the decay of 1858 is the raw material out of which the growth of 1859 is furnished. To pulverise the clay in lands heavy with it, it is necessary to back-furrow and ridge them during the fall. If they have been manured, just before back-furrowing, all the better—then the manure is held between the back-furrows and the decomposition goes on all winter. The exposed surface of the soil, thawing and freezing alternately, falls into powder, and not one atom of the decayed manure, or of the fertilizing elements in the rain or snow, is lost—the alumina retains it all, till the roots of plants in the spring are ready to absorb and elaborate it. A light sandy soil, or a sandy loam, lacking clay, of course, wants different treatment. That should be left flat—some even roll it with benefit. A clayey loam must be treated according to the amount of clay, and the crops to be raised. He would back-furrow and ridge a place into which he meant to put deep crops, but not potatoes.

Prof. Mapes enlarged upon the properties of alumina. Bury a fishy duck in a clayey soil, said he, and to-morrow you may cook and eat it without perceiving a remnant of the fishy flavor. Pulverized clay finely moistened will disinfect a place almost equal to chloride of lime. Stables with clay bottoms never smell. It was this property of absorbing and retaining which made it true that farmers sometimes by carting on two inches of clay upon a light sandy soil, made a barren field more productive than if the same amount of manure had been spread upon it. The Professor then proceeded to show how land would bear to be more heavy with clay, if well underdrained, than otherwise. He preferred drains five feet deep and eighty feet apart to those three feet deep and twenty feet apart. Generally his plan cost no more than the other. The land never puddles near the drain, above the bottom of the drain. The water enters the drain from below—never from the sides. Between the drains the water of falling showers forms an arch in the earth, below which, for a short distance, the earth is saturated, but above it never. Until this arch is flattened to the lower level of the drain the water will continue to issue from the drains. The five feet drain then secures two feet more of earth in depth that is never saturated than the three feet drains. He urged the necessity of keeping both ends of the drain open to the admission of air—the upper end being secured so by a pile of large stones reaching to the surface—and the circulation of air through it should be sufficient to extinguish the light of a candle placed at the upper opening. Another use of the drain was that it made a mulch in effect of the upper inch of soil over the whole field.

The Professor digressed here to insist on the value of mulching ground with refuse hay, salt hay, anything. Sometimes farmers discover that a thick coat of barnyard manure spread on in the fall is of great service to their land, and think that it is all a mistake about the ammonia's being wasted when manure is spread in the fall. But the ammonia is all wasted, and a coat of shavings would have done just as much good. The chief value of the manure was as a mulch, keeping the ground from early freezing.

The remarks of Prof. Mapes were received with several manifestations of applause.

He remarked on Gurneyism—that the ground covered for a time gathers fertility—if it was floored over for a time it would prove so. He spoke of an ingenious gardener who used slabs with their barks on, cutting notches in them to correspond. He laid them over the beds, flat side down, and set strawberry plants in the notch holes—the crop was excellent. After some time he lifted these slabs and dug up the ground, and then replaced them. By this kind of mulching, he gained all the benefit of Gurneyism, and had *perfect command over all weeds.*

He mentioned with great respect the late Dr. Enderlin, a most distinguished pupil of Leibig's, whose researches in chemistry were giving promise of rich rewards, in the system of producing flowers, almost if not quite equal to those of nature, in perfumes and tastes. A subject which still engages Prof. Mapes.

Mr. Burgess, of Long Island, related some facts illustrating these statements.

The club adopted the following questions for next meeting: " Winter treatment of manures ;" "Root feed for stock ;" "Effect of winter on clay and on sandy soils, ridged in the fall of the year ;" " Sorghum compared with corn stalks, as winter fodder."

The club unanimously requested that the meetings hereafter be on Tuesday, of each week.

The still and the sparkling Scuppernong white wines, and the Red Pamlico Mish grape wine of North Carolina, were tasted, and considered good, but having too much sugar. A fine sample of pure alcohol from the Scuppernong wine, was also presented by Dr. Gallagher.

A member asked about the production of brandy.

Prof. Mapes said that brandy was made, better in quality from Claret wine worth *only ten dollars a hogshead,* than from pure Maderia wine worth *five dollars a bottle.*

The club then adjourned.   H. MEIGS, *Secretary.*

December 14, 1858.

Present—Messrs. Prof. Nash, Chilson, Doughty and Pike, of Jersey; Prof. Mapes, Hon. Hugh Maxwell, Hon. Frank Tuthill, of the Assembly; Dr. Adamson, B. Silliman, Esq., Mr. Davol, Daniel C. Robinson, Mr.

Witt, of Williamsburgh; Olcott, Lawton, of New Rochelle, and others.—27 members.

William Lawton in the chair. Henry Meigs, *Secretary.*

The Secretary read the following papers, viz:

[Societe Imperial, &c. August, 1858.]

PLUMS.

M. G. Liegel, in the *Monatschrift fur Pomologie,* a distinguished pomologist, says, by profoundly studying the varieties of the plum, he has discovered that the plum stones furnish by their forms more precise knowledge of the true character of the fruit they belong to than external examination of the fruit itself can do, especially as to its size and color, and a collection of the pitt's nuts will always serve to determine the fruit. That he uses it with great advantage. He says:

1st. I examine the nut to ascertain whether the point of it is in the middle of the upper and lower shells, or a little on one side of the center; whether it is long or short, sharp or obtuse, or prominent.

2d. The upper shell has three angular ridges, one in the middle and one on each side, sometimes well separated, sometimes lightly marked, sometimes near each other, sometimes quite prominent, as in apricot nuts, widely spaced, &c., &c.

He advises that the nuts of the best plums should be preserved; their forms, as well as that of their fruits, be exactly drawn. That such models will always be valuable to fruit raisers.

Extracts from Mr. D. K. Minor's letter from Australia.

MELBOURN, AUSTRALIA, *August*, 13, 1858.

GEN. CHANDLER, of the American Institute. Dear sir—I have now been in this city four weeks, during which time I have been constantly engaged in getting our machinery on shore and in store, and preparing for its transport to the mines, where I intend to engage in working a quartz gold mine. It will take me about two months, probably, to select a location and get fifteen or twenty tons of machinery there and in operation. Of course I have had, thus far, very little opportunity to investigate the agricultural progress here, nor shall I be able to give much thought to it. From what I have seen, heard of and tasted, I have a very exalted idea of the capability of this country of large crops of the very best wheat, oats and other grain, of potatoes and other vegetables, superior to any I ever saw except in California, and same of Apples, pears, peaches, figs, and a great variety of the finest grapes. Excellent beef, superior to your New York beef, at 6 to 4½ pence; choice corned beef 3½ to 4 pence, or from 16 cents to 7.

I have rarely seen such fine oats and corn. I hope to send samples to the American Institute. Here I am in the midst of winter. A plowing match came off the other day; the plows were very long, made of wrought iron, yokes of wood with iron bows. I should like to see the Yankee yoke along side of them. I wish to become instrumental in exchanges between this and home of the best things, through the American Institute. You must have our grains to plant, we want such agricultural works as you can spare us, agricultural implements, &c. We will present all to the agricultural societies of Australia. Send to me through R. W. Cameron, agent, No. 6, Bowling Green, New York, to Wilkinson Brothers, Melbourne, for me.

I find this climate delightful. Our police here are excellent, the city a lovely one ; prospects of business bright. We have a million and a quarter of inhabitants in this large territory. We want ten millions of people, and in twenty or thirty years we shall employ forty millions of people.

I send a printed meteorological table, showing our weather and temperature, which I wish you to hand to Mr. Meriam.

D. K. MINOR.

SORGHUM SUGAR.

At Springfield, Illinois, a sugar mill is running day and night; it yields near 300 gallons a day of the molasses ; no sugar made yet ; the syrup is not so good as usual, owing to too much wet. The cane syrup of last year yielded *ten per cent saccharine.*

[Journal de la Societe Imperial et Centrale d'Horticulture. Napoleon III. Protecteur. August, 1858.]

THE PAULOWNIA IMPERIALIS.

At Alfort, on the river Seine, on the property of one of our colleagues, Mons. Rousset, we transplanted, last December, a very large paulownia, about twenty-six feet high, with a round head of considerable extent. I had to take off some of the branches, especially such as were broken. These branches were left all winter in the garden. On the 16th of May last we were much surprised to see all the extremities of those branches covered with numerous flower buds, which grew and flowered at the same time as the buds on the tree to which they belonged. None of the buds failed, and, I may say, were more numerous than those on the parent tree, and the flowers preserved their color and their sweet agreeable odor which exhales at their blooming. This is a remarkable fact, for few ornamental trees, whose branches are cut off and left in open air five months before the period of flowering, were ever known to survive so long.

Prof. Nash said that however strictly science and labor are applied to cultivation, it may be considered to be experimental, for nature acts in many ways which we cannot define.

The Chairman called up one of the subjects—" Winter treatment of Manure."

Mr. Meigs.—My old friend, Mr. Amos, of Greenwich village, cultivated a large garden there, where the old State prison long afterwards stood. Mr. Amos was one of the very energetic farmers of that day. In winter, when most men do little out doors, he carted out his large masses of manure upon the snow or the ground, and has loaded up 100 loads, one horse cart, in a day, and put it out on the land, by which great industry he probably lost by the air more than one half of its value, but he thought, as most farmers did and do now, that the essences of his manure filtered into the soil.

Professor Mapes, in answer to the question, how sandy a soil must be to make it improper to back furrow and ridge it, answered that any land which was sandy enough to be "blowy" ought not to be ridged; the flatter that lay the better. A New Jersey farmer mucked a sandy field in the winter, raised a green crop, turned it in and rolled the field; after that he was troubled no more with the drifting, though before half the fence would sometimes be buried. But when he came to put in corn on the field, he would hill it. The hills were very high, and of course through the winter it was left very much in the condition that it would have been in if ridged. The frost and sun alternating powdered the whole surface, and next spring it was as blowy as ever again. Now, any soil so sandy as that should be left flat. Another rule was a good one: any land that is improved by plowing in wet weather ought not to be ridged in the fall. Clayey soils are badly damaged by wet plowing, sandy ones improved.

The regular text of the day was the "Winter treatment of Manures." Prof. Mapes said that the value of barn yard manure was not dependent so much on the constituents of the manure as on the condition of those constituents. One pound of potash in that manure was worth more to the land than 100 pounds of potash taken from a feldspar rock, though the chemist could detect no difference in the two articles. The organic constituents of a cord of barn yard manure, when it has been burned, may be put in your hat, but that little is worth a ton of chemically the same materials that have been through none of its organic changes. Take a dose of sulphate of magnesia directly from the rock, and if it dont kill it will terribly gripe you. But let the chemist take it and subject it to frequent crystalizations, and then a very much smaller dose will act as a gentle cathartic, and prove an invaluable medicine. But neither analysis nor the microscope exhibits any difference between the two articles. No chemist living can tell the difference between carbonate of lime taken from a piece of Westchester limestone and taken from a chalk cliff of England; yet 1,000 bushels of the former spread on an acre of land makes it barren for years, while the chalky fields of England are fertile. The latter is formed of the debris of animals, the other is not, and hence the difference. Hence it is evident that it is not enough that you have certain substances in certain quantities in your manure to make it valuable; its value is enhanced with every new manipulation it receives. Chemistry is always at work in the manure heap, winter and summer. There is no winter in it except on the surface. In the open dished barn yard, see how every little pool gives out its carburetted hydrogen gas, how the bubbles of gas are constantly rising, and the strong currents of air sweep them away, wasting them. Every bent straw is a syphon to give new points of surface and facilitate the evaporation. No one looking intelligently at it can doubt the waste. The heap should have but one surface, should be sheltered from the wind—see how much sooner a wet blanket dries in the wind than in a calm—should always be under cover. Practically, the best arrangement was to make one end of the floor of the heap a little lower than the other, and at the lower corner to sink a hogshead. Into this hogshead put a chain pump. Every week, every day if you prefer, pump back the liquor upon the heap. If it has no fluid to drain off, put water into the hogshead and pump it on the heap. No fear of adding too much unless the hogshead overflows. The heat within and the moisture will not allow anything in the heap to escape decomposition, and very speedily the whole interior will be homogeneous. Turning it over with a fork is nothing to this turning over that chemistry is effecting for you. Into the hogshead turn the slops of the house ; on to the heap turn all waste stuff, leaves, muck, straw, night soil, it will all be worked up. The drainage into the hogshead is the most valuable manure, to be applied directly to the land, if you choose. But every time it goes through the heap it secures a new change, and improves the character of the whole. If you want to hurry up the mass for use, pour into the hogshead hot water and pump that on. Such a heap does not deteriorate in quantity, either, as a common, unwetted muck heap does ; a plenty of water will prevent its burning. If your soil is especially deficient in any one element, put that into the hogshead and put it on to the heap, and your whole field will get it.

Benjamin Pike, of Jersey, said there was a special benefit arising out of Prof. Mapes' mode, and that is the moisture and heat causes the weed seeds to swell so as to be killed. I find this in a tank of twelve feet deep and twelve feet wide, into which I cause all the liquor of my manure to run, and the seeds of the weeds go in, fall to the bottom and there be destroyed.

Prof. Mapes said he would discharge a man who spread manure in the morning upon a field that he did not mean to plow till afternoon. Yet some insist that spreading the manure in the fall on fields to be plowed next spring, brought good crops. So they do, but the greater part of the good got out of the manure was the mulch that its long litter furnished ; and long litter was too valuable to be used for such purpose, when thatch, or even shavings, would answer just as well. The manure, to be of service to the next crop, must be finely divided. Composting it, in the manner above stated, did this ; plowing it under of course could not. Putting soil on the manure heap did good, but only so far as the soil acted as a divisor to the manure.

For the next meeting, Mr. Olcott proposed " The National Value of the Chinese Sugar-Cane." Not an agricultural paper turns up that does not report at least one experiment in its neighborhood with this imported cane. Very extensively, this year, the farmers are raising this article—and in the west, successfully. Here, added Prof. Mapes, it cannot be very much raised for sugar—it wants a longer season than our climate permits— though so much as can be manufactured within two or three weeks, the New York State farmers can profitably raise and manufacture into molasses.

For fodder, the cane was too hard when dry—though by the aid of Blanchard's mill, (which he explained,) it was eaten by cattle with avidity.

Prof. Mapes said that experience proves that sugar cane juice turns acid very soon after being cut, while that of Chinese sugar cane, the sorghum, may be kept a considerable length of time, and it will not acetify. I have samples of the sugar made from the sorghum, equal in quality to the best white refined sugar of the Stuarts.

Mr. Olcott found the sorghum question important in Europe, whence he has just arrived, and its superior importance here will soon become very manifest by its magnitude and value.

Prof. Mapes spoke of the sorghum as having too hard a skin to please stock when it was dry—that Blanchard's new mill divides that skin into filaments as fine as timothy hay, rendering it very palatable to stock. That the operation of the steel disks of this mill is to slice up grain without mashing the globules—so that the dough made of this flour rises without leaven or yeast, and the bread sweeter than other bread and keeps sweet a long time—has kept so *four months!* I have two of his mills in operation as I want them, at my farm.

The *minute rings* cut or rather sheared off from grain by this disk mill, fall on an *agitated sifter* which shakes out the flour and separates the bran.

Dr. Adamson, from South Africa, said that about 600 lbs. of sugar could be obtained from cane, per acre.

Prof. Mapes said that 1,500 lbs. per acre was yielded under favorable circumstances.

The club adopted for next meeting the subjects—By Mr. Olcott, "The National Value of the Chinese Sugar-Cane;" by Prof. Mapes, "Root Feeding."

The club then adjourned.

H. MEIGS, *Secretary.*

December 21, 1858.

Present—Rev. J. Adamson, late of South Africa; Prof. James J. Mapes, Rev. Benjamin Pike, of Jersey; Fuller, Kavanach, Bruce, of Williamsburgh; Henry S. Olcott, Chilson, Prof. Nash, Provost, of Williamsburgh; Lawton, of New Rochelle, and others—33 members.

Rev. Mr. Adamson in the chair. Henry Meigs, Secretary.

The Chairman gave a letter to read on the Sorghum. Balfour, (Fish river, South Africa,) October 13, 1832, to the Chairman, at Capetown.

KAFFER REED—CHINESE SUGAR CANE AND AFRICAN CANES.

The Rev. J. Adamson, recently from South Africa, where he has resided twenty-six years, presented the following extracts from a letter received by him in 1832, from the Rev. W. K. Thompson, from Balfour, (head of Fish river, South Africa,) relative to the sugar cane of that region. He calls it the

Kaffer sugar cane, or *Sweet reed.* It was difficult to obtain the seed from it because the cultivation of it picked off the seed spikes before they were ripe, (except that left to ripen for seed,) to increase the saccharine in the stalks. He however sent a small bag of the ripe seed to Mr. Adamson, and also a sample of sugar which he made from it. He supposed it might yield 500 lbs. per acre, while sugar cane yields twice as much and stands on the ground two seasons, while the Kaffer reed stands but one season. But the Kaffer reed is comparatively easier of culture and less liable to casualties, so that it will perhaps appear to come nearer in value to the sugar cane than it seems at first view, we are disposed to admit.

Chairman.—Chinese sugar cane is the first question to-day.

Henry S. Olcott.—We propose to-day, Mr. Chairman, to consider the Chinese sugar cane in a national point of view ; as a great staple crop which, from unostentatious beginnings, but with amazing rapidity, has pushed its way into a position of real national importance. It would be difficult to find throughout the whole range of cultivated plants, one which of equal value to this has had a parallel history. We have in our time seen almost the whole nation mad upon the subject of silk worm culture, and fortunes made and lost in a week in speculations with the *Morus Multicaulis;* and in a past generation the value of immense estates was paid for a single tulip bulb during the prevalence of the tulipomania in Holland. But in both of these cases the speculation was based upon plants of but very limited use, and that false value once removed, the deluded victims had nothing left to realize upon. The bulb was fit only to please the cultivated eye of a florist, and the discarded mulberry tree would not even make good cord-wood.

When I first published a translation of Louis Vilmorin's pamphlet, the sorgho was comparatively unknown in this country ; and when shortly afterwards I more directly called public attention to the plant, it was widely hinted that a parallel to the *Morus Multicaulis* and *Kobar Potato* humbugs was about being introduced. The idea that from one of the same plant various alcoholic products, as well as sirup, sugar, vinegar, paper, starch, and dye stuffs, could be, and had been produced, seemed ridiculous. Some editors amused themselves greatly thereat, and strove to throw contempt upon the whole thing. Time, however, Mr. Chairman, has proved that it is well not to judge too hastily. In three seasons the area under cultivation has increased from five acres to more than *one hundred thousand;* and so much sirup has been made in the various sections of country, that it has been claimed that in Illinois sorgho sirup is one of the very first crops in point of value already.

It is almost impossible to take up an agricultural journal from any part of the United States, which does not contain some certificate of successful sorgho culture. And it is quite certain that with this year's experience to aid us, the next we shall be enabled to record far better results.

Now there is not the slightest doubt but that the value of this plant is by many over estimated. Farmers making a first experiment on a patch of a few rods square, conceive the idea that large fortunes may be made in cultivating it for sugar in their district; and, without apparatus, capital, or especially experience, they nevertheless count on great results. A single season's practical trial will suffice to undeceive them, and they will then be ready to take a sensible view of the real value of the plant, and the proper mode to make it available.

The national value of the sorgho is shown in its adaptability to so wide a range of territory. As a forage and syrup crop, it will yield from Maine to Texas. It is not injured by frosts which would kill Indian corn; and as for the summer drouth, why the hotter the weather the more it seems to flourish. And here we have one of its very greatest recommendations.

There is a season of the year when the excessive heat of the sun sometimes completely parches our pasture lots, and causes the corn leaves to curl and droop. Just at the time when our animals are taxed with heavy labor, and when fresh green food is most necessary for their comfort; just when our cows are in their greatest flow of milk and need succulent pasture to maintain it; just when the roots of the grasses in the pasture by close cropping are exposed to the fierce heat and killed, and the next year's crop seriously lessened; just at this time, the Chinese Sugar Cane grows and thrives, and elaborates its saccharine juices, more rapidly than at any other time of the year. It strikes its roots deep into the moist cool subsoil, and obtains abundant moisture. The chemical transformations of the gases into starch, and sugar, and woody fibre, are more active as the dog star increases, and the farmer may be completely relieved from all the wonted ill effects of the drought, by having a field sown broadcast with sorgho, and at this hot season cutting it up and feeding it to his animals. One acre of the dried up pasture, if it had been sown with sorgho for fodder, would now give sustenance to thirty head of cattle for forty-five days. I say this confidently, for I can point you to a case where it was actually done, and give you the exact figures. In this respect, the sorgho bears an analogy to Indian corn, similar to that between the turnip and the mangold wurzel, the English farmers finding that the latter is unaffected by heats similar to that of the past season, which proved very destructive to their turnips.

The burthen of green fodder which may be cut on a single acre sown broadcast with sorgho, is immense, forty tons having actually been obtained in France; and in this country 19,844 lbs. of dry fodder, the weight being taken after the stalks had been drying for three months.

I have considered it first as a forage crop, from a desire to show that, entirely ignoring the question of sugar, syrup, and alcohol production, we have here a great point in its favor to fall back upon. But I would not be understood as wishing to undervalue its other capabilities; on the contrary, we should, with all due conservatism and moderation, set them prominently before us in estimating the national value of the cane. Our Patent Office Report for 1855 says, that "without wishing to present the question in an extravagant light, it may be stated that this crop is capable of being cultivated within the territory of the United States to an extent equal to that of Indian corn, say 25,000,000 acres per annum ; and estimating the average yield of dry or cured fodder to the acre at *two tons*, the yearly amount produced would be 50,000,000 tons, which, to keep within bounds, would be worth at least $500,000,000, besides the profits derived from the animals in milk, flesh, labor, and wool."

Now, of course, this estimate, like all other numerical castles built upon foundations of only the thickness of a sheet of paper, looks very fair and very wonderful, but it is an exaggeration—for the writer assumes that all the area at present under Indian corn, is to be put into sorgho fodder, and that if so and so be allowed, why then it is plain that the country gains $500,000,000 per annum from the Chinese sugar cane culture. But, although we do not wish to go to any extremes for arguments in favor of the cane, we may assume that the country is this year richer by a great many dollars, because of the introduction and popularization of sorgho and imphee ; and this advantage will be more and more considerable each succeeding year as their culture increases, and farmers learn better what to do with the crop after it is harvested.

It has been said that both the plant stalks and seeds were poisonous to cattle. This may be so, but I have seen Governor Hammond feeding several hundred cattle and five hundred hogs on imphee stalks, day after day and week after week, and with no ill effects, except that perhaps the animals eat so greedily as to surfeit themselves if not checked. I have fed my own horses, cows and swine on it, and with the reverse of injurious effects. In particular, a team of heavy horses, which subsisted for some two months principally on cut sorgho stalks, and although engaged at heavy labor the whole time, were fat and sleek throughout.

Mr. George W. Kendall, writing to the *N. O. Picayune*, says that the cultivation is widely extending in Texas, and is a perfect success; that it stands the drouth as a salamander does fire ; that it has entirely escaped the ravages of grasshoppers, although neighboring corn fields have been devastated ; that he has fed his stock on it regularly, and should be very happy to receive any that any timid experimenter may have to spare or throw away.

A. H. Wren says in the *Ohio Farmer* of November 20th, that he has proved to his satisfaction "that one acre of Chinese sugar cane will go as far for feeding hogs alone, as an acre of from 75 to 100 bushels of corn, cut up and thrown to their hogs as farmers do their green corn."

It seems that this cry of the sorgho being poisonous originated in France, and found its way over here. To show how well it is to search out these stories up to the fountain head, I may mention that whilst in London recently, I received a letter from the illustrious Monsieur L. Vilmorin, dated " Gien, 28th October," and in it he makes use of expressions of which the following is a translation: "I am visiting in this district a large cultivator, who informed me of his having had several sheep poisoned by eating sorgho. This is the fourth or fifth example of the kind which has come under my observation, and in every case where I could get at the details and sift the evidence, I have found that if poisoned, the animals had been fed with very small plants, scarcely a foot in height. At the same time, and since, this same cultivator had given to his cattle sorgho stalks, and has been very well satisfied with its use. I advised several French journalists to investigate the several cases, before laying them before the public, but they did not choose to do so, preferring, as is their wont, to make a great noise about it."

Now, looking at the plant in the light of its saccharine productions, I think we shall find abundant reasons for congratulating ourselves with having been instrumental in introducing it to public notice. There was a time when it was not believed that the sorgho and imphee contained crystallizable sugar, and when so great a chemist as Dr. Augustus A. Hayes declared that his microscopes and evaporating glasses, proved the existence only of *glucose* in the juice. But those theories have now been exploded, and Dr. Hayes has himself written for my book, "SORGHO AND IMPHEE," a very candid retraction of his former assumptions, and claims to have discovered a new fact in chemistry, no less an one than the actual *conversion* of grape sugar into true cane crystals, in the juice of sorgho.

Be this as it may, our friend Lovering, at Philadelphia, has made as beautiful cane sugar as ever left the shores of the "Queen of the Antilles," or rejoiced the heart of a Louisiana planter. And, profiting by his published statements, many others, in various parts of the United States, have this year duplicated his success. If this be so, it will be asked, "Will not the production of northern and north-western sugar seriously affect the imports from abroad ?" It will certainly have its influence, but for many years, the planters in the Mauritius, in Cuba, and in the Straits settlements, may enjoy their rest undisturbed ; for rest assured that so long as they, with their slave laborers, can put sugars on board vessels at three cents per pound, and make a living profit, we northern men cannot compete with them to any great extent. But, we shall find this to be the case. Our small farmers will use the spare time of their men, and their families, to make enough sorgho and imphee syrup to last throughout the winter. The more careful and intelligent ones will make sugar, and thus, in many hundreds of families in districts removed from the sea-board, no sugar, or at any rate, only the best qualities, will be purchased at the store. This increased production will, by degrees, have its effect upon the prices of foreign sugars, and if the tide of immigration should materially diminish, it would react to a considerable extent upon the sugar growers of the tropics.

I think we shall see, at no distant date, large mills erected in the centres of agricultural districts, to which the crops of small farmers will be carried for manufacture ; but there is no doubt but that a vast number of small mills will be purchased by single farmers for their sole use. The editor of the *North-Western Prairie Farmer*, in a very candid article, says that he believes that in five years the north-west will be a large exporter of sugars, and that it is quite possible, that in 1870 steamers will land at Cairo, Ill., for cargoes of it for the New Orleans market. Statistics show that in France the consumption of sugars has doubled in the last thirty years. It has increased more than fifty per cent in England, in the last fifteen years. In the German States, embraced in the Zollverein, it has quadrupled in the same period. The consumption in this country is something more than twenty pounds, annually, per head. And it is a remarkable fact, that, large as is the consumption in France, twenty millions, or nearly two-thirds of its population, do not use sugar at all. From 1801 to 1857, the increase in the use of sugar has been enormous in this country. In the former year we imported 21,376 tons; in the latter, 241,765, which, added to 39,000 from Louisiana, made an aggregate consumption of 280,765 tons. The consumption of England in 1801, was 114.542; in 1857, 355,719 tons. In France, the figures are only complete as far back as 1831, in which year its consumption was 91,671 tons; in 1857, it had reached 180,032 tons.

Now, we have entirely neglected one branch of manufacture, which in France I find to be principally pursued at the present day, viz.: the making of alcohol and brandies. Whenever our people fully realize that the miserable stuffs they are now drinking under the names of "Cognac Brandy," "Old Jamaica Rum," "London Dock Port," and "Amontillado Sherry," are nothing but common pure spirits disguised with different poisonous and nauseating essential oils, and find that from pure sorgho juice fine brandy, rum, alcohol, cider and beer can be easily made at a very low price, we shall suddenly awaken to the fact that our friends from China and Africa have still another recommendation to favor.

I will say nothing of the excellent vinegar, of the paper made from the macerated fibers of the stalk, of the nutritious flour from the seeds, and the value of the seeds themselves as a substitute for oats for horses, nor of the brilliant dyes for which Doctor Sicard has taken out a patent in France, for these, as compared with the forage, the sugar syrup and alcohols are of minor importance. But I think that from what has already been enumerated, you will agree with me that "the national value of the Chinese Sugar Cane" is very considerable.

Mr. W. Lawton said that the statistics given in Mr. Olcott's paper showed that we use here one-tenth as much sugar as flour, and this would show to the Club the magnitude of the interest which was before them for discussion. If we considered this new cane in any one of the aspects presented, he felt sure that we would see that the greatest satisfaction must be felt from its domestication amongst us. The attention of the farmers, although much attracted to it, should be still more so. It is no delusive humbug, nor any longer a mere experiment of questionable value.

The chairman said that in Africa he had seen the natives plucking out the spikelets to increase the quantity of saccharine in the stalk. As to its being poisonous to stock he did not believe it; for in Africa the natives had suffered their goats, sheep, and cattle, to eat it, for ages past. In fact they could not prevent it if it had been desired, for the cane grows wild in every part of the country.

Mr. Olcott did not think it at all a good practice to pull out the heads, for he had seen in Georgia and South Carolina stalks so treated, on which the following curious result was produced. The seed head being removed, the vigor of the plant was turned to the production of small branches, which shot up from each joint of the stalk, and the cane was rendered unfit for crushing.

Professor Nash thought the national value of sorgho and imphee, as sugar producers, depended upon the great physiological question, how much sugar should be eaten by a man. An excessive quantity would prove detrimental rather than otherwise.

The chairman said he recollected the investigation made to determine this point, by the celebrated Dr. Lyon Playfair, in London, some years ago. It was found that a full grown man in a state of health, required sixty-two ounces of food per week, if all his food were reduced to a solid state; and that of this quantity two-thirds must be of a carbonaceous nature, either starch or sugar, to furnish the material for combustion in his lungs, and keep up the proper degree of animal warmth. The remaining one-third must be of nitrogenous or flesh-forming character.

Professor Nash thought too much sugar was not good; the ill effects of excessive quantities are to be noticed in the constitutions of pampered children of rich parents. He thought that Mr. Olcott had omitted in his calculations, the amount of domestic maple sugar, which amounted to a large quantity in the aggregate. The maple sugar of Vermont is absorbed by Boston refiners to make the better qualities of sugar.

Prof. Mapes said that this did not amount to the thousandth of one per cent of the sugar annually refined in the United States. As to the nutritive value of sugar, it was shown in the fat, sleek condition of the negroes and animals during the boiling season in Cuba. At this period they subsist almost entirely upon it, and at no time of the year are they in such perfect condition. The Emperor of China makes it a duty of the men of his body guard to eat a certain quantity of sugar every day to keep them fat, fat being their greatest recommendation. If he were there, he did not doubt but that his corpulence would ensure his being made at the very least a *corporal* of the guard.

In China there was a popular legend that the introduction of the sugar cane was due to the fact that a man, left by his shipmates to die on the island of Borneo, was found three years afterwards to have entirely subsisted on sugar cane, and the crew in taking him back to China, took at the same time some of this valuable plant.

Prof. M. knew by experience that sorgho was an excellent forage plant, and was, in its green state, preferred by cattle to Stowell's evergreen corn; but when both are thoroughly dried, they refuse the sorghum, because of the hardness of the outer part of the stalk. This was scarcely an objection, since the introduction of Blanchard's slitting mill, which worked with perfect success, rendering the stalks in a hay-like form. He had tested the sorgho juice, and found it to mark as high as $10\frac{1}{2}$ degrees Beaume, which was richer than an average of the Louisiana cane. There was neither a difficulty in making sugar from it, nor of getting a paying quantity per acre. The best qualities of loaf sugar can be made directly from the cane. All sorgho sugars have a finer flavor than cane sugar. This flavor is entirely *sui generis*. He did not believe that large refineries would be established for working up the crops of small farmers, because the sugar making season is too short to warrant the necessary expenditure of capital, $100,000 being the *minimum* cost of a large sugar refinery. It would also be impracticable to maintain a large force of skilled sugar makers throughout the entire year, for the sake of using them for the few weeks in the fall when sugar could be made. But thousands and thousands of small farmers could profitably make the sugar needed for their families, and this would be done. By Kneller's "blast process" it was within the reach of small farmers to become sugar makers. A set of small pans, with leaf filter and all apparatus complete (except the mill), could be set up for about $100.

The vinegar made from sorgho would prove a great source of profit. There are concerns in this city making several thousand gallons of vinegar per day. He proceeded to describe the process of vinegar making at present in vogue.

He thought it would be necessary to concentrate the juice into a weak molasses before making vinegar, as this would give it any desired strength. The sorgho vinegar would be equal in quality to best cider vinegar.

As to rum, that from sorgho will be as much better than Santa Cruz rum, as the latter excels new England "thunder and lightning." It might not be pleasing to the friends of temperance that this plant should be cultivated for that purpose, but so long as people will drink alcoholic liquors, we may as well give them unadulterated.

Subjects for next Tuesday, by Prof. Mapes, "Root Feeding." "What principle is involved in the disintegration of soils and the various implements for doing it."

By Mr. Olcott, "The management of agricultural fairs."

The Club adjourned.   H. MEIGS, *Secretary.*

December 28, 1858.

Present—Messrs. Professor Mapes, Lawton, Bruce, Chambers, Leonard, Chilson, Pike, Doughty, Witt, Pardee, Johnson, and others—thirty-seven members.

William Lawton, of New Rochelle, in the chair. Henry Meigs, Secretary.

The Secretary read the following papers and translations made by him, viz:

GOOD NEWS FROM ENGLAND.
[London Farmers' Magazine, December 1858.]

Not many years ago the landlord was simply the recipient of rent, with very little knowledge of the details by which this rent was created. How great is the change in all this ! It has come to pass with a rapidity almost inconceivable—from the Prince Consort to the Governor of the Scilly Islands—from the Woolsack to the youngest Bishop—from the Speaker to the last Peer's son, borough born into the "House"—through every grade of upper life, farming is a thing more familiar than the catechism—far more generally practised than the Decalogue.

I have seen Ireland's first Duke stand over a tank, on a model farm, exquisite in its extreme filth, while one of England's best classic scholars, eloquently, as a labor of love, gave to us the primary compounds of the horrid composition.

Vast progress is made—the beef, mutton and corn are now literally the result of system based on pure science. Great improvement in tenants and landlords. The care-worn soil may indeed deplore the days of long fallows, easy farming—*for it knows no rest !*—but it is grateful.

One article in the Journal impeaches the theory of close keeping of manures. Asserts that barn-yard manure exposed on the field to rain, snow, wind and all weathers—bean straw serves that purpose as well—has in every case proved superior to manure used in the ordinary way. This clashes with the doctrines of chemistry.

A farmer on the Wabash made 400 gallons of molasses from one acre of Chinese sugar cane, this season. It is worth 50 cents a gallon !

[Athenæum, London, November 1858.]

Van Thaer, founder of scientific agriculture in Germany—a monument is being made. Statue of bronze, by Ranch, on a proper base.

FAIRS.

France has held twelve large ones since 1798—that was attended by 110 exhibiters ; in 1819, there were 1,662 exhibiters ; in 1849, 4,494 exhibiters ; in 1855, 9,790. *French exhibiters only.*

The Royal Agricultural Society of England, has held twenty consecutive fairs from 1839 to 1858.

A great Metropolitan exhibition of cattle and implements, is contemplated for 1861.

The Royal Agricultural Society of England, offers the following prizes for 1859 :

1. Microscopic investigation—*fifty sovereigns* for the best report on the results of the microscopic observation of the vegetable physiology of agriculture.

3. Steam cultivation—*twenty-five sovereigns.*

4. Tillage, a substitute for manure—*twenty sovereigns.*

5. Modifications of the four course system—*twenty sovereigns.*

7. Failure of the turnip crop—*twenty sovereigns.*

8. The comparative cost of cattle food and manure—*twenty sovereigns.*

9. Best essay on agriculture—*ten sovereigns.*

All reports, &c., must be sent to the Secretary, James Hudson, 12 Hanover Square. Contributors will keep copies of their essays, as the Secretary cannot be responsible for their return.

The following extracts are from Part I, of Volume 19, of the Journal of the Royal Agricultural Society of England, just received by the American Institute:

PRIZE ESSAY ON THE POTATO, ITS CULTURE, PRODUCTION, AND DISEASE.

By Jeffery Lang, M. D.

In July, 1845, standing on an eminence on the north-east side of the orchard of four acres, I was surprised at seeing a *broad band of blackened leaves* running diagonally across the orchard, bearing the direction of south-west to north-east, and in which band the apple trees looked as if they had been scorched with fire. Within the lines of the band there did not appear to be a green leaf; the smell was fœtid, and very disgusting. Passing downward by the road fence, to make a closer investigation, I found that the band of blackened leaves was about a thousand feet wide, resolvable into three, like stripes on a ribbon; of considerable intensity in the middle, shading out at the edges. The leaves on the trees in the band were shrivelled and blackened, but firmly adherent; and, although I did not notice it then, I have since found it to be the fact, that numbers of the long shoots were strangely contorted. The grass in the orchard was very high. It was attributed to lightning, as there had been a violent south-west gale, four or five days before. The leaves of the black-thorn, in the hedges, were blackened, like the apple leaves.

The potatoes in the nursery plot, at the southern end of the orchard, were much discolored *within the line of the band, but not at all beyond it.* We traced this black band fourteen or fifteen miles in a *straight line.* Every field of potatoes within the line were much shrivelled and cut; those without, unaffected at the time. In about a fortnight, or three weeks, the disease was almost universal, fœtid and offensive. When dug up, the sound ones soon had the disease with increased virulence. The disease had appeared in certain localities before, one or two years; but in 1845, all accounts agree as to its extent and malignity.

The opinion that the disease originates in the tuber planted, or in the stem growing from it, *is a delusion.* It always originates in the leaf.

The way the potato is produced from the tuber, has been investigated. Dry, clean potatoes, were placed on a chimney piece, in a seldom used room. They threw up stalks, short, thick, and studded with minute leaves; while on the summit of the stalk, were three or four larger, but still minute, leaves, forming a tuft. Speedily from the axils of the minute leaves, a shoot was thrown forth, terminating in two *leaves*, closely enwrapped, the one by the other. This was the germ of the future potato, whose formation can by any one be rendered evident, the *inner leaf forming, apparently, the cells of the potato in which the starch is deposited*, while the *enwrapping leaf* forms the *skin.* When this shoot is about two inches long, we introduce it carefully into a large bunch of soft moist moss, and in ten days or a fortnight, a minute potato, not larger than a duck-shot, will be found instead of the two terminal leaves before mentioned.

CHRYSANTHEMUM.

By H. Meigs.

This interesting plant is now cultivated in many varieties, extensively. From being a *gold-flower*, as its name implies, it has become of many colors. The metal-like durability of its buds and full blown flowers caused it to be call the Eternal and Immortal. Lindley, in his Vegetable Kingdom, places it among the *Asteraceæ*, making about *sixty* in number under the title Chrysanthemum only, and of the whole class of *Asters* he makes *one hundred and one genera.*

Genus Chrysanthemum contains Steiroglossa, Lidbeckia, Gamolepis, Lasthenia, Hologymne, Psilothamnus, Jacquemoutia, Spiridanthus, Coinogyne, Egletes, Xerobius, Eyselia, Venegasia, Leucopsidium, Xanthocephalum, Phymaspermum, Hisutsua, Bracanthemum, Nananthea, Leucanthemum, Phalacrodiscus, Phalacroglossum, Diabasis, Enuchoglossum, Phalacrocarpum, Prolongoa, Adenachæna, Matricaria, Pyrethrum, Gymnocline, Xanthoglossa, Coleostephus, Tridactylina, Dendrathema, Allardia, Chrysanthemum, Ismelia, Pinardia, Centrospermum, Heteranthemis, Centrachæna, Spermoptera, Mayarsa, Preauxia, Monoptera, Stigmatotheca, Argyranthemum, Dimosphotheca, Meteorina, Gattenhofia, Cardispermum, Lestibodia, Blaxium, Castalis, Rutidocarpæa, Arnoldia, Triplocarpœa, Acanthotheca, Monolopia, Steirodiscus, Schistostemium, Chlamysperma, Villanova, Brachymeris, Brachystylis and Jacosta.

I have Chrysanthemum buds and full blown flowers from my garden thirty years ago, and not more faded than if made of any metal except gold.

Journal of the Royal Agricultural Society of England. Part 1. No. 41. Vol. 19. Presented by the Society to the American Institute.

We are always pleased with this journal, and extract good from it.

ON THE MANAGEMENT OF BREEDING CATTLE.—A Prize Essay.

By Edward Bowly.

"Success depends on good forms and constitutions. I refer on this point to a letter written on this subject, by Major Rudd, to an American friend, many years since, on pure Short-horns, which is equally applicable to any breed of cattle at the present time, viz:

"A small and fine head, a capacious chest, the shoulders lying back in the body, the ribs round and barrel-like, the back straight from the neck to the top of the tail, the loins wide, the hind quarters long and straight, the twist full and deep, the bones small, and the offal light; to these points of shape, must be added the great essential of good handling, which is the index of the propensity to fatten. A knowledge of handling cannot be communicated by letter, and is acquired only by practice; it consists in a peculiar feel of the flesh under the skin. The skin should be rather loose, and under it the flesh should feel *rather soft, yet firm and elastic*; when a beast has this particular handling, and has long soft silky hair, it indicates the propensity to fatten. The animals must be screened from the great variations of climate, avoiding extremes always—better in open sheds with yards to them, than in entirely closed houses—not too many together, lest the stronger tyrannize over the weaker, preventing them from obtaining their proper share of food and shelter. *Four, selected for agreeing together*, are enough for one shed and yard. Shade in summer, and pure water, are most essential to their well being. Young animals require the most care, their growth must not be checked—on the three first years will success depend principally. I have bred Short-horns these twenty years. My early calves, i. e., from December to February, suck the cows for one fortnight. I then give skimmed milk and thick gruel made from boiled linseed, in equal proportions, twice a day. As soon as they are inclined to eat, I give them oil cake, carrots and hay. When three months old I reduce the milk and linseed to once a day, and in three weeks after discontinue it altogether, *continuing the food* until they are turned out to grass. Then I give them two pounds of oil cake daily, which I continue in addition to their other food for twelve months, that is, till they go to grass the following year; in July and August of which year, they are served by the bull, so that they will calve the year following, just before going to grass, when they will be about two years and four months old. I allow their calves to run with them during the summer—when four or five months old I take the calves away and dry the dams, by which means the heifers get a much larger rest than the older cows before they calve again, thereby encouraging their growth, and under this system they can produce calves at an early age without interfering with their full development of their forms.

I never give any artificial food to animals after they have completed their growth, and not often after eighteen months old, up to which age I consider it profitable to the breeder to give a moderate quantity of oil cake, thereby increasing the size of the animal and the value of the manure. My cows have grass alone during the summer; late in autumn a little hay at night and morning, and hay and roots when in milk, in winter; the dry cattle have pulped roots and straw-chaff during that season. This is one of the *greatest improvements of the present day*. Formerly, when they were fed on roots and straw, they ate too many of the former and not sufficient of the latter. I have now several dry cows in excellent condition, being fed on 45 lbs. of pulped Swedes and a bushel and an half of straw-chaff, each, daily, and no other food whatever. My calves of last year, now eleven to thirteen months old, are in a very thriving condition with 28 lbs.

of pulped Swedes, one bushel of straw-chaff, with two lbs. of oil cake, each, daily. I mix the roots and chaff but a short time before giving them to the animals. Some allow the mixture to rest, but it is apt to turn acid, and that is unfavorable to their health. There is no advantage in steaming the food. Straw alone often causes obstructions in the *second stomach*, and is one of the most dangerous maladies we have to contend with, in cows.

I have no faith in the *roughing calves* to make them hardy—it weakens instead of strengthening their constitutions, and in two or three generations that *roughing* will ruin the best breed of catle in the country. There is no real reason for forcing show animals—good judges know all that—there is no necessity for such extreme fat, as seen at nearly all our shows.

Lord Ducie's herd was brought to the hammer only in ordinary condition. Some of his heifer calves were really too poor, yet this did not detract from their value in the eyes of breeders. Lord Ducie gave over a thousand guineas for six animals, one of them a calf. He was right, for at his sale, a bull for which he gave 200 guineas, sold for 700 guineas, and others in proportion.

In selecting a bull, so much depends on the character of the female he is required for, that it is almost impossible to lay down a rule. It is better that he should be too coarse rather than too fine. When a herd of cattle are approaching perfection the greatest care and judgment are required; for having reached this point, there is always a disposition to degenerate. What is called *breeding in and in* will, no doubt, ensure greater certainty as to the produce, but beyond *one* or *two* generations, it is objectionable. Some of our best men, among them the late Sir John Lebright, found it injurious. The term *breeding in and in* is very indefinite. Some applying it to *all near relations*, whereas, strictly speaking, it should only be applied to animals of *precisely the same blood*, such as *own brother and sister*. Now the daughter is only half the blood of the father, and th son only half that of the mother, and breeding from such relationship as this last, if watched with care, may be carried to a moderate extent without injury, and perhaps with some advantage. But as good males can now easily be had, no man need *breed in and in*.

Cleanliness is important. A brush made of whalebone, to scrub occasionally, particularly places not easily reached by the tongue of the animal.

ERGOT

Is found not only on grain but on many grasses. Rye grass is particularly subject to it when it has run to seed. Almost all the grasses are subject to it. It produces abortion in females. Grazed land is more subject to it.

Mr. Pike, of New Jersey, (eighty-four years old,) was asked what he thought of the turnip for feed. Said that he thought rutabagas profitable. I feed to my stock and they prosper. I get as much feed from five acres as I do of hay off of fifteen. I have a patent machine for chopping roots for stock but I find a *tub* better. Carrots are excellent feed; better, however for a horse than for cattle. Ruta bagas do not give taste to milk, but common turnips do.

Mr. Meigs mentioned the alarm in England as to the failure of the turnip from disease. That about ten years ago a report to Parliament estimated the agricultural product of England at *three thousand millions of dollars*—of which the *turnip in all its uses* formed *fifteen hundred millions of dollars!*

The Chairman had found advantages in giving to his stock a variety of food. That the animals have excellent memories, and demand as much punctuality in their meals as we do.

Mr. Provoost found a great advantage in the Russia turnip crop, because he first took off his land good crops of peas, beans, and the like, and then comes the turnip.

Mr. Pardee wanted for digging up roots such a fork as was not made. It should be eighteen or twenty inches long in the three or four tines, and so strong as to bear the leverage at that depth under the carrots, beets, &c.

Subjects for next meeting, prepared by Prof. Mapes : " Root feeding;" "Spring management of fruit trees." By Mr. Olcott : " The management of agricultural fairs."

Adjourned.   H. MEIGS, *Secretary.*

January 4, 1859.

John M. Crowell, M. D., in the chair. Henry Meigs, Secretary.

The Secretary read extracts and translations made by him from foreign and domestic papers, lately received by the Institute :

THE OSTRICH.

[The Societe Imperiale Zoologique d'Acclimatation, July, 1858.]

This powerful society uses its means in causing all animals of utility or beauty, to be brought into France and acclimated there. The ostrich is one which they have already taken seriously in hand. The knowledge they have acquired relative to that great bird, surpasses all former. Through the instrumentality of their agents in Algeria, &c., they have commenced the domestication in the central nursery of the government, at Hamma, near Algiers. A flock of them was gathered, by officers, civil and military, during the last twelve years. Some of the birds were sent to the Museum of Natural History, at Paris—some of these were afterwards sent to the Zoological gardens of Marseilles and Antwerp. At the Paris Museum they were put into a circular spot, fifty feet in diameter, having sheds all around the interior. Into these sheds the birds never entered, be the weather ever so bad. The males were perpetually fighting. At length one became conqueror, and never allowed his enemy a moment's peace, whether he was eating or loving. The females began to lay eggs quite regularly, beginning about the middle of January, and continuing until the latter part of March. Sometimes they re-commence laying in September and October. The male crows (it may be called)—the skin of his neck and thighs turn bright red, his gullet swells, his neck bends back, and sounds come from the bottom of his breast, deep, rough, contracted and strange, forming a sort of guttural thunder. They made several nests by making a hole in the hard earth full of stones and gravel—a nest of about three and a half feet in diameter. In these hollows, however, they never laid eggs, but any where else, hap-hazard. Heavy rains made a sort of mortar in the nests—the birds abandoned it—sand was heaped in one of the nests and they made a hollow in that. About the second of July they began to sit regularly—guarding it for hours. On the second of September the first young ostrich came out of the nest, walking around it. In four days more they quit the nest to take care of this new born chick, which was a male, and is now (June, 1858,) as large as its parents—that is, from September, 1857—nine months. All sorts of food was offered by the parents, but *salads* were preferred to all other food. The female lays about fifty eggs a year, one of which contains as much as twenty-four Spanish hen's eggs— they are good to eat—not quite so delicate as hen's eggs. Two points are settled : 1st. The ostrich bears domestication and reproduces. 2d. Never abandons its nest, and is *monogamous.*

[Societe Imperiale Zoologique D'Acclimatation. Paris, Juillet, 1858.]

THE OSTRICH.

By Mr. Hardy, Director General of the Central Nursery of the Government at Hamma, near Algiers.

For about a dozen years past, ostriches have been kept here in a rather narrow inclosure. The flock was gathered from various persons of the army and of civil government. There were many more males than females in it, and these were continually fighting each other. The females did not lay any eggs, whether because they were too young or because the place did not suit them.

This flock became reduced by sending some as presents to the Museum of Natural History of Paris, to the Zoological Gardens of Marseilles and of Antwerp. Only two males and two females were retained. In 1852 these were put into a circular inclosure in the middle of one of the main walks of the nursery ; this space was about fifty feet in diameter ; around it is a shed, but the ostriches never enter it even to eat or sleep, but always stay out, no matter how bad the weather may be. They appeared to be mated, but the males were always fighting, until at last one conquered the other, and never gave him one moment's respite whether he was eating or loving. However, the females began to lay pretty regularly. They always began to lay in about the middle of January, and left off in the latter half of March. Sometimes they laid again in September and October. The moment of laying was always preceded by the rutting of the male, with peculiar action. The skin of his neck and thighs (which have no feathers) turn bright red ; he crows or sings with sounds from the bottom of his breast and gullet ; sounds rough, concentrated and strange. To produce them, he bends back his neck, shuts his bill, and by spasmodic movements, produced at his will, in his whole body, he forces the air from his lungs, his gullet swells to an extraordinary size, and then we hear three sorts of guttural thunder, the second of which is several notes higher than the first, and the third much deeper, and is prolonged and gradually extinguished. This crowing is frequently repeated It is a savage sound. and has some analogy with the roar of the lion. It is heard day and night, chiefly in the morning. The rut is manifested by his performing a kind of dance, by crouching before the female upon his hams, and balancing himself in a tottering manner some eight or ten minutes, while his head strikes, with the back part of it, his body on both sides and in front of his wings, which shake feverishly, and his whole body trembles, while from his gullet we hear a kind of cooing, dull and shaky, and his whole system seems to be in a hysterical delirium These symptoms precede his *treading*, which he does often in a day, principally in the morning, and during the tread we hear a deep rumbling sound, indicating the violence of his passion. When laying time comes, they form a hollow in the ground, *both* working at it. They throw earth out, the wings are agitated—they will make a hollow in the hardest ground. The place where they did it, in their park, was full of stones, gravel, &c., in a sort of mortar. Stones of considerable size were thrown out by them. The hollow was made about three feet and an half in diameter. They had made many such hollows without choosing to lay in them. Notwithstanding all this preparation, the eggs were never laid in any of the hollows, but any where else, hap-hazard. In December 1856, I put a couple into a larger and more retired park, about an acre, half of it covered with trees and richly grown plants ; the other side sheltered from the west by a high building, along which they were sheltered from wind and rain in winter. In January they dug a nest in the thick woods, exactly where they were thickest, the ground being an ochrey clay. About the 15th, the laying began, the two first eggs being laid in the park hap-hazard, but afterwards she deposited them in the nest. She thus laid a dozen, and in the fore part of March began to sit. A week after we had heavy rains, the water got into the nest and the eggs were in a sort of mortar—the poor birds abandoned the nest. I knew that they laid twice a year. I ordered a large hillock of sand to be made where the hole was and surrounded it at a distance with mats so that persons could not see it. Towards the middle of May I was gratified by seeing the ostriches digging a new nest on the top of this sand hill, and soon the laying began. About the last of June they began to guard the nest some hours every day, and after July 2d, began to sit regularly. On the 2d of September, I first saw a little ostrich walking about the outside of the nest ; four days after, they ceased to sit, and busied themselves with their *new born chick!* I afterwards broke the remaining eggs and found three dead chicks in them, two eggs perfectly unchanged, and two rotten. The young one was a male and is now as *large as its parents*, that is, from 2d *September* 1857 *to June* 1858.

Last January they laid again, 14 eggs, ending in first days of March, 1858. One egg was first put out of the nest, and remained untouched by the ostriches. Every time they began to set, they turned every egg over, and changed their position. When it rained, both male and female united their wings to cover the nest. On May 11, some young ones were seen. On the 13th, in the morning, both quit the nest, having a flock of nine young ones. The younger moved with unsteady steps; the older ones picked and eat tender plants, the father and mother both watching them with anxious vigilance, the father especially, and he sheltered them with his wings at night. All sorts of eatables were offered to them by the parents, but they preferred salads to all others. They eat bread, but in very small quantities. When hatched, they were covered with long thick down. The other couple were set on a dozen eggs. They first wondered at them. After several days, pecked them, seeming to count them; at last they began to set. The female lays about fifty eggs a year. These eggs weigh about three pounds each; so that the ostrich lays about 150 lbs. of eggs per annum. Twenty-four eggs of the Spanish hen are about equal to one ostrich egg. The ostrich egg is less delicate to taste, but they are perfectly eatable. Their feed is grains and herbs; they love to swallow shining articles, pebbly metal, &c.

Two points are settled. 1. The ostrich bears domestication and reproduces; 2. Never abandons the nest; 3. It is monogamous, or if polygamous, that is an exception.

[Journal de la Societe Imperiale et Centrale d'Horticulture. Paris, Juillet, 1858.]

CHINESE YAM. (*Dioscorea batatas.*)

Excellent drawings are given of the male and female vines, fruit, seed, &c., by Mons. Duchartre.

The vine can grow 14 or 17 feet in length, and about one-quarter of an inch in diameter. It entwines from left to right; sends out branches voluble, like itself; leaves bright green above, pale below; it is *dioique*, that is, some vines have male flowers only; others, female only. Until 1856, we had in Europe, none but male flowers; these are very small and green, growing in little groups of two and three. The female flowers are disposed by four and five at spaces. The fruit is a capsule of fawn color, about two-eighths of an inch long, with three concave sides. The seed is fawn colored, and is in the middle of a sort of wing, very thin, with irregular light plaits radiating from the seed, but not reaching the border of the wing; the whole seed is nearly semi-circular; the seed is a little oily; the seed remains attached to the vine, sometimes for three months and an half; the seed sowed in a pot in the beginning of April, came up at about the end of it, and most of them formed young plants in May and June. The crop from tubes is more convenient and a better crop.

The most interesting experiment in this, was made by Mons. Leveau-Vallée, of Rome, 1858. He planted in thumb pots cuttings of the tuber one-eighth or less of an inch, and like ones in open ground. From 470 of the first, he obtained about five lbs. of tubers ; from the second, of 430 in open ground, he obtained nearly as much. He planted these, and from 88 square metres of ground he obtained *nearly* 300 lbs. weight of excellent tubers. So that the crop is much the best from tubers—far better than from the seed or the *bulbilles*, (little tubers at the foot of leaf stalks.)

MISTLETOE OF GREAT BRITAIN.

Lindley, in his Vegetable Kingdom, says it is of the Loranthaceæ order, 302. Plants of a shrubby character, in almost all cases growing into the tissue of other plants, as true parasites. Leaves opposite, (but sometimes alternate,) veinless, fleshy, without stipules (at the feet of leaf stalks or petioles) ; seed solitary ; fruit succulent. When on the apple tree, its wood contains twice as much potash and five times as much phosphoric acid as the wood of the foster tree. Exceedingly curious Loranths are found in Guatemala. Dutrochet *Sur la Motilile* tried many curious experiments with Mistletoe. Loranths are about equally dispersed through the equinoctial regions of Asia and America, but are much more rare on the continent of Africa, only two from its equinoctial regions, and five or six from the Cape of Good Hope, two from the South Seas, and one from New Holland, (Australia.)

The bark of Mistletoe is astringent, as it is in the Mistletoe of the oak tree. The berries contain a viscid matter like bird-lime, and is insoluble in water or in alcohol. The habit of the common Mistletoe gives an idea of all excepting the tubular richly colored calyx. They are of small moment in medicine. The Mistletoe of the oak, *Viscum Album*, was consecrated by the Druids—(The priests of the Oak, as the name implies.)

Some doubt has been entertained, in modern times, whether the modern Mistletoe on the apple tree was the oak plant of the Druids ; but it has recently been found on the oak in the west of England, leaving no doubt about it. The powder of its leaves and shoots has been used for epilepsy.

[Journal of the Royal Agricultural Society of England, No. 41, Part 1, 1858.]

From this valuable work, just received from the society as a gift, we extract the following :

ON THE TRANSFORMATION OF ÆGILOPS INTO WHEAT.
By Prof. Henfry.

In our 15th volume of this Journal, (page 167) we published a translation of a paper written by Mr. Fabre, of Agde, in the south of France, on this subject. [We translated the same article in 1854, and it is in our printed transactions.—H. Meigs.]

Mr. Fabre endeavored to show that our cultivated wheat (the origin of which is obscure,) had been produced from the grass called *Ægilops ovata*, through the influence of cultivation. His explanations do not appear to be conclusive, by the experiments of Dr. Godson. Mr. Regel, director of the Botanical garden at Moscow, appears to have been earliest in the discovery that the Ægilops (Αιγιλωψ) triticoides (like wheat,) (*wild oats,*) which formed the first stage of transition from Ægilops ovata, towards wheat, was a hybrid, but Mr. Godson was first to give practical, and as it appears, decisive proof in favor of that view.

Prof. Planchon, of Montpelier, has repeated the hybridizing experiments of Mr. Godson with success ; so also have Messrs. Groenland and Vilmorin, near Paris. Prof. Henslaw has also found a *triticoid* form of *Ægilops squarrosa*, which proved barren, affording rather a presumption that it was a hybrid. Mr. Brown, of Colchester, has given an account of a similar form, which was fertile, and was cultivated for four years, without however, becoming wheat. The French botanists now call this hybrid *Ægilops speltæformis*, as it appears in its wild state.

DR. GODSON ON THE NATURAL AND ARTIFICIAL FERTILIZATION OF ÆGILOPS BY TRITICUM. (*Wheat.*)

Hybridity excited the attention of naturalists more than a century ago, but it has been long neglected, although very interesting and important, at least in a scientific point of view. On one hand, *crossing* renders certain species of plants very " critical," and the determination of these becomes almost impossible, if we do not carefully distinguish the forms arising through hybridation from those which constitute genuine specific types. By this means, Messrs. A. Braun, Koch, Wimmer, Fries, Nageli, Lang, &c., have succeeded in elucidating certain genera of plants previously almost inextricable, and which were the despair of descriptive botanists. Of this we have examples in the genera *Cirsium* and *Carduum* (thistle), *Mentha* (mints), *Verbascum* (mulleins), *Polygonum* (docks), and *Salix* (willows).

On the other hand, hybrids, when fertile, tend to return, after a certain number of generations, to one of the two types which have given them birth ; and, as the crossings may take place in opposite directions, we sometimes meet with complete series of intermediate forms between two perfectly distinct species. Thus, Mons. Grenier has gathered in a meadow, in the environs of Pontarlia, such a series of forms between *Narcissus pseudo-narcissus* and *Narcissus-poeticus;* and Mons. De Solis has likewise observed a complete set of individuals, presenting. all the modifications which can exist between *Ulex-nanus* and *U-europæus* (beans), comprehending in the midst of them *U-gallii*. Other exactly similar instances might be cited. The origin of cultivated wheat, *which has not, up to this time, been found in a wild state in any part of the world*, occupied the attention of naturalists in ancient times ; it was attributed by the Greeks to Ægilops as its parent plant. The spike of the Ægilops ovata breaks at its base when mature, that it does not become separated into pieces, and that it preserves its seeds tightly fixed to its floral envelopes.

TOO MANY PLANTS IN ONE FRAME.

I had not been long a gardener when Mr. Knight, director of the Exotic nursery, reproached me for stuffing my frames and hot house with too many plants. He said that I was worse than a plant vender for that. He gave me the wise advice, "Not to put *many, nor a variety*, of plants in one frame or hot house, if I wished to gain premiums for plants." When Mr. Knight said this, I had young beans (Flageolets), strawberries and cucumbers fit to eat; potted vines in full bloom, others in bud; my fig trees on the walls vigorous; melons in pots blooming, and in the shade of my cucumbers (on trellis) a quantity of budded plants in pots. The first thing that I condemned was my fig trees, which gave me a luxuriant growth of leaves and stones, but no figs, being in too much shade and too much heat. By altering this state of things I had the pleasure of having fine figs, grapes, peaches, &c. I have used guano water with benefit. My cucumbers succeed well, especially the *Kenyon* and the *Sion-house* sorts. I have no doubt but that I can raise from a *pot* a weight of cucumbers greater than that of the soil in the *pot*.

[From the Gardener's Chronicle.]

CALCEOLARIAS

Have gained in figure, size and colors of the flowers, much in a few years past. We now have innumerable varieties, many of which, however, are not worth the trouble of cultivation. The flowers are very easily obtained, with proper care. The great secret of success with them, is keeping them free from moisture in winter, and from frost, by as little heat as possible. In summer it wants watering frequently, and some shelter from the burning rays of the sun. They do well in frames along walls. The tops being fixed by hinges so that they are readily opened and kept open when necessary. In winter give them but little water. After they have done flowering, cut off the tops, manure them, water them often, and they will put out side shoots.

Although our herbaceous calceolarias are pretty plants, yet, they are displaced, now, almost everywhere, by the tree calceolaria, which gives many more flowers and is more hardy and more easy to cultivate. Of these we recommend the Boven orange, Roi des Jaunes, Roi de Sardaigne (crimson), Pierre Précieuse (yellow with a touch of brown), Prince d' Orange (yellow), Beauty of Montreal (light crimson), Perfection (orange), Eclipse (scarlet), Falcon (orange, spotted with brown), Nain Jaune (yellow dwarf), Heywood Hawkins (orange brown), Aurea floribunda (gold flower).

The Club adjourned.

HENRY MEIGS, *Secretary.*

TUESDAY, *January* 11, 1859.

Present—Prof. Mapes, Prof. Nash, Dr. Crowell, Mr. Hardenbrook, of Greenwich, Ct.; Bruce, Witt, Doughty, and others.

Andrew S. Fuller, Horticulturist, of Williamsburgh, in the chair. Henry Meigs, Secretary.

The Secretary read the following translations, &c., made by him from the works last received from abroad and home, viz.:

[Bulletin Mensuel De La Société Impériale Zoologique D'Acclimatation, Paris, Nov., 1858.]

Mons. Drouyn de Lhuys, Vice-President of the society, and the Chevalier Debranz, Counsellor of the Emperor of Austria, a member of this society, communicated to the President the desire expressed by the Counts Castellani and Freschi, to obtain the aid of this society in a scientific expedition to China, with a view to endeavor to regenerate the silk worm, which has recently shown an alarming evidence of a falling off by disease. A meeting was held on the 17th of September, 1858. The Counts Castellain and Freschi were present by invitation and explained the object in view, and the necessity of fully examining the silk worm and importing eggs on the largest scale, should they find that the disease does not exist there. These learned Italians exhibit great self-devotion, courage, and patriotism in this undertaking. They do it under the auspices of his serene highness the Archduke Ferdinand Maximilian of Austria, together with the assistance of the French and English governments. These commissioners in the silk interest of the world, are to examine how the worm has been managed for the last *forty centuries*, and to learn how to do so in Europe. The Counts are proprietors of very extensive silkworm nurseries and are equally rich in knowledge of silk both scientifically and practically. They propose to send packages of from two to five ounces weight of the eggs, and as many of the packages as may be wanted for experiment in Europe, upon the largest scale, from Asia and China. This society subscribes 2000 francs

The Minister of Commerce, Agriculture and Public Works, has addressed a circular to the chambers of commerce, and the learned societies inviting subscriptions for packages at $4 per ounce of eggs. Address for subscription the Chevalier Debranz.

Messrs. Castellani and Freschi have tried many experiments to feed the silk worm. They pulverized dry mulberry leaves and rice for feed with some success.

As to the silk worm of the ash tree, it is now certain that it is the true Bombyx Cynthia.

Camels are being introduced into Brazil. The Marquis D'Olinda interests himself much in the plan.

Gambras partridges, and some Gangas, are received from Algeria for acclimation. Sent home by General Gastu.

Mons. Gaguin, president of a committee on pisciculture, established by the agricultural society of Louhans, announces a donation of one thousand francs to the committee.

Mons. Jules Poinsard, from Texas, presented seeds, and the book, "Army Meteorological Register," and the "Reports on the purchase, the importation and use of Camels and Dromedaries," by Major Henry C. Wayne, of the regular army of the United States.

A specimen of *Pyrethrum Caucasian, Chamomile of Mount Caucasus*, now first grown in France, was presented.

M. Graindorge, of Bagiolet, has *fifty* varieties of strawberries, twenty of gooseberries, seven of raspberries, and ten of the finest kinds of grapes.

Mons. Pepin said that the Caucasian Pyrethrum differed from the Pyrethrum roseum and the P. carneum used in Persia and in Russia, where they pulverize the flowers for medical use, and to *kill insects*, which it is energetic in doing. Some members doubted this singular property of the powdered chamomile. Others had proved its power over insects.

M. Varaskine says it is daily employed in Russia for that purpose.

The Imperial Society has purchased a suitable building for its use in *Grenelle St. Germain street*, No. 84, having about 13,000 square feet, with very solid walls, for 200,000 francs ($40,000).

[Revue Horticole, Paris, Nov. 1858.]

PALMA CHRISTI. (*Ricinus Sanguinus*, or *Ricinus Obermanni*.)

This variety grows ten feet high, and differs materially from our common Palma Christi. It is well worth cultivation.

LENORMAND CAULIFLOWER.

It is not a new species, but admirably cultivated. At the exhibition at Lyons it is distinguished. Grown on a field of peas they, the heads, measured in circumference upwards of four feet. They are the most hardy and finest of the class.

The subject of the day, "Root Feeding," and "Fruit Trees in Spring," was called up, and Prof. Mapes was requested to speak.

Prof. Mapes deemed it best to use a few minutes in considering certain new doctrines uttered in England, on the mode of applying manures. A strong writer, *J. D.*, appears in the London Farmers' Magazine, who insists upon it that the method of making compost manure heaps is all wrong; that the same materials, straw, &c., &c., spread over a field and suffered to dry there by sun and wind, lets down into the soil, ammonia and the other fertilizing constituents, doing more to enrich the ground than if it was buried in the soil. We all recollect the Gurney system— the enriching the soil by covering it for a time with hay, straw, boards, or anything else! He called it a mulch. You have all noticed the effect. *J. D.* decides that the long straw of barnyard manure being washed by rains, thus fertilizes the soil! True mulching is just as perfect in keeping land when the hay, straw, boards or other material, is *first washed perfectly clean!* An acre, therefore, *covered all over* by a *floor of clean dry boards*, is far more effectually fertilized than by the *clean dry straw.* Ammonia placed in a vessel *in ice*, ascends into the air as readily as from soil or manure, and that contained in soil is arrested at the surface better by the board than it is by the straw!

A German chemist has come out in England, where his novelties will take much better than among the chemists of Germany, and he blazons the discovery that manure does not lose by a winter's exposure spread on land. I have tried weight for weight, green manure and clean salt hay, and found them equal as to surface manuring; but when plowed in I find them thirty per cent better in three years after, than the surface application. Carpenters' shavings are as good a mulch as hay and straw. It is said, too, that under-drained ground gives potatoes and no rot! That is not so; for on my well under-drained land, I boasted of sound potatoes for several years, until they testified against that notion by getting the rot. These new fangled notions are illustrated by one of mine. Feeling confident that I could excel everybody in preserving fruit fresh a longer time than has been done by anybody. I have tried it, as I told the club I would, and I now tell the members that my finest pears, the Duchesse D'Angouleme and others, did keep all their external freshness, and plumpness, and beauty, but lost all their flavor! Good for nothing, and immediately commenced rotting!

A member asked as to the benefit of electricity applied to plants.

Prof. Mapes described the experiments which have been tried, and could not discover the slightest benefit from it, except in one or two instances. One was a gardener, who dug trenches close together over his garden, and laid wires in them, with copper and zinc plates,&c. His garden was improved precisely as much by *like trenching, without any wires at all!* One man insisted on a marvellous electric growth of a vine entwined about a lightening rod. I found on examination, that the iron rod which absorbed *much more heat* than any wooden trellis, had helped the vine to grow!

A Member.—That is the milk of the cocoa nut!

Prof. Mapes.—Which is said to be put in them by young monkies!

Mr. Hardenbrook.—I own a small patch of thirty-eight acres at Greenwich, Connecticut, and want to make the most of it; and I ask the club at next meeting, to tell me how to do it.

Prof. Nash.—Grow oats and carrots—the latter as good and better for horses—sleek hair, good digestion, with more strength for work.

Prof. Mapes talked up carrot many years ago. The pectic acid in them is excellent for digestion; they will make your cow give as good butter as she can from grass. The Dutch grate carrot fine to put in the churn to help the butter.

I get 1,500 bushels of carrots per acre. I can't afford to raise corn near New York for $2.00; wheat for $4.00; rye for $2.00; nor oats for $2.50 per bushel. Root crops will pay. Celery is good—I stow it in my mushroom caves, where it keeps well, handy for market.

I ask you to taste wine from rhubarb plant, and wine from currants. (They were tasted first without their names,) and pleased palates. The rhubarb wine, color of champagne; currant of carmine color, very beautiful.

Messrs. Fowler & Wells presented copies of their paper *Life Illustrated,* having good lessons on *diseased eating, &c.*

By Mr. Hardenbrook.—Subject for next meeting : "The most profitable management of small farms near great cities."

The Mistletoe of England, with its fruit on, was on the table.

The club adjourned to Tuesday, January 18th, at noon. It meets every Tuesday, at noon.

H. MEIGS, *Secretary.*

———

January 18, 1859.

Present—Messrs. Benjamin Pike and Mr. Doughty, of Jersey ; Fuller, of Brooklyn ; Burgess, Bruce, Witt and Kavanach, of Williamsburgh ; Dr. Shelton, Dr. Crowell, Hardenbrook, of Greenwich, Conn. ; Judge H. E. French, of Exeter, New Hampshire ; Prof. Mapes, of Jersey ; Prof. Nash, Messrs. Wells, Chilson, Patrick, Lawton, Pardee, Chambers, Pierce, Daniel C. Robinson, R. L. Pell and others—41 members.

President Pell in the chair.   Henry Meigs, Secretary.

The Secretary read the following translations and extracts from works of home and abroad, received by the American Institute since last meeting, viz :

[Journal de la Societe Imperiale et Centrale d'Horticulture, Paris, November 1858.]

Seeds of the Chamomiles, Pyrethrum roseum, and Carneum have been planted, and two or three varieties raised, called Gloire de Nimy and Tom-Pouce—(Glory of Minny and Tom Thumb,) very beautiful flowers. These Chamomiles, when their flowers are dried, are used as Insecticides—*Insect Destroyers.*

CUSCUTE OR DODDER, A PARASITE.

In temperate latitudes, some climb and twist around large trees—some of them gigantic.   In Affghanistan there is one that half buries the tree it is attached to.   Valmont de Bomare, in his Dictionaire d'Histoire Naturelle, speaks of it growing like hair on grapes.   It was called a monster by Fortunatus Licetus, and by Aldrovandus, long ago.   It is occasionally found thick as on the human head and upwards of three feet long. *Keteler* has caused it to grow on bunches of grapes.   It is thought to be a large growth of that terrible pest the Oidium—and that it may spread.

EGGS.

Mons. De Sora, on a farm near Paris, raises poultry, and has eggs on a great scale.   He feeds them with horse flesh, raw, minced, &c.   He began with 300 hens, who gave him in the first year 300 eggs each.   In 1857, he had 100,000 hens, laying at a like rate, or 40 million eggs.   The old fashioned barnyard fowls are preferred to the modern fancy Shanghai, Cochin, &c., being easier fed, and giving better flesh and eggs.   The minced meat is seasoned very slightly with salt and ground pepper—for these hens are somewhat epicures !   Sora clears $17,500 per annum by his eggs, &c.

Pecan nuts fatten wild turkies. *Horse chesnuts* steeped a while in lime water, then well washed in pure water and boiled to a paste, are very fattening to sheep! Deer eat them raw—they enrich cow's milk—they cure a horse's cough—hence the name *The Horses' chesnut.*

Physic for stock, is as bad as it is for man.

STABLES.

Keep them as clean as possible. In an open field where the stock live very much according to nature, they cannot suffer from their own manure and bad air. Their stables therefore ought to be as clean in all respects as the *open pasture,* if possible. And feed them with punctual regularity. They feel a breakfast, dinner, and supper at too early or too late hours more than any alderman ever did. They suffer, and your pocket pays the loss.

Giant Pea, of Himalaya, grows six feet high, have large pods with large peas, very fine eating.

Mr. Fuller, a gardener of Brooklyn, exhibited to the Club a *new seedling* pear from France, of rich color and weighing one pound six ounces. Mr. Fuller read extracts made by him relative to fruit.

[Journal De Maine'et Loire, November, 1858.]

Mons. Caulaincourt gave a splendid dinner yesterday which was truly a grand affair. On the table there were seven pears which cost three hundred francs ($60,) a piece—a diplomat's dinner of the first order.

At another dinner, in the saloon of the Provencaux brothers, six persons had for their dessert, fruits and wine at the cost of 1,500 francs.

In passing the fruit store of Madame Chévét, in the Palais Royale, I saw pears in the window marked with their prices, *sixty francs* each. I walked in and asked Madame Chévét if she could sell the pears readily at such prices? Her reply was "certainly, and we sell some pears for much more; we have some that cost *one hundred and twenty francs* each. We let them at *five francs* each, to figure on the tables, at gentlemen's dinners, where they occupy the post of honor on the tables, to be looked at but not eaten or even touched. Paper ones would answer the same purpose except in that fragrance given off by the real pears."

Mr. Pell.—Apples were put into barrels with cider to keep well. On arriving in Europe they were admired for their beautiful appearance, but they had lost all their flavor and tasted of nothing but cider!

Mr. Lawton remarked that he was pleased with the lesson on physic for stock, and thought it as bad for men.

Prof. Mapes.—Yet it is often wanted for both, and has very useful results.

Prof. Nash.—When young, I used to wait on my father's stock of thirty or forty cattle, among whom sickness was unknown. They were always fed with great regularity but never pampered.

Mr. Meigs.—Our best butchers advised me long ago not to buy beef for my family unless certified to be of cattle with healthy *livers,* for many of them were as badly diseased as any men, in that vital organ. I followed that injunction.

Prof. Mapes had sold his pears this year for $8.50 per hundred. Last year for $12.50. On Jersey city ferry only, last season, ninety thousand baskets of strawberries in one day. Peaches incumbered steamboat decks, and often are numerous baskets of them emptied into the river because the prices were too low; at the same time good ones sold readily at $2.50 per basket. The dealers drowned peaches as some do kittens, to make cats more valuable.

Mr. Lawton.—I sold my strawberries for 75 cents a quart. I have now one acre of Wilson's seedlings, and another acre of Peabody's.

Prof. Mapes.—My *Napoleon pears* prove always good; they often do not on other fields. Pomological conventions have condemned them. I do not. The causes of failure I do not know—the causes may be many.

Mr. Fuller exhibited Cedar of Lebanon, with its cone, from his place on Long Island. It has been found difficult to cultivate. I do not find it so. It hates standing in wet.

The President called up the question of the day "Small farms near large cities," and invited Prof. Mapes to speak.

Prof. Mapes said that he was happy to find others willing to hear him, but for his own part he was almost tired of hearing himself talk.

Land near large cities necessarily rises to high prices, and can no longer afford to bear the grand staples of a country—its bread and meat. It must become diminished in size of farm, and must be converted into gardens, receive the most perfect tillage and fertilization to make it profitable. He illustrated, on the black board, by figures, the comparative values of the lands and their crops, showing mathematically, that an acre at $5, giving Indian corn at thirty bushels, worth fifty cents per bushel, is but $15, while gardens, at Aharsimus, Jersey, near us, of only five or ten acres, being carefully cultivated, make money. The gardeners from them carry loads of vegetables to market and return to the gardens with *loads of manure always*. They raise vegetables that cannot bear, well, long transportation to market, and other crops like carrots and others, giving vast yield per acre. They can sell all the cabbages to spare for our southern markets. They cannot grow *apples*, or *corn*, or *wheat*, or *rye*, or *oats*, or *hay!* They can raise seeds of all, and when of best kinds, sell well. When I first raised the Stowell ever-green corn on my farm near Newark, I sold the seed at the rate of $32 a bushel. Seed of our late Bergen cabbage can hardly be bought for $10 a pound. The best tools and all of them must be had, and mules or horses taught to work in drills. Where I have them work, a single well taught mule with a "weeder," doing more work in the root fields in one day, than forty men with hoes can do. I had once 20 men, and more; what with high pay and some *barratry*, I did not profit so much as I now do, on more ground, with my all sorts of tools, and *seven men*. I keep the *weeder moving*, not so much to kill weeds already grown as to cut them up in their incipient stages. Mr. Reed, of Elizabethtown, calls a *weed* on his place a *curiosity*. He never waits for them to grow. Labor and science can do all, but a mere laborer and mere chemist cannot do it.

Judge French of New Hampshire, who is here, just returned from agricultural study of Europe, is now about to give us lessons of high value in his book ; it goes the whole depth in the drainage system, and without that I would not accept as a gift the best farm in our republic. We do make some *beautiful cottages*, and about them nothing to eat (comparatively).

Hon. H. E. French, of Exeter, was called up, and said, that England had convinced him of one thing, and that is, that successful agriculture demands capital. He had admired a Lincoln Heath farm, where a lighthouse was maintained ninety years ago, sixty feet high, to direct travellers over its gloomy and barren wilds. A farm of a thousand acres costs, for rent and taxes, about ten thousand dollars per annum, and requires a capital of fifty thousand dollars to render it profitable. Strict calculations are made of every thing, especially as to the manures. When by their system an acre is made to yield thirty bushels of wheat, they find that to raise two bushels more costs, in manures, &c., too much for profit. I saw land reclaimed from the sea water raising fifty-six bushels of wheat an acre. We have lost all knowledge of the inglorious art so long triumphant among us, that of *skinning land !* get all its vegetable element out of it, sell them all and leave the land to starve ! We formerly skinned New England. but starving not being as good as eating, we have got to work among our numberless rocks and boulders, tilled, manured, and got up to *more bushels of wheat on an acre than the glorious west !* Some people wonder how we can build such nice houses and live in them ! We have left off skinning the land and taken to manure, to drainage and thorough tillage, and with all these well done, we all can build those beautiful cottages so fitly mentioned by my learned friend Professor Mapes, and have beautiful farms all around them to load their tables with the *world's* best things.

President Pell.—I have made on my farm one hundred miles of drain, chiefly with stone ; I have also tiles, some of them glazed, others porous. I found that chesnut planks, two inches thick, laid on the bottoms of my ditches, to build upon, are good. I have, in some spots, made drains seven feet deep !

Prof. Nash.—Plants, occasionally, fill drains with their roots.

Mr. Meigs.—A well near a willow was filled with roots so that water could not be drawn by the pump, near the corner of Twenty-first street and Eighth avenue, some years ago.

President has traced roots eighty feet !

Mr. Bruce.—A poplar tree choked a well in Wall street, near it, fifty years ago ! Spoiled the water !

Mr. Lawton moved as subjects for the next meeting " Drains and Small farms." Adopted.

Mr. Fuller received for *experimental culture* the fruit of the mistletoe from the Club.

The Club adjourned.

H. MEIGS, *Secretary.*

January 25, 1859.

Present—Messrs. President Pell, Bruce, Prof. Mapes, Prof. Nash, Dr. Holton, Benj. Pike, Dr. Crowell, Brower, Witt, Kavanach, Roberts, Stacey, Geo. E. Waring, Fuller, Doughty, Leonard, Burgess, Lawton, Steele, Dr. Shelton, of Long Island; Chilson, Judge Scoville, and others, 41 members.

President Pell in the chair. Henry Meigs, Secretary.

The Secretary read the following translations, &c., made by him from works received by the Institute from foreign countries and home, viz:

MAISON RUSTIQUE

Gives the following as means of anticipating changes of weather, besides the barometer, thermometer, &c., &c.

The Stars.—If the sun rises pale and remains reddish, and its disk very large, the indication is of violent wind. Stars bright and sparkling, clear, cool weather, &c.

Vegetables.—When chick-weed, bird-weed, and some others, close their flowers, look for rain. Chick-weed is called the poor man's barometer.

Birds are, from their hollow bones, &c., more sensible of changes in the atmosphere than other animals. They afford many indications. Aquatic birds beat the water, especially in the morning; ducks are much affected by an approaching change; crows are playful on the banks of streams, &c., and fly high in air; fishes leap out of water often before a storm; the king-fisher returns to the sea while the gale still blows, moles coming out of their holes. The little bird's song and the dolphin's play foretell calm.

Signs of Rain.—Birds come to land from the sea; geese and ducks take to the water, and are noisy; crows and blackbirds assemble and suddenly separate; magpies and jackdaws get together and are noisy; herons and buzzards fly low; swallows sweep the surface of the water; pigeons stay at home; poultry and partridges roll in the sand and shake their wings; the rooster crows morning and evening, and claps his wings; the lark and the sparrow sing earlier than usual in the morning; the chaffinch is noisy near dwelling houses; peacocks and owls make more noise than usual; asses bray more than common; cattle open their nostrils wider than usual, lie down and lick themselves; horses neigh violently and gambol; goats and sheep leap much and are quarrelsome; cats clean their paws and ears; dogs paw up the earth, and noises proceed from their bellies; rats and mice make more noise than common; frogs croak; earth-worms come to the surface more than usual; spiders move about little, keeping in their holes; flies are dull; ants hasten to their holes; so do the bees.

Signs of weather from inanimate bodies are numberless; such as swelling of wood, sweat on iron and stones, strings of musical instruments breaking, circles around lights, ponds become thick and muddy, &c. &c. I hope that our good people will follow up the observations.

On the expansion and contraction of the air, physical and mechanical action. When the air becomes heavy, as it is said, (in truth, light,) animals suffer, and vegetables are relaxed. To this circumstance we, in part, attribute the low growth of plants on mountains; and we add that to the expansion and contraction of the air, its spring and its weight, are the means employed by nature to determine the movement of the sap.

BONES.

There are many questions not yet settled, as to the proper management of bones for manure. When fresh from the animal, whole or divided, their natural decomposition is always, almost, too slow; and enormous differences are found by experience, in the time required to decompose them when pulverized.

USES OF SALT IN AGRICULTURE.

Cadwallader Ford, of Boston Society for promoting agriculture in 1790, observes that he left his farming to his sons, and they never used any salt until 1785. That year on an acre of flax we sowed a bushel of salt, after the plants had grown a finger's length. It had a good effect. My neighbors for two miles around had no flax worth the trouble of pulling, while I got nearly ten bushels of seed to my acre. I advise the trying it on rye, oats, Indian corn, and at the rate of two bushels per acre. They may depend on it that every bushel of salt will produce more than five times the cost of the salt, and perhaps as much as ten times.

[American Academy of Arts and Sciences.]

Joseph Greenleaf, Esq., of Boston, says, (1790,) that in his part of the country, the farmers say that whoever raises Indian corn, pays more for the labor than the corn is worth. To convince them of their error, I bought a piece of land from one of them which he affirmed was worn out and would not produce a crop of any thing. The land was dry, not a stone in it, very light, shallow, inclining to sand, overrun with briars, weeds, St. John's wort, and here and there a spire of coarse wild grass.

I got a plow made with a sharp coulter, a share of about one-fourth the size and weight of the common plows, with a furrow board on a new construction; it followed the coulter edgewise, turning the furrow over in rather a spiral form. With this plow, requiring but one horse, I plowed the full length of the field, and returning I turned up a furrow against the first one. At four feet from this I turned up another similar double furrow; so leaving four feet space between every double furrow through the whole field. On these double furrows I planted potatoes four feet apart between each hill. The field contained two acres and an half, and was about forty rods in length. It was plowed and planted in *one day*, with one horse and two boys. When the potatoes came up, the same boys with the same plow and horse, turned another furrow of the *unplowed space*, towards the potatoes on each side, and dressed the potatoes with hoes. They did this in *one day*. At half hilling the potatoes, this plowing towards them was repeated, so, now, the whole field was plowed. At hilling they cross-plowed, throwing the earth towards the potatoes, and then dressing with the hoe. By this method the two acres and an half were completely tilled in *four days*, with the labor of *one horse* and *two boys*—which in the common way of managing ground would have required the labor of *a man, one boy and two horses for ten days.* I had a good crop and next year one of Indian corn.

CARROTS.

By Major Spooner, of Roxbury, 1790.

I raised them in good deep rich soil, and got four or five hundred bushels off one acre. They will *increase* the milk of cows, keep horses in as good condition *as grain*.

CHEMICAL RESULTS.

Leibig said some time ago "That it would be pronounced one of the greatest wonders of the age if any one would succeed in condensing coal-gas into a white, dry, solid, odourless substance, portable, capable of being placed on a candlestick, or burned in a lamp."

That greatest of discoveries has been made. A mineral oil flows out of coal in Derbyshire, which is obviously produced by a slow process of distillation from the coal; it consists, as fuel, of solid paraffine, (a tasteless, inodorous fatty matter, fusible at 112°, it resists the action of acids and alkalies—seems to be a hydro-carbon. The name is from *parum*, (little) and *affinitas*, (affinity) to denote the remarkable indifference, which is its characteristic feature,) dissolved in a liquid oil. A consideration of the conditions under which this material product is formed has led Mr. James Young, of Manchester, to the discovery of a method (which he has patented,) of readily obtaining the paraffine in any quantity desired, and at a cheap rate (compared with common candles,) from *ordinary coal gas*.

M. Derode, of Paris, has patented a process for uniting cast iron to cast iron and other metals, by electricity, either magnetic or galvanic; also to soldering.

[Wilson's Farmers' Dictionary or Cyclopedia.]
LIQUID MANURE.

Urine or any other liquid manure which mainly consists of urine, ought not to be applied to vegetables in a fresh state. It scorches the grass and other plants on which it falls, fresh from the animal, in a dry time. The liquid manure should be strained or filtered through straw or coarse sand in order to extract pieces or straw and anything else which would injure the equal distribution of the fluid, and thus diminish its aggregate effect on the crop. The quantity to be applied is according to its strength, crop, soil, &c. Liquid manure containing ten per cent of the saline and organic principles of urine and farm-yard drainings, may ordinarily be applied at the rate of from twenty tons to thirty tons on an acre. Sprengel (a celebrated agricultural chemist,) says, that to a German acre, (about two-thirds of the English acre,) there should be applied from 20,000 to 30,000 pounds weight of the urine, &c. The effect lasts but one year. The Flemish farmers use 2,840 gallons on an English acre, for flax. They do it clumsily. The English do it much as we sprinkle streets with water, from suitable carts. It is always more efficient on light sandy than on heavy clay soils and loams. Swiss farmers, after every mowing of their grass, sprinkle with their mist-wasser, liquid manure, for a new growth of grass. Some grass fields manured in this way by Harley, the proprietor of the celebrated Willowbank dairy, at Glasgow, cut grass on some of his fields six times in one season, and at each cutting the grass was about fifteen inches long. Singular, but it does more harm than good to barley. It makes potatoes large, but sometimes watery. Not so good for turnips as barn-yard manure.

Liquid manure, such as *night soil* and water, was practiced by the Chinese from the earliest period. Cato says the Romans mixed grape stones with water to fertilize their olive trees. Columella says, (1800 years ago,) that putrid stale urine and lees of oil are good for grape vines and apple trees.

Evelyn, of modern times, proposed artificial mixtures, dung, urine, salt, lime, nitre, in the following proportions: Salt, one part, lime, two parts, mixed in a heap, to lay so two or three months, turned over sometimes. When used, add twenty to thirty bushels of it to ten or fifteen tons of water, and apply to one acre. All manures, organic or inorganic, should be dissolved for the use of plants. Artificial liquid manures is largely used on the continent of Europe, and was so before the English farmers used it. Swiss farmers call it gulle, the French call it lizier, and the Germans call it mist-wasser. In the German states and in the Netherlands, they sweep the dung of their stall fed cattle into reservoirs underground, mixing it with four or five times its bulk of water, according to the richness of the manure. Five reservoirs are provided, large enough each to receive the manure made in one week, so that each may have four weeks to foment; then it is pumped into water carts or large open vessels. Same practice in northern Italy. It should be spread very even on the land. The potatoe thrives remarkably with five or six bushels of salt an acre. The liquid manure is injured by clear sunshine, and we should always, if we can, apply it in cloudy weather. Human urine, says Berzelius, contains almost everything a vegetable requires, viz.:

Water,.................................... .... 93.300
Urea, ... 3.010

Henry Steele, of Jersey city, exhibited his patent *Bee-hive Moth Preventer*. Small metallic doors over the entrances are readily managed by the bees, but no moth understands it, and can't get in.

Mr. Pell.—Will not these doors brush off the wax material?

Steele.—Not at all. Bees know how to enter without any damage.

Mr. Pell.—Bees are stationed at the holes to fan with their wings, so as to keep the queen bee cool. He described the copulation of the queen.

H. L. Young, of Poughkeepsie, exhibited apples and desired to know what name they have in pomology. They are very free from worms, the tree a bountiful bearer. He will give grafts of it. It bears every year.

Mr. Pell.—It is probably originally from the Greening, but our apples are mixed up so that we count some 800 varieties already. Naturally, apple trees bear biennially, because its bearing is generally too profuse to bear annually and perfect fruit buds for the next year. The tree will last 200 years.

Prof. Nash.—Why should we not have apples plenty, every year, although the trees may live less long ?

Mr. Pell objects to that system. The pear is liable to injury from curculio which perfects itself in it.

Mr. Fuller.—The curculio pierces it, deposits a worm which leaves the fruit, and is not perfected in the pear.

Prof. Nash.—Insects attack the fruit of trees which have more or less disease, in preference to those in perfect health.

Peter W. Wendover laid on the table ears of sweet corn, flint, and others from his farm in Jersey. His object is to show that by his method corn can be grown with smaller cobs than usual, with heavier corn on them. Common corn weighs about fifty-four to fifty-seven pounds per bushel, while mine weighs sixty-one pounds per bushel. I grow it in *drills*, and I think it does better than in *hills*.

President Pell read his paper on drainage in part; will read the remainder at next meeting. He illustrated his plans upon the black-board.

Prof. Mapes.—I want to get rid of the stone drains and have tiles in their place. Roots of plants obstruct water-ways in a remarkable manner occasionally, by an excessive mass of them; but *all roots hate clay;* never enter it, or a clay pipe, if possible, especially that containing foetid limestone. Drains require for their best effects on soil, to be open at both ends; and at the upper end they should be kept open by a sort of chimney, or bit of pipe or other tube, to let the air which enters at the lower end escape at the top, where you will ordinarily find it strong enough to blow out a lighted candle. This produces fine effects in the land, by *æration* (airing it); it renders the temperature of it warmer. I get my drains dug preparatory to fixing the pipe, for twenty-five cents a rod, which makes my cost of drains per acre, about $40. When the well known William Cobbett was here, he had, for a time, a farm on Long Island, and I, as a boy, was with him for a while. He planted rows of turnips, and that the turnips were superior in *eight rows* on each side of a drain. Drained land shows it better after the first year. I get as good drainage at eighty feet apart as forty. Five feet deep makes it better than twenty by three. The proffessor illustrated this on the black-board. I use an iron wheel resembling a cheese with its contents out. This has a little plow, cutting two inches at a time; the earth is carried by it to the surface at every revolution and thrown off sideways. This cheese of mine works down three feet. It cost $140. A deep subsoil plow first run on the line of a drain, prepares well for digging the drain. I have one of my pupils here, who is engineer of our great Central Park—he is directing its drainage—Mr. Waring.

George E. Waring.—Has tried drainage on a swamp with heavy, dense clay, and, generally, water requiring wading. I made drains eighty feet apart and five feet deep. In the next year its corn crop was among the best. At the Central Park we are making drains as near as we can, forty feet apart and four feet deep; using tiles of inch and a half bore, having collars to cover the joints, made of burned clay like the pipes. These answer better than anything else. We tried hay, grass, &c., even twisted like ropes, but that would not do. We now find that what little silt gets into our pipes can be removed, and then hardly any can again get into them. We begin by a careful survey of our field; ascertain where the out-fall of the water must be; establish a bee line from thence to the upper end, running at a depth of four feet above this line, without regard to the uneveness of the surface, this line being well marked by stakes; then we drive down pegs on which to fix points for observation. We then dig down to our bee line, however deep that may be, in a few places. (We have dug down thirteen feet, in a place or so. The tiles are then laid, with their collars firmly and properly covered up. We find that the heaviest rains are drained off by these small tubes. It acts constantly and moderately, so that bodies of water apparently far too large for them to carry off, are not only taken away, as it were, by uninterrupted *retail*, but I find these little pipes never full, or even half full of water at any time. We have *silt basins*, which we can clean out, so that our pipes will always be clean. *Test-holes* are made before draining, to show the water in the land. I recommend that tiles be used for the *test-holes*. Our tiles are from Albany, made for us at $14 per 1000; will soon be made for $7 or $8.

Prof. Mapes.—At the Canandaigua works they are made for $2.38 per thousand. Judge French says they can be afforded at $5 00.

Mr. Waring.—Our collars cost half as much as the pipes. We use *saddles*, too, in some cases. Collars are stronger. We have drained fifteen acres already. Over our silt basins, we have cast iron covers. I find that our present plan was in use long ago, at Auberge, in France, on a field always remarkable for its fertility. It has been found out recently that it had been drained about four feet deep, by burned tiles of clay, of small bore, glazed, and each end of pipe *whittled* away (tapered) to fit the next one, all laid at about *forty feet apart*! as near as our modern measurements go. This was done in 1620, 238 years ago.

Dr. Crowell.—What angle of inclination do you adopt?

Mr. Waring.—*That of our bee line* from the upper to the lower ends of the drains.

Subjects for next meeting—by Prof. Mapes, " Drainage, and the value city manure," and " Small farms near large cities."

The club adjourned.

H. MEIGS, *Secretary.*

February 1, 1859.

Present—Messrs. President Pell, Dr. Shelton, of Jamaica ; Dr. Holton, Dr. Crowell, Messrs. Bruce, Witt, Pierce, Doughty and his son, John V. Brower and Benjamin Pike, of Jersey ; Kavanach, Field, Burgess, Fuller, Provost, Roberts, Hon. John G. Bergen, Adrian Bergen, Pardee, Lawton, Rev. Dr. Adamson, Bowman, Dr. R. T. Underhill, of Croton Point ; Prof. Nash, Wm. B. Leonard, John W. Chambers, Mr. McCarthy, Skidmore, of Long Island ; Stacey, and others—fifty-one members in all.

President Pell in the chair. Henry Meigs, Secretary.

Mr. Meigs.—The fact is now established that agriculture, the heretofore most neglected of all human arts, has been subjected to a great modern revolution. The French style an intelligent farmer an Agronome, a Greek word meaning the *law of land*, or the science of land.

Nature is so bountiful, that man and beast, and insect and fish, all find something to feed upon, in the pleasant lands of the earth, almost without work or talent of any sort. But man, whose dominion was assigned by the Almighty, over all the earth, must use his immortal reason to conquer his lands, from ice to ice from north to south. He lives, therefore, where all out door life is, with a half dozen exceptions, torpid or extinguished.

ON THE APPLICATION OF SEWER WATER AND OTHER TOWN MANURES TO AGRICULTURAL PRODUCTIONS.

Mr. Pell.—Within the city of New York we find many of the streets and houses perfectly filthy, the atmosphere fœtid ; disease, small pox, typhus and sundry other epidemics, rife among the people, bringing as a necessary consequence in their train destitution, and the absolute need of not only pecuniary, but medical relief ; all attributable to the presence of the very richest materials of production ; the total absence of which, would, in a great degree, restore health, avert the recurrence of disease, and if applied to land in the several districts, not only cheapen food, and increase labor, but promote abundance. As we pass through our streets, the chief seats of insalubrity are indicated to our senses by sickening, depressing, and deadening sensations, produced by inhaling air rendered impure by the admixture of organic vapors arising from decay of vegetable substances, as well as offensive and pungent smells, caused by foul air.

In these districts the vegetable and animal excreta from houses are discharged through drains into sewers, and thence into the rivers, occasioning the entire loss of the manure. In other sections the manure is accumulated in and about dwellings, occasioning excessive sickness and mortality, even though the natural climate may be superior. The people in these 'quarters likewise live and sleep in confined habitations, constantly polluted by the emanations from large quantities of cess pool water retained beneath them. This is removed in closed receptacles, but the decomposition of matter contained in them goes on, and the noxious gases escape, causing inconvenience and annoyance to all those living on the thoroughfares through which they pass. Numerous palliations for the evils arising from retention of manures near dwellings, have been often tried; chemical agents have been used to deodorize and disinfect them, to fix the ammonia and arrest decomposition. The value of these disinfectants have been examined, and their complete sanitary efficacy proved doubtful, their addition to the manure useless if not detrimental, and where muck as absorbents have been used, the bulk was so augmented, that the expense of removal became great. In some instances air shafts from cess pools have been used as expedients to carry off the product of decomposition, but they only increase the amount of evaporation, and although they diminish the intensity of the effluvia on the spot, they spread among the inhabitants of the neighborhood the gaseous impurity more widely, and waste the valuable properties of the manure, the pecuniary loss of which is trivial, compared to the mortality occasioned by the retention of filth in the cess pools.

While none of these expedients have been successful in the removal of the sanitary evils, they would have cost as much had they been practicable on a large scale, as would a complete system of house and city drainage. The investigations so far made as to the means of improving the sanitary condition of our population, created by the inconvenience and expense of cleansing by hand labor, have firmly established the conclusion, that the refuse is received best, most easily preserved, least offensively and most thoroughly and economically removed by water, in impermeable pipes, leading into covered receptacles. The principle of the removal of the refuse in suspension in water may be applied universally at a far lower rate than the expense of cleaning cess pools; that until the principle is applied, until the obstacles created by the expense of hand labor and cartage in the removal of excrementitious matters are overcome, until cess pools are abolished, and all substances, liable to run into putrefactive fermentation, is immediately removed from among habitations, until the surface cleansing of alleys, streets, and particularly markets, in thickly inhabited communities is effected more quickly, a positive improvement in the public health of the districts occupied by the majority of the population, cannot possibly be expected. The average quantity of cess pool manure is at least two loads per annum for each house.

But if cess pools be superseded, and the water closet principle generally introduced, as it has been in a large number of houses in the city, then as the old practice of engineering converts the East and North rivers into great sewers, they will become far more polluted than they at present are.

At this stage of investigation, which brings us to the dilemma of either polluting our noble rivers, by the discharge of the refuse of the city into them, or of polluting the atmosphere by the retention and accumulation of the refuse near to our habitations, we are driven in the search for the means of relief, to enquire into the necessities of agriculture, and to consider the various means of applying our excrementitious matters, suspended, or dissolved in water, as a fertilizer.

I have examined various important examples hereinafter cited, and in my own mind have established the fact, that by the application of manures in the liquid form, a degree of continuous and constantly increasing fertility may be obtained, such as has been produced by no other method. Still the examination of the practice with sewer water has brought to notice objections, on sanitary grounds, to the practice as sometimes pursued near towns, on account of the offensive, and no doubt injurious, emanations which the water emits when placed on and permitted to stand upon the fields. The probable evils, I think, are assuredly much less than the decomposition and discharge of the emanations within a town, from badly arranged sewers, and within habitations from cesspools, ill-constructed drains, or from accumulations on the surface. The emanations from irrigation with sewer water, I am sure, from experiment, is far less than the usual top dressing with manure in the solid form. Any soil may be manured with city sewage, and decomposing animalized manures with impunity, and without the fear of causing fevers, agues, &c., provided it is so located that the wind may have access to it. If, on the contrary, the free motion of the air is prevented by trees, or other obstacles, there ague abounds, and its effects may be readily discovered by the haggard appearance of the inhabitants who are exposed to the influence of the rising pollution. Injurious effects upon health of the prolonged retention of excessive moisture on a surface of vegetable mould, where the ground becomes most thoroughly saturated, is established by the production of rot among sheep, red water among cattle, and fever among men; which diseases appear and disappear coincident with the operations of flooding and drying. It is certain that wheresoever water is laid on the land in larger quantities than it can soon absorb, or where there is alternate wetting in excess, particularly in situations protected from atmospheric influences, malaria invariably arises.

The fact is, that no irrigated land is safe for sheep, or cattle in the fall, to graze upon, unless it has been previously thoroughly under-drained. I have had my sheep affected slightly, and my cattle lamed, on such land before drainage—never after. But the general conclusion as to the unsalubrity of the common irrigations on undrained lands, and their unfitness for proximity to towns, is corroborated by the fact that in the Lombardo-Venetian provinces, where there is some of the oldest, most extensive and skillfully conducted irrigation in all Europe, the government has long found it necessary to interfere for the protection of the health of towns. I was informed by the Grand Duke, in Milan, that permanent irrigation, on undrained land, was prohibited within five miles' distance of all the towns under his rule. I proposed to him a plan, which I have practiced successfully since, under many varied circumstances, in horticultural field and garden cultivation, and have invariably found it perfectly free from inconvenience of any kind; and that is to dilute the liquids intended for irrigation to such a degree as almost to extinguish smell. In that state I have always found it admirable when applied to plants, because it is readily carried beneath the surface of the ground in minute subdivision, facilitating rapid decomposition, and complete absorption by the roots, and believe that a single load of solid manure sufficiently liquified, will have ten times the fertilizing power that it would applied in the solid form. The miscellaneous refuse of any house in the country, containing ten persons, will be found amply sufficient, if properly diluted with water, to irrigate and make rich, five acres of land, to an extent of fertility far beyond anything ever yet obtained, or possible to obtain, by top dressings. There are hundreds of farms within a few miles of us, capable of producing an abundance of straw and some grass, with a small supply of water. All the owner of such land has to do, is to place stock upon it, they will eat the straw, and convert it into solid manure; the water will liquify it, and gravitation convey it to the fields. The only labor required throughout this beautiful operation will be to open and shut the sluices.

It seems to me important to remember the fact already stated, that an extent of dilution sufficient to almost extinguish smell, and so clear that if you did not know its contents you would not refuse to drink it, is the best condition for the assimilation and absorption by the roots of plants. The more I dilute the better I appear to progress in my horticultural improvements, because the fibrous particles are entirely gotten rid of, and there is nothing left to clog the mouths of the rootlets, which are so small that I have never discovered them with the microscope. I have even found that it is a good plan, after irrigating with this liquid twice each week, to irrigate once with pure water, which so completely washes the fibrous matter, that there is no nidus left for animalcules in the soil. Therefore be assured that your liquid manure is not in a condition fit for assimilation by the plant, so long as there are particles in it, visible to the naked eye. You cannot induce the roots of plants to take in solid bodies in a division so minute as to be held in suspension in water, because they are filters, formed by God, so perfect that those employed in the laboratories of men will never compare with them. Furthermore, the weakest solutions of manures that can be made are not altogether absorbed by the spongioles of plants; a separation invariably takes place; a certain portion of the dissolved salt leaves the water the instant it enters the spungiole. If you will make very thin solutions of sugar, gum or starch, and place plants in them, they will grow; make them thick, and they will block up the pores of the vegetable tissue, and the plant will die. All the plans for the precipitation of sewer water, which have been examined, precipitate some portions only of the manure, leaving the most valuable in solution.

There is no doubt but that the experience derived from garden cultivation, forms the very best basis for culture on the farm, inasmuch as the results are mainly derived from observation on individual plants, under much more varied circumstances, than generally occur within the same period of time in respect to whole fields. The greatest advancement in horticultural productions, and those that were most eminently successful, when I was competing for the prizes of the American Institute and State Society, were by the application of liquified manures formed from water-closets, liquid from the cow and horse stables, laundry, waste from bathing-tubs, and other sources to be found on small farms, which were placed in a brick manure cistern, where they immediately passed into a state of incipient decomposition, and rapidly became fit for use. When drawn off, it was excessively diluted with water, and applied to the plants when they were in a state of active growth ; at any other period the effects would be prejudicial. I used this composition on a squash vine, and obtained many specimens of squash weighing from one hundred and seventy-five to two hundred and one pounds, melons eighty pounds, cucumbers six feet long, corn fourteen feet high, bearing fourteen full ears to the hill, &c. ; all of which were publicly exhibited, and are mentioned in the State Agricultural Report.

The produce in favor of liquid manures, over solid, preponderates greatly in favor of liquid, in size, quantity, quality, flavor, color and weight. Experience has fully proved to me, that for all crops ordinarily raised, sewage is the most valuable manure that has yet been introduced to farmers. I have often lost my strawberries, gooseberries, and raspberries by an application of solid manure, which forced the leaves to grow, but not so liquid, which I applied when the flower buds were forming, and as a consequence produced fruit in place of leaves. Liquid manure may be misapplied in wet weather, and is of course subject to the casualties of rain storms, but far less so than solid manure top dressings. While liquid applications are immediate on the growth of vegetation, they have been practically found not transient in the soil, as was anticipated they would be at the commencement of their use. At all events my experiments with liquid manures have been most successful, from the fact that all the efficacious elements contained in them have been so combined as not to be washed away, thus doubling their efficacy, and placing that most important of all sciences, farming, on principles as sure, as well conducted manufactories, and enabling the farmer to carry on the operations of agriculture, with more security, and less anxiety, than any other of the pursuits of man. I have positively satisfied myself by experiment that land thoroughly underdrained never deteriorates, but constantly increases in fertility from year to year, though it may be washed every week through and through by heavy rains, because the fertilizing elements in the soil, as well as the liquid substances added, are retained by it chemically, for the use of plants. To prove this fact, I put 120 lbs. of pulverized clay in a keg and bored a tap hole at the bottom, then poured in seventy quarts of strong urine and sewage water, of the most offensive character, and the result was a pellucid stream of water perfectly free from odor from the bottom.

Liquid manure or sewage water may be applied to the land when it is fallow, with the certainty of perfect incorporation, and that the deposit will be available for the following crop, and at any time during the growth of vegetation it will be cumulative, and increase the fertility of the soil continually. Such has been the case at Edinburgh, Milan, and many other places, where liquid manure has been applied scientifically, always producing a superabundance of crops, which has continued for fifty years without any exhaustion of soil or deterioration of the herbage. The average yield at Edinburgh has been four full crops a year of grass, eighteen inches high, and the collective weight cut amounted to eighty tons per acre, and with all cruciferous and leguminous plants, fruits, &c., heavier and more rapid crops have been obtained by liquid manure than by any other.

I once applied dilute sewage water to wheat; the result was so great a weight of grain, that the straw could not sustain it, and the crop lodged. The following season I macerated wheat straw in a liquid, in one experiment, and in another used a soluble silicate, both results were most satisfactory. The miscellaneous nature of town sewage is more favorable to vegetable production than any other manure.

The sanatary results of collecting, removing and applying New York city manure, appears—

1. That it is far better to submit to the entire loss as manure, of the ordure, animal and vegetable refuse, than permit it to be retained for removal at some remote period, and during the intervening time to create noxious impurities, amidst a thickly populated district.

2. That there have not been any disinfectants invented as satisfactory preventives; those known are so expensive, that they exceed the cost of immediate removal of all offensive substances.

3. That it is the first condition of salubrity, that all town manures should be at once taken from habitations, and that the object can be most economically effected by being removed in water.

4. That it would be of less injury to the health of the public, to use our magnificent rivers as great sewers, than to permit the refuse to remain underneath our habitations.

5. That manure applied to the surface of land by irrigation is of less injury than would be the application of manure as top dressing.

6. That the necessity of exposure can be prevented by conveying sewer water in close impermeable underground pipes, and by its distribution through the medium of gravitation or steam power.

As agricultural results—

1. That the application of city sewage has produced finer crops than any other species of manure; and that a four fold yield of grass above the ordinary growth, on like soils, has been maintained for fifty years, by means of the sewer manure of Milan and Edinburgh.

2. That an equal fertility by the application of liquified farm manures has been obtained by a similar application.

3. That the greatest increase of the fertilizing principle of manures by a judicious application in a liquid form, on various descriptions of sand, loams, and clays, has been displayed, and that the quantity and quality has been greatly improved.

4. That the usual augmentation of crops by the application of liquid manures on green crops has been four fold above the ordinary production.

5. That the principal advantages of the application of liquid manure consists in its prompt action, quick absorption, and readiness with which it is carried to the roots of plants.

6. That the distribution of street sewage through pipes is cheaper and far more effectual than any other mode of manuring land.

7. That by this mode manure can be applied with less waste and danger to the public health, than by any other.

When we take into consideration the nature of the effluvia escaping from cess pools and other similar places, we will find that the principal gas given out from these deposits is sulphuretted hydrogen, the most deadly of the gaseous poisons, two or three inches causing death immediately if injected into a vein, or beneath the skin of an animal.

You may place the body of a cat, or any similar creature, in a bag containing sulphuretted hydrogen, and though you leave his head out, he will die in eight or ten minutes ; ten quarts injected into the intestines of a cow, will kill her in a minute ; and it is utterly impossible to keep any animal in high condition in the neighborhood of large privies, where sulphuretted hydrogen is given out in quantities. You can scarcely so dilute it with atmospheric air as to deprive it of its noxious propensities. If one part is mixed with eight hundred parts of common atmospheric air, and a dog is compelled to inhale it, he will die immediately. Various instances are recorded in which immediate death followed the incautious inhalation of this gas by persons engaged in removing the contents from cess pools. And still these effluvia are constantly breathed by those inhabiting back alleys and streets, though in extreme dilution, still to the prejudice of their health.

Now all these matters can be gotten rid of in a cheap, easy manner, thus ; it has been shown, year after year, in our city, that at least two-thirds of the annual expense of street cleaning, and cleansing cesspools, is the charge for cartage, which the sewers as now constructed may be made to render entirely unnecessary. The refuse of the streets, courts, alleys, and other filthy places, might be removed in the same way as the refuse of houses, to wit : through pipes. This is the most convenient, cheap, and rapid mode of removing the refuse from houses ; in like manner the refuse of the streets and thoroughfares might be swept at once into the sewers and discharged by water ; the streets might be swept at night and the sewers flushed in the morning, thus conveying the silt to proper reservoirs, wherever it may be found convenient to erect them, as their contents may be raised by steam power over heights of several hundred feet, and conveyed through iron pipes 14 miles for about five cents per ton. The expense of this mode of cleansing the streets of New York city, would not cost more than that of conveying the Croton into the city, after the mains are laid and that will not be a tenth part of the cost of cartage alone. Thus the richest materials of production, that now accumulate in our streets and houses, invariably and inevitably tainting the air, and rendering it pestilential, might be promptly removed, daily, and spread out on the surface of the surrounding country, after having first enriched the Central Park with inexhaustible fertility, and clothed its rocks with verdure, so that it might everlastingly be maintained in a state of purity and richness.

Sewers constructed and managed in the way that ours are, accumulate great deposits, which are more noxious than they formerly were, from the fact that cesspools from houses are now deposited in them, the gases from which escape into the streets, as well as habitations where the drains are not well trapped. The deposits in many street sewers are allowed to remain several years, during which time the public are constantly exposed to the poisonous emanations evolving from them. Moreover, at certain periods the accumulations reach a certain point, when private drains become choked; then, for the first time, the foul state of the sewer manifests itself, and the occupants of private dwellings are put to annoyance and expense, gratuitously inflicted upon them by the authorities, who will not adopt the proper system, which is to flush the sewers regularly, and thus prevent them from becoming laboratories to generate poison on an immense scale, and conduits to spread them abroad most effectually, to an extent that may be actually measured by every inch of drain not regularly washed by a stream of Croton, which is, in reality, the most essential part of a good system of house and street drainage.

And there is not the least difficulty in such a system, less, in fact, in this city, than any other city in the world. All we require is good sewers, proper shoots, and the ample supply of water always at hand. The height of the Croton above the tide is 115 feet, 105 feet above the lowest, and 60 feet above the highest grade of streets, below Murray Hill, and the loss of head by friction in the pipes is only about twenty-five feet, while the city is drawing. At Harlem River Valley, a twelve inch pipe, with a six inch jet, throws water 110 feet high, the city fountains throw from sixty to seventy feet, and the water is kept on at high pressure in all the streets at all times. Since we have had this abundant supply of pure water, I have noticed that habits of cleanliness, not only inside but outside of the houses, as well as the health of the people, has increased beyond comparison with former times, besides perceptibly producing temperance among the lower orders. And if I had the direction of Croton distribution, with the present quantity to back me, which amounts to four times the supply, to 600,-000 persons, as enters London for 2,500,000, I would cleanse the surfaces of the yards, streets and pavements, with water, in preference to the broom, which only reduces the bulk of dirt without removing it, and when it is wet, spreads it over the surface, stirs it up, and much increases the extent of deleterious evaporation; whereas, water would remove the whole by a single movement, into the sewers, and at the same time, flush them to the receiving reservoirs, thus saving manures for agricultural purposes, without raising a particle of offensive dust, double in value, for what is now paid for the water, preventing disease, suffering and death. There are certain adjustments established between the organic and physical kingdoms, and between the two great divisions of the organic kingdom, which we ought to bear in mind in the practical consideration of this matter. We are certain that atmospheric air is necessary, in an equal degree, to the life of animals and plants, but that they produce opposite changes in the construction of the air, chemically speaking : the plant gives off, as excrementitious, that principle of the air on which the animal subsists, and lives upon that part of it the animal rejects as excrementitious ; while the animal, in turn, restores to the atmosphere the principle which constitutes the pabulum of the plant, and subsists upon that which the plant has rejected as of no further use to it. In this peculiar manner these two great classes of organized beings renovate the air for each other, and forever maintain it in a state of richness and purity.

On this magnificent adjustment depends the further principle, equally at the foundation of all proper sanatary regulations, to wit : that the refuse of the substances which have served not only for food but clothing to the inhabitants of the city, and which is permitted to accumulate there, inevitably taint the air, and render it thoroughly pestilential, promptly removed to the rural districts, would avert disease, promote abundance, cheapen food, and increase the demand for beneficial labor. The Legislature should prohibit, under certain penalties, the letting of any dwelling in which the Croton is not let in, and sewer arrangements made from the cesspool to the main. A good supply of water, and cesspool so constructed as to be readily cleaned, are absolutely essential to the preservation of the public health and morals. The humanizing influence of habits of cleanliness has never been sufficiently acted upon. A clean, well ordered house, exercises over its occupants a moral and physical influence, which has a tendency to make the members of the household sober, peaceable and considerate of the feelings of each other, besides imbuing them with a respect for property, for the laws in general, and even for higher duties and obligations, the observance of which no laws can possibly enforce. Whereas, a squalid, filthy, unwholesome dwelling, devoid of water, and other necessary comforts, tends to make every dweller regardless of the happiness and feelings of each other, sensual and selfish, leading them to form habits of dishonesty, idleness, violence and debauchery, besides training them to every degree of ruffianism and brutality, the truth of which may be easily demonstrated from the fact, that these districts always send forth thieves, pickpockets, reckless and violent men, who perpetrate deeds in cold blood that fill the city and country with disgust and horror. I know of places in the great city of New York that it would be utterly impossible to convey by description any conception of their poisonous and disgusting condition ; they must be seen to be understood, and when seen, you would exclaim, involuntarily, can such a place exist in a city that has made any progress in civilization. Even so long ago as in 1844, thirty-four thousand of our population lived in alleys and courts, and seven thousand in cellars, so constructed as to cut off all circulation of air, being dark, damp, and chilly, the inmates suffering from the effects of rheumatism, fevers, contagious and inflammatory diseases, affections of the skin, lungs, eyes, ears; degenerate in morals, degraded in habits. Fathers, mothers, children, and strangers, sometimes to the number of thirty, crowded in a single apartment of small dimensions.

Half of these creatures die before the fifth year, the mean age of death does not exceed twenty, and the remainder die under forty-five. Now, there are limits to the denseness of population, which, when passed, invariably lead to disease and death. To prevent this, pass a law to forbid crowding of population, by adjusting, to superficial limits, the size and number of dwellings, employ scavengers to remove solid bulky matters, construct sewers and drains, with a sufficient supply of water to carry to the receiving reservoirs, the comminuted solids, and adopt proper modes of ventilation for aerial matters, which latter subject is so little attended to, that even the magnificent houses of our city, in which the wealthy and intelligent reside, have no provision for a systematic mode of ventilation; and is this to be wondered at, when we know that there are whole Encyclopædias of Architecture and Building, in which the topic of ventilation, and warming, even does not occur. I would recommend some capable Yankee to give these matters attention, and publish a good book on the subject, and thus spread general knowledge among the building community. And let him bear in mind that a large part of the bulk of the human frame is occupied with apparatus intended expressly for the purpose of ventilating the blood, or exposing it to the action of pure atmospheric air; this part is the chest, which has to work incessantly, from the instant we enter the world, until the moment we leave it. To shut up, therefore, four thousand persons in the Academy of Music, nearly closed against the admission of air, would render useless this extraordinary breathing apparatus, so admirably formed by nature, as each individual would vitiate, in the course of two hours, seventy-five cubic feet of atmospheric air, rendering it unfit for the purposes of respiration. Therefore, the four thousand pair of lungs will render three hundred thousand cubic feet of air noxious, causing them to be prone to the attacks of each other's diseases, besides deteriorating the general health. Even while the individuals who generate poison, not by their respiration only, but by the poisonous emanations arising from their bodies, may remain free from its effects themselves, still communicate it to others, as was the case in the Black Assize, at Oxford, in 1577, where the Lord Chief Baron, the sheriff, and about three hundred more, (all who were present in the court,) were infected, by the prisoners, with fatal typhus, and died in forty hours. The lungs afford a ready and ample means by which effluvia may be conveyed into the circulating current, entailing diseases which essentially depend on a vitiated state of blood, caused by stench and effluvia arising from defective drainage. Even cattle are affected, if every drain entering a stable has not a stink-trap, a sufficient supply of water to cleanse it, careful drainage, and a superior exit for the escape of the vitiated air; these, in nine stables out of ten, are defective, much too small, and untrapped. The effect of emanations of animal and vegetable refuse, as from horses and cattle which are confined in such ill-cleansed, ill-ventilated stables, is first to depress their appetites and general condition, and put them off their feed; then low fever follows, leading on to various forms of inflammatory attacks and epidemics, which often prove fatal.

The plain practical questions that I now intend to bring before the club are—

1. The comparative extent to which town sewage, refuse, and liquid manures are valued.
2. The modes of application.
3. The cost and expenses of such application.
4. The agricultural, sanitary, and financial results.
5. The facilities for extended application.

Irrigation with sewage water is carried to a great extent in Milan, by means of a covered canal, known as the Sevese, built by the Romans, and the Navaglio, constructed during the middle ages remains open, and serves for navigation as well as drainage. All the streets of the city have in the centre a subterranean sewer, in brick work, into which the houses discharge liquid materials from the laboratories and water closets, and these are carried by the Sevese into the Navaglio, and then to the Vettabbia, which flows out of the southern part of the city, and, after a course of ten miles, discharges itself into the river Lambro, fertilizing prodigiously a great extent of meadow land, which the fertilizing matter borne by these several waters raises the surface in such a manner, that the deposit has to be removed frequently by the neighboring agriculturists as a fertilizer to preserve the level of irrigation. These meadows are mowed in November, January, March and April, for stable feeding; and in September they furnish an abundant pasture for cattle until the beginning of winter irrigation.

In Wiltshire, England, in the vicinity of Salisbury, along the valley of the river Willy to beyond the town of Warminster, a distance of twenty-two miles, is an almost continuous series of meadows irrigated with water and town refuse; the whole area is three thousand acres. These meadows are watered seven days and nights in succession, and then the water is turned off for the same length of time, during winter. In spring it is turned four days on and four off; in summer three days on and six off. The whole of these meadows, therefore, during half the year, form one large evaporating surface, as much as would be the case if the whole area constituted an immense lake. Even when the water is off, the ground is so saturated that the evaporation still goes on.

The cost of this system of irrigation is about thirty dollars per acre per annum, and the yield four immense crops of grass in twelve months. A portion of this land has not been plowed, drained, leveled, or in any way broken up from its original, or native state. The liquid and liquified manures, have been turned upon the moss, heather, rushes, and weeds, converting them all into decayed vegetable matter, and producing instead a luxuriant and sweet grass. After two liquid dressings of three days each, a deposit of black mould was found amidst the roots nearly two inches thick; this had been carried in suspension in the water. On another portion growing Italian rye grass, it was found to have grown two inches in twenty-four hours, and within seven months seventy tons was cut from an acre, without the slightest appearance of exhaustion in the land; on the contrary, its fertility increases constantly. Before the town sewage was used it would only keep five sheep to the acre, now it will maintain five oxen and twenty sheep, if the crop is cut and carried to them.

MR. TELFER'S FARM, NEAR AYR.

This is a small dairy farm of forty acres, about one and a half miles west of the town. The sub-soil is beach gravel with a slight admixture of clay. Water is too abundant, lying dead within twenty inches of the surface. The whole arrangement of the stable, steaming room, dairy, &c., are so admirable that it would delight any of you to visit the establishment. I have drawn on the black board a section of the barn, erected to contain forty-eight milk cows, the number kept on the farm.

No bedding or litter is used here. The cows lie on cocoanut mats. The ventilation is perfect, and the air sweeter than in the majority of the dwelling houses in New York.

It will be seen that behind the cattle there is a long row of perforated plates eighteen inches wide; the liquid passes through these, and is conveyed in the hollow semi-circular channels to the tank, placed at the end of the barn, where it is diluted with four times its bulk of water. The cost of the tank did not exceed $150. An engine, of three horse power, is used to raise the fluid, and also for churning, grinding oats, chopping hay, pumping water to supply the cattle, &c. The comparatively small extent of land only requires the engine to be occasionally used for irrigation; and as the surface is flat, and the height to which the liquid manure has to be lifted is small, the engine, when in use, is capable of doing the other work of the farm at the same time. The cost of the engine was $300, and there are two pumps for liquid manure, having four inch barrels, and fourteen inch stroke, making twenty-five strokes per minute; the capability of the pumps is therefore about 31¾ gallons per minute, or about 19,000 gallons per day of ten hours. The quantity of the liquid laid on at each application is about 5,000 gallons per acre, so that the whole farm could be covered in ten days if required, so far as the power of the pumps are concerned.

Iron pipes three inches diameter extend from the engine pumps through the field, not exceeding in cost $12.00 per acre. The hose pipe is of gutta percha, 150 yards long, costing with discharge pipe $100. The engine is used six hours per week at an expense of about $22.00.

The following then is the cost of carrying out Mr. Telfer's farm:

Tank,	$150 00
Engine,	300 00
Iron pipes and hydrants,	500 00
Distributing hose and pipe,	100 00
	$1,060 00
Annual interest,	74 20
Wages and fuel,	55 00
Total,	$1,189 20

The liquid manure is applied to all kinds of crops upon Mr. Telfer's farm; and, though rye grass is the favorite, it is also used for turnips, mangel wurzel, cabbages, rhubarb and fruit.

The hay and grain purchased during the year, amounted to $1,115; the other food is produced on the farm. The first cutting of grass is in the latter part of March, eighteen inches high; the second two feet high; the third four feet; the fourth four feet; the fifth two feet, and the sixth eighteen inches. Taking the mean, the aggregate height of grass grown and cut off this farm, within seven months, was fifteen feet in height. All this is eaten upon the premises, and the whole marketable produce is represented by milk and butter. Two hundred and thirty-four pounds were

made each week, amounting to,	$3,042 00
per annum; and the milk sold for,	2,535 00
Total receipts for milk and butter,	$5,577 00

I only need add, that previously to the adoption of the present system of farming, these forty acres of land were barely sufficient to support eight cows.

A Mr. Ralston, in Ayrshire, made all the necessary arrangements for the application of liquid manure in three years, on a farm of forty acres, and produced the following year eighty stacks of hay, where more than twelve had never been made before. He cut two crops of grass at the same time in the same ten acre field; before he finished the first cutting of nine inches high, there was a second cutting ready of six inches when he commenced.

On the Marquis of Ailsa's property, near Ayr, thirty acres have been brought under irrigation by gravitation. The field pipes from the tanks are all made of glazed earthenware. The work was contracted for, and the contractor was bound to maintain them in good order, for twelve months, under thirty feet pressure. I have written to learn with what success, and will report to the Club in due time.

Robert Harvey has a dairy farm near Glasgow, of 400 acres, and keeps a thousand cows, and has five miles of under-ground pipes, through which he forces the fertilizing liquid from his cow stables, and sells to the neighboring farmers 2,000 tons of solid manure, annually, for a dollar and a half per ton.

On this farm the liquid is applied with great advantage to all crops. It produces fine oats, wheat, turnips, mangel wurzel, cabbages, &c., but has the most wonderful effect on Italian rye grass, which is first cut when four feet high; the second, four feet three inches; and the third, eighteen inches.

The fluid is applied immediately after cutting, and if the cattle are turned on seven days afterward, they eat most greedily, and invariably select the portions of the field that has received the largest dose.

The Metropolitan Sewage company, at Fulham, England, have a station on the west bank of the Kensington canal, at Stanley bridge, where they have erected a steam engine to pump the sewage water of the town over the top of a stand pipe seventy-five feet high. This altitude gives a sufficient pressure for the whole contiguous district, and the fertilizing fluid is conveyed from the stand pipe, and distributed, by about fifteen miles of mains and services, varying from fourteen inches diameter at the works, down to two inches diameter in the fields and gardens where it is used. The consumers have plugs or hydrants fixed at convenient distances in their lands, and with their own servants, and hose and jet pipe, apply it when they please; paying to the company the sum of seventeen and a half dollars per acre per annum. And they found the fertilizing power of extremely diluted city sewage extraordinary, absolutely augmenting the ordinary large crops more than half. The sea meadows near Edinburgh, worthless twenty years ago, are enriched by sewage water, by gravitation, and open gutters, at an expense of twelve dollars per acre, and are now worth two thousand six hundred dollars per acre. Irrespective, therefore, of the extraordinary pecuniary value of city sewage, the expeditious removal of all organic fertilizing excreta from our city is so necessary to health, that every facility should be given by the Legislature to the corporation, for the most efficient arrangements for stations, reservoirs, mains and service pipes, necessary to distribute sewage waters in the rural districts. I would respectfully recommend that the corporation of New York, offer to pay the sum expended last year for cleansing the city, for the next ten years, to any company, who will engage to wash every street, and flush every drain, between the hours of one and four o'clock, after sundown, without permitting any portion of the same to enter either the North or East river, from the first of March to the first of December. This plan would save all the excrementitious matter of our population, and return it to the soil, enabling it to maintain in fertility as many acres as there are inhabitants, with the addition of two elements, silica and nitrogen ; the former of which may be supplied by the proper disintegration of the earth, the latter by ammonia, always present in the rain.

Prof. Nash described as he saw it, the management of liquid manure on Mr. Mechi's farms. One man, with a hose of gutta percha, parts the standing grain, and in one day gives a shower of liquid manure to eleven acres. The fluid is forced by steam power, some forty to fifty feet high, and thence falls in a fine shower.

The cleansing of this great city can be done by an intelligent capitalist with large profit to himself and vast benefit to the adjacent farms and gardens.

Mr. Lawton.—Vide his paper.

Dr. Underhill, of Croton Point, gave samples of his wines, the pure juice of his Isabella and Catawbas, saying that our taste was wrong as to wines, all requiring them to be what nature has not made them, that is, sweet! Some mistaken persons have strongly asserted that American wine differs from European, in having no cream of tartar in it! when in fact, it contains as much as any wine in the world, and *it would not be wine without it*. If neutralized it was injured and rendered suitable to depraved tastes. I found seventeen pounds of tartar in one cask of my wine. The far famed Madeira wine was always twenty per cent brandy. Europe says that our Catawba is a strong wine. You know what large quantities of our whisky goes to France to return in other names of wines and brandies.

Mr. Meigs.—All who visit Europe find that all the masses drink sour wine. Such is always the case with their " Vin du Pais."

Mr. Pardee moved that the Board of Agriculture alter the meetings to Mondays, and that, believing there would be no objection, we adjourn to Monday! Carried.

Question for next meeting, by Mr. Lawton, " Our national loss of fertility by exports of produce ;" also, " Small farms near cities ; Drainage ; and City manures."

The Club adjourned.

H. MEIGS, *Secretary.*

February 7, 1859.

Present—Messrs. President Pell, Bruce, Burgess, Fuller, Leonard, Chambers, Pike, Pardee, Stacey, Witt, Solon Robinson, D. C. Robinson, Veeder, Judge Livington, Chilson, Doughty, Lawton, Dr. Crowell, and others—thirty-nine members in all.

President Pell in the chair. Henry Meigs, Secretary.

The Secretary read the following translations, &c., made by him since the last meeting, viz.:

[Revue Horticole. Paris, 16th December, 1858.]

New Zealand spinach is one of the best vegetables we meet with. The ends of the leaves and stems are slightly acid, and have a very agreeable taste. It has succeeded wherever it has been planted ; product abundant. A small bed of it gives enough all summer for an ordinary family. The reason for its not yet becoming more known, is, that its growth is rather uncertain. Sow it where you will, in hot bed or open air, transplant or any way. Mons. Joigneaux says, he pours boiling water on the seeds, lets them cool gradually, and after some days, sows them in open air. Let the beds have all the sun and don't let the plants be very near each other—a distance of sixteen or seventeen centimetres—about *ten inches apart*. When once planted, the root bears one winter and shoots new leaves, so it wants but one planting.

EDWARD REGEL,

Director of the Botanic Garden of St. Petersburgh.

[Begonia Rex. From Japan.]

Brilliant foliage ; original in Assam. The upper face of the leaf of a deep metallic green, on it a brilliant white silvery zone. Lower side of the leaf, beautiful velvety red. Flowers fine rose color. Easily propagated by the slips, &c.

We have received, in exchanges, many of the Transactions of the societies of the United States. Among them we notice those of Maine, whose practice in draining deserves our study. They appear to possess all the knowledge necessary, and the industry in execution. In raising corn, we may all learn something from Maine.

J. C. Clements, of Kenduskeag, has a vat in his barn, water tight, ten feet deep, twenty-one by thirty-two feet square, for compost. Puts in ten or fifteen loads of muck. His hogs root in it, to get a little of the corn which he occasionally throws in the vat ; his privy and hen-roost are situated over it, and all the refuse of the house runs in, all the dung of his horses, fifteen cattle, twenty sheep, and, occasionally, plaster, ashes and salt. This compost is worth double that made in the old way ; for with that which had been exposed to the weather a year, I got fifty bushels of corn, while, with my new compost, I raised, in 1856, 107 bushels of good, sound, shelled corn, on one acre, and last year, 1857, 125½ bushels of good corn on an acre, measured by disinterested men. I used eight rowed. I I always select the best ears for seed. I select a piece of warm land, spread four or five cords of manure, one-half first, and plow it in four or five days before I plant. I put the other half in the hills. Before planting, I level the ground with a *fine-tooth* harrow, then furrow with a large seed-plow to the depth of *ten* inches ; rows three feet apart, and always from *north to south*. I leave two feet between the drills ; cover the manure in them as soon as possible, and an inch thick of the loam over that, *pressing it down hard with the foot*, drop three or four grains of corn in each hill, and cover them one inch and a half deep. I leave the surface of the field as nearly level as possible.

It is hard to say which is worst, scarcity or excess of water. Draining makes ground warmer ; it, the land, saves warmth, admits air, prevents, in great degree, drought. Subsoiling necessary, and should always accompany draining. It is not near so valuable in wet land.

On four acres, 285 rods of stone drain, three feet four inches deep. Cost $62.50 per acre, or $250 the four acres. In 1857, it was miry and springy. August 30, 1858, its crops remarkably good. The amount of water draining off ascertained to be 17,280 gallons a day.

They use the small pipe, with collar.

CULTIVATION OF THE CRANBERRY ON LONG ISLAND.

Mr. Wiles.—I will give you a short history of my cranberry cultivation. After all the information I could obtain about soil, location and profit, I got plants, and started one-eighth of an acre, two years ago last spring ; and, by the way the plants grew and flourished, I became satisfied it would pay, and made it up to one acre—part of it year ago last spring, and the balance this last spring. You see by this account, that only the eighth of an acre came into bearing this past season, or what they call the first bearing year. True, I gathered a few berries last year, but this is what cultivators call the first bearing year, and I am informed they are not in their prime until the plants are five or six years old. I know nothing about it myself, by experience, but state only the information I have obtained from others. Now for the result, the facts that came under my own observation. Since I saw you, I have received account of sales, and also received the money, for the product of the eighth of an acre. After deducting all expenses, paid freight, commissions, &c., I received $14.50. At this rate, an acre will pay, the third year from planting, $116 per acre. Now, one fact must be borne in mind ; I was unacquainted with the cultivation of them, and I am satisfied, to begin with, I did not get the best variety of vines—the upland is the best, I bought mine for the upland, but am convined I did not get them ; and, in the next place, experience has taught me I did not give them proper cultivation. I am now satisfied, that with the upland vines, and proper cultivation in the beginning, the third year the yield will be full $200 per acre.

The subject of the day, viz : " Loss of fertility to our land by the export of its products."

Mr. Pell remarked as follows :—Agriculture may justly be considered the art of obtaining from the soil the necessary food for the sustenance of man and his animals, and is consequently the parent of all other arts.

And, at the first blush, it would appear that man possesses entire control over all the means of subsistence. But when we come to thoroughly investigate the matter, we are obliged to confess that the desired results can only be obtained by performing, in a peculiar manner, certain processes, at certain periods, and that agriculture is, in reality, an experimental art, and has been brought to its present perfection, mainly without the aid of science, but with the view of obtaining the greatest possible produce, at the smallest expense of labor and manure. In this manner, Great Britain has gradually increased her production from five millions of dollars per annum, in the time of the Roman invasion, to one thousand millions, at the present time. And this enormous sum is a mere fraction of what her soil may be made capable of producing, when she calls science to her aid, and returns to the land the loss of fertility by the exportation of her products. She is the largest exporter of agricultural productions in the world, which has, so far, rendered her people wealthy, happy and powerful, and will continue so long as her nobles, and monarchs, encourage, as they now do, agriculture. When I think of this all-important subject, and realize the dependence of human life upon it, and call to mind the fact that one year's failure would depopulate the universe as surely as the flood did, I grieve that so little has been accomplished by us, that our government fails to organize a proper dissemination of agricultural information among the people through the medium of agricultural colleges, and that there is no sympathy among legislators for the farmer. In the whole United States, there is not a single agricultural college of any great distinction, while in the territory of Prussia, there are several, where the students are taught that perfect husbandry consists in graduating the pabulum to the nutritive powers, satisfying the entire capabilities of plants at the proper period of time, giving them the heat, moisture, and climate suited to their constitutions, making their condition in the ground perfect, always placing within the reach of their roots, the assimilating elements composing them, and thus, without the possibility of a failure, ensuring productive returns. All this requires knowledge which we, as a people, really do not possess.

What we desire to learn in our agricultural college, is, to supply the necessary enrichers without waste, restricting them to the kind and quantity required by the plants cultivated, so that there might be nothing left to wash away, or escape into the atmosphere in a gaseous form, and that the product may be obtained with the least expenditure of labor. To learn this requires study, and a thorough insight into the physiology of vegetation, which would be best acquired in an institution endowed for the purpose, and, I think, might be easily afforded by a people, the value of whose real and personal estate amounts to seven billion, one hundred and thirty-five million, seven hundred and eighty thousand, two hundred and twenty-eight dollars. The land that yields crops in the United States, if divided among its inhabitants, would give to each seven and a third acres, and amount in value to three billion, two hundred and seventy million, seven hundred and thirty-three thousand, one hundred and ninety-three. The loss of fertility, to which by the exportation of animal and other products, I will endeavor to show. There were in the United States, in the year 1850, eighty-five million, two hundred and ninety-three thousand, one hundred and fifty animals, including horses, asses, mules, horned cattle, sheep and swine. If all the excrementitious matter derived from these animals were returned to the soil from which they derived sustenance, they would retain in fertility, by the application, perhaps, of nitrogen, forty-two million, one hundred and forty-five thousand, one hundred and seventy-five acres.

Wheat is the most important among the cultivated cerealia, whether we regard the value of its produce to the agriculturist, or the very important uses to which it may be applied, in culinary, baking and confectionary arts. It has followed the progress of man's civilization, in all the countries suitable to its growth, from the earliest times, and is, probably, coeval with the creation. It was first sown in this country on the Elizabeth islands, in Massachusetts, by Gosnold, in 1602. In 1776 the Hessian fly was introduced in some straw, on the west end of Long Island; from that point it spread at the rate of twenty-five to thirty miles a day, and is now everywhere, and in some places more congenial to it than others, the ravages have become so great as to induce growers to abandon the cultivation of this important grain. Still, prior to 1850, there was an increase in the United States of about fifteen million, six hundred and forty-five thousand, three hundred and seventy-eight bushels.

In 1850 we raised one hundred millon, five hundred and three thousand, eight hundred and ninety-nine bushels, notwithstanding, in some of the largest wheat growing States the crop of 1849 fell far below the average. At the London exhibition there was no wheat exhibited superior to that grown in Genesee county, this State, which received the prize medal.

Now 44,400 lbs. of wheat, grown on twenty-five acres, would be all the farinaceous food required to be consumed by one hundred adult persons in a year, and it would contain

Potass and soda,..	368 pounds.
Lime and magnesia,...	177
Phosphoric acid,..	486
Silica,..	21
Metallic oxides,...	5
Nitrogen,...	1,021
Sulphur and chlorine,.......................................	a fraction.
	2,078

In order, then, to grow a crop of wheat, annually, on the same twenty-five acres, it would be necessary to return these elements removed by the crop; if it is exported, the loss of fertility will be equal to the quantity of valuable chemicals taken away in the wheat.

Rye.—This grain was cultivated in America shortly after the arrival of the English, and yields from twenty to thirty bushels to the acre, weighing from forty-eight to fifty-six pounds. In the aggregate, its production in the United States has decreased four million, four hundred and fifty-seven thousand, except in New York, where, owing to the wheat insect, and demand for distilling, it has increased about forty per cent. This grain has never entered to much extent into our foreign commerce, as we consume it as fast as raised. In 1850 two million, one hundred and forty-four thousand bushels were manufactured into spirituous liquors. This grain delights in a sandy soil, devoid of much vegetable matter, and in which manure is not abundant. The loss of fertility by the export of this grain would not be as much felt as that of wheat. The product of the whole country in 1850, was about fourteen million, one hundred and eighty-eight thousand, six hundred and thirty-seven bushels. The straw is highly esteemed for manure, and is more generally thus applied than that of any other cereal except, perhaps, Indian corn.

Indian corn takes precedence in the United States in the scale of crops, and is probably much better adapted to the soil and climate than any other, besides furnishing to the people much the largest percentage of nourishing food. It is of American origin, and is found growing from the Rocky Mountains to Paraguay. It was first cultivated as a crop on James river, in Virginia, in 1608; the yield then was a thousand fold. When properly cultivated east of the Rocky Mountains, the yield varies from 25 to 135 bushels per acre. The increase of production from 1840 to 1850 was two hundred and fourteen millions of bushels, about fifty-six per cent. In Illinois the increase has been equal to sixty per cent. In 1851 we exported three million, four hundred and twenty-six thousand, eight hundred and eleven bushels, and a million of barrels of Indian meal, and manufactured eleven and a half million of bushels in spirituous liquors. In 1850 the crop grown amounted to five hundred and ninety-two million, three hundred and twenty-six thousand, six hundred and twelve bushels; in every forty-four thousand pounds of which, were the elements of fertility, in sufficient quantity to enrich twenty-five acres of land, from which may be deduced the loss of fertility to the amount of the quantity exported and manufactured. The corn stalks, fortunately, remain upon the farm, and form a principal ingredient in the composition of barn-yard manure, and is found very valuable, not so much, perhaps, from the nourishment which it is of itself capable of imparting to the soil, as from the value it acquires, by combining with excrement, and absorbing urine, in its different stages of decomposition.

The oat crop may justly be considered one of the most important that we raise, when we take into consideration the improvement and nourishment it affords to live stock. This grain was first sown by Gosnold, on Elizabeth Island, Massachusetts, in 1602. It is a hardy grain, growing in climates too hot and too cold for wheat or rye. Like rye, it has not entered to a great extent into our foreign commerce, as the consumption at home has generally been equal to the quantity raised. In 1845, 1846 and 1847, during the famine in Ireland, occasioned by the rot in potatoes, we exported a larger quantity than ever before or since. In the year 1850, the total produce of the United States amounted to one hundred and forty-six million, six hundred and seventy-eight thousand, eight hundred and seventy-nine bushels.

Barley has never been exported largely from this country, as we consume all we raise for the manufacture of spirituous liquors. Gosnold, likewise, introduced this grain. And although it is indigenous to the regions bordering on the torrid zone, it flourishes near the fiftieth parallel of north latitude. In 1850 we raised five million, one hundred and sixty-seven thousand, one hundred and sixteen bushels. This crop not being exported, the loss of fertility to the soil is not great, as the straw is generally returned to the field from which the crop is taken.

Buckwheat is cultivated throughout the civilized world, and affords a delicious article of diet to a very large portion of the human family. It is also found to be an excellent food for milch cows. It has never entered into the list of our exportations, and is, consequently, an important enricher of the soil. We grew in 1850, eight million, nine hundred and fifty-six thousand, nine hundred and sixteen bushels.

Tobacco assuredly exhibits one of the most striking features in man's history. It is indigenous to the tropical regions, and was cultivated by the savages. When Columbus arrived, in 1492, he was invited by an Indian chief, on the Island of Cuba, to take a smoke. Its importance in commerce, and the many modes of employing it to gratify the senses of the poor and rich throughout the world, from the burning sands of Africa to the Arctic regions is amazing. In 1611 it was first cultivated in Virginia, by the use of the spade, and in 1616, its cultivation increased to such an extent that even the public streets in Jamestown were plowed up and planted with it. James the 1st, attempted to restrain its use, but was entirely unsuccessful. Its culture spread from Virginia into Louisiana, Carolina, Georgia and Maryland, and they supplied all Europe. In 1840 the United States raised two hundred and nineteen millions, one hundred and sixty-three thousand, three hundred and nineteen pounds. In 1850, one hundred and ninety-nine millions, seven hundred and fifty-two thousand, six hundred and forty-six pounds. Showing a falling off in its cultivation of nineteen million, four hundred and ten thousand, six hundred and seventy-three pounds. There is no crop grown that has rendered more land sterile than tobacco, as the roots even are removed from the soil.

For manure we mainly depend upon our hay, and fodder crops, including dried Indian corn blades, straw, haulm of peas, beans, &c. The eastern and middle states are the principal raisers of hay, which instead of retaining, they ship in large quantities pressed in bales to southern markets, thus entailing upon our soils loss of fertility by the exportation of our products.

In 1840 the hay crop of the United States was ten millions, two hundred and forty-eight thousand, one hundred and eight tons. In 1850, thirteen millions, eight hundred and thirty-eight thousand, five hundred and seventy-nine tons. Showing an increase of three millions, five hundred and ninety tons.

We raise in the United States, besides the productions named, the following, nearly all of which are exported from the land, to the cost of its fertility : 2,468,624 lbs. of cotton ; 52,788,174 lbs. of wool ; 9,219,975 bushels of peas and beans ; 65,796,793 bushels of Irish potatoes ; 38,259,-196 bushels of sweet potatoes ; 7,723,326 bushels of orchard products ; 221,240 gallons of wine ; 5,269,930 bushels garden productions ; 313,266,-962 lbs. of butter ; 105,535,219 lbs. of cheese ; 468,977 bushels of clover seed ; 416,811 bushels of timothy and other seed ; 3,496,029 lbs. of hops ; 7,715,961 lbs. of flax ; 462,312 bush. of flax seed ; 10,843 lbs. of cocoons ; 34,249,886 lbs. of maple sugar ; 247,581 hhds. of cane sugar ; 12,700,606 gallons of molasses ; 14,853,857 lbs. of beeswax and honey. $27,481,399 is the value of home manufactures ; $109,485,757 is the value of slaughtered animals.

The loss of fertility by the exportation of crops, will be shown by the following table of the average produce of nutritive substances of different kinds from an acre of the ordinary cultivated crops, in the order that I have mentioned them :

	Gross produce.		Woody fibre.	Starch, sugar.	Gluten.	Oil.	Saline matter.
	Bush.	Pounds.	Pounds.	Pounds.	Pounds.	Pounds.	Pounds.
Wheat, ...	25	1,500	225	825	220	50	30
Rye, ...	25	1,300	130	780	190	40	13
Indian corn, . . .	30	1,800	270	900	216	170	27
Oats, ...	40	1,700	340	850	230	95	60
Barley, ...	35	1,800	270	1,080	216	45	36
Buckwheat, ...	30	1,300	320	650	180	5	21
	Tons.						
Meadow hay, . . .	1½	3,400	1,020	1,360	240	170	220
Wheat straw, . .	. .	3,000	1,500	900	40	15	150
Rye straw, ...	. .	4,000	1,800	1,500	53	20	120
Oat straw, ...	. .	2,700	1,210	950	36	20	135
Barley straw, . .	. .	2,100	1,050	630	28	16	105

The following table will show the quantities of the elements of food removed from one hundred acres of land by the usual system of farming ; and the quantities which would be returned by one hundred adult persons :

	Twenty-five acres of wheat.	Twenty-five acres of barley	From the land in the flesh of forty lambs, weighing 90 lbs. each.	Four young cows.	Excretions of 100 adult persons returned to the soil.
	lbs.	lbs.	lbs.	lbs.	lbs.
Nitrogen,.....................	1,860	1,030	128	23	2,312
Sulphur and chlorine, ...	Trace.	Trace.	12	......	87
Metallic oxides, ...	4	......	4	......	6
Silica.	30	420	......	......	166
Potash and soda.................	470	395	8	4	827
Phosphoric acid,................	680	430	210	42	1,713
Lime and magnesia, ...	350	225	144	250	3,158

This table shows conclusively, that if all the excrementitious matters of our population could be returned to the soil, instead of being wasted in the rivers, it would maintain in fertility as many acres as there are inhabitants. The refuse of New York contains an immense quantity of valuable substances not included in the above table.

For example, refuse from manufactories, alkali contained in soap makers waste, manure of cows, pigs, cattle, horses, blood from the butchers' shambles, etc.

And if we were permitted to use these manures, the amount of food which a given field could be made to yield, would depend upon the crop raised. For instance, thirty bushels of wheat will produce fourteen hundred pounds of extra flour, while a crop of twelve thousand pounds of potatoes will give four thousand four hundred pounds of agreeable mealy food. Thus you perceive the gross weight of production in the one case is three times what it is in the other.

You will find further, that if you enrich two fields precisely alike, and grow upon one grass, and upon the other potatoes, turnips, or cabbages, you will have three times as much food from the latter as from the former. But from experience, notwithstanding more food is raised by cultivating the land to arable purposes, and more persons may be sustained by it, yet, more money may be made by converting the land into meadow, particularly where a ready market is at hand for the hay, and where an abundance of manure can be obtained to top dress the meadow, annually. Farmers at a distance, from hay markets, will find it more profitable to rear and fatten cattle, and make butter and cheese, than to raise and export the fertility of their lands in the shape of cereal grains. Farmers find that the influence of seasons have a great effect upon crops, and cannot be overcome; the enormous crop of one year may not be gathered the next, because a warm, cold, wet, or dry season may interfere with its growth. And yet science seems to say that superior husbandry and experimental research, will do much, even here, to prevent intelligent and diligent agriculturists from meeting with failures.

Mr. Pardee proposed, as subjects for next meeting, "Spring flowers," "Seeds, plants and trees."

Wm. Lawton inquired if there could not be created, from the soil and air, a power of recuperation, to balance the loss of exportation of fertility with grain, and other products. He said: I believe that a simple process would restore fertility to waste places. He even thought Canada thistles a blessing, rather than a curse, and that a growth of them would serve to restore fertility to worn out fields. Mr. Lawton eloquently said, that the land within twenty miles around this city, ought to be made beautiful, lovely homes, so happy as to prevent the people from running away to distant regions, as they now do.

Andrew S. Fuller.—I believe that it is a principle of nature, for all plants to deposit upon the earth enough to keep up fertility. Look at forests. The first growth was upon sterile land, and a continuous growth has enriched the earth. If we will keep and apply all straw to the land, we can take away the grain. The excrement of any animal will produce more than the animal can consume. This has been proved by experiments, and so it has in the growth of trees. I think that we can export all that others will take from us, if we use the proper means to keep up the fertility of our land. The *larch* put on barren land, soon enriches it, and makes feed for cows. The natural power of plants to enrich land enables us to spare some of its products without loss of fertility.

Mr. Meigs reminded the club of the enriching doctrine and practice of the admired John Taylor, of Caroline, Virginia, whose little manual, the "Arator," (plowman,) deserves immortality. He converted the barrens, caused by a depraved wasting tillage, into thirty bushels of wheat acres. He put everything into the soil, except its mere fruit and grain; every leaf, bit of wood, weed, straw, stump—everything. He thought we could have the grain only, the tender leaf of cabbage only, *not the stumps and coarse parts*, nor the skins of apples, or stems, or cores, but the flesh of the apple only, &c. Another wise and good man, James Madison, after his presidential term expired, became president of a farmers' club (agricultural society), and there taught a doctrine in agriculture which I cannot forget, viz: "That God ordered it that on level lands, bearing forests for ages, could not create a soil over *about one foot deep*, because having created man of such a size that he could *till that depth with his spade or plow, and no more.* That the deep soils washed into the vallies are only exceptions, and of no use." Indeed, we have found, lately, that when, on some of the worn out soils, cultivated hitherto four inches deep, we thoroughly spade up, or plow, ten inches deep, we find fertility in it.

Mr. Pardee was glad to see lessons on fertility increasing in value, and hoped we should soon have a system of undoubted rules as to manures.

Mr. John P. Veeder.—Every resource that is at hand I find important, and necessary, to apply, to keep up fertility—everything to increase the bulk of manure. Quantity is more important than the time of application. Any vegetable matter added to the manure, I find profitable. So I dig much from the swamp, and I have made an accumulation of nearly three feet deep of good compost, in one season, in my barnyard. In some sandy soils, plants can find no substance to live upon, yet will grow well when the necessary pabulum is added. Then it is not worth while to transfer the muck from worthless swamps to worthless sandy plains, to enable them to produce useful vegetation.

Benjamin F. Pike.—I have used all the muck and scrapings I can obtain, to increase my compost in my barnyard, and I collect all the drainage water from the road that I can, and hold it in a cistern, to moisten my compost heap. The overflowing waters of the cistern I convey to a pond, the sediment all being retained in the cistern, and is pumped up on to the manure heaps, and any excess runs back again into the same reservoir, so that nothing is lost. By my pump, too, I can irrigate a portion of my farm with this liquid manure, the value of which I am well satisfied of, having used it for many years. I have never seen as good asparagus anywhere, as I have grown by the use of liquid manure. I have also found great advantage from irrigation from a mountain stream. One advantage of my cistern supplied by open drain, is that it washes in a great many seeds of weeds, which are there destroyed.

Mrs. Elizabeth Langdon, of Long Island, who owns over 300 acres at Thompson, gave a little of her experience in farming. She stated that she had broken up thirty-seven acres of scrub oak land, and tried to demonstrate what a woman could do at farming. I have planted pears, and other fruit trees, and have succeeded admirably. I find no difficulty in growing anything that I wish. My grapes are doing very well, and so are all small fruits, particularly the Lawton blackberry. My potatoes have done well on the scrub oak land, cleared in the February before planting the crop. Clover grows beautifully, and so do all kinds of grass. As soon as the oak roots are rotten, I use the subsoil plow. In plowing out the roots, I use a large plow, that runs near a foot and a half deep. My great object has been to show that a woman can live upon a farm, and conduct her own affairs, and that these cheap lands of Long Island, offer good, healthy situations for making comfortable homes. She thought that some of the feeble women of the city, might improve their health by just such a course as she is pursuing. Mrs. Langdon believed that fruits and flowers could be better managed by ladies than men; that as much open air exercise in garden and farm would increase the health and strength of the fair sex, she was satisfied as to her own experience. She had expended, in her farm and garden, about ten thousand dollars, and was determined to try the establishment of an agricultural school, or college, for ladies only, at her place. She requested the club to send committees to examine and report on her farm and garden.

THE BAKER APPLE.

Solon Robinson presented specimens of the Baker apple, a very handsome red fruit, highly aromatic, and something like the Baldwin apple in size and color. Mr. Robinson stated that it was one of the best apples, for all purposes, that he was acquainted with, being good to eat out of hand, and good to cook. It is remarkably good when baked, and is universally esteemed where known, which is only in a little circle near where it originated, in Ridgefield, Conn.

The club then adjourned.

H. MEIGS, *Secretary.*

February, 14, 1859.

Present—Messrs. R. L. Pell, Dr. Holton, Prof. Nash, Dr. Crowell, Chilson, Stacey, Hon. John G. Bergen, Adrian Bergen, Roberts, Pardee, Solon Robinson. Witt, Hardenbrook, Fuller, Burgess, sen., and Burgess, jr., Doughty, Benjamin Pike—48 in all.

Robert L. Pell in the chair. Henry Meigs, secretary.

Secretary Meigs read papers selected and translated by him, viz.:

[Bulletin Mensuel de la Societe Imperiale Zoologique d'Acclimatation. Dec., 1858.]

WOOL.

The history of the Angora goat is given. It descends from the magnificent Buck of Falcona, which originated in the high mountains of Thibet; then to the central plains of Asia; from Armenia to Chinese-Tartary, from whence, through Chang-Hai, it is exported, both raw and manufactured. At the Exhibition of all Nations, London, there was Angora wool from the Kalmouk territory, on the river Don, between the Black sea and the Caspian, north of Caucasus. These goats are scattered all over the surface of Asia. They arrived in Asia Minor, in the 11th and 12th centuries, along with the Turks. It was totally unknown to the ancients.

Belon, the naturalist, in the 16th century, first made it known, describing its fleece as fine as silk, and white as snow; used to make camlets. The goat fattens as easily as a sheep. Repeated observations shows that there is no similarity to our common goat in them. It is said to be impossible to transform, by crossing, common sheep into Merinos. Now, Læhner, in his remarkable *Anleitung zur Schafzucht*, declares, that after successive generations of crosses, the original type reappears the moment you cease to use the pure blood Merino rams.

Angora produces, annually, from about 500,000 goats, near one million and a half pounds of wool, much of which is made into strong cloth, for men, fine cloth, for women, and for stockings and gloves. The rest of this wool all goes to England. Some think this is below the truth. The flesh of this goat is valued as being infinitely better than that of the common goat. They carry young five months, and seldom bear more than two young ones.

The Spanish government made the first importation of them.   In 1765, they disappeared, and in 1787, the president de la Tour d'Aignes introduced several hundred of them, from the lower Alps, upon the Leberon chain.   These flourished under the guardianship of their Turkish masters, who came to Spain with them, in order to teach the methods of spinning and weaving their wool.   The unfortunate Louis XVI, about the close of last century, imported them to Rambouillet.   Ferdinand VII, had a hundred of them at his *El Retiro* park, in 1830.   In 1849, Dr. J. B. Davis, of South Carolina, imported there six females, and two rams; in 1855, he had fifty of pure blood.   These goats prefer hay to grass.

PEACH WOOD FOR FUEL.

The "Prairie Farmer," Chicago, Illinois, Feb. 3, 1859.   S. M. G. says his fine peach orchard was killed by the cold of 1855–1856.   He left the trees standing till the following winter.   The wood was then thoroughly seasoned, and he used it as fuel, and heard no scolding in the house all that winter, about wood.   It is excellent fuel, and soon raised.   We have forest trees near us, but we prefer the peach.   For fuel, I would grow the peach trees as near as corn.

Mr. Lawton.—The farmer who may have devoted his life to the cultivation of the soil, following in the footsteps of intelligent progenitors, with satisfactory results, may undervalue science in connection with his business, and, to a superficial observer, with some propriety; but the case is precisely similar to the mechanic arts, in which many unlearned men have acquired great proficiency.   The scientific farmer avails himself quietly and promptly of all the improvements of the age; the merely practical one walks in the beaten track of his forefathers, and, by physical labor, produces satisfactory results, without a proper knowledge of the cause of this success.   The practical and theoretical farmer should be constantly associated, and the mental and physical energies of both thus advance.

Nearly all the results in agricultural labors, have their foundation in certain facts and principles connected with chemistry, and vegetable physiology, which afford the sure means of advancing agriculture almost to perfection.   We would not deny that without a knowledge of principles, much has been done, but rather regret that science had not shortened the method and labor.   The subject under discussion this day, is deeply interesting to a large class of persons, who, in their yearnings for a rural life, have their little farms, which must be made productive to enable them to retain their homes in the country, while a large portion of their time is passed in the business walks in life of our towns and cities.   Let us, then, take into consideration a proper preparation of the soil for all crops, the adaptation of crops for the nearest market, and our wants; and this brings us at once to drainage, which, on a bottom of loamy soil, is almost as indispensable to the health of the farmer, as to his success in cultivation. We cannot expect that the whole of even a small farm will be immediately drained by two inch tiles, in the approved method now adopted.   Where we have stiff, clay soils, we have generally plenty of stone; in such cases, the best drains can be formed with these stone, by making them five feet deep, and one hundred feet apart, and filling in three feet with stone. The value and necessity of drainage, is a fixed fact, and no further experiments are required; all the farmer has to consider, is economy in the method and adaptation to his position, and the profile of his grounds.

Except for line fences, or woodland, I would remove division fences upon small farms, and depend upon stall feeding for all my stock; and thus gradually, by drainage and subsoiling, bring every acre in proper condition for the most profitable crops. The word *adaptation* should be constantly presented to the mind of the agriculturist, taking in view, geographical position, facilities for markets, and their extent for various products of the garden and farm; and it will require but a little reflection to adapt the cultivation of both to the most profitable results.

In this connection may be considered the rural embellishment of the farm by the proper cultivation of valuable fruit trees, and by the grouping and arrangments of trees and shrubbery, so as to produce ample returns of delicious fruit, for home consumption and sale, and the luxurious enjoyment of shade and fragrance, without impairing the productiveness, to a great extent, of the soil which sustains them.

Much has been said of our " worn out lands," and " exhausted soils;" and when nature has garnered, for ages, her rich deposits of nitrogen, in connection with all the fertilizing properties with which it is always connected in our soils, we have rudely broken in upon those rich treasures, and wantonly and carelessly used them, by the sale of our crops, so as to prepare this beautiful portion of the globe for a desert, instead of a rich and glorious inheritance for our successors. Are we continuing this system, so unbecoming, and in mockery of the intelligence of the age? or are there remedies, by change of crops, and compensating principles (if I may use the expression), by which changes may be effected to perpetuate, for ever, the productiveness of all soils for the needful fruits to sustain life?

Mr. John V. Brower, of Jersey city, exhibited a sample of pumpkin meal or flour, from a manufactory recently established there. The pumpkin is taken freshly ripe, subjected to a drying process which extracts all the moisture, leaving all the saccharine, so that when wanted for pies, &c., milk only is added, and no water, making a superior pie. Squash is also manufactured. All the refuse, skins, seeds, &c., are separately treated for feed to stock.

Solon Robinson.—We have had that before.

Prof. Nash.—It is not new. I wish, if the Club pleases, to say a few words more on drainage, before we take up the subject of the day. Draining land constitutes a *special study of every acre.* No two are in *all respects alike.* A farmer should avail himself of all the knowledge he can get adapted to his particular case. The adopted practice of deep tile or other drainage, costs too much to be done by our farmers. I talked with an intelligent farmer in Buckinghamshire, England, lately, on this subject. He showed me his whole operation. Divide his farm into plats, four rods square; take a borer, same as we bore post holes with, but a foot in diameter; two men can bore, five feet deep, forty holes on an acre, in one day; fill these holes with small sized pebbles, nearly full, and the land will be drained at the cost of the labor of two men's work and something for putting in the pebbles. A suitable borer can be made for six dollars. In this way we drain an acre completely for less than *five* dollars, in place of probably never less than *forty* dollars the common way. Generally, English farmers have stiff rules and obey them. This was a bold and valuable departure. Very few acres of land need any better drainage than these pebble holes, through which all the surface water perpetually settles below the ordinary roots of our crops.

Hon. John G. Bergen, of Long Island.—We farmers sometimes say of land which will not pay us well for cultivation: *It is sick !* Such lands require Doctor Drainage & Co. to cure them. Much the greater part of our Long Island land is perfectly well and wants no doctor. We should not give out from our Club the idea that no farming can be done on our island without the costly processes of draining. Let particular acres be examined and drained ; the general whole is very well and not sick.

Mr. Pardee.—Still it is perfectly well known to wise agriculturists, that all arable land whatever, as a general rule, is rendered much more valuable by drainage, which, although expensive at first, continues for a very long time to keep that land in order for the best cultivation.

Prof. Nash.—There is very little land like that of Long Island, ever reputed for quick absorption of the rains ; but much land retains too much water near its surface, and all such must be drained. Clay is exceedingly common in soils, and in all ages been covered with soils; then, as a sub-soil, retains too much water, such must be bored through to let the water go below, out of the way of roots of our crops, for none but water plants can stand having their roots in water long. Trenches, deep, by powerful plows, pebbles in the bottoms of them, and the surface soil plowed back to cover the pebbles deep enough to be out of the reach of the common plow-share, make cheap drains, effectual in such lands as have not stiff sub-soil under that. Much soil on the hills of New England are loamy, with gravelly sub-soil, needs no drainage better than it has naturally. On that land the farmer can hoe his corn in thirty minutes after a smart shower. There is but little land, however, anywhere, but what may be greatly benefited by draining.

The Chairman called up the regular subjects.

Mr. Pardee remarked that the selection of those flowers, plants, and trees, best suited for a garden or farm, was of the greatest importance, and not without difficulty in obtaining them. We must not only have best kinds but such as are in full health. Take no peach tree from a nursery or elsewhere, where the yellows exist ; no pear tree where the fruit is poor as the crack in Virgalieu, &c., &c.; have no apples but such as are delicious. Why encumber the garden with an indifferent one, or with a shy bearer instead of an abundant one. I have endeavored to prepare a list of such as I should like to have. Others can add to it.

It is important in selecting trees to get healthy ones. Fruit that will succeed in one place fails in another. There are 1,200 kinds of apples, and 8,000 sorts of pears, and yet a dozen or twenty sorts is all that one wants. There are 60 or 70 sorts of cherries, but half a dozen is all that I would recommend any one man to plant. Large varieties are kept in nurseries, because there are people who are foolish or vain enough to have this great variety.

A New Jersey friend who desired to stock a place of some four acres with useful fruits, shrubs, and flowers, asked me, a short time since, to make out a list of such things as I would plant myself, for family use. Now, as I suppose that some others may be similarly situated, I will read that list for their benefit. It is not perfect, of course, but it will serve as a chart in place of a better one.

The figures prefixed to each name, indicate the number of trees or plants of that sort which I would plant, to make a well proportioned orchard or garden.

Apples.—8 Early Harvest, 2 Red Astrachan, 3 Sweet Bough, 3 Fall Pippin, 2 Gravenstein, 2 Porter, 6 Baldwin, 6 Rhode Island Greening, 2 King Apples, 2 Norton's Melon, 2 Roxbury Russet, 2 Tallman Sweeting—Total 38.

Pears.—2 Beurre Giffard, 2 Madelaine, 1 Osburn's Summer, 3 Bartlett, 6 Duchess D'Angouleme, 3 Flemish Beauty, 3 Seckel, 2 Sheldon, 2 Virgalieu, 3 Easter Beurre, 2 Lawrence—Total 29.

Cherries.—4 Black Tartarian, 1 Black Eagle, 1 Elton, 2 Early Purple Georgia, 2 Yellow Spanish.

Peaches.—2 Crawford Early, 2 Crawford Late, 2 Oldmixon Free, 1 Sweet Water, 2 Morris White.

Quinces.—4 Orange Quince.

Grapes.—2 Catawba, 1 Delaware, 1 Rebecca, 2 Diana, 1 Hartford Prolific, 4 Isabella, 1 Northern Muscadine.

Gooseberry.—6 Houghton's Seedling.

Raspberries.—2 dozen Franconi, 2 dozen Orange, 1 Fastolff.

Strawberries.—100 Boston Pine, 100 Hovey Seedling, 100 Hooker Seedling, 200 Wilson's Seedling.

Rhubarb.—2 Caboon's Mammoth, 1 Victoria.

Roses.—Madam Laffay and La Reine, Geant de Battailes, Baron Caroline de Sausal, Prince Albert, Lord Raglan, Blanch Vibert, Mad. Boranquet, Glori de Dijon, Souvenir de Malmaison, Persian Yellow, Queen of the Prairies, Baltimore Belle, Created Moss and Lanci Moss.

Shrubs.—Wigelia Rosea and Amabalis, Forsythia Virdimence, Spirea Prunifolia, Spirea Reessie, Spirea Sinensis Pendula, Pyrus Japonica, Mahonia Aquifolia, Hardy Azalea, Double Almond, Double Althea Var, Double fl Currant, Siberian Lilac, Large flowering Lilac, Evergreens, Pompone Chrysanthemums, Hardy Phlox, &c.

Ornamental Trees.—Magnolia Glauca, Magnolia Soulangiana, Magnolia, Macrophylla, Magnolia Tripetala, Pawlonia, Copper-leaved Beech, New Weeping Beech, Maple Sycamore, Horse Chestnut, Judas Tree, Purple Fringe Tree, Purple English Oak, Variagated Oak, Ring Willow, Variagated L. Willow, American Linden, Tulip Tree, Curl-leaved Elm, Weeping Elm, Japan Jinko Tree.

Currants.—6 Cherry Currant, 6 Large White Province, 2 Versailles.

Climbers.—8 Variegated Honeysuckles, 1 Glycine, 1 Bigonia Grandiflora, 1 Irish Broad Leaf Ivy.

Peoni.—1 Peonia Albida pleno, Peonia Odorata, Peonia Moutan Banksii.

Plums.—1 Smith's Orlean, 1 Washington, 1 Jefferson.

Apricot.—1 Dubois' Golden, 1 Moorpark, 1 Large Early.

Flowers.—Dielytra Spectabilis, Petunias, Verbenas, Dahlias, &c.

I must add to this list the Lawton Blackberry.

Mr. Lawton.—I find my Black Tartarian cherry very fine. The Early Richmond also; but I think the Black Eagle is an improvement on the Black Tartarian. Bloodgood's Honey cherry is fine.

Solon Robinson.—We should get hold of that delicious grape, the *Ohio Delaware;* it is exceedingly rich, of a medium size, and of a rich purple color.

Mr. J. G. Bergen.—I see no tart cherry on the list.

Mr. Pardee.—That tree is so liable to the *black knot* I cannot recommend it. I have been plagued with it and found no cure. Not even by cutting away branches having it on. My young trees are as liable as others.

Mr. J. G. Bergen.—We have lost our tart cherries by it. It attacked some trees of near 100 *years old!* It got on one of our best cherry trees, the Mayduke.

Mr. Lawton.—I like that cherry. It comes early; is beautiful to look at; ripens nearly ten days before others; and when fully ripe has a dark color and very rich taste.

Mr. Underhill advised putting on the list of good things the *Governor Wood cherry,* named after the Governor of Ohio.

Mr. Pardee.—Its flavor is very fine.

Mr. J. G. Bergen.—I have watched the black knot on my farm, on Long Island. I have tried to get rid of it. I could not. It is as bad as the peach yellow or the Virgalieu *pear crack.*

Mr. Meigs.—Has any insect been found to be the cause of it. I have examined for years in vain. I have found insects in the cavities but I believe they were not the cause of the knot.

Mr. Fuller.—I always find *grubs in the knots!*

Mr. Adrian Bergen.—We of Long Island have sustained a severe loss of our *pie cherries* from the black knot, and we have no cherry yet, or a substitute for it. The knot renders the branches so brittle that they break off very easily by wind, ice, snow, &c. It seems to me to be a disease in the tree which all our art fails to cure, and it is getting into our other kinds of cherry trees.

The season for sowing seed and planting trees and plants will soon be at hand, and it is very important that we should take up this subject early in the season, collect as many facts, draw out as many useful hints upon this branch of science as possible. No good builder would commence laying the foundation of a building without having a plan drawn of its shape, size, and proportion, accompanied with an estimate of its cost, and what is more important, the materials to be used properly selected.

If it is important to the builder to select his materials before commencing his building, it certainly is of the greatest importance to the farmer and gardener to have the materials *selected* with care for the structure he is about to build in the form of trees and plants.

A large majority of cultivators wait until the season arrives for planting before they even enquire where the seed and plants which they want can be obtained. Then often the particular varieties which are wanted most can not be had in their immediate vicinity; if they send to a distant part of of the country to obtain them, they will, in nine cases out of ten, arrive too late in the season to be of any use.

Suppose you want a variety of vegetable seeds to sow in April or May; if obtained now, you can put a few into a flower-pot filled with good soil, and place it in your hot bed or greenhouse; if you have neither of these at your command, the window of a warm room will answer. In a few days you will have an opportunity of seeing what proportion of them are good, and by making a note of the quantity sown, and what per cent, of them were made to grow, you will obtain a guide that will be of service to you when you come to sow your main crop.

Various plans have been given to the public by our agricultural and horticultural journals, by which we might tell good seeds from bad. Many of the plans suggested are valuable; but after several years' experience, we have found no test so good as that of planting a small quantity a few weeks before the general planting time.

The vitality of many kinds of seeds can be readily ascertained by putting them into hot water; the onion, for example, if good, will sprout in a very few minutes, but you can not tell whether the onion will be red, white, or yellow.

We once had a little experience in the onion line; and for the benefit of others we will relate it. We wanted to sow an acre of fine newly cleared land to onions; we went to a seed store and bought a sufficient quantity of red onion seed (so the package was labelled), tried the scalding process, and found them good; sowed them and they came up beautifully; but in a few weeks we were supprised that our acre of red onions was nothing but leeks—a variety of onion that was of no more value to us than so many Canada thistles. There is a slight difference between the common onion seed and the leek, but it would not be noticed by a person unacquainted with the latter.

With some varieties of shrub and tree seeds the process of testing their vitality can not be done quite as readily as with vegetable seeds, as some are covered with a much harder covering, such as the peach, plum, and cherry. With such as these we must resort to some method of expanding this hard, bony covering and make it sufficiently porous to admit moisture, for no seed will grow without it. If we let the seed become so dry that there is not sufficient moisture contained within to keep the pores open, then we must employ some agent that will act either chemically or mechanically in opening them again.

The Locust has often been mentioned as one of that class of seeds that is generally found difficult to make grow; scalding them has been reccommended as the best means of aiding their germinating powers, and very probably it is, although we have never found any difficulty in making the seeds of the yellow locust (Robinia pseudacacia) or the honey locust (Gleditschia tricanthos) grow readily without freezing or scalding, but we gather the seed before they are what is generally termed ripe; the carbonaceous matter which incloses the seed at this time is in a state easily acted upon by moisture, and therefore it offers no impedient to its entering to the germ of the seed.

If the seed of either of these varieties are examined when the pods are just commencing to turn a brown color, they will be found that they are nearly double the size they are when the pods have become dry and fallen from the tree. When such seeds are full grown, they contain all the elements necessary for the proper development into a new individual plant.

The change that takes place after this while on the tree is merely a hardening process, the covering of the seed, as the watery parts are given off, shrinks, closes up the pores, and compresses the albumen into a much smaller space than it was when in a green state. All the seed of leguminous plants undergo this change to a greater degree than any other class we have examined, and to those who have found it difficult to grow this class of seeds we would recommend gathering early. But it must be borne in mind that nature gave them this covering for their protection, and if gathered before it has become fully matured, they will not bear the rough usage or changes of climate as well as when left to thoroughly ripen.

We have practiced this plan of gathering seeds early upon many kinds not leguminous, and in most cases we have been well satisfied with the result. It will be remembered by the Club that I exhibited here last season cones, seed, and plants of the great tree of California (Sequoia giantea); the cones were taken from the tree before they were full grown, and sent with the seeds in them; yet they grew readily, and the young plants to this day are vigorous and healthy.

There has been much disappointment experienced by those receiving evergreen seeds from the Pacific coast, and we would suggest to them to have the cones gathered before they open (but let them be full grown), and have them sent immediately, and we think they will find it cheaper in the end to have them sent in this way although the cost of transportation be considerably more. It is not always the largest and most hardy appearing seeds that preserve their vitality the longest. Some of the most delicate in appearance will keep good to almost an indefinite period. Wheat, taken from the tombs of Egypt, where it had been for at least three thousand years, as it is well known, has been made to grow; but the peach, with its coarse shell, would not, under the same circumstances, remain sound a dozen years. While some may be imbedded in the earth excluded entirely from the air, and yet remain perfectly sound for ages, others, if so treated, would be destroyed in a few hours.

Seed of the same species exhibits a great diversity of character. The sugar-maple (Acer saccharinum) will keep for a year or two with very little trouble, but the silver maple (Acer dusycarpum) with the same care, would become worthless in a few days. The silver maple being one of that class of indigenous trees that ripen their seeds early in the season, Nature designed that they should fall to the earth, take root, and grow to a size sufficient to withstand the rigors of the coming winter; this fact might become the basis of a very good theory, and that is, all trees of our climate that ripen their seeds in the spring or early part of summer must be allowed to grow the same season or not at all. In a majority of cases this would be found correct, but there would be exceptions to this theory as with most others. For instance, the seeds of the American elm (Ulmus americana), if gathered as soon as they commence falling from the tree, and sown immediately, will grow in a few days, and make fine plants by the following autumn; but if allowed to become dry, they will not grow until the next year. Not so with the silver maple; it must grow soon after it comes from the tree, or never; it seems that its life is measured like that of the animal creation. Some writers on vegetable physiology have advanced the theory, that all seeds may be kept under proper care perfectly sound for any length of time we may desire. We hope they will perfect their discovery and let the facts be known, for if there is one branch of agriculture or horticulture upon which we need light more than another, it is this one—the preservation of seeds.

ORNAMENTAL SHRUBS.

Very few really good hardy new shrubs have been brought out in the past year; in fact, we think there is no year in the past ten that has produced so little to attract attention in the way of shrubs as the one just past.

The English and French horticultural papers mention a few, but from the description given we conclude they possess but very little merit.

We have many really splendid varieties that were brought to notice several years ago, that are to this day seldom met with except in the grounds of nurserymen.

The double dwarf white flowering almond is a beautiful plant, and equal in beauty to our old and universal favorite, the pink flowering.

The double red flowering currant, double red Pyrus Japonica, with the Spiræas, Billardii, Calloso, and double Revesii, should not be forgotten by those who are about to ornament their gardens. The Wiegelia, Rosea, and Amabilis are becoming general favorites; there is a new variety, with yellow flowers, said to be very fine.   Many of our native shrubs are worthy of a place by the side of these much admired foreigners, such as the Palmias, Rhododendrons, Clethra, Iteas, Stuartias, Azalias, and a host of others that deserve a place in every garden where shrubs are cultivated.

In roses we have a goodly number of new ones; some improvements have been made in the form of the flowers, but very little in color.   Several new American seedlings have been announced, but it is to be regretted that most of the seedlings raised in this country have to go to Europe, and be there offered for sale, before the people of this country will notice them.

ORNAMENTAL TREES.

With ornamental trees we display the same weakness that we do in many other things, by importing too much.   Living as we do in a country having a greater and more beautiful variety of trees than any other country in the temperate zone on the globe, yet we still cling to that foolish vanity of preferring the trees of foreign lands to those of our own.   With our forty varieties of oak, a dozen or more of poplar, a half dozen of elm, as many of maple, three or four of beech, ten to fifteen of birch, five or six of magnolias, catalpa, tulip tree, Kentucky coffee, liquid amber, with over fifty varieties of evergreen trees, it is very strange that we cannot be suited at home, and give up planting such vile trash as the Ailanthus and silver leaf Abele.

We believe in ornamenting our homes with everything that is either useful or beautiful, whether native or foreign; but this giving preference to a thing that has no other recommendation but that of coming from a foreign country, is simply ridiculous, and we believe there is no nation on earth that displays so much zeal in admiring the products of other countrys as we Americans do.   Better close our seaports at once, and wrap ourselves up in our dignity (if we have enough left), like the Japanese, than to be forever spending our time and money in gathering the production of foreign countries, and *neglecting* those of our own.

GRAPES.

The number of hardy native grapes that have been brought to notice in the past four or five years, is a sure indication that our pomologists are fully awakened to the importance of improving our native varieties.

Over one hundred varieties are now claiming the attention of those who desire to cultivate the grape.   If their numbers increase with the same rapidity for the next ten as they have for the past five years, we certainly shall have no scarcity in number of varieties.

Those who like a very sweet grape will find in the Delaware a perfection of flavor.   The Rebecca, Anna, and several other white varieties, are worthy of special attention.

There is one variety that has been neglected, which we think has some very good qualities—we refer to the Hartford Prolific.   Although it has been several years in cultivation, and the vine can be had very cheap, yet it seems to be but very little known. Perhaps it is owing to the fact of our Pomological Convention passing some very unfavorable resolutions in regard to it; but the *resolutions* did not change the good qualities of the grape.

It is a black grape with medium size bunches, the berry nearly as large as the Isabella, quite sweet, with a musky flavor, perfectly hardy, and ripens the middle to last of August. Its greatest merit is in bearing an immense quantity of fruit under circumstances that many other varieties would not bear at all. It has, however, one fault—that of falling from the bunches as soon as fairly ripe.

CURRANTS.

In size of the fruit at least there is a decided improvement. Among the red varieties that deserve notice are the two varieties of the cherry currant, one with long bunches, the other with larger fruit but shorter bunches, the La Versaillaise, Fertile d'Angers and Red Imperial. The Prince Albert has pale red fruit. Gloire des Sablons is a *new* variety with striped fruit. Imperial Jaune, or yellow Imperial, is a beautiful, large, pale yellow variety. There are several new white varieties, but whether they are superior to our old favorites we are not prepared to say.

There is probably no fruit of our gardens that is so universally neglected as the currant, yet we know of none that shows the effects of good culture as soon. All that is necessary is to give them a good soil. Shortening the young wood, thinning out the old, keep the grass and weeds away from around the plants, and you will be surprised to see the amount of fruit that can be grown on a few rods of land.

There are several new varieties of raspberries, strawberries, pears, and cherries that are worthy of our attention, but we will not weary your patience by noticing them to-day.

Mr. Fuller illustrated on the black board his method of transplanting trees. The hole sometimes five feet deep; the bottom of the hole never left *concave* for that holds water, but always convex on the upper side; that figure tends to convey the surplus water laterally off from the roots, and for better security, I set a tree not in the hole but near to it, so that the hole is my special drain for that tree. Roots standing in too much water are very apt to rot. All bruised roots, big and little, must be cut above the wounds with a perfectly sharp knife! Doing all this you are sure of a good tree and not without it.

Mr. Pardee wished that the Chairman and Mr. Burgess senior, would, at the next meeting, give us more of their theory and practice of draining.

Mr. Fuller.—The Delaware grape vine has been held at three dollars— too much! A too common practice largely prevails of customers to a nursery insisting on great reduction of the prices of all the best plants in it, so that some nurserymen feel compelled to comply, on *pain of having no sales;* consequently the reduction does greatly happen in the *quality of the plants.*

Give your nurseryman *good prices* and you will afterwards, for years, be glad you did, for you will have *noble trees*, and he a *soothed conscience.*

Mr. Lawton spoke of the value of means to restore fertility to exhauted land, or give it to land which never had it, by sowing such plants as will begin in them, such as the Canada thistle, which will open the ground by its roots and rapidly add its organism to the poor land.

Mr. Robinson.—To exterminate them from the land which they have settled in is one of those works of celebrity like those of the fabled *Sisiphus.* For in a good settlement of these thistles, let a smart man set down along side of them and cut them up with his knife for three years, and he shall have a good plenty left! The least bit of root springs up again.

Subjects for next meeting.—"Spring flowers, seeds, plants and trees " continued, and " Drainage."

The Club adjourned.

H. MEIGS, *Secretary.*

February 21, 1859.

Present—Messrs. Pell, Bullock, Bruce, Chilson, Lawton, Solon Robinson, Daniel C. Robinson, Peters, Fuller, Veeder, Gore, J. D. Wright, J. B. Wright, Doughty, B. Pike, Stacey, Roberts, Witt, Hardenbrook, Brower, Pardee, Clark, Jennings, Burgess, sen., Dr. Shelton, Dr. Holton, Prof. Nash—seventy-five members in all.

R. L. Pell in the chair. Henry Meigs, secretary.

[Revue Horticole. Paris, Jan. 1859.]

DES FRUITS VEREUX. (*Wormy Fruit.*)

Fruits with pits are destroyed, in great numbers, by Lepidoptera, (four-winged, their larvæ are caterpillars,) which prick the fruit when it has about one-fourth of its growth, in the month of May (in France), in order to put an egg in each. The insect always selects the finest fruit. From a worm it becomes a caterpillar, then forms a cocoon, then is a butterfly. The most common enemy is *Carpocapsa Pomona*, whose butterfly is hardly larger than the winged moth which has fed on woolen cloth. Whether the fruit stays on its branch or falls off, is immaterial in the development of this insect. What makes it the most disastrous enemy of garden fruit, is that immediately after its birth, which always precedes the complete maturity of most pears and apples, it begins to lay its eggs, and this causes greater damage than the first generation did. The larvæ thus laid, towards the end of summer, hide in the crevices of bark, in their cocoons, till next season. The only way to save our fruit from their ravages, is to hunt for and destroy them, in every tree. Perseverance will do it. Small trees are easily saved ; large ones are more difficult, and ought to be examined twice a day from May to the harvest, and to make it a law not to leave a fallen fruit on the ground ; there the worm crawls out, if the season be unfavorable, becomes a chrysalis, and a butterfly next May.

Lately entomologists have discovered another fruit enemy of *pit-fruits*, a very small insect, the *Tipula*. The female puts an egg into the head of pear, when it is as large as a hazel-nut. The worm, of *microscopic size*, opens a gallery to the centre of the fruit, and afterwards makes another gallery leading out of the pear; it falls, and the worm buries itself in the earth, and afterwards becomes a butterfly. the *perfect insect.* Raise the soil around the trees, and Tipula is destroyed, for he is only two centimeters (seven-eighths of an inch) deep, and cannot escape when covered deeper. YSABEAU.

[From the London Times.]
THE UPS AND DOWNS OF WHEAT.

Mr. C. Wren Hopkins writes to the Times: "For a period of no less than thirty-two years, ever since 1827, the price of wheat has moved in quadrennial periods. Four years up and four years down, with a regularity so steady and invariable that it is difficult to cast one's eyes over the scale of "annual averages" and escape the impression that it is a perfect natural cycle.

"No expression of words will do justice like the diagram of annual prices. It is as follows:"

From 1827 to 1831, price rose from.....58s. to 66s.

    1831 to 1835, price fell from.....66s. to 58s., 52s., 46s., and 39s.

    1835 to 1839, price rose from.....48s. to 55s., 64s., 70s.

    1839 to 1843, price fell from.....66s. to 64s., 57s., 50s.

    1843 to 1847, price rose from.....50s. to 51s., 54s., 69s.

    1847 to 1851, price fell from.....50s. to 44s., 40s , 38s.

    1851 to 1855, price rose from.....41s. to 53s., 72s., 74s.

    1855 to 1859, price fell from.....69s. to 56s., to the lower rate.

In the retrospect of the prices long ago, we find these ebbs and flows of prices recorded, but not so exactly in quadrennial periods.—H. MEIGS.

A NEW MOWING MACHINE.

Chester Bullock of Jamestown, New York.. exhibited a model of a new plan of mowing machine. The blades work from the point in such a manner as to give a more perfect, shear-cutting motion. The idea is that it will work with less power, and will not clog in any kind of grass.

AN IMPROVED REAPING MACHINE

Which is claimed to be an improvement upon Jerome's machine, was exhibited. One of the principal improvements is, the raker sits upon a seat and rakes the grain off, so as to be out of the way of the next round.

Prof. Nash explained that the principle upon which nearly all mowing machines cut, is that of shears, whether the knives move on a bar or swing from a pivot at the point or heel. He thought there must be a positive advantage in the principle of Mr. Bullock's machines. The motion gives a greater drawing out.

FRUITS, TREES, FLOWERS, &c.,

R. G. Pardee.—Every one would engage in growing fruits and flowers, if each thought he could excel in any one thing. That is the stimulus to grow something that is better than he has grown before, or better than any of his neighbors can grow? Perhaps to gain a great notoriety as the producer of a new seedling, new rarity, or more perfect fruit or flower. The great lack of every one is the want of knowledge how to do—how to plant, cultivate, and produce. It is just about as easy to do this thing well as ill, if one only knew how. Gardening is a kind of work particularly suited to females. One of the best hands I ever knew at budding, grafting, and pruning, was a woman. And it is the duty, as it is the privilege of every woman who has a little spot of ground, to learn how to cultivate fruit and flowers. They should inform themselves so as to be able to excel. It is very easy. It is not necessary to pay a gardener, or buy largely of seeds. Each one should know how. And then only hire a laborer, that the employer could tell how to work, as well as a woman can, or should tell the servant in the kitchen.

Mr. Burgess, a practical gardener.—In relation to planting trees I would always fill the bottom of the hole a foot deep with stones, shells, or rubble, and break down the edges of the hole. When the tree is set in place and the roots all carefully straightened out and bedded in the soft, fine earth, I lay a couple of rods across each other and over the roots, and stake them down. This makes the tree stand firm, and obviates, the need of a post to support the body. If the ground is trenched all over, the trees may be set with less care about rubble in the holes.

Starting seeds early, can be done in thumb pots, under bell glasses. Always put sand in the bottom of pots or boxes in which you start seeds. Put good clean soil in the box to plant seed in. The soil must be kept moist and warm. Seeds start best in darkness. I lay a slate over seed boxes. That gets warm without letting the sun shine directly on the earth. The slate should not cover the box or pot tightly. I would set trees the first week in October. It is an excellent rule to adopt in setting trees, of "a southerly wind and a cloudy sky," for the air is moist, and the roots do not dry up so fast as in weather when the air is dry.

RAISING MELONS.

R. G. Pardee.—I wish Mr. Burgess would tell us how he has managed to grow very fine melons.

Mr Burgess.—When my ground is prepared all right, by deep digging, and manuring with fine compost, I set four bricks, and plant the seeds between, with a sheet of glass over. Pinch off the heart of the plant, when you get three leaves, and that will make the roots stronger, and throw out laterals, which always produce the finest fruit. As soon as a melon begins to give off aroma, pick it off and take it to a cool dry place, in a fruit room, and set it on a slate, stone or brick, and cover it with an earthen pot, and it will greatly improve its quality. I have so kept a melon thirteen days, and have used seed thirteen years old.

Mr. Pardee.—A successful grower of melons of my acquaintance throws out the earth of a large hole and suns it, and then throws it back another day, and so on several times; and before planting he puts a lot of good, fine manure in the bottom, so that the hill is a little higher than the ground around; then plants the seed as Mr. Burgess does, and always carefully pinches out the center buds of the first stalk, and also the laterals, when two or three feet long.

Mr. Wright, a farmer of New Jersey, gave his experience in raising melons. He said that he was careful not to raise the hills; he would prefer to have the hills a little below rather than above.

Mr. Burgess.—It would improve the melons to cover the ground thinly with straw for vines to run over.

Andrew S. Fuller.—I agree with Mr. Burgess about his mode of planting melons, and setting trees. He presented illustrations to show how trees may be anchored down with hooked stakes. Also the plan of digging holes with a cone-shaped bottom, so as to give the lateral roots a chance to run deeper than the bottom of the hole under the tree, and also drains away the water from the tree. His plan of staking down the roots obviates all necessity of setting up a post and tying the tree to it, or using wires to brace the tree as is common in France. No injury occurs to the roots from the stakes, if driven firmly, so as to hold the roots fast on the ground.

TRANSPLANTING PINE AND OTHER TREES.

Mr. Veeder.—I have many trees upon my place, and of late I have been very successful. I once lost 99 out of 100 pines. Now I lose few, if any. The pine tree must be carefully taken up. Cut the roots all smooth, with a square of earth attached to the roots. Use no manure. It grows best in sandy or poor soil. From May 15 to August 1 is the best time in the latitude of Albany. I have been successful in transplanting all sorts of forest trees. I am careful to dig large holes, and put the top soil with the roots. If the hole is in sod, I invert the sods at the bottom. Sometimes I borrow good earth from some other place. I am careful to embed the roots in fine earth. Afterward, I pour on a pail of water if the earth is very dry. I tramp down the earth hard above the roots. I seldom cut off a branch of a fruit or forest tree in transplanting. I have the best success in not pruning, and I never stake a tree. I put weight of earth enough on the roots to hold them firmly. If drouth comes on, I always use mulching. Transplanting requires a great deal of care and attention, but by it I have a grove of 6,000 or 7,000 trees to protect my house from cold winds. I only use water to compact the earth around the small roots.

GERMINATION OF SEEDS.

Mr. Pell addressed the Club upon the subject. Moisture, air and heat are all required to make any seeds germinate. Soil, mechanically speaking, ranges from rocks to powder, and it is that kind of soil best fitted to give the requisites to the seeds that will cause them to germinate readily. Some soils may be supplied with water but destitute of air. Another may be supplied with air and no water. Soil that make seeds germinate be t, makes plants grow best throughout. Soil must be finely pulverized, and light and porous. All soil must have moisture and air freely passing through it to be in a healthy condition. Pulverization and draining are the indispensable requisites in the preparation of any soil to get it in a perfect condition. It is one of the most valuable improvements in agriculture. We can easily see that fine pulverization is of the utmost importance to the ready germination of seeds, and why not see the same necessity for keeping the soil in the same condition throughout the growing season ?

The hour of adjournment having arrived, Mr. Pell postponed a continuation of his remarks until next week, when the discussion of the subject of tree planting, fruits and flowers and draining will be continued.

Solon Robinson moved that, " How and when to prune grape vines" should be added, as many persons are anxious just now for information upon that subject.

Mr. Burgess.—I get boxes which have been used to hold tin plates for *three cents* each, and use them to start plants in—they last several years. In England I got a silver medal for my melons, *Persian*, like the Cantelope somewhat. I kept the seed *thirteen* years. When the melons were ripe I put them in a dark cellar on *slates*, and each melon covered by an earthen pot for thirteen days. (It will not do to lay them on wood, unless that was perfectly dry; on other wood the melons would be tainted with the smell of the wood, *as of pine*, for inst nce.) At the end of the thirteen days they are in a perfect order for table. For such melons I got the silver medal and the applause, with hurrah ! three times three. I kept the seed in cartridge paper and that in a tight tin box.

Mr. Fuller, in answer to questions.—A tree dislikes confinement by being tied to stakes, or otherwise. It demands *all that exercise which the winds give it*, from its root to its topmost branch ! Its bark is often hurt by ties to stakes. And trees with stakes *don't look well* on a lawn, or elsewhere.

J. D. Wright.—Is it a good practice to put potatoes in the hole with the roots ?

Mr. Fuller.—No ! Never put in any raw, crude, vegetable matter. I have now got some new and very choice Camellias, from France; much valued.

Mr. Lawton.—The Camellias of our distinguished friend Marshall P. Wilder, have sold—a single plant—as high as $250.

Mr. Pell spoke on the germination of seeds.

The term germination is applied to the phenomena through which seed passes after having reached the state of maturity. Unripe seeds rarely germinate, for the reason that their parts are not prepared to combine chemically, on which germination mainly depends. Close examination has incontestibly proved that germination essentially consists of numerous chemical changes, which, for their development, require the presence of a certain amount of heat, moisture, and air ; and to comprehend these processes, it is necessary we should understand the conditions under which they act. After discovering these, we will comprehend precisely what is necessary to make a seed grow successfully. These, we have seen, are moisture, air, and heat ; consequently, whenever a seed is so placed, germination must take place.

Soil does not act chemically in the process of germination, but is merely the vehicle through which a constant supply of moisture, heat and air may be kept up.

Keeping this statement in view, we can readily understand the conditions of soil necessary to influence the future prospect of the crops. We must, therefore examine into the mechanical relations of soil. This can best be done by the aid of figures.

Soil, mechanically speaking, consists of particles, which assume all sizes and forms, from rocks to stones, pebbles, and finally, powder ; in all which stages they are of such irregular shape that they cannot possibly lie so close together as to prevent passages between them, owing to which fact soil, in the mass, is always porous. I have frequently placed the smallest particle of which soil is composed, under the magnifier, and have invariably found it porous, and generally composed of broken vegetable tissue. Even the finest dust from the road-side, presented every imaginable variety of structure and shape.

Fig. 1.

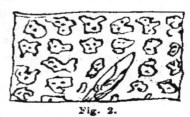

Fig. 2.

Fig. 3.

Fig. 4.

You will observe delineated on the black-board, four figures, giving a rude representation of what the glass exhibited to me in my examinations of soil, by which I may be enabled partially to illustrate the properties of soil, mechanically speaking.

By examining figure 1, you will observe that there are two classes of pores, consisting of large ones, which may be seen between the particles of earth, and the small ones, which occur by themselves; while the large pores form canals between themselves, the small ones have no direct connection with the pore sof the encircling particles. The effect is, as you perceive in figure 1, that the pores and canals are all perfectly empty, the soil being dry, and consequently permitting the canals to communicate at the surface with the air, and thus filling them with it. In this condition you observe the seed *a*, which is abundantly supplied with air, but no moisture, consequently it cannot grow.

In figure 2, you will notice that both canals and pores are filled with water, which has completely taken the place of atmospheric air, and the soil may justly be denominated wet, the seed is therefore thoroughly supplied with water, but no air, consequently it cannot germinate. This never exactly occurs, for the reason that water dissolves air, to some extent, and the seed does germinate under certain circumstances, but not by any means so advantageously as it would if the soil was in a better condition.

Figure 3 presents a very different state of soil. The canals, being open, are admirably supplied with air, while, at the same time, the pores are completely filled with water. The seed *a*, therefore, has sufficient air from the canals, and an abundant supply of water, as every particle of soil coming in contact with it abounds with this necessary quality. This may then be considered the exact condition of soil requisite for every period of the plant's growth, and invariably occurs when the soil is merely moist, but not wet, and when it presents the appearance of being well watered, and will still crumble in the hand without attaching particles to it.

Figure 4 presents for your consideration another condition of a healthy soil, as far as water is concerned, as it is moist, but not wet, the pores only being supplied with water. Still there are only a few canals, the soil having adhered together, and so shut out the interstitial canals that they present the appearance of pores. This may be termed an uncultivated clod, into which the roots of plants are incapable of extending their fibres.

I will now apply the four conditions of soil represented to you, practically, so that you may ascertain when they occur on your farms, and how to obviate them.

The first condition, then, generally occurs in coarse sand, which contains few pores, and wide canals, owing to the large size of individual particles, which allows a free circulation of air, and consequent dryness. In this case I would permit all the stones found on the surface to remain, as they retain evaporation by casting shades.

Figure 2 represents a condition of soil that occurs much more frequently in nature, than figure 1. When a quantity of water is added to a dry soil, it immediately fills the interstitial canals, and then enters the pores of each individual particle, which if the supply is not excessive, soon empty the canals, and thus form a perfectly healthy condition of soil. If the supply of water is very great through the medium of a spring, or otherwise, the canals become filled, as well as the pores, and form what may be called an undrained soil, when the whole entire process of germination of the seed is interfered with. At this period thorough draining is absolutely essential if you would improve your soil. Excess of water always reduces the temperature of the earth to the extent of seven degrees fahrenheit in summer, which is fully equivalent to an elevation above the ocean of two thousand feet. And in the winter the temperature is very high, whereas there should be a difference between summer and winter of at least thirty-five degrees to produce vigor in vegetation. If a soil is excessively wet, the thermometer will vary throughout the year about ten degrees. Complete draining, and thorough pulverization of the soil, will entirely overcome all these difficulties, by establishing a direct communication between the drains and interstitial canals—thus rendering it impossible for water to remain in the canals, without finding the drains by gravitation.

Figure 4 certainly indicates a soil badly cultivated, in which unbroken clods, but little better than rocks exist, being not only impermeable to the fibres of plants, but even the atmosphere. Therefore it would be impossible to say too much in favor of completely pulverizing the soil ; even the most thorough draining will not supersede the absolute necessity of properly and effectually performing this necessary operation. The acknowledged superiority of garden, over field cultivation, is referable to the great perfection to which pulverizing is carried. The celebrated Jethro Tull was the first man who directed the farmers attention to this important subject. He imagined that the use of manure might be entirely superseded by pulverizing effectually. The success of drill husbandry is owing to the fact that the soil becomes well stirred during the progress of the crop, which pulverizing increases the number and size of the interstitial canals. In conversation with a farmer some time since, he remarked that the interstitial canals must be so small, that their amount could be of very little consequence. I replied that in a soil only half pulverized, they amount to not less than a quarter of the whole bulk of the soil, and that two hundred cubic inches of moist soil (that is to say. one in which the pores are full of water, while the canals are filled with air,) contain at least fifty cubic inches of air. If this calculation be correct, in a field pulverized to the depth of eight inches, every acre will retain under its surface 25,090,560 cubic inches of air. You are all aware that a disturbed soil more than fills the space it previously occupied. Deep pulverization, combined with a thorough system of drainage, is without doubt one of the most valuable improvements in modern agriculture, and is particularly applicable on all soils lying upon retentive subsoils. Before the introduction of this principle, such soils were exceedingly difficult to manage, but after being drained, and pulverized by the subsoil plow, they became very valuable, easily tilled, and produced remunerating crops, from the fact that in time of drought they retained a greater supply of moisture and nourished the plants well, at the same time they possessed the power of draining off a superabundance of water during excessively heavy rains.

The chemical effect produced by pulverizing the soil is in two ways advantageous; it enables the roots to penetrate to a proper depth, and renders it permeable by atmospheric influence, thus supplying the roots with oxygen gas, and moisture, not only from the soil, but atmosphere. This power to absorb moisture from the air depends upon the division of the particles of soil, their absorbing powers increasing in proportion to the disintegration; when this power is great, moisture is abundantly supplied even during drought. The most fertile and highly cultivated soils possess the greatest absorbent powers. An imperfectly pulverized soil invariably exposes a large surface to the wind and sun, which of course facilitates by evaporation the loss of moisture, and directly aggravates the injurious influence of drought, in every stage of the growth of plants.

We have seen, then, that to insure the growth of the seeds we place in the earth, a proper cultivation of the soil is of the most importance, and that minute pulverization is indispensable to admit air, and drainage to remove superfluous water, which would otherwise destroy the seed.

The next important step is sowing the seed, and although they will vegetate in a moist atmosphere on the surface of the earth, and also even when too deeply covered, it does not certainly follow that the depth at which they are planted is unimportant; too much covering is very detrimental, and entirely at variance with the wonderful process of nature. You will

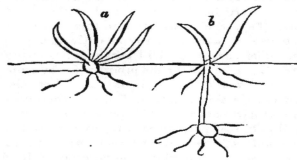 observe on the black board two rye plants; *a* represents a seed planted at the proper distance below the surface of the earth, and *b* one that was too deeply covered; *b* vegetated notwithstanding the mistake in planting, and threw out two sickly leaves above the ground, where they remained stationary until new roots were formed near the surface superseding the first. While *a* being properly planted far surpassed *b*. Those practising the drill system find that seeds can be more uniformly planted than when sown broadcast promiscuously and harrowed in; and should therefore be generally practiced in all expedient cases.

The most critical period in the life of a plant appears to be, when the seed has completely expended its nourishment in its development, as may be detected, by the yellow appearance presented by it, immediately after being weaned, and left to seek in the earth a new kind of food. At this period all sickly individuals die, and by their decomposition strengthen and invigorate the healthy advancement of the rest, which progress rapidly to maturity, if the disintegration of the earth has been thorough. The injurious consequences of the often extreme variations of seasons are mitigated when the land is thoroughly and perfectly drained, and cultivated with liquid manures. Drainage will be found to compensate even for the deficiency of solar heat in a backward summer, besides increasing the fertility of the soil from year to year; though constantly washed by heavy rains, the liquid manures applied never escape through the soil, but are invariably retained by it chemically. When solid manures will be washed bodily into the nearest ditches, and water courses, so that the outfalls from top dressed undrained lands will invariably be found turbid, when those from the richly manured with liquid will be pellucid and transparent. If farmers were to examine the solid manures before they placed them upon their fields, with the microscope, they would find all the fibrous portions composing them, filled with devastating insects, and thousands of seeds of injurious and unsuspected weeds. Besides all the particles that are visible to the eye, must be entirely decomposed before the plant can absorb them. I know this is so, from the fact that I have failed with the most powerful microscope to detect the least aperture to the roots of any plants, consequently the fact is conclusive to my mind, that no manure, even in the shape of an impalpable powder can be assimilated by any plant except in a liquid form.

Besides, if land is properly drained, and cultivated with liquid manure, the usual risk of injury when the season is wet, is much diminished, as the superabundance of water can immediately run off, and drought need not be at all dreaded when an artificial shower of liquid manure is at hand.

Thorough drainage, and command of liquid manure, will, to a great extent, compensate for the want of solar heat in summer, as the removal of water saves heat that would be required otherwise for its evaporation, and liquid manure stimulates and nourishes vegetation. The two principal causes of fluctuations in crops, are deficiency or excess of moisture, which we can thus to a great extent control. Lands irrigated with simple water may be readily distinguished by the soft and spongy texture of the vegetable tissues, but that obtained by the use of liquid manure is preferred by cattle and greedily devoured. It yields prompt nourishment to the growing plant, saves loss by immediate passage into the soil, comes into action in two months, instead of two years, as is the case with solid manure. Repairs, at once, the failure of other composts, changes leaves that were yellow into a beautiful green color, and is the only manure that does not cause exhaustion of the land, because it not only dissolves and spreads, but conveys, without loss of time, nutrition to vegetation. You farmers well know, from dear bought experience, what bad results attend the expenditure and labor of manuring fields with solid compost in dry weather, and ought, by all means, to resort to liquid manure as the proper basis of cultivation. The best time to apply it is on the first snow that falls in December, before the hard frost sets in, and the last snow in the spring, that it may be ready for the roots when they first begin to grow, as, according to vegetable physiology, they possess the wonderful faculty of selecting the food most suitable to them, and do not take up, indiscriminately, everything that is presented.

Farmers, generally, mismanage their solid manures, by their long retention on the surface, and consequent evaporation of their fertilizing qualities, to the extent, frequently, of more than two-thirds, and their liquid manures are, invariably, directed to the nearest stream, being considered a nuisance in the barn-yard.

Take it for granted that in every case where the dung of the stable, and of the cattle yards, are exposed in heaps to the atmosphere, and where the washings from it, with the urine of the cattle, are permitted to run off, that the loss of production that might be derived from a different application of the manures, is fully equal to the rent of the farm.

You have always considered that only as manure that you could raise into your wagons with a fork, but you must now consider that which may be applied with the scoop, the main stay of your agricultural operations. And, instead of requiring it dark, strong and fœtid, let it be light, transparent, and devoid of smell.

There are certain adjustments established between the physical and organic kingdom, which it would be well to bear in mind. We are aware that atmospheric air is equally necessary to the life of animals and plants, but that they produce opposite changes in the chemical constitution of the air. The plant gives off as excrementitious that principle of the air on which the animal mainly subsists, and lives upon that part which the animal rejects as excrementitious, while the animal, in turn, gives back to the air the precise principle which constitutes the food of the plant, and subsists on that which the plant has rejected as no longer of service to it. In this way these two classes of organized beings renovate the atmosphere for each other, and eternally maintain it for each other in a state of richness and purity. On this magnificent adjustment depends the principle that the refuse of the materials which have served us as food and clothing, and which, if permitted to accumulate, invariably taint the atmosphere, and cause it to become pestilential, if liquified and promptly spread on the surface of the ground, not only give it fruitfulness, but clothe it with luxuriance, and endue it with inexhaustible healthfulness. A due conformity to these great laws of nature would bring us happiness, plenty, health and wealth, but which we cannot disregard any more than any other physical law of nature without suffering. As is instanced, daily, in this great city of New York, here we find the streets abounding with filth, the air fœtid, typhus and other epidemic diseases rife among the people, bringing in their train destitution, want and misery, all arising from the presence of the very richest materials of production, the absence of which would restore health, avert disease, and if applied to the land, cheapen food by promoting abundance. Our suburbs are poor, and thinly clad with vegetation, except plants favored by moisture, the population few, and they afflicted with rheumatism and other kindred diseases, arising from an excess of water, which might be drained by some well considered plan, that would not press with severity on any of the owners, and thus benefit posterity as well as the present generation. The moral influence of filth and discomfort in our streets has not been sufficiently attended to, and is, in the greatest degree anti-social. The wretched homes generally correspond with the streets, and when the man returns from his labor, exhausted, and requires refreshment and quiet, he finds discomfort, squalor, and filth around him, and gets away from it as fast as possible, to spend his hard earned wages in selfish gratifications.

The neglect of the decencies of life invariably debases the human mind, to the same extent that hopeless want produces recklessness. The power of the poor of obtaining bread, and maintaining their progeny, is much diminished by the neglect of the city authorities to drain, sewer, and cleanse the localities they are forced to inhabit. It has been taught, by large experience, that there are certain epochs of life, that three-quarters of the persons who die at those epochs, die of acute fevers, to which humanity is subject at the period which intervenes after the dangers of infancy and childhood have been passed, or between puberty and old age. This precious term of life may be extended almost indefinitely, by human wisdom and precaution, because it arises from the dirty state of the streets, and the forlorn condition of the houses in which they reside; sewage, ventilation and cleanliness being unknown, pernicious poison is unceasingly generated in such quantities as to predispose the systems of the inhabitants to fatal maladies, by the decomposition of vegetable and animal matters, which always exist where many persons are congregated together. Remove these to the rural districts before putrefaction commences, and they will fit the soil for the reception and germination of seed, and become not only a primary, but fundamental means of preventing the production of fever. It may not be generally known, but even so far back as 1845, thirty-four thousand of our population lived in alleys and cellars, of which number seven thousand occupied damp, cold, underground apartments, and most of them were afflicted with contagious affections of the skin, rheumatism and other inflammatory diseases, and all of them with more or less fever, induced by the nauseous effluvium arising from their dirty condition, and the want of pure unrespired air; half of the children of these wretched people die before they reach the fifth year, and the mean age of death does not exceed twenty years.

The means of remedying these evils are simple: First, by employing the labor of scavengers, for bulky matter; second, by the use of drains, with a full supply of water, to carry off comminuted solids; and thirdly, ventilation for aerial matters. Attention to these simple rules will annihilate the sad influences which now debilitate constitutions, cause epidemics, and drive thousands of citizens to hospitals and death, besides affording those matters so necessary for fitting the soil to receive and germinate seeds.

The formation of all soils for this purpose may be traced, without much difficulty, to the disintegration of rocks, by chemical and mechanical agencies, that contain alkaline earths and alkalies. Yellow clay is undoubtely formed from granite, blue clay from greenstone and sienite, other clays by the disintegration of felspars. The red clays of New Jersey contain protoxide of iron, and are great absorbents of oxygen ; they do not become fertile until the protoxide is converted into peroxide. Soils thus being formed for the reception of seeds by the disintegration of rocks, their properties are dependent upon the component parts of the rocks, and the effects produced upon them by the action of the water and air to which they are exposed. The constituents of these soils, are clay, lime and sand ; the first, being produced by the disintegration of mica, felspar, and other aluminous minerals, possess the fructifying element of all soils ; the sand contains no inorganic substance, except carbonate and silicate of lime, and consequently afford no nourishment for vegetation. The lime acts with great efficacy upon land containing vegetable or animal substances, and frequently produces more durable and nourishing effects, than the application of barnyard manure, because it renders every particle of them useful to the preparation of the soil, and germination of the seed. Of saline substances used as a preparation of the soil for the reception of seed, chloride of sodium has received the most attention, and has been extensively applied, but I am opposed to its use in large quantities, from the fact that the shores of the ocean are generally sterile. There is great diversity of opinion among agriculturists as to its value as a manure, and no data has been given regarding the quantity to be applied, or the proper season for applying it. My experiments lead me to believe that six bushels to the acre should never be exceeded. Saltpetre has been effectually tried as a manure, but, being expensive, experiments are required to confirm its value.

The whole subject of the germination of seed, and the fitness of soil for its reception, is one of engrossing interest to the agriculturist, and deeply interesting to the physiologist, who can make but little proficiency in the study without investigating the means by which plants derive their nourishments from the soil, and how they are admitted into the interior of them. We find by examination, that essentially a plant consists of three parts— roots, stems, and leaves. The former push themselves great distances, in every imaginable direction, through the earth, to obtain food, in order to increase the stem and leaves, which make a corresponding advancement through the atmosphere, and increase their leaves and luxuriance in proportion to the extension of the roots.

The stems of plants consist of the pith, wood, bark, and medullary rays. The pith and rays are extensions of the same substance. The pith forms the centre of the stem, the wood encircles it, and the bark completes the cylinder. The stem is fitted with capillary tubes of various sizes, through which the liquid and gaseous substances are conveyed to the branches. The roots and branches of a tree are capable of being reversed, and made to bear on their changed prolongations. I once, by degrees, reversed a currant bush, and in due course of time, the roots became branches, and bore fruit, while the branches became roots, and sustained them. The banana tree is a familiar example of this convertible power contained in rees. Cherries, plums, apples, &c., may be made to produce the same results.

The leaf of a tree is merely the expansion of the bark, and acts upon the atmosphere in the same manner that the root does upon the soil, and it is an expansion of the bark likewise, changed at its extremity into a spongy mass, which possesses the power of absorbing a very large quantity of water, and extracting the gases which it contains for the benefit of the plant, besides soda, lime, potash, and even silica. But decidedly the most important function that roots possess, is their power of selecting those matters from the soil best calculated to maintain their growth and healthy condition. You may present to the roots of a plant, acetate of lime, or strontia, in a liquid form, and they will not absorb either; if they did, immediate death would ensue. Men and animals do not possess this power, and often swallow, unwittingly, substances that prove fatal. Sheep will eat various poisons, such as the five-finger vine, laurel, &c., and men, opium, arsenic, &c. Water appears to possess the power of selecting; if you present nitrogen, oxygen, and carbonic acid gas, it will give preference to the latter, and absorb it first.

Roots in my mind are constituted to choose from the earth, and give decided preference to those matters which are the most essential to their natures, and if they are not there, the plant will no doubt admit matters that may be injurious. These however are never found in the natural soil or climate of any plant, and therefore the roots cannot encounter any poison, unless administered by man. I have invariably advanced the theory that all plants throw off excretory matters, which has often been denied by those with whom the subject was discussed. To satisfy myself, last summer, I caused a few kernels of wheat to germinate in a powder of perfectly pure chalk, and found in it afterwards aceate of lime, showing that they do excrete. Yet notwithstanding, by experiments for several seasons, I am unable to satisfy myself that there is a positive benefit to be obtained by a rotation of crops, which I have always advocated and practiced faithfully heretofore. Last year I plowed up a clover field, which had grown that crop successfully for three years, and sowed it to rye; the yield was splendid, and I at first attributed it to the excrementitious substances thrown off by the clover. But upon thoroughly examining the soil, found it full of decomposing roots, and was obliged, I must confess unwillingly, to yield my favorite theory, and give the credit where it was justly due. The next field, with a fine growth of rye sown the previous fall, was plowed under, and sown with oats; this crop was equal in quantity and quality to the rye or clover, the rye giving to it the requisite quantity of green manure, it not yet having had growth enough to throw off any large amount of excrement. We have too few experiments upon this very important subject to permit us to decide with any degree of certainty; I intend however to continue them, and will from time to time report progress, as the earth continues to reveal the phenomena of her vegetable mysteries to my experiments upon her bosom.

THE COURSE OF THE SAP.

To observe this beautiful process I cut a small tree down near the ground, and thrust it into a vessel of prepared madder, which in a few minutes ascended through the capillary tubes of the tree, and not only tinged them, but even the leaves were sensibly affected, after which the return sap colored the bark. This shows plainly, that. the sap from the roots passes through the tubes in the wood, by capillary attraction, to the leaves, over which it spreads itself, and then descends again through the bark, and passes off at the roots' extremities.

Of the the importance of leaves in the economy of vegetation, I once had sufficient proof. A new gardener stripped all the leaves from a few grape vines that were in full bearing, and the result was total destruction of the fruit. On another occasion early frost destroyed the leaves of some peach trees that were full of fruit, and the result was entire loss of crop. Mildew attacked the leaves of a small quince plantation, and deterioration of the fruit followed.

The functions of the stems of plants are as various as those connected with the roots, and they appear to possess the same discriminating power of admitting into their circulation the numerous substances in the soil. I found that the trunks of some trees which I thrust into the liquid madder, rejected it entirely, in the spring of the year, but accepted it readily in the fall. How will physiologists explain this? I suppose the reason is that the sap flows less rapidly in the fall than spring, and confines itself more to the internal part of the tree, consequently I never attempt to impregnate wood with kyanizing solutions, except in the autumn. The pine, and I imagine all other evergreens, circulate sap throughout the year, as by experiment I find they will receive liquid coloring solutions, or salt, at any time.

You may always discover the age of a tree, by examining the zones annually formed. Though this has been denied by a learned man belonging to this Institute, I am convinced, after making one hundred experiments, that it is true. The zone formed the first year around the pith, consists entirely of woody fibre, firm on the exterior, but intermixed with rays on the interior, tending towards the centre. The following season, another similar zone is formed, which does not undergo any alteration of structure afterwards, and always remains as long as the tree lives to mark its age. The formation of the wood of a tree, is entirely different from that of the bark ; the latter grows by addition to its internal economy, and the former by deposits upon its external.

There are very many conditions requisite to sustain the life of plants, and besides those of each genus, require without a doubt, special conditions, and if by any accident one of these is entirely deficient, though all the rest are present, the plant will fail to mature.

How then shall we restore fertility to our sods, and fit them for the reception and germination of the seed ?

If we undertake to effect the object by draining, the amelioration will be indebted to the removal of superfluous matter. If by burning turf, the ashes will be the restoring principle. If by the rotation of crops, the roots of the previous crop will act as the restorer of the fertilizing conditions requisite. If we summer fallow, restored fertility will no doubt be due, to the decomposition of the matters, not removed by the crop, which increase the vegetable mould.

If all these fail, as they sometimes do, there is no way left but to analyze the soil, and make a direct application of the missing ingredients, remembering that plants invariably derive from a rich soil a certain proportion of their organic food, of their nitrogen nearly all, of their inorganic food all.

When you find a corn, wheat, or rye crop injured by insects, you may rest assured that they will descend in the earth to the subsoil to deposit their eggs, and if undisturbed, will appear in such multitudes the ensuing season as to destroy the crop entirely. To obviate this difficulty, plow your stubble deeper than usual in the fall, which will bring them to the surface, where exposed to the influence of a winter's frost will insure their destruction. I have frequently heard farmers rail against deep plowing in the spring for summer grain, which they say is generally destroyed by insects. And I have given as a reason, that the insects of the previous crop, that had deposited their eggs below the reach of shallow plowing, had been brought to the surface by deep spring plowing, and exposed to the vivifying influence of the sun, arose in countless thousands to destroy the crop.

Professor Brown has stated before the United States Agricultural Society, in Washington, that the State of Maryland lost annually fifteen millions of dollars by the ravages of the wheat midge. If so small a state as Maryland, loses fifteen millions per annum, by this single species of insect, what must the loss be throughout the United States, by all the insect tribes combined.

From long experience, I am perfectly convinced, that deep plowing in the fall, in all our northern states, will destroy the larvæ of so large a proportion of insects that the crop will be saved.

And in the southern states, an application of lime on plowed land, will prove fatal to all insects, worms, and slugs, injurious to agricultural productions. It possesses the wonderful property of falling into extremely minute particles, which are carried downward through the pores of the soil by the rain, until they reach the impervious layer, near which the insects have deposited their ova, coming in contact with these, they immediately dissolve them and gradually produce a fine mould, which may again be brought to the surface, together with the lime, by sowing deep rooted clover, or lucerne. And when these are again plowed under, the soil will be prepared for the germination of seed and its reception.

Subjects.—" Spring flowers, plants, seeds, trees, drainage, and pruning the grape vine."

The Club then adjourned. H. MEIGS, *Secretary.*

Present—Messrs. Pell, Solon Robinson, Wm. Lawton, Bruee, of Williamsburgh; Fuller, Field, Adrian Bergen, Hon. John G. Bergen, Kavanach, of Brooklyn; Coleman, of Canandaigua; Doughty, of Jersey city; Pike, do; Chilson, Stacey, Dr. Holton, Veeder, R. G. Pardee, Prof. James J. Mapes, McCarty, Prof. Nash, Mr. Wright, Judge Livingston, Wilson, Gore, Witt, J. M Bixby, Dr. Shelton, of Jamaica, Long Island; Judge French, of Massachusetts—fifty-five members in all.

Mr. R. L. Pell in the chair. Henry Meigs, Secretary.

The Secretary read the following extracts, from works received by the Institute since the last meeting, viz:

[London Farmers' Magazine, Feb. 1859.]

STEEPING SEEDS.

Cuthbert W. Johnson, on steeping seeds, tried eighteen distinct steeps, and found—

1. That turnip seed did best when moistened occasionally with nothing but pure water.

2. Very dilute sulphuric acid killed seeds; Peruvian guano as bad as sulphate of ammonia.

3. Superphosphate of lime retarded instead of hastening germination of seeds.

What conclusion.—Mix artificial manures, such as guano and superphosphate with as much ashes as is practicable, if sown dry, or with much water for liquid manuring. Superphosphate made plants when fairly up, grow much more vigorously and twice as big as the rest.

The *California Farmer*, of January 21st, 1858, quotes the Southern Planter, saying that peach trees into which a few ten penny nails have been driven near the roots, are not subject to injury from the borer—the oxydation of the iron evolving ammonia, which penetrates every part of the tree, leaves and all.

He recommends planting peach trees for fire wood.

The editor calls attention to the true Lawton blackberry,—very superior plant, just imported by Messrs. Graves and Williams, Merchant st., San Francisco.

He says, don't kill the birds. The farmers are now sowing in San Jose, waited on by *myriads* of black birds, crows and other pensioners of the farm. Let them alone—there are far more destructive agents than the birds, ever ready to devour our crops.

The principal, if not indeed the only attraction, which the birds find in our newly plowed fields, is, the plentiful supply of worms turned out by the plow. A friend tells us he omitted slaughtering birds, and had excellent crops of grain while his neighbors' crops were overrun and ruined by worms; and an examination of the craws of the birds slain in the act of supposed depredation settles the question.

STUMPS OF TREES.

Dig a trench around a stump, six or eight inches wide and eight or ten inches deep; fill it with wheat-chaff, into which a fire-stick (punk) is put lighted. A slow mouldering combustion takes place and burns all the stump to the depth of eight or ten inches, out of the reach of our plowshare. Do this in the heat of summer, in dry time, and begin in calm weather or the wind will blow some of your chaff away from the stump.

By the last steamer from Europe, we have received, among other things, "An extract from the catalogue of plants," for sale by " Oudin, Ainee ;" Mr. Oudin Larin at Lisieux.

He recommends his *Prédome*, a dwarf bean yielding 1,000 for 1. They grow like bushes. Also, his "*Abundance Pea.*" Also, his curly-headed or frizzled Drum-head cabbage.

DISEASES OF WHEAT.

Boussingault gave his opinion that sulphate of copper was a cure for parasitic diseases of wheat. He says, " I can assure the reader that our fields of wheat in Alsace are never infected where sulphate of copper is used. One hundred grammes, equal to three and one-quarter ounces, troy weight, ore applied to three bushels (a sack,) of wheat, by dissolving it in water enough to cover the grain, for three-quarters of an hour. The grain is wet with it, in a basket,.allowed to drain, and then spread out on a floor to dry before sowing it." Sulphate of copper is commonly called blue vitriol.

Some have put four quarts of slaked lime to the bushel of wheat, wet it, stir three or four times, and have no *smut*. Charles W. Gilbert, of Knox county, Illinois, had smut on his wheat nineteen years ago. Used the lime, and has clean wheat ever since.

The Illinois State Horticultural Society is attended by many ladies. The culture of flowers and fruits, under their care, is urged, for blooming cheeks, rich health, and making home delightful.

The most suitable trees, for the dress of the naked prairies, are pointed out, and their planting, by seeds or young trees, strongly urged. In a few years those plains will lose their peculiar character. Fires will be prevented from ravaging the country, by divisions of the surface, in place of one continuous ocean like level covered with tall grass, the burning of which, for ages, has prevented any trees from growing.

CANADA THISTLES.

Solon Robinson.—I have received a pile of letters upon destroying this pest of Northern farmers, and, as it would seem from a letter from Frederick, Md., Southern ones, too. L. Rainsford, of that place, says he had an acre of land badly infected with Canada thistles, which he extirpated by hard labor. " We employed two men, who went over the ground with grubbing-hoes, and took out every plant and root, as they supposed, leaving them on the surface. The ground was afterwards raked, and plowed and raked again, and afterwards the sprouts kept cut off with long chisels."

Wm. P. Gates write from Windham, Conn., that he extirpated the thistles by plowing, planting corn, and careful hoeing for three years, and then sowing the land to oats and grass.

E. Marks of Camillus, N. Y., writes to the same effect. He says if you will prevent the growth of leaves the plant must die:

"Large patches may be destroyed by thoroughly plowing as often as the plant appears above the turface. Small and scattered patches may be killed with the hoe. With the plow I have killed many acres of 'simon pure' Canada thistles and quack grass."

QUACK GRASS.

T. W. Field.—I have a little story to tell about quack grass. In filling in a hollow, I burried quack grass several feet deep, and it lay burried five years, when I dug up a portion of the ground and found the roots alive and ready to grow as soon as exposed to the atmosphere.

Adrian Bergen.—By plowing and hoeing continually, we may extirpate and keep down weeds, there is no other way. We have a great variety of weeds on Long Island, and I don't know where we get them, except it is from city manures. We are compelled to keep stirring our land to keep them under control.

T. W. Field.—If the land is stony, so that the plow cannot move them, it is nearly impossible to kill Canada thistles by the plow. If the top is kept cut, it will not always kill the root. But, if left till nearly ripe, and then cut at a time when rain happens to follow, the most of them will die.

Mr. Gore, of New Jersey, said that he had succeeded in extirpating Canada thistles by cutting them in August, and following it up the next year.

Wm. Lawton spoke of the value of the common thistle in the compost heap. I am very glad that this question was, in a measure, unintentionally brought up, since it has elicited so much valuable information.

QUANTITY OF HAY PER ACRE.

Solon Robinson.—I hold a letter from Charles Taylor, of Wilmington, Vt., who wants to know "What is the greatest number of tons of hay that has been raised on one acre of land in England during one year? and what kind of hay was it?" Perhaps the Chairman or some other person here will give him and the rest of mankind an answer.

Robert L. Pell.—It has been published that, upon the Earl of Derby's land, a field of 100 acres was watered by liquid manure, by a steam-engine and pipes, and a hydrant and hose to each ten acres, and this land was mowed seven times, and gave upon one acre 100 tons weight of grass, and estimated an average of 75 tons upon each acres. The meadows near Edinburgh, watered with sewage water, grew 14 feet of grass a year, which cut at several times, weighed 80 tons. In Ayrshire, similar treatment of forty acres of land has enabled its owner to feed 100 cows.

Prof. Nash.—I have seen two farms in England conducted on this principle. Mr. Mechi's farm is 175 acres, with a hydrant at each 11 acres, with a hose 80 feet long, by which all crops were watered with liquid manure. The results pay well, but, from what I saw, I am not prepared to believe that 100 tons of grass were ever cut from an acre in one year, except it is weighed with a deal of water in it. The way the grass is reported to have been weighed on the Ayrshire meadows showed that half the weight must have been water. I never have seen anything to induce me to believe that over eight tuns of dry hay have ever been raised upon any one acre.

Judge French, of New Hampshire, said that he had never seen anything to induce him to swallow those big stories about great hay crops. We cut sometimes in New England three tons per acre of dry hay. I have averaged that upon some acres, at one cutting. Ordinarily a second crop is made upon such land. With irrigation perhaps two tons could be cut at the second mowing. Perhaps the rye grass, which is the kind grown in England, and weighed very wet, may weigh 100 tons, and perhaps it would not make over twelve tons an acre of dry hay. I doubt if it would.

Prof. Mapes.—I suppose that twelve tons can be grown in this country by irrigation with sewerage water. Mr. Lincoln, of Worcester, has done something like this.

Prof. Nash.—I must dissent from all stories about grass crops that produce over 8 tons of dry hay per acre.

T. W. Field.—I cannot believe in a grass crop that weighs more than the rain-water falling upon the land in one season. The weight of rain-water that falls upon an acre is 45 tons. It is true more than that quantity can be put on by irrigation, but I don't know about growing more than that weight of grass.

DRAINAGE.

This question of the day being called up Prof. Mapes asked Judge French to state what he had seen in England about tile draining. The question of the necessity of silt basins is important, and also about inserting small tiles into leading drains. The English engineers say that there is no bed equal to the natural condition of the earth for laying down tiles. They open a little cavity at the bottom of the ditch with a tool so as to fit the tile, where it rests easy and firm. We should like to know at what depth English experience has found it best to lay drains. Judge French has lately travelled in England, and examined the subject of draining in all its bearings, and is now engaged in putting a book to press, containing his views upon the subject, and is therefore undoubtedly competent to give us some information upon this, the most important question of American agriculture.

Judge French.—The best depth of drain, it is thought, is four feet; and that is so, according to my observations, though it depends upon circumstances. Where tiles are dear and labor cheap, the less tiles we can use the better. Drains three feet deep, at forty feet apart, are not so effective as at five feet deep and fifty feet apart. Tiles in this country must be laid below frost and sub-soil plows, and that should be at least three feet deep.

Nobody contends now in England for less than three feet depth of drains, and those who advocate three feet are called shallow drainers.

As a general rule, it costs as much to dig the fourth foot as it does the other three feet. A four-foot drain is opened in England only one foot wide at the top, and just wide enough to lay the tile at the bottom. I open my drains four inches wide at the bottom, because that is as narrow as I can dig with a pick. The digger must have room for his foot at the bottom to work with that tool, and our soil is so hard that nothing else will do. As to the size of tiles, I never would use a one-inch tile, because I do not believe it is sufficient to carry off the great amount of rain water that falls in this country, which is much greater than falls in England, and it does not come in that gentle, drizzling way, but with a rush, just as we do many things, and the pipes must be large enough to carry it all off. We have no sufficient tables as yet, but we are getting posted up, and from what I have seen, I think we have got to provide against a rain fall of 45 inches a year. Our New England showers are sometimes little deluges. In 1852, we had 6 inches in one hour. Often we have 2, 3, or 4 inches in 24 hours. Just before planting we have a flood of rain, and this must be carried off, and that immediately. I have drained some of my land at 50 feet apart, five feet deep. We need, as a general thing, larger tiles in this country than in England, simply because we have more water to carry off in a short time. As to the water going through the pores of the tile, there is ten times as much goes through the joints as through the pores, so that making them porous is not so very important. The joints will take in all the water in the ground. I would have my tiles about as well burnt as good wall brick. They are then strong enough, and can be cut, and are not likely to break in the earth. They should be hard enough not to dissolve, and the clay should be compressed enough to make the tile strong enough, without such hard burning as will melt the clay. I prefer collars three inches long, and always would use collars on small pipes, because they keep the pipes in line ; and I would not use less than $1\frac{1}{2}$ inch tiles. As to the shape of the orifice, if you have a low head, an egg shape, with small end down, is the best ; but a round hole is generally good enough. So is a tile that is round on the outside. The difficulty in round tiles is, that they are apt to bend in drying, and it is important to have the line of pipes straight. The round tile is the form adopted by the Land-draining Company in England—a company of competent men, who work scientifically. They never use less than $1\frac{1}{4}$ inch pipe, and those always with collars ; but they prefer 2 inch tile, without collars.

As to joining brook drains, I would have a pipe made purposely, and never bring in the side drain at right angles, and always give it a fall into the main pipe.

As to silt basins, if you want to inspect your drains, a silt basin may be of use ; but simpler things than such silt basins as are made in the Central Park, will answer. A large, strong made pipe, set up over the drain pipe, where the branches join, will enable any one to inspect a drain to see where the stoppage is. My impression is that two-inch tiles, fifty feet apart, in ditches 200 yards long, will carry off all the water necessary. Pipes should be as smooth as possible. Two-inch pipes are probably more economical than one and a half inch pipes with collars, since the collars cost in England half as much as pipes. But there is some land in which it will not answer to lay pipes of any size without collars or some substitute. I use pieces of wood, such as the Yankee boot-makers use to stiffen the bottoms of thick boots, which I put under the joints of the tiles, and that effectually keeps one pipe from settling below the other.

Recollect, I speak of this Yankee way of saving leather, and making stiff boot soles, perfectly confidentially. But these pieces of board being cheaper than anything else, I find it good economy to use them under my tile, whether it is or not under the boot soles. The most of the draining-tile used in this country are two and a half to three and a half inches in diameter, and, generally, of the most expensive kind.

Prof. Mapes.—There is a new tool that is a substitute for a pick, that will dig five feet deep by horse power, narrow enough for tile draining. I dig seventy rods long in a day, three feet deep, with a yoke of oxen, with Pratt's digging machine. Then, with a sub-soil plow and the horse-pick I do the most of the work the other two feet. All my drains are five feet deep. Our tile makers have ascertained that tile can be made more porous by mixing dust of anthracite coal with the clay. The pipes, too, are stronger when so mixed.

Salisbury's machine for making drain tile is easily adapted to the wants of any farmer, and can be worked upon any farm, it is so simple. It also makes better tile than the expensive machinery. One can make 3,000 tile a day. It is very easy, too, to set up a kiln of tile upon any farm so as to burn them.

Messrs. R. P. Wilson & Co., by letter, invite the members to see a boy make *one hundred pounds of butter in five minutes*, by their new process, *the air pump churn*, at No. 37 Park Row, on Wednesday next, at three o'clock, P. M.

Dr. Grant, of Iona Island, North river, near Peekskill, will give his views upon pruning grape vine.

Subjects continued.—" Spring flowers, seeds, plants, trees, drainage, and pruning grape vine."

The Club adjourned.

H. MEIGS, *Secretary.*

March 7, 1859.

Present—Messrs. R. L. Pell, Hon. Robert Swift Livingston, John M. Bixby, John Campbell, Hon. Hugh Maxwell, R. G. Pardee, Rev. Mr. Campbell, Benjamin Pike, Judge French, of Massachusetts; Prof. Nash, Amos Gore, Hon. John G. Bergen, Solon Robinson, Mr. Atwood, Mr. Brower and Mr. Doughty, of Jersey; Bruce, Witt, Burgess, Fuller,

Kavanach, of Brooklyn ; Mr. Leonard, Mr. Chambers, D. C. Robinson, Mr. Roberts, Mr. Wright, Chilson, Dr. Grant, of Iona ; Dr. Griscom, Dr. Ward, of Jersey ; about ninety in all

Robert L. Pell in the chair.   Henry Meigs, Secretary.

The Secretary read the following translations, &c., made by him from the last works received from home and abroad, viz.:

[Le Bon Jardinier Almanach Horticole for 1859.   By Vilmorin.   1,555 pages, with some illustrations.   Paris.

From this valuable work, just presented to the American Institute by the author, we translate the following, viz.:   •

THE WEATHER.

While we are waiting for meteorology to become a science it concerns every farmer and gardener to study, carefully, the weather of his own location, that he may work profitably.   He should note down, daily, such changes as occur there.   Common sayings and proverbs, repeated with so great confidence, are pure prejudices which long experience has not sanctioned ; they are not worthy of faith.

DURATION OF VITALITY OF SEEDS.

Wheat—germinating power very short.   That of France and middle Europe, in a warm season, when the grain is completely matured, only three or four years.   The wheat of Algeria and of the south of Spain, has germinated after nine years.   The seed was from Abyssinia ; but of these kept *nine* years *only one or two* out of *one hundred*, germinated, and their plants were miserable, and killed by rust before the grain ripened.   From nine years to the thousands of years of the mummy wheat is a very long step.   Those who are the most strongly inclined to believe, are obliged to suppose that its preservation is due to the painted mummy cases where it is found ; the absence of air, of too much humidity, or too great desiccation, and to temperature, of very slight variation.   The vapor of the bitumen is injurious to the grain.   I do not believe that the ancient mummy wheat can germinate.   Those who have believed it must have been deceived.   To satisfy myself, I baked soil in a bread oven, for six hours, so that no seed could possibly grow in it except those I planted.   Mummy wheat would not grow in it.   My precaution was caused by the result of my experiments on Ægilops.   I planted wheat in 163 pots of *baked soil.* I found, still, two wheat and one rye plants.   Lastly, as to mummy wheats, the oldest of them received and circulated by the Horticultural Society of Paris, is, the *Blé de Miracle*—miraculous wheat—*Triticum compositum* variety *still growing in Egypt*, and which, on account of its strange growth, is now found in all the collections of grain.

THE HALTICA.   (*Turnip Flea.*)

Make a little car on wheels, suited to the drills ; smear it with tar or glue ; draw it through the field ; the flea jumps and is caught.   Immense numbers are readily destroyed by it.   This flea gnaws the cotyledons, it makes a sieve of the leaf, and its larvæ, which come a month before it, are almost as injurious.   Steeping seed in tobacco, &c., have all been tried, but there is a better way, and that is, if you have time, let them eat the first crop, and then you plant another (Mr. Bergen's method with cucumbers) ; before that, put straw on and fire it, to destroy the larvæ.

We have a *Pine Apple Pear* like the Doyenné ; has yellow skin, spotted, red cheek, fine, melting, sugary, juicy, musk perfume. First quality. Pine apple odor ; ripe in September and October.

We now have fifty-six kinds of pine apples.

We have the Celery radish which ought to be better known. It is excellent, very tender, like marrow.

Bokhara clover grows from six to eight feet high.

John Campbell, formerly a vice-president of the Institute, presented ears of white flint corn, fully grown, having 600 grains on each, and Yellow King Pillip, with smaller grains, 14 rows, having 740 grains.

THE OYSTERS OF VIRGINIA.

Mr. Meigs.—The city of New York is said to pay more for oysters than for meat ; and the State of Virginia gives them. Virginia has said that she is robbed of her oysters, and should derive a large income from their sale !

New York gives back to Virginia more money in oyster shells, than we pay for the oysters. The shells are mixed with the otherwise useless dust of coal, in kilns, burned to lime, and shipped to Virginia in vast quantities, where it is used for top dressing grass and crops, giving durable fertility to the land.

The oysters estimated to be taken from there by the first of July, 1859, are *eight million eight hundred and eight thousand four hundred and ninety-two bushels.* That *amount of shells* will be left, after we have swallowed the tenants, to go on the dry land for the use of vegetables !

PLUMS ON PEACH STOCKS.

The *Michigan Farmer*, of Feb. 26, 1859, says, that at the nursery of Mr. Allen, of Walpole, there are plum trees, of twenty years' growth, on *peach stocks*, all free from warts, while the plum trees in the neighborhood are covered with warts.

BRICK FENCE POSTS.

William Lyman, of Moscow, Livingston county, proposes to make fence posts out of clay ; burn them hard ; that they will be strong ; will last forever ; and that that the boards secured to them will last fifty years !

Vide the *Genesee Farmer*, of Rochester, March, 1859. He has cast them of six feet length, and five inches square, and some only two by five inches square. Believes they can be stood on end in kilns and burned hard—i. e., the silex in them melted—become very strong, impenetrable by water. Cast with suitable holes in them, for fence-making.

Note by H. Meigs.—They can be burned, but at a cost far beyond our wooden posts ; but they are indestructible. Violence will break them, and so it will any one we can make of iron, or anything else.

THE DELAWARE GRAPE.

Josiah Salter, of Rochester.—We have been engaged in the cultivation of this grape for more than twenty (20) years, and we can fully indorse the remarks made by Mr. Robinson at the last meeting, by asserting that the Delaware is the best grape that we have ever seen for out of door culture in this latitude, because it possesses the following qualities:

1. *Great hardiness.*—It has been known to stand uninjured, where Isabella, Catawba, and Clinton, have been killed to the ground.

2. *Productiveness.*—It is a great bearer. The berries and bunches increase in size as the well cultivated vine grows older; and it probably will produce more pounds of fruit to the acre than any other sort that we know of.

3. *Earliness.*—It is said to ripen in Delaware, Ohio, about the middle of August, and in Western New York, early in September. There is no other native grape nearly as good that ripens so early, that we know of.

4. *Quality is best.*—Whenever and wherever compared with other varieties, Delaware always bears off the palm.

Now, my dear sir, these grapes are so scarce, for two reasons:

1. The above mentioned excellent qualities cause them to be in great demand, and prices rise in proportion.

2. Those who have the genuine stock find it is extremely difficult to multiply; more than twice as hard to make the plants grow as to start any other sort, yet, when once started, it is as good a grower as any grape vine with which we are acquainted. In fact, we have found it the most difficult to multiply of all the grape vines at present known. We have been engaged for some years, in propagating grape vines for sale. We got all our original stock plants direct from the first disseminator in Delaware, Ohio; but from our experience with hundreds of stock plants, and from the universal testimony of gentlemen in the trade, we are sure that these two reasons, namely, great demand, and the difficulty of multiplying, will combine to render the Delaware a scarce sort of vine for some years to come.

RED CATTLE OF NEW ENGLAND.

Joseph Arnold.—In all I have read of the importers of stock, I have not heard the name of Col. Jeremiah Wadsworth, who, in my opinion, has done more in forming the character of those cattle, than perhaps all others.

Wadsworth imported from England to Hartford, Conn., as I suppose, soon after 1790, I being young, and not a resident there until 1796 or '97. The importation consisted of studs and mares, a bull or bulls, a cow or cows. Of these I have seen one bull and two studs, and I believe, some of the mares. One of the studs, a black—a noble animal for draft—I do not know that I have seen his equal. The other a grey, noted for speed.

The bull was said at that time, to be of the best stock in England. He was kept upon a farm adjoining my father's. Although spotted, his stock were a large proportion red. The oxen were those large broad-horned, spoken of in your discussions. The red were the preferred colors among the farmers. The Bissel ox, of East Windsor, Conn., noted at the time as being the largest in the States, if not in the world, was of this stock of red cattle—a noble animal. My brother saw him, and to exhibit his dimensions, a one-half bushel was placed upon his back, between his pipe, and a peck measure on each side of it, and stood without assistance. His weight was between 3,000 and 4,000 lbs. The bull, when killed, weighed 1,700 or 1,800, and was said not to be fat. My father had killed, of mixed breed, that weighed over 1,100.

Col. Wadsworth was a farmer, considered at that time of large fortune, owning many farms about Hartford, on which this stock was kept. He owned, besides, a large tract of land in the Genesee country of this State, which, as I understood, he employed two of his nephews to survey and dispose of, giving them the privilege to select as much and where they chose, for themselves. Somewhere between 1800 and 1806, or 1808, they at several times, visited Hartford, to get of this stock of cattle and horses from their uncle's farm. My father was selected by the parties to appraise the stock they took home with them, as well as some purchased of my father—his being red.

In after years, droves of these, or from this stock, were driven through the country, which the drovers reported were purchased from these Genesee Wadsworths. There was exhibited at the State fair at Poughkeepsie, a number of yoke of working oxen—perhaps as many as ten—that appeared to be of this same stock, owned, as was said, by these western Wadsworths, who at this time, I believe, are neither of them living. And the principal part of those familiar with this important importation having passed away, is my apology for these remarks. I might add that this Col. Wadsworth was said to belong to General Washington's staff; probably had charge of the commissary department.

I might add to a subject on which a great deal has been said—that of corn ground in the ear, called cob-meal—that from forty years' experience, it is a favorite of mine for fattening oxen and working horses, and especially in fattening swine, after they are five or six months old, previous to which I prefer rye, ground, or its bran—corn, at that age, being too hearty. After this age they want as much as they will eat, and I consider the cob-meal will do them as much good as clear meal, which is apt to clog, being more than they can digest, and is wasted, passing the stomach more readily than cob-meal, and yet the cob contains more or less nourishment.

Experiments of forty years convinced me that pork can be made for four cents per pound, feeding corn at fifty cents per bushel, ground as above, when the farmer has a market for his corn, deliver one load a day at a seaport market, saving his manure and cartage for the trouble of feeding. This by selecting hogs that will fatten young, such as the Barryfield; the Suffolk appears much like them, yet, I think, smaller. Such hogs, with proper attention, will make from 200 to 300 lbs. of pork, at from eight to ten months old.

I fattened two pigs the last season, that I consider did not cost me the amount I have fixed. They were kept in a stye, and fed not beyond good order, until after corn harvest, when it was ground in the ear; wet up two or three days' feed at a time, thick enough to feed with a shovel, and nothing else except some apples, and no drink, until seven and a half months old, when I killed them, weighing 279 and 275. My neighbors had of the same litter, fed the corn in the ear, and I suppose ate more than mine, and did not weigh over 150 lbs.

A member requested the Chairman to state his experience in bees.

Mr. Pell complied, accounting for the production of drone bees, workers and queens. The virgin queen, he believes, lays eggs that produce drones. After association with the male, the eggs produce workers, or queen bees, according to the size of the cells the eggs are hatched in.

Solon Robinson read several letters and extracts, asking information; some of which called up interesting discussions. Here is one:

HOW TO TREAT AN OLD ORCHARD.

Wm. P. Gates, of Windham, Conn., wants to know how to treat the soil in an old orchard, or where trees have been planted ten years. Plowing cuts and bruises the roots, and, he thinks, must injure the trees. How then, shall the soil be loosened?

Judge French, of New Hampshire.—We generally keep our orchards plowed two-thirds of the time, and work the land at first as deep as possible. We don't think it good policy to ripen grain in an orchard. Sow with oats and cut them for green fodder. Plant with corn and cut green. Potatoes are the best hoed crop for an orchard, old or young.

Thomas W. Field.—I have been trying to answer this question a long time. Some orchards on long Island that are plowed often, have ceased to bear, while trees in the hedges and walls continue to bear fruit abundantly. Some pomologists contend that orchards should not be disturbed by the plow. Trees derive very little nourishment from deep soil; it nearly all comes from the fibrous roots near the surface. If we can keep the surface loose it will be useful; but plowing I believe is injurious.

Prof. Nash.—I concur generally with Mr. Field in this; but, for naturally drained land, I have no doubt it is the best practice to let the land lie in grass. No general rule can be given, but it must be adapted to the situation and circumstances of each orchard.

Mr. Pell.—My experience is that all orchards require plowing. I have found roots in my orchards as large as my arm, extending fourteen feet deep. Rye will kill an orchard quicker than anything else. I never stop to inquire whether my plow is cutting the apple roots or not. It does not injure them.

The subject was still further discussed, without coming to any conclusion whether an orchard should be plowed or not.

TO RENOVATE OLD TREES.

Andrew S. Fuller.—I generally take old trees and find how far out the roots extend, and dig so as to cut off three or four feet of the out ends of all the roots, by a ditch three feet deep and three feet wide, which I fill with good soil and manure. It will almost always renovate them. If trees are mossy, scrape it off with a hoe.

Thomas W. Field.—I agree with Mr. Fuller in this recommendation.

WHORTLEBERRIES.

Wm. T. Morse, of Lanawa, Chautauque county, New York, wants to know if the seed of whortleberries will grow after being dried, and if so, how should it be prepared and planted? Can the bushes be transplanted and made to grow successfully?

Mr. Fuller, Mr. Field, Mr. Pell and others, gave answers to this question, the gist of which is, that the seed will grow best planted fresh from the berries. If that cannot be done, wash it out from the pulp and put it in earth, not moist enough to vegetate the seed, nor yet very dry. Transport the mass as soon as possible, and plant the seeds in rows in nursery beds, from which the bushes can be transplanted. They do not live well when transplanted from the woods to other localities.

Solon Robinson.—Here is another letter of inquiry:

THE POULTRY BUSINESS.

C. Upson, of West Meriden, Connecticut, wants information about establishing a great poultry and egg-producing business, to supply city markets; also, what breed of hens are the best for eggs.

R. G. Pardee.—I have tried almost all varieties of hens, and have settled upon the Black Spanish, or crosses of them upon the old stock, such as I can pick up in market at fifty cents a piece. I have also tried the experiment of keeping hens in the city and the cost of eggs. I keep them in a house at the back of the yard, letting them out for exercise just before roosting time, feeding them on scraps from the kitchen—potatoes, meat, &c., and corn, and find my eggs cost just three cents a dozen on an average through the year.

Solon Robinson.—I recommend to the inquirer the account of the business in France, where dead horses are converted into eggs and chickens.

Thomas W. Field.—The less hens I keep, I think the better for me. I have fed them with dead horses and all sorts of food, but I can't make it profitable to myself or neighbors either.

Solon Robinson.—I have one more letter, a part of which I will read.

CANADA THISTLES.

A Vermont boy writes a feeling letter about Canada thistles; for, as he says, " I was once a barefooted Vermont boy, and suffered so much from this same *Carduus arvensis*, that I can feel them to this day. About subduing them, he says:

" The hoe will *not* discommode it, only preventing its going to seed, and I make no doubt that the roots are stronger in the fall, after a hoed crop, than they were in the spring before; for the hoe can reach only the top of the upright rhizoma, thereby heading it back, to its advantage, as any gardener knows. It cannot be destroyed by being torn into pieces by the plow or harrow; for its long, rope-like roots—both the rhizoma, and true roots—reaching from two to six feet below the surface of the ground, swarm with buds, and a short fragment answers the purpose of producing a perfect plant, as well as a potato does a potato plant.

"Then, if we cannot subdue the thistle by force, we must, Pelissier-like, smother it in its den. And this, luckily, is easily done. Leave the foe alone during the spring, when they, as though thinking they have the field to themselves, will put forth all their forces, and, in June, the strength and vigor of the plant will be above, or near the surface of the ground. Then put a 'green-sward plow' among them, and carefully turn them under in their pride, and you have subdued them. This will uttarly clear them from fields that can be plowed; and buckwheat or turnips are just in time to take the place of the thistles. Clover is prized for soiling, because the roots bear seed: but thistle roots seem to have no end. Rocky pastures must smart or prick, unless close mowing before a heavy rain, while the thistles are in blossom, may help them."

GRAPE CULTURE.

This was one of the questions of the day, and was called up in preference to any other, for the purpose of getting Dr. Grant, of Iona, an island in the Hudson, near Peekskill, to give the Club his views. The Doctor has devoted a great deal of attention to grape culture, and has read all that has been published, and his remarks were listened to with an attention that showed how deep an interest is taken in this question. We can only give a few brief notes of what he said, all of which he illustrated with well executed drawings, and with real vines. His discourse was one abounding with practical information. Several grape-growers present gathered near to catch every word, often putting questions that elicited valuable information.

Pruning.—Cut off the first year's growth above two buds, and next year cut back so as to leave two buds of that year's growth. In nature a vine grows both branch and roots to a great length, before bearing fruit, as it can bear no fruit until its leaves and branches reach the air and sun at the top of the tree. In cultivation we must train vines to new habits. We cannot depend upon any but native varieties. A well grown vine will reach five or six feet the first year, and ten or twelve feet the second year, and its success as a bearer will mainly depend upon the manner of training, and pruning it the first year. No untrimmed vine can remain healthy and be productive. Fruit buds grow upon the same branches but once. Ten feet square of ground is required for a root, and six or seven times that for the vine. Mildew is the great enemy to contend with, and the vine must have air and vigorous growth, for that tends to prevent mildew, and it must have room so as to expose every leaf to the sun. On the third year two bunches to a cane, or branch, is all that can be grown to perfection; all others must be plucked off. The leaves naturally develop themselves to

the sun, and no more leaves must be left than will fill the space. No healthy leaf grows in the shade. Vines suffered to bear too full the third year are ruined ever after.

The fourth year, train up four upright canes, and these will each produce three bunches, and the horizontal shoots will produce twenty-four bunches and bud out new shoots. Only three bunches to a shoot should be grown, and a bunch never should be exposed to the noon-day sun. Training vines upon the trellis is best for the vineyard. The arbor gives shade, and may give satisfaction; but the trellis gives the most fruit. Four feet length of elevation of canes is as much as will produce perfect fruit.

At the end of the seventh year the vine is fully established, with three branches on each shoot, which will give six bunches, three on each arm between each upright. At the base of each shoot is a bud for the fruit-bearing shoot next year. The ends of the fruit-bearing branches must be stopped at about two feet from the base. It will shoot again, and must be stopped again, and this stopping is best done by merely pinching the vine at the right point with thumb and fingers, leaving one leaf. The best thing to tie vines to the trellis wires is basket willow. Bulrushes are also good. Hatters' trimmings are also recommended.

If all the buds are permitted to grow, the vine will soon be ruined. The best bunches always grow nearest the stalk. November is the best time to shorten back a vine to the buds that are to be left for bearing. It is an object with the young vine to cut back or stop the growth of branches, to give strength to the root. Pinching the bud of a growing vine is to give vigor to the root, as well as the buds that are to furnish the canes for fruit next year.

The doctor exhibited vines one year old six feet long, and two years old twelve feet long, grown from two-eyed cuttings of the Diana Grape, which is considered a slow grower. Long cuttings should never be planted. Take a cutting with three eyes and set it in the ground, so that the upper one is half an inch under the surface. Two or three eyes are better; two eyes are best. A serpentine form given to a young vine makes it grow stronger. The best plan to get new vines is by layers. It makes vines that will bear earlier. I have seen five bunches upon a Delaware cane of one year, grow perfect. But three bunches to a cane, generally, is as much as can be depended upon. A vine must not be made to overbear, or over-produce wood. Sparing the knife spoils the vine. I think, in this country, that the trellis form of growing vines, both for wine and market fruit, will be the best plan—better than growing upon stakes. On posts seven or eight feet high place five wires, and set the rows ten feet apart, and running north and south if convenient. Grapes can be grown to advantage in the city. A vigorous vine can be carried up six or eight feet a year, without bearing until it reaches the top of the house, and there trained upon a trellis, and produce good fruit many years. Vines can, also, be trained upon brick walls, or in yards, that have four hours of sun a day. It is not necessary that the sun shine on the ground where a vine is rooted, so that it reaches up to a sunny spot for leaves and fruit. I have trained vines up a house-side three stories high.

All sides of a house may be used, but on the north side the fruit will not ripen well. A northeast exposure, on the sea coast, is not a good one for grapes. One objection to an eastern exposure is bright suns after frosts. Summer pruning is indispensable. In the angle between the leaves, two buds start, and if one is not pinched out it will produce a shoot that will bear green grapes in the fall. Care must be taken not to cut off the vines in the hard wood in the summer. The shoot must be stopped in the bud, by pinching, and not by cutting away hard wood. Vines never should be trimmed with ordinary shears, but by a very keen knife, with a smooth cut.

The bunch next to the main stem covers the bud of the fruit-bearing branch for next year. In pruning in the fall all of the fruit-bearing arm is cut away to one bud. It is better to prune in November than later, on account of the exuding of the sap, which is considerable if pruning is done in March, which damages the vine more the second year than the present year. There are many advantages in pruning in November, but if neglected then, it must not be neglected altogether, for upon that, and also plucking off all excess of fruit, depends the success of grape-growing.

NATIVE WINES.

Mr. Rockwell, of Ridgefield, Conn., exhibited a large number of samples of Connecticut made wine, which were tested and several of them approved. To our notion, the fault of this manufacture is that he uses too much sugar.

RHUBARB WINE.

Solon Robinson announced that he had a bottle of native wine that very strongly resembled Sherry, which he would offer to the ladies and gentlemen, in the beautiful silver goblet which "the friends of progress in Connecticut" presented him for telling them they could better grow grapes than corn upon their hard rocky hillsides. This wine was drank with great satisfaction, and highly praised ; and then he told those who admired its good qualities, that it was made from the juice of rhubarb (pie plant), at the rate of 800 gallons per acre, in Wisconsin.

Dr. Grant said the osier (or basket willow,) was best for training the vines on, that his German vine-dressers fixed them firmly in their places very quickly and beautifully !

Amos Gore had found hatter's shavings very good (the trimmings off the edges of hats).

Dr. Grant.—They are excellent. November is the best time to prune the grape vine.

Mr. Pardee.—Do grapes love the sun ?

Dr. Grant.—Six hours in a day is enough for them. The brick walls of your cities are favorable for the grapes because they are heated by the sun and retain it well.

Mr. Pell read the following remarks on drainage:

The ordinary expectations of the results from thorough draining varies much according to the nature and previous condition of the land. A sixth of increase in produce of grain crops may be considered as the very lowest estimate, and in actual result it is rarely less than one-fourth.

In numerous cases, after one year's cultivation, the yield is doubled, while the expense of preparing and working the land is considerably lessened. There is, in every case, a very great increase of straw, for adding to the manure heap, and a far less quantity of manure placed upon the land, in its changed condition, produces wonderful effect. The complete cleaning of the land is facilitated; the pulverization and disintegration is, at all times, more completely attained, and at far less expense; and the labor of the farmer is rarely interrupted when rain has not recently fallen. On nearly all lands, the actual result in a few years will enable the tenant to pay ten per cent on the cost of drainage, besides being himself well repaid. I have known instances on my farm where thirty per cent on the expenditure has been realized.

You will not consider such returns exaggerated when you consider the various items of which the improvement consists; such, for example, as the increased quantity of every crop, the earlier cultivation, earlier seeding, earlier maturity of grain, and, as a consequence, its improvement in weight and quantity; the facility it affords of cultivating the earth early in the spring and late at the fall; the preservation of manures, particularly if they are liquid, and consequent economy in their application, besides other advantages which are productive of considerable profits.

Still it is difficult to state accurately what returns may not be actually realized, owing to the numerous circumstances of the natures of soils, height of the land drained, proximity of population, etc. Other considerations are likewise involved with the expense of drains, fencing, clearing the land, and above all this cost, capital is required to thoroughly cultivate the land, without which drainage, of itself, would not repay the outlay involved.

I have qualified a thin clay soil, which in parts was covered with water, and consequently unfit for cultivation, to grow not only green crops in profusion, but grow crops superior to those on the dry and cultivated lands in the neighborhood—a result attributable to drainage, which will most assuredly pave the way for the introduction of the most perfect system of garden culture, facilitate the growing of a succession of crops the same summer; likewise the use of manure in the liquid form, which is the only way it should be applied, and finally afford immense advantages in the application of irrigation on grass land, which cannot possibly permeate the soil unless it is effectually underdrained. Without this preparation, irrigated meadows are rapidly converted into swamps, and soon contaminate the atmosphere by depositing dress on the surface.

Drainage, besides benefiting the land, ameliorates the climate and purifies the air, as it is well known that shallow, stagnant water, and water mechanically separated, as it is in the soil, is far more susceptible of evaporation than when in motion, as a creek, or combined as a pond; and that evaporation is invariably accompanied with a diminution of the temperature from objects from which it takes place. When water is evaporated, each drop divides itself into a thousand parts, which are borne up by the friction of atmosphere. Drainage keeps water in constant motion, and removes it so far below the surface as to prevent the sun from acting upon it, which of necessity prevents excessive evaporation with its usual reduction of temperature.

And if ammonia and other gaseous substances, the result of vegetable and animal decomposition, are, as they are believed to be, the origin of miasma, and the source of fevers, their retention near the surface will be great in proportion to the amount of water.

In my practice, by way of experiment, I have used cylindrical pipes fourteen inches long, of several sizes, adapted to the quantity of water to be removed, and joined together at the junction by a collar, which centres each pair of pipes, and maintains the line of the bore. I have likewise placed small stones in the bottom of the drain, and on these arranged cylindrical pipe tiles of two inch bore. I have also tried the horse-shoe tile with sole, and the pipe tile of two inch tube without collars, which latter would run a much larger quantity of water in a stated time than the horse-shoe tile, and carry with it, to its terminus, more earthy matter taken in at the junctions. Pipes are one-third less weighty than tiles with soles, and cost less at the tilery. I would therefore give them the preference, next to stone, of all other materials for general drainage.

Open or horse-shoe tiles should always be laid on flat tile soles or slate. Pipe tiles of less than 1½ inches should be laid with collars, and for large sizes, scoop out the bottom of the drain to fit the periphery of the tile, or an unobstructed run of water will not be secured. Tiles ought always to be laid by a man in whom you can place unbounded confidence, with strict orders on no account to hurry the work, but to lay them perfectly even and firm.

. Drains 12 feet apart require for an acre :

		12 inch tile.	15 inch.
12 feet apart,	....	3,630	2,904
18 "	....	2,420	1,936
21 "	....	2,074	1,659
30 "	....	1,452	1,161
36 "	....	1,210	968

The cutting of tile drains requires precise work, and should be performed with tools made expressly for it, consisting of a narrow spade, long in the blade, which turns the sides of the drain and throws out the loose soil readily. Connected with this instrument there are two other tools that will be found indispensable, a narrow hoe to remove small stones, and narrow scoop to remove wet earth. I usually finish the beds of the drain with a trowel, before laying the pipe.

The cost of land drainage per acre, with tiles 1¼ inches, at $7 per 1,000, may be approximated as follows:

Tenacious gravelly clay soils, drains 15 ft. apart, 2 ft. 6 in. deep,....$40
Friable clay,..................... 18 ft. apart, 2 ft. 9 in. deep,.... 29
Clayey loam, ... 22 ft. apart, 3 ft. deep, ... 25
Light gravelly loam,............. 33 ft. apart, 3 ft. 6 in. deep,.... 20
Sandy loam, ... 39 ft. apart, 4 ft. deep, ... 15
Sandy soil, ... 45 ft. apart, 4 ft. deep, ... 14
Coarse gravel, ... 60 ft. apart, 4 ft. 6 in. deep,.... 13
Loose gravel, ... 66 ft. apart, 4 ft. 6 in. deep,.... 11

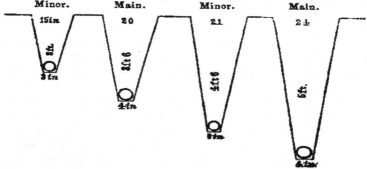

The smaller the quantity of water to be discharged, the greater care you must take, not only in the concentration of the flow, but exactitude of the construction of your pipes, as it is of far more importance than smoothness of surface. A perfectly smooth glass pipe, with a wavy surface, will discharge far less water at the same inclination, than clay pipes of perfect construction.

I have observed a great error made by farmers in common practice, which is to form the junctions of their drains at right angles, with pieces projecting, which impedes the flow nearly as follows: Equal quantities of water running in a straight line at the rate of eighty seconds, with a turn at right angles, the discharge will be effected in 130 seconds, while with a moderate curve, in 100 seconds.

In calculating the expense of forming ditches or drains, one of the principal items is the quantity of dirt that has to be thrown out, which of course depends on the size of the ditch. The cost of labor increases with the weight of earth to be removed; therefore it is well to know the number of cubic yards of cutting in a ditch of any given dimensions. This, may be readily found by multiplying together the mean width, depth, and length. For example, if your drain is three hundred yards long, and the cutting three feet deep, twenty inches wide at the top, and four inches at the bottom, the mean width would be twelve inches, (or the half of the sum, twenty and four,) and if you multiply one hundred, the length, by one, the depth in yards, and by one-third, the mean width in yards, the product would be one hundred cubic yards.

Draining on solid clay, free from stones, may be made at a cheaper rate per rod, in length, than on any other variety of soil, as its firmness permits the labor to be accomplished with narrow spades, and the removal of small quantities of soil.

Draining sands, gravels, or clays, in which veins of sand are found, is much more expensive, because broad spades are used and a large amount of soil must be removed. And draining stony soils is more expensive still, because it becomes necessary to use the pick, which adds much to the expense. If the first six inches is turned up by the plow, a man will dig 100 rods of drain through wet, stony, hard ground, three feet deep, twenty inches wide at the top, and three inches wide at the bottom, in thirty days, counting ten hours to the day. One man in two days will lay the tiles, and in eight days fill up the drain.

On a loam soil with a clay subsoil, drained to the depth of four feet, the upper six inches plowed out, one man can easily dig, one day with another, three and a half rods per day, throwing out ten and a half cubic yards of soil.

There was a draining plow exhibited at the World's Fair in London, which was considered to hold the next place to the American reaper. It was worked by two horses attached to a capstan, which, by an invisible wire rope, drew towards it a low framework, leaving a narrow slit cut on the surface of the ground. On examination it proved to have dragged through the slit, behind it, a string of pipes at the depth of four feet below the surface, which were firmly fixed in the ground, but it did not give the drain a uniform decline. After the first trial before the committee, in a clay subsoil with a gentle descent, the success was perfect. And it drained an acre with $1\frac{3}{4}$ inch pipes, 33 feet apart, $2\frac{1}{2}$ feet deep, for 12.62½.

I had occasion once to take up some pipes, through which a spring run of thirty gallons per minute, and I found to my amazement the roots of the Canada thistle growing luxuriantly thirty feet long, and a willow forty, which would soon have entirely choked the pipe.

You will find that the more vegetable matter and clay that a soil has in it, the more it will contract and swell, in alternate dry and wet weather. This contraction in clay soils, frequently presses upon tender roots injuriously; while a sandy soil has the same bulk, whether wet or dry, and therefore the roots are compressed uniformly in all weather, and may be thrown out, undisturbed, in all directions.

There are thousands of farmers who have never had any opportunities of observing the effects of perfect drainage, and the great difference between undrained and drained land, and they consequently cannot judge when land needs drainage. When such is the case, it dries up in the summer season, the soil cracks, and forms open fissures in every direction, the surface becomes too hard to plow, is inelastic, and entirely too dry for the growth of vegetables.

In the fall, the cracks fill with water, and, having no outlet, become soft and wet, sinking under foot like a sponge, and entirely unfit for advantageous cropping.

In the spring, there is no vigor in the plants, they appear sickly, their color is bad, their parts undeveloped, and if they grow at all, ripen unequally, and if stock are turned in to graze, they will invariably avoid the undrained portions.

The condition of the soil, and drainage that may be required, can always be ascertained by test-holes, dug here and there, from four to eight feet deep, and wide enough for a man to work readily in. The water issuing from the sides, will invariably show at what levels it is accumulated, and the necessary depth of drains to carry it away.

Drains frequently fail to produce the desired effect, from the want of a perfectly regular inclination. If, instead of a gradual and uniform fall, they rise in the bed, the descending water will of course accumulate, until it reaches the level of the rising, and there form permanent stagnation. Therefore do not, on any consideration, fail to make the bottom of your drain, perfectly straight to the out-fall, which may be accomplished with three staves of wood, two of them two feet long, and the third as much more than two feet as the drain is deep ; place one of the short ones on the ground at the head of the drain, and the other at the lower extremity. A second party then holds the long one in an upright position, touching the bottom of the drain, and if the tops of the three are on a line, the fall is uniform. In the alluvial clay districts, west, where the drainage is effected by open ditches, ague and fever is periodically prevalent ; rheumatism and scrofulous affections, also abound. The country is subject to dense fogs, which invariably communicate a chilly feeling to the people, and the cattle suffer with a disease known as " red water," all of which bad effects immediately disappear when the drains are covered in.

The depth and distances of drains that are in general use are various, arising from the difference necessary to suit the different nature of the soils, and the difference in opinion of practical farmers. The soils, likewise, are so varied in character, that no settled rule can be established.

The depths in use since the introduction of thorough draining, have varied from two to three, four, five, six, and seven feet ; the distances apart have ranged from ten to sixty feet, with success. For years it was almost impossible to persuade practical men that depths from eighteen inches to two feet would be effectual in clay soils, at whatever distances they might be placed ; but in the course of experience, depths from two and a half to three feet, in clays, and compacted drift soils, have led to general adoption of such depths. Where beds of gravel, sand, or other loose soils, occur within five or six feet of the surface, if the out-fall will allow, it is best to cut down to them, but never so deep unless under such circumstances. Deep drains arrest the ascent of water and noxious substances from beneath, whether by the force of springs or capillary action, and will be permanent only so long as you keep them in good order; the moment they are neglected, the original state of the field will return again. When rain enters the earth, it displaces the air with which it comes in contact, which either rises into the atmosphere or descends to the drains. When it ceases to fall, the water sinks, and the pores are left open to take in fresh air. Efficient drainage protects the farmer from the uncertain duration of the seasons, by carrying off the water so rapidly as to render the soil workable so soon as the rain ceases to fall. If a man will undertake to drain thoroughly, say ten acres of land, he will find himself repaid in three years. He may, then, gradually drain any amount by the repeated use of the same money. In draining, remember that water does not run into drains by instinct, but completely saturates the soil, and can only be drawn off by drains made deep. A three foot drain will only drain land two feet six inches, and it is usual for rye and wheat to extend as deep in the soil as they do above it. A well authenticated case has come to my knowledge, where the roots of rye have extended, on the bank of the Wall-kill river, to the depth of seventy-two feet, for water. If you make two sets of drains, one deep and the other shallow, the shallow one will be useless, except to aerate the soil. On low lying soils, if you have a sufficient out-fall, and can reach gravel by going down six, eight, or even ten feet, do not fail to do so, and it will affect favorably all the land on the same level, even if it be ten miles square, and all the mill sites within the same area, unfavorably, by bringing the water to a point at which it will be useless to fill mill ponds. And notwithstanding I am the owner of some of the finest mill sites in the country, I would be willing to see them all demolished throughout the land for the sake of agriculture, and steam power substituted, and have no doubt but that, in a majority of cases, this arrangement would prove not only economical to the farmer, but to the manufacturer, as it would restore the streams to their natural beds, and thus open them as arteries for drainage, and enable farmers, millers and manufacturers, to reclaim, and bring under cultivation, at a moderate cost, thousands of acres now overflowed and destroyed by mill dams. I believe if nine out of ten of the mill streams in the United States, were surveyed from the ocean to their source, and the mills upon them valued, the land injured or benefited by such mill dams ascertained, and the question of advantage or disadvantage to the landholder and manufacturer appraised, it would be found that the injury done would far exceed the rental of the mills; and it would be a measure of national economy, to buy up the mills and give the owners steam power, in all densely inhabited districts.

Thorough drainage will be the means of introducing many important improvements by the extended cultivation of green and root crops, giving employment to the laboring population, increasing the quantity and reducing the price of food, raising the value of land by lessening the expense of labor, increasing the number of cattle, which will multiply the substantial manures, besides ameliorating the climate, as has been proved, and bringing cereal crops to early maturity.

My gardens have been very deeply drained with stone, and though a high sandy loam, with uniform beneficial results; and, notwithstanding they necessarily contain many trees and plants, not annuals, no obstructions have occurred during eighteen years from the roots of trees, or biennials, besides their forwardness, early productiveness, and perfection of crops, have been greatly increased. Fruit trees and grape vines that were previously entirely barren, became great fruit bearers, and not only so, but the elevated temperature caused them to ripen their fruit two weeks earlier than the same varieties not so favorably circumstanced.

I have applied drainage to wood lands, and thus produced a most vigorous growth, but find very old decaying trees are immediately destroyed by it, when sound trees are wonderfully improved, no matter what their age may be, or whether they stand alone, or in clumps. But young plantations thrive astonishingly, and the contrast between a drained and undrained orchard would be remarked by the most casual observer, the one being vigorous in growth, healthy in the bark, and free from moss; the other precisely the reverse. Nearly all the old orchards in the United States may be classed with the latter,—not one in a hundred of which has probably ever been drained, and the consequence is their present forlorn appearance, and rapid advancement towards destruction. I hazard the opinion, that in a few short years, that noble fruit will be very scarce in our country, and all through the neglect of proper drainage. And if my experiments prove true, that drainage quickly destroys old and decaying trees, it is too late with many of them to adopt this mode of renovation; but I would strenuously urge all those, who are so fortunate as to have thriving old orchards, to lose no time in constructing deep stone underdrains between each, or every other row of trees, according to the nature of the soil. And here, they will find an immense advantage in stone over every other substance, from the fact that they will if proper precautions are taken in their arrangement, not only dry the ground, and elevate the temperature, but what is next in importance aerate the roots, so that the atmosphere, which is always laden with moisture, and the gases essential to their existence may freely find them. When water falls on undrained land it runs off rapidly, but if drained, it trickles along the surface short distances, absorbs gaseous matters, and then penetrates the ground, conveying them immediately to the roots of trees and into their circulation, thus ministering to their nourishment and growth. Rain water in falling to the earth washes the atmosphere of the solid matter that had previously risen into it in the form of vapor, and as it passes into well drained ground dissolves other solid substances, which are conveyed in a liquid form to the roots of plants, and ascend with the sap through the stalks.

I have heard farmers regret that they had drained their clay lands, because they crack and become dure, still I scarcely ever knew weather so hot as entirely to exhaust the clay, which has a great affinity for moisture, of its water, and have generally noticed that the grain crops and grass on such land, was flourishing when that on lighter lands was burned up.

It will be well to remember that all bodies on the surface of the earth radiate rays of heat in perfectly straight lines, warm bodies to cold bodies ; and the whole surface is eternally casting rays into space through the atmosphere, both striving for an equilibrium of heat. Different substances on the earth radiate heat with different degrees of rapidity, and those which become cool first, attract the falling dew first. Thus you may observe in summer, your pastures will be perfectly wet, while your gravelled road will be dry, and your thoroughly drained field will delight the falling dew, which will only expend its superfluity upon the undrained clod. Who can contemplate with indifference the unbounded munificence of the Great Impartial.

Let two adjoining fields be wet in different degrees, that which is wettest will, invariably give off the largest quantity of moisture, and will, consequently, be the coldest. When spring arrives it will warm and prepare the one for cultivation by the heating rays of the sun, while the other will swallow them up, and cause them to re-ascend in the form of vapor. The remedy for this state of things is effectual drainage.

Soil has great capillary power, as may be instanced by pouring water on the soil of a flower pot, which the earth gradually absorbs until the surface becomes moist. The same operation is constantly performed in your open fields. The water from beneath is drawn to the surface, and where it is present in large quantities, the capillary action keeps the top moist, and consequently cold. This tendency to ascend is not the same in all earth by any means. In soils that contain a large percentage of vegetable matter, and in porous, sandy soils, it ascends readily, but not so in stiff clays. The capillary action above mentioned is of very great importance, as it renders the earth the power to produce remunerating crops, by bringing with it the soluble matters that rest in the subsoil, which, when they reach the surface, evaporate the water, and leave the saline matters to accumulate behind them.

A proper drain covered in, of the same depth as an open ditch, will drain a much greater breadth of soil than the open ditch can possibly effect, because their absorptive power is inferior to the blind drain. from the fact that their sides become covered with vegetation. Besides, during dry seasons, the water moves sluggishly over the uneven bottoms, frequently lodging in pools, becomes stagnant, and gives off an offensive, insalubrious effluvia, highly noxious to the inhabitants in the vicinity, and sometimes causing fatal diseases.

If drainage can be directed into natural streams, you may diminish the friction and accelerate the discharge, by straightening and thereby shortening the drains, and concentrating the flow.

You frequently find districts below high water mark, where there is no outfall; in fact there are millions of acres in New Jersey, within a short distance of this city, that might be drained by steam power for a very small sum per acre. For example: a single pumping engine, in England, made by Harvey, upon the expansive principle, working twenty-four hours per day, seven days per week, mean power ninety-five horses, raised four million, one hundred and seven thousand, eight hundred and twenty-five gallons of water per diem. With regard to the Jersey meadows, there is a want of natural outfall, and the ditches are alternately filled and emptied as the tide flows and ebbs.

Were I to attempt to drain these immense areas of valuable land, all of which are destined, at no distant day, to be reclaimed, I would prevent the river water from oozing through the soil as it now does, by digging a wide ditch; parallel to the river, of a depth greater than the proposed drainage, and fill it completely with rammed clay incorporated with gravel, which forms a composition not apt to crack or contract, as much as clay would alone.

After having progressed so far, I would next secure an outfall, by conveying the water to the river, at low tide, by drains having sluice boxes so arranged as entirely to exclude the entrance of the river water at flood tide; and if the supply of water from the land proved greater than could be gotten rid of thus, I would collect it in deep reservoirs and eject it by mechanical force, or steam. Setting aside the mooted question as to the depth at which water ought to be retained, I do not so much object to depths greater than three feet, as I do to greater distances in all soils, as I have universally found, from long experience, that wherever distances more than twenty-four or thirty feet, in compact soils, have been adopted, there has not been, uniformly, a perfectly dry condition of soil, particularly after recent rain. If you would have quick drainage and complete aeration of your land, incur the expense of stone, and place your drains twenty feet apart.

Same subjects ordered to be continued.

The Club then adjourned.

H. MEIGS, Secretary.

March 14, 1859.

Present—Messrs. R. L. Pell, Rev. Dr. Adamson, of the Cape of Good Hope; Solon Robinson, Fowler, Bruce, Witt, Lawton, Chilson, Provoost, Fuller, Doughty, Haines, Veeder, Wright, jr., Van Houghton, Darling, Dr. Holton, Hon. J. G. Bergen, Wm. B. Leonard, John W. Chambers, Manning, Daniel C. Robinson, Mrs. Fowler, Mrs. Roberts, and nine other ladies, Hon. R. S. Livingston, Godwin, Alex. S. Rowley, Prof. Nash, and others—88 members.

Robert L. Pell, in the chair. Henry Meigs, Secretary.

The Secretary read a translation by him from

La Révue Horticole. Paris, 1859.

LES RAISINS BARBUS. (*Bearded Grapes.*)

A short time ago we gave an account of this phenomenon, and we now give a note from F. Boncenne, a judge of the civil tribunal of Fontenoy-Compté (Vendée), stating that this wonderful beard, gazed at as an approaching old age of grape, denoting the end, is, after all, an invention entirely human; pardon me the saying, "a little horticole recreation" which the greater part of our gardeners have done to make merry those who come to look at the gardens.

BLACK SWEET CORN.

Wm. Lawton.—I present some curious specimens of dark-husked corn. All the leaves and stalks are purple, and so is the cob, while the grains are white. Now, this dark color may have some effect upon the ripening of the seed, on account of the color absorbing the rays of heat more freely. Other ears were exhibited, the grains of which were dark, which grew upon white cobs and white stalks.

ROCKY MOUNTAIN CORN.

Mr. Doughty exhibited specimens of the corn with every kernel covered with a husk, and also ears from the same seed, grown on the same stalk, entirely free from these surperfluous husks.

Secretary Meigs.—I grew the Jersey sweet corn, of shrivelled grains, more than forty years ago. I found the growth very uniform. The ears small, and quality for the table when green, very fine. I procured some of the Mandan corn, brought by Lewis & Clark, and first made known to the Atlantic States. It was white, ears quite small, not more than seven inches long, and the earliest we had seen. I had ears fit for table by the fourth of July, on this island.

R. G. Pardee.—I grew the black sweet corn ten years ago, and found it much sweeter than the old sort. I don't know that it has any other advantages, and its color is objectionable.

TANNERS' WASTE FOR MANURE.

Solon Robinson.—I hold in my hand a letter from Samuel R. Eells, of Northampton, Penn., who wants to know if tanners' scraps (skivings) are good for manure, and how to use them. Also, if horns and horn piths are or can be used to advantage? He says: "I receive a great many good ideas from your club, through the columns of the Tribune, hence my application."

Now I say, that the information that may be given here to this individual, may be beneficial to a great many other people.

The Chairman.—When I first used these tanners' scraps, I found that they injured the crops. Now, I consider a ton of these scraps, properly decomposed by the aid of the oil of vitriol, and composted with swamp muck, worth as much as three-fourths of a ton of Peruvian guano. The horns and piths are also very valuable, as they contain much phosphate of lime. Bone earth is so valuable, that if applied to a lot covered with five-finger vines, it will renovate and make the field productive. Any way to decompose these tan-yard substances, will make them very valuable, more so than any farm-yard manure, and they are easily managed.

Prof. Nash.—I have seen some wonderful results produced from application of bones to the earth. I have seen the spongioles cling around bones in great masses, to extract sustenance. I believe that crops will use up the substance of bones, in time, without previously dissolving them in acid or otherwise.

The Chairman stated a very pointed result from the buried bones of an animal in causing a grape vine to produce fruit.

Mr. Meigs reminded the club of the system of Columella, 1700 years ago. Make trenches three feet deep and three feet wide; put in some pieces of stones, bones broken up, especially put in skulls of animals, broken up; fill the trench with the best soil suited to the grape; set the vines in it, at suitable distances; let nothing grow; let the surface of the ground be sandy, and not a weed or a plant on it. Such success attended Columella's grapes, and all his crops, that the *Land Skinners* of *Italy* cried out (as our own may well do), " Columella deals with the devil! for Italy has been so long cultivated, that her land is worn out, and cannot be restored by natural means. Columella gets his secret help from the devil!"

It was with that learned farmer as it was, some thirteen hundred years afterwards, with the father of printing. Oh! the devil and Dr. Faustus!

Mr. Pardee enquired what depth bones should be placed around grape vines.

The Chairman.—No matter how far off the bones are, the vine roots will find them if it can get no phosphates from any other source. All crops must have phosphates, and grapes cannot grow without a supply. Roots spread abroad in search of food; if they can find it at home they will not spread.

LIQUID MANURE.

Dr. Holton read a letter from Dr. Brown, from Wisconsin, inquiring about the mode of sending liquid manure from the vats to the field, and whether it was in a fit condition to apply to crops as it would naturally exist in the vat.

The Chairman stated that liquid manure should only be used in a very diluted state. All manure should be liquefied before applying it to the land.

John G. Bergen said it was utterly impracticable to apply liquid manure upon farms in general. He had heard a great deal about this thing, but he had no faith in it. The best way was to put the manure well composted in our barn yards, upon the field, and the usual rain will dilute it as fast as the wheat and other crops want it. Liquid manure is doubtless good on grass and some other crops; but we shall never find the farm labor conducted with the costly steam and other machinery of Mechi or any other great moneyed man until the millennium.

Solon Robinson.—I am satisfied that the correct method of treating all manure is to put it in solution in tanks at the barn, and send it to the field by steam power, just as has been repeatedly described here as practiced by Mr. Mechi and others in England. Upon any farm, level or hilly, where the amount of team work to haul manure is large enough to justify the first outlay, there is no doubt in my mind that steam power is the cheapest of any that can be used, and the time will come when carting manure will be looked upon as a very slovenly way of farming. It will be found far more economical to dissolve it where it is made, and send it to the field through pipes, by a stationary engine. The people that come after us will look back upon this age of the world as we do upon the dark ages of the past, and wonder how it is possible that we could have been so stupid as to cart manure with oxen and horses, when it would be so much better and cheaper done by dissolving it, and using steam.

Mr. Van Houton, of Paterson, thought the application of coarse manure tended to keep the soil porous, and would be more productive than when fed with liquid manure. A neighbor used flax on a field to great advantage.

Wm. Lawton advocated the old practice of applying manure in bulk. He was afraid of these daring innovations.

Prof. Nash.—It is very difficult to get people to understand the use of liquid manure. The writer of the letter read to us don't appear to understand the theory of liquid manuring. Manure applied in a liquid state must be very much diluted to enable him to spread it over all the land. And he cannot do it to effect in the manner he speaks of, with troughs. It costs in England $100 an acre to prepare the farm with pipes and engines to send liquid manure to the field. I have not much doubt of the economy of this method of applying manure.

The Chairman said that he was satisfied that the time would come when an opinion, different from that now common about applying liquid manure, would prevail.

FLOWER CULTURE.

This question having been some weeks on the docket, was called up.

R. G. Pardee.—I urge all to try to raise seedlings. A lady sent to Boston for some seeds, and out of twenty-five cents' worth, she obtained a great number of valuable verbenas, beside other flowers. Some of our finest flowers are so perfect in the flower that they do not produce perfect seeds without destroying the flower. This is the case with the Aster—the centre must be plucked out to give room for seeds. The finest flower in nature is produced from a seed too small to be seen by the naked eye. It grows two feet across. This is the *Rafflesia.* If a lady can excel in the production of a single flower, she will have a stimulus to go on improving. It is this educated love of flowers that has been the cause of producing the fine flowers that now adorn the world.

LICE ON PLANTS.

The best thing to cure this difficulty, probably, is tobacco-water Solution of aloes is also recommended.

Dr. Grant, the great grape culturist, said that he would state, for the benefit of amateur florists, how to rid them of these troublesome insects. Prepare a tub or some deep vessel full of soap suds, or what you might term almost a sort of diluted soap, and let the pot stand in it half an hour, and then rinse off with clear water. Take the pot in the hands, and reverse and dip the plant in the suds. For plants in the garden a syringe must be used with the soapy mixture, which is also a good fertilizer for the plants. Care must be taken to wash well with clear water afterwards.

Andrew S. Fuller.—I have talked flowers so much that I have talked out, but I am willing to answer questions. I have killed the plant aphis in green-houses by burning tobacco and cayenne pepper. A house plant may be smoked by a common pipe, reversed and blown through. Put a small coal of fire into a pipe, tobacco on that, and then blow through it on to the insects, but be careful to wash the plants well afterwards! they love to have all their pores open and clear. Pure water put on with great force will wash off insects.

JARS FOR PLANTS.

Dont't use a glazed jar for plants under any circumstances.

SWEET WILLIAMS.

This is one of the finest, hardy, fragrant flowers that we have, and grows from seeds, though not always perfect. I have got 30 fine double flowers from 500 seed; the others were single.

THE WARDER CASE

is a fine parlor ornament, and succeeds well.

Mr. Meigs.—The Rafflesia was so called after Governor Raffles, of the Island of Java, who first brought it to European notice.

DOUBLE FLOWERS.

Dr. Adams said, many of the flowers that we esteem so much are works of art—they do not exist in nature. It would be a very important inquiry what is the cause of this great increase of petals, which makes the double flowers, whether the change originates in the seed, or how it is produced. Take the common Marygold, for instance, and it sometimes produces flowers that may be called monstrosities. However common and simple some of these things may be, they afford subjects for valuable studies.

SEEDLINGS.

Mr. Fuller.—We want a good yellow verbena and a good double one, and the lady that succeeds in this will confer a great favor upon the world.

Sow verbena seeds now in good soil and you will get good flowers this season. Select seeds from the best flowers and plant them until you may get what you are in pursuit of. Seeds kept some years are more likely to produce double flowers than new seed. It is a work of time, but nearly all the flowers we have may be improved.

Dr. Grant.—Forty years ago I had two hollyhock seeds, of two sorts. From the flowers of these two seeds I saved seeds, and continued to plant till I got the most beautiful double flowers, by a continued progression. A hollyhock may be made perennial by not allowing the flowers to go to seed.

PREPARATION OF FLOWER BEDS.

R. G. Pardee.—The soil must be finely prepared. I sift some of it for the surface of a flower bed, and make it very level. Sow the flower seeds on the sifted soil, and then sift about one-sixteenth of an inch of the soil over them. I would cover the soil of a new bed with boards, or cloth, to prevent disturbing them in a hard rain. It is also useful to shade it from very hot sunshine. Some seeds need scalding to make them vegetate.

Mr. Meigs.—I planted seed of the Cypress vine, more than forty years ago, which did not vegetate for one year !

Dr. Adamson gave an interesting description of the Rafflesia, which, he said, is a very curious plant. It is of a sort of mushroom character. It is not fragrant. Its shape is of a basin form. Its uses and value are not very apparent. It is always attached to the root of a tree. It originated in the Island of Sumatra, and was named in honor of Gov. Raffle, who sent it over to England, where it has been propagated. It does not properly belong to the fungus order of plants, although it resembles them. It is only grown as a curiosity, in large gardens.

The flowers, when decayed, have a fœtid odor, like decayed flesh. Its seeds are microscopic.

Mr. Pardee.—Mr. Charlton, the horticulturist, of Staten Island, grows several stump parasites, of curious character.

Mr. A. M. Powell, of Columbia, recommended parlor flower portable conservatories, as being very beautiful ornaments.

Mr. Fuller.—They are ; very much so.

Dr. Grant.—I entirely coincide !

Dr. Adamson.—The difficulty of transporting some valuable seeds to great distances, led to the adoption of these portable conservatories, by which the growing plant can be taken long voyages successfully. They became common, as parlor ornaments, in London, five years ago. The ferns and mosses grow well in them. Many flowers not existing in nature, are now produced by art. Stamens become, under culture, petals, as we see in the Hyacinth. Is the change to improvement in the seed ? We sow seeds of single petals, which become double. We have an illustration in the Rocky Mountain corn before us, where the grains are each closely covered with their separate husks originally ; but here, while *one ear* still wears that wild mountain overcoat, *another ear, on the same stalk*, grown by Mr. Doughty in the mild climate of New Jersey, has dropped the overcoat altogether. Such modifications of plants teach us perseverance in the creation of novel flowers, fruits, &c.

Mr. Fuller.—We want a good yellow and a good double Verbenum, and now is the time to sow the seed. The ladies ought to try it. I have raised from flower seeds, 2,000 plants, all differing from the originals, and from each other. When you find a good variety, stick to it. Grow it year after year ; eight, nine—yes, ten years ! The longer the better. You will find that when a deformed flower shows itself, it is ready for doubling. Keep flower seeds three years, or longer. Sow them every year from the same package. We want hardy perennial double Phloxes. I raised 1,000 good for nothing.

JENKINS' CAST IRON FENCE POSTS.

Mr. Alexander S. Rowley exhibited a model of it. The posts six feet long ; with mortises for boards, two inches ; bottom mortise ten inches, next nine, next eight, the fourth seven inches wide. The posts are driven into the ground two feet ; each post having a transverse plate of iron, which is settled to the surface to steady the post.

Mr. Doughty, of Jersey, presented from his farm, Discorea Batatas, of two feet in length.

Mr. Godwin proposed as a question, " The best kind of earth, and the required depth to fill in on streets, for proper culture of shade trees, especially in the avenues around the Central Park; and the best mode of obtaining best turf for the ball-grounds of that park."

Subjects for next meeting—by Mr. Pardee, " Spring flowers, seeds, plants, trees ;" by Mr. Robinson, " Pruning the grape vine ;" by Prof. Nash, " Drainage."

The club adjourned.

H. MEIGS, *Secretary.*

March 21, 1859.

Present—Messrs. Hon. Robert Swift Livingston, Thaddeus Selleck, Fuller, Lawton, Solon Robinson, Daniel C. Robinson, Hon. John G. Bergen, Adrian Bergen, Chilson, Witt, Dr. Peck, Leonard, Chambers, Hardenbrook Wright, Jr., of Flushing, Roberts, Pike, Doughty, Hughes, Paine, John Campbell, Pierce, Geissenhainer, Atwood, Prof. Mapes, Rowe, Spear, Stacey, Absalom Peters, Bruce, Hite, Provoort, French, Dr. Holton, Haines, Pardee, Roberts, Mrs. Fowler, Mrs. Roberts, and 16 other ladies—ninety-nine members in all.

The Hon. R. S. Livingston in the chair. Henry Meigs, Secretary.

The Secretary read the following papers :

[Year Book of Facts of 1859.]

Extract from this very valuable little book.

PISCICULTURE.

M. Coste, who has devoted many years to this interesting subject, has presented to the French Academy of Sciences some specimens of trout, hatched at the College de France, and then transferred to a pond in the Emperor's domain of Villeneuve-l'Etang, near St. Cloud.

The trout of one year old in that pond were about twenty centimetres (about 8½ inches) in length, and between two and three ounces in weight ; so that, in the Paris market, they would fetch from 1 franc (about 20 cents) to 1¼ (about 25 cents) each.

Those of the age of thirty-three months were between 45 and 50 centimetres (17¼ inches) to 19½ inches in length, and weighed from one pound to two pounds and upwards ; so that their market value was between 3 and 4 francs (60 to 80 cents) each. They were so numerous in the small piece of water where they had been reared, that it was impossible to take them with a dredging net without killing some, so that a casting net had to be used. M. Coste added, that they had no other nourishment but worms, insects and tadpoles.

SALMON.

On the 26th of July, 1858, the net fisheries, on the river Tweed, had the largest take of salmon ever remembered by the oldest fisherman, in the same space. From 6 o'clock A. M. till night, they took 3,500 full grown salmon, and about half as many grilses and trout, making in all 5,000 fish.

OBSERVATIONS ON THE CEREALIA.

Mr. Pell spoke on the subject of materials of which we make bread.

The various products of the vegetable kingdom are distinguished from each other, as to their nourishing properties, by the proportion of gluten, starch, mucilage, sugar, oils and acids, that they contain. The first three named are the most valuable, because they abound in farinaceous principles, which, on being dried and ground, produce farina that can be easily converted into bread.

Among farinaceous plants the most important undoubtedly are the corn-bearing grasses, and next to them the leguminosæ, or pods bearing seeds, such as peas, beans, &c. God has kindly distributed the corn plants over the entire world, inhabited by man ; and they consist of Indian corn, wheat, rye, oats, rice and millet. In other countries the term corn is applied to all varieties of grain, but with us, maize alone is called corn. The only grain that will make light bread is wheat, and where this will not grow, the others are called into requisition as food for man.

All grain plants, supported upon hollow straw, are annuals, and known as culmiferous, bearing a leaf from each joint. The stems are covered with fluid, which is extracted from the earth and dissolved by some mysterious process unknown to man, probably ammonia.

Grain-bearing plants are all remarkable for the wonderful power they possess of multiplying themselves indefinitely, according to the circumstances under which they are grown. Their stalks are increased by tillering, which is performed by throwing out a set of coronal roots, above the seminal. One seed has been known to throw up two hundred and fifty stalks, bearing nineteen thousand seeds, and the stalks were divided and planted until they had multiplied to five hundred and ten, sustaining twenty-one thousand two hundred ears, yielding six hundred thousand grains. Cereal plants have been cultivated for so long a period of time, that it is not known where they originated, but it is most probable that most of them came from India, as nearly all our vegetables and fruits. At all events they were all unknown in America when it was discovered, except Indian corn.

The cerealia do not grow equally well in all climates. Rice requires the warmest climate of all, and a totally different mode of cultivation; then next in order comes Indian corn, followed in succession by wheat, rye, barley, and finally oats. Rice, corn and wheat are more extensively cultivated thoughout the world than either of the others, though corn has much the greatest range of temperature; rice supports by far the greatest number of the human family; oats and barley extend farther north than any other grain. In Liberia, rye grows to 60 deg., in Kamtschatka no cereal will grow, and in America 52 deg. appears to be the limit, but in Lapland, 70 deg. In Western Asia, rye will not grow, but wheat succeeds admirably, and furnishes bread for the inhabitants. In China and Japan, rice abounds. In the South Sea Islands no variety of grain will grow, and its place is supplied by the bread fruit tree. In New Holland, agriculture disappears entirely, except in the temperate part, and the people live upon sago. In South America, Indian corn predominates between 4,000 and 6,000 feet of elevation, and not much below or above; but potatoes succeed well at 12,000 feet. Wheat does pretty well in Van Diemen's Land and New Zealand.

In all countries where wheat will succeed at all, it is raised in preference to all other cerealia. It contains more gluten and starch than any other grain, which qualities make it by far the best for bread. During the reign of Henry VIII. wheat flour was only used by the rich, and rye, oats and barley, was the chief food of the poorer classes.

There are several varieties of wheat, but two are mainly cultivated, to wit : Triticum, hybernicum, winter wheat, white and red ; and triticum, astivum, spring, or summer wheat. It is sown in April and ripens in the fall, about two weeks before winter wheat. The grain is small, and does not yield quite as much flour as the winter variety, and is less productive and uncertain in some districts; the straw is used for hats, being easily plaited. Botanists think that the varieties of wheat are produced by peculiarities of soil and climate, and have been divided into hard and soft wheats. The hard wheats are produced in warm climates; the soft wheats in cold. The hard wheats are solid, compact, and almost transparent, and when broken in two present a very white appearance. The soft wheats have no opaque coat, and yield to the pressure of the finger and thumb, they are best fitted for vinous fermentation in distilling and brewing, because they contain the most starch. Wheat varies much according to the different countries in which it is grown ; northern Europe is not favorable to its cultivation. In Sweden, home grown wheat is rarely met with ; rye flour is common, but is baked into bread only in the spring and fall, consequently it is difficult to masticate.

Wheat rolls may sometimes be seen on the tables of the rich, but this is of rare occurrence. A baker was once requested to make five dollars worth for a sea captain, and he required security for the payment, for fear if so large a quantity was left upon his hands he could not dispose of it, even though the town contained twenty-five thousand people. The finest wheat in Europe grows in Sicily, and is of two kinds, the one is a long, plump grain, and is generally boiled for the table, as a substitute for rice ; the other is soft, very white, and is manufactured into bread. Neither variety is exported, owing to government restrictions.

Wheat is, unfortunately, liable to smut, mildew, and blight, principally occasioned by fungi, which may be observed through the medium of the microscope, attached to the ears and stems, constantly engaged in introducing a deleterious matter which destroys the nourishing principle of the grain. Wheat injures, immediately, if stacked before quite dry, or if a wet harvest prevents cutting in proper season ; the sweetest and best is always that which is thrashed as taken from the field.

BARLEY.

Next in importance to wheat may be classed barley, which possesses one great advantage over it, and that is, it may be grown in a far greater range of climate, bearing drought, cold and heat, with impunity, grows on a light soil, comes early to maturity in northern climates, where wheat will not flourish at all. The inhabitants of Lapland grow it in six weeks. The Spaniards have two crops in a season. Its native country is unknown, but I imagine it was Egypt, from the fact that they have grown it from the earliest antiquity. The Romans used it for bread, as do the inhabitants of Scotland, Wales, and several counties in England at the present time. In the south of Great Britain it is principally raised for malt liquors, and is found the best for that purpose, when grown on light chalk soils, which causes the grain to be thin in skin and rich in color ; consequently the barley grown in Norfolk is quite celebrated for its malting properties, and the brewers cannot be induced to purchase the barley raised in Durham, even at a much lower price, if the Norfolk is in market, it is, when unfit for malting, used in those districts for the purposes of fattening hogs and horned stock. If grown on clay soils it will be found coarse and unfit for malting ; on loam, plump, full of meal, and fine for bread. Good malting barley always increases during germination, in the process, one-half in bulk, in twenty-four hours, and when dried, diminishes to the bulk of the grain, but when finally prepared yields eighty pounds of malt to one hundred pounds of barley.

Agriculturists and botanists enumerate many varieties of barley, but those chiefly cultivated are summer (hordeum vulgare,) in which the kernels are disposed in two rows, one on either side, with erect awns, thin husk and large grains. And the winter (hordeum hexasticon,) or double rowed, which is more hardy than the summer variety, ripens earlier, and is better calculated for cold, bleak situations. At the same time it possesses far less saccharine matter than those growing under a more genial sun.

The gluten of barley is soluble in cold water, but coagulates at 130°, it contains a minute quantity of green oily matter, in taste resembling whiskey, and from which it, no doubt, receives its flavor, besides a small percentage of nitrate of soda, capable of crystalizing.

Barley is not so nutritious as wheat, has but one-third as much gluten, as much sugar, more mucilage, and the same quantity of starch. These qualities make it a less stimulating and lighter food than wheat, though much less nutritive. When barley is cut it should be housed immediately, from the fact that if it becomes wet it sprouts and is unfit for bread.

OATS—(*Avena Latina.*)

Is, no doubt the hardiest of all the cereal family, and enjoys a cold climate, so much so that it cannot be cultivated in the southern parts of Europe. I never saw it south of Paris. It possesses one important advantage over all the other grains, and that is, it will succeed where they will not. Crude soils, and stiff clays, if only dry, will grow it; its flavor for food is improved when the soil is poor, and exposure bleak and cold. The relative proportions of meal and husk, in the several varieties of oats, differ in a greater degree than any other cereal. The potato oat is rich in meal, and the Tartary oat, in husk; the former is grown in Scotland for banocks, and the latter in England for bread, and the two in this country for horses. Soil, climate, season, variety, and manure applied, all effect the produce and chemical composition of the grain. Its native country is unknown. Lord Anson discovered it growing luxuriantly on the island of Juan Fernandez. By analysis, in 1,000 parts were found 641 parts of starch, 87 gluten, 15 saccharine matter, showing that it contains less nutritive matter than corn, rye, wheat or barley, and still the laboring people of Scotland, Derbyshire, Lancashire and Wales, subsist mainly, and retain their strength upon bread and sundry other preparations made from it. Those people infinitely prefer bread made from oats than from any other cereal, and it actually occupies the same place in Scotland that the potato does in Ireland, and rye in Germany. When the ground is foul and badly prepared twenty bushels to the acre may be considered a fair yield, but in a rich, well managed, thoroughly drained piece of sandy loam, I have raised eighty bushels to the acre, weighing forty-five pounds to the bushel, and have caused the same oats, sown in drills, to weigh forty-eight pounds, yielding eight pounds of meal to fourteen pounds of oats.

Land intended for this grain should be plowed in the autumn, and again early in the spring, if a full crop is desired; it will, however, grow with less cultivation and on a greater variety of soil than any other of the cereal grasses, but succeeds the best on newly broken up pastures, and fresh soils abounding in organic substances. A wretched custom prevails in this country and Great Britain, of taking two crops of oats in succession, or an oat crop after a barley or wheat crop, which is bad husbandry.

The spikelets of oats contain three seeds, and the florets are furnished with awns. It differs from wheat in the form of the ear; it is not a spike with a single sachis, but a panicle, resembling pine branches; the grains hang with the open extremities downward, and are covered with chaff which defends them from rain, and renders it less liable to some diseases that wheat is subject to.

RYE—(*Secale Cereale.*)

This grain approaches the nearest to that of wheat in its glutenous properties, and ranks next to it in the fitness of its flour for baking into bread. It has probably been noticed by you that have eaten rye bread, that it has a sweet taste, which shows that the flour contains much saccharine matter. Rye flour absorbes much more moisture from the atmosphere than that made from any other grain. The husk contains an aromatic acidulous flavour, and if the bran is not entirely separated when ground into flour, it gives the bread an agreeable taste. It is a singular fact that in the baking, it undergoes an acetous fermentation, which renders the bread sour a short time after it is made, and often has a gentle aperient action upon the bowels. If, however, it is mixed with wheat flour, say two-thirds wheat and one-third rye, it makes a far better bread than either would alone, and is greatly preferred to any other by those accustomed to use it. It is solid and firm, retains its moisture for a long time, and is very nutritious and healthy. To obtain this result readily, sow rye and wheat together.

Rye contains a sufficient quantity of sugar to be easily converted into malt, and consequently spirits and beer. Two parts of unmalted rye meal, mixed with one part barley, is used in Holland for the distillation of Geneva, and it is imagined that an essential oil in the husk imparts to it its flavor.

But this grain which is so much cultivated for bread, is subject to a disagreeable disease known as ergot, which consists of an enlargement of the grain by a fungous; it is a deadly poison, and produces upon the human constitution a dreadful effect, causing in some cases epilepsy, which soon ends fatally. Some are rendered crazy, and others still suffer with mortification of the legs, arms, &c. Its use has proved particularly fatal in parts of Germany and France, but seldom in England or this country. When sown for a crop, two and half bushels per acre is the proper quantity, but if for straw plait, four bushels would not be too much, as it vegetates slowly. It is best always to sow it when the earth is dry, otherwise it may rot before germination takes place. No opinion can ever be formed respecting the prospect of a crop until the period of flowering is past. It ripens earlier than wheat, and if permitted to stand in a shower of rain when quite ripe, it will sprout on the stem. It produces a much larger quantity of straw than any other grain, grows higher, and is stronger than wheat. Besides being cultivated for grain, it is grown as spring food for cattle, and if permitted to come to maturity in a young orchard two years in succession, will destroy it.

INDIAN CORN—(*Zea Maize.*)

This native of the American continent is the most noble of the cereal grasses, and at the present time constitutes the bread corn of North America, Mexico, and a portion of Africa. It is not indigenous in any part of the European continent ; it is probably nearly as extensively used for the food of man as rice, and is celebrated for the large return it yields from a given extent of land. I have raised one hundred bushels of shelled corn to the acre. It is remarkably fattening when fed to pigs, poultry and cattle, and the people who live upon it are hearty, healthy, strong, and think no bread more strengthening. The athletic American Indians sufficiently demonstrate its wholesomeness. It grows well, and prospers in low swampy situations, where it dries up the superfluous moisture, and causes the soil to become firm. It acquires the height of eight or ten feet in favorable localities. I have grown it fifteen feet by the application of specific manures, and when ripe, all the roots of a hill might be placed in a half peck measure. Give the roots of any plant the requisite manures for its growth, and they will not extend themselves ; place them seventy feet off, and they will be sure to find them if the season is long enough.

RICE—(*Oryza Sativa.*)

This grain has formed the principal food of the inhabitants of India, China and Japan, for centuries, and the enormous quantities they consume annually, always surprises other nations. The reason, undoubtedly, is, that it contains so minute a percentage of gluten, that small quantities would be entirely insufficient to sustain the body, when no other food was used, therefore inordinate quantities are found necessary. It is, probably, more extensively grown and consumed than any other species of grain. It is light and exceedingly wholesome, but contains much less nutritive principle than wheat. When in the husk, it is called paddy, that which is exported from Bengal is called cargo rice. It is red, coarse, large grained, and sweet, and is preferred by the natives to all other varieties. It is not kiln-dried before exportation, but parboiled, in earthen vessels, to destroy the vegetative principle, that it may be preserved better, and to facilitate the husking process. Patna rice is much esteemed in Europe, but, nevertheless, that raised on the marshy flats of South Carolina, is, without doubt, superior to any other, no matter where grown.

Rice raised on land, artificially or naturally irrigated, produces twelve times more than that on dry soil. Owing to droughts and other unexplained causes, there is far greater variation in the crops of rice than any other known grain. The reason why the inhabitants of Hindostan suffer more from famine than any other people is, that they depend entirely on rice for subsistence, and when it is cut off their situation is precarious indeed. We export large quantities of rice from Carolina to Europe, with the husk on, by which means the foreign purchaser saves three and a half dollars per hundred weight, duty, besides preserving its sweetness and flavor better, during long voyages, than when shelled.

Rice, when growing, more nearly resembles barley than any other cereal grass; it branches out into several stems, at the tops of which the grains form in large clusters, but grow on separate pedicles, which spring from the main stalk; each grain is terminated by an awn, and is covered with a yellow husk.

In South Carolina the rice is planted in rows, seventeen inches apart, from center to center, by negro women, water is then permitted to flow over the fields for fifteen days, to the depth of three inches or less, to sprout the seeds. It is then drawn off until the rice plants grow four inches, which requires thirty days, the fields are then again flooded for two weeks, to destroy the weeds. These processes cease on or about the 17th of May, after which the ground is permitted to remain dry until the 16th of July, during which period it is frequently hoed, to kill weeds and pulverize the earth; the water is then again introduced to mature the rice, and it ripens while standing in the water. The harvesting extends from August to October. The male slaves cut it with a sickle, and the females put it up in bundles. The cultivation of this grain is exceedingly unhealthy; the slaves are compelled to stand ankle deep in mud, with their bare heads exposed to the sun, which destroys great numbers of them.

Rice, when properly cooked, forms a cheap and valuable addition to our food, and has often been called into requisition to lessen the consumption of wheat flour, in years of scarcity. It should be boiled soft, without breaking the grains. This can only be accomplished in simmering, not boiling water.

BUCKWHEAT—(*Polygonum Fagopyrum.*)

Is known in almost every part of the world; it was first introduced into Europe after the time of the crusades. It is eaten in Russia, Switzerland, China, Japan, the United States, and other countries, but does not properly belong to the cerealia; its leaves resemble ivy, with purplish flowers, and the seeds, beech-mast, being triangular in shape, and of a brown color. It contains a small percentage of gluten and starch, and considerable sugar. In the United States it is chiefly made into cakes, and baked on a griddle; they are sweet and agreeable.

In Silesia, Ukraine, Saxony and France, it is boiled and made into puddings, pottage, or tarts. In Tuscany it is mixed with barley meal and baked into bread. In some parts of our country spirit is distilled from it, in flavor resembling French brandy, which is shipped to France, but not landed, brought back, placed in a bonded warehouse, and sold under debenture as the veritable article.

The cultivation of buckwheat is neglected except in certain districts, notwithstanding it grows upon light sandy soils, eradicates weeds, and enriches the land, besides admirably preparing it for the reception of many other grains. Its growth is very rapid, but, being a native of a warm climate, early frosts have a serious effect upon it. As a food for poultry, hogs, cows, &c., it stands high, and communicates a fine flavor to milk.

MILLET—(*Panicum Sorghum.*)

Bears smaller seeds than any other cereal grass; the number of seeds, however, compensate for their size; it grows well in a sandy soil, and forms the chief article of food for the sandy parts of Nubia, Syria, Arabia and India. It is very productive, and not unfrequently fermented into beer. It is employed for bread, puddings, &c., and sometimes substituted for sago and rice. In our climate it seldom ripens its seeds perfectly, and therefore cannot be cultivated advantageously. The panicum arborescens is reported by Linnæus to equal in height the tallest trees in the East Indies, though the culin is but little thicker than a goose's quill.

Solon Robinson.—I have, as usual, an accumulation of letters upon various interesting subjects, that are interesting because they elicit remarks that are not only useful to the persons who make inquiries, or give information, but to many others who read the reports of these meetings.

WEEDY GRASS PLATS.

Here is a letter from Edwin F. Torrey, of Honesdale, Wayne county, Penn., who wants information upon a difficulty that troubles many other persons. He says:

"I have a grass plat, or rather, it was a grass plat once; but for the last two years the sorrel and plantain have almost run the grass out. I have raked it up every spring with a sharp iron rake, and planted lawn grass seed profusely, and used horse manure, plaster and poudrette, but neither of them seem to produce the desired effect. As I have rose bushes, dwarf fruit trees, &c., planted around in it, I do not wish to spade it up if I can avoid it. If you can suggest any fertilzer that will supply the chemical deficiency, you will confer a favor which will be duly appreciated."

Mr. Robinson then asked some one to tell this man, and so tell hundreds of others, what to do with his grass plat.

Andrew S. Fuller.—I think the difficulty may be cured with lime and salt.

Prof. Mapes afterwards suggested that he should use the "lime and salt mixture," so often described here—that is, lime slaked by water saturated with salt, and left to effervesce in a pile, using the outside as it forms into dry powder, and applying it liberally.

Solon Robinson.—Here is a letter that gives us some useful hints about potatoes. S. W. Brown, of Brimfield, Hampden county, Mass., says:

"The Peach Blows have been our standard article for the last half dozen years, but for two or three years back they have proved a failure, on account of blasting. About the last of August the tops turn perfectly black, and all die off in two days' time. The Prince Albert yielded almost as well as the Peach Blow, but is inclined to be soggy toward spring. The Davis Seedling is now, all things considered, the best potato we raise. It is a good yielder, fair and uniform size, growing better from digging time to spring, and nearly free from rot—the most so of any raised here. We have another potato, a seedling of this county, called by us Wood's potato, and in Boston the Jenny Lind. It is a large, long, reddish potato, not good for the table until midwinter, then fair; yield great. I have dug a bushel in from six to eight hills often. It is the best potato to feed, all things considered, that is raised, and is growing better, as an eating potato, every year, and sells as high, within six or eight cents, as the Peach Blow."

In answer to the question from Mr. Robinson, Joseph G. French said the statement was correct about the feeding quality and value of the Jenny Lind potato.

John G. Bergen.—For the purpose of experiment, I planted 14 pieces of land with potatoes last year, and dug the crop in July, with the following results: The eye end portion of the tuber gave 11 lbs. with the least stalks, and the potatoes averaging largest. The seed of the middle end gave 18½ lbs. and had too many stalks. The bud end gave 14¾ lbs. and had too many stalks. The potatoes were the largest where the fewest stalks grew.

ILLINOIS BUTTER.

Solon Robinson said: Townsend Seeley, of Kendall, Ill., which is on Fox River, south of Ausable Grove, speaks of the country as much better adapted to grass than grain, and thinks if farmers could be induced to plow less and plow better, and seed more land to grass for hay and pasture, and make beef and butter, it would be better for them; but he says that butter makers are discouraged on account of the prejudice in this city against Illinois butter. He wants farmers advised what to do. This prejudice against Illinois butter is no greater than it is against all western butter. In fact, no greater than it would be against any butter that comes to market in the same bad condition, or that is made in a country where the water will not answer for washing in the laundry; because, butter to keep well, not only needs to be made from sweet grass, grown upon a soil where no lime abounds, and to be washed in soft cold water, just as surely as a dirty garment needs to be washed in soft hot water. Illinois butter is, when well made, good while new, but the best of it does not keep as well after it comes here as some of our home made. That is one reason why butter making cannot be depended upon for profit in that State.

GROWING RADISHES.

Here is a little piece of information that may be useful to many persons. Thomas Jones, of Centre county, Mich., wants to tell others how to raise radishes without their being troubled with weeds or worms. It is simply trenching the eaath two feet deep and reversing the soil—that from that depth below the surface being free from weed seeds and worms. If necessary, enrich the ground with liquid manure. He says the idea occurred to him from seeing how well these plants grew upon dirt thrown out of a well.

LIQUID MANURE.

The allusion to liquid manure started a little discussion upon this subject, which was talked upon at the last meeting.

John G. Bergen.—I still contend that all manures cannot be applied in a liquid state to advantage.

Prof. Nash.—The cost of transferring manure from the barn to the crops, is the cost of fuel and interest on the cost of appliances to send the liquid to the field, and that is not over three mills per ton. There is no necessity of using coarse manure on land well underdrained. All weed seeds are dissolved in the vats of liquid manure, and by the use of lime and acids. Mr. Mechi told me he could dissolve a whole wagon load of dead horses in a few days.

AMERICAN GUANO.

Solon Robinson read a letter of inquiry about the value of "American Guano," that is, the guano from Baker's and Jarvis' Islands. The farmers upon Long Island are anxious to know what it is worth as a fertilizer.

Adrian Bergen thought this as good as any other guano that he had tried.

Mr. Doughty, of New Jersey.—I tried this guano on a crop of carrots against stable manure, and found the guano equal in all respects to the manure. I cannot tell the rate per acre at which I used it.

John G. Bergen.—We have, sometimes, found great benefit in the use of Peruvian guano, on Long Island, and at other times we have not been able to perceive the least benefit. Perhaps it is because the quality varies.

Prof. Nash.—The farmer wants to know what the fertilizer is worth. The value of this American guano is based upon eighty per cent of insoluble phosphates. Now, what is bone phosphate worth to the farmer for some particular crop?

Andrew S. Fuller.—I tried this guano and several other phosphatic appliances, and found no difference, but come to the conclusion that I would not give a cent for any of them. I had rather have a whole bone than any superphosphate, and, if broken, it is, of course, still better. But the best crop was obtained upon deeply tilled land, without manure, alongside of the same kind of plants dressed with American guano.

GREEN SAND MARL.

Prof. Nash.—There is no ton of manure equal to Peruvian guano, but we have a fertilizer worth twice as much, according to its cost, and that is the green sand marl of New Jersey. It affords food for plants and adds permanent value to the soil. One man using it, at a cost of fifteen cents a bushel, thought others foolish who neglect its use at that cost. He grew

300 bushels of potatoes per acre by using this marl where he could grow none before. Even the sea-shore sand, slightly impregnated with green sand, has been used with wonderful effect.

R. G. Pardee.—A man on Long Island put on a very large dressing of this green sand marl, and it produced nothing. He thought it was because the land was already charged with saline matters. I advise all to try experiments carefully before investing largely.

John G. Bergen.—There is a great difference in the quality of this marl. Some of it would pay transportation. Some of my neighbors have tried this marl and give it up as not worth the cost.

Andrew S. Fuller.—What do we use this marl for ? Is it for the value of the lime and potash ? I don't know of any thing else that is claimed for it. Well, I can't afford to buy it, nor even pay transportation of the marl, because I can buy crude potash and lime at a cheaper rate.

Solon Robinson.—I have two more little presentations to make.

A NEW GRAPE.

B. B. Wiggins, of Greenpoint, L. I., sends us some seeds of a new variety of native grape, which grows in the swamps of that part of the island, which is of a purple color, and larger than the Isabella, and ripens two weeks earlier. These seeds I propose to give to Andrew S. Fuller. to propagate and prove their value.

BLACKBERRY WINE.

George Seymour, of Norwalk, Conn., presented a sample of his blackberry wine, made from the juice of 2½ bushels of New Rochelle blackberries and 90 pounds of refined sugar to the barrel, adding water to make up the quantity. This sample is only six months old. With age, it would be a delicious cordial.

This wine was tasted by the persons present, both men and women, and very much admired. It was thought quite superior to some grape wines presented by Mr. Provoost, of Williamsburgh.

CULTIVATION OF FLOWERS.

This, one of the regular questions, being called up, R. G. Pardee said that he had a list of 25 varieties of flowers that he had made out for a lady, and if that was not full enough he would recommend a little book lately published by Fowler & Wells. The following is the list referred to:

Select list of Flowers—25 Species.—Best select Verbenas ; best select Petunias ; best select Pansies ; best select Asters, French Truffant ; Peoniflower Aster ; Chycantheme flora Aster ; Phlox Drummondi, alba, criterion and Victoria ; Portulacas, best varieties ; Double Balsams in variety ; China Pink, new-marbled, &c.; Cypress Vine ; Canary-bird flower ; Amaranths ; tri-colored, &c.; Sweet Williams, double ; best Lupines, perennial ; best Digitalis or Fox Gloves ; best Delphinum or Garkshur-vine ; Phlox perennial, Roi Leopold, &c.; Hollyhocks, double ; Dyelytra spectabilis ; best Chrysanthemums Dwarfs ; Dahlias, select ; Peony ; Yucca filamentosa ; Roses in variety.

Mr. Pardee gave interesting descriptions of some of the flowers named, particularly recommending the Dyelytra, on account of its hardiness and beautiful flowers.

Andrew S. Fuller.—I want to call attention to the Yucca plant. It is so common that nobody knows of it. Here are two plants that I grew from seed. They stood out all winter, entirely green, and are two years old, and will bear beautiful flowers at three years old. As to Verbena seed, I advise all to save seeds, but you must attend to it early in the morning. Pansy seed has been generally imported, but it can be grown here, and the plants prove to be better than from imported seed. Mr. Fuller made a free distribution of some hundreds of papers of flower seeds of his own raising, at his Brooklyn nursery and gardens, to the ladies who attend the Club.

THE GRAPE VINE.

Mr. Provoost, of Williamsburgh, gave his views upon vine pruning, which differs widely from the ordinary mode. He turns down the branches and lets them take root. He said : I do not prune at all in the fall, and only cut away dead wood in the spring, or where the vines are too thick. I have grown 28 bunches upon a single branch. I spread salt hay over the ground to kill the weeds. I train vines upon trellises eight feet high, and I carry down layers between the tows for new vines. The vine represented in the plan exhibited is 22 years old. I prefer wooden slats instead of wires. Upon vines chafed on wires, so as to bleed, I have applied hot pitch with success. The rows of trellis are eight feet apart, but I have vines between the rows supported upon stakes. I have made 1,500 gallons of wine from an acre in one year. I never dig up the ground in my vineyard with anything but a hoe. I apply manure, and also sand, which I find very beneficial.

Prof. Mapes.—I should like to find out where the advantage of this method of training lies. Is it from the number of roots ? If so, I think there is a better way, by growing more vines, and not such large, old vines. I dig my holes four feet deep and four feet wide, to set a vine, and that is filled with suitable soil, and I manure afterward with such things as the vine and fruit need. I don't find barn-yard manure as good as bone manure and potash. I find no difficulty in training upon wires. I fasten the vines to the wires with leaden wires. I trim the first branches horizontally to the lower wire, and rub off all the upright branches but four, and in trimming, I cut down in November, two of these upright shoots to a single bud, and let the other two shoots grow next year, and cut them back in the fall, so as to grow the odd and even number shoots alternate years for fruit bearing. Never trim vines in the spring. The cutting of the fall can be kept for use, if required, by burying in earth or sand.

A grape vine is a rank feeder. You may, if you like, bury a horse near the roots of a vine, and it will use it up in time. As to summer pruning, I pinch off twice, the shoots of bearing canes, at the third leaf, beyond the bunch.

John Rowe exhibited a specimen of improved pruning shears, that were much approved by the grape culturists present, as they were so constructed as to make a smooth cut.

Hon. John G. Bergen gave grafts from his choice seedlings, the *Bergen pear* and the *Island pear*.

Mr. Spear exhibited his patent Corn Husking machine; and a man can husk 25 ears per minute with it. By more effort he can husk 60 per minute. The machine costs about ten dollars, and must be very useful on middle sized farms.

Mr. Doughty exhibited Dioscorea Batatas from his farm in New Jersey. They are about two feet long, were somewhat embarrassed by the stones in his subsoil. He planted them on raised ridges.

Mr. Provoost, of Williamsburgh, near Green Point ferry, exhibited wine and brandy from his vineyard. The wine sells as sacramental pure wine, for six dollars a gallon. The brandy for seven dollars a gallon. He raises on one acre fifteen hundred gallons of *pure grape juice*.

. Mr. Pardee requested the ladies to prepare for the next meeting such questions as they desire to have answered, and leave them with Secretary Meigs.

Subjects for next meeting.—Spring flowers; peach tree; soil, &c., suitable for central park shade trees, also, for our avenues.

The Club adjourned at 2 o'clock P. M.

H. MEIGS, *Secretary.*

March 28, 1849.

Present—Messrs. Captain Lawton, of Newport, R. I., Robert L. Pell, late President of the Institute, Solon Robinson, Daniel C. Robinson, Chilson, Bruce, Witt, Fuller, Stacey, Hardenbrooke, John V. Brower, Roberts, Wright, Jr., Haines, Benjamin Pike, John Johnson, Hon. Hugh Maxwell, Adrian Bergen of Gowanus, Doughty, Prof. Mapes, of Jersey, Dunn, of Newark, R. G. Pardee, Prof. Nash, Hon. Robert Swift Livingston, N. R. French, Dr. Holton, Dr. Crowell, Thomas Godwin, John W. Chambers, Ezekiel A. Harris, Wm. Lawton—108 members.

Hon. R. S. Livingston in the chair. H. Meigs, Secretary.

The Secretary read the following translations, made by him from the works received by the American Institute since the last meeting, viz:

[Journal de la Société Impériale d'Horticulture Napoleon III., Protecteur. Paris, December, 1858.]

THE RAINVILLE POTATO.

Is superior to all the varieties hitherto obtained. It ripens between the 10th and 15th of August. Its flowers are lilac color; the tuber long, with few eyes in it; of a light yellow colored skin, and yellowish white flesh. It is distinguished for its fine grain, cooks quick, and is full of starch.

Many members of this Society, who have tasted them, all agree to their good quality. They produce 20 or 30 for 1.

PEACH TREES,

They find to do best when set out in November. The roots, during winter, are being made ready in their small ones and spongioles for spring. Straw spread around the tree in burning hot weather, helps them much.

THE POMOLOGICAL CONGRESS OF LYONS, 1856, 1857, & 1858,

Consisted of 200 members, of whom 113 are practical men, and the rest proprietors and officers of societies for agriculture and horticulture.

The Prefect of the Seine, at their request, gave the Congress the place No. 84 in Grenelle, St. Germain street, for their meetings hereafter.

The *Fragaria lucida*, a transparent strawberry from California, has not flourished in France. The Secretary General announced the receipt of many works from the Smithsonian Institute. The Congress met at $2\frac{1}{4}$ and adjourned at 3 o'clock P. M.

[From the Transactions of the Batavian Society of Arts and Sciences.]

" Verhandlungen van Het Bataviaasch Genootschap van Kunsten en Wetenschappen, Batavia, 1857." Just received from Java, through Hon. Mr. Burlage, Consul General of the Netherlands.

ICTHYOLOGY OF JAPAN—By Dr. P. Bleeker.

" After I had, in two articles, brought together all the knowledge we have of the fishes of Japan worth remark, we obtained a greater collection from the city of Nagasaki, for which our thanks are due to Mr. A. I. I. Wolff, who made this costly collection of 120 species, chiefly from the Bay of Nagasaki."

We recommend this work to all who love knowledge, and also as it leads to profit in commerce. The Society sends us also some periodicals which they have published, relating to the language, governments, history, and natural history, of the surrounding region, the great Archipelago, under the title of " Tijdschrift voor Indische Taal, Land en Volkenkunde." Periodical relative to the language and people of India."

Prof. Mapes.—I always plant peach trees carefully, with points down. In taking the tree from the nursery, I cut of all the limbs, and set it an inch higher in its new place than it stood before. I shorten in all the limbs next year two-thirds the length by cutting off always at a leaf bud, and not a fruit bud ; and I let the trees branch from near the ground. Natural seedlings are longer lived than budded trees. It is positively necessary to disturb the ground as early as possible in the spring. All peach limbs should be shortened in so as not to be pendant. No organic matter will answer for peach trees. Barn-yard manures will kill them. Nothing but inorganic manures will answer. Trees should be trimmed early in the spring, as soon as the weather is warm enough to make the limbs supple.

The Peach Worm is frequently destroyed, or rather prevented, by using the caustic soda wash—an application accidentally discovered by a New Jersey gardener, a few years ago, to be the best thing ever applied to kill issects and make smooth bark.

William Lawton.—Nothing but a sharp knife to cut out the worm, after well seated, will cure that difficulty.

Prof. Mapes.—This remedy is something like the Frenchman's flea powder—"catch the flea and force it down his throat." The only easy remedy is boiling water. Put a cloth around the tree and pour boiling hot water on, and the steam will kill the worms. I find no difficulty in killing peach worms in my trees with hot water. It would not hurt the tree to apply a jet of steam direct to the worm-affected part, but it will hurt the worm. It would be impossible to pick out the worms in an orchard, such as some in Jersey, of 80,000 trees. The best cure for the yellows is to give the trees as vigorous a growth as possible, by the use of inorganic fertilizers.

Solon Robinson.—Will Prof. Mapes please give the direction once more for making the caustic soda wash? I have had many applications for it lately.

Prof. Mapes.—Take common sal soda and put it in any old iron pot or other vessel red hot, and then put it hot into water, one pound to one gallon, and let it stand till cool, and use it with a brush or swab to the body or limbs of the trees you wish to clean, and it kills all insects it comes in contact with, and makes the bark assume a smooth, polished appearance. It will not injure any growing plants.

Solon Robinson.—Joel Parker, of Cambridge, Mass., wants to know how much of the lime and salt mixture to apply to a strawberry bed, and when; and another person wants to know how much to apply to grass land.

R. G. Pardee.—I used one bushel of lime and one peck of salt, prepared as directed, to a piece 30 feet square, two weeks before setting out the plants.

Prof. Mapes—If a soil is very full of vegetable matter and tannic acid, that quantity may answer. Upon grass land six to ten bushels may be applied. But understand, lime and salt separate, or merely mixed, are not the mixture that I mean. It is three bushels of lime slaked with water, completely saturated, with one bushel of salt, and left in a pile until the air produces an efflorescence and a light chlorine and soda powder on the outside, which, being swept off, is the article to apply to the land. Then the air produces more on the outside, and it may be necessary to turn the pile several times, and wait weeks for it all to change; but that is the substance that produces such marked effect upon soils which are deficient, as most old fields are, of chlorine and soda.

R. L. Pell.—At the last meeting of the Farmers' Club, I stated that it would be well for agriculturists, invariably, to use liquid manures, if possible, instead of solid, for the reason that a plant could not imbibe manure, through its capillaries, in any other than a liquid form. Several remarks were made to which I desired to reply, but the hour for miscellaneous business having expired, I was compelled to delay until this meeting.

It has been proved, that by mismanagement of solid manures, whether from farms or from towns, by their retention on the surface, by the evaporation of their most fertilizing portions, and by mismanagement of them in the ground, as much as two-thirds, and often more, of their fertilizing powers are commonly lost, and that the loss of the liquid manures is generally total.

The American and English farmer have, hitherto, only considered that as manure, which he could raise with his fork; but the time is coming, as I said at the last meeting, when that only will be considered regular manure which he may apply with the scoop.

Dark deep color, and rank consistencies, are the chief qualities he now seeks in liquid manures as proper conditions for their use.

The further advance, according to horticultural experience, will be in liquid applications of perfect transparency and void of smell. The fibrous or solid matter which farmers now most regard, is of little comparative value, and the difficulty will hereafter be how to dispose of it, and prevent it being injurious.

Experience in England, with respect to the application of liquid manures, is corroborated by agriculturists in Germany and elsewhere; especially by the practical experience of the celebrated De Candolle, whose statement on the subject emphatically declares "It is to be desired that the practical use of liquid manure, which serves at one and the same time as manure and for watering, should become more universal and more popular in a great part of Europe."

The eminent German agriculturist Schwerze, gives the following as the advantages which he had experienced, and observed generally in practice from the application of manure in the liquid form.

1st. The advantage of manure applied in the liquid instead of the solid consists first, and above all, in the promptitude of its action. For a great number of plants, such as cabbages, turnips, rape, hemp, flax, for fodder plants, and all others that require prompt nourishment, and which cannot wait the slow decomposition of solid manure for the food which is suitable to them, liquid manure is most important.

2d. In the saving of loss from less emanation by the immediate passage of the manure into the soil.

3d. In hastening production. Whilst solid manure requires several years to bring the whole of its force into action, manure applied in the liquid form comes into action in a few weeks. Thus the returns of capital for the manure in the liquid form will be made in half the time.

4. Liquid manure is immediately available, relieves the plants at once, changes the color to a deep green, and creates a metamorphosis which it is impossible to effect with solid manure.

5. For grasses and clovers, liquid manure, well treated, is the only substance that does not occasion any exhaustion of the soil; for besides the addition of the water, which is in itself a good thing for fodder plants, it serves to dissolve and spread, and, without loss of time, convey nutritive

matter to vegetation. Those agriculturists who have, for a long time, manured fields with the ordinary manure, know how little result attends the labor and expenditure of solids in dry weather, for when in that form it is nearly all lost.

There is no doubt but that liquid manure gains in quantity and quality, and in other conditions; that the results from that method of preparing enriches a greater quantity than with the ordinary method; that the farmer may with it always assist a failing vegetation; that it may be given abundantly of a sufficient quantity; that liquid manure is particularly suitable for fodder plants, and that those who can ought to resort to it as the basis of their cultivation.

Having given evidence as to the fertilizing powers of liquid manure, I will now relate the expense of several mechanical means of distribution, and will first state the practical disadvantages of liquids, so that you will be compelled to allow that I am fair. The expense of the re-arrangement of stables and cattle sheds, and the construction of new tanks and reservoirs; the expense of the carriage of the liquids to distant fields, over bad roads; that many young plants do not bear the application of liquid manure, except in moist weather, when the ground will not sustain the passage of loaded carts. Though it may always be put on when the weather is frosty to advantage. A further inconvenience is that the solid residue will not rise in the pumps, and must therefore be cleansed out three or four times a year, and treated as compost; lime must then be used to decompose the fibrous matters. In Belgium, and many parts of Germany, some of the inconveniencies of the delivery from the water cart are obviated by conveying it into the fields in casks, borne by laborers, on their backs, from whence they distribute it by hand, which I have often seen them do, and been assured by them that it paid. This distribution, either by water cart or hand carriage, is attended by the inconvenience of delivery in too high a state of concentration, in order to avoid the increased bulk and weight of carriage by proper dilution, which would often be with eight or ten parts of water. But by the method of distribution through pipes, with hose and jet (by steam power where there is not sufficient fall,) the objections above named are obviated and many advantages gained, as will be perceived by the practical examples that I will furnish.

In Mr. Holland's experiments, three tons of night soil, diluted with seventeen tons of water, produced a more fertilizing effect than a top dressing of fifteen loads of stable manure. The weight of grass on the irrigated land was fifty per cent greater. With an eight horse power steam engine, with the labor of one engineman and four distributors with hose and jets, three hundred loads of liquid manure were distributed in ten hours, about half which time was occupied in shifting the hose. He has used hose 1,000 feet long over elevations of thirty and forty feet with ease.

On Mr. Kennedy's farm, the quantity delivered by a jet worked by a twelve-horse steam engine, at an extreme length of three-quarters of a mile, or over four hundred acres, was about 40,000 gallons, or 180 tons per day, at the expense for labour of less than half a cent per ton. Two of his men distribute a very heavy dressing of liquid manure on ten acres per diem.

Trial was made of the distribution of liquid manure, by a steam engine on a barge belonging to the Metropolitan Commissioners of Sewers, in a canal in London. It appeared that within a quarter of a mile from the banks, 100 tons were distributed at a rate of expense of 41 cents. One hundred tons would cover an acre to about an inch in depth; a good shower would cover it to about the depth of an eighth of an inch. The removal of manure liquified, is a removal in a form in which it may be applied at once; whereas the removal by hand labor and cartage of the solid or semi-fluid manure, from the town to the suburb, or from the barn to the farm, is a removal in a form requiring a troublesome and offensive manipulation. The offensiveness of night soil, is one great reason why it is not more used. The convenience in the application of guano has diminished and lowered the demand for this valuable substance. If this could be diluted and distributed by pipe in the form of sewage, it would have the superiority in convenience.

The cheapness of lifting and removal on a large scale, by the power of steam, renders the question of levels much less important than it has generally been considered. The expense of raising 45,000 gallons a hundred feet high, by a twenty-five horse power engine, is only two shillings.

Whatever be the manure, it must be carried to the height of the land, and wheresoever solid manure is carried, liquid manure could be raised at a far cheaper rate.

There appears to be some misconception in relation to the power of pumping, and apprehensions are often expressed that mixtures of common dung would clog the pipes, and could not be pumped. This is a mistake, as thick mud, filled with fibrous matter, has been pumped through a hose twenty-four hundred feet long. I believe that the dirt in our streets might be made to cover the Central Park, through pipes by means of a steam engine, at the rate of six shillings per inch of depth per acre, (equal to 134 cubic yards,) which could not be carried and spread by man and horse power for less than six dollars per inch of depth per acre.

The distribution of liquid manure may be accomplished through flexible hose with lateral openings, like the eyelet holes of a lady's stays, very rapidly, and with much less power than is required to discharge by the jet, and at a less expense, with more equal distribution. One man and a boy, with the aid of a twelve-horse power steam engine, would be enabled to distribute more liquids in a given time than twenty water carts, each requiring a horse and driver.

While the method with the engine is available at all times, the water cart cannot be got on the land without injury, and at some seasons it would be impracticable to use a cart at all. At such times, if the liquid were carried on by the method in use in Belgium and Germany, the labor of two hundred men would be required to effect the distribution, which, by the engine, is effected by one man and a boy.

If earthen pipes are used, the expense of irrigating may be reduced $5 per acre ; and I do not know why they should not, as we are aware the Romans used earthenware for the distribution of water, at 100 feet of pressure, and some laid down by them in the first century are still in use. In France, at the present day, such pipes are in use at 120 feet of pressure. At Weymouth they have been in use for more than 20 years, at an intermittent pressure of sixty feet ; but neither engineers nor pipe manufacturers appear generally to care to master so economical an apparatus, apparontly considering them impracticable.

The power derivable from the prompt application of plain water to arrable land, is unknown to the agriculture of the United States, and but little known in garden culture, and scarcely practiced in horticulture. In the market garden cultivation of Paris and Naples, effects are produced by skillful watering, which we, as a people, know nothing about. At Naples the water is distributed by regular channels of irrigation. At the market gardens of Paris it is distributed by hand labor, by the use of the scoop, at a tremendous expense, but for which the extra produce amply compensates. The cheap power of distributing water may often be of immense importance to the farmer, to facilitate the working of the land at those periods when it is hardened by drought, and when, for plowing or other work, extra labor, often more than double the ordinary amount, is necessary. On such occasions, laborers wet the ground to facilitate the working with the spade. Where water is available, and when the ground may be thoroughly wetted at a small expense, the farmer may, by such an application, work in two horses, where otherwise five might be required. A tank 60 feet long, 12 feet wide, and 13 feet deep, furnished with lever agitators, holding 60,000 gallons, may be built for one thousand dollars.

With solid manure the farmer frequently spreads the larvæ of devastating insects, and provides for their sustenation. By distributing manure in the liquid form, this mischief is avoided. Moreover the fixed distributary apparatus will be on a large scale, what the garden engine is on a small scale to the horticulturist, a powerful arm to the agriculturists against insect devastators, by the rapid distribution, in water, of cheap substances which are destructive to them. By distributing a shower of muck-water over a turnip field, the fly will immediately disappear. If you would illustrate this question fairly, as to the expense, place a man at your liquid manure cistern and let him pump through a hose, and you will find that the same labor required to lift a given quantity of manure into a water cart, might convey the same liquid as far as the hose need extend on the same level. Mr. Neilson, of Halewood farm, England, having some time since had his attention called to the facilities of this method of distribution by hand pump and hose, as against the water cart, used a hose of four hundred feet long, and found that he could, within the range of the hose, by hand labor, distribute manure at less than one-third the expense of distribution by the water cart. By applications of liquid manure by this method, he accomplished the feat of raising, on a well drained acre of ground, previously in good condition, one hundred tons of green crop of Italian rye grass and clover within a year. For the distribution of plain water, as well as manure, taking into account the expense of the original formation of water meadows, as well as other expenses, it now appears to be decided in England, that this method of distribution by hose will be found to be cheaper, particularly when carried out on a large scale, and when the collateral economies are considered, than by the cheapest instances of the water meadow system.

Mr. Mechi says, in a recent report made by him : I have already one hundred acres finished for liquid manure distribution, and shall finish one hundred and seventy acres in about a fortnight. There will be about 1,100 iron three inch pipes, three yards long, making a total length of nearly two miles ; each pipe weighs 119 lbs., so that 55 tons of iron piping will be about the quantity. My pair of pumps are of 20 inch stroke and 5½ inches diameter, capable of raising and discharging about 80 gallons per minute. My great tank is about the size of a small chapel, 30 feet deep and 30 feet diameter at the widest part. My bog spring, of 80,000 gallons per diem, falls into the tank. I shall expend $3,000 for the one hundred and seventy acres, which will cover the expense of tank, pumps, pipage, gutta percha hose, and every expense except the steam engine, which I have already. The pipes are joined with tarred rope and boiling lead, like the common street water pipes, and placed in the ground 18 inches deep. There will be one hydrant or iron supply post for every 11 acres ; 200 yards of gutta percha pipe (half two inch, half one and a half inch,) will reach any part of the farm. The pumps will be enabled by means of various taps, to distribute either liquid manure or plain water, as may be found desirable. A man and lad dispose of six hundred hogsheads per diem, enough for ten acres. The cost of the application, including interest on capital, engineer's pay, man and boy in the field, and coals would be 13 shillings, $3,25 ; about 33 cents per acre, will more than cover the whole cost of applying 150 tons of manure on 10 acres of land. This expense is ridiculously small, in comparison with the ordinary cost and waste.

Mr. Mechi says : " How frequently I am told by observant agriculturists, that although they have constructed tanks for the preservation of liquid manure, they could never perceive any good result from its application. To doubt the value of liquid excrements, would be to deny the utility of the sheepfold, and to disbelieve in the science of agriculture. The great mistake, he says, is in using it insufficiently diluted, on a growing crop. Its strength and pungency are injurious to the roots of growing plants. The urine of a cow, or horse, falling in dry, hot weather, on young clover, destroys it. With respect to the necessary dilution of our manure, you can hardly dilute it too much ; say one hogshead of liquid manure to fifty hogsheads of water. The soluble form is the only true and profitable principle, searching, warming, and fructifying the barren subsoil by aëration, irrigation, and disintegration. When we, as agriculturists, understand chemistry in its relation to agriculture, which shows us that there is no difference between a bullock and a shower of rain, except in organics ; when we comprehend that three-quarters of the weight of our bodies is water, that nine-tenths of our turnips is water, then shall we believe that water is manure. The seeds of weeds are quickly destroyed by saturation in liquid manure ; the maceration of our manure will prevent the increase of weeds. The cost per ton is about one cent, delivered on the land. Although the irrigation with liquid manure has only been in operation for eight months, it is telling, very unmistakably, on the profits of my farm. For instance, a piece of red clover, of eight acres, being an imperfect plant, was condemned to be plowed up early ; but, on the application of the jet it produced enough to maintain 13 sheep per acre, all the summer, thus setting free my other fields for hay. It has greatly increased my produce of roots, both Swedes and mangold-wurzel. The time is fast approaching when the farmer will receive back, weekly, from our towns and cities, his supplies of food, altered in form but scarcely in value. How reasonable and delightful to trace the bullock of to-day returning this day week, and passing through the jet, to produce on the morrow the food for another bullock.''

There are 260 acres of land one and a half miles southeast of Edinburgh, which are irrigated with city sewage, and takes fourteen days to irrigate. The produce of the land is sold by auction on the grounds, to the cow feeders of the city, at $155 per acre, between the middle of April and the first of October ; they are shut up and regularly irrigated through the winter. The collective weight of grass cut within those periods is 80 tons per acre. The cost of maintaining these meadows, independent of the engine, consists in the employment of two hands to turn on and off the water. There are other similar meadows on the west side of Edinburgh.

In the immediate vicinity of Glasgow, there is a farm which is supplied with liquid manure from a dairy of seven hundred cows, attached to a large distillery, the entire drainage from which flows in a full continuous stream into a tank containing forty thousand gallons, whence it is pumped up immediately by a 12 horse power engine, into large cisterns placed on the highest points of the land to be irrigated ; from these it descends by gravitation, through systems of pipes wherever required, the furthest point being two miles, and the highest elevation 80 feet above the engine. This is a farm under a nineteen years' lease, and the tenant only uses the liquid and sells his solid manures, amounting to three thousand tons a year, for $1.75 cents per ton.

Near Maybole, in Ayrshire, there is a farm of four hundred acres belonging to a gentleman whose name has escaped me, laid down with pipes, through which superphosphate of lime and guano have been transmitted in solution. The water made use of on this farm has to be raised from wells 70 feet deep, and four hundred yards from the tanks ; still, the liquid is delivered on the land at the rate of 4,000 gallons an hour, that being the usual portion allowed here to an acre. At certain points are hydrants to which gutta percha hose is attached in lengths of twenty yards, at the end of which is a sharp nozzle, with an orifice ranging from one to one and a half inches, according to the pressure laid on, from which the liquid makes its exit with a jet of from twelve to fifteen yards. All the labor required is that of a man and a boy to adjust the hose and direct the disposition of the liquid, and eight or ten acres may thus be fertilized in a day; the total extent of delivery is about 1,900,000 yards. On this farm, one hundred and thirty acres of root crops, dressed with liquid manure, was ready for the hoe twelve days earlier than another lot dressed with double the amount of solid manure. The yield from the former was twenty tons to the acre, and of the latter fifty tons, and the limit of fertility was not reached, as was plainly shown in one part of the field, which had, accidentally, received more than its allowance of liquid, and which showed a marked increase of luxuriance over that around it. The cost of purchasing and laying down the pipes on this farm was at the rate of $12 per acre.

Mr. Telfer has a small farm in the town of Ayer, containing fifty acres, which was formerly a sandy waste, but by the application of liquid manure, with a three horse power engine, diluted with sea water, he has raised the fertility of the soil to the extent of supporting forty-eight cows, where previously eight only were kept; the produce from three and a half acres yielded keep for thirty-six cows for four months. Besides the enormous increase in the quantity of produce of this farm, its quality was so much improved by the liquid, that four cents per pound above the current price in the district was paid for the butter; this difference amounting to a sum more than equal to the whole previous rent of the farm.

There are irrigated meadows along the river Weley, twenty-two miles in extent, containing three thousand acres, belonging to several owners; it is all grass land, and yields four heavy crops a year. They are watered with pure water from the river, several times each year, at an expense of fifty cents per acre for each watering, and one dollar and twenty-five cents is expended annually for cleaning out the water courses, carriers, and leveling the soil.

The Duke of Bedford owns nineteen-twentieths of the land upon which the town of Tavistock stands, containing a population of eight thousand persons. The Duke, at his own cost, in 1846, sewered the whole town, and conveyed the liquid on to his contiguous land, a portion of which he had previously drained to the depth of six feet. An account of the annual money value derived from twenty-five acres of this land, that under the old process of solid manures was considered of little value, is as follows:

Grass sold,...	$350 00
Hay,...	225 00
Fourteen cows pastured for seventeen weeks,.................	235 00
Fourteen young cattle for thirty-five weeks, ...	185 00
One hundred ewes for four weeks,........................	80 00
Horse keeping,..	50 00

Thirteen bullocks, four weeks,.............................	$40 00
Eighty-eight sheep, two weeks, ...	10 00
	$1,175 00

If a farm has a stream of water upon it, I would recommend that peat, lime, clay, loam, all sorts of manures, organic, mineral, soluble and insoluble, be applied by water, rather than any other process; because it can be done at much less cost, and with better agricultural results in solution and suspension. And it will be found better for the interest of farmers to cultivate a small piece of ground well, rather than a large piece ill. One acre of market garden has produced twelve hundred and fifty dollars, and I do not believe the average annual return of the arable land in the whole United States is twenty dollars per acre; and the reason is, that the surplus capital of our country is invested in railroad shares, mining companies, &c., instead of agriculture. We are truly an agricultural people, still agriculture does not form in our general or college education, as it ought, an honorable portion; the consequence is, the honest farmer is looked down upon even by the honest blacksmith, and in the busy city is called a bumpkin, in the legislative halls, an ass. This would not be the case if a department of agriculture was appended to our schools and colleges, where a patient professor might explain the most judicious modes of drainage, irrigation, tillage, course of crops, feeding stock, arranging buildings, &c. Then when our merchant princes retired from the toils of business, the want of agricultural knowledge would not be felt, and their theoretical information would lead to practical experiments of value.

The grand error of the farmers of this country, is their inordinate desire to grasp a territory of land on which to commence their operations, instead of concentrating capital, talent and exertion, within circumscribed limits. It would be well to bear in mind that it is next to impossible to improve, effectually, stiff clay land without buildings, for a less sum than one hundred dollars per acre. For example, drainage will cost $35, subsoiling, fallowing, &c., $35, manuring $30. You may travel all over our country, and then over Europe, and you will generally find that all farms might be more profitably cultivated than they are, from the fact that all men are prone to commit the error above mentioned. In our country, when a gentleman makes up his mind to become a farmer, he purchases a farm, and then puts out at interest all his available funds, and because the farm that has been worked fifty years without manure, will not support his cattle, horses, dogs, and himself, soon becomes disgusted. How different is this management, from that of our European friends, who never undertake farming without capital. A tenant of Lord Leicester expended on a farm of 1,200 acres, in twenty-six years, one hundred thousand dollars in artificial enrichers, and two hundred thousand dollars for oil cake.

Mr. Hudson, another of Lord Leicester's tenants, expended in thirty years, two hundred and fifty thousand dollars for oil cake, and one hundred and twenty-five thousand dollars for artificial manures. He uses the teeth of sheep and cattle for scythes, and fattens them with oil cake. The proprietor of Canning Park applies nearly one hundred tons of water, with five hundred pounds of guano dissolved in it, at a single dressing, upon a Scotch acre of land growing rye grass, and he makes five such applications in a season with profit.

On a hilly portion of my farm the land was top-dressed with solid stable manure, on both sides of an irrigating gutter. Pure water was shed over the lower part immediately, and the manure washed in; while that on the upper side, above the water, consolidated into hard lumps, and the herbage became brown, coarse, yellow, sickly and useless, that on the lower side presented the most beautiful green, luxuriant appearance imaginable. Toward fall I turned up a spit on the lower side, and found a rich black deposit of mould three-quarters of an inch thick, and a darkened soil six inches below. I then turned a spit above the gutter, and found the soil the same from the surface downwards, a pale gray, without the least sign of penetrating manure. It is entirely unnecessary to make any comment on the great contrast presented in the same field, with the same quantities of like manure, growing the same variety of grass, only separated by a water gutter twenty inches wide,—the only difference being the use of liquified manure on the lower side, and solid on the upper. There are many thousands of acres of land, within a few miles circuit of this great city, now considered as waste, that may be immediately, cheaply, and profitably cultivated by draining, and the distribution and application of lime, soils, and manures in solution and suspension in water, moved to any part where they may be required, even where the plow, harrow and cart cannot penetrate. Enterprise, capital, and water, being the chief requirements to convert these barren lands into fields of green and nutritious grasses.

I am at a loss to know why it is that the capitalists of our country are always ready to loan money for every hazardous scheme that can be desired by the art of man, except where agricultural improvement is the object. Can it be for the want of confidence in our farmers, or do they not desire to see our soils improved, or is it because the laws of the land do not authorize a proper channel for the investment of money in the improvement of agriculture? Let a company be formed, with sufficient capital to purchase the waste lands of New Jersey, Long Island, and Westchester county, which can be bought for a song, comparatively speaking, and drain, clear, plow, and crop them, then rent them. Let this company receive from the corporation of New York, the amount expended last year for cleansing the city, for the term of ten years, with the promise to construct proper receiving reservoirs connected with the sewers, to flush all the filth of the city into the sewers with Croton water, between the hours of twelve and four in the morning, and never, on any consideration, to permit one quart of it to flow into either of our rivers. Let these enrichers be placed upon their lands, and every acre of it will yield a clear profit, to speak immeasurably within bounds, of one hundred dollars.

The child is born who will see a totally different state of agriculture than that which now pervades our country ; he will see not only the sewage of our great city, but all the towns in our land, flow back to the source from whence the production that made it came. Our millers and manufacturers will use steam, and our streams will irrigate our fields. Our children will receive at college an agricultural as well as collegiate education, and consequently rank far higher than we, in an enlightened and social scale. The plow and the harrow, both injurious to land, will give way to mighty improvements in the agricultural art. The hungry soil will be torn from its depths, and thrown into the atmosphere in disintegrated particles, and return not only aerated, but saturated with nitrogen and ammonia. And capital now withheld from us on account of our pernicious and penurious system, will be proud to develope its immense strength in our behalf.

The most permanent source of national wealth arises from its agricultural prosperity. The encouragement of agriculture should be a main object with every well constituted government, and it is the duty of every man composing it to use his best endeavors, at all times, thus to promote the prosperity of his country.

What I have principally attempted to describe in my remarks to-day is a general outline of practice. To recommend any system as proper, in all cases, and in every situation, would certainly be an act of folly as well as mischief, because particular circumstances must always guide the practice of the agriculturist. Agricultural theories, I find, much more frequently mislead than instruct ; they may, possibly, contribute to the advancement of agricultural science, abstractedly considered from the practice, but to the generality of farmers, they frequently prove more injurious than beneficial. Ignorance is always dazzled by the lureing charms of novelty. A theory appears which looks plausible ; agriculturists adopt it, anticipate immense gains, and find themselves deceived. The inevitable consequence is, that they afterwards, invariably, treat what they call book farming, with disdain and contempt, and with disgust reject every improvement that bears any feature of novelty.

When surface drainage became general, in consequence of extended cultivation of the country, and the improvement of waste lands, and more especially when open drains were extensively adopted, it is notorious that the excess of floods increased greatly, and that the streams dried more rapidly in drought.

The introduction of thorough draining, in place of open drains, has, on the contrary, had a tendency to prevent the excess of flood, because the drops of rain falling on the surface have to fill the vacant places in the drained soil, and consequently require many hours to fully drain off after the shower has fallen, so that the crisis of the flood from water on the surface of the land undrained has passed long before the percolating water arrives to increase its volume. Consequently, thorough drainage will diminish the excess of flood in streams, whilst the mud carried off will be reduced. The water from thorough drains, as is well known, usually runs free from apparent suspended substances.

During drought in summer, the water in streams is much reduced by thorough drainage; the dry soil receives and absorbs the rain of showers unless they continue for a long time and are very heavy.

Sluggish rivers and streams throughout our western country oppose obstacles to proper land drainage, being generally kept full to the banks by mill dams erected one below another, for miles in extent, rendering it utterly impossible to drain vast rich alluvial meadows, without embankments or other artificial and costly means; as I said before, they should be demolished for the benefit of agriculture, and steam substituted. A very striking example of the economical and beneficial result arising from the destruction of mill dams, and the substitution of steam for water power, has been exhibited under the operation of the Rye and Derwent Drainage Act, resulting from the wise co-operation of the Earl of Carlisle to knock down three mill dams and give the mills steam, thereby restoring the river to its natural bed and proper functions as the great artery of drainage, and enabling thousands of acres of valuable land to be drained and reclaimed at a moderate cost.

Every old authority, and all modern writers on drainage of land in Europe, have condemned mill dams and water mills. The effect of extensive drainage on main water courses is that of increasing the height of their rise or flood times, and rendering the flow and subsidence more rapid than before.

Wherever it is practicable to collect the drainage water from higher lands in ponds, and there storing it for irrigating lower lands, it should always be done, as it contains valuable soluble manures in solution and suspension, the fertilizing properties of which will render grass fields on lower levels exceedingly luxuriant, and can be carried out on all farms having surfaces at different altitudes; besides, in many cases it may be made to drive a water wheel, and do all the threshing, sawing and milling of the farm before it is used for agricultural purposes. It will be found profitable on all farms where drainage is carried on extensively, to form a pond at the lowest level, and with a small steam engine convey the water in pipes for irrigating higher levels during dry seasons. You would thus return to them the enriching properties carried off in the drains.

I had the water which was drawn by drains from a very large area of land that had been most thoroughly manured with barn yard manure, guano, lime, crushed bones, salt, plaster of Paris, &c., analyzed, the object being to discover, for my own satisfaction, the total amount of these enriching matters carried off from land most thoroughly drained as this was. A gallon of bright, clear, colorless water was collected and evaporated to dryness, and the residue weighed a little over twelve grains, and contained the following ingredients:

Alkaline sulphates, ... A trace
Silicious substances,................................. .... A trace

Chloride of magnesium, ...	A trace	
Common salts, ...	3 grains	
Sulphate of lime, ...	2	do
Vegetable and animal matter, ...	2	do
Magnesia and carbonate of lime,...................	5	do

$$\overline{ 12 \text{ grains}}$$

I was astonished to find by this experiment how small a quantity of vegetable and animal substances in the earth had been carried away by the water, where they exist in solution, and cannot be separated by filtration on account of the insignificant quantity mechanically suspended. This water was, as may be observed by the foregoing analysis, entirely free from metalic impregnations or deleterious gases ; consequently it did not become offensive, or give rise to noxious effluvia on being kept a considerable length of time, and consequently would not have contributed to disease, even had it been collected in reservoirs for agricultural irrigation. There was nothing in it to render it unfit as a beverage ; still it was insipid, from the small percentage of lime and salt contained in it, as well as deficiency of fixed carbonic acid gas.

This is by no means the case with the generality of drainage water obtained from springs, rivers, creeks, &c. ; they are often impregnated to a less or greater degree with foreign matters, which they hold in suspension, and they usually consist of four varieties :

1st. The mineral ;
2d. The animal ;
3d. The vegetable ;
4th The mechanical.

Filtration separates the mechanical ; the saline matter may be distinguished as alkaline ; the gypsum and salt as neutral.

The alkaline consists of bicarbonates, such as magnesia and lime. These earthy salts cause water containing them to be termed hard, and when used for manufacturing purposes through the medium of steam boilers, encrusts them, frequently causing explosions, and if used for washing, consumes an enormous quantity of soap. Rain water, as it drops from the heavens, is probably the most pure of all varieties of water, containing chiefly ammonia. The animal, earthy and vegetable matters found in it, after having passed through the drains, are extracted from the soil in its passage through it, and the amount of them depends upon the constituents of the soil through which it passes, and the time the water is maintained in communication with the earth.

The average annual fall of rain water in the State of New York, is about twenty-six inches, half of which remains in the soil, and the other half is carried off by evaporation. Therefore a cubic foot of water would be annually retained on every square foot of surface, equal to forty-three thousand five hundred and sixty cubic feet on every square acre. It will always be found that the quantity of evaporation from land is far more limited than from water, the one depending upon the capillary action and retentive power of the surface soil, while the other arises from a comparative inexhaustible source. The rate of evaporation from land depends in a measure upon temperature, and is invariably accelerated by the effects of a hot sun upon the earth's surface; then again the temperature is affected by elevation. The supply of water is somewhat dependent upon the geography of the district; close proximity, for example, to a large river, lake, or sea, promotes the fall of rain. Thus one side of a mountain range, exposed to oblique showers, will require much more draining than the other side, not so exposed. So one country requires far more draining than another, owing to the quantity of rain that falls annually. In England, the fall ranges between twe ty-one and thirty-two inches; in Brazil, 280 inches; in Bombay, 78 inches; in South Carolina, 50 inches; in Cumana, 8 inches. The rain falls in large quantities near the equator, and diminishes toward the poles.

The agriculturist, before he commences to make his drains, must first calculate the quantity of water required for the district in which he lives, and its position relative to the surrounding country. If it is elevated, the water will run off rapidly. Even before sowing, the germination of the seed planted in it, if in a low situation, and the soil is of a retentive character, the earth may become so saturated as to prevent the entrance of air, and consequently impede if not prevent the germination of seed.

All soils exist in one of three conditions:

1st. Clay, which is a dense close mass of particles finely comminuted, of an exceedingly tenacious kind, and when wet forms a paste impermeable to water, and is rarely devoid of moisture under any circumstances, even when its constituent particles are readily separable.

2d. In the sandy or gravelly form, the particles are rarely if ever united, consequently the soil is full of interstitial canals and passages for water, and does not possess the power to retain or prevent its admission.

3d. This soil is made up of calcareous or aluminous elements, sometimes silicious, in an incalculable variety of proportions, and is filled with pores for the ingress of air and water.

In the first named soil, wet weather in the spring or fall frequently retards the sowing of grain, even if partially drained, but if undrained, it most completely prevents it, and absolutely compels the agriculturist to change his system of farming, and sow other grains when the season is more advanced. In this case efficient drainage would carry off the water rapidly, and rescue the farmer from the dominion of late or early seasons, and prevent the failure of his crop, besides repaying the entire cost in two or three years, particularly if his drains are deep and have a ready escape, as this renders the soil available to deep-rooted plants, and enables them to send down their fibres to the stores of abundant nourishment, which they help to increase in permanent value by the excrementitious emanations from themselves.

The man who drains his own lands, confers a benefit upon his neighbors. This is true in regard to the exercise of human skill in all the walks of life. We are no doubt all mutually dependent upon each other—as much so in draining as perhaps any other ; for if we do not meet with kindly co-operation, we may be prevented from using a contiguous outfall, and thus prevent the improvement of an immense area of land. I have known several such cases among people who ought gratefully to acknowledge the value of such improvements, which render homes salubrious, and fields fruitful that were before barren, besides promoting the general happiness and comfort of the entire inhabitants of the district.

Draining is undoubtedly equivalent to an entire change of soil as well as climate, in reference not only to the growth of plants, but the health of the people. It deepens the earth, removes the water, and washes out noxious substances from the subsoil, thus aiding the roots to descend. Where there is no outlet under a sandy soil, or in fact any other variety of soil, the poisonous matters sink down from above, or ooze up from below, and remain for a considerable time in the soil, rendering it not only unwholesome, but unfit for the growth of plants. A proper drain will arrest those poisons that descend from above, as well as those arising from below, and every rain will wash the deleterious matters from the soil as deep as the bottom of the drains, and the air will follow in sufficient quantities to produce beneficial results, carrying oxygen, hydrogen and nitrogen where most required and best known. Still, man, with all his knowledge of nature, cannot discern any difference between them, as they are destitute of smell, taste and color ; yet Science, with a lighted match, immediately indicates that they are entirely different from each other. In fact, gasses of various kinds form a very large share of the solid parts of animals and plants. When separated they are invisible. Atmospheric air, when united constitutes a large portion of the magnificent productions of nature. Farmers rarely see the reason of very many of their most common operations, and they have comparatively but little control over agricultural results, because they do not employ their senses of thought as diligently as they do their hands. You often hear farmers say their farms are exhausted by frequent cropping, and I have asked them what exhaustion means, how it takes place, how it can be remedied, and if under any circumstances nature would remedy it if man left it to her ? They pleaded ignorance and failed to answer. If you doubt this, look at the practice of agriculturists generally ; observe the thousands of acres on Long Island and in New Jersey, exhibiting a degree of unproductiveness certainly not natural to the soil, which was fertile by nature but rendered infertile by art. Chemistry may enable them gradually to restore these tracts again to fertility. Drainage, irrigation, lime and gypsum, will produce an abundant growth of vegetation.

The agriculturist must recollect that in the drainage of land two objects must be attained. In very rainy locations he desires to remove the surface water from his fields immediately ; but in districts not so situated, that which ascends from the springs beneath the surface should share his regard.

When rain falls, a portion escapes into the streams, and a portion sinks into the soil; the latter descends in a straight line through the loose materials of the earth until it reaches rocks or impervious subsoil. If the rocks are porous, or have cracks in them, it continues to sink until it reaches indurated clay, or some compact material, over which it spreads laterally, and finally accumulates in beds and gives rise to natural springs, which we are enabled to bring to the surface by means of wells, making lands inhabitable that would not be so were it not for this wise provision of nature. When such lands are hardened by drought, the well will enable the farmer to distribute water over them, and thus facilitate plow or spade culture. The proper situation of the drain is the line where wetness first begins, which is usually rendered perceptible by a change of color in the soil; and the course the drain should follow is indicated by the growth of sub-aquatic plants. By cutting a drain in nearly this line, of sufficient depth to reach the sandy or porous stratum in which the water percolates, you can intercept and remove it to some convenient neighboring outlet. In this case draining is effected without much difficulty. But moisture arises to the surface in different manners, which requires the judgment of the drainer to adapt the direction of his drain to the change of circumstances. When the soil and subsoil are of a mixed nature, draining becomes far more tedious and sometimes extremely difficult. In such soils the collections of water are separated from each other by beds of clay, and, when heavy rains occur, rise to the level of the surrounding surface, where it overflows and saturates the ground, rendering it sour and unproductive. These mixed soils frequently have no connection with each other, and will consequently require as many deep drains as there are beds, in order to draw the water. To drain such a field, you must commence at the lowest part and work up to the most elevated, in such a direction as to pass through the beds of porous materials as well as the clay.

No rule is strictly applicable to mixed soils. The drainer must study the cause of injury, and adapt his remedy to meet the exigency, aiming constantly to reach the reservoir in which the water is retained. If the ground to be drained is flat comparatively, a ditch carried through the hollowest part will act as a desiccative to the land for a great distance on each side of it, for the reason that the shape resembles a basin, formed generally by a clay subsoil, which holds the water to be supplied to the superincumbent soil. Land, rendered wet, however, by water springing from beneath, bears but a small proportion to that injured by the fall of rain upon its surface; consequently those soils that are considered dry, frequently render cultivation precarious by the imperfect escape of rain water from their surface. When soil is incumbent upon beds of sand, the water is rapidly absorbed. When on beds of impervious clay, the water saturates every particle of earth as it runs slowly over the surface. When on partially pervious subsoils, by good management, in a favorable season, crops may be produced. But when on rock, filled with numerous fissures, the land is generally fertile, and universally produces good crops. Therefore to produce results analagous to those of Nature, you must make uniform channels for the water to escape through, as she did in the example last named. When drains, located near each other, have been constructed some time, you will observe an immense number of small fissures between the drains, which frequently reach to the bottom of the drain, and are caused by the contraction of the earth, arising from its dryer condition. These form channels for the percolation of rain water from all parts of the surface immediately to the level of the drains. To evolve this property of the soil to the greatest extent, the drains must be placed near each other, so as to absorb the moisture retained between them. · In forming drains, the very first object that presents itself to the consideration of the drainer, is the nature of the subsoil. If it consists of tenacious clay, the distance from drain to drain should be from twelve to eighteen feet; if a porous or sandy subsoil, from twenty to thirty feet will be sufficiently near; and in gravelly soils, a still greater distance asunder will answer the purpose. Longitudinal direction should be given to all drains, if possible, as the chances of being choked by depositions of mud or sand are thereby much diminished; and if by any chance it should become stopped, the water, by its altitudinal pressure, will overcome the impediment, or it will burst at the surface of the ground, and show where the evil exists. Thorough draining cannot be considered complete, however perfect it may be, until subsoil plowing accomplishes entire disintegration of soil. Drainage must not be considered, as usual, a completed task, but merely a part of the system. Subsoil plowing is alike indispensable to stir the subsoil, that it may offer no obstruction to the water until it reaches the drains. When deep draining and subsoil plowing are properly and scientifically accomplished, no limits can possibly be assigned to the amazing productiveness of the soil. Still subsoil plowing may be injudiciously performed, particularly when the ground is in a soft pliant condition, and instead of crumbling to pieces, adheres to the plow, and forms a paste, impervious to water and destructive to roots. Therefore the desired amelioration can only be obtained by a judicious application of this all-important implement. All practical agriculturists know that land resting upon a retentive clay subsoil becomes consolidated to such a degree, from the action of winters' snow and rain, that many plowings are often found necessary to bring it to a proper state of cultivation, and if a wet spring follows, the whole is often converted into a thoroughly indurated, unmanageable, compact mass.

Draining is certainly equivalent to a complete and lasting change of soil, as well as a similar change of climate, both in reference to the health of the population and growth of vegetation. It not only deepens the soil, but removes the water, and with it the noxious ingredients found in many soils highly pernicious to the descending roots. All soils are benefited by draining, even light, porous, sandy soils, lying on a sloping surface, are greatly improved. In nearly all sandy soils, where no outlet exists, noxious matters either form above or below, render it unfit for cultivated plants. Who has not seen swamps on our highest mountains, beneath which unwholesome waters linger, thus inducing hopeless barrenness ? They find it necessary to drain the sandy Steppes of Hungary and Russia, shortly after which the daisy and dandelion appear ; then in turn the wholesome and nutritive grasses take their place. The operations of the agriculturist, in causing changes upon land, are either chemical or mechanical. When he plows, subsoils, and drains, he alters the physical character of his soil,— when he manures, limes, marls, &c., he changes its chemical constitution. These operations, therefore, are distinct. When a soil will grow all the crops we desire, mechanical operations are all that are required to retain it in fertility. If inorganic constituents are wanting, draining will prepare it for further operations, but will not remove sterility. All the older drainage in this country and Europe, was chiefly surface drainage, by furrow and ridge. This, besides leaving the soil surcharged with water, carried off the finer particles of earth, and with them such manures and fertilizing substances as were removable from the surface in suspension. When heavy rain storms occurred, a large portion of the manure top-dressing was carried into the ditches and streams. The modern method, instead of draining over the surface, does away entirely with ridges and furrows, makes the surface level, and causes the water to drain downward through the land to the under-ground channels. In its course through the soil, the fine earthy powder of the mold, and the particles of manure or loose vegetable matter are left in it, and the soluble manure is carried down for the sustenance of vegetation. This saving of fertilizing mold greatly increases the productiveness of thoroughly drained land, apart from the permeability, increased temperature, and finer condition of the soil, induced by drainage.

Estimating the thorough drainage of land by the cubic contents of the soil, calculating from the level of the bottom of the drainage to the surface of the soil, cannot possibly give any exposition of the agricultural effect ; because it has not yet been fully determined, by experiment or practice, how far it is beneficial to the growth of plants to remove free water from the lower portion of the subsoil. In some localities the results of experiments are in favor of moderate depths of drains, showing that the most beneficial distance from the surface for the free water is two feet ; when below that, in dry summers, the crops are found to suffer, and it is customary to dam up the water to that level. Water will rise some inches in soil by capillary or molecular attraction, but in such cases rarely fills the interstices to such an extent as to exclude atmospheric air, but attaches itself merely to the surface of the particles, where it remains available to the roots of plants, without any of the bad effects resulting from stagnant free water. Until agriculturists, by experiment, fully and practically determine as to the proper distance for retaining a supply, the depth to which land should be drained cannot be determined. When ascertained, the rule will be found to vary with the nature and condition of the soil.

We do not desire that our drains should deprive the land of moisture, but merely adjust the quantity so as to produce the highest state of fertility ; and we have invariably found, in all varieties of soil, whether on high or low ground, that drainage has remunerated us well for the outlay. You will find that the if the annual increase of trees on undrained land is five per cent., the increase on drained land will be ten per cent., and on land drained and irrigated, twelve per cent. In perfect drainage, twenty-four hours' rain should percolate through, and leave the land in twenty-two hours from the time the drains began to perform their duty. This can only be effected by forming a large subterranean area of porosity. The continuation of water in the soil for a longer period than capillary retention could allow it to remain, is mechanically and chemically hurtful, from the fact that it causes density and sediment. A narrow and deep drain will afford much porocity at the least cost.

The material with which the drains are filled should be durable, without possessing much capillary attraction. If circumstances compelled me to use pipes instead of stones for a drain, I would place hard, round stones under them, to prevent choking by superincumbent soil, and to resist side pressure. Stones scarcely have any mechanical affinity for water, and do not offer obstructions to its passage. Every eighty yards in length, a drain should open into one somewhat larger, or percolation will be delayed. I would recommend that no perishable material should be placed in a drain. I have used bushes, straw, stalks, hay, &c., but find reverted bogs the best, and next, sods, with the grass side down. In every ten acres there should be one main open ditch for the closed drains to empty into. The absence of such an artery renders many drains perfectly useless. While water enters drains at the sides, its most rapid and constant entrance is at the bottom, where the main pressure is. The deeper the drain, the greater will be the weight of the column of water, and the more quick the filtration, which at two feet will be double that of one ; at six feet, six times as great, and so on, in proportion to the superincumbent weight of water.

I once cut drains through a piece of wet land, four feet deep, and although the ground was exceedingly wet to within ten inches of the surface, no water flowed through them ; I then added another foot, which permitted gravity to overcome the suspensive power, and they rapidly filled with water to the depth of eleven inches, and continued permanently to perform their duty ; showing plainly that the deeper the drain, the higher the water will be compelled to ascend, and the more time it will take to reach the surface, the active delaying forces being space, gravity, and friction, causing slow evaporation, and consequently a dry and warm soil. On undrained land, water is the greatest enemy the agriculturist has to contend with, but on a well drained soil it is his very best friend ; and he can never have too much of it, as it is our richest manure, and percolates the soil loaded with heat, carbonic acid gas, ammonia, and other chemical combinations. You all are aware that in summer, if you place the thermometer one inch below the surface of the ground, it will immediately indicate one hundred and thirty-seven degrees, and of four feet six inches, only forty-four degrees. After a heavy rain of twenty-four hours, try the same experiment, and you will probably find, as I did, that the heat on the surface was one hundred, while that at four feet deep was ninety; showing that the rain had carried the heat down with it, where it will remain for a long time to invigorate the roots of the crops. This shows the exceeding great folly of making open water courses on the surface of the ground to carry it off, instead of making drains below to save the heat, gases, and moisture in the earth, which may be compared, if properly drained, to an immense spunge, always ready not only to absorb, but retain, an enormous quantity of water, with a single drop of which it will not part, until all the molecules and pores have taken in more than they can possibly hold by capillary attraction. This I have often observed by examining the outlets of my drains after a tremendous rain during the summer, and frequently find no water issuing from them. If dry, after the rain, it will be drawn again to the surface of the field by evaporation, acting upon capillary attraction before it has time to reach the drains. I have frequently heard good farmers say that they do not believe in subsoil plowing, because they invariably raise better crops on land plowed five inches, than they do from that plowed eighteen. Still these same men are all inconsistent, because they invariably till their drained gardens eighteen inches, and if you ask them why they do so, will reply that they obtain much better crops in their gardens by deep cultivation, never for a moment considering, that if their fields were drained and subsoil plowed, the result would be the same. The fact is, the generality of land should on no account be subsoil plowed before it is thoroughly underdrained, because at the bottom of the furrow left by the subsoil plow will become a living lake, and ruin every crop he sows upon the ground.

There are but few soils that do not require draining and subsoil plowing, I do not know of any. Strong tenacious clays of every description require deep cultivation. Sandy, gravelly and silty soils generally, if not invariably, have hard bottoms of pebbles mixed with protoxide of iron, masses of conglomerated pudding stone, with veins of clay running through them in sufficient quantities to head back, or retentively hold, spring water; therefore they require deep cultivation. If proper attention was paid to these matters, you would never hear the eternal complaint of the destruction of the roots of clover, wheat and rye, by freezing out. Let me assure you this never would be the case if the soil was sufficiently deep. The roots of the cereal crops, clovers and grasses, will run a great distance down if the soil will permit, and the roots of the White and Swede turnip will extend many feet in a friable soil; the root of a common field parsnip has been traced over thirteen feet, and then broken off, perhaps several feet from its extreme point.

I sincerely hope that a few of us at least who now compose this assembly of agriculturists, may live to see the day when this penurious and pinching economy in farming shall succumb to more enlarged views, and permit capital to develop its circumscribed strength. Let our motto, manufactures, science and the arts, unite in one common interest for the welfare of our entire agricultural people, remembering that there is no occupation in which one-quarter of the amount of capital is invested, and that the better the farmer does, the cheaper will be bread.

SPRING FLOWERS.

R. G. Pardee.—One of the readiest and most useful liquid manures for flowers is soap suds. Sulphate of potash, an ounce or two dissolved in a pail of water, makes a valuable liquid manure for flowers. Hen manure should always be dissolved, and applied in liquid form. Cow manure should be treated in the same way. This is the best application for rose bushes. I use nothing on my garden but liquid manure. Such things as I can buy and dissolve, such as sulphate of pota-h, nitrate of potash, nitrate of soda, glauber salts, guano, &c; almost everything of the manure kind may be put in an old cask set in the ground, and used upon the flowers and plants of a small garden. Only dilute it well, and there is no danger or trouble about liquid manure killing plants.

Judge Meigs.—I have some questions from a lady, Miss Randall, of Lexington avenue, about flowers. She asks—Is the Dielytra a hardy plant?

Andrew S. Fuller.—Yes, perfectly—as hardy as the Peona.

Judge Meigs.—Will the Hydrangea grow from cuttings?

Mr. Pardee.—Yes, but every one cannot make it grow. Will common garden soil grow cranberries?

R. G. Pardee.—I have not been successful. I have some doubts about cranberry-growing in garden soil being made profitable, though some persons succeed pretty well.

Will the currant bear best in the tree shape? Mr. Pardee and Mr. Pell say tree shape. Mr. Fuller says the tree shape will want renewing every three years. Will the Holly grow well here? Several gentlemen answered Yes, the American Holly. It grows back of Brooklyn.

VITALITY OF SEEDS.

R. G. Pardee.—Much inquiry is made as to the length of time in which seeds may be safely trusted to germinate. If properly kept, I reply as follows: Parsnips and rhubarb, two years; beans and peas, two or three years; carrot, nasturstiums, mustard, parsley and lettuce, three to four years; pepper, cabbage, spinach, tomato, turnip, salsify, radish, and egg plant, four to five years; asparagus, onion, celery, okra, broccoli, and cauliflower, five to six years; beets, cucumber, gourd, melon, squash, pumpkins, corn and other grains, six to ten years and longer. The great secret of keeping seeds is to have them well matured, and kept cool and dry. It is impossible to say how long seeds may be made to preserve vitality, with proper care; but it is certain that any sort may be spoiled in any year by damp and heat.

FERTILIZING SEEDS.

Solon Robinson.—I have the following communication from D. B. Taylor of this city, upon a new use of sugar for fertilizing seeds. He writes:

"According to the published letters of John Ronald, Esq., of Glasgow, Scotland, a gentleman who has given to the subject the most thorough investigation, sugar mixed with chimney soot forms the very best manure for coating seed wheat and other cereals, as well as garden seeds, before planting, that has ever yet been tried. Chemists have discovered that a seed of wheat, immediately after life has been given to the embryo plant, is by some inscrutable law of nature, changed chiefly into sugar, by which the infant plant is kept alive and nourished, until it is able to send out fibres or suckers in search of other nourishment. The sugar enriches, and being, when dissolved, of a glutinous nature, adheres to the seed ; and soot is said to be a certain preventive to the worm. The soot and sugar should be mixed in water to the thickness of good cream, say to six bushels of seed grain put three pounds of sugar, and soot to make it like thick black ink; after mixing it well with the seed grain, let it stand quiet in a tub from 20 to 40 hours. By this treatment of large sized seed, which should always be selected, an increased crop of full 30 per cent can be safely calculated upon by the farmer."

NEW VARIETIES OF POTATOES.

Judge Meigs.—The Paris Journal of Horticulture says the Rainville potato is superior to any other new variety. Its flowers are lilac; tubers long, with few eyes; skin light yellowish; flesh light and fine grained, full of starch, cooks quick, is of a pleasant taste, ripens in August, and produces well.

Dr. Holton exhibited a sample of a new French potato, called the Decaisne, the seed of which he sent from Paris a couple of years ago to P. M. Forward, of Southwick, Mass., who thinks them remarkably fine. In form they are like the English Whites—roundish, with deep eyes.

N. R. French exhibited two samples, one of English Flukes and one of Prince Albert, and asked the club to see if there was any difference. He stated that the Flukes were selling at high prices as a new variety. To him, and others who had examined them, they appeared identical.

Solon Robinson.—Here is a letter from Champlain, March 25, which recommends something new in potato growing. The writer says :

" Last Spring, my brother, a neophyte in farm-life, planted a few rows of potatoes in the garden, and planted them so deeply that his assistant— a Nestor in farm duties—declared they would 'never come up at all.' But more important matters claimed attention, and, despite old Joe's remonstrance, the poor potatoes were suffered to remain in their deep prison-bed. Well, in the fall, our potatoes generally proved 'small and few in a hill,' and the digger declared the hills which my brother had manipulated to be entirely destitute, until, in his investigations, he chanced to penetrate the compact soil below the loose earth. Here, to his surprise, he stumbled on a perfect potato-mine, a deposit of tubers, so imbedded in the soil that their dislodgment was no small labor—the soil was so packed you'd have thought it never saw a spade—and they were the largest, brightest, smoothest skinned, and soundest-cored potatoes that ever the earth rolled out.   And, one thing worthy of note ; while those surface-grown were tainted with rot, these were like ivory, and now are as sound as when first taken from the ground.   It is not my intention to theorize much, but is it not fair to suppose that potatoes planted near the surface are affected by the changes of the weather ; that the blistering sun and drenching rain contribute in no small degree to their decay ; while those deeper planted draw their sustenance from a soil whose temperature is more equal, nestle, as it were, in the cool, moist bosom of earth, and, sucking her deep founts, are protected from the extremes of heat and cold, of wet and drouth. But enough of speculation.   I have given the facts, and potato growers can draw their own conclusions.   In any event, however, will it not be well enough for them to try the experiment this year of planting a row or two of their potatoes at twice their usual depth.   The result in the Fall may impel them to adopt the experiment as a rule, and give them cause to gratefully remember the suggestion of   C. H. W."

Solon Robinson.—Here is another letter asking for information about another new potato ; and as I see the author of it present, I shall call upon him to give the desired information.   It is the " Pelham seedling."   Will Robert L. Pell give some account of it ?

Mr. Pell said : I started this seedling ten years ago, and have carefully cultivated the product to obtain an early and dry variety.   It is now the earliest potato known.   I have manured this potato with liquid manure, as well as other crops, and the result has been highly beneficial.   I look upon it as a valuable acquisition.   A sample of it, both cooked and in its natural condition, I will place before you.

Judge Meigs.—Here are some of the potatoes boiled, and I will pass them around to be tasted.

They were all cracked open, and almost as dry as meal, of a good flavor, and grow of a good size, roundish in form, white color, and very sound and heavy.   The Club made the following resolution in regard to these potatoes :

Resolved, That the Pelham Seedling potatoes exhibited to the Farmers' Club to-day in a raw and boiled state, are fine, large, white, mealy, of good flavor, and an acquisition of value to the present stock.

GRAPE-GROWING IN CONNECTICUT.

Solon Robinson.—Nath. Dustin of Uncasville, on the Thames River, wants to know if he can grow grapes successfully, and what sort, and what situation.

Several persons answered that they would grow the Isabella, Diana, Delaware, Concord and Hartford Prolific, on the south side of hills without shelter, and with certain success, by laying down the vines in the Fall.

HALLOCK'S PATENT FRUIT BOXES.

N. Hallock exhibited specimens of his new style of fruit boxes, made for two cents each, of thin shavings of wood, to hold a quart of berries, and for 1½ cents to hold a pint, and full strong enough to bear transportation, with any kind of market berries. They will be a good substitute for baskets, and for more expensive boxes.

Mr. Maxwell asked if there was a remedy for the yellows in peach leaves.

Prof. Mapes.—The best method is to restore the health of the tree by using *inorganic fertilizers only*, for the common barn yard manures are unsuited to the peach. By this and good treatment the constitution of the tree is regained, and a vigorous growth throwing off the yellows. While I am up, I wish to state my experience in the origin of the tree. I take the peach pit and set it *sharp point down*, for the same reason that I set the eye side of a Lima bean down; because then the plant comes straight up out of the ground; whereas, if they happen to be wrong end up, the plants suffer in rising by trying to turn over; the peach tree then gets an *unhappy twist*, which it never recovers from.

The Professor illustrated his mode of trimming peach trees, in relation to the *fruit* and to the *wood buds*. on the blackboard. He related the thriving condition of a peach tree, standing near enough to a stable window for a horse to bite off about the proper amount of its branches, doing it with a skill and taste utterly unknown to his master. A peach limb should not, with its fruit, bend down below level, for then it is very apt to perish. Never apply any nitrogenous manure to peach trees.

Mr. Maxwell.—Does that rule also govern as to the apricot tree?

Prof. Mapes.—Yes, sir, and to nectarine. I find budding very easy, as follows : Select a limb to bud another of like size. With a perfectly sharp knife scoop out a slice from the tree, and another from the graft—exactly alike. *Fit in on and bind up quick.*

Mr. Doughty exhibited dioscorea batata—the Chinese yam, from his farm—about two feet in length.

QUESTIONS FOR NEXT MEETING.

Solon Robinson.—" Lawns and how to revive old orchards."

Prof. Mapes.—" Spring and summer treatment of strawberries."

Mr. Pardee.—" Spring flowers, seeds, plants, trees."

Thomas Godwin.—" Proper soil and its depth for shade trees in the Central Park and in our avenues."

The Club then adjourned.

H. MEIGS, *Secretary.*

April 4th, 1859.

Present.—Messrs. Robert L. Pell, Hon. Judge Livingston, Lawton, Chilson, Pardee, Prof. J. J. Mapes, Olcott, Davoll, Roberts, Heermance, Hon. John G. Bergen, Fuller, Witt, Bruce, Wm. B. Leonard, John W. Chambers, Isidore Bernhard, J. A. Bunting, J. V. Brower, Thos. Godwin, Veeder, Stuart, James Renwick, President of the Institute, McCready, Vice President, Aycrigg, Vice-President Gen. Hall, Dr. Moffat, Rev. Mr. Gardiner, Charles Turell, Doughty, Pierce, Wright, Jr., Daniel C. Robinson, Solon Robinson, R. Van Houten, of Paterson, Jersey, Van Brunt, of Jersey, Dr. Crowell, Ezekiel Harris—100 members in all.

Mr. Meigs read the following article, received since last meeting—extracts prepared by him, viz:

UNITED STATES GUANO.

Some time ago the guano of Jarvis' and of Baker's islands, in the Pacific Ocean, was discovered by an American citizen, and the attention of this Club strongly drawn to it by Mr. Benson, the representative of the discoverer. This Club issued a circular, inviting all the farming interest of our country to join in petitioning our government to examine the islands, and if valuable in guano, and out of the dominion of any nation, to plant our stars and stripes on them. The government promptly dispatched a frigate to take possession of those islands. They are ours.

Doubts have subsequently hung over the question of the agricultural value of that guano. But now we have the positive undeniable evidence of their great value, decided by the most honorable and learned chemists of our country, viz: by John C. Draper, Analytical Chemist of the University of New York; by R. Ogden Doremus, Prof. of Analytical Chemistry of the New York Medical College; by George Scaffor, M. D., and B. Fanueil Craig, M. D., for Jas. Henry, Secretary of the Smithsonian Institution.

The comparison of it with barn yard manure is as follows, in that main point, "phosphate of lime." Barn yard manure in this stands below guano.

By Prof. Draper:
Phosphate and sulphate of lime,.............................. 72.50
By Prof. Doremus:
Sulphate of lime and phosphate 78.75
Drs. Scafforth and Craig:
Residue of fixed salts, ... 71.57

The value of this ingredient to grain crops is fully admitted. The quantity of this guano is very great; and let us remember that in using it we are paying our own people for the ships and the labor, instead of foreigners; that it is United States guano. H. MEIGS.

[Sciota Valley Farmer, March 18, 1859.]

BAKING WITHOUT SCORCHING.

A bowl with two quarts of water, set in an oven when baking, will prevent pies, cakes, &c., from being scorched. Try it, ladies.

[Ohio Valley Farmer, Cincinnati, April, 1859.]

Dioscorea Batata, Chinese Yam, is excellent.

RENOVATION OF PEACH TREES.

Remove the soil from around the tree, and put on charcoal. Great renovation.

[California Farmer, San Francisco, March 5, 1859.]

Peach in bloom yesterday. Apple buds opening.

[North Western Prairie Farmer, Chicago, March 26, 1859.

SEEDLING POTATO.

Make a hole in the ground a foot deep, put in potato balls, put a mark on the spot; dig them up next spring and sow the seed as you do radish. When grown large enough, transplant them.

[Journal of Agriculture, and the Transactions of the Highland Agricultural Society of Scotland, March, 1859.]

The members of this society are in number 3,658. The Emperor Napoleon and Prince Albert head the list—the Emperor as Honorary *Associate*, elected in 1856; the Prince Consort as Honorary *Member*, elected in 1841. A great number of the nobility are members; the Duke of Athole is now President. Ordinary annual member fee, £1 3s. 6d. Life membership varying from £12 12s. to £7 1s. Tenant farmers and members of local associations, 10s. annually, or £5 5s. for life.

GUANO.

Phospho-Peruvian guano and Sombrero guano, seem to have lost their former power as manure. Whether the land is guano-sick, the fact is that wherever Peruvian guano has been extensively used, its effects are certainly much diminished, as the phospho proves better for turnips. Farmers also find benefit from using less of it than formerly.

This phospho guano is found on the West India Islands, Sombrero, on Monk's Islands, &c., occupied by multitudes of sea fowl.

TO PREVENT GRAIN FROM LODGING.

Sow several varieties together. The reason is that some bend least in storm, and help the weaker to stand up and get up, and a larger crop of grain is had.

[Prof. Anderson, Chemist of the Society—Address February, 1859, before the Society.]

ARTIFICAL MANURES.

Notwithstanding all that has been done, and the many careful experiments, I am sometimes inclined to think we take credit to ourselves for knowing more about artificial manures than our knowledge justifies. We find the *worse* the artificial manure, the *louder* are the praises. Defective analyses mislead farmers much. Those in the books are generally quite erroneous.

In regard to agricultural institutions, the crowning one is the Royal Agricultural Society of England, under the auspices of Prince Albert, with its income of £10,000 a year; commencing under George III., grandfather of the Queen.

The *Prairie Farmer*, Chicago, March 31, joins numbers of the wise who lesson us to spare the birds.

It says: "The birds pay rent; spare them, feed them, pay them! They prove the best workers on the farm!"

Another says: "I carefully examined robins, and found that they all live on insects and worms.   They are very fond of the wire-worm fly.   Occasionally, by way of dessert, they pick a few strawberries and cherries; but they earn it by killing millions of our enemies of crops!"   [See Transactions of the Massachusetts Horticultural Society in 1858.]

By O. B. Galusha.—Moss, to pack trees and plants for long journeys, put up damp and lightly, grafts in pure sawdust, from bass or from hard wood, will keep *fifteen months.*

Seeds of most of the evergreens grow best in a mixture of *sand and leaf mold.*   Cover the surface of the soil with moss, as a mulch, water lightly, keep under the shade of a fence or a raised platform, free access to air. Some sorts of the evergreens will grow the first year.

We notice that a New York city lady is establishing a horticultural school for girls.   We sadly want such schools in the West, not only for girls but for boys.   Our gardeners are all foreigners.   Somebody may make money by it here.

Mr. Heermance, of Geneva, Ontario county, exhibited a model farm gate, which is readily opened and shut by a person on horseback or in a carriage, by means of a hanging drop, accessible to the hand, by which the gate divides, each part running on an inclined bar above, and as readily meet again as the bar inclines both ways to the centre.

CULTIVATION OF FLOWERS AND LAWNS.

Solon Robinson.—I have two letters from two noble women—women who improve and beautify the earth.   I will read them, and promised that they will be listened to with pleasure.   The first is from one who signs herself " Housewife," of Colchester, Vt.

We give the most of it as follows :

While other housewives are enriching your columns with accounts of their experience in cooking, I will pen a few lines in behalf of the flower garden, which should be attended to as well as the " creature comforts,'t last that love of the beautiful which is implanted in every heart, should perish through neglect.   Many housewifes are so entirely devoted to cooking, house-cleaning and sewing that they cannot have a minute's time even for reading except on Sundays, and then they " are so tired they had rather rest than read."

I hereby advise them not to cook so much, not to scrub so much, and sew with a machine.   Others will say they have so many human flowers to attend to that they cannot cultivate any others, and these will let their door-yards run to waste and weeds, instead of having them seeded down, and flower-beds cut in the rich, green turf.

I have cultivated a few of the common kinds of flowers ever since I was a child, but have lost the delight of seeing some new, strange flower expand its beauties to my view, because I know not how nor where to procure an assortment of choice, rare seed.   Last Spring, I accidentally looke i over a flower-seed catalogue with much interest, because it was the first of the kind I had ever seen.   I found I could have new and lovely flowers at a very triffling expense. My ambition was fired; I gave my husband no peace until he had the kitchen garden removed to the rear of the house, and removed the fence which separated the old kitchen garden and the door-yard, thus making a fine little lawn. I got a man to help me—not a gardener—we have no professed gardeners within ten miles. I drew the plan of my flower-beds myself, and had the man cut them out of the turf in the desired orms.

Previous to this, I persuaded three or four housewives—all mothers of families, with plenty to do—to join me in sending for flower seeds and roots. There we exchanged with each other, thus obtaining a fine variety at a small expense. We followed the directions given in the catalogue, and were very successful with the most delicate seeds. My lawn was beautiful; indeed, so rich and varied were the effects of French and German asters. German balsams, German stocks, English pansies, phloxes, verbenas and dahlias, *from seed the first season*, that my husband, who had at first ridiculed my flower-venture, was obliged to acknowledge its success.

Last Fall I sent for a few hyacinth, crocus, and early tulip bulbs, and had a fine display of flowers in our living room, during the dreary Winter months. My room is even now filled with the exquisite fragrance of hyacinths, which still continue in bloom. I hope this article will attract the attention of my toil-worn sisters: they can have no idea what a source of purest enjoyment the cultivation of flowers will be to them. Its influence has been very beneficial to my little ones, who watch the expansion of the delicate and wonderful buds with an interest fully equal to my own.

Mr. Robinson continued.—I hope this pleasant letter will stimulate a great many other housewives not to give husbands any peace until they give their wives lawns and flower gardens.

The next letter is from Ruth Lynde, of New Bedford, Mass., about the cause of grass near the house running out. It says:

I read with interest the account of the Farmers' Club meetings, and noticed in the last, complaints about weedy grass plots.

I will give you the result of my observations, and you may communicate them if you think them of sufficient importance to the Club.

I have had the grass destroyed in the manner described at two different places where I have resided, and found the same cause productive of the same result at each.

During the Winter and Spring, the servant girls were in the habit of throwing soaps suds after washing clothes or dishes, upon the grass plot, and I noticed invariably that the plantain and sorrel came up instead of the grass. Here at my mother's, I have a bit of garden, and there is a grass plot also, and since I urged upon her notice the ill effect of soap suds upon the grass, and she commanded its discontinuance, the grass has come in again, and much white clover with it. Most houses in the country have a patch of plantain around the kitchen doors, and the same habit of throwing out sudsy water is the cause of its growth.

If you like, I will write you about plants and flowers, and my method of killing the slugs (or their parents) which are such a blight to rose bushes.

I am very fond of gardening, and have quite a nice selection of herbaceous plants not in general cultivation. This year I expect some great results from the application of some new dressing to the hyacinths and tulips.

STRAWBERRIES.

R. G. Pardee.—It depends upon fair treatment to make this plant bear abundantly every year. But it needs experience of the different sorts, to be successful, because the varieties have different habits. In Spring, rake back the straw from the crown of the plants, and let it lie between rows. Sprinkle with soap suds every few days. Pull out the weeds as fast as they appear.

I never cut off runners. In October, I rake off all the lightly struck runners, and then select vigorous old or new plants to stand for bearers next year, and turn under the others, and cover in the fall again with straw or leaves. The ground being well prepared in the first place, don't need continual working. The most prolific bearer is the Wilson seedling. I do do not esteem Peabody's seedling as a fine flavored berry. Hovey's seedling is not so good as his Boston pine. Very few know what a good strawberry is. I once simulated my vines so much that they grew all leaves and stems, and no fruit. In preparing ground for a bed, I would fork it very deep, say two feet, and dress with ashes or leaf mold—never with animal manure. I would put rare plants in rows three feet apart, and two feet in the rows. Cover the ground half an inch deep with tan bark. If I could not get tan I would use sawdust or leaves from the woods. Straw or salt hay, or rowen, will do for a mulch. There are four things that will prevent you from growing strawberries.

1st. You do not prepare the ground well.

2d. You must have a good variety of plants.

3d. You must not use any kind of animal manure, and nothing that will make the vines grow rankly.

4th. You must keep the ground clear, but you must not use the hoe; hoeing destroys more strawberry plants than anything else. Use your fingers and the fork to get out weeds and loosen the soil.

In preparing for a bed use the lime and salt mixture freely. While growing use soap suds; also, solution of sulphate of potash, one or two ounces to a pail full of water. Nitrate of soda in the same proportion, is a good substance also to apply to strawberries.

Wm. Lawton.—I think a great deal of Peabody's new strawberry. It is a prodigious strong grower. The leaf stalk is long and fruit stem short. I think the flavor excellent. It has a peculiar aroma and flavor. I know many persons utterly condemn it; I do not.

SOIL FOR STRAWBERRIES.

Solon Robinson.—There is this one fact to be borne in mind in regard to good soil for strawberries. In any southern exposure, where the soil is loamy and rich in leaf mold, strawberries can be successfully grown by simply digging the ground deep before setting out the plants, without using any manurial substance whatever.

R. G. Pardee.—High manuring will force runners and leaves, and such plants will not bear fruit well. It never injures plants to cut off runners. Don't let your varieties of berries run together. The strongest growers will drive out the best bearers. The Early Scarlet sends out runners very strong. I would set a board between varieties, to prevent their running together. To fructify Hovey's seedling, I would not require staminate plants nearer than thirty feet. I would have a bed ten feet square of staminates to one of 100 feet of pistilates.

Prof. Mapes.—An excellent thing for a strawberry bed is a tanbark liquor, not too strong. The reason that field strawberries are high flavored is probably because there is more tannic acid to be obtained by the plants in the fields than in the garden. A good plan for field culture is alternate beds and paths. Prepare the paths well in Spring, and let the runners set in them, and then turn under the old vines. Mulch is particularly useful. A gentleman at Derby, Conn., covered his beds with slabs, edged to a width of four feet long, and laid them down bark up, with notches in the edges through which the plants grow. The plants grew well, and have produced well and kept clean. After bearing the crop, he lifts the slabs and loosens the soil, and lays down the slabs again. If runners are wanted for new plants, the slabs are taken away.

Mr. Pardee.—I arranged a mound of earth with clam shells all around, with strawberry plants between them, watering at the top and letting it run down. It is upon the same principle as the slab theory, and makes a very pretty ornament, and the crop was very large. April is the best time to set plants for Autumn. One who will attend to it will succeed best in the season after fruiting. I can transplant plants all the Summer months.

Prof. Mapes.—I find potash, phosphate, soda, all excellent for strawberries.

Judge Meigs.—I have found the broken bark of the wood pile an excellent dressing for strawberries owing to the tannin in the bark.

RENOVATING OLD ORCHARDS.

Prof. Mapes.—There was an old orchard on my place that had ceased bearing, which I fully renovated and afterward cut down, because I cannot afford the shade. The land is to valuable to grow large trees upon. I can produce fruit upon dwarfs more economically. All old apple orchards are deficient in lime, but the lime must be properly prepared to be of use. The caustic soda wash spoken of last week will clear them of insects and fungi. I subsoiled the old orchard which was in grass, and applied lime. I recommend ten bushels per acre, sowed in a caustic state on the surface. Lime is only soluble in large quantities of water. The next Spring I applied phosphate of lime. This orchard was then in vigorous bearing, and had not before borne for years. The grass crop was also more than doubled. Run the subsoil plow up and down hill, and it will serve to drain the land.

A Jersey farmer said that he had pursued the course recommended by Prof. Mapes, in an old orchard, but without success. I would be very glad to know what to do to prevent the decay of apple trees. I have not used the subsoil plow, nor under-draining.

Prof. Mapes.—I only run the subsoil lifter furrows some four feet apart, without disturbing the soil. Lime and manure should not be applied at the same time to orchards. The plowing is an important part of the treatment.

Mr. Veeder — A German, working for me, practices removing the earth from the apple tree roots in the Fall, and that has completely renovated an old tree on my farm. I have great faith in the value of cutting off the long runners of tree roots.

Adrian Bergen.—I wish I could make the apple trees on Long Island produce as they did thirty years ago. The trees have generally failed. I believe apple trees are failing all over the land. It is not all owing to want of lime. There is something beside this that affects apple trees.

Mr. Veeder.—I know one apple tree that bore, two years ago, in Schenectady County, seventy barrels of apples.

Richard Van Houten, of Paterson, New Jersey.—My father loved an orchard, and made one, of our most valuable apples, chiefly pippins, about forty years ago. Of late years it has, as well as many other orchards, shown unequivocal marks of defect and decay. Having heard of the successful renovation of the apple trees, by Prof. Mapes, I followed his example and used all the knowledge I could get, but I failed ; and there is extensive failure in Jersey, the causes of which, and the remedy, are much wanted.

The questions for next meeting the same.

The Club adjourned.   H. MEIGS, *Secretary*.

April 11, 1859.

Present—Messrs. Pell, Pardee, Solon Robinson, Wright, Clough, Lawton, Livingston, Steele, Roberts, Brewster, Adrian Bergen, John G. Bergen, Prof. Nash, Fuller, Lowe, Dr. Holton, Freeman, Stacey, Ross, Col. Travers, John Campbell—50 in all.

Judge R. S. Livingston in the chair. H. Meigs, Secretary.

The Secretary read the following papers :

[Journal de la Société Imperiale et Centrale d'Horticulture, Napoleon III., Protecteur. Paris, 1859.]

This noble society includes in it 1,854 members. S. A. I. Princess Jerome Napoleon and the Prince Napoleon, the Princess Mathilde, the two Kings of Siam, S. A. Datu-Tummong-Gong Daing Ibrahim. In. Marajah de Singapour, et caetera, S. A. Tuanvin van Thoobeker, the eldest son of Datu Tummong, S. A. Tuanvin van Abdulrahman, the second son, and a large number of the nobility of Europe. It has 112 corresponding societies, of which two are in the United States, viz : the American Institute and the Smithsonian Institute.

JAPAN.

The American Institute, at its meeting on the 7th of April inst., elected *Dr. Simmons*, a surgeon in the missionary service, who will reside in Japan, a corresponding member. He will give all desired knowledge of the agriculture, mechanic arts, &c., of that remarkable country.

THE BIRDS AGAIN.

The *Prairie Farmer*, of Chicago. Illinois, of the 7th of April, 1859, says : " Wilson, the ornithologist, computes that each red-winged blackbird destroys, on an average, fifty grubs a day in summer. The robin, woodthrush, bluebird, catbird, sparrow, oriole, woodpecker, and many other birds. are equally useful. While hoeing my garden the other day, I saw a little bird alight near a row of cabbages. He commenced at one end of the row, and making the entire circuit of every plant, and examining carefully the under surface of every leaf, went through to the other end. His search was not unsuccessful, for he found and devoured worms and insects from almost every plant. Now, no gold could buy the service which the scores of these *winged gardeners* labor so diligently and effectually to render, without money and without price, and besides that, giving me sweet songs without number in addition. Reader, encourage the birds."

DEEP PREJUDICE.

During the severe panic in Ireland, a few years ago, when a U. S. ship of war was loaded with provisions and sent there, free of charge, we endeavored to teach them the value of our noble native Indian corn. Our late associate, Joseph Cowdin, Consul at Glasgow, exerted himself to bring it into fashion, by all our styles of cooking it. He treated rich and poor at his own expense for a long time. He succeeded more extensively than it had ever been done before. Still the deep prejudice remains. They cannot find out yet, as our Indians had done, that while wheat bread alone *will not sustain man*, Indian corn will, for the flinty part contains oil, and the rest flour, which, together, sustains life.

This prejudice reminds us of the deep prejudice against potatoes. More than two hundred years elapsed from its introduction by Raleigh, before it was understood. Even within the last fifty years, the well known Englishman, Cobbet, published to the world that *potatoes were not fit for men*— that they should be left in the ground for the hogs to root them out with their snouts ! Now the most desirable article on any table, well named by the French " *Pomme de Tèrre*"—*Apple of the Earth*—and it is far superior in value to the *Gold apple* of the Romans ; their " *Aurantia*"—our *Orange.*

LAWTON BLACKBERRY.

A London publication speaks of the Lawton blackberry in high terms, and says that it is about to be introduced widely into England. It is spoken of as a distinct variety of this kind of fruit, heretofore unknown. The plants are sold in London at 2s. 6d. sterling—62 cents each, and seem likely to be as popular there as here.

Mr. Pardee.—Mr. Underhill, of Yonkers, says that this is the sweetest of all blackberries when ripe. The berries never should be pulled from the bush, but suffered to hang until ripe enough to fall by a little shake.

Solon Robinson.—These berries should rather be tickled from the bush, and then they will tickle the palate. There is no blackberry grown in the world that I ever saw equal to the Lawton or New Rochelle variety. They are very rich and sweet, as well as great bearers.

COBBET ON POTATOES.

William Lawton.—In regard to what the Secretary has said about Cobbet on potatoes, his strong and truthful assertion was that no nation could prosper where its people were confined to a single article of food.

Solon Robinson.—Cobbet also prophesied that the famine would come upon Ireland, as it did, whenever the potato crop happened to fail for a single year. I have several letters from persons who read the proceedings of these meetings, some of which I will read. The first is from a seeker after knowledge.

THE HORSE HOE.

A. J. Hope, of Sharon Springs, had read so much about the "horse hoe," that he has been at last awakened sufficiently to inquire "whether it will hoe corn? and is it capable of hoeing corn as effectually as a man with a hoe?" He is evidently astonished at what is said here about its capability to do the work of twenty men, and "wants to know what is the price of this new labor-saving tool in the improved art of farming, and where is it to be had?"

For his benefit, and the benefit of ten thousand other benighted American farmers, I will answer these inquiries briefly. The implement was contrived a few years ago by Mr. Knox, pattern maker for Nourse, Mason & Co., the great implement manufacturers at Worcester, Mass., (the greatest in this country—perhaps in the world), and is known as "Knox's horse hoe." Our correspondent may rest assured that it will hoe corn and every other crop, all that is needed, except picking the weeds from among the plants, and it will do (if not the work of twenty men), as good work as the hand hoe, just as fast as a horse can walk. And this invaluable implement, indispensable to a y man who plants an acre, costs only $7.

Considerable discussion sprung up on this horse hoe question, but all who have ever seen the implement at work, concurred in the above statement of its value.

GROUND NUTS.

Solon Robinson.—Here is a letter of inquiry about a plant that I never saw cultivated, but hope it can be, for I remember it well as one of the pleasant reminiscences of boyhood life in Connecticut, where I was taught to dig and roast and eat the "Indian ground nuts," by an old squaw. The letter I hold in my hand is from Jackson, Michigan, which, after speaking of the satisfaction which the reports of these meetings give the writer, inbuires "if any one can tell him whether the ground nut that grows about old neglected fields, along decayed logs or old decaying fences, or on the borders of wood tracts, can be cultivated." It is commonly about the size of a nutmeg, but round, the outside black; when roasted, the inside is white and mealy, and resembles a boiled chestnut, but more savory. The plant shoots up a little vine, which quirls round a weed or hazel, or whatever it may get hold of, and reaches up, in its growth, a foot and a half or two feet; has a near resemblance to what is called cornbind.

Andrew S. Fuller.—This plant is the *Apios tuberosum*, and it can and should be cultivated. I have it growing in my garden, and it does well. I grew mine from the seed, and have tubers near an inch in diameter. I was attracted to it by reading of it in Eaton and Wright's old work on botany, which recommended it highly as a much neglected American plant.

Solon Robinson.—I recommend those who try its cultivation, to follow nature as near as may be, and use wood, mold leaves, and rotten wood for manure.

CURCULIO REMEDY.

Judge Meigs.—Here is an article that gives a recipe for keeping off curculio: One pound of whale oil soap, four ounces of sulphur, mixed in twelve gallons of water; a half peck of lime in four gallons of water; pour off the clear water after the lime is dissolved, and add it to the other water, adding four gallons of strong tobacco water. Apply the mixture with a syringe.

Henry Steele, Jersey City, said that he had prevented curculio by the use of black soap from the tallow chandlers, dissolved in water, and much diluted, with which the trees are syringed directly after the blossoms fall, after a rain, and repeated, if necessary, in consequence of being washed off.

R. G. Pardee.—A person present assures me that a neighbor of his yarded his hogs around his plum trees, and that saved them from the curculio. Mr. Pardee said that he thought that fresh cow or pig manure, dissolved, and the water sprinkled over plum trees, would prevent curculio. They dislike any strong smelling substances.

Wm. Lawton.—You may apply cow or pig manure raw to all fruits and berries, but not horse manure; that never should be used fresh—make it first into compost.

NEW BEE HIVE.

E. W. Phelps exhibited his plan of bee hive, the principal feature of which is, that the comb is fastened to slats in the hive, so as to take out any one frame and sheet of comb without disturbing any other part of the comb. Old comb can also be taken out of any part of the hive. The cost of a hive is about $3.50. One hive in a room in this city made 60 pounds of fine honey one season. This hive differs from other slat hives in this, that the frames are in sections so as to divide a sheet of comb into small squares. He also exhibited a very ingenious protection against bee-moths.

EGG EXAMINERS.

Mr. Clough exhibited a little contrivance, called the eoniscope, to detect bad eggs. The egg is placed in a hole of a box, and the light reflects on a mirror inside, and tells unerringly the true condition of the egg. A little practice enables any one to discover whether eggs are fresh or not.

A NEW FLY CATCHER.

Mr. Clough, who appears to be a genuine Yankee, exhibited a new contrivance for catching flies. A wheel is wound up and runs by clock-work, and cages all the flies that light upon a molasses-covered surface. The caged are used to feed hens with, being valued as high as corn by the bushel.

THE JENNY LIND OR WOOD'S POTATO.

Solon Robinson.—Here is an interesting letter from John C. Polley, dated Dewitt, Clinton county, Iowa, April 2, 1859, giving the origin of the Wood's potato. The writer says :

"In reading the report of the American Institute Farmers' Club, of March 21, I noticed in a letter of S. W. Brown of Brimfield, Hampden county, Mass., that the potato known in market as the 'Jenny Lind' is Wood's seedling. I have often seen the Jenny Lind potato advertised, but did not know it was only another name for the Wood potato. Perhaps your Club will take an interest in the history of that potato, and as I am intimately acquainted with it, I will give it in brief. Isaac N. Wood, a farmer, living in Holland, Hampden county, Mass., in the fall of 1845 or '46, gathered a few potato balls from the vines of the Peachblow potato, and the following spring planted some of the seeds. They grew feebly the first year, the tops bearing very little resemblance to those of potatoes. In the fall he harvested about two quarts, varying in size from that of a grape to a crow's egg. There were three distinct varieties in this first crop. The following spring he planted them in a sandy soil, and raised from one kind about ninety pounds, most of them of large size. The two other varieties yielded very little, and were not preserved; the former were carefully stored for seed. Their appearance the second year, from the original seed, was the same as it is to-day; and it seemed as mature then as it was after years of cultivation. It had the same rough appearance then that it has now; the eyes were numerous and deep set. The next year, he cut these ninety pounds of seed in such a way as to leave but one eye on a piece, and put three pieces in a hill. The hills were 1½ feet apart one way, and 3½ the other. Seeding in this way, he had enough to plant one-fourth of an acre. The ground was dry and sandy, and highly manured. I saw them several times during the season, and have never seen a greater growth of tops than on that piece. It was impossible to tell, by the tops, which way the rows went, even while they were standing up, and before they were thrown down by the wind and their own weight. He harvested from that piece 130 bushels of potatoes; some of them were remarkably large, weighing from two to three pounds. He used of this crop only enough to test thoroughly their quality. The next spring he sold them in small quantities to his neighbors for seed, at an extra price. My father procured some of the seed, and raised them for many years, and always considered them a valuable kind to raise, especially for feeding stock. They were not so good for table use as many other kinds; but they grow better toward spring, and perhaps at that season of the year they are on an equality with our best varieties. They will go further in seeding than any other kind I now remember, and yield much better than the average. I think them a valuable addition to the already numerous varieties."

Mr. Robinson continued.—This is very interesting and valuable information—this tracing varieties back to their origin, and proving that things sold for new are only some old ones with new names.

RENOVATING OLD ORCHARDS.

I will now read you a very valuable letter from a woman, upon the treatment of old orchards, plum trees, rosebushes and flowers. It is from Ruth H. Lynde, of New Bedford, Mass., who has written us a very sensible letter upon renovating old orchards, and other things. Here is what she says about what she did with the old apple trees:

"Some years ago I lived on a small farm in New York State, and one of the inducements held out for hiring it was, that there was a fine apple orchard of choice grafted fruit. This decided—but the trees were in a miserably sickly condition, and the fruit scanty and mean, knotty and wormy. In the fall, a circle was dug around every apple tree, nearly two feet from the crown and over a foot and a half in depth. Dressing from the hog-pen was put into each hole, until within half a foot of the top, and anthracite coal ashes spread over up to the crown. In the spring the trees were pruned, the orchard plowed, oats sown, and the crop of oats was fair; the trees bloomed more, but fruit was scarce and still poor. That fall, after the leaves had fallen, the trees were scraped—the trunks, branches and boughs—and the grubs scraped off that were in the loose bark, sufficed to feed for two days a hundred fowls, consisting of turkeys, hens and Guinea fowls. The fowls, generally, were in an inclosed place, and corn kept in a trough for their daily use; as the corn was untouched, and the fowls healthy, my statement can be relied on. Next spring the orchard was a a mass of blossoms, and so beautiful I never wearied looking at it. The trees were so laden with fruit that two of them split in the fork, and a person could not walk upright under them. I never saw such quantities of fruit, and fine fruit, too—Bell Flowers, Fall Pippins, Seek-no-Furthers, Summer Pie Apples, and so forth. This was fourteen or fifteen years ago.

"*Plum Trees—How to treat the Black Knot.*—On this place were plum trees in as diseased a condition as the apple trees. The worse ones were cut down and burned, the curculio knots all cut off and burned. In the fall, salt from the pickled meat barrels was put around the trunks, not quite close to the crown, and in the spring the trunks and branches were carefully scraped, and soft-soap melted and applied all over with a brush. It was gratifying to see the good effect of this upon the bark of the trees. The windfalls I always burned up, as I ever had more faith in the destroying power of fire than any thing else—a curculio germ seems to live through everything but fire. These trees afterward bore fine fruit, and abundantly.

"*The Rose-slug Destroyer—How Destroyed.*—With regard to the insects that infest rosebushes, the most troublesome with us have been the slugs, which cause the bushes to look as if they had been burned. In trying to destroy the grub or the cock-chafer, I stumbled into a plan that proved quite effectual in destroying the black glossy fly, which is the progenitor of the slugs. This is the remedy: Scatter air-slaked lime upon the ground, as far as the branches of the bush extends, and apply it twice a year, at the two periods of growth when the leaves first open, and when the second growth commences. There are two crops of flies at these periods. Let this remain upon the ground some days, and then dig it under. When these insects first come out of the ground they are very sluggish, and can be killed with the thumb and finger. I have never seen them attack anything but rosebushes. For three years I have pursued this plan, and while my friends' bushes are all shabby and sickly-looking, mine are fresh and green. One need not neglect cooking or housework to have a garden. The garden is the play, and when work-weary, it refreshes one to be in it.

"*Flowering Plants.*—The Dielytra Spectabilis is quite common in Massachusetts, is very handsome and hardy, and, as one jocosely remarked, 'it is the better for a little frost.' Yuccas are in almost every garden.

"There is more pleasure in cultivating herbaceous plants; they require less care than annuals, and always are sure to flower. The various kinds of *penstemon fraxinella* (dictamnus), double red and white lychnis, hardy veronicas, buglars, rather a coarse-growing plant, but when in flower, beautiful—color clear, heavenly blue, and it is like looking into the sky to look at it when in bloom; double white and purple sweet rocket (*Hesperis matronalia*), perfume delicious as a violet; upright clematis; helleborus Nigre, or Christmas rose, very choice, low habit of growth, leaves evergreen, bears our winters, and blooms under the snow and ice—not a great bloomer, but is desirable in a collection.

"Of vernal flowers, *cardamine pratensis*, or cuckoo flower; *cynoglossum* (hound's tongue), lungworth (*pulmonaria*), *anemone hepatica* and *anemone aconiti folium*, are also fine flowers. But the finest of all garden flowers, perfectly hard, and but little known, is the *dodecatheon media*, or American cowslip—the flowers vary in color, from pure white to dark lilac, and have reflexed petals like the cyclamen. The flower stalk is long, and from the top project these beautiful flowers, the whole like an elegantly formed chandelier. Seeds of this plant are not to be relied on, but they propagate rapidly, and in the fall three plants can be taken from one root."

Andrew S. Fuller.—The plant spoken of last, the *dodecatheon media*, as the American cowslip, is not the one that grows in wet places all over New England, bearing a yellow flower and known as cowslip, but an upland plant, which is very common at the West, and is worthy all the praise given to it by the writer.

LIME FOR FRUIT TREES.

Solon Robinson.—Here is another inquirer after knowledge. F. Hotchkin, of Sullivan county, N. Y., wants to know if "lime in a liquid state is injurious to fruit trees?" He does not say how he wants to apply it, nor what he means by liquid lime, but he may be assured that lime will not injure fruit trees in any way that he pleases to apply it, on the ground, at the roots, or in powder on the tops, or in a liquid state on the trunks.

FRUIT TREES—TO PROTECT FROM ANTS.

Wm. Davis, Marengo, Morrow Co., O., offer the following plan for protecting fruit trees from ants, which, he says, have killed many trees for him. It is the same plan pursued in this city to make loafers, and then get rid of them——that is, feed them with whisky, and make them drunk, and then wipe them out. He says: "Mix whisky, molasses and water, in equal parts, and fill a tumbler about two-thirds full, and set it partly in the ground at the foot of the tree infested by ants. When it gets full of the drunkards, scoop them out and kill them." We suggest feeding them to fowls.

KEEPING WHEAT FLOUR.

A. Mr. Ross stated that he manufactures wheat flour that will keep sweet ten years——that he has flour now ten years old as sweet as when it was first ground. He has taken numerous medals and prizes for his flour, as the finest, handsomest exhibited. He grinds upon a convex and concave pair of stones of only a foot diameter, and has so little wheat in the mill at once that it does not heat, which is what injures flour ground in the ordinary way. The flour of his mill comes so cold from the mill that it is ready to pack immediately without cooling.

A committee was appointed to visit his mill, at No. 211 Centre street, and examine the process by which he alleges he makes flour that is so much better than that ground in ordinary mills, and report the facts to a future meeting of the Club.

The next meeting will be held next Monday noon, at the Union (Cooper building), and one of the questions to be discussed is, the relative value of various fertilizers.

Adjourned.

HENRY MEIGS, *Secretary.*

April 25th, 1859.

Present.—Messrs. Senator Crolius, Renwick, our President, Dr. Holton, Mrs. Holton, Solon Robinson, Witt, Bruce, Mr. Leonard, Wm. Lawton,

Chilson, Rev. Dr. Gardiner, Mr. Pardee, Van Houten, of Paterson, Jersey, Moffat, Atwater, of Springfield, Wright, Jr.—8 more ladies—45 members in all.

William Lawton, of New Rochelle, in the chair; Henry Meigs, Secretary.

The Secretary read the following very interesting paper from Professor James J. Mapes, being proof of the important truth so long taught by the Professor, who is the entirely original discoverer of it—the high value in agricultural science of the "*progression of primaries*," viz:

MINERAL PHOSPHATES AS COMPARED WITH THE PHOSPHATES OF BONE, BLOOD, ETC.

Until within a few months we have stood alone in advocating "*the progression of primaries in organic life*," and now we are only sustained by others in the extent, that the French Academy of Science after a series of experiment has declared, what we have so often asserted, that phosphates from the rocks, or those of volcanic origin, have no value as fertilizers. Since the increase in the consumption of phosphate of lime, thousands of tons of phosphates of the kinds we have named, have been introduced into the United States, and have been manufactured into supposed superphosphates of lime, manipulated guanos, etc., and strange to say, these mixtures have received the endorsement of many chemists. Suppose, as an instance, that that we should grind together the phosphatic rock, of Estremadura, or that of Dover, New Jersey, or of Crown Point, Lake Champlain, or the volcanic phosphates covering some of the small islands of the Carribbean Sea, and elswhere, and brought here under the name of *guano*, phosphatic guano, etc., and mix this powder with eight or ten per cent of sulphate of ammonia, or treat the ground phosphatic rock or phosphatic guano (so called) with sulphuric acid, and then send such mixtures to the inspectors at Baltimore for analysis, what would be their report as to its value? Why, they would pronounce it to contain 80 per cent of soluble and insoluble phosphate of lime, and a large percentage of ammonia. They could not do otherwise under the present erroneous doctrines, than to suppose it to be more valuable than any other mixture containing less phosphate and ammonia. Send at the same time another specimen, composed of 100 lbs. of calcined bones, treated with 56 lbs. of sulphuric acid and mixed with 36 lbs. of Peruvian guano and 20 lbs. of sulphate of ammonia, to which is added 212 lbs. of dried blood, what will they say of this latter mixture? Why, on the present doctrine, that "fertilizers owe their value to their phosphate of lime and ammonia," without taking into account the *source* of either, they cannot but pronounce the first worth $70 per ton, and the latter less than half that sum, and still in fact 100 lbs. of the latter will produce more plant-growth than will any known quantity of the former.

Phosphates have no value for agricultural purposes, unless taken from *organic life*, like the blood and bones of animals. The phosphates from the phosphatic rocks and volcanic deposits, *miscalled guanos*, although ground and treated with sulphuric acid, *have no value as fertilizers*, and cannot be absorbed into the higher class of plants, such as are now required for the use of men and animals. They must first be taken up by lichens and mosses, and be progressed by them in a way which chemistry as yet has failed to discover, and on their decay and re-deposit of their phosphates in the soil, be absorbed by a higher class of plants for further progression, and so on through nature's laboratory, until we find the progressed phosphates occupying the bones of animals.

Man might as well try to exist on dissolved rocks instead of the same constituents composing plants in a progressed state, as to attempt to feed plants or primitive phosphates, no matter how manipulated by grinding and acids. We know this experimentally and practically, and this new discovery of the French Academy only serves to endorse our oft-told views to the extent of their investigations.

ON THE DIFFERENT KINDS OF PHOSPHATES OF LIME.

Translated from the French by H. Meigs.

The Academy has charged M. Boussingault and me with the examination of a note of M. Moride, containing observations, and the results of many experiments, on the phosphates of lime employed as manure, and particularly on those of the compositions called *minerals*, massses of which, more or less considerable, are found burried in the soil.

It is not the first time that this important question has called for the investigation of science: a great work, now in a course of publication, of our illustrious permanent secretary, M. Elie de Beaumont, is at this moment drawing the attention of the public to the same subject.

There would indeed be an immense benefit to agriculture in obtaining phosphates of lime, assimilable by plants, to the same extent as phosphate of ground bones acidified, imperfectly carbonized, or mixed with organic azotous substances, such as are present in the refuse of sugar refineries.

Under these conditions phosphate of lime, by virtue of its interposition in the midst of organic tissue, presents itself in a state of extreme division easily assailable by acids.

In England its divisibility, as well as it is dissolubility, are still further increased by treating the bones with sulphuric acid, which forms sulphate and bisulphate of lime, attacking even the organic tissue, so that the ossous fragments become soft and friable.

In presence of the carbonate limestone of the soil, or of that which is added to the bones thus disintegrated, the excess of acid is found saturated, the organic azotous matter becomes spontaneously changeable, and the ammoniacal products of its decomposition coöperate of themselves to the nutrition of plants.

Effects analogous to these take place when we employ carbonized bones in powder, mixed with the blood used in effecting the clarification of sugar or sirups; there are added to them reactions equally favorable, dependent on the porosity of that animal charcoal, capable of condensing the ambient gas, and of yielding them gradually afterwards to the absorbent organs of the vegetables.

It is not known to be entirely the same with mineral phosphates; endowed with a very strong cohesion, the mechanical means by which, even to this day, we are only able to treat them, are insufficient to reduce them to a state of division comparable to that of phosphate of bones.

Besides, the importations of mineral phosphates from Estremadura into Great Britain, have not produced amongst the agriculturist all the favorable results where expected from them. One of us, M. Dumas, had the opportunity, in 1850, of stating this fact, during a mission with which he was charged by the Minister of Agriculture and Commerce, relative to the agricultural improvements introduced into England, Scotland, and Ireland:* it does not appear that they have since succeeded in obtaining in Great Britain as good effects from the mineral phosphates as from bones, or the black residues of the refineries.

All the above clearly admits, is the inferiority of the *mineral* phosphates, while their after experiments more clearly show their entire worthlessness.

The worthy Secretary is in error, when he supposes that the difference between mineral phosphate and bone phosphate is due to the *mechanical condition* or *porosity* of the two: for if he had dissolved portions of each in dilute muriatic acid, so that each would have been in solution, and then applied them respectively to the soil, he would have found that the dissolved phosphate from bones would fertilize plants and be readily assimilated by them, while the dissolved mineral phosphate would have produced no effect at all. We know that unless these mineral phosphate be first made into crystallizable salts, and be then redissolved and crystalized a great number of times, they cannot be made to answer any useful purpose in agriculture for the use of the generation living at the time of their pplication. This is just as true as that finely ground feldspar, although may contain 17 per cent, of potash, still it will not fertilize those plants requiring potash. One pound of potash taken from the ashes of plants, is worth more as a fertilizer, than tons of ground feldspar: and this is equally true of every primary in nature. An analysis as now made, of either soils or fertilizers, is an analysis of its powers for *all time*, and not of its available constituents for one, five, or ten years.

The translation to which we have referred then goes on to say:

On his part, M. Moride, who, with M Bohierre, has rendered indisputable services to agriculture, by analyzing the manures deposited in the government dock-yards, and exposing certain frauds in commercial manures, has proved, by direct experiment, the insolubility of many mineral phosphates in the weak acids, in the state in which they are now offered to ag-

* See the Reports on Drainage, the Retting of Flax, the Peat Mosses, the Bakeries, and the Commercial Manures, published by the Minister, and the Memoirs of the Central Society of Agriculture in 1850.

riculturists; * and he has thought it his duty to caution these last, by pointing out to them the means of detecting the mineral phosphates mixed, whether it be with organic matters or with the phosphate of bones, or with the bone black of the refineries. For this purpose he recommends particularly the employment of acetic acid in a boiling state, which attacks and dissolves these last, whilst it leaves the others intact, and the incineration of which yields, with the phosphate of bones or the black of the refineries, white ashes; whilst the mineral phosphates produce red or brown ashes.

We shall render to agriculture a still greater service if we discover the means of economically dividing the mineral phosphates to the state in which they readily become assimilable by plants.

M. Morin thinks that we shall attain it by dissolving these natural phosphates by powerful mineral acids, in order to separate them from the sand; then by precipitating the solution with ammoniacal and magnesian liquids, afterwards adding to it animal or fermentable matters.

This process, probably efficacious, would undoubtedly be too expensive; at least it could not be executed in localities where they have not the opportunity of applying to it the dissipated vapors of chlorhydrate acid, and add to it afterwards either magnesian sea-water or ammoniacal water condensed in the refrigerators of oil gas or hydrate of lime; and everything leads us to hope that we may succeed in reuniting economic conditions of this kind which admit of utilizing the natural phosphates.

Whatever may happen, M. Moride will have effected a useful object at this moment, on which we perhaps found, upon the incomplete preparation of mineral phosphates, great expectations, by calling the attention of agriculturists to facts which were little known to them.

We have, in consequence, the honor of proposing to you to address to this young scholar the thanks of the Academy, recommending him to follow up his useful investigation.†

PAYEN,
Member of the Academy of Sciences, and Permanent Secretary of the Central Society of Ag.

* In order to demonstrate the solubility of certain pulverized phosphates, M. Moride has taken of each of them 0.05 gr., and treated them with 10 cubic centimetres of acetic acid during ten minutes at 65 degrees. The filtered liquid was precipitated by ammoniac, and the phosphoric acid sought for in the calcined precipitates, by adding some drops of azotic acid, and taking up again by distilled water, in which they add azotate of silver. The following are the results obtained thus:

Specimens.	Phosphate of lime.	Phosphate dissolved by acetic acid.
Phosphate (pure or calcined) powder (bones),	89.20	0.254
Bone dust, calcined white,	92.00	0.285
Bone charcoal fit for refining,	75.10	0.300
Black residue of refinery,	63.40	0.340
Apatite of logrosan (Estramadura),	94.25	0.000
Nodules from the Ardennes,	66.00	0.000
Do. in black dust of commerce,	70.00	0.000
Do. of the Ardennes calcined,	62.00	0.000

The apatite had left dissolved by the acid 26 millièmes of oxyde of iron. The three following specimens had yielded 34, 26, and 28 millièmes of oxyde of iron and alumina.

M. Moride has further stated that the phosphates of bones are soluble in seltzwater, sucrate of lime, and in peat animalized by means of fermentation; whilst the natural phosphates which he has examined are insoluble in them.

† The recommendations of this report are adopted.

This testing by acetic acid may be very well, and we sincerely hope that chemists in Baltimore and elsewhere will try it, and if found correct, will adopt it, and cease recommending the mixtures made of valueless, miscalled phosphatic guanos, mineral phosphates, etc., merely because they contain a quantity of *unprogressed* mineral phosphates. Many phosphates are now in the market, which are not the residuum of the excretiæ of birds. Those phosphates derived from birds are of organic origin, and have value, but we have tried all the kinds thus far imported, and have found the Peruvian and one single importation of Carribbean imbued with rotten coral or progressed carbonate of lime, to be the only useful guanos, and even these are much less so per pound than true nitrogenized superphosphate of lime, made of burned bones, sulphuric acid, Peruvian guano, sulphate of ammonia, and dried blood, one hundred pounds of which will equal in value, when both its power and lasting effects are taken into account, one hundred and eighty-five pounds of even the best Peruvian guano.

To the President and Members of the Farmers' Club, American Institute, New-York.

Gentlemen : I beg your acceptance of a sample of the Decaisne potatoes, below described. Of their edible qualities, the accompanying sample will enable you to judge. Allow me to assure you, Gentlemen of the Farmers' Club, that they exceed in prolificness all other kinds known to me, and I have found them less subject to decay than any others.

> I am, gentlemen, very respectfully yours,
>   PLINY M. FORWARD.

Southwick, *Hampden Co., Mass.*

DECAISNE POTATOES.

The subscriber offers to Gentlemen of the Farmers' Club, samples of a very remarkable potato, recently introduced from Europe. Combining as it does, in a high degree, superior edible qualities, with remarkable prolificness, this potato needs only to be known to secure it a widespread popularity.

The means by which the subscriber came into possession of this potato were as follows :—In the spring of 1856, Dr. D. P. Holton, of New York city, then residing in Paris, and attending lectures at the various colleges, of that city, heard Prof. Decaisne (Professor of Horticulture at the Garden of Plants) give a lecture upon this potato, and in such high terms did he speak of its merits, so flatteringly of its wonderful qualities, that he was induced to solicit of the Professor (who politely granted the favor) a couple of them for a transatlantic friend, to serve as an introduction of them into this country.

From these two potatoes, of medium size, the subscriber raised about three-fourths of a bushel of potatoes, of large size and of excellent quality, notwithstanding a considerable loss had been occasioned by the depredations of mice. The last year, he raised from scarcely more than a half bushel of the same, and under somewhat unfavorable circumstances, between 24 and 25 bushels, large measure.

WHEAT FROM THE BATTLE FIELD OF WATERLOO.

Mr. President: While the nations of Europe are meditating human slaughter, the genius of America is developing the arts of peace. Visiting Belgium a year ago last July, I made the two hours' coach route S. W. from Brussels to the battle field of Waterloo, and ascended the central earth-mound elevated by the victors, one hundred and fifty feet, and crowned by the bronze colossal lion, turned France-ward in a threatening posture.

With the maps and drawings, and the vivid descriptions of our guide, who had himself been a participator in the events of 18th June, 1815, we surveyed the fields of carnage and blood.

The present occupants of the land enriched by human flesh and bone, urged their sale of balls, bayonets, bullets, and various fragments of guns and other reliques of the implements of war, and of bones, which continue to be found at every turning of the soil.

I preferred rather to bring samples of the products of the arts of peace— the bountiful fruits of earth, graciously given by Him who causeth seed time and harvest while the earth remaineth ; who maketh his sun to rise on the evil and on the good, and sendeth rain on the just and on the unjust. Accept, Mr. President, this wheat from Waterloo.

Mr. Meigs was happy to announce that Poland has just founded her *first agricultural society.*

Mr. Lawton adverted to the value of marl.

Dr. Holton had listened, at Berlin, with the greatest pleasure and instruction, to the admirable lectures of the justly celebrated Elwenberg, to large classes, having movable microscopes enough to enable every scholar to view the subjects of the learned Professor's discourse. The Doctor had visited the battle ground of Waterloo, and the mound there, raised in commemoration of that great fight which has fertilized the ground *for wheat*, of which he gave samples to the Club.

Solon Robinson called the attention of members to the great importance of the American Institute's next cattle show, which, instead of being, as heretofore, too limited and merely secondary at its annual fair, ought to be a distinct exhibition at which all the neighboring States will assist, by reason of the great accessibility of New York, and the great advantages of our great metropolis, for the reception and entertainment of visitors from everywhere.

President Renwick saw that matter in the same light, and had no doubt the Institute would so order it as to render the next cattle show eminent for its greatness.

Mr. Atwater, of Springfield.—The United States Agricultural Society hold their cattle show this year in the West. The American Institute has a clear field in all the East, for such a cattle show as never was held here before. Springfield will do her best to supply the show of horses with best and largest contributions. All New England will join in the effort to create a memorable Eastern Show of Live Stock, which fears no competition with the world.

President Renwick.—The Waterloo wheat, laid on the table, probably owes its goodly growth to the human manure to which Flanders is indebted for filling her granaries.

Solon Robinson read an inquiry from one of his correspondents, on the notions of the moon affecting planting parks, &c.

Mr. Meigs.—The influences attributed to the moon are idle, and have vanished before science. Vilmorin, in his last Almanac, declares to France that there is no meteorological knowledge useful generally, but that each district has its own. While fog buries London, Paris is all bright. Mr. Meigs had recorded meteorological observations from 1795 to this day, first as assistant to his father, professor of mathematics and natural philosophy in Yale college, who was also secretary of the Philoshphical Society. On reading Strabo's Geography nearly forty years ago, I remarked his distinct account of the fog of London above 1800 years ago, as being identical with the fog of to-day. Herschell gave rules of observation by phases of the moon, which are unavailing. Weather predictions are vain. The old English alma- nac maker's printer's devil, for sport, printed *snow in June*, on a certain day, and it happened! So that the credit of the old almanac became firmly established.

President Renwick.—The weather conforms, in a measure, to the phases of the moon, so far as storms are concerned—the great rotary storms reaching the coasts of Ireland, Norway, &c.

Mr. Pardee.—Millions of money are lost by the absurd regard to old superstitious weather wisdom.

Solon Robinson.—One correspondent wants to know whether woolen rags are useful as manure.

Mr. Meigs.—I always valued them, and put them about the roots of valued vines or plants.

President Renwick.—Red rags are selected to obtain lake color.

Solon Robinson.—Country farmers hoot at a barometer, and often lose their hay for want of one.

Mr. Van Houten, of Paterson.—I am a farmer. Let the great papers tell farmers about the barometer; it will do good. I have a neighbor farmer who always cuts his grass by the moon, and of course is sometimes caught. Science is of no use without practice. The Institute should sup- ply the useful knowledge.

The Chairman called up the regular subject—Lime.

Mr. Meigs remarked on the error to which we are sometimes putting on lime where there is already enough or too much. That mistake was made by our late distinguished President Talmage, who put lime on some of his land which already held enough, and so spoiled its fertility for some years.

Mr. Atwater stated his experience in lime as manure. Sandy land wants it. I add three bushels of slaked lime and one bushel of salt to a cord of common manure, with good effect. Twenty bushels of lime on an acre of rather heavy land is good.

Mr. Moody, of New Jersey.—I have been benefited by sixty bushels of lime per acre, on my *clay loam* land. Lime and bone dust eradicate the sorrel and moss on sour lands. I put lime on new land, make grass, then two bushels of gypsum broadcast in moist weather. On 18 acres I have kept 22 cattle and a horse. I grow the Lawton blackberry. Although I am only a shoemaker, you see I have some of the glorious blessings of the farm about me. It is true that I practice law, too.

Mr. Robinson.—Thirty bushels of slaked lime every year for four years, on an acre of suitable land, will make it fertile for fourteen years afterwards.

Mr. Atwater.—Sixty bushels of slaked lime fertilizes more than one hundred and twenty bushels of unslaked. We use shell. *I bury lime in clay pits for winter ;* it improves it for next year's use.

President Renwick stated that he had visited the Club simply for the purpose of showing his respect for it, and manifesting the interest he took in its proceedings. He had hoped to have heard a discussion from the proposer of the question. As that gentleman was not present, and as the subject before the Club was one to which he had in former days given some attention, he would draw upon his memory for the points, which, at the request of the late James Wadsworth, of Geneseo, he had laid down in an edition published by that patron of agriculture, of Ruffin's Treatise on the use of lime as a manure. It will be recollected that this publication was made many years ago, and before the day of Liebig and Johnson. What he stated, therefore, of the condition of chemical science, was to be considered as applicable at the time these authors began to write.

He then went on to say that the reasons usually assigned for the use of lime in agriculture, were three in number :

1. To render argillaceous soils friable, thus rendering their tillage more easy, allowing the surface water in wet weather to sink through them, and preventing them from baking into stiff clods in seasons of drought.

2. To render sandy soils more retentive of moisture ; and,

3. To act upon inert organic matter, promoting its decomposition, and fitting it to become the food of plants.

The results of the action of lime upon the growth of plants, and of some species in particular, are so wonderful that the three reasons thus stated will not account for them. Those others are, however, very obvious, although not usually stated in treatises on chemistry, These, continuing the order of numbers, are :

4. Lime is an essential constituent of a number of vegetable products, if it be not of many vegetable principles. Chemists have usually limited the elements of the vegetable kingdom to oxygen, hydrogen and carbon, as universal, and nitrogen as occasional. The ashes of plants, with the exception of their soluble portions, were long neglected, and only figured among the results as *earthy matter.* Now so far from being unworthy of notice, it was in this earthy material that the distinctive character of the vegetable, in its applications, lay. Thus the ashes of wheat contain the sulphate, phosphate and carbonate of lime. The two former, in particular, constitute its value as the food of man, and warrant its epithet of " the

staff of life." Not to mention many others, the peach contains compounds of lime, as does the locust tree. Now neither of these three plants will flourish in a soil that contains no lime. The first will run to straw, and have empty ears; the second will be unhealthy; the third will be liable to the attack of insects, and will not acquire any useful dimensions.

5. The next reason for the use of lime is to be found in its power to neutralize acids. Practical men long spoke of sour soils before scientific men were willing to admit of their existence. These soils are marked by the growth of useless or noxious plants, the most characteristic of which is sheep sorrel. The presence of this plant manifests the existence of oxalic acid in the soil, and for this acid lime in any or every state of combination, is a remedy. Under the same head may be classed the use of lime in soils which contain sulphate of iron. This is the case with many of the fields overlying gneiss and mica slate rocks in Westchester county, and on our own island. This salt of iron is decomposed by lime and its carbonate, forming the valuable compound sulphate of lime.

6. The carbonate of lime, in a state of fine powder, has a strong mechanical attraction for the gases which are yielded by decomposing vegetable and animal substances. When soils contain this earthy constituent, these gases remain, to be taken up as they are needed by plants; but where the soil is sandy, and no carbonate of lime is present, these gases are rapidly dissipated in the air. It may thus happen that the manure spread by one farmer upon his sand, shall enrich the field of his neighbor who has charged his soil with carbonate of lime, and maintains it in fine tilth. The value of fallowing is due to the absorption of gases by the soil, and will be much greater in soils containing carbonate of lime, than in those which do not.

He proceeded in the second place to consider the manner of applying lime in agriculture. As an introduction to this branch of the subject, he thought it expedient to state to his hearers not versed in science, a few chemical facts. Lime is an earth, which, when free from combination, is alkaline and highly caustic. It has necessarily a very high affinity for acids, with which it combines to form compounds, which are styled *neutral*, because they manifest the characters of *neither* of their compounds. He thought it proper to refer to this familiar fact, because one of the gentlemen who preceded him, had, in speaking of plaster, referred to the presence of sulphuric acid in it, in a way which might have left the impression that acid properties were still manifest in that compound.

The compounds of lime, connected with our subject, are, the carbonate, the sulphate, and the phosphate. The two first occur in nature in combination with water, which forms a notable portion of their solid mass. Both part with this water when heated, but the sulphate of lime is not decomposed, while the carbonic acid is driven off from the carbonate by heat. The sulphate of lime, after being deprived of its water and permitted to cool, attracts that substance with great avidity, insomuch that if it be raised with water to the consistence of a thick cream, the mixture speedily becomes solid. Hence the use of sulphate of lime in the mechanic and fine arts, and its familiar name of plaster.

The principal sources of lime in agriculture are limestones, chalk, calcareous marls, and the shells of crustaceous animals. In all of these, the lime exists in combination with carbonic acid and water, being mild, almost inert, and hardly soluable in water. To render these forms fit for use in agriculture, it is necessary that they be reduced to fine powder. In the softer chalks and marls, this is effected readily by mere exposure to frost. Limestones might be pulverized by mechanical means, but as a general rule they can be more readily and cheaply reduced to powder by burning to quick-lime, and slaking by the effusion of water. The powder thus obtained attracts carbonic acid from the atmosphere, and finally becomes as mild as the limestone whence it was prepared. This method, however, ought not to be applied to shells. They contain an animal matter, highly valuable as a manure, which is destroyed by heat; they therefore ought to be crushed—and there are cases, as in planting trees, when the entire shells, buried deep in the earth, are to be preferred.

Except in the third of the cases for which lime had been said to be useful, namely, to hasten the decomposition of inert organic matter, lime ought to be rendered perfectly mild by the absorption of water and carbonic acid, before it is mixed with the soil. In conformity with this rule, it is usual to leave the slaked lime in heaps, until it is thoroughly deprived of its causticity by the absorption of carbonic acid from the atmosphere. Even for the correction of acidity, the mild form is to be preferred, unless the soil is also covered with moss and other vegetables difficult of eradication, in which case the caustic lime speedily destroys them.

The President next went on to remark that although lime, except in small quantities, did not enter into the material of plants, it was, notwithstanding, absolutely essential to the constitution of a soil fertile in the cereal gramina, and particularly in wheat. This was remarked first by Sir Humphrey Davy, who stated that he had examined no soil of acknowledged fertility, which did not show indications of the presence of carbonate of lime. These indications consist in effervescence with acids. But lime in some other form, as for instance the sulphate and oxalate, may be present, although no effervescence take place.

The President was inclined to refer the well known fact, that lands cultivated by farmers of German descent in Pennsylvania, were maintained in good heart by the application of lime, although the plow often turned up fragments of limestone, to the conversion of the carbonate into sulphate and iron, probably oxalate. How oxalic acid might be generated in the soil, would require him to enter into a discussion of probabilities, instead of facts, both too tedious and too vague for the present occasion.

He next proceeded to the third branch of his subject—the proper quantity of lime to be applied. In some countries, as in England, Scotland and Belgium, the application of lime served as the basis of all cultivation. It was, however, well understood that of itself it was of little value, and might be positively hurtful, were no putrescent manures largely and habitually used on the lands previously limed. The application of lime took place in those countries at long intervals, say of 21 years, and it was a proverb in respect to calcareous marls, that no farmer ever lived to see his field marled a second time. The quantity of slaked lime applied at such intervals, in Scotland, was, according to Sir John Sinclair, as much as 600 bushels per acre, to stiff clay, and 200 bushels per acre to sand. In other cases, however, it was well known that the application of far less quantities rendered soils barren for several years. Chemical investigation has shown that where such was the case, the limestone contained the cabonate of magnesia, as well as that of lime. Such a limestone does not fall to powder on the effusion of water, but although broken by it into lumps, may, if buried in the ground, remain caustic for months, destroying the organic matter which may come in contact with it. The magnesia also, does not appear to enter, except in exceedingly minute quantities, into the constitution of plants, and if absorbed, affects their vitality. Now, all the limestones in the region in Pennsylvania in which lime is so advantageously used, are magnesium, and experience has limited the application of the lime obtained from them to 20 or 30 bushels per acre.

Except in the case of reclaiming the lands which yield peat or turf, such as the *mosses* of Scotland and the *bogs* of Ireland, where 200 or 300 bushels of caustic lime per acre have been found beneficial, large quantities, even of a pure slaked lime, are unnecessary. In some portions of France, distant from quarries of limestone, and where fuel is scarce, necessity has taught the most economic use of lime. This consists in forming it into compost with sods and refuse vegetable matter. The heaps are frequently turned by the plow, and when the incorporation is complete, are carted out and spread upon the ground. In this way it is said that seven bushels per acre are ample, but the application must be repeated in advance of every wheat crop.

In continuation, he stated that the carbonate of lime, except in small quantities, did not enter into the constitution of any plants, and was not a proper food for many of them. It therefore was not a manure, in the farmer's sense of the word, except for the cereal gramina, to which it also yielded the base of the phosphate of lime, which seemed essential to the filling of the ears. The carbonate of lime, however, permitted larger quantities of putrescent manures to be applied to the soils which contain it, naturally or applied, and prolonged their effect by retaining the gases generated by their decomposition.

He, in conclusion, said that the subject would not be complete, did he not say something in reference to the use of sulphate of lime, *gypsum*, or as more familiarly known, *plaster*. He had already referred to the mode of preparing it for the use of the agriculturist by mechanical crushing, and not by heat. This statement set at naught the explanation of its action given by some, namely, that the plaster absorbed moisture from the air, and gave it out slowly to the plants. The true theory of the use of plaster is the same as that of the 4th reason assigned by him for the use of lime, namely, that it is an essential constituent of some plants. Thus it has been found in small proportion in wheat and in the potato, but in red clover it is the only constituent that is not destroyed by fire. No other earthy matter has ever been found in the ashes of red clover, and hence, as far as that plant is concerned, sulphate of lime cannot be replaced by any other substance. Red clover appears to derive none of its food from the constituents of the soil, except at the very act of ripening its seeds, and thus the application of plaster to a soil in which nothing else would grow, has, in well known instances, produced a luxuriant growth of red clover. The President had himself, when a director of the Mohawk and Hudson (now the eastern portion of the Central) railroad, advised that the slopes of the deep cuts, and the sides of the embankments, constructed of a flowing sand, be sown with a red clover seed and plaster, to prevent their destruction by the wind. The experiment was successful in the production of a luxuriant growth of the plant, but was more beneficial than could have been anticipated, for under the shelter of the red clover the white clover and the seeds of true grasses took root ; and these slopes are to the present day, after a lapse of more than thirty years, covered with a green sward, in which the red clover is seen, if it be seen at all.

It may be laid down as a rule that, in all but a few excepted positions, if even a straggling growth of summer grain can be obtained, the application of plaster will cause a tolerable growth of clover, and that this, if returned to the soil while in a succulent state, may furnish the material of a more plentiful harvest. But the clover must be returned to the soil, or employed in feeding cattle whose manure is made use of on the farm, otherwise the stimulus of plaster upon one particular growth may render the ground so barren that it cannot be restored except at great cost. The exceptions to the use of plaster are found in soils which already contain sulphate of lime, and in those in which free oxalic acid exists. The former can never be benefited by plaster ; the latter may be prepared for its beneficial use by the application of lime. The President then referred to the very interesting account which had been given, by a gentleman who preceded him, of his successful treatment of a sour and mossy soil, by slaked lime and plaster. This instance he characterized as a most successful application of a chemical principle under the direction of practical intelligence.

Another exception, he stated, was usually made to the beneficial use of plaster, namely, to the prevalence of sea air. He did not, however, think that the action of the air of the sea could possibly produce such an effect, and was inclined to ascribe it to the other causes already assigned. He had seen plaster used to advantage upon clover on ground almost surrounded by the tide ; and in villas around New York, plaster had improved grass plats. The instance to which he referred was on the Kingsbridge farm, once held by Robert Macomb. The substratum was white marble, and the soil abounded in carbonate of lime. On this farm large crops of clover were obtained by the use of plaster, while on the ridges to the east and west of the marble formation, the subsoil of which rested on gneiss and moca slate, no beneficial effect followed the application of gypsum. Chemical considerations, too long to be entered upon, show the great probability that the latter soils must have already contained sulphate of lime, and therefore could not be benefited by adding more. As to the quantity of sulphate of lime necessary to ensure a good crop of old clover, it need not exceed the weight of the ashes of the plant, and the practical gentleman who had limited it to eighty pounds per acre, seemed to have reached in practice a result corresponding to theory. Beyond such a quantity, plaster does no good ; if in large excess, it does positive injury.

Subjects for next meeting, Spring Fruits, Renovation of Orchards, &c.

Adjourned.   H. MEIGS, *Secretary*.

MECHANICS' CLUB.

Organized March 2, 1854—Name changed to Polytechnic Association, March 16, 1859.

RULES ESTABLISHED BY THE BOARD OF SCIENCE AND THE ARTS, MARCH 2, 1854.

First—A club for the promotion of manufactures, arts, and for the discussion of mechanical subjects, is created under the name of the Mechanics' Club.

Second—The Mechanics' Club is an agent of the committee of arts and sciences, and is under its entire control, in the same manner as the Farmers' Club is of the committee of agriculture. The transactions of the Club are in the name of the American Institute.

Third—The committee of arts and sciences appoint annually the Chairman and Secretary of the Mechanics' Club. In the absence of the Chairman and Secretary, persons to supply their places will be chosen at the meetings of the Club.

Fourth—Such papers read at the Mechanics' Club as are accepted for that purpose, will be printed under the direction and at the expense of the American Institute, which also provides a place of meeting, lights and fires. No other expenses are to be incurred, except by special appropriation of the American Institute, according to the rules and by-laws; nor any liability incurred by the Institute, except on special resolution.

Fifth—The meetings of the Mechanics' Club are free of all expense to those who attend them.

Sixth—The Mechanics' Club shall select, in advance, a subject for discussion at each of its meetings, which subject shall be announced in the call of meetings.

Seventh—Written communications to the Club are to be read by the Secretary, unless objection is made; and if objected to, will be read, if it be ordered by a majority of the members present.

Eighth—The Mechanics' Club will recommend what papers read before them, or what part of other transactions they judge worthy of publication, to the committee of arts and sciences, by which the publications may be ordered in its discretion.

Ninth—No person attending the meetings of the Club shall speak more than once on any one subject, nor shall occupy in such speech more than fifteen minutes, except by permission of the Club.

Tenth—No argument is allowed between members. Facts alone are to be stated.

Eleventh—All questions of order are decided without appeal, by the presiding officer.

Twelfth—The meetings of the Mechanics' Club are held at the Repository of the American Institute, No. 351 Broadway, in the city of New York, on the second and fourth Wednesday of each month, at 7½ o'clock P. M.

May 12, 1858.

Present—Messrs. T. B. Stillman, Stetson, Seeley, Fisher, Godwin, Pell, and others.

Thomas B. Stillman in the chair. T. D. Stetson, Secretary pro tem.

A member gave a long and full description of his Electric Engine, accompanied by a working model of the same style as that exhibited in the Crystal Palace, but with some improvements.

The regular question of the evening was opened by the chairman, who, on taking his seat however, called for a report from the committee on the Origin of Photographic Portraiture.

Mr. Stetson made a verbal report of the progress of this time, which was simply the preparing of several letters, and the reception of a reply from Prof. J. W. Draper, which he read, with a few comments.

Mr. Fisher knew Messrs. Wolcott & Johnson at that date, and thought Mr. Wolcott very familiar with light and with manipulations at that date, and as likely to succeed in a first experiment as any other man.

Mr. Stillman said of boiler setting, that great care should be taken not to allow the earth to absorb the heat from the fire. Had set a boiler with a very deep space or chamber for the products of combustion to revolve and circulate in.   It was very wasteful of fuel, but the waste was avoided by the introduction of a platform above the bottom and near the boiler.

Mr. Pell had observed the same kind of effect in ice houses.

Mr. Godwin had known great beneficial results in ice houses, from the introduction of non-conducting material at the base.

Mr. Stetson explained the Aldridge Hot Blast Furnace for steam boilers, illustrating on the blackboard by diagrams.

Mr. Fisher claimed for the Baker Furnace the credit of using the Hot Blast as long ago as 1854.

Mr. ——— proposed that Aldrid e's would be better if fed with fresh air warmed in a pipe in the chimney

Mr. Stillman gave some interesting facts concerning the utilizing of heat on North river steamboats.

Mr. Godwin advocated Cross Flue Boilers.   He illustrated on the blackboard the setting of domestic boilers.

The question for the next meeting was announced to be " The setting of steam boilers."

Adjourned.   **T. D. STETSON,** *Sec'y pro tem.*

May 26, 1858.

A meeting of the Mechanics' Club was held this Wednesday, May 26, 1858, at 8 o'clock P. M.

Present—Messrs. Leonard, Stetson, Johnson, Seeley, Amory, Hedrick, and others.

Mr. Wm. B. Leonard in the chair.   The Secretary, Mr. Meigs, being absent, on motion of Mr. Stetson, Mr. John W. Chambers was appointed Secretary pro tem.

The following extracts, by Mr. Meigs, in relation to the Traction Engine, were read :

[London Artisan, April, 1858.]

A new Traction Steam Engine, on Boydell's plan, has just been made at Lincoln (England), by Messrs. Clayton & Shuttleworth, who are about to send it to Odessa.   It has been tried, and its action was perfectly satisfactory.   It is constructed on Boydell's principle, but is different in several parts—as for instance, it moves on *three* instead of *five* wheels.   The weight of the boiler resting on two wheels of immense strength ; the third wheel being a steering or guiding one, placed in front, something after the fashion of a perambulator.   Behind this wheel is a box for the steersman, who, by a very simple apparatus, is enabled to turn the proderous vehicle in any direction, and with the utmost facility.   The average speed along good roads is stated at the rate of *three miles* per hour, though it can go *four miles* per hour.

A new patent Traction Engine for the farm, by William Bray, chief engineer of the steamer Lord Warden, South-Eastern Railroad Company.

For particulars I refer to the Artisan, but note its action.   With two hours' supply of fuel (coal) and water on board, it weighs about *five tons.*

It is almost as handy as a lady's perambulator in the streets and crooked lanes of our town. To-day it climbed Folkstone Hill, on the old Dover road, 1½ miles winding road, having a total ascent of 300 feet, and in some parts a gradient of 1 in 8. This it did to the satisfaction of all present, with two four-wheeled farm wagons loaded with stone, weighing in all about *ten tons*. The steam pressure used was from 40 lbs. to 60. lbs. per inch. It took the load up without any apparent difficulty in thirty-five minutes. The engine was then disconnected from the load, the pinion shifted into the first motion, and it run off about two miles at the rate of six miles per hour and back. The pinion was again shifted on to the slow motion, all the wagon wheels were shiddid, and but little steam used in descending. The parts of this machine are few and simple.

The question for consideration for this evening, viz : "The setting of steam boilers," was then called up.

Mr. Stetson, one of the committee to examine the Amory furnace, stated that the committee were not ready to report this evening—that Mr. Amory was present and could explain the nature of the improvement. I should like Mr. Amory to illustrate the plan upon the black board.

Mr. Amory then illustrated upon the black board the plan of setting their boilers. The principle is as follows : Under the boilers are erected several curved bridges, forming chambers, which give the flame and heat a reverbatory motion. The ash receiver in these boilers is closed, and hot air is supplied by a pipe under the heat reservoir ; by this method a great saving of fuel is effected, for after all, the question resolves itself into the fact of the amount of evaporation produced by one pound of coal. A thermometer had been placed in the chimney at the end of the boiler, and it was found that it ranged from 300 to 400 degrees—showing that a large portion of the heat had been expended under the boiler.

The boilers at the Bible House, in this city, are set on this plan, where they can be viewed. A window has been inserted in the masonry so that the effect of the mixture of the oxygen of the atmosphere with the various gases generated in the combustion of the fuel can be inspected.

The Chairman.—At what distance is the bottom of the receiver from the boilers ? and what portion of the circle of the boiler is exposed to the flame ?

Mr. Amory.—The bottom of the receiver is about three feet from the water, and about one-third of the circle of the boiler is exposed to the heat. By experiments made by Mr. Haswell, for the government, the space was not over eighteen inches. A saving of 15 per cent was reported by him. After deepening the reservoir to about three feet, a saving of 33½ was obtained.

Mr. Seeley thought the thermometer was not an accurate test at such a high heat. He suggested alloys of different metals, as a safer guide— these alloys might be made of substances that would melt at known heats.

Mr. Stetson alluded to his examination of the mode of setting the boilers used at the tunnel at Bergen Hill ; a hot blast was there used. In testing the degree of heat escaping from the chimney, he found the thermometer indicated about 500 degrees of heat.

Subject for the next meeting : "Warming and ventilating of buildings."

Adjourned.   JOHN W. CHAMBERS, *Sec'y pro tem.*

June 9, 1858.

A meeting of the Mechanics' Club, was held this, Wednesday, June 9, 1858, at 8 o'clock.

Present—Messrs. Fisher, Stetson, Johnson, Brown, Seeley, Butler, Reynolds, Hedrick, Main, Ingolls—18 in all.

Mr. Fisher in the chair.   Mr. John W. Chambers was appointed Secretary pro tem.

The following extracts, by Mr. Meigs, from scientific journals were read :

[London Athenæum, Feb. 1858.   Royal Institution, Jan. 29, 1858.]

ON MOLECULAR IMPRESSIONS BY LIGHT AND ELECTRICITY.

The remarkable relations existing between the physical structure of matter and its effect upon heat, light, electricity, magnetism, &c., seem, until the present century, to have attracted little attention : thus, to take the two agents, light and electricity, how manifestly their effects depend upon the malecular organization of the bodies subjected to their influence. *Carbon* as diamond, transmits light but *stops electricity!* as coke, or graphite, into which heat transforms diamond, transmits electricity, but *stops light!*

The celebrated photographer, Mons. Niepce de St. Victor, recently tried the following experiment, viz : An engraving after having been some time in the dark, was then exposed to the light of the sun as to *one-half* while the other half was covered by an opaque screen. It was then taken into a dark room, the screen removed, and the whole engraving placed in close proximity to a sheet of highly sensitive photographic paper, that half of the engraving which had been exposed to the light was reproduced on the photographic paper, while no effect was produced by the other half.

Mr. Grove had little doubt that if this discourse was in summer instead of mid winter, he could have literally realized in this theatre, the Laputa problem of extracting *sunbeams from cucumbers.* While fishing last autumn, at Fontenay, he observed some white patches on the skin of a trout, which he was satisfied were not there when he was taken out of the water. The trout had been rolling about in some leaves, at the foot of a tree, and this gave him the notion that the effect might be photographic ! He placed a serrated leaf on each side of a fresh fish, laid him down on his side, that one leaf might be exposed to sun light while the other was in dark. After an hour or so, a well defined image of the leaf was apparent on the exposed side, and none on the dark side.   Electricity effects molecular changes.

Of the practical results to science, of the molecular changes, a beautiful illustration was afforded by the photography of the moon, by Mr. De la Rue, which, afforded by the aid of the electric lamp, images of the moon, *six feet in diameter*, in which the details of the surface were well defined. The cone in Tycho, the double cone in Copernicus, and even the ridge of

Aristarchus could be detected. The bright lines radiating from the mountains were clear and distinct. One of Jupiter, showed his belts very well marked, and his satellites visible. Now, assuming a high degree of perfection in astronomical photography, they may be illuminated to an indefinite degree of brilliancy by adventitious, light to detect impressions invisible without it ?

The distinguished astronomer, Le Verrier (glass-founder), has laid before the Academy of Sciences, his great work La Reduction des Observations faites aux Instruments Méridiens de l'Observatoire de Paris, depuis 1800, jusqu'a 1829.

SPEED ON RAILWAYS.

At a recent meeting at Birmingham, one of the most distinguished men in the world (Lord Brougham,) suggested that " the speed of trains should be limited to twenty-five or thirty miles an hour." Now, with proper care and good management, a speed of seventy miles an hour can be made as safe as one of seventeen. Accidents do not arise from the degree of speed, but from bad construction or mismanagement. *Good workmanship* and *good* management are required. To prevent a horse running away we should not tie his legs, but *put a good rider upon his back!*

[From the American Mining Journal.]
GRINDING QUARTZ FOR GOLD.

In Piedmont, Italy, there are now gold quartz works which have been in operation the last *thousand years!* Not rich enough to pay by the methods used elsewhere, here they roast the rock, then break it with a hammer to lumps about $1\frac{1}{4}$ inches square; these are fed to revolving millstones, so set as to grind the quartz as small as Indian corn! which is then fed to other mill-stones so set as to grind these to the finest powder. This they amalgamate in the usual manner. The stones are common burr, and last several months.

[Geological Institute of Vienna.]
STRENGTHENING ELECTRO MAGNETS.

M. Schefzik, Engineer of the Austrian Imperial Telegraphs, has perfectly succeeded in this by *using* (instead of the copper wire of inconsiderable diameter, in wrapping the iron cores,) ribbons of copper, *presenting the edges to the core.*

GRANTHAM ON IRON SHIP BUILDING

Speaks of Shortridge, Howell & Jessop's homogeneous metal, and its advantages for plating iron ships. An inch bar of it has been tested at the Liverpool Cable Testing Machine. It broke under a strain of fifty-three tons; rather more than double the best English bar iron. This metal is ductile, malleable, and welds with facility. It resists oxidation and fire far better than common iron.

Mr. John Laird, the great pioneer of iron ship building, has taken the initiative in the use of this homogeneous metal, for ship building purposes, in building the iron vessel for carrying Dr. Livingston on his mission to the very heart of the almost unknown regions of Africa.

ECONOMY OF STEAM.

All the steam engines now extensively in use, are practically, in fact, Watt's engines, more or less developed and improved, and it appears that, in some instances, an economy has been now attained that the consumption of coal is only from two to two and one-half pounds per hour per indicated horse power; and theory shows that this is almost the greatest economy we can arrive at; and if we want to economize further, we must introduce some new principle, such as the use of superheated steam, (the late Mr. Frost's *stame*,) or heated air, which is analagous to it, inasmuch as it can be worked at a high temperature *without attaining a dangerous pressure!* (Quere.) The theory of this is now well understood, and the only difficulty that exists, is as to its convenient practical application.

[London Artisan. April, 1858.]

INSTITUTION OF CIVIL ENGINEERS.

Sawyer on "The Self-acting Tools employed in the construction of Steam Engines," &c.

The new mode of forging rivets for boilers; making a ton of well formed rivets, exactly alike, in ten hours, and apparatus for forging nuts exactly.

Mr. Richard Roberts has made his Jacquard or Multifarious Perforating Machine, and it is now employed at the Canada Works, Birkenhead, for punching the boiler plates for making the Victoria bridge over the river St. Lawrence. It punches 72 holes in each plate of ten feet long and $3\frac{1}{4}$ wide and 5-16th of an inch thick; does 90 such plates in $10\frac{1}{2}$ hours by one mechanic, three laborers and one boy. The same work by hand takes 4 men to work with the templates, and 8 men at the machine, and do much less work in a day than the machine does.

It was stated that great care should be taken in using the rivet machines, as, if undue pressure is employed, the rivets are too much compressed; and instances were given in which the plates were split in riveting throughout their length. The *cunning hand* of man is truly admirable! A good workman would not do that.

ELECTRO-MAGNETIC ENGINES

are under consideration; and to show that these are not mere matters of speculation, for they are actually used in France for driving small and delicate machinery, for which they are well adapted, being *clean, easily managed* and *cool.* But they cost more than steam engines. To produce a given total amount of energy, it consumes 32 lbs. of zinc for every six pounds of coal that a steam engine consumes.

COLORING MATTER FROM COAL TAR, GUANO AND GRASS.

London, April, 1858.

The products of coal tar have long been looked to as a valuable source of *fine dyes* and *colors,* and we are now enabled to show that this view ha been to a great extent satisfactorily realized in commercial practice. Messrs. Perkins & Church have obtained from the alkaloids of coal tar, and one from napthaline, several blue coloring substances of great value. They are named by the discoverers, Nitroso-phenyline and Nitroso-napthyline. They are beautiful purple-blue colors; some of them have been success-fully fixed on silk. One, in particular, fairly rivals the delicate orchil color, or that made from lichens, while it has the great advantage of resisting the action of light.

The process is dissolving in water the sulphates of aniline, of cuminine, of taluidine, adding bi-chromate of potash sufficient to neutralize the sul-phuric acid in these sulphates. The whole is left to stand for twelve hours, when a brown substance is precipitated, which is washed with coal-tar nap-tha, and then dissolved in methylated spirits. This solution, with the addition of a little tartaric or oxalic acid, forms the *dyeing liquor*.

Messrs. Low and Calvert have conjointly produced from coal tar, colors resembling safflower pinks and cochineal crimsons; and on a piece of calico, mordanted for madder, all the various colors and shades derived from the madder root, violet, purple, chocolate, pink and red, can be obtained in this way. The safflower imitation stands the action of soap and light; the real, of course, does not.

Guano has produced in the laboratory of the French chemist, M. de Pouilly, a very beautiful crimson called murexide, (like the *murex Tyrian* purple,) and has fixed it on silk by dipping the silk in a concentrated solu-tion of bi-chloride of mercury, mixed with the murexide, squeezing the silk well and hanging it in the air, a magnificent crimson *insoluble com-pound* is thus fixed on the silk.

Wool Dyed Green with Grass.—Mr. Schlumberger has fixed the green *chlorophylle* of grass and leaves permanently on wool.

HOMES TO BE HAPPY MUST BE HEALTHY.

Mr. John Johnson.—Volumes have been written by learned and scien-tific men, anxious for the public good, not only on the advantages of ven-tilation, but on the absolute necessity of it for the preservation of health. Practical men come to the aid of science, and invent contrivances for effecting the object; and those of real utility can only be considered, which admit of being adapted to our present mode of constructing our dwellings, halls, &c., having due regard to the cost as well as efficiency. The phy-sician knows too well, the difficulties which are in his path in his daily practice, where ventilation cannot be had, or where it can be, and is not effected; fresh, pure air, being more important, even, than unwholesome food. At any rate, a time must come when fresh air will be so regarded—the latter being the invisible one, we know; but, facts well considered, the result will prove this of the first importance, and will stand in the scale higher than the visible, tangible, necessaries of life.

The invisible agent, then, of health or disease, demands, like other natu-ral agents, to be brought under proper management and control, in order that it may be subservient to the real purposes of life. Without this pure element, it is impossible that our homes can be healthy.

Many of our houses have been built with what would appear a most surprising ignorance of this want of the principal necessary of life ; and many bedrooms are without fire-places, or other means for ingress or egress of air. Such buildings are often filled to overflowing with their living contents, ignorant that each and all of them are poisoning each other. The committee on public health should be aroused to this important question, and the ball should be kept in motion, till no habitation for man or beast be constructed which should be unfit for the occupancy of the tenant who is to inhabit the same.

Each inspiration requires about twenty cubic inches ; fifteen inspirations per minute, requiring 300 cubic inches, or nearly one-sixth of a foot. This quantity, mixing with the air, would render about two feet unfit for respiration. Under ordinary circumstances, the respired air is near the temperature of the body, or 98°. This is specifically higher than the surrounding air, generally.

In dry air, heated to 240°, D. Dobson found the heat of the body 99.5°. He remained in air 210°, ten minutes ; his temperature was 101.5°.

Fillit and Marantin, that air was respired at 300° to 325°.

In Quito, Bonpland and Humboldt, found fishes in volcanic water, at 210°

In Germany, some bath girls have breathed air at 288°, for ten minutes, without inconvenience ; one girl inhaled it at 325°, for five minutes. Sir Joseph Banks moved about in a room at 211°, and Sir Charles Bladger at 260°. Sir E. Parry, Capt. Kane, and others, at 50° below zero.

Mr. Stetson thought the subject a very important one. He alluded to the warming of the Cooper Union, viz., through perforations in the floor ; and also to the plan adopted by Mr. Rutan, admitting the hot air at the top, and forcing it out near the floor. Perfect ventilation, is admitting pure air imperceptibly into the room.

Mr. Seeley.—I do not approve of the plan of admitting air at the ceiling. I am of opinion that air should be admitted at the floor, in imperceptible streams.

Mr. Stetson.—Breathing produces carbonic acid gas. Gas light destroys a vast amount of air.

Mr. Butler thought that carbonic acid gas was the trouble. Chemists, by some mode, could get rid of that. The pure and impure air might be separated.

Mr. Seeley thought that we should study nature. Carbonic acid gas was continually forming by breathing, and by our mode of lighting. The winds constantly change it ; plants consume a vast deal. Plants in aquariums, render the water pure, and prevent the changing of the water.

Mr. Reynolds being called upon to explain the system of ventilation in the Cooper Union, stated that, firstly, a pair of locomotive boilers and an engine, propelling fans ten feet in diameter. In winter, the air is taken some distance up. The air is forced through coils of pipes, 1,800 feet ;

,the pipes are filled with steam, and the air then passes into ventilators, or through perforations in the floors. I think the method adopted is very excellent, and seems to give g·eat satisfaction.

Mr. John Johnson spoke of the want of practical thought, in the arrangement of ventilators.

Table containing the Velocity and Force of the Wind.

—Velocity of the wind.—		Pependicular force on 1 foot area in pounds avoirdupois.	
Miles in 1 hour.	Feet in a second.		
1	1.47	.005	Hardly perceptible.
2	2.93	.020 }	Just perceptible.
8	4 40	.044 }	
4	5.87	.079 }	Gentle, pleasant wind.
5	7.33	.123 }	
10	14.67	.492 }	Pleasant, brisk gale.
15	22.00	1.107 }	
20	29.34	1.968 }	Very brisk.
25	36.67	3.975 }	
30	44.01	4.429 }	High wind.
35	51.34	6.027 }	
40	58.68	7.873 }	Very high wind.
45	66.01	9.963 }	
50	73.35	12.300	A storm, or tempest.
60	88.02	17.715	Great storm.
80	117.36	31.490	A hurricane.
100	146.70	49.200	A hurricane that tears up trees, and carries buildings before it.

For ventilation in mines, the air is moved at about five miles per hour.

On motion of Mr. Stetson, the subject was continued for the next meeting, and hoping some practical men will furnish estimates of relative cost of warming and ventilation.

Adjourned.

JOHN W. CHAMBERS, Sec'y pro tem.

June 28, 1858.

Present—Messrs. Backus, Cohen, Johnson, Godwin, Seeley, Disturnell, Leonard, Chambers, Upfield, of Lancaster, Ohio; Mr. Maine and others— 24 members in all.

The regular chairman, Thomas B. Stillman, being absent, Samuel D. Backus, was chosen chairman *pro tem.* Henry Meigs, Secretary.

Mr. Cohen moved that our meetings during summer, be held at 5 o'clock P. M., and that when we adjourn, that it be until after the fair, unless sooner called by the Chairman.

Mr. Leonard seconded the motion, which was carried unanimously.

The Chairman called up miscellaneous business. None being then offered, he stated some remarks he had made on the cause of exfoliation of paint from brick walls, even from often painted, old hard brick walls. Was it uniformly so? What is the rationale of it?

Mr. Johnson inclined to think it due to the action of frost upon the moisture in the bricks, and that hard pressed brick, from dry clay, were apt to be disintegrated and peel the paint off of course.

Mr. Seeley thought that the lime contained in them had the power to produce the stated effects—and that (as is usual,) the brick has moisture in it—oil paint cannot penetrate it.

Mr. Cohen.—It is due to the moisture absorbed by the brick.

Mr. Leonard.—It is most observed on walls relative to their exposure, *north*, *south*, *east* or *west?* It is produced by the moisture absorbed by the bricks.

Mr. Meigs.—Are the bricks in our buildings ever dry, even those hard burned. Do they not all, readily imbibe moisture and retain it long ?

Mr. Leonard.—Brick-makers use small coal dust to mix with their brick clay. This when burned leaves the brick quite porous.

The Chairman.—I have the mastic which had been painted on brick wall exfoliate in large sheets.

M. Disturnell introduced Mr. Upfield, of Lancaster, Ohio, who exhibited and explained his new system of measurement for shoes and boots—saving some 20 per cent in leather. His drawings, lithographed, are on a large scale. His work costs six dollars. He can be found at 34 Spruce street, New York. He states that his rules are infallible in all cases where the foot and leg are in common natural condition. He thinks his plan is a sure one in place of the *uncertain fancy measure and cut of the makers.*

Mr. Meigs adverted to recent successful measures used by our best tailors

The Chairman called up the regular question : " Warming and ventilation of buildings.

Mr. Johnson illustrated by drawings on the black board Faraday's mode of conduction of heat, for the double purpose of ventilating and lighting, as it has been tried in the New Parliament House—House of Lords, London—where Mr. Johnson examined it in 1851. The difficulty in the gas flames was that by sudden breezes, it often cracked the glass tubes containing it. There is nothing new in it however.

Mr. Godwin examined the Parliament House, with an engineer, in 1852. Did not notice the arrangement spoken of by Mr. Johnson. The ventilation was by Reid. Mr. Godwin illustrated on black board, his own system of warming and ventilating buildings, in this city, many years ago.

Mr. Meigs asked the chairman if he had examined the warming and ventilation of the Capitol at Albany, he, Mr. Backus, having recently been a member of the House of Representatives there.

Mr. Chairman.—Had not, but had discovered that the Capitol was badly off in the ventilation and warming.

Mr. Meigs said that he was a member in 1818, and then a body of pure air was admitted to the heater from the outside of the building, and when warmed it came into the hall of representatives through large iron tubes, causing a slight pressure of the air of the hall outward, the doors opening inward with difficulty as the air endeavored to escape. *That is the true principle ; not to heat the same air*, but to *have the external air warmed constantly and so poured into the building.* Many large representatives from the country sat without their coats, while the insides of the windows of the hall of representatives were covered an inch thick with ice, formed of the moisture of the air in the hall, by the external cold.

The Chairman asked Mr. Johnson to take the chair while he took the floor, and illustrated on the blackboard his views of the system of heat and air, as easily executed in small buildings by means of double walls and roof. That the lighting of buildings should be made. if possible, to operate like daylight, so that in assemblies the play of countenance may be seen, which cannot be when light comes from several different quarters at once.

Mr. Maine recommends summer ventilation of churches by means of a chimney with a furnace, and numerous pipes from all parts of the building connecting with the chimney.

Mr. Disturnell.—The whole difficulty in ventilation is in the smallness of our rooms.

Mr. Maine.—No matter how large the room, if it be close there can be no ventilation or comfort in it.

Mr. Seeley remarked further on the Faraday Burner, and moved that this same subject be continued at next meeting.

The Club then adjourned. **H. MEIGS,** *Secretary.*

November 24, 1858.

Present—Messrs. Butler, Leonard, Veeder, Seeley, and others.

John P. Veeder in the chair. Henry Meigs, Secretary.

The Secretary remarked that the Club is organized not only for discovery and improvement of all useful works in the vast round of mechanism, but also in all the fine arts, which of necessity includes the Art of Design.

I believe it will be useful for us to keep before our eyes all that has been done in this delightful department of human genius, and to avail ourselves of all in them which is desirable, as so many steps towards the perfection of the Art of Design. With this view let us look back to the beginning, for at certain periods the art has found glorious adepts long ago.

The Romans held the painter and sculptor in great esteem and honor at the earliest time. Of the illustrious family of the *Fabii*, whose ancestors were famous for fine crops of the best *beans*, there arose an artist, *Fabius Pictor*, (Fabius the painter) in the year 450, ab urbe condita. His pictures were so much admired that some of them were placed for safe keeping and public exhibition in the sixth quarter of the city of Rome, in a temple, where they were exhibited until the temple was burned in the reign of the Emperor Claudius, several hundred years.

The next artist of great distinction was also a distinguished poet. *Pacuvius,* who painted the Temple of Hercules in the cattle market in the eighth quarter of the city of Rome. It was called the Temple of Hercules Victor. It was a small round building. Pacuvius was a nephew of Ennius, of ancient celebrity. The glory he gained by his pencil was greatly nrcased by his highly successful dramas. *Antisteus Labeon,* who was

Pro-consul in Narbonese Gaul, was an admired miniature painter. *Quintus Pedius*, a nobleman, born dumb, was advised by the orator Messala to learn the art of painting.   The Emperor Augustus Cæsar approved of it. Pedius soon gave strong evidence of great ability as an artist, but died while yet a young man.

Marcus Valerius Maximus Messala first exhibited on the side wall of the *Curia Hostilia*, the Court of Argument by counsellors at law, a picture of the Battle in Sicily, where he conquered King Hiero and the Carthagenians in the year 490, ab urbe condita.   *Lucius Scipio* placed in the capitol a picture of his great Asiatic Victory, and thus displeased his bro.her, Scipio Africanus, whose son had been taken prisoner by him at that battle. *Claudius Pulcher* had a curtain in the theatre, representing a house with its tiled roof, drawn with so much truth that crows tried to alight upon it. After the plunder of the Acheans, Rome became fond of foreign paintings. They took noble pictures among the spoils.   One of Bacchus, painted by Aristides, was valued by King Attalus at $12,000.   Subsequently a great many pictures were exhibited in Rome.   Julius Cæsar and Marcus Agrippa made painting fashionable.   Agrippa paid for a picture of an Ajax and a Venus $2,400.   Augustus Cæsar exhibited in the most public place in his market two pictures—one of the Battle of Actium, and the other of his great Triumph held in the city of Rome.

The Greeks in their criticisms on painting first called the gradation of light in a picture its TONE, because it was a *harmonious* mixing of light and shadow.   The old artists used a red called sinopis, which was cheap, costing but twenty-five cents a pound ; they used it in making bright skies. They used *white lead*, as well as several other white pigments.   The ship builders used white lead in painting their vessels.   The various ochres, sandarach. (of which we make pounce,) syriacum, lampblack, a black like India ink, made of burnt lees of wine.   The celebrated artists Polygnotus and Mycon, of Athens, used it.   Apelles (whose fine dresses and manners gave him the appellation of *Abrodiaitos*, or the *Beau*,) first burned ivory to get a black.   Alexander the Great was very fond of him and went often to his studio ; he forbade all other artists making portraits of him.   A Venus painted by Apelles, lasted more than four hundred years ; it was last in the possession of the Emperor Nero, who displaced it at last and put a picture of Dorothea there.   Nero ordered a painting to be executed *on cloth* a hundred and twenty feet high, which was hardly finished when it was struck by lightning and consumed, together with the greater part of his garden of Maia, where the picture was.

Apollodorus, of Athens, painted a picture of Ajax in flames, caused by lightning ; also, a priest in the act of adoration ; both of them were captivating pictures.   Zeuxis followed Apelles about 350 years before our Saviour. After painting some time for money he painted gratis, saying that no sum of money could induce him to paint a picture.

His painting of Penelope was surprising by its admirable expression of modesty.   His drawings were rigidly exact.   In painting his Lacinian Juno, the people of the city of Agrgentum, iñ Sicily, provided him with views of their most beautiful daughters, *naked*, to draw from. He selected five of them and thus drew his Juno. Some persons admired his picture of a *child with a bunch of grapes* because the birds pecked at the grapes. But Zeuxis said he was mortified at that, because if he had done justice to the child the birds would not have dared to come near enough to it to peck the grapes in its hands. He painted Alexander the Great holding a thunderbolt in his hand, for the temple of Diana in Ephesus. That picture was valued at over $9,000. Zeuxis used a subtle varnish that gave great luster to his paintings.

The art of design is, in other words, drawing. which is indispensible in almost every human work ; a building, a fence, a vehicle, a ship, dress, cloth, implements, from a spade to a steam engine, everywhere the art of drawing is demanded. It is a great business in all civilized nations, and that nation which excels in it leads all others in the sale of her manufactures and works of all sorts. Schools to teach design are necessary. This Club should do all in its power to stimulate its growth among us, so that in due time American works may bear the palm of excellence in design and perfection of mechanism. Already the art is exerted here admirably in drawing machinery, in which very valuable work Europe is also excellent, and we are now following rapidly in painting, engraving, sculpture, &c.

The secretary calls the attention of the club to the Atlantic cable, which has realized the difficulties which the club anticipated long ago, regretting, as all men must, the failure of such an enterprise, stamped as one of the noblest and most bold of any scientific problem ever solved by men, entitled to all the merit that the utmost success could have gained. The club will recall their suggestion of the surest path for the World's telegram, that by Behring's straits, as it appears by the map, drawn from authentic data by the club, that course is now under exploration by the Emperor of Russia, as the club then supposed it would. The narrow water, there dividing the two great continents, is only 200 feet deep, hardly 50 miles wide, and no ice islands can injure the cables, because the current is perpetual through the straits from the Pacific ocean to the Arctic. That the effort made to lay a cable under 2,000 miles of ocean, was a giant work, and the men who did it had merited all the praise the world had given them. They had deserved success ! The miracle all but done !

We are glad to see that Frenchmen view it thus, and we give their own language as follows :

"Ainsi donc la pose du câble télégraphique est maintenant un fait accompli. Qu'un accident en occasion la rupture, on que des defectuosités du genre de celles qui retardent aujourd'hui les communications entre l'Amerique et l'Europe se découvre dans sa structure, dans le premier cas, le succès qui a couronné les efforts de la compagnie ne pourra manquer d'accompagna ceux que l'on fera desormais dans le même but, et, dans le seconde cas, le génie inventeur de l'epoque trouvera certainment mille

moyens de perfectionner le fil conducteur. Le Rêve était magnifique ;
Dieu a permis qu'il se soit realisé que sa volonté nous permette d'on profiter.
Les noms des deux frères Field, des Morse, des Peter Cooper, des Moses
Taylor, des Marshall O. Roberts, et des Chandler White, appartiennent
desormais a l'histoire ; apres Dieu ils sont les auteurs de l'union fraternelle
de deux continents.   ' *Audaces fortuna juvat*.' La réussité de leur
audacieux projet les a tout-a-coup fait sortir de l'ombre pour leur donner
relief glorieux de Héros de la Science.''

The great agent, electricity, so long a study, yielding more and more
development, wants great attention still.   Let us look back upon our first
steps in this great science, and now earnestly look for more light !   It
extends in all directions.   It is attraction and repulsion ; it is vitreous,
positive, resinous, negative, electro-magnetic, frictional, animal (flesh or
fish), chemical, thermo, and why not psycho (for ice at one end and heat at
the other, of a metal rod, produce it,) cohesion also, for electricity results
from all chemical solution and aggregation, as well as from all *motion*.
Heat and light are parts, but as latent heat, it belongs to all bodies.
Cabeus, more than 200 years ago, gave us the natural magneto-elect icity
of the earth ; it was one grand *magnet;* it is so called from Magnesia, where
they believed the *loadstone* was first found.   Lucretius says,

> " Quem magnetem vocant nomine Graii,
> Magnetem quia sit patrus in montibus ortus.''

Plato said that the power of the magnet to communicate its virtue to iron
was understood ; they formed a chain of iron rings, which, when magnetized, adhered to each other.   The Chinese understood both its adhesive power and its polarity, many centuries before the Christian
era.   Pliny thought that the magnet had medical virtues—that it cured
sore eyes and *burns !* William Gilbert's " Essay on a New Physiology of
Magnetic Bodies," was published in London in 1600, and at *Sedan*, in
1630, and it is the most remarkable work on the subject that had yet
appeared.   He has never had the credit he deserved.

A magnet, like certain polypes, has, when divided, the same positive and
negative poles, so that supposing one magnetized *atom divided*, each part
would still have its poles, or anode and cathode.   We test this by the common experiment. of piercing a card with electricity ; the hole is not made
as by all mechanical processes, i. e., from either side through, but we find
a burr on both sides, showing that the positive and negative parted in the
centre of the card and exploded in opposite directions.   So the atom of
water, composed as it is of two parts of hydrogen and one of oxygen, is
formed into water by the electricities, and one drop of which (says Faraday), contains enough of them to make a *thunder storm*, when suitably
separated.

Gravitation, or as La Place calls it, pésanteur, which we translate by the
word weight, has a velocity of not less than *fifty millions of times greater
than that of light !* So that while light requires $9\frac{1}{2}$ years to reach us
from one of the nearest fixed stars—No. 61, in Cygni—pésanteur reaches
us in *five seconds*.

All the stars send us light which appears to be the same (except trifling shades of color in some,) in all, and we see, with good telescopes, *one hundred millions of them.* What follows—all the electricities are in them all.

It is not impossible that we may discover the powers of the electricities and use them for all manner of force! The resources, as above shown, are near enough to infinite for all that man can want. Let us hope and work them, until we have not only put a girdle around the whole earth but set in motion every wanted engine and machinery on land and sea, maintained light and warmth like a summer's day, over all mankind.

OUR STREET PAVEMENTS—FALL OF OUR HORSES.

An hourly infliction upon our horses and the feelings of citizens, so striking, so hurtful, and yet so easily prevented.

Some months ago the Mechanics' Club of the American Institute, feeling, with our citizens, the very strongest sympathy for our most valued friend, the horse, was induced to think of a preventive. It concluded by offering (gratis,) to our worthy mayor, its plan, viz.: The pavement needs to be kept rough enough, at all times, to prevent slipping. This it proposes to do in the most perfect and economical manner. Carriages, strong enough to carry *upright pounders shod with steel points*, operated by the movement of the carriage itself, driven by one man, to pass with other vehicles, freely, through our streets, pecking as it goes, the smooth surfaces of our pavement; the depth and amount of the *pecking* or *roughening* to be regulated at pleasure. Such pavement pecking carriages can work at all times and at an expense not *one-tenth that of an omnibus!*

The Club is desired to consider this remedy for a serious street evil, and if best, recommend its adoption.

Subjects for next meeting.—"Warming and ventilation of buildings;" "Canal steam navigation."

Mr. Seeley called attention to some of the properties of gutta percha, relative to its insulation of electricity. That it suffered great alteration. When coated on wires it became very brittle and was readily rubbed all off. It should be attended to when we are about trusting it with insulation on long cables.

The Club adjourned.

H. MEIGS, *Secretary.*

December 8, 1858.

Present—Messrs. Johnson, Clough, of Indiana; Brown, Jones, Seeley, Reynolds, Leonard, Veeder, Woodward, Stetson, and others.

John Johnson in the chair. Henry Meigs, Secretary.

Miscellaneous business being still in order the Secretary read the following papers:

[Journal of the Society of Arts. London.]

This society has more than 350 societies in union with it, from all of which a weekly journal is published in London. From such abundant streams of knowledge we derive most interesting views of the progress of art and industry. We extract the following on iron, far more important than all the gold of the world :

The 21st ordinary meeting of the one hundred and fourth session, Sir Thomas Phillips, member of the council, in the chair.

Charles Sanderson introduced the subject of iron.

Metallurgy is a science of vast extent in its application. In England the application of science to it has been so successful that our iron works now stand models of intelligence and ingenuity, marked by the diligent researches of men of high capacity, whose united efforts have produced the comparatively perfect system we now employ.

The immense iron establishments of England stand pre-eminent both in mechanical skill and practical management. It is in the immense laboratory of the blast furnace that the first result comes—pig iron, as pure as possible. When chemical analysis has given the quantity and quality of the earthy contents of the ore, other substances are added in such proportions as will secure a *perfect vitrification of the whole.* These other substances are called fluxes. The iron ore is charged into the furnace as a calcined peroxide. Limestone is added as a flux to unite with the earthy matter which the *ore* and the *fuel* may contain. During five or six feet of their descent in the furnace the moisture is expelled, the ore becomes then gradually heated to redness and is prepared for reduction in the *first zone* of the furnace. Here the ore loses a portion of its oxide, and becomes reduced to a protoxide. They now enter the *second zone,* which ends at the *boshes* or widest part of the furnace. At this point the ores are not only completely deoxidized, but become partially cemented. The limestone has now parted with its carbonic acid and the alkaline part of it unites with the earthy matter, together forming *slag.* The whole now gradually but slowly descends through this part of the furnace which is made wider in order that the materials may take a longer time in passing through this space, thus leaving them for a longer time subjected to the *action of the carbon.* The metallic portion becomes gradually developed and acted upon by the carbon of the fuel, and the highly carbonizing gases it meets with in the lower region of the furnace. It then passes the direct action of the blast at the tuyers and falling into the dam, separates itself by its superior specific gravity from the vitreous earthy matter which covers it and *protects it from the oxidizing influence of the blast.* The air blown into the furnace is composed, in round numbers, of 79 nitrogen and 21 oxygen. Before this air has risen three feet from the tuyere it is converted into 65 nitrogen and 27 carbonic oxide, &c.

Sir Francis Knowles proposes to introduce potash, felspar or soda, into the furnace charges. He adds lime equal to two-thirds of the weight of the silica contained in the felspar ; the bases then become lime, alumina, and the alkali, which being in excess, is released to form the cyanide required. He states that his trials have given him a cinder entirely free from iron.

Cold blast pig iron is most likely to produce the strongest iron for castings. I submit a new form of rail; it is made from a thick plate of iron and steel united. The plate, when hot, is bent up into the form of a rail, the steel coating outside before the bar is cold. It is hardened by being plunged into cold water and tempered the usual way. By these means are obtained great combined strength of the two metals, and an addition of thirty-three per cent. by hardening and tempering the steel, which not only prevents its running surface from rapid wear, but prevents all *lamination*, and they are much stronger. M. Chenot, of France, uses an electro-magnetic machine to separate iron from deleterious matter. He then adds thick lime water and produces cast steel.

Sir Francis Knowles has a patent for making cast steel from iron ore direct.

France imports iron from England. In 1856, nearly 85,000 tons of pig; in 1857, 89,000 tons. The United States imported from us, in ——, 58,000 tons of pig; in 1856, in rails, bars, &c., 231,000 tons; in 1857, 221,000 tons. In the United States, many iron works are not in operation, and others, like ours, doing very little. Our exports to all countries, so far this year, show decrease, from 1857, of 149,000 tons, of which 118,000 tons are of the United States.

England now exports iron, and articles made of it, to the value of £22,994,671. This export will continue while we are able to make iron at our cheap rates. Were I to look back into the private history of many of our large works from their commencement, I should find large sums *devoted to projects* of which no vestige now remains; while the erection of the requisite machinery had cost more than double the original estimates, they are not worth half the money they cost.

Whilst England may, at present, look round with some security upon the efforts of other nations, do not let us forget that knowledge expands among them as among us. We have the power, let us have the will, to bring our Eastern Metropolis in direct communication with the rulers of that vast empire at home; let us hope to see her rivers, which every where stretch their arms throughout this land, teeming with riches and prolific vegetation, covered with light-draught steamboats; let railroads open out the immense resources of a country which has successively enriched many European nations, and England's wealth and energy will then draw from this long neglected portion of our empire, those benefits which she ought long ere this to have enjoyed.

Our rails, generally speaking, are not so good as they can be made, and the almost daily reports which we hear of the defects of our iron-built steamships, are proof that this kind of iron might be improved; and this can *only be done by giving the maker a better price.*

[London Artisan, August, 1858.

ON BOILER EXPLOSIONS. By EDWARD STRONG.

Extracts by H. Meigs.

The theory that hydrogen gas is produced in a boiler (whether of iron or copper) by too much heat decomposing water—or, secondly, that overheating causes water to take a *spheroidical* form, are *mysteries*. Engineers have often said that when the metal is heated to redness from shortness of water, the gas is formed and exploded, with force equal to that of gunpowder. Hydrogen gas is generated in the boiler but it is harmless until mixed with certain amount of air, or of oxygen gas, neither of which *should be* present in boilers when working. *Iron*, red hot, decomposes water, but red hot *copper* does not, nor will do it at any temperature, however high. A copper fire-box, with tubes of brass, cannot decompose water. Copper has proved to be superior to iron for raising steam, and it will not blow up.

Water in the Spheroidical form.—If a plate of iron be heated to boiling water, it gives steam, but when heated beyond 212° Fahrenheit, water on it does not form steam, but takes the spheroidical form, at 340°, rolling in globular forms ; when the heat diminishes to 212°, then steam is formed. It is said that the heat being reduced to 212°, after the water has taken the spheroidical form, steam is produced so as to produce explosion of the boiler. This theory has never been proved. The ordinary working pressure on locomotive boilers, is 120 lbs. per inch. Such pressure requires 343° of heat, at which the water must be in spheroidical form, so that whenever the pressure falls to 110 lbs. per inch, that form ceases and we ought to have an explosion, which, however, does not take place. Further, engines have been worked at 200 lbs. with perfect safety, with temperature of 385°. These facts show the absurdity of the theory of explosion from the spheroidical form of water. Locomotives are frequently so inclined as to have part overheated without explosion ! The two theories being disposed of, the rest is simple ; it is the *mechanical strength of the boiler only !* The boiler maker, therefore, should not merely make it strong enough while it is new but allow enough to *allow for wear during the number of years which it is decided to be workable* It should first be tested by hydraulic pressure of at least double its working pressure ; and the boiler should be so tested once, at least, every year of its employment. *Neglected leakage* leads to mischief, for it rapidly reduces the strength of the plate there. Dirt, &c., bad.

SAFETY VALVES.

Every boiler should have one. On no account should two or more boilers (as is sometimes done,) have but one for all. Each boiler is fitted with a stop cock, so that if one cock should happen to be closed that boiler would inevitably explode. This *one valve* for several boilers, is, however, allowed in government service even, sometimes. The valve, sometimes, becomes *locked* through some defect, and then an explosion follows. Their free working must be often tried by the engineer. The *lead plug* must be attended to. It should be renewed every month.

SUMMARY.

Boiler tested properly; leakage stopped; boiler clean; two valves and a lead plug to each boiler; kept in order; and an explosion may be said to be an impossibility. A locomotive boiler on being tested for the first time, at the builders', (Messrs. Sharp, Stewart & Co.,) exploded, destroying life, attributed to imperfect rivets fixed by machinery, so as to reduce the strength from 490 lbs. per inch to 100 lbs.

FIRST LOCOMOTIVES IN THE UNITED STATES.

Horatio Allen, of our Novelty Works, brought here, from England, in 1829, the first locomotives, one of which was used on the Delaware and Hudson railroad, at Carbondale, in Pennsylvania, and was taken off, being too heavy for that *road*. The first one made in the United States, was at the West Point foundry, in 1830, for the South Carolina railroad, and was called the *Phœnix;* a second one was called the *West Point.* In the spring of 1831, the third one, built for the Mohawk and Hudson railroad from Albany to Schenectady, was called the *De Witt Clinton*, the first one run in the State of New York.

Mr. Clough, of Indiana, exhibited and explained his new steam meter.

Mr. Meigs had examined in the large stores of Messrs. Bowen & McNamee, in Broadway, Gold's method of warming buildings. Three furnaces in the lower story, each about six feet high by four or five diameter, make steam. The steam regulates, automatically, the supply of water and that of air to the furnaces whose fire valves close when the steam is high enough, and deaden the fires. Pipes lead the steam to radiators placed where wanted in every part. The radiators are plates of sheet iron quilted together (by rivits) at short intervals, leaving space between them for a very thin stratum of steam. Such double plates are placed within a few inches of each other, in masses as required. The pipes reconduct to the boilers the water of the condensed steam, these pipes being a little inclined, so as to carry off all water and so prevent rust when the radiators are unemployed. The stores have seven floors, each 150 feet long and 50 feet wide. So that there is space warmed equal to eighty-four rooms of twenty-five feet square, and the whole warmed by sixty tons of coal per annum, or each room of 25 feet square is warmed by three-quarters or one ton per annum.

Mr. Leonard had large experience in extensive factories, and had found the physician's bill large when dry heat was employed, and when he introduced steam warmth, health rose among the people of the factories, while doctor's bills fell. He attributed this salutary change to tho moisture accompanying the steam heat. Such, however, was the result of experience.

The Club unanimously requested that its meetings be every Wednesday evening. Mr. Leonard, of the Board, assented.

Adjourned to Wednesday, December 22, at 7 o'clock, P. M.

                                        H. MEIGS, *Secretary*.

––––––––

                                        December 15, 1858.

Present—Messrs. Johnson, Butler, Brown, Seeley, Leonard, Hathaway, Veeder, Bruce, Witt, and others—20 members.

John Johnson in the chair.   Henry Meigs, Secretary.

Mr. Seeley stated the first question, ventilation, intimating that the known properties of vitiated air from breathing, &c., so hazardous to health and life, were not known to the mass of men, that even the carbonic acid produced from burning charcoal, so fatal in close apartments, or that naturally formed at the bottom of wells, and are still not popularly understood. Our purpose is to help in expanding this knowledge.

Mr. Clough, of Indiana, added his views. That a man vitiated sixty hogsheads of air every day. He adverted to the sad effects of such air on general health, often producing bad effects, which some constitutions throw off with great difficulty if ever. Admit pure air! by every feasible method.

Mr. Seeley called for a paper on this subject, in the collection of the Chairman—a scientific article. It was read.

The Chairman adverted to methods used to remove carbonic acid gas from floors, &c.

Mr. Veeder.—Heat from furnaces, grates, stoves, &c., was commonly wasted to a large amount without rendering the temperature what was steadily wanted. That slow combustion obviated the evil by a well graduated uniform steady supply of warmth not over-drying the air. That stoves for such purpose kept the fuel always sufficiently charred to light up quick when oxygen is admitted. He strongly advocated the careful ventilation of rooms.

Chairman.—The Cooper Institute building is warmed by warm air; pure air is taken twenty feet above the sidewalk, forced downwards into the basement, is warmed, and ascends of course, being warmed by steam pipes. He desired that a paper on the carbonic acid and oxygen be prepared for next meeting.

Mr. Meigs.—I was brought up in free air. The great fire places! the *pure sweet heat* of hickory, pine, &c. No shutters or curtains! If air must be scientifically admitted into a building it ought not to be from near the ground but from upper air!

Mr. Veeder spoke of the advantage of double walls in keeping uniform warmth.

Mr. Meigs.—For that purpose rooms for making sulphuric acid have double walls, the inner one of lead, and by having between the two this *jacket of air*, as it is called, the temperature is maintained twenty-four hours longer than in single walls.

Mr. Veeder again spoke of combustion, of the effect of blowers on furnaces, causing the hydrogen at the tops of flues to burn blue.

Mr. Seeley.—Currents of air in rooms are well shown by smoke—but no room can be without currents of air—but they must not be strong.

Mr. Brown summed up arguments and showed plainly that the several methods were adapted each to a different class of buildings. He explained the ready freezing of steam pipes, and the great care and engineer skill demanded in the management of the apparatus, puts it above private buildings. He reviewed all the processes of heating and ventilation, and said that it was essential that he who found any want of either must then seek the remedy for his own special circumstances, or in plain terms, each must have suitable appliances in his own case, no other case being precisely the same. That enough was known to some men to suit every case; but it *was* like the doctor among patients of very diverse habits and constitutions! Mr. Brown had repeated his own remarks, but the community would require repetition on repetition in order to *practice* the most established laws of temperature and ventilation.

The Club proposed, for next meeting, the subjects of "Boilers and Combustion," and "Canal Steam Navigation."

The Club adjourned.

H. MEIGS, *Secretary.*

December, 22, 1858.

Present—Messrs. Butler, Johnson, Brown, Seeley, Bruce, Cohen, and others—16 members.

Mr. Butler in the chair. Henry Meigs, Secretary.

The Secretary read the following papers, viz:

[Society of Arts. London, 1858.]

ELECTRO-MAGNETISM AS A MOTIVE POWER.

Would it not be reasonable to compare it with the steam engine when Watt took it in hand, and before he had found a Bolton to assist him with capital? Had Watt not found a capitalist, he might have died and made no sign, and the gigantic improvements resulting from his genius would have remained undeveloped. The question is confessedly a very great one, and admits of a division of labor; and if chemists would turn their attention to the discovery of a cheaper substance than zinc in the battery, a material point would be gained. I think the three following improvements may be justly claimed by Mr. Thomas Allen:

1st. The application of the magnetic force *direct*, and not tangentially.

2d. The use only of the most powerful portion of the geometric curve, formed by the rapidly decreasing magnetic power in proportion to distance.

3d. The continuations of motion or stroke, in the same direction, over any required space by means of successive groups of magnets.

I am aware that these points cannot well be understood without an explanatory diagram, but I will endeavor to explain how a model might be constructed which would illustrate these three points.

Let us suppose that three groups of four magnets each will be sufficient for illustration. Cotton reels will very aptly represent magnets with the wire coil. By a series of disks arranged at suitable distances from each other, the force is continued from one to another so as to produce a stroke of adequate length. Thus by continuing the power through a sufficient number of magnets, the force is obtained for useful purposes.

It has been considered too costly, but when the power is fully attained it will be far cheaper than steam. Prof. Liebig goes out of his way (Agricultural Chemistry) to run a tilt against electro-motive power. He says it is altogether fallacious ; that zinc is represented by an equivalent of carbon (coal), so that, according to the experiments of Despretz, *six pounds of zinc*, in combining with oxygen, develop no more heat than *one pound of coal*, he maintains that the heating power of the current is the equivalent or the mechanical power through electro-magnetism, or in other words, that the heat developed by the passage of the current, ought to raise steam enough to furnish a power equivalent to the electro-magnetic power of the same current, and from the fact that the mechanical force derived from the steam raised by the heating power of the current is so small, compared with that obtained by the combustion of coal, he arrives at the conclusion that electro-magnetic power " can never be used."

Those who choose to think for themselves are not turned aside from investigations by the discouragements thrown in the path, but heedless of the dried leaves of theory of those who, without the comparative anatomy of thought, beg the question, seek to apply the dynamic effects of magnetism to machinery.

A powerful magnet resembles a steam engine with an enormous piston, with an exceedingly short stroke. Hitherto every application of electro-magnetism that has been put to a practical trial, has been at variance with the laws of electricity or of mechanics ; and also, that the power of electricity, when applied in the form of an electro-magnet, is wonderfully *great* from *small* means. The difficulties will in due time yield to knowledge. What a grand problem will be solved when electro-motive power shall everywhere supplant all other motive powers,—a motive power *without fire*, and applicable everywhere it is wanted.

The triumphs of science should be ever regarded as the manifestations from a higher Providence, developing new powers for men, and preparing the instrumentalities by which it is brought about.

Mr. Hearder said that Mr. Hjorth, of Copenhagen, had lately constructed an electro-magnet of large size, with an attractive force of some hundred pounds at *a distance of upwards of three inches.*

Iron is only susceptible of a certain amount of magnetism.

Mr. Henley said he had expended hundreds of pounds of his own, and several thousands of other people's, without success. He had made a magnet which sustained the weight of *fifteen thousand pounds*, which, at the distance of three or four inches, was only *four or five pounds.* That the cost of half a horse power per day was nearly £5 ($25).

Mr. Siemens has said the cost, compared with steam, was 300 to 1.

Mr. Newton said that a rotary was made 20 years ago which showed some power.

Mr. Henry Revely states in a letter, that Mr. Palmer, of No. 122 Newgate street, (Horn & Thornthwaite's,) about 1840, made for him a polyzonal piston rod, armed with many keepers, passing up and down between an indefinite number of stages of powerful horse-shoe magnets, combined with a new mode of instantaneously making and breaking any number of circuits by means of cranks and jointed levers. Palmer found that only 6¼ per cent. of the holding power of the electro-magnet was available as motive power at the distance of the thickness of letter paper—or that a magnet of 100 lbs. holding power would only *pull 16 lbs.* at that distance.

[From the same Journal.]
PUDDLED STEEL.

Mr. Barlow states, that in addition to that quality of which the tensile strength is stated at 160,000 lbs. per inch, and in one sample 173,817 lbs., other samples, representing a different quality of the material, exhibited a strength of 112,000 lbs. per inch, or about *twice the strength of iron.*

A girder of 289 tons would possess the same effective strength as the *Menai tube,* which weighs 1,553 tons. This shows the great importance of obtaining more accurate knowledge of this new material, and whether the strength of puddled steel can be uniformly depended on, or what variations it is liable to.

Applied to roads, although capable of great duration, steel rails will not last forever; and when worn out, are more difficult than iron to repair.

The question is made whether *oil* is not a better *fuel* than *coal* for steam engines.

Wood is talked of for bearings of shafts, especially propellers, as with certain pressures it is many times more durable than metal.

Mr. Johnson.—I and my partner, Mr. Wolcott, made an electro-magnetic machine, many years ago; rotating and fixed magnets; the power exerted tangentially. Time is an element in this power, for iron is not capable of receiving the magnetic power instantaneously, but slowly. The magnets are, therefore, not charged suddenly, as is generally believed.

Mr. Seeley.—The softest iron is soonest charged; and that is so with the coils. I think that there is no hope for success with the electro machine, unless a material greatly cheaper than zinc be substituted.

Mr. Johnson.—I suggest for the reflection of members, that electricity may be available without magnetism, for motive power.

Mr. Leonard adverted to Paine's electro-magnetic engine, exhibited in in this repository some time ago, as exhibiting, by dynamometer, about one-seventh of one horse.

Mr. Seeley recommended the supply of scientific works by the Institute, for our library. It is now wanting in many.

Mr. Johnson advised the trying of experiments on production of electricity by means of combustion.

Mr. Meigs reminded members of the remarkable experiments tried by Dr. Perkins, Jr., in London, on heating water *red hot ;* using a strong iron cylinder, with a piston. The water in the cylinder, compressed by the piston, was heated red hot, and no force exhibited ! Yet, probably, if in such a state the water was allowed one inch of space more, it would have taken a mile ! by conversion into air.

Mr. Seeley.—One lb. of hydrogen is equivalent in furnishing caloric to six lbs. of coal. It is well known that copper will not decompose water nor iron either. There are no cases of explosion which can be imputed to anything but the expansive power of steam.

Mr. Brown had earnestly investigated explosions and was convinced that the mixture of explosive character is never present and cannot be produced. Expansion only does it.

Mr. Johnson called attention to the peculiar liability to explosion at the start of an engine.

Mr. Meigs asked, what is the effect on the strength of iron boilers, of the successive heatings and coolings it is subjected to ? Does it granulate the iron as in cases of percussion, as in carriage axles, &c.? The water and steam being at a given state before the engine moves, exerts no unusual force, but the moment the engine starts, steam is drawn, space made, and an effort instantly made to supply more and supplies too much ! Steam as well as water, can be heated to combustion. Our old friend Frost, with his *stame* could do it !

Mr. Cohen.—Wood, on some of our locomotive engines, is burned by the heat of the steam.

Mr. Meigs.—I melted a cannon ball in anthracite fire, the coals white hot, yet retains inside its native color and quality.

Mr. Cohen.—I have examined the iron of burst boilers and found the metal as tough as when new.

Mr. Brown.—Put a weak bar of iron on end, in a corner, for a while, and it becomes tough.

Subjects for next meeting.—" Steam or Caloric for Canal Navigation."
Adjourned.   H. MEIGS, *Secretary.*

December, 29, 1858.

Present—Messrs. Leonard, Fisher, Seeley, Chilson, Witt, Geissenhainer, Finell, Veeder, Sykes, and others—16 members.

Frederick W. Geissenhainer, jr., in the chair. Henry Meigs, Secretary.

The Secretary read the following extracts from the last works received from home and from Europe, since the last meeting, viz :

In May, 1857, this Club recommended the route proposed below :

WORLD'S TELEGRAM.

The *Invalide Russe* announces a telegram to America, across the regions of Siberia. From Portland at the mouth of the Columbia, in the Pacific, to Moscow, is only 7,000 miles, the line to extend to Kiachta, so that news from Pekin, in China, could he had in a week. He says that all the nations who want to speak to China will be obliged to do it through this line.

The cable from England to Holland has four copper wires covered with gutta percha, and that with 10 wires No. 00, thus making the cable 5 inches in circumference and ⅝ths in diameter, and weighing 8 tons 12 cwt per mile. In September last a screw steamer of 918 tons took 150 miles of it, and in three days landed the end—4 to 6 miles per hour, high wind, with a heavy sea.

[London Mechanics' Magazine. November, 1858.]

HUGHES'S TELEGRAPH—PRINTING.

We visited Mr. Henley's works at East Greenwich, and saw his instruments in operation. We believe that there is even better cause than the *Times* announced, for believing that the Atlantic cable may yet be rendered the channel for perfect communication between England and America, in both directions. What the *Times* said respecting the earth's currents is founded on fact, and we have no doubt whatever, that the Hughes instrument, as modified to suit the circumstances of the Atlantic cable, is thoroughly well adapted to the faint currents now sent through it. He has, in addition to the printing apparatus, an invention by which the faintest conceivable currents may be utilized—a battery of a couple of fragments of wire excited to an extremely low degree only. The current from this battery was, of course, so faint as to be entirely incapable of producing anything like a deflection in the needle of a fine Henly Galvanometer, even when the instrument was placed in the circuit, close to the battery. Yet, this extremely faint current, when passed through two hundred and forty miles of the Australian cable, now shipping *from* Mr. Henley's works, worked the apparatus perfectly. The conclusion is, that not only the currents obtained, at Valentia, from Newfoundland, sufficient to record signals, but may, by Hughes's apparatus, be worked, and signals recorded perfectly, even long after all currents, perceptible by the ordinary instruments, have ceased to exist.

GUTTA PERCHA AND SUBMARINE CABLES.

When the temperature is low it becomes brittle ; the consequence is, that it will break from the conducting wire when any *extra strain* occurs. It is perfectly pliable at 212° Fahrenheit. India rubber is superior to it as a covering. Spun yarn, saturated with tar, has a tendency to dissolve gutta percha or India rubber.

Vessels on Tovell's plan have marvellous speed. Two have been built and proved. The *Margaret* and the *Laughing Water*. Bishop is now building another of about 150 tons.

TALBOT—PHOTOGLYPHIC ENGRAVING.

Cover the plate with *gelatine*—that used by confectioners—a quarter of an ounce dissolved in eight or ten ounces of water, by aid of heat. To this solution add about one ounce of a saturated solution of bichromate of potash in water, all strained through linen cloth. This mixture keeps for several months. In cold weather it becomes a jelly and must be warmed for use—should be kept in a dark place. Pour a little on the plate to be engraved, spread it all over, then hold up the plate vertically and let the superfluous gelatin run off at a corner, then hold it level over a spirit lamp and dry it; it is then a yellowish film on the plate, with narrow borders of primative colors. The object to be engraved is screwed down on it in a photographic copying frame,—laces, leaves, writing, &c. Put the whole in the sunshine from one to several minutes. A faint image appears on the plate. Finely powdered gum copal is carefully, evenly spread over the plate, then hold the plate level over a spirit lamp to melt the copal—it requires considerable heat. Muriatic acid, commonly called hydrochloric, is saturated with peroxide of iron, by heat. Strain it, then evaporate some of it and bottle it. It solidifies in a brown semi-crystalline mass,—cork it well. It attracts moisture very quickly; place a powder of it spread over the plate and it deliquesces quickly. In two or three minutes it etches the plate; then wipe all off with cotton wool; pour a rapid stream of cold water on it; wipe clean with linen cloth; rub with soft whiting and water to get rid of the gelatin.

At the Royal Institution, November 2d, Mr. Malone exhibited photo-lithographs, by Poitevin's process, which are very effective for breadth and accuracy.

Carbon Printing is a subject to be brought before the Institution next meeting.

ENGRAVING COPIES.

At the positive pole of a galvanic battery a plate of iron is placed, and immersed in a proper iron solution, and on a copper plate placed at the opposite pole and likewise immersed; if the solution be properly saturated, a deposit of iron, bright and perfectly smooth, is formed on the copper plate.

SUBMARINE CABLES.

Mr. Hearder has patented one, coating the conductors with cotton, silk, wool, hair, flax, or other suitable fibrous or porous substance or substances, previous to the coat of insulating material, then the like over that, then another coat of insulating material; alternate coats as many as are requisite.

ALUMINIUM.

Luizi Ferrari Corbelli, of Florence, Italy. Patent for obtaining aluminium cheaply.

100 grammes of well washed clay; dry it, dissolve it in about six times its weight of concentrated sulphuric acid, or very strong hydrochloric acid;

dry it ; heat it in an earthen vessel up to 450° or 500° centigrade ; after which mix it with 200 grammes of yellow prussiate of potash, quite dry and pulverized. The quantity of this to be added depends, in some measure, on the quantity of siliceous matter contained in the clay. To this mixture add 150 grammes of common salt, put all in the crucible, heat to white heat. When it cools, the aluminium will be found at the bottom. I claim, particularly, the application of prussiate of potash.

SEA CABLES.

Sievier, of Middlesex. Patent. Coat copper conductors with bismuth or tin, iron, lead, brass, antimony, zinc, nickel, or any alloy of any two or more of them, previous to insulating coat. The copper conductor then is more easily insulated. Electrotype the conductors.

Mr. Seeley remarked that the rings formed of the smoke on discharges of cannon are readily produced by means of a sprinkle of hydrochloric acid over the bottom of an earthen or glass jar, and a phial of ammonia, open, placed on the bottom ; a covering of paper over the mouth of the jar, with a circular hole in the middle of it as large as a cent piece. Smoke remains in the jar, if undisturbed, but on gently tapping on the paper cover, rings are ejected at every tap.

Chairman.—The regular subject is now in order—" Canal Steam or Caloric Navigation."

Mr. Seeley.—Steam was tried on a canal boat at Rochester, on the Erie canal, some fifteen years ago. The boat and machinery were brought from Europe. It was abandoned. I have thought much on this question, and believe that steam will be found best.

Chairman.—Members will recollect that steam was tried on the Delaware canal and discontinued.

Mr. Seeley.—The well known difficulty of damage to canals by much agitation of the water, is to be always carefully provided for, let the movement of the boat be from any motor whatever.

Mr. C. W. Sykes has entertained the theory of propulsion on canals by forced jets, or sheets of air in the water, beneath the surface.

Mr. William B. Leonard.—The policy of this State, in deepening the canals, has rendered them capable of the reception of motors, other than the tedious, slow tug of horses, and therefore greatly enhanced their value, as they may now perform the work of two years in one. Mr. Paine, of Worcester, is now engaged in the construction of an engine, which, perhaps, may turn out to be very well adapted to canal navigation. Water is imbibed by loosely twisted cords of cotton, from whose capillary moisture the engine receives sufficient vapor to produce power. The contrivance is not yet finished, but seems, so far, to promise a cheap, safe and adequate power for engines for canal boats, if not for greater vessels and machinery. Some who know more about it than I do, think it will work well.

Mr. Finell had long pondered this question, and had formed a plan, the principle of which he explained and illustrated upon the blackboard. It consists of an iron plate projected in front of the boat, edgewise, under the water, and then drawn to the boat, causing little or no commotion in the water, and yet having powerful hold of the water.

Mr. Seeley observed that side paddles have one advantage, which is to break up and destroy the wave always raised by the bow of the boat, thus doing little if any damage to the banks of the canal. That the movement of that wave is estimated at from 9 to 10 miles per hour ; that if the boat could be propelled at that speed, it would ride on the wave and do very little if any injury to the banks. The experiment has been tried in Great Britain recently. Perhaps a horizontal engine, *with piston* acting horizontally, might be found best to gain motion through canals.

Mr. Leonard mentioned a machine he had seen at Albany, having belts over drums, causing a steady pull of the paddles, vertically dropt into the water. We do not hear of its practical utility, although it gave no backwater. He reminded members that the Rotary Engine, on Barrow's plan, has been tried. The perfect compactness of this form of engine greatly recommends it for canal boats, if in all other respects suitable. But the Club well knows the very great objections found to all engines formed on the principle of rotation.

Mr. Seeley.—Some of the sections of our Erie canal have banks of so firm a character that they sustain far less damage from commotion of the waters than others—the swamps, for instance, where the banks are much more easily damaged by commotion. Perhaps locomotive engines on a railroad along the sides of the canals, could tug the barges through the canal !

Chairman.—Philadelphia tried that and it proved a total failure.

A member remarked that if our canals require locomotives on rails we had better take the cargo out of the boat and put it on freight cars !

Subjects for next meeting.—" Canal Steam Navigation " continued, and, by Mr. Seeley, " Motors."

The Club adjourned at 9 o'clock, P. M., to Wednesday next, at 7 o'clock, P. M. H. MEIGS, *Secretary.*

––––––

January 5th, 1859.

John Johnson in the chair ; Henry Meigs, Secretary.

Present.—27 members.

The Secretary read an article from the London Society of Arts, speaking of the ability of Mr. Soule in steam machinery.

Frederick W. Geissenhainer, Jr., read the following paper prepared by him on the propulsion of vessels, viz:

HISTORY OF PROPULSION OF VESSELS PRIOR TO 1810.

Although no means of propulsion for vessels had ever come into extensive use, except in connection with the steam engine, yet we are not to imagine that the ancients cast no thoughts on this subject.

The *first* method of moving a vessel against wind and tide, seems to have been the art of sailing, the invention of which, as well as of letters, and astronomy, belong to the Phoenicians or inhabitants of *Tyre* and *Sidon*. For *Jason*, and the Argonauts who first sailed under *Jason*, from *Greece* to *Colchis*, in the ship "*Argo*," in quest of the *Golden fleece*,— that is, of commerce, flourished long after the Phoenicians were a powerful nation. The invention of sails is ascribed to Æolus, the "God of the Winds;" by others to Dædalus. These sails were first made of skins, which the Veneti, a people of Gaul, used even in the time of Julius Cæsar.

The next and most common method of moving vessels among the ancients was the well known system of rowing, exerting the manual strength of from one to three hundred men, according to the size of the boat, and having two, three, four and five rows or banks of oars, and called Biremes, Triremes, quadremes, quinqueremes. The Grecians, however, had vessels by sixteen tiers of oars.

While we incline to the idea that the vessels of the ancients were very small, compared with those of modern times, and are somewhat fortified in the idea by the mention made by Cicero that a vessel of 2,000 amphoræ, viz., 56 tons, was considered a large ship, (Cic. Fam., 12, 15), we are told by other authors that Ptolemy built a vessel 280 cubits, i. e., 420 feet long ; another 300 feet ; the former 7,182, the latter 3,197 tons burthen ; and we are told by Pliny, the ship which brought from Egypt the great obelisk that stood in the circus of the Vatican, in the time of Caligula, beside the obelisk, carried about 1,138 tons of ballast.

It has been asserted that boats with paddle wheels, turned by oxen within the vessel, were known to the ancient Egyptians, and it is said that there are representations of such vessels in some of the Egyptian tombs.

Boats, impelled by horses, oxen or men, were known to the Romans, Vulturius, in his rare and curious work, De Re Militari, published in 1472, gives representations of two wheel boats, one having a pair, the other five pair of wheels. These wheels, containing four paddles each, were turned by a crank in their axles, and in the one with five pair of wheels, the cranks were connected by ropes, so as to give simultaneous motion.

Wheel boats were known to the Chinese, and in the 8th vol. of the "Memoirs of the Jesuit Missionaries at Pekin," published at Paris, 1782, is an engraving and description of a vessel of war with two paddle wheels on a side, turned by men.

Many writers recommended the use of paddle wheels, or revolving oars, for the propulsion of vessels, long before the experiment arising from the use of steam. Some proposed to work them by capstans ; others by a tread-wheel ; others by a crank turned by hand ; and as far back as 1682, a wheel boat, propelled by horses, was used on the Thames.

Blasco de Garray is mentioned as the first who exhibited, in 1543, "an engine by which ships and vessels of the largest size could be propelled, even in a calm, without the aid of sails or oars."

Beyond the fact that Garray used a pair of side wheels, and a large cauldron or vessel for boiling water, we have no authentic record. It has been suggested, however, that he may have used a modification of the engine of Hero, the elder, who lived 130 years before the Christian era ; and in his works he shows beyond doubt a recognition of the two properties of steam ; expansion, and contraction, applied nearly 2,000 years before being made available for any practical purposes.

The engine of the Marquis of Worcester, although claimed by him to draw or haul boats up rivers against the stream, is entitled to little attention.

Papins' project next follows. Although he is entitled to the invention of the safety valve for boilers, and for a machine containing some of the rudiments of a condensing engine, he wholly failed to put his project of navigation to a practical test. He employed two or three steam cylinders ; a rack was placed on the piston rod, working into a pinion fastened on the axle of the revolving paddles. When one piston was ascending, the others were working downwards, and as they would give contrary motions, one was detached while the other was in action, and by these means the motion was made continuous and regular.

In 1731, Dr. John Allen proposed a plan for propelling vessels, by forcing a stream of water or air out of a tunnel or pipe at the stern of a vessel, which was to be urged forward by its reaction, imitating says Dr. Allen, what the Author of nature has shown us in the swimming of fishes, who proceed in their progressive motion not by the vibration of their fins as oars, but by protusion with their tails ; and water fowls swim forward by paddling their feet beyond their bodies. This plan, although modified from time to time, has not proved by experiment to posses any advantage.

Jonathan Hull, in 1737, published a description and draught of a new machine to carry ships out of harbor against wind and tide. This plan does not seem to have been put in practice, nor does he seem to have added anything new to the known method of propulsion, except the crank motion, of which he was the inventor and patentee. Hull proposed placing an atmospheric engine in a tug boat, and to communicate its power by means of ropes to the axis of a kind of paddle wheel, mounted in a frame-work projecting from the stern of the vessel. A contrivance was added for continuing the motion of the paddles, by the descent of counter-balancing weights in the intervals of the stroke of the piston.

To guard against the injury of the fans, or paddles, by the violence of the waves, Hull proposed to lay pieces of timber so as to swim on each side of them.

He also suggested that in inland rivers, where the bottom could possibly be reached, the fans or paddles might be taken out, and cranks placed on the hinder axis, on which the paddles were usually fixed, to strike a shaft to the bottom of the river and drive the vessel forward.

The difficulty in counter balancing the ascending stroke of the single action engine, proved an insurmountable objection to Hull's plan, and, as has been observed, a ship containing such a propelling machine would be so cumbersome as to be useless, and he advances the idea that such machinery should be placed in a separate vessel, to be used for towing vessels.

The ideas of Hull were lost sight of and forgetten, until Watt (like many others of the present day, being ignorant of previous inventions,) actually took out a patent for the application of the crank to the steam engine, patented seven years before by Hull.

Genevois, of Geneva, in 1759, published a scheme for improvement in navigation, and proposed the use of a jointed propeller, or oar wheel, which should be extended while actually propelling the boat, but should fold together so as to pass through the water with very little resistance while being moved forward to make a fresh stroke.

The propellers he intended to work by the reaction of springs, proposing the use of Newcomen's steam engine for this purpose.

In 1774, Comte d'Auxiron constructed a steamboat, but as his engine was inadequate to move the wheels, no practical advancement in the art resulted from it.

Peirer Fris resumed the d'Auxiron experiment the next year, but laboring under the same difficulty, obtained only power enough to stem the current of the Seine.

The Marquis de Jauffray, in 1778, constructed a boat 46½ inches long and 4½ broad. This vessel had a single paddle wheel on each side, with skillful machinery, but too weak for the purposes intended. Political disturbances caused the Marquis to abandon his experiments.

M. de Blanc, a French watchmaker, patented, in 1796, a method of propelling vessels by steam. This method, Jauffray claimed, was obtained from communications made by him to Blanc. Both experiments were tried on the Seine, and the method of propulsion was by means of paddles, or float boards, attached to an endless chain stretched over two wheels projecting from the side of the vessel.

While these experiments were being made in Europe, Fitch and Rumsey were making experiments in the same line in the United States. In 1783, Fitch succeeded in moving a boat on the Delaware, by means of paddles set in motion by a steam engine. Rumsey, his rival, about the same time, exhibited models of a boat which he proposed moving by *wheels, cranks* and *poles.*

In 1787, he made a voyage on the Potomac with a boat 50 feet long, propelled by the *reaction of a stream of water* drawn in at the *bow* and forced out at the *stern,* by means of a pump worked by a steam engine, which it is said made three or four miles an hour, carrying 3 tons, besides her engine, which was one-third of a ton in weight. The boiler held only 5 gallons of water, and consumed 4 to 6 bushels of coal in 12 hours.

He afterwards proposed long poles, reaching to the bed of the river, when going against rapid currents.

Becoming discontented in his rivalry with Fitch, he went to England and constructed a vessel similar to that used on the Potomac, and although he died before its completion, yet his associates completed it, and obtained a speed of 4 miles an hour against wind and tide on the Thames.

Patrick Miller, of Dumfrieshire, James Taylor and William Symington, each made experiments in the boat, the paddle wheel, and reciprocating motion of the steam engine, each having a beneficial tendency to the future introduction of steam navigation.

Miller proposed two hulls, with a paddle wheel between, so as to enable the vessel to bear sail.

In 1789, Miller constructed a large double barge, with a paddle wheel in the centre, driven by a 12 horse power engine, which made 7 miles an hour on the Forth and Clyde canal.

Symington, in 1801, commenced experimenting in steam navigation under the auspices of Lord Dundas. His object seems to have been the introduction of tug boats, instead of horses, for drawing boats on canals. In 1802, one of his boats drew, on the Forth and Clyde canal, two loaded vessels of 70 tons burden, each 19 miles, in 6½ hours, against a head wind so strong that no other vessel could move to the windward that day.

This tug boat was a short vessel with a single paddle wheel in the stern, driven by a horizontal engine, connected directly with the crank, having a cylinder 22 inches diameter and 4 feet stroke.

In this case the success of the vessel was beyond all doubt, but the project was abandoned in consequence of the injury to the banks of the canal from the undulation of the water, caused by the paddle wheel. The speed of the boat, alone, is said to have been 6 miles an hour.

In 1791, John Stevens, of Hoboken, commenced his experiments, which although more perfect than his predecessors, were unsuccessful in the great object. He succeded in impelling boats at 5 or 6 miles an hour. During these experiments he invented the *first tubular boiler*.

In 1793, the Earl of Stanhope constructed a boat on the plan of Genevois, with a propeller similar to a duck's foot, but being unable to obtain more than 3 miles an hour, it was abandoned. We find Fulton advising him to use the paddle wheel, but he declined so doing.

Chancellor Livingston now took up the subject, and constructed a boat propelled by a system of paddles resembling a chain pump, and in 1797 applied to the Legislature of New York for an exclusive grant to navigate boats by a steam engine, which was granted on condition that he should, within twelve months, produce a steam vessel that should attain a mean rate of 4 miles an hour. Although assisted by Nesbitt and Brunel, he failed to accomplish it, and being appointed minister plenipotentiary of the United States to France, he suspended his operations.

In 1801, Oliver Evans, of Philadelphia, made an experiment which may be mentioned in this connection. He built for the corporation of the city of Philadelphia, a dredging machine, weighing twenty-one tons, which he mounted on wheels, and gearing the engine to the axle, propelled the machine from his shop one and a half miles to the Delaware river. He then placed a wheel in the stern of the vessel, and propelled it on the Delaware to its point of destination.

One great improvement made by Evans, was in the form of his boiler, he being the first to make it in the form of a cylinder.

Up to this time steam navigation was in embryo, and we now come to the dawn of that great invention which has advanced civilization far beyond the hopes of its then most sanguine friends, and which, considering the immense rivers, bays, gulfs and lakes with which the United States are surrounded, seems to have been reserved by a good Providence as a part of that advancement which the *Anglo Saxon* was to achieve in carrying on the work of civilization to the westward bounds of the earth, and to bring into close proximity the distant nations of the globe, in trade, commerce, manners and customs, as well as the *advancement* of the *gospel*.

Livingston met Fulton at Paris, and the result of the interview was a series of experiments as to the best mode of propulsion. After repeated experiments the paddle wheel was found to possess the greatest advantage. Fulton simplified the engine of Watt, and contrary to those who preceded him, made the relation of the force of the engine and velocity of the wheels and the resistance of the water to the motion of the vessel, a preliminary calculation. So exact were his calculations, that the speed of his vessels were told while only the plan had been drawn. Fulton constructed his boat, called the Clermont, which was 133 feet long, 7 feet deep, and 18 feet breadth. The cylinder of the engine (one made by Watt and Bolton) was two feet in diameter and four feet stroke; the wheels (side paddles), fifteen feet in diameter and four feet face, dipping two feet in the water. Vessel 160 tons burden.

After several experimental trips, the Clermont, in 1807, was started as a passenger boat to Albany. Her first passage was performed in thirty-two hours, there being a head wind and adverse tide each way. The trip was performed wholly by steam. Thus, by the talent, energy and perseverance of Fulton, the crude and previously abortive schemes of other inventors were carried into practical and beneficial operation.

It would be interesting to follow the progress of steamboats from that time to the present, but I have only adduced the application of steam to navigation to show what has been done up to Fulton's time, and more particularly in reference to the propulsion of small boats; for of this class all canal boats are necessarily rated.

Steam on canals will be seen had been tried to some extent, and the side wheel and stern wheel had been found impracticable. About 1838 the screw was introduced. "The screw of Archimedes" was the designation given to it, but it will be noticed that it differs essentially from the Archimedean screw, probably so called from the fact that it was first tried in a yacht called the "Archimedes." The vessel built in 1839 had a screw applied and placed in the dead wood under its counter, between the keel and stern post. The screw consisted of a helix, making one revolution about a horizontal axle passing longitudinally through the ship, and put in motion by a steam engine ; and it was found on experiment to work well, and to have a propelling power equal to the paddle wheel.

This screw has undergone various modifications. In one improvement the helix is made of two parts, each equal to half a revolution, placed at a small distance from each other on the same axle. By this disposition it is supposed that the escape of the water, after it has been acted upon by the screw to propel the vessel, will be facilitated, and, I may add, all the disadvantages of back water overcome by perforations in the arms near the " hub," as recently patented in England.

In regard to the navigation of our canals by steam, the washing of the banks seems to be one of the great points to be accomplished. I do not hesitate to say that it cannot be *entirely* avoided. It is impossible to move any body, be it ever so small, in water without displacing it to some extent. Drop a piece of stone in a glass of water, you displace it in every part just in proportion to the bulk of the stone. So a vessel passing displaces the water on either side in proportion to its bulk in the water. This causes a rise and fall or undulated wave on the shore—not so much attributable to the motion caused by its propelling power, as to the displacement following the passage of the cut-water through the water. Various modes might be proposed to get rid of the motion caused by the wheels or propellers, could we get rid of the displacement. Setting the wheels at such an angle as to throw the motion on the center of the canal, or the more recent and scientific plan, as shown on Montgomery's Archmedean propeller, being the ordinary screw propeller, with a rim controlling the flow of water in a line parallel, or rather consequentive with the shaft.

The use of the propeller on the Delaware and Raritan canal, will show that, in order to make steam profitable to canal navigation, the canal must be made suitable first ; and unless the banks of the canal are secured by sheet piling, stone or masonry, all methods to introduce steam will be found more or less objectionable, inasmuch as it will be impossible to acquire any considerable speed without washing the banks just in proportion to such speed ; and the most we can hope for will be a slow speed, but a little beyond that of horse power.

Mr. Stetson said that we can learn much from Soule, of Manchester, whose researches are highly valued for scientific and practical character. We find that out of all the power we make, we only *realize* from five to ten per cent of it in utilizing it.

Mr. Reed.—Steam will extinguish incandescent coals, and when applied in the holds of ships or any tight rooms, will reach every particle of fire and put it out—it abstracts all the oxygen, so that fire cannot live in it.

Mr. Sewall.—Pipes to carry steam from the boiler to the interior of the vessel, were tried in our steam frigate Mississippi.

Mr. Seeley.—Steam for extinguishing fire was suggested twenty-five years ago. Flame is extinguished by steam—heat remains. Difficult in application to buildings, on account of the access of air.

Mr. Fisher.—Valuable goods receive much damage from steam. A cleanly gas would do better if it could be applied—the carbonic acid gas might be generated by acid or crushed marble, ready in the lower part of the building. Water does great damage!

Mr. Seeley.—No person could enter the building while the gas was in it.

Mr. Meigs.—Would the gas be generated fast enough to arrest the fire?

Mr. Butler.—Cotton mills have tried them—pipes from the boilers to the picking rooms, especially—where the cotton is in a very inflammable form.

Mr. Stetson.—There is a patent for steam extinguishers. I examined boats at the west which had pipes from the boilers leading through the decks to the interior of the boat, to force in steam. I have not heard of such a boat being burned.

Mr. Reed.—I saw it succeed in a wood yard on fire—as far as the steam could reach it.

Mr. Butler.—Timber on fire and well charred extinguished by steam arising from water on the floors making steam. As a fire extinguisher it has been talked of some years ago.

Mr. Sewall.—As an engineer, I have recommended it for ships—but the owners will not adopt any plan of the sort.

Mr. Fisher.—If those owners were prosecuted and damages recovered for *lost lives*, means to prevent fires in ships would be immediately *provided.* Applause.

The Chairman.—At sea the velocity of the ship through the water has been made to serve as a power to force water through a tube by the side of the ship above her deck, and a large and steady stream discharged upon her deck! A water ram may be used with effect.

Mr. Reed.—The steam apparatus is to be put into the new ship *Karnak.*

Mr. Henry, of Flushing, exhibited his model of canal boat and Archimedean screw propeller.

Mr. Fisher proposed as a subject for next meeting, "Steam fire engines." Adopted by the club.

Mr. Henry spoke of Paine's new hot air engine with its partial supply of water, through the capillary attraction of cords of loose twisted cotton, whose moisture united with the hot air, &c.

Mr. Sewall.—Lord Stirling made a hot air engine twenty-five years ago; it worked for some two years and cracked. It first expanded the air and then contracted it, using the difference for power.

At 10¼ P. M., the Club adjourned.

H. MEIGS, *Secretary.*

January 12, 1858.

Present—Messrs. S. D. Tillman, Rev. Mr. Adamson, Stetson, Seeley, Manning, Eunson, Fisher, Cohen, Edgerly, Bruce, Witt, Johnson, Leonard, and others—twenty-nine members in all.

S. D. Tillman in the chair. Henry Meigs, Secretary.

The Secretary read the following extracts from scientific works last received from abroad and home, viz:

PAINTED STATUARY.

Sir J. Gardner Wilkinson has examined the question and finds that it was universal among the ancients. Bas relievos or alto relievos all painted. The earliest statues were all painted red. They could not bear the naked bright white marble statuary. The Romans gave an annual coating of vermillion to their statues—gave colored eyes and colored dress. They also used metallic compounds to color the bronze statues. The colored marble busts in the Capitol Museum, show that their now white faces were once painted to correspond. The old wooden colossal acroliths, (wooden bodies with stone heads and feet) of the time of Phidias, were covered with real drapery, and the faces colored (probably) to life. Etruscan bas relief, flesh colored figures. Spain now has colored statues of kings, martyrs, saints, &c. The Greeks sometimes gilded as well as painted statues, and sometimes left them without.

ARCHITECTURE.

It has been supposed that the ancients did not understand the use and properties of the arch. There are round arches made of brick at Thebes, built 1490 years before our Saviour !

SCHOOL OF ART.

Ruskin, in his inaugural address before the Cambridge School of Art, October 29, 1858, said : " Examine the history of nations and you will find this great fact, clear and unmistakable on the front of it. That *good art has only* been produced by nations who rejoiced in it, fed themselves with it as if it were bread ; basked in it, as if it were sunshine ; shouted at the sight of it ; danced with the delight of it ; quarrelled for it ; fought for it ; starved for it ; did in fact precisely the opposite with it of what we want to do with it—*they made it to keep, and we to sell !*" We have made a great fuss about the patterns of silk lately, wanting to vie with Lyons ! Well, we may try forever, so long as we don't really enjoy silk patterns we shall never get any, and we don't enjoy them. We make a dress to fit well, but we don't enjoy the beauty of the silk ! I have the weakness to enjoy (as all good students and all good painters do,) the dress patterns, whether of Fra Angelico, Perugino, John Bellini, Giorgione, Titian, Tintoret, Veronese, Leonardo da Vinci. The Queen is one of the loveliest of Veronese's female figures. I was one day upwards of two hours *vainly* trying to render with perfect accuracy, the *curves of two leaves of the brocaded silk of her dress !*

PHOTOGRAPH.

Mr. George Downes, of the Photographic Institution, (London, November 1858,) has produced in the manner of M. Le Grai, four stereoscopic marine views, singularly bright and instantaneous in effect. The surf breaks on the shore with the tumultuous crash and white silvery glitter of live sea.

Mr. Tillman called for the reading of an article in the American Journal of Science and Arts, for November last, relative to the claim of originality in the inventions of *Physionometer*, for accuracy in making moulds from objects in relief, a great aid to statuaries; also the screw propeller and the reducer, a pantograph for the sculptor. Those are (in France,) ascribed to Frederick Sauvage, a native of Boulogne, sur mer, in September, 1785. In 1811 he was employed to construct steamboats to run between Boulogne and London. He became discouraged and died insane in 1857.

Several members—Stetson, Leonard and others, claimed for steam navigation an American origin, and the condensation of steam by the methods ascribed to Alexis Sauvage—the supply of distilled or pure water to prevent incrustation, burning of the boiler, waste of fuel, and explosion of the boilers. Stephen A. Gold, an American, constructed a steamboat for ocean navigation, in which the steam was condensed in a hollow metal keel, with perfect success.

Mr. Stetson stated that Pierson, of New York, made a condenser, still in use, better than Hall's, of England, and it is now on the ship Adriatic, and in some of our war vessels.

Mr. R. G. Eunson explained the condensation and air pump as applied to some western steamers. The air pump cannot be dispensed with, and high steam can be more easily condensed than the low steam—150 pounds on a square inch than 50 pounds.

Mr. Stetson.—It requires air pump to work it. In 1852, or '53, Joshua Lowe tried it here on a stationary engine, but his valves necessarily worked with such great rapidity, striking like sledge hammers, that they soon ruined the machine. The atmospheric air always contained in water must be pumped out, and some water with it.

Mr. Eunson.—I use a hydrostatic pump. There can be no condensing in high pressure engine without air pump.

Mr. Seeley.—Common water always contains atmospheric air. A *cubic inch* of water forms *a cubic foot of steam* or about 1728 times more volume. Is there an intermediate stage between them?

Mr. Cohen.—None. At the right moment of absorption of heat by water, it *flashes into steam!* and in freezing, it also may be said to *flash into ice!* There is no intermediate state.

The subject of the day: "Steam Fire Engines," was taken up.

Mr. Fisher explained the construction of the Lee and Larned engine, of the principal parts of which he was the inventor. A steam carriage with locomotive engine modified is the steam fire engine. The character of boiler most suitable, was discussed. It is not yet satisfactorily developed, but it can be made to do much greater work than any hand engine—to be kept in readiness with its fire and steam—run faster to the fire than the hand engine!—pour on a larger and steadier stream of water. Although heavy, its steering apparatus, which I govern by a screw, is perfectly capable of controlling it.   It is practicable to make one as light as a hand engine.

Mr. Manning said the noise alarmed cattle and horses very much, and that in its noise and speed it would be dangerous in such a street as Broadway and very difficult to work in our narrow streets.   Its noise must be smothered in some way.   I have ridden on Dudgeon's engine—it was very manageable in Broadway among omnibuses, carts and carriages.

Mr. Fisher.—It weighs 3,000 lbs.

Mr. Leonard.—I rode through the city on Dudgeon's engine—occasionally at a speed of *eighteen miles an hour.*   Horses were much alarmed by its noise, as they usually are by engines, until used to it on our railways. It was easy to start, to turn and to stop.

The Chairman.—Good steam fire engines are now made in considerable numbers at the Seneca Falls factories—cost $5,000 each—to be drawn by two horses.   The steam is got up in them in five minutes.

Mr. Edgerly.—We have no buildings over one hundred feet high !   Our hand engines always get to a fire before you hear a fire bell toll the district !   More harm is often done to goods by water instead of fire.   The most powerful steam fire engine could only deaden a heavy fire.

The Chairman.—Cincinnati has tried them and now has a corps paid, with their steam fire engines.

Mr. Manning.—The city of St. Louis also.

Mr. Fisher.—On a smooth McAdamized road the engines can run forty miles an hour.

Mr. Seeley mentioned expansion and contraction of metal as a source of motive power.

Mr. Stetson.—Berdan availed himself of it in heating the ovens of his Automatic bakery, by using brass rods connected with the cast iron valves, so as to open or close them as the heat increased or diminished.   How many steam fire engines have been made ?

Mr. Manning.—One was burned in its house in Boston.

Mr. Fisher.—Denied by the mayor of that city.   It was one of Latta's.

Subject for next meeting : " The form and style of a suitable building for the American Institute."

The Club meets every Wednesday, at 7 o'clock P. M.

Adjourned.   H. MEIGS, *Secretary.*

————

January 19, 1858.

Present—Messrs. Stetson, Sewall, Cohen, Dr. Treadwell, Mr. Treadwell, Veeder, Brower, Haskell, Bruce, Rev. Dr. Adamson, Sherry, Seeley, Sykes, Chambers, and others—29 members in all.

John P. Veeder in the chair.   Henry Meigs, Secretary.

The Secretary read the following extract:

[London Society of Arts, November 24, 1858.]

Mr. F. Joubert read a paper on a method of rendering copper engraved plates capable of producing a greatly increased number of impressions. The valued engravings of the last century, Hogarth, Strange, Heath, and others, were in great demand, and as copper would not supply it, steel plates were substituted for engravings some forty years ago. We now harden the face of copper plate engravings by coating them with a thin film of iron, effected by placing the plate at the negative pole of the galvanic battery, and a plate of iron at the positive pole, and both plates immersed in a proper iron solution—a deposit of iron, bright and perfectly smooth, is thrown upon the copper plate. This coat can be removed and renewed as often as is required. It is said that twelve thousand impressions from one copper plate can be taken.

The subject of erecting a " a suitable edifice for the American Institute " being called up,

Mr. Leonard said that his idea of it was one extensive floor, safe for crowds of persons, presenting the whole exhibition at a glance—such a view was always interesting. His long experience in fairs satisfied him that no building for such crowds and such exhibitions should be much elevated. He acted a part in the management of the late Crystal Palace, while it held the World's Fair, as well as that of the American Institute. He has examined the edifices for like purposes in other cities. That in addition to the great works of our people in still life, in the composition of the fair, few were more interesting than the magnificent machinery of our people in full action, from the smallest moving powers to the most massive—from a card-printer to a Hoe's printing press—from a watch movement to the most powerful steam motor, or perhaps the turning and boring of 30 ton shafts or Dahlgreen cannon of many tons weight. All this demands space and perfect strength, while the spectators in tens of thousands can examine all with as much feeling of safety as if they were in an open garden.

When this Institute, in its infancy, held a fair in one room in the former Masonic Hall, on Broadway, opposite to the New York Hospital, it required power to put some small machinery in motion, and was actually obliged to hide a stout negro man to turn a crank for a loom weaving woolen cloth—the first power loom ever used for woolen. We have attracted, by our fairs, hundreds of thousands of persons to the city, whose money remained for our benefit. This city demands such exhibitions, and to refuse us a place to hold them on, would make the very stones in our streets *cry out shame.*

Mr. Sykes thought an entire block would be necessary, with stores, &c., on its exterior to let, while the whole interior could be occupied with the fair.

Dr. Holton read an extract from the Caen Stone Series, written in 1858, describing a union between the American Institute, Lyceum of Natural History, Historical Society, Observatory, and kindred associations, seeking at the present time a permanent depository for their treasures of nature, science and art. This union is represented as already effected and the buildings completed. For these societies the State and city governments had erected a substantial four story fire proof building, one thousand feet long, terminated by two pavilions, accessible by cars uniting the Hudson and East rivers, and the railroad lines extending from the southern to the northern limits of Manhattan Island.

For the cultivation and sale of plants, seeds and flowers, the basement, the first and second stories, were rented to florists, having uniform, lofty rooms of the height of two stories, projecting east and west, with roof and walls of glass. The third story was occupied by the American Institute, and contained models of furnaces, steam engines, locomotives, bake-houses, iron foundries, wash-houses, roofing, iron promenade roofs overlaid with asphaltum, apparatus for heating and lighting, turning-lathes, capstans, cranes, freight-arms, bridges, markets, stewards' depots, carpentry, pulleys, diving-bells, printing presses, looms, spinning machines, ropewalks, a collection of weights and measures of countries with which the great emporium is commercially connected, agricultural implements, astronomical instruments, &c.; also a library on subjects connected with agriculture, arts, and trades.

The fourth story was to be occupied, one half by the Horticultural Society, and the other by the New York Lyceum of Natural History, rent free, on condition that they there open a perpetual exhibition, free to the public from sunrise till sunset, except on the Sabbath; a suitable police guard and other attendants being furnished by the city.

Each of these societies established a co-ordinate department, auxiliary to the Exchange Lyceum, reciprocating in products of nature and art with individuals, and with corresponding societies in all the States of the Union, and in remote parts of the earth.

On the right and left rose two pavilions, on square bases, of which one side exceeded the breadth of the main building, surmounted by towers.

The pavilion of the south was remarkable for the beauty of its proportions, and the character of solidity it at the same time possessed. On the first floor were the central offices of the police telegraphs, establishing instantaneous communication with all the watch-towers.

The second and third stories united, made a large room for public lectures, for the public meetings of the American Institute, the associations and societies located in the pavilions, and in the other parts of the city, and for the exhibitions of the Horticultural Society. Here the annual course of lectures on Astronomy attracted auditors from a great distance.

On the fourth story was a select library of mathematical, philosophical, geographical, and astronomical works.

Here was a bureau of longitudes and triangulations, co-operating with similar bureaux in other cities, greatly aided by the net-work of telegraphs throughout the land. Here, also, was a school for navigation and civil engineering, sustained by the Legislature, and free to pupils from every State and nation. These subjects were seen to be of increasing importance.

Here were rooms for the professors, assistants, and students of the Observatory. The fifth and sixth stories were especially devoted to the purposes of the Observatory, and private study in the grand problems relating thereto.

On the roof, at the four corners, were turrets opening downward to the Observatory rooms, and crowned with rotary cupolas, by means of which the astronomers might safely direct their instruments to any part of the heavens, without inconvenience from the weather.

On the roof were several pluviameters, for ascertaining the quantity of rain, and two anemometers, which indicated the direction of the wind upon duplicate dials; one pair of which was in the Observatory room, and the other in the lecture room below.

Above this pavilion rose the tower, ascended by winding stairs within, having platforms at three several heights, with exterior balustraded promenades. Next above was a circular apartment, presenting on the northern, western, southern and eastern faces dials, marking the hour to citizens.

This was crowned with a dome, in manner and for purposes similar to those on the turrets described, and under the direction of a principal, with assistants, one of whom (by reason of the advantages of this position) was charged with the special and constant duty of city watch, who, by a speaking-tube, and also by telegraphic wires, was in easy communication with the fire and police departments on the first floor, and through them with all the city.

The northern pavilion was for purposes connected with a new order of city interests, for a detailed description of which reference should be had to the Caen Stone Series. This temple of science had also a central pavilion, bearing a lofty tower, upon each of the four corners of which stood colossal statues.

On the south-west angle stood Washington, ever hopefully regarding the full development of the institutions of freedom in these United Republics.

On the south-east stood Fulton, gratefully beholding the triumphs of steam navigation, emanating from this city, the future centre of the commercial world.

On the north-west stood Clinton, looking complacently at the enlargement of our canals and the extension of his sagacious schemes; not did he view with a jealous eye the ship canal from Buffalo to Lake Ontario.

On the north-east angle stood Morse, joyfully contemplating the success of national and international telegraphs, reciprocating the movements of thought.

Mr. Stetson.—The edifice should be central as to population. That as theaters are usually located by the proprietors with that view exclusively, we may well follow their example.

Mr. Seeley.—Broadway, lower part, best. That the edifice should be made more attractive, and do more public good, by clubs, lectures, library, reading rooms, repository for works of genius, art, industry, always open to the world, free of charge, than by one annual fair.

Dr. Treadwell described the building of the Maryland Institute at Baltimore. It has not a quarter of the space we had at the Crystal Palace. I prefer Reservoir Square here for our building; population grows rapidly out to it, and it will soon become central enough.

Mr. Brower.—The center of population of the whole surrounding country moves down town ; our park and city hall are already near it.

Mr. Treadwell, Jr.—All admit the superiority of one floor to hold the whole exhibition, and our people will not, and ought not, to trust themselves in such crowds—tens of thousands—much above the solid earth. As to centrality, a great change will be effected every five or ten years.

Secretary Meigs.—It is proper that we should avail ourselves of all knowledge, and experience is best of all. The Romans, after several centuries of steady industry, by Cato and others gardeners, while, as Juvenal says, " all the men were brave and all the women chaste," no public shows or theatres were wanted ; but when they began to be wealthy, towards the Christian era, they would have theatres. Their best rulers, whether consuls or emperors, always opposed them. Yet they came, first small, then movable, of wood, and at last a freeman of Rome formed a company to build a large one of wood. He selected for its site " the Greenwich village of Rome," viz., Fidenæ, about the same distance from Rome that the late Crystal Palace was. He said he could make it large and strong enough for all Rome to get in and be safe. He procured timbers, some of which were the largest then known ; they *squared four feet*. On the completion of it all Rome was in exstacy. Fifty thousand of the people could get in at once! They got in. It fell and killed about *nine thousand* of the best society ! This checked *bad* building and shows for some time. But in the time of Vespasian, against his wish, they clamored for a theatre. The wise and good Emperor said, If you will have a theatre, I will build you a proper one. He gave Rome the Coliseum, with ground room five and a quarter acres ; stone seats for 87,000 persons, and standing room for 22,000, with vomitories (passages) enough to let all out in a few minutes ; without a roof, having sheets of cloth to keep off water, &c. This was the acme of theatrical glory, Rome said of it, " Dum stat Coliseum stet Roma. Qundo cadit Coliseum cadet Roma." Their sublime law, " Salus populi suprema lex," should be our law.

Mr. Sherry.—Safety is near the ground. Country people visit you more than citizens do. Provide where you will, the country people will come to see it.

Mr Meigs had been consulted by a large landholder, as to the centre of this population. Had been commissioner on streets and avenues, and considered the growth of this city, and that, singular as it may now seem, that centre was about our battery, looking to the certain immense growth of Brooklyn and to adjacent Jersey ; and he had no doubt but Brooklyn would rapidly reach, and very far surpass, this city in population, owing to its admirable location, facilities, &c.

Mr. Sykes thought that a lofty and splendid building of glazed brick, of variegated color, should be erected on Broadway, *seven stories high!*

Dr. Holton described the Conservatoire des Arts et Métiérs of Paris, as worthy of imitation as a permanent exhibition.

Mr. Seeley liked that plan, and premiums for best articles could always be awarded.

Mr. Sperry spoke of the permanently great leader of the country as being New York. Nature decreed it. It is leader, and should prove its pre-eminence by suitable institutions of such character and magnitude as became the most illustrious city in the world.

Mr. Sherry exhibited his new propeller, a *screw of four blades* within, and attached to a suitable cylindric section, to give much greater strength to the blades, contract the body of water while acted upon by them, and defend them from floating logs and other things to break the blades.

Mr. Stetson.—This propeller band is not new. The points of screw blades have been secured by bands. The Philadelphia propeller blades are inclined towards the point of delivery, and their points are slightly curved towards the immersion, the propeller being something tunnel formed. England has talked of and used in propellor blades the parabolic form, which have found patents.

Mr. Sewall.—It is found that a small number of blades is best, for friction must be avoided, and in rapid revolution the screw has little power, for it *breaks the water all to pieces!* Two blades are probably better than four, up to a certain velocity.

Mr. Haskell held the same opinion, assigning manifest reasons for that fault in screw propulsion.

Mr. Seeley justified in some measure the title *Archimedean*, given to a propeller.

Mr. Sewall.—When our distinguished citizen, John Stevens, of Hoboken, first used a screw propeller, he called it a scull, the blade of the oar acting alternately like the blades of the screw.

Rev. Dr. Adamson proposed, as a good question for the Club, " Escapes from buildings on fire." " The telescope," " A suitable edifice for the American Institute," and " Motors," continued.

At 10½ o'clock P. M. adjourned.   H. MEIGS, *Secretary.*

———

January 26, 1859.

Present — Messrs. President Pell, Rev. Dr. Adamson, Chambers, Bruce, Butler, Stetson, Cohen, Leonard, Dr. Holton, Tillman, Seeley, Manning, John Johnson, Breisach, Brower, Sykes, Fitz, and others—33 members.

Mr. Pell in the chair. Henry Meigs, Secretary.

Mr. Stetson spoke of the present uncertainty in the Steam Fire Engine, compared with the hand engines. Our experience in them is, however, narrow. I believe, however, in their ultimate success.

Mr. Edgerly.—They burst their hose in consequence of the suddenness with which they force the water, notwithstanding their air chambers, which are unequal to the power of steam, yet manageable in hand engines.

Mr. Leonard.—Lee & Larned's Steam Fire Engine has air chambers, but it appears to me that they are not large enough to give the requisite elasticity.

Mr. Edgerly.—Fire companies are prejudiced against them, as tending to supplant our volunteer system by paid companies, as in New Orleans, St. Louis and Philadelphia. Our firemen's fund of $100,000 will suffer. The steam power, propelling the engines to fires through our crowded streets, is very objectionable. It must be done by men or horses, or by hand.

The subject of the evening being called up, the Chairman said that he would open the subject.

The Telescope is derived from the Greek words τηλη, distant; σκοπεω, I look at; and is an optical instrument used for the purpose of viewing distant objects.

I intend this evening to trace human progress and intelligence, as far as this great invention is concerned, from the commencement to the present time. It was no doubt invented by Baptista Porta, but did not, in his hands, assume sufficient maturity to be usefully applied for celestial and terrestrial examinations. It has, however, been ascribed by Descartes to James Metius, a citizen of Alkmaer, in Holland; by Huygens, to John Jeppersey; by Prof. Moll, after thoroughly examining the official papers in the archives at the Hague, to Jacob Adriaancy, on the 17th of October, 1608, with whom the art died. In 1609, the renowned Gallileo invented a telescope that magnified three times; he increased the power in subsequent trials, and in 1610 observed the satellites of Jupiter.

Sir Isaac Newton, in the year 1671, discovered and made the reflecting telescope; its speculum was two inches and three-tenths in diameter, its focal length six inches, and it magnified 38 times. It is now in possession of the Royal Society of England. When I saw it the eye-glass was gone, and it looked as if it had passed through the wars.

The next telescope was constructed by Hadley, in 1723, the speculum of which was 6 inches, its focal length 63 inches, and magnified 230 times. It is also owned by the Royal Society, and is in a dilapidated condition.

Short succeeded Hadley, and greatly excelled him; but when he died, destroyed his tools, and all that he had made, that posterity might not be aided by the knowledge he had acquired. He made short work of it.

Next came the immortal Herschel, whose unhampered thought made a bold attempt to explore the extent of God's works, but his great reflector only enabled him to see a mere speck, space being infinite. Were the great Architect of the skies to permit him to place his telescope on his namesake, additional revelations would be impressed upon his telescopic sphere, garnished with suns and starry configurations, marvellous as those we now behold to-night.

Watson followed, and his telescopes, in composition, polish, and figure, were truly exquisite. His largest did not exceed nine inches aperture, but they were never equalled before him.

Tully was contemporary to Watson, though his telescopes were superior to Short's, they were inferior to Watson's.

Ramage, in 1820, constructed a telescope 15 inches in diameter and 25 feet focal length, which remained for many years in the Royal Observatory at Greenwich, where its performances were ridiculed. It is now in the Observatory of Glasgow.

Lord Oxmantown's telescope has overcome many of Herschel's difficulties, and carried to an extent he did not dare contemplate the illuminating power, together with a sharpness of definition, little, if at all, inferior to that of the achromatic. The moon's appearance, through his instrument, was magnificent beyond expression.

In 1853, an immense telescope was constructed in England, under the supervision of M. Gavatt. The tube was 76 feet long, slung at the side of a brick tower 64 feet high, and 15 feet in diameter. It resembles a cigar, with the eye-piece at the narrow end, and a dew cap at the other; making the total length, when in use, 85 feet. The design of the dew cap is to prevent obscuration by the condensation of moisture, which takes place during night when the instrument is in use. The exterior is of bright metal, while the interior is black. The tube, at its greatest circumference, measures 18 feet, and this part is 24 feet from the object glass. The optical works and the object glasses were executed by Slater. Two glasses are used, one of flint and the other plate. The plate glass lens has a positive focal length of 30 feet $1\frac{1}{2}$ inches; the flint glass lens has a negative focal length of 49 feet $10\frac{1}{2}$ inches. These two lenses placed in contact, are used in combination, and constitute the achromatic object of glass. The magnifying powers of this instrument range from five hundred to three thousand. A letter a quarter of an inch high can be read at a distance of half a mile; still its performances in that year were confused and unsatisfactory.

But of all the telescopes ever invented, the world-renowned Lord Rosse's possesses peculiar qualities of superiority, which enable those having access to it to collect light, and penetrate into regions of previously unknown space. It enters into indefinite nebulous forms, which can only be observed generally by other instruments, and exhibits wonderful configurations altogether unimagined before—actually converting what we consider nebulous fields of light, into superb clusters of stars. And it promises to be of immense importance in reference to the dynamical principles on which remote suns are sustained, while whirling about within their respective orbits. By its revelations thousands of nebulæ have already been cata-logued, and tens of thousands are still to be.

The tube of this wonderful telescope is 56 feet long, made of wood one inch thick, and hooped with iron ; its diameter is 7 feet. It is placed be-tween two walls, and commands a view for half an hour on each side of the meridian ; that is, its whole motion, from east to west, is limited to fifteen degrees. It has a reflecting surface of 4,071 square inches, while that of Herschel's forty-foot telescope had only 1,811.

Sir James South made a trial of this instrument in 1845, and said, "Never before in my life did I see such glorious sidereal pictures. The nebulæ in the Canes Vevatici was resolved into a large globular cluster of stars, not unlike that in Hercules."

The great nebulæ of Orion has been examined with every telescope made since the first inventor, without the remotest aspect of a stellar con-stillation.

But in March, 1846, Lord Rosse reported that he plainly saw through his telescope, a mass of stars about the trapezium, and that the rest of the nebulæ abounded with stars. It has proved that the bright stars, com-prized between the first and fourth magnitudes, are one quarter physically double ; that is to say, one out of four. The probability is, that the num-ber of compound systems is less than the number of insulated stars. Such is admitted to be the power of Rosse's telescope, that if a star of the first magnitude were removed to such a distance that its light would require three millions of years to reach us, this marvelous instrument would show it to our eye. The range opened to us by Rosse's telescope may be appre-hended by the measurement, not of distances in leagues, or tens of millions of leagues or diameters of our little earth's orbit, but of the advancement of light in free space. It requires one hundred and thirty-five years for the flight of light from a fixed star of the sixth magnitude to reach us.

Leon Foucault formed a telescope speculum of silvered glass, in which experiment he used glass that was not transparent, but in fact imperfect, but still free from air bubbles. On this he deposited a film of silver of uniform thickness, and found it became transparent, transmitting a blue light, and the reflecting surface was exceedingly brilliant. Dr. Greer often examined, and looked through the different mirrors constructed on this novel principle, and actually put them to a severe test, by comparing one of seven inches with an achromatic of fine quality, and pronounced Mr. Foucault's superior.

I have so frequently used the term achromatic, and may so often use it again before bringing this subject to a close, that I will in this connection say a few words concerning it.

Achromatism, means the destruction of primary colors, which invariably accompany the image of any object seen through a lens or prism. Light is compounded of rays unequally refrangible and is not homogeneous. In passing into a telescope, some of the rays are refracted and bent out of their course more than others ; when the image of an object, seen through it was indistinct, compressed and encircled by a colored ring. This was for years the chief and most formidable obstacle presented to the manufacturers of telescopes, who brought to their aid mathematicians, artists and chemists ; all of whom for a long period of ti ue, believed and reported that achromatism was utterly impossible, and that light could not be deflected, without being decomposed. Even the great men were led to this conclusion, by imperfect and badly conducted experiments. Subsequent discoveries have proved that the rays of light may be curved without being separated. But notwithstanding the progress that has been made in the theory of light and colors, the subject of achromatism is still one of the most embarrassing in regard to theory and practice. Plato considered it to be an usurpation of the rights of God, to attempt the investigation of this mystery of nature. At length Sir Isaac Newton brought his great mind to bear upon the subject, and demonstrated, by many decisive experiments, that color depends not on any modification of light acquired by reflection or refraction, but is inherent in the light itself; the solar rays being composed of rays of all the colors contained in the spectrum, which are differently affected while passing through refracting medea. The merit of the discovery of achromatic compensation is now supposed, and generally conceded to belong to John Dolland, who reasoning from the construction of the eye, which is a perfect achromatic instrument, and skillful experiment tend to the practical improvement, and the subsequent discoveries of Fraunhofer have opened up a new view of the composition of the spectrum.

The vision of telescopes must always be more or less impaired by natural occurrences that are forever happening. Every living animal moving on the earth causes vibrations, some of which were so fine as to be utterly unknown before high magnifying powers incontestibly proved their existence. Early on any Sunday morning, you may place your ear close to the ground at Fourth street, corner of the Sixth avenue, and hear the first car leave its depot at Forty-first, which if there were no other occurrences of the same character, happening at the same time, would effect the high powers of a telescope at Fourth street. Thunder, percussions, wind, roaring of the ocean, are always occurring, so that the surface of the earth is never free from vibrations, sufficient to disturb the passage of light through telescopes, and cause the heavenly bodies to twinkle into large diameters, and this will limit high powers.

A water telescope has been invented arranged for two eyes, with which instrument objects have been distinctly seen on the bottom of the ocean where the water was seventy-two feet deep.

The reason why we rarely see the bottom of a clear lake, or sea, where the depth is within the power of vision, is not that the light is reflected from objects at the bottom so feeble as to be imperceptible to us from their passage through the dense medium of water, but from the irregular refractions given to the rays in passing out of the water into the atmosphere, caused by the ripple on the surface, where the refraction takes place; when these obstructions are removed, we can distinctly see the bottom. The tube of the marine telescope screens the eyes from reflection, because the water comes in contact with the glass plate, so that the person looking through the tube, sees distinctly the objects at the bottom.

Light passing through salt water, loses half of its intensity for every fifteen feet through which it passes.

A new reflecting telescope has been constructed by Mr. Lyman of Lenox, Massachusetts, the tube of which is composed of thick Russia iron. Up to 1852, this telescope, in point of optical power, was in advance of anything before achieved in this country. It separated double stars, distant from each other half a second of arc.

Yale College has a telescope made by Dolland, of London; it has a focal length of ten feet, and an aperture of five inches. The object glass is perfectly achromatic, and for objects that require a fine light it is a superior instrument.

In 1852, an achromatic refracting telescope, manufactured by Clark, of Boston, was presented to Williams College. It is mounted equatorially, and has a clock movement. The sixth star in the trapezium of Orion, has been seen by it, which is certainly an indication of its superiority.

The Hudson Observatory, in Ohio, has an equatorial telescope, with a transit circle and clock; it was made by Simms, of London, and clock by Molineux, and has a mercurial pendulum.

The Philadelphia High School have an equatorial telescope, made by Merz and Mahler, of Munich. It is of eight feet focal length, and six inches aperture, with clock-work movement, and has a variety of powers to 480 with micrometers. This instrument was the most superior that had been imported from Europe up to 1840, and introduced Munich to America.

The Philadelphia Observatory became celebrated at home and abroad for having furnished 436 moon culminations, and 120 star occultations, together with a series of observations for latitude.

At West Point we have a large equatorial telescope, made by Lerebours, of Paris. It is a refractor, of eight feet focal length, and six inches aperture, and is moved by clock-work.

The Washington Observatory have a refracting telescope, made by Merz and Mahler, of Munich. It has a repeating filar micrometer, with eight eye pieces, magnifying from 100 to 1,000 times. The cost of this instrument was $6,000; its object glass is valued at $3,600.

The Georgetown Observatory has an equatorial instrument, made by Simms, of London, at a cost of $2,000.

Cincinnati Observatory was so fortunate as to secure, through the medium of Professor Mitchell, a superior object glass, twelve inches aperture, found at Munich, which has been pronounced, by those who ought to know, one of the best ever manufactured. It cost, when mounted, nine thousand four hundred and thirty-seven dollars.

At the Cambridge Observatory there is a telescope that has eighteen different powers, ranging from 103 to 2,000. It was made at Munich.

The Tuscaloosa Observatory has a superior instrument, made by Simms, of London, which has magnifying powers ranging from 44 to 1,640. Cost four thousand dollars.

Mr. Rutherford, of this city, owns a refracting telescope, made by Henry Fitz, of New York. The aperture of the object glass is nine inches, and its focal length nine and a half feet. It is mounted equatorially, with clock work like the Dorpat telescope made by Gregg and Rupp, of New York. The hour circle is eighteen inches in diameter, and the declination circle eleven inches. It has four eye pieces, the highest magnifying six hundred times. It cost, including clock work and micrometer, two thousand two hundred dollars. It rests upon a brick column, surrounded by a revolving dome twelve feet in diameter.

Mr. John Campbell has an observatory on the top of his honse in New York. The dome is twelve feet in diameter, the opening in which for the instrument is fifteen inches, and extends a little beyond the zenith. It is an achromatic refractor, eight inches aperture, and ten and a half feet focal length. It has six negative eye pieces, magnifying from 60 to 480 times. Made by Henry Fitz.

Mr. Van Arsdale, of New Jersey, has a fine telescope. So has Charleston, South Carolina ; Kentucky University, Dartmouth College, Shelby College, Michigan ; Buffalo Observatory, Cloverden Observatory, Hamilton College, and the Dudley Observatory, the telescopes contained in which are all worthy of a description.

In accordance with a recommendation made by Sir John Herschel, in 1854, to the British Association, that daily photographic pictures be taken of the sun's disk, for the purpose of studying by comparison its physical changes, a photographic telescope has been constructed and placed in the Kew Observatory. The proportions of the instrument are as follows : Diameter of the object glass, 34 inches, and its focal length 50 inches. The eye glass magnifies 25 times. The object glass is under-connected in such a manner as to produce a practical coincidence of the chemical and visual foci. Other accurate and careful experiments have been made to regulate the light, time of producing the image, and measuring the diameter of the spots.

Mr. Henry Fitz said that he cheerfully complied with the invitation of the Club to speak of telescopes and their construction. The instrument has lately been employed to take photographs of the heavenly bodies. Here are some of the moon, taken lately at Boston.

Photographs of Jupiter, show his belts imperfectly—perhaps we may do better before long. A German spectacle maker having combined a convex and a concave lens, found that it furnished a superior view of distant objects;

this fact became known to Galileo, who used it in his discoveries. That instrument was not a telescope—it was like our modern opera glass, to which our own eye is the eye piece. Our telescope depends on a single lens. Galileo saw the moons of Jupiter with his opera glass, magnifying *only three or four times.* Huygens saw *one* of Saturn's moons with his glass. Cassini's telescope was composed of an object glass placed on top of a pole, made managable in connection with a short tube below by means of cords, so that he could by means of the tube at focus catch views of planets and stars. He had a negative eye piece on the tube, composed of two lenses. He saw four of the moons of Saturn. Herschel saw the sixth moon of Saturn. Sir John Herschel, at the Cape of Good Hope, saw the sixth, but not the seventh certainly—only a glimpse! the atmosphere very clear too. The moon is caught in the motion of Saturn past a star, being with its planet, so that we thus discover it to be not a star, and therefore a moon of Saturn's. Lassell's Liverpool Reflector, shows Saturn's eighth satellite. That telescope is more *space penetrating* than Herschel's great forty feet reflector.

Lord Rosse, with his great reflector of six feet diameter, has said nothing about the moons of the planet Herschel. Rutherford's has seen two of those satellites. Mitchell's twelve inch object glass, at Cincinnati, sees Saturn's three rings, two solid and one apparently nebulous—as some think all matter was before it condensed into the present bodies. Some suppose that the present nebulous ring of Saturn will ultimately break up into satellites.

The question is ofter repeated, why have we not larger and more powerful telescopes? I will assign the reasons as at present understood. An object glass of great size is exceedingly difficult to make of adequate purity and perfectly homogeneous. One of fifteen inches, one of twenty-four at Paris, but not in useful condition, and one of twenty-nine inches at the Crystal Palace, England, on exhibition. Glass has been poured on an iron table, then rolled out by metal roller as true as possible. Craig made object glasses of this by cutting out a piece and placing it so that while heated to sufficient pliability atmospheric pressure would give it proper form—there were striæ in it. He said that Saturn was discrete looking, something like our pavement. He searched for Venus' moon in vain. The Cambridge fifteen inch reflector gives fine view of Orion, &c.

To make good object glasses we melt about 800 lbs. of glass in a crucible, heat it so high that it will pour like water almost, and keep stirring it in order to make it homogeneous and of as uniform density as possible. This stirring is difficult because the metals become too soft, and as we use *stirrers* of pipe clay, which occasionally touching the sides of the crucible, rub off particles which injure the glass—the effect is seen in the form of spots with three tails, streaks, &c. To render this glass strong it is left to cool gradually, which anneals it. When cold we break it to pieces and out of the purest piece in it, we make the object glass (the flint half of it). The other half is made of greenish tinted crown glass—why called *crown* I never could tell. We put the flint glass inside and the crown out, because the flint glass is liable to injury, being much weaker—in fact a wafer put on it, with paper over it, will when dry pull off some of the glass with it. Rock crystal is best if we could have that throne of a single one four feet thick, mentioned by Bayard Taylor, we could saw out an object glass of great power. You all know that it takes two kinds of glass to make one. He described the experiments of Newton and others on colors of the rays of light, their various reflexibility and refrangibility, and the fact that the red ray passes more directly through any translucent medium, and the experiments made to get rid of the prismatic colors entirely, so as to form lenses perfectly achromatic, (*a-chroma*, *without color*). Dolland, a silk weaver, made by circumstances an astronomical instrument maker, discovered that the bottoms of green and white glass tumblers together gave colorless light, and he made an object glass of the two—crown and flint, ground to fit each other so exactly as to appear but one to the eye—it proved achromatic and remains still the best refractor. You all know the great reflectors; Lord Rosse's, weighs about three tons. All these solid mirrors are difficult to manage in celestial observations, on account of the serious difficulty of difference of temperature between them and air, for when air is warmer the moisture is immediately condensed on the mirror, so that very often the observer becomes disappointed, wipes it clean, and the polish of it suffers. He described the proceeding relative to the manufacture of the object glass in England. A mathematician first determined its figure by angular investigations—the practical grinder follows them, &c. I grind my object glasses without any such trouble. My largest object glass, 12⅜ inches, is at the Ann Arbour Observatory, on a rising ground, where the winds from the prairies are felt in the observatory. I can make such a telescope for $6,750.

Mr. Meigs.—I had a correspondence twenty years ago with Messrs. Frauenhoffer and Utzschneider, relative to one of their refractors for New York—ten inch aperture. They required ten thousand dollars, to be deposited in Europe for it. It embraced equatorial movement.

Mr. Fitz in reply to a question of Mr. Meigs, said he preferred the refractors to the reflectors, even those of only four inch aperture. As to the intense heat required in melting the glass, the potash in it makes it necessary to its vitrification.

Mr. Butler.—Why will not platinum, covered with burned clay, make a good stirrer of the melted glass?

Rev. Mr. Adamson.—Was at the the Herschel Observatory, at Good Hope, and tried the power of Sir John's telescope. Although the air is clear there, yet doubtless more perfect view would be at elevated position, even a mile and an half high, above general cloud, &c., more perfect definition of objects can be obtained.

Mr. Fitz.—A dull atmosphere, yet clear, is best for a very clear night when the stars seem peculiarly sparkling, causes the object to *dance*, I may say.

A conversation ensued relative to tremor of the earth affecting observations.

Mr. Sykes.—Why not suspend the telescope by cords ?

Mr. Fitz.—It has been tried.

Mr. Seeley.—Why not fluid lenses ? Why not oxide of zinc instead of lead in the glass ?

Mr. Fitz.—Fully tried and failed. Has succeeded on a small scale, not over three inches diameter for lens. No advantage in the zinc.

Mr. Leonard moved thanks to Mr. Fitz. Given unanimously.

Mr. Stetson.—As to tremor—put glass under the legs of piano.

Mr. Adamson.—Materials of different substance check it.

Mr. Seeley.—The glass keeps the tone of the piano. Elastic bodies alone vibrate.

Mr. Adamson.—This great city ought to have an observatory of the first order, if it was only to regulate time. That of Edinburgh is founded on Tufa rock.

Mr. Tillman.—The glass insulates and electrises the piano · perhaps. Place a person so—touch his hair, and you can light gas with your finger.

Mr. Seeley.—Why not have pocket telescopes ?

Mr. Fitz.—The Germans make them, so that by doubling up they fit the pocket, although their focal range is nine inches, but they are of little use on account of the great difficulty in finding the object. With one of them a man's features have been distinguished at a mile off. Our whalemen have such—they can at mast-head hold one of them and spy the distant whale or other object.

Mr. Cohen recommended the employment of proper reporters by the Institute to take every word said, and these afterwards rendered to a report for our published transactions. He will move it at the next meeting of the Institute.

The committee on questions, continued " The Telescope" with the "Microscope." Adjourned.

H. MEIGS, *Secretary.*

February 2, 1859.

Present—Messrs. President Pell, Veeder, Leonard, Haskell, Chambers, Pierce. Cohen, Finell, Syks, Stetson, Breisach, Butler, Seeley, Tillman, Bruce, Witt, Johnson, Fitz, Holton, Prof. Hedrick and others—thirty-one members.

President Pell in the chair. Henry Meigs, Secretary.

The Secretary read the following extracts from publications received by the Institute since the last meeting, viz :

MECHANICS.

Two Greens, in England, have just patented a new apparatus for superheating steam, i. e., our old friend Frost's " Stame."

NEW PADDLE WHEELS.

A. V. Newton, patent.—To adjust at pleasure the angle at which the paddles strike the water.

FIRE ESCAPE.

J. F. M. Carpentier, patent 939.—Wicker basket on a flat board—two strong iron loops fastened to the board through which are passed two strong ropes, two ends of which are fixed by eyes to a small beam fixed inside of the room. This basket, with person in it, is to descend, while persons in the street hold the lower ends of the two ropes.

Mr. Hughes, a patent, April 27, 1858.—Chief object being to expedite a succession of electric currents over one line wire.

H. A. De Saegher, patent, to prevent incrustation of boilers. Wood ashes, $\frac{2}{10}$; charcoal powdered, $\frac{1}{10}$; resin or pitch, $\frac{6}{10}$; stearine, $\frac{1}{8}$. Or soft soap, $\frac{2}{10}$; tallow, $\frac{1}{13}$, and $\frac{2}{10}$ of $\frac{3}{4}$ powdered charcoal and $\frac{1}{4}$ soot or lamp-black, formed into balls or cakes, for use.

George C. Barney invited the club to examine his new patent whiffletree, on the table.

Mr. Leonard explained its object—detaching from a vehicle when the horses became unmanageable, by drawing a bolt passing through the looped ends of the whiffletree, and leaving the vehicle free. Each end of the whiffletree is then drawn by the horses without striking against their legs.

Mr. Veeder approved of this plan.

Mr. Stetson also, with the proviso that in case when the horses are going at full speed it would generally be more dangerous (if it was readily done,) to detach them than to trust to their being ultimately arrested. A detached carriage when at full speed would prove very dangerous to persons in it.

The Secretary mentioned a *new butter making machine*, now shown and seen by a member.

Mr. Pierce described it as composed of a pair of iron rollers whose contact is regulated by a fine screw capable of bringing them near enough together to crush the butter globules of milk passing between them with a rapid dasher below. It was said that the milk was heated to about 70° Fahrenheit before passing it through the rollers.

Mr. Leonard.—The machine or churn was at the Palace. It was there said to make the butter in one minute.

Mr. Pell referred to a churn exhibited to the Institute a few years ago, making butter in three minutes. It was done by heating the milk. The public took it up and the owner made a fortune of it. No public good! It takes one and a half hours to make butter from cold milk.

Mr. Pierce.—The roller machine is said to make fifteen to eighteen per cent more butter than a common churn.

Prof. Hedrick explained the globules which are visible in cream through a microscope.

Mr. Pell has examined them with a microscope, and although minute, its power reveals them as it does now in its modern application to business purposes—the discovery of adulteration in provisions and drugs—more effectually than chemistry. I move for a committee to examine the new butter machine, and report to the next meeting.

Mr. Veeder.—When I was young, and on my father's farm, my good mother employed me ocasionally to churn the cream. I had discovered that heating it saved much labor, and I sometimes put in some hot water to make the butter come quicker. Butter composed of stearic and margaric acids, or hydrogen and carbon, if crushed to a certain degree, would be entirely decomposed—the hydrogen escaping, while the carbon remains totally different substances from butter. The oil of butter, called *elain* or *butyrine*, when used to make a soap, gives three odorous compounds, *butyric, capric*, and *capronic* acids—the two last so called from the *goatish smell*. Perhaps the sudden production of butter in the machine, is an electrical effect from the metalic rollers. I once had a quantity of lard, which had been in a vessel laden with wheat, leaky; the wheat heated by fermentation, caused the lard to undergo an alteration, deemed destructive to it, but was beneficial. It was beautifully granulated, and was stearic acid. The lard had been three weeks under the wheat.

Mr. Seeley.—Milk put on bibulous paper, passes through, leaving the butter on the paper. In churning, atmospheric air is dashed in. The globule of butter has no sack; heat softens it, and it therefore more readily collects in masses. It is the casein in butter which renders it difficult to keep. If that was all out, the butter would keep a century.

Mr. Leonard.—Any material improvement in butter and its manufacture, is of such great importance to the world, that I must ask the Club to examine this new machine, by their special committee.

Mr. Stetson.—The theory of churning the globules of butter between rollers will appear, by calculation, to be absurd. The diameter of the globule, instead of being, as magnified, one-eighth of an inch, must be 13 inches to be crushed by the rollers, however fine the thread of the adjusting screw, even 32 per inch. Heat is injurious to butter. The roller machine should not receive justification from this club, which, that it may be useful to the world, must be mathematically exact, if it is possible.

Mr. Seeley moved an amendment, viz: that the committee also examine and report on *Hill's Air Light*. Lost.

A committee was then ordered to be appointed by the President, who appointed Messrs. Tillman, Hedrick and Veeder.

THE TELESCOPE.

Mr. Henry Fitz continued his remarks from the last meeting. He had made a mistake as to Gallileo's telescope. It was composed of two glasses, plano-concave and double convex. The tube about two feet long, magnified about 30 *areal*, not diametrical—making about 6 times. The eye-glass magnifies. A telescope with its object glass, or reflector, is perfect as a telescope. The eye pieces of our varying magnifying powers take the place of our own eyes, which they resemble, except in power; they are microscopes. The motion of Venus, giving to her the phases of our moon, can almost be seen by the naked eye. When Gallileo first saw that, he felt the conclusion of her and our earth's revolution around the sun. It established the truth of the Copernican system. He saw with it, for the first time, the satellites of Jupiter, and their revolutions around the planet—another parallel demonstration of the revolution of the planets around the sun. Huygens went further; he discovered the brightest of Saturn's moons, *Titan.* He adopted the negative eye-piece, except when spider lines are used for measurement. Many persons ask, how large does the moon look to you? One says, "as big as a hogshead;" one, "a dinner plate;" another, "a saucer." Hold up your *little finger*, with your arm straight, and it covers the moon at full. Photography is now employed to take the faces of planets. Here is one of the moon. Our maps of the moon are far superior to the photograph. Jupiter's belt and Saturn's rings, too—the latter you know when its edge presents itself to our view—is but a luminous fibre stretched across the face of Saturn—a mere spider's web.

Gregory's reflecting telescope has two concave mirrors, the large one at the lower end, with a small one above—the rays passing through a hole in the centre of the large one from the smaller one, to the eye, give two reflections. The parabolic curve is the true surface for an object glass or a mirror.

Mr. Meigs.—This conic section is, therefore, not only the true path of a projectile, but the best pathway of light for our eyes.

The curvature of the small mirror should be elliptic, but is commonly made spherical; and then the curve of the large mirror should be the hyperbola to counteract the aberration of the small one. Herschel's large mirror was 4 feet in diameter by three inches thick. This was not invented by Messier. Lord Rosse's reflector is 6 feet diameter and 6 inches thick; 45 per cent of the light is absorbed by the mirror. Silver has been proposed for mirrors, but it readily turns dark, as you see on all your plate. Prof. Steinhiel has electrotyped silver on a mirror; this forms a beautiful surface, and can of course be renewed as often as you please. The most diaphanous substance reflects some 12 per cent of light, 1-12th of every incident ray. Flint glass disperses light more than crown glass. Refracting telescopes are preferable to reflectors. Great expectations grew, as to celestial discoveries, from Lord Rosse's, but they have not been met. Rutherford's refractor, of 11 inches aperture, shows Saturn's seventh satellite mirror. An object glass of large size might, perhaps, be sawed off from a mass in shallow crucible, say 2 to 3 feet; but with all our care, one part of the melted mass will differ from the other. Dolland's 4 feet tube, and 4 inches aperture, is a very good telescope. Watson, of Ann Arbor Observatory, is a very good observer; he determined the true path of the recent comet.

Mr. Meigs.—Can reflectors be maintained by artificial means at the temperature of the air during observations, to prevent condensation of moisture on their surfaces?

Mr. Fitz.—It has been thought of.

Mr. Stetson.—You speak of the absorption of light by the reflectors, do they not also absorb heat?

Mr. Fitz.—None; polished surfaces do not. Parker's lens melted gold in a decanter of water. The lower strata of air abound in impurities, and injure observations.

Prof. Hedrick described Steinhiel's silvering of glass speculums, as on the side opposite to the light, as in common mirrors; so that a fine polish is presented.

Mr. Fitz.—Outside the glass.

Mr. Tillman.—Glass has one advantage over the metals, for telescopic purposes, being less expansible, and strong enough to be made greatly lighter than the brittle alloy used for reflectors; and consequently it would be much less liable to condense moisture on its surface, and would not be injured, as they are, by wiping it off.

Mr. Fitz.—The alloy reflectors are very sensitive; the touch of the finger affects them—slight variation of temperature cracks them.

Mr. John Johnson.—What is the largest reflector now?

Mr. Fitz.—There is one in Paris of 19 or 20 inches; it may prove the best observer. To get rid of chromatic glasses, monochromatic have been tried—yellow and red, for instance. We see better through misty air with the red glass than the white one; yet color is unfriendly to our most interesting views, that is, the most remote, for we have fallen in love with nebulæ.

Mr. Butler.—What is the actual power of the large lens?

Mr. Fitz.—It is according to its area. Rutherford's has a power of 900 times; it magnifies a moon of Jupiter as large as our moon, and the spots upon it.

Mr. Tillman.—The question for next meeting—"Coal Oil."

At 10½ o'clock P. M., the Club adjourned.

H. MEIGS, *Secretary.*

February 9, 1859.

Present—Messrs. President Pell, Leonard, Bruce, Witt, Seeley, Veeder, Haskell, John Johnson, Shephard, of Chicago, Sykes, Stetson, Palmer, Breisach, Prof. Mason, of Poughkeepsie, Mr. Dwight, of New Haven, Prof. Hedrick, Tillman, Reid, and others—40 in all.

President Pell in the chair. Henry Meigs, Secretary.

The Secretary read the following papers, selected by him, viz:

COAL OIL.

A gentleman in Baltimore is said to have invented a new retort for the production of the oil, by which the light and heavy oils are separated from each other in the retort, and nearly one-third more oil is obtained than by the present process. The danger from the incondensible gases is also prevented by his plan. Patent for distillation of coal oil, N. B. Hatch, of Lawrenceville, Penn.

LIGHT HEALTHY.

Experiments conducted by Sir James Wylie, late Physician to the Emperor of Russia, in the Hospital of St. Petersburgh, proved that the number of patients cured in rooms properly lighted, was four to one more than in the dark rooms. This produced reformation in lighting the hospitals of Russia, with most beneficial results, in all the places visited by the cholera. Patients on the shaded sides of streets, &c., died in greater number than those on the sunny side. Persons are more healthy on southerly than on northerly slopes of mountains, and they are better developed. Those in secluded valleys are subject to deformities and peculiar diseases, more than on the high, open ground. Plants suffer as well as animals. It is thought that scrofula prevails in the valleys, &c.

AMERICAN AND ENGLISH IRON COMPARED.

A distinguished railroad engineer of Chili, South America, writes, on the 14th of last October, (1858,)—"I trust to be able to interest some of my friends to send orders for iron to the States, instead of to England, where we are pretty sure to get poor iron. The whole of the iron sent out to me for railroad repairs on a road in Peru, which I built, and which iron came from the company in England that *owned the road*, (that is, the iron was ordered by them in England,) was not fit for the purpose. The fact is, I have been suffering from the effects of trash, sent to me from England. I am heartily sick of it, and will now see what can be done in the States."

FROM LONDON TO AMERICA,

By iron steamers, now building on the Tyne, in 110 hours—four days and fourteen hours.

The Atlantic Royal Mail Steam Navigation Company say that, and are building three powerful iron steamers to do it, at New-Castle-upon-Tyne. They are 330 feet long by 38 feet beam. Three oscillating cylinders of 75 inches diameter, each 2,200 horse power. Minimum speed, 20 miles per hour or more.

WHO INVENTED THE SCREW PROPELLER ?

The London Artisan, of Jan. 1st, 1859, has a deposition of Francis Pettit Smith, stating that he applied a portion of the Archimedean screw to propel a model boat in 1835 ; has been constantly employed by government, from 1840 to 1851, in fitting screw propellers; has a *pension of* £200, *or* $1,000, for his long gratuitous exertions connected with the introduction of them into the naval service.

Telegraph companies are treating with Turkey to make lines in Europe, Asia, and on the coasts.

Two companies are announced, one for London, the other for connecting India, Australia and China.

YANKEE LOCOMOTIVES IN EGYPT.

On the railroad between Alexandria and Suez, there are four locomotives, two of which were built at Mason's Works, Taunton, Massachusetts, on a difference between the English and American locomotives. The American told the Pasha, that instead of being weak, as the English had said, he would haul as many loaded cars as would reach from one end of the road to the other. The Pasha, to try it, had all the cars he had, 75 of them, heavily loaded, and his own car hooked on. The American locomotives hauled the whole of them *two hundred miles to Suez in twelve hours*, stopping for fuel and water. This being done, the Pasha cried, " God is great. A Yankee is very near perfection." The Pasha now uses the *Taunton* engines altogether.

The first patent for making coal oil was taken in England by James Young, of Manchester, Oct. 7, 1850, and here March 23, 1852.

The Chairman called for the report of the committee on the new Chicago churn.

Mr. Stillman reported that the two rollers are set so closely that paper hardly passes through, one roller moving with double velocity. The power (hand) strong ; paddle beneath in rapid motion. The milk, after being warmed to about 75° Fahr., was poured on the rollers, and butter was formed in two minutes and a half. The machine is not as perfect as it may be made.

Mr. Shepard, of Chicago, said that he had the churn under his charge. It was invented by Daniel Johnson, of New York.

Mr. Seeley.—Why put warm water into the churn ?

Mr. Shepard.—To keep the butter as it forms from sticking to the sides of the churn.

Mr. Veeder.—The subject is interesting. Let President Pell be added to the committee, and the examination be continued. Carried.

Mr. Pell had ascertained by his microscopes that each globule of butter was contained in double sacks, the inner one very delicate, *the outer one casein*, as he thinks.

Mr. Seeley.—I have examined globules of mercury in soap-suds. They will gather into small piles resembling piles of shot.

The President called up the regular subject, coal oil.

Mr. Tillman.—This subject has not yet been examined, as it must be, by our most able chemists. The late Professor Ellet had made much progress in the analysis of the products of coal of various formations.

Mr. Veeder called on manufacturers of coal oil who were present to give us information.

Mr. Palmer.—I am now engaged in it, and came here to obtain more knowledge, for I am deeply sensible that we lack a great deal that may yet be known in the extraction of the valuable products from coal. As far as I know now, there are no successful works as yet.

Mr. Stetson.—As an engineer, I prefer to make myself thoroughly acquainted with all that has been done before attempting further plans. The extraction of the valuable matters contained in our vast coal mines, in such economical way as to supply *light only* for millions of people, has a vast value.

John Johnson.—A difficulty in causing a uniform heat in masses of coal for distillation, must be overcome before we can be successful. That heat must be so moderate as not to destroy the products wanted, for it is so readily gassified that we readily lose our results.

Mr. Seeley has had some practical acquaintance with this matter. Bituminous coal yields the desired products to some extent. Asphaltum may be dissolved in alcohol, giving opportunity to examine its constituents more perfectly. By heat they readily become gas instead of oil. Tubes of considerable length will be necessary for condensation of the coal products. I believe the gas tar comes over first, then the valuable constituents, beurzole, paraffine, kerosine and naphtaline. I have experimented the last five years on this subject. To make suitable extraction, we must contrive to heat the mass of coal equally at the center and outside. *Bars of iron heated outside of the mass*, may conduct sufficient heat to its center.

Mr. Meigs.—In all cases should not the mass be well reduced in its pieces—pulverized, or nearly so ?

Mr. Seeley.—No doubt. And all the products must be drawn off together, and subsequently separated.

Mr. Veeder has dealt in oils and devoted attention to coal oil, &c. We want the views of men of science and practice too, on this occasion. We must get at the fundamental principles—the philosophy of the thing—before we can succeed. Gas is the usual product, and that at no very high temperature. Each particle of oil (as I understand it) is composed of hydrogen and carbon, at a certain temperature. The New Brunswick Cannel and the Bituminous coal, give out gas and oil at about 700° to 900° Fahr. Benzole (in the distillation) comes off *first*, naphtaline *second*, oil *third*, paraffine *last*. When the heat continues twenty-four hours, we get the largest quantity of oil. Sulphur is a troublesome constituent of the coal, and must be got rid of. It goes along with the other products through all the processes. There is an establishment here using in one mass of about twenty-five tons of coal, and are about using *sixty tons*. I advised the use of fifty tons in one mass two years ago. I advise the establishment of the works at the mouths of the coal mines. We can cheaply carry the products to market, but not the coals to our works. Coal oil, to be a national blessing, must be cheap.

Mr. Dwight, of New Haven, asked the constituents of benzole.

Mr. Reid illustrated on the black-board, and explained the construction of works with the spiral tube or worm, similar to the distillery process, for receiving and condensing the coal products. The wood fired on top of the coal, air sucked downward through the coal, actual combustion prevented as in the pyroligneous retort.

Mr. Veeder repeated the necessity of a slow combustion, which might, if required, be maintained for a year, But, as you well know, oxygen is admitted, the charred body inflames instantly, and of course consumes. Salt, lime and coal have been fluxed together to get the oil.

S. D. Tillman stated that many oils smoke when used in lamps, because there is an excess of carbon in their composition. When there is an *equal* number of atoms of carbon and hydrogen there will be *no smoke.* Our common burning gas is chiefly composed of olifiant gas, in which the carbon and hydrogen atoms are as 4 to 4; in gas from oil they are as 8 to 8; in spermaceti as 32 to 32; in turpentine, camphene, and rosin oil, the proportions are 20 of carbon to 16 of hydrogen, or as 5 to 4. When sufficient oxygen can be obtained from the air to burn this extra carbon, the light produced is of the most brilliant quality. Mr. T. proposed to obtain from coal a product containing 16 C. to 16 H. It will be a fluid, and will burn in a lamp without smoke. It will also be a valuable lubricator.

Prof. Hedrick.—It will be found necessary to determine precisely the various temperatures at which the several products of the coal come off; they must be chemically taken to pieces, each treated per se, and in this the process must proceed, for it cannot recede. We must thus separate what we want from useless products. Chevreuil's fine and laborious experiments on fatty acids will help our chemical investigations.

Prof. Mason.—The bitumen of the Dead sea is organic; all like bodies will more or less serve our purpose, as asphaltum, Cannel coal, or like bodies. I think the term coal is misapplied to the Cannel; it appears to be an extract from coal, rather than coal in itself.

Prof. Hedrick.—Anthracite coal contains no hydrogen, for that was driven out in its last formation. All are organic, from first to last formations.

Prof. Mason.—The subject before us possesses deep interest. I used it in an address some twenty years ago. We *pagana* dwellers out of cities, (for I live two miles from Poughkeepsie,) have lately found out the darkness visible in which we have lived in the country, for when we tried to light up our country parlor for a party, as we do our city parlor, we found that by setting fire to all the spermaceti candles in the house, we groped in the dark, in comparison with the brilliant illumination of our city gas-burners. So that I thought of laying two miles of pipe, to draw light from the city to my country parlors. Some citizens spend $900, others $1,500. If I understand what benefactors are, let me say that those who give to us the best food, clothing, fuel and light, will be entitled to that noble name, Benefactors. These great blessings must be cheap, so that all can share. Monopolies are natural enemies to the common people. Gas companies shine gloriously upon the rich; cheap light is to them odious. When a good man (as the world says) becomes president of a (light) gas company, his nature receives, exofficio, an alterative—*he can no longer shine for the poor!* To attain our great object, let me advise our numerous ingenious men, those who are ever striving for something new, not to waste their time and money on this coal oil, or any other great object, without first calling in all the help to be obtained from thorough science—the chemist, the miner, &c. We want effective and cheap retorts for making light, even more than we do those helps of humanity, the modern sewing machines.

Mr. Veeder.—Bituminous coal yields about ten gallons of oil, Cannel is reported to give 100 gallons, per ton. May not the coke be rendered of value to the oil extractor—both are wanted.

Mr. Mason.—We cannot bring coal to market to get the oil out of it. The coal at the mouth of the mine is worth but a shilling a ton, or a little more. We must make the oil at the mine. Anthracite has none; it all hardens as we near our sea coasts. Bituminous coal has too little.

Mr. Tillman.—The veins of the Breckenridge mine are shallow.

Mr. Mason.—Only $2\frac{1}{2}$ to 4 feet thick.

Mr. Dwight.—Some 5 feet.

Mr. Veeder.—The Kerosine oil is now somewhat in market, and is valued. The New Brunswick coal costs $18 a ton. There are not many suitable mines—even those Breckenridge veins are rather limited.

Mr. Johnson.—How is it as to coal oil patents?

Mr. Haskell.—I know but *the one* mentioned by the Secretary that is of much value.

Mr. Mason doubted whether *nature will submit to some of the patents!* "Si naturam expellas—tamen usque recurrit."

Mr. Veeder moved that the main subject be the exclusive one next meeting.

Mr. Leonard from the committee on questions: " *Coal oil,*" *only*, for next meeting.

The Club adjourned.　　　　　　　　　H. MEIGS, *Secretary.*

———

February 16, 1859.

Present— Messrs. R. L. Pell, Bruce, Witt, John Johnson, Davoll, Benjamin Pike, Butler, Seeley, Veeder, Conolly, Finell, Lawton, Palmer, Pierce, Breisach, Prof. Mason, Prof. Hedrick ; Engineers Stetson, Cohen, Tillman, Everitt, Haskell, Reid and others—fifty-five members in all.

Mr. Pell in the chair. Henry Meigs, Secretary.

The Secretary read the following papers prepared by him, viz :

He called attention to the pamphlet of the Engineer, Charles B. Stuart, on Civil and Military Engineering, Feb. 1859, Buffalo.

He states that the United States have expended during the present century not less than three thousand millions of dollars on their public works. He proposes to publish at the earliest day practicable, The History of American Engineering, with the biography of Engineers, with illustrations. He desires to ascertain the names and residence of *all* American engineers, that he may send his circulars to them, and he will return to them, before the first of July, a printed *directory* of all the civil and military engineers of America. All communications to be addressed to Geneva, Ontario co., New York.

Our corresponding member, Mons. L. A. Huguet Latour, of Montreal, from whom we have received almost all the valuable public works of Canada, sends since our last meeting several more, among them an octavo volume relative to the crown lands; another octavo, relative to the roads of the Canadas, by a special committee of the Legislature.

Mr. Pell.—Our subject this evening is one of vast importance, from the fact that we are naturally led to believe that coal is a substance inexhaustible in the world. We are told that the United States contains 129,230 square miles of coal; Great Britain, 11,850; Spain, 3,408; France, 1,719; Belgium, 518; and that the actual annual product in 1852, in Great Britain, was 31,500,000 tons; Belgium, 4,960,000; United States, 4,000,000, and France, 4,140,000 tons. The opinion that these fields and others to be discovered are inexhaustible, it appears to me rests altogether upon assumed data, rather than upon accurate statistical accounts, upon which alone it would be safe to warrant an opinion, entitled to respect. And I assure you, that unless we can found our calculations upon a much firmer basis, than we can now, this question will become one of serious concern. You will all allow that there is nothing easier than to assume, that available coal seams of great thickness extend over innumerable square leagues, yet when we come seriously to contemplate the only data given as to found these estimates upon, how perfectly unsatisfactory they are. We must not take into consideration, the mere quantity of coal, but the extent, depth, position, and thickness. Hundreds of inferior seams can only be worked to repay the expense from nine to eighteen hundred feet, in conjunction with those of superior quality. Inferior coal cannot be raised from such depths unless its price is raised to that now asked for the best quality of coal. The vital question to be considered is the additional expense and increased difficulty of mining, and not the exhaustion of mines so much, but the point at which they can be profitably worked; this needs immediate attention. If these inferior seams are not now worked in conjunction with the richer seams, they will inevitably be lost. Much of our coal is anthracite, and incapable of yielding more than a trace of oil; it is different in its properties from all others, and consists almost entirely of carbon, with very little hydrogen, consequently it gives no flame nor smoke, neither does it afford gas. You may almost term it mineral charcoal, it is not unlike coke, which it resembles in its properties, but not in appearance. It has a high shining lustre, but is smooth in its fracture, and is without a doubt superior to the very best Newcastle.

Cannel coal by means of super heated steam, may be made to yield a beautiful oil, which has been successfully substituted for turpentine in painting. This liquid is perfectly colorless, completely volatile, and very fluid, is not altered in the least by exposure to the light, and leaves no stain upon paper; it has however a pungent smell, something like coal gas, which, when evaporation takes place, disappears. Very many comparative experiments have been made, with the view of comparing it with turpentine, which have resulted in showing satisfactorily, that wood work, painted with paints mixed with this coal essence, dried quickly, and the smell disappeared more rapidly than when turpentine was used. The introduction of this into general use would be of great importance commercially speaking.

By simple distillation we obtain from bituminous coal a very fine oil for burning in lamps, and by a second process, a much heavier product, admirable for lubricating machinery, particularly if mixed with a saponified animal, or fish oil.

A very fine oil may be obtained by mixing sulphuric and nitric acid with coal naphtha, which oil when exposed twelve hours to the action of oxygen, becomes a crystalline solid, and if this is permitted to come in contact with potassa, both in aqueous and alchoholic solution, has a great analogy with the oil of bitter almonds. Coal oil obtained by the distillation of coal tar, mixed with a corresponding bulk of water, forms an admirable fuel, and when passed through a nozzle perforated with small holes, gives intense heat; when rectified, it is extensively used for dissolving india rubber, in making the varnish of water proof cloth, and likewise for burning in lamps, peculiarly constructed for the purpose.

Coal oil separated from the thick tar, yields first the light essential oil; and afterwards a denser oil, by progressively increasing the heat, tructuous oil, fit for lubricating and greasing will be produced. There will be left in the cucurbit a liquid tar, which may be converted into black grease by mixing it with caustic soda; after stirring this product at a temperature of eighty-five degrees Fahrenheit for three hours, saponification takes place, and paraffinised grease is produced.

The heat for the production of oily matters must on no account be carried beyond 600 degrees Fahrenheit, if it is, all the gas will be immediately converted into carbonated hydrogen and carbonic oxide, to the injury of the hydro-carbonated and hydro-carburetted liquids. Seven gallons of coal oil mixed with one gallon of turpentine, and stirred until thoroughly incorporated, makes not only a good lubricating oil, but a safe burning oil.

If you fill an air-tight vessel with water, overlying a small quantity of the oil of coal tar, you may place in it flesh, birds with the feathers on, or any other thing you may feel disposed to preserve for an indefinite period of time, and success will attend the operation, so long as they remain immersed in the water, which becomes charged with the vapor of the oil evaporating at the ordinary temperature. I am led to believe that Breckenridge coal, found in Kentucky, yields a superior oil for lubricating purposes.

Various other products of coal when distilled, are turned to account; from the ammoniacal liquor, muriate of ammonia is manufactured; 400 lbs. of coal afford 84 lbs. of coal tar, which again contains in 200 lbs. 52 lbs. of coal oil, 96 lbs. of pitch. I have employed the tar as paint, with the view of preserving wood, and found to my surprise, as it was highly recommended, that a more injurious compound cannot possibly be used; it will completely destroy a shingle roof in five years, that would last thirty-five without its use. I have likewise used the pitch, but consider it infinitely inferior to that made from the pine tree. Coal gas, impregnated with coal naphtha, affords a more brilliant light than coal gas alone, besides effecting a saving of eighteen per cent. To accomplish this end, coal gas may be passed through a sponge or pumice stone saturated with naphtha.

Peach Mountain anthracite coal contains bitumen and volatile matter, 2 per cent; Lehigh coal, 5 per cent; Lackawana, 3 per cent; Semi bituminous coal, Maryland, 12 per cent; Blosburgh, 14 per cent; Bituminous coal, New Castle, 35 per cent; Liverpool, 39 per cent; Richmond, Virginia, 32 per cent; Cannelton, Indiana, 34 per cent.

Notwithstanding these several coals are so rich in volatile matters, I am really surprised to find that the principal part of all the gas consumed in the United States and Great Britain, is obtained from bituminous coal, and that the average product from five of the best varieties is 2.70 cubic feet from the pound; whereas bitumen yields five cubic feet to the pound. The cost of coal now used for the supply of gas burned in New York, is one dollar for every thousand cubic feet of gas. And bitumen may be supplied at five dollars per ton; the cost of bitumen would then be 38 cents for one thousand cubic feet of gas. Consequently by substituting bitumen for coal, the gas might be supplied to us for less than half its present cost and leave a remunerating profit to the manufacturer.

The inquiry immediately suggests itself, What are the resources of bitumen? I reply, inexhaustible from a single source. There is a lake of bitumen in Trinidad that would supply the world to the end of time. Besides, it abounds on the coasts of Mexico, Texas and South America. In the island of Cuba, six miles from Havana, there is is a stratum 144 feet in thickness, and so far, I am not aware that it has been profitably used for any purpose—certainly not for gas.

	Volatile matter.	Coke. Volatile matter
The bitumen of Trinidad contains, ...	65 per cent.	36 per cent.
Cuba do	63 do	
Yucatan do	62 do	
Cannel coal do	44 do	
Liverpool, do	40 do	

It has several advantages over coal; it does not contain sulphur, and consequently does not produce noxious gases. There is no nitrogen in it; therefore ammonia is not formed. Gas escapes from a retort filled with coal in eight hours, at a bright red heat. Bitumen, by the use of bitumen as fuel, will be discharged in two hours, and yield double the quantity of gas, with half the labor in handling materials. Near the village of Amiano, in the State of Parma, there is a spring that yields liquid bitumen in quantities ample to illuminate the entire city of Genoa, for which purpose it has been for some time employed. It has a singular odor, and yellow color, but can readily be rendered colorless by a simple distilling process. It boils at 160°, is highly inflammable, being compounded of 36 carbon with 5 hydrogen, and is consequently a pure hydro-carbon. There are wells of bitumen in the Birman Empire, that yield 400,000 hogsheads annually. It is burned in lamps for light, notwithstanding its unpleasant odor.

Paraffine is another property obtained from coal, which possesses the power of resisting the action of highly concentrated alkalies and acids, and potassium even, at a boiling temperature. Its flame is brilliantly white, and deposits no soot. Its translucency and lubricating quality recommend it for numerous technical applications. A ton of Cannel coal will yield thirteen pounds, besides thirty pounds of lubricating oil, saturated with paraffine, which surpasses all other fatty substances as an anti-frictional. A Mr. Young, in England, now supplies London weekly with eight thousand gallons of this valuable substance.

Kerosene oil is a product of the distillation of Bituminous coal, and has come into use as a source of light. It is exceedingly rich in carbon, and produces a fine light, does not vaporize, and is consequently not explosive. When not ignited it emits an empyreumatic odor, which is not perceived during combustion.

When coal is placed in tight iron retorts, and heated to redness by external fire, the high heat decomposes the coal enclosed, producing a great many compounds, the principal of which are coke, or the solid residue of the coal, a black oil known as coal tar, water, several compounds of ammonia, among which are sulphurous acid, sulphuretted hydrogen, carbonic acid, carbonic oxide, heavy carburetted hydrogen, light carburetted hydrogen, or olefiant gas, and a vapor known as sulphuret of carbon. There are likewise traces of numerous other substances. One cubic foot of light carburetted hydrogen consumes in its combustion two cubic feet of oxygen, and generates one cubic foot of carbonic acid. This produces sufficient heat to raise 2,500 feet of air from sixty to eighty degrees.

By different degrees of temperature products of an entirely different character are produced. The lower you cause the temperature to be, the less gas and the more liquid will be formed ; and the higher the temperature, the greater will be the quantity of gas. Distillation may be greatly facilitated by allowing a jet of heated hydrogen gas to be admitted into the retort. In this manner the liquids are distilled in an atmosphere of hydrogen, and thus preserved from igneous decomposition, while the hydrogen takes up a large portion of the ammonia and sulphur contained in the coal.

It would be really difficult to find a matter of so great importance to the public as the procurement of a proper oil for the purpose of lubricating machinery. Man's works are all inanimate, and made as near as may be in imitation of the works of the Almighty ; and it is an incontestible fact that the nearer the imitation approaches, the nearer we must arrive at perfection. Who does not know that God never made an animal without supplying his joints with a lubricator, and not only so, but likewise an oily substance externally, perfectly adapted to the density of the element in which he intended it to move ? Who will deny, then, that all mechanism intended to possess motion, must be governed precisely by the same laws, which can be done only in one way, by selecting an oil possessing pure chemical properties for lubrication.   Where can we find this theory more splendidly developed than in the wonderful mechanism of a cotton factory, governed by the strict laws of motion and force ?   The consequence is, the wearing of the working parts are so inconceivably small, that I can only compare them to the unequalled motion of man's body.   In these admirably managed establishments, the largest proportion of the very best sperm oil imported into the country is used.   Even on my farm I find economy in using the most expensive oils for my mowing and threshing machines, as well as cart and wagon axles.

We all know that marine engines and locomotives suffer inconceivably from oscillation, and its most intimate companion, friction, and will continue so to do until engine drivers are engaged to work by contract, when they will govern themselves by the same law that governs cotton spinners, and steam locomotion will for the first time fully develop its power.   Precisely the same remarks will apply to marine engines.   They being company concerns, are not aware that the substances now used by their agents are chemically unfitted for the purposes to which they are applied, and in nine cases out of ten offer resistance to the working of the machinery, instead of aid.   If it is necessary that any lubricating oil should be pure, that applied to them must necessarily be so, because there are immense surfaces exposed to friction, many of them composed of copper, tin and zinc alloys, and all of them susceptible to the influence of electricity, which, when exerted, produces heat, expansion the resulting consequences.   I think coal oil, if properly prepared, may be made fully equal, if not superior, to any other for lubricating purposes.   And if I were the unfortunate owner of a steamship, I would not only lubricate her machinery with coal oil, but the ship herself, which would increase her velocity through her native element at least twenty per cent.

Mr. Tillman suggested difficulty in revolving large masses.   It will be found an objection.

Secretary Leonard.—The methods of giving and sustaining such revolution are all within the power of mechanics.   Like cylinders, containing large masses of rags, are used in our paper mills with entire facility.

Mr. Reid illustrated on the black-board the bowl, (like a pipe bowl,) made of fire bricks, to hold many tons of coal, with wood on top to give heat ; worms, like distillers', leading to three vats to receive the condensed products ; an air pump at the end of the worm to draw air down through the coal in the bowl.

Mr. Tillman illustrated the atomic compounds of the coal products on the board.

Mr. Everitt.—The heat in the bowl must be under perfect control, or the process will be ruined.   A low heat only must be employed.

Mr. Reid.—Cover at pleasure with iron caps.   The required condensation is light, not heavy, as in common distillation.   The unpleasant odor complained of in the coal oil is not found when the heat of the mass does not exceed 450° or 500° Fahr.

Mr. Veeder, whose business is in oils, desired to know how to rid coal oil of its sulphur.

Mr. Reid.—Pass it through lime water.

Mr. Everitt.—The odors resulting from combustion are very difficult to remove.

Mr. Stetson.—May not surplus heat in the mass be regulated by suitable introduction of cold air ? The *various products* of the coal come off at *different temperatures*, and we must find out what those are.

Mr. Everitt.—600° brings out all, leaving coke alone.

Mr. Seeley.—Men knew nearly as much *one hundred years ago as we do now* on the subject before us, as to the oils, the temperatures. Heat the oils. One boils at 200°; another at 300°, and so on to 300°, 400°, 500°. Young's patent is mistaken. Laboratories of chemists have given us as accurate results as Young. Coal tar products were better examined before. Mr. Seeley draws the atomic symbols of some of the materials. Heat diminishes the carbon in all of them.

Secretary Meigs tried the Anthracite coal when first brought here. He examined the coals after they had gone through white heat, and was then somewhat surprised to find, when cold, the inside of the coal as black as ever, and as good to burn. We have thrown away such coals, because the outsides were ashes, these thirty years past, by millions tons! Not knowing that the carbon in them sustains any degree of heat, it enters the substance of iron in the furnace.

Secretary Leonard.—I do not see why perforated plates may not be used to pass the gases. The journals can be worked gas-tight, and breaks within the cylinder will stir the mass properly for admission of heat uniformly.

Mr. Stetson.—The Pittsburgh engineers are doing their best to improve the coal products, finding difficulties enough. Common sense finds in bodies differences which the atomic symbols do not satisfy inquiry. Is paraffine commercially valuable ? As a candle it does not burn well and correctly.

Mr. Seeley.—A patent has been granted this week for paraffine candles.

Mr. Everitt.—They are now made in Boston and elsewhere. They burn well in that climate, but when warmer, they are apt to bend like asphaltum.

Prof. Hedrick.—The coal oils are not pure chemical compounds. Analysis cannot tell us precisely what is combined with them. Some say they are binary compounds, one dissolving the other. We want to separate the oils. That would be worth the trouble of severe analysis. The boiling point of water tells us much, and the various degrees of heat are capable of further analysis. German chemists are doing much in this article.

Mr. Tillman had objections to the revolving cylinder. Pittsburgh is now beginning to despair of success. He justifies the symbolic atom method of definition. *Weight* cannot tell us. When the atomic compound is equal, as in stearine, spermaceti, and some others, the burning is best. The question before us ought to first go through the chemical inquiry before the expenditure of time and money. It would be sound policy to give our best chemists five thousand dollars for advice before we begin our works.

Mr. Veeder.—Heat the mass of coal to 300° slowly ; then, by the admission of oxygen, the heat would rise, if necessary, to 600° in a few minutes.

Mr. Seeley.—How low price per gallon ? said to be $1.50.

Mr. Everitt.—Never less than 75 cents.

Mr. Stetson.—A Pittsburgh manufacturer will sell it crude at one shilling a gallon. It might be refined here.

Mr. Reid.—There is much difficulty in refining it. We may use several vats for condensation at the several temperatures, viz., vat 1 at the highest ; at 2, 3, 4, 5, 6 in succession as the combined product passes through the worms in the order given.

Mr. Everitt approved that plan.

Mr. Veeder.—It coincides with the principle I have found relative to the different temperatures.

Prof. Mason rose to ask questions. The subject before us is of great importance. Those who know will please to answer. Question.—How near to sperm oil for lubrication has coal oil been brought ?

Mr. Everitt.—Not one-half.

Prof. Mason.—Our railroads want all our best oils. What is the objection to the coal oil ?

Mr. Everitt.—The acids in it.

Prof. Mason.—Your city gas costs $2.50 per $1,000 feet ; ours of Poughkeepsie costs $4.00. What will an equal illuminating power from coal cost ?

Mr. Everitt.—Six dollars a gallon.

Mr. Seeley.—In its best state it has more illuminating power than our common gas.

Prof. Mason.—Has coal oil been well tested on railroads ?

Mr. Veeder.—Some of the western roads use it, and it is used on some rough machinery. The oil particles are quite different from the fish oils. Whale oil is 600°, and coal 300°. The paraffine in coal oil,chills too easily for lubrication. Even in printing offices, in vaults where it is quite warm, the machinery oiled with the coal oil with the paraffine in it, makes bad work sometimes by chilling up, and so breaking down the press work suddenly. The more dense coal oil, with paraffine out, does much better. I believe that a very valuable lubricator will yet be made of it. I have experimented with the Trinidad asphaltum of the lake, and it does not yield very good light. It is not safe to recommend as yet anything before sperm oil for lubrication. Its oil particles are minute, but little carbonaceous matter combined witn it, and in use it leaves the metallic lustre on the journals, &c. Whale oil, and most others, tarnish them, and leave a film of fibrinous matter on them like a varnish.

Prof. Mason.—What matter is that ?

Mr. Veeder.—I believe it to be composed of the sacks holding the oil—the envelopes of the particles of oil.

Prof. Mason.—Who will say what it is ?

Prof. Hedrick.—It is resinous.

Prof. Mason.—It is fibrine, gluten, higher purification of the oil makes it cost $3 a gallon.

Mr. Veeder.—We use caustic alkali in purifying fish oils, soda or potash as strong as 52°. The various secretions of the animal pass through the oil seize the fibrine and settle it to the bottom. We call this *bleaching the oil.* A woolen blanket put in will be eaten up by this process. The best will form a film on glass—it answers for some painting.

Prof. Mason.—All fibrine originates in the blood—its particles are intensely minute—it is carried into the fat of the animal. There is less fibrine formed in the blood in cold regions than in warm. Tropical oils are fine lubricators—Palm oil for example. Good oil of tar has foreign matter in mechanical mixture with it.

Mr. Seeley.—The tendency of oils to thicken is resinification, the gradual drying down is not to fibrine but to resin. Camphene combines with oxygen, and goes back to resin. Oils tend the same way, and there is no remedy.

The Chairman.—Why not among the yet unknown products of coal, Ottar of Roses ?

Mr. Meigs.—Chemistry now gives us *perfumes from dung* and from base subjects.

Mr. Veeder.—I have not found any gum in coal oil, which has the singular property of creeping up the sides of its vessels—lamps, &c., and creeping out. No fish oil can do that, and it differs greatly from resin oil, which requires time only to resume its resin form.

Mr. Tillman.—Benzole contains too much carbon for a lubricator. Watchmakers have for the delicate movements, oil of some small fish—I do not know what fish. Our sea fish are now largely used for oil for lubrication, and their refuse for a guano, in Nova Scotia.

Mr. Haskell.—And on Long Island from the *moss bunkers.*

Prof. Mann objected to the fish manures on account of their lack of durable fertilization.

Mr. Stetson.—Heat is slow in penetrating masses of coal—the outside may be (as bakers would say) burnt while the inside is raw. A revolving cylinder to heat it, as we burn coffee, is a French patent, is used at Pittsburgh. A large cylinder is easily supported by friction wheels. The heat must be continuous and so may the supply of coal be.

Mr. Everitt.—Berge & Gillespie, of Freeport, Pennsylvania, use it.

Mr. Seeley read the following paper, viz:

It is manifest to me that we have a hard race before us after the great point, *good cheap coal oil !* There is a very wide field here for our ingenuity. We shall have to find out how far we can profitably conduct gas from the gas works to our homes, in pipes, &c.

The Chairman.—I predict that in ten years from this coal oil will be used all over the civilized world.

Mr. Leonard, from the committee on questions, gave for next meeting: " The Microscope."

At 10½ o'clock P. M., the Club adjourned.

H. MEIGS, *Secretary.*

February 23, 1859.

Present—Messrs. R. L. Pell, Bruce, Godwin, A. Nash, Judge Scoville, Stetson, Seeley, John Johnson, Breisach, Finell, Veeder, Griscom, Haskell, Lawton, Jerome, Nowlan, Prof. Mason, Prof. Hedrick and others ers—45 members.

R. L. Pell in the chair. Henry Meigs, Secretary.

The Secretary read the following extracts :

STOPPING RAILROAD TRAIN.

Mr. E. Palmer, of Woodford Green, Essex, Ohio—a series of transverse rollers under the engine and cars. The circumferences are a short distance above the rails. If the wheels get off the track, these rollers are immediately in operation, and having flanges on their inner ends, act as a series of wheels, &c. Also, a drag-carriage behind, self acting.

J. Lubbock.—Bees make circular cells in the circumference of the comb, and afterwards, when they had worked a row next to them, they made the first row hexagonal like all the rest. Wasps always built hexagonal cells from the beginning.

HELIOSTAT.

F. Galton's, as cheap and as portable as a common ship's compass. Light can be flashed from it so as to attract attention from the most careless person, at ten miles distance—can be used anywhere the sun shines, and convey messages known only to the person seeing the flash. Another Heliostat can flash the response.

Mr. Nowlan exhibits his plan of a bridge over the East river, and explains the construction of it.

G. F. Jerome exhibits mowing and reaping machine, and explains its operation. A castor wheel on the left side supports the cutting frame so as to adapt it to irregular surfaces. Its shear movement is claimed to act without clogging. It cuts five feet swathe. One horse can do mowing on six or eight acres a day. At Mineola, Queens county, on Long Island.

Mr. Godwin moves for the reading by the Chairman of his paper on the Microscope. Carried.

Mr. Pell complied, as follows:

MICROSCOPE.

Two of the most noble instruments presented by scientific men to the world we inhabit, are the telescope and microscope. With them we control the universe, and are enabled to gaze upon existences hitherto unknown to us. Through the medium of the telescope creations millions of miles beyond our globe are revealed. While the microscope brings to light those that the unassisted eye never could have beheld. The telescope carries us to the illimitable fields of space, and unfolds to us systems of suns like our own, rushing with the same inconceivable speed amidst attendant glittering worlds.

While the microscope opens to us fields of instinct life enshrined in regions of infinitude, and aggregated by myriads, so mysterious as scarcely to be grasped by the intellect of man.

As the astronomer with his telescope sweeps over the star spangled heavens in a cloudless night, and trembles at the power and majesty of the Supreme God, so the microcopist sweeps over a drop of water, which immediately becomes an ocean, teeming with groups of symmetrical figures, sporting at will through their spacious domain, and he holds his breath for fear of disturbing them. The term microscope is derived from μικρος, small, and σκοπεω, I view, and was first suggested by Demisianus.

Aristophanes, five hundred years before the birth of our Saviour, speaks of a burning sphere. Seneca, born the first year of the Christian æra, writes that small objects might be seen through a glass filled with water. Pliny speakes of lenses made of glass. Ptolemy uses the word refraction in his writings. Lenses of a convex figure were used in the fourth century. The English, however say, that Roger Bacon, in the thirteenth century, invented the telescope, microscope, camera obscura, gunpowder, and the reading glass. Huyghen, gives Cornelius Drebbel, a Dutchman, the credit of inventing the compound microscopes in 1621. While Fontana, in 1618, claims the discovery. Be that as it may, Zacharias Jansen, in 1590, presented the first microscope, to Charles Albert, Arch Duke of Austria. Viviani, in his life of Galileo, says he invented the microscope from his knowledge of the telescope, and that in 1612, he sent one to Sigismund, King of Poland. In 1667, Robert Hooke published a work on philosophical descriptions of bodies made by a magnifying glass. He was the first who made globule lenses of high power.

The solar microscope, is admirably adapted to illustrate popular subjects rather than accurate investigations, as its construction is inferior to the compound. It has a condensing lens, mirror, and object glass. When used it is passed through a hole in a window shutter, and the tube with its lenses fastened on the inside; the mirror receives the rays of the sun, and reflects them along the tube, where they are condensed by the lens, and concentrated upon the object, placed near the principal focus. On account of the powerful concentration of light upon the object, the image may be seen by all the room ; an ignited jet of oxygen and hydrogen gases upon carbonate of lime, as well as light produced by the galvanic battery, has been used advantageously in place of the solar rays.

The Polytechnic Institution, in England, have a new oxyhydrogen microscope, made by Carey, consisting of six powers, ranging from one hundred to seventy-four millions of times. The second power magnifies the wings of the locust to twenty-six feet in length ; the fourth power magnifies the sting of the honey bee to twenty-five feet ; by the sixth power the eye of the house fly is magnified to such an extent, that each lens appears to be 12½ inches in diameter, and the human hair 17 inches in diameter.

If day light is made use of as the illuminating agent, your instrument must be placed so as not to be exposed to the direct rays of the sun. A white cloud opposite that great luminary, is the point from which the most intense light is given off. A dark cloud in the same position is one from which the fewest rays proceed.

You may always estimate the magnifying power of either simple or compound lenses, by comparing any object of known size, that can be perfectly seen ; this distance is called the standard of distinct vision, and with it you may compare all the magnifying powers of your lenses. Opticians now adopt ten inches as the standard. And this decimal is certainly a useful number, because with it as a standard, the magnifying power of lenses, of any focal length, can be easily determined. If the lens under examination be of one inch focus, we have only to add a cipher to the denominator of the fraction, which expresses the focal length of the lens, and the result will necessarily be the magnifying power. Thus if the lens be half an inch focal length, the magnifying power will be twenty diameters.

Every object desired to be examined by the microscope belong to one of two classes, the opaque or transparent, and the methods of illumination differ for each class. In the former the light is reflected upon them by means of a convex mirror, whilst in the latter it is condensed upon them by a lens.

THE SINGLE MICROSCOPE.

In this instrument an object becomes visible by rays of light emanating on its surface, which are received by the eye and concentrated upon the retina, thus forming a perfect image on the inner posterior surface of the eye, provided it is at the focal distance of the lens. A single microscope may be made by piercing a circular hole in a piece of metal, and introducing into it a drop of water, which immediately assumes a spherical form on both sides of the metal. Rock crystal makes the best microscopic lenses. Flint glass is not fitted for them, because it possesses too great a dispersive power. The crystalline lenses of small fish give a perfect image of minute objects.

COMPOUND MICROSCOPE.

This instrument is formed by combining two converging lenses, whose axis are placed in the same line, and possesses the power of developing exeeedingly minute objects. It is furnished with object lenses and eye-glasses which may be used in combination or singly. When it magnifies an object five hundred times, it becomes very distinct, but if four thousand times, the outlines are not perfectly preserved. The mirror consists of a frame of brass, in which two silvered glasses are set, one plane and the other concave, which should not be less than two inches in diameter. In the former the light is reflected in converging rays; the latter in parallel rays.

Very little is generally known of the management of modern compound microscopes; consequently many of those who have good ones cannot use them advantageously, finding great difficulty generally in overcoming the spherical aberrations of the light's rays. Even manufacturers sometimes err in the principles of their construction, and find to their surprise that the glass disperses the rays, and produces prismatic colors. The coloring of images may be easily prevented by a proper achromatic lens; and to overcome spherical aberration, the object glass must be arranged so as to neutralize the negative and positive rays, of which spherical aberration consists. The microscope manufacturer, when arranging his instrument for illuminating objects, and requires a condenser of light, should imitate nature, as there is no better condenser than a white cloud between the earth and the sun. He may use a white disc of plaster for this purpose. A mirror is generally made use of, but is bad, because it reflects the rays through the object, confuses the vision, and prevents a good definition through the medium of a glare of light. The construction of a magnifying power for a compound microscope is complicated, because several lenses must necessarily be employed to form one magnifier; and not only that, two different kinds of glass must be used for one lens of such a magnifier; and perhaps there is no single problem throughout the range of this noble science that has occupied the mind of the learned throughout all lands as that of achromatism, and achromatic combinations; all the first attempts were unsuccessful, and even within the last twenty-five years, such great men as Wallaston and Biot actually predicted that the compound microscope would never be superior to the simple when supplied with doublets. Notwithstanding the opinion of these great philosophers, within the last few years the compound microscope has become the most important instrument ever bestowed by science upon nature's investigator, man.

With it nature has become widely explored; the gushing brook, rippling stream, and quiet lake, have exposed to its magnifying power their congregated myriads of insect life; before its invention, when we examined one species of water it was red, another orange, another green, but we knew not the cause; we now know the colors are formed by living bodies, and that they swarm throughout all seas, and all lands; mud brought from the bottom of the ocean, by the lead, full fifteen hundred feet in depth, was found full to repletion of organic life. The air we breathe abounds not only with living animalcules, but their eggs, raised by evaporation from the surface of the earth, and borne unseen by the naked eye into the atmosphere, ready to develope life when circumstances are favorable, which sometimes does not occur until they have crossed not only oceans, but continents, and thus by the will of the Great Supreme, become disseminated throughout the universe. Naturalists, with untiring labor, have recognized, grouped and delineated, eight hundred different species of animalcules, and become acquainted with their modes of reproduction, habits and forms. One variety can change their forms at will, and assume many grotesque shapes; others shoot up in the form of plants, have round shaped flowers, fringed with hair, and are instinct with life, even to the remotest branch. The Monad is the most minute of all living matter; five hundred millions may exist in a single drop of water; the largest ever examined, had only attained the length of the twelve-thousandth part of an inch. In a cubic inch of dirt forty-one millions of distinct animalcules have been estimated to exist.

By the aid of the microscope naturalists have been able to discover eyes in the entire family of rotatorial animalcules, always supposed to be blind, and thus proving the existence of a nervous system in those atoms of creation. Who can fail, knowing such facts, to be astounded at the amazing perfection the Creator has bestowed upon these minute creatures!

They multiply in various ways; some are brought forth alive, some proceed from eggs, others increase by the growth of buds, issuing from the body of the parent, and become perfect animalcules; others still divide themselves into several individual beings. A single infusoria was kept in water for eighteen days, during which time it laid four eggs each day, and the young ones when two days old, laid the same number; in ten days the offspring of this single insect amounted to a million; in twelve days to sixteen millions.

There are others that increase much more rapidly. Naturalists have affirmed that the box chain animalcule (Gallionella,) increases in one day to the number of one hundred and forty million millions. When water containing the wheel animalcule evaporates, the creature apparently dies and becomes hard and dry, and may in this state be preserved for many years in sand. When placed in water it revives at once, and swims with its accustomed activity. The most intense poisons mingled with water full of animalcules does not affect them, neither does the cold of the arctic regions, where they are found alive in solid ice.

The twilight Monad is only the twenty-four thousandth of an inch long, and a single shot, one-tenth of an inch in diameter, is said to occupy more space than seventeen hundred millions of these living monads.

In the harbor of Wismar, on the Baltic, there is deposited every season 228,854 cubic feet of mud, which accumulation has continued for one hundred years; at this rate 22,885,400 cubic feet—equal to 3,240,000 hundred weight. The compound microscope being brought to bear upon it, announced the fact, that one-quarter of it was composed of living infusoria, and a large portion of the balance of microscopic forms. The farther we progress with the microscope, the more curious and interesting will be the forms that will meet our gaze at every step.

Professor Kelland, of Paris, has executed some extraordinary microscopic writing, on a spot the size of a pin head. The Professor shows, by means of powerful microscopes, several specimens of distinct and beautiful writing, one of them containing the whole of the Lord's Prayer, executed within this small compass.   Layard's last work on Nineveh, shows that the national records of Assyria, were written on square bricks, in characters so small as to be scarcely legible without a microscope ; and that a microscope was actually found in the ruins.

The evidence of microscopic life is not confined to the earth's surface. The same formation of rocks from the siliceous or calcareous shells of animalcules which is seen in the chalk formation of Europe, occurs also on the most gigantic scale, in East and West Africa, Asia, North America, and Russia; demonstrating that microscopic life in the formation of the earth, has been in the hands of the Deity a most important agent, and has produced the following remarkable results, to wit : That microscopic life, and the forms which constitute masses of rock and earth, exist precisely in the same manner throughout the whole surface of the earth, in all climates, zones, and situations—in low valleys, on high mountains, at the bottom of all seas, oceans, and rivers ; and what is very extraordinary, both those of vegetable and animal origin, present a perfect resemblance in characters, whether found in Europe, or this country, and without regard to the Fauna and Flora of the localities.   The Navicula, Himantidum arcus, Pinnularia viridis, and Eunotia amphioxys, appear to be exceedingly important as far as the economy of nature is concerned.   The constituents of their bodies and shells are principally silica, carbon, lime, iron, manganese, and alumina, united with silica.   Iron abounds in the minutest animalcules, and appears to be combined mechanically.   The development of organic life exerts a great and important influence upon the earth's surface, especially upon the formation of humus in the valleys.

Microscopic life is not confined to the surface of the earth, but is found on a gigantic scale in the chalk formations of Europe, on the mountains in Africa, and under the coal formations in Russia, and different parts of the United States. At Richmond, Virginia, there is an infusorial strata twenty feet deep ; and at Berlin, in Prussia, sixty feet in depth, endangering the solidity of buildings above it. In Bilin, in Bohemia, a series of slate strata, fourteen feet thick, has been examined with the microscope, and proved to contain by estimation, forty thousand millions of distinct organic forms in a cubic inch weighing 220 grains.

The microscope has proved that coal is of vegetable origin.   In an examination of slices of polished Newcastle coal, by means of transmitted light, cellular structure, or vegetable cells, which were supposed to contain the oil and gas of the coal were found, and in specimens of anthracite coal these cells were empty. Upon examining the ashes of coal, abundant traces of vegetable structure were discovered, consisting of woody fibre imbedded in tissue of plants, which favors the idea that coal was formed of the plants growing on the spot, and not by drifting, as is usually supposed.   The microscope has proved that the substance which forms the elementary membranes of the tissue of all plants, is the same in every species of vegetable.

The snow flake, under the microscope, presents the appearance of the most exquisitely formed crystals, in such diversity of figures as to amaze and delight all beholders; single crystals unite, and form double stars, of the most delicate structure, and of several hundred distinct varieties, which enables them to fall lightly upon the tender plants, and effectually protect them from the wintry blast. Suppose it had been ordered differently, and all the water that now falls in this manner, was showered upon us in the form of hail, what would be the consequence?

With the microscope I have plainly observed crystals in great abundance within the cells of many plants, and throughout the entire bark of many trees, such as the apple, pear, peach, plum, and likewise forest trees, also in the potato, onion, &c.

As far as my investigations have gone, microscopically speaking, the wonderful structure of the eyes of insects have amazed me the most. In the common spider, I have counted six in one species, and eight in another. In the centipede, eighteen; in the horse fly, 3,000—and Hooke says there are 7,000; in the dragon fly, 3,000; and Lenenhoeck says there are 12,000, and that they each shine with the brilliancy of the choicest gems, and gleam with the most magnificent hues of light, displaying colors of surpassing beauty. I consider the diamond beetle, one of the most brilliant creatures in existence—when brought under the microscope—his whole entire body glows resplendently with the dazzling colors of the emerald and ruby, the eye fairly quails under their radiance. The scales of fishes, as objects for the microscope, are exceedingly beautiful, and present an immense number of elegant forms; even on the same fish, I have found scales from different parts of the body, differing not only in form, but structure.

The fine dust that you often see on flowers, known as pollen, when examined by the microscope, presents to the astonished view, an immense number of highly organized bodies, of every form, size, shape and color, according to the plants from which they are extracted—it is white, blue, purple and yellow; it is imprisoned in the anther, which opens at the proper season and sets the imprisoned impregnator free to be borne by the atmosphere wherever required to fructify plants of the same genus. I have crushed them when ripe, and have invariably found them full of oil, and if thrown upon water, will cover it with oleaginous particles—this is the matter which fructifies. The pollen of corn, zea mays, looks precisely like buckwheat when magnified, and contains within each atom, a cell, less in size than the three-thousandth part of an inch, filled with oil.

A few years since I made a paste of flour and water, by boiling, and placed it in a room where the thermometer ranged at about seventy degrees Fahrenheit, and in five days it was completely alive with minute light brown creatures, much resembling eels. If this experiment is performed in the fall, these eels are oviparous, and produce their young from eggs; if on the contrary, in the spring, they are viviparous, and a single female frequently contains more than one hundred long eels. The vinegar eel is larger, and more tapering, which enables it to move with great celerity in its native element. It is oviparous and viviparous.

One of the most beautiful discoveries of the microscope is that which reveals to us the strange fact that bodies when they pass slowly to the solid state from the liquid, assume singular forms of great beauty and elegance, termed crystallizations, each having the form of the primitive crystal; many of which frequently combine and give rise to a magnificent collection of perfectly symmetrical figures. A very large portion of the mineral crust of our earth is in a crystallized condition. Take the granite for example, which the microscope informs us is composed of crystals of mica, quartz, and feldspar. All the clay slate hills are mainly constituted of regular forms. Fluid bodies become crystals. Salt may be converted into brine, so that no separate particle can be observed, and when evaporated, will immediately form crystals. Sulphur may be melted, and allowed to cool gradually, when it forms beautiful crystals, at first so minute that they almost elude the most powerful microscope, but as they unite the most magnificent configurations are seen branching out in all directions, with perfect symmetry, representing foliage crowded together in rich clusters. Nitrate of potash may be dissolved, spread on a piece of glass, and subjected to heat, when six-sided prisms, perfectly transparent, will spring up under the microscope, throw out lateral spurs, and finally spread over the surface of the glass in beautiful lines of crystallized net work. In the East Indies, nitrate of potash forms in the same manner upon the earth's surface, and are swept into piles, and leached, as we do ashes—the liquid is then evaporated, and the result is the crystalized nitre of commerce. A drop of benzoic acid exhibits the most splendid crystallizations under a powerful microscope; transparent sharp crystals, perfectly colorless are first seen, and they afterwards rapidly run into vines and lovely foliage, which spreads its glittering branches on every side, gleaming like sprays of silver. If you would be perfectly delighted, dissolve the acid in alcohol, and spread the liquid upon a pane of glass, then bring your microscope immediately to bear, as the evaporation is rapid ; in an instant, the chaotic surface becomes studded profusely with every imaginable combination of exquisitely beautiful crystalline figures, the crystals composing which are only one seven hundredth part of an inch in size.

Copperas crystallizes in rhomboidal transparent prisms of a sea green color, and when observed under the microscope exhibit very interesting combinations. Crystals at first display themselves in a vertical position, and then branches push from them on every side, with great order and precision, and look like bristling arrows, which at length apparently form a massive structure, still revealing the primitive crystal, through the mingled shadows and lights that fall upon the crystalized surface, and these may be varied by adjusting the mirror, when the illumination will shine brightly upon some magnificent cluster, and again falls subdued upon the minute gems, crowned in a mass of crystallizations, resembling the bastions of fortifications.

Camphor dissolved in alcohol, and spread upon glass, forms first, under the microscope, a misty looking surface, which, in the twinkling of an eye, becomes perfectly studded with splendid stars, starting forth in perfect form, radiating from centers in six branches of the same length, formed like fern leaves, tapering to a point from a wide base. The crystals are small, being only the one hundred and twenty-sixth part of an inch, and last for a short time only, as the camphor and alcohol are both very volatile.

But the most beautiful crystals that can be revealed by the microscope, are those prepared from solutions of muriate of ammonia, which, when liquified and placed upon a pane of glass, throws up first from the edges, short dagger-shaped crystals in every direction, perfectly transparent. From these, as they advance, other crystals shoot out in irregular lengths, but perfectly parallel to each other, and at right angles to the main shaft. These are again studded with crystals, which likewise shoot out at right angles ; and from these again others proceed to an indefinite number ; and when the light is caused to fall upon them in the right direction, rich prismatic colors are displayed, really beautiful to behold—so much so, that no description by words, or delineation by an artist, can convey a full conception of the richness and elegance of the resulting configurations to the mind.

MURIATE OF BARYTES.

When this substance is dissolved in water, a clean solution is formed devoid of color, which crystallizes immediately on glass, with a moderate heat, and by the power of the microscope presents to the eye figures of exquisite grace and astonishing delicacy ; but the fluid crystallizes so rapidly, and the glittering filaments, of whose rare beauty I cannot convey adequately an idea, with instantaneous flashes simultaneously disappear, but not before the observer has seen crystals rise, form branches, divide and subdivide into sprays and limbs, spreading their fairy boughs over the entire field of view, exhibiting a magnificent appearance if seen by a single light, when every crystal separately acts as a prism in the decomposition of the rays, and the field of view becomes immediately illuminated with the splendor of the rainbow.

Bichromate of potassa produces crystals in the form of four-sided prisms, of a transparent cherry color, which rapidly advance under the microscope into various configurations, forming single stems first, which heap into thousands of curved shoots, that entwine and interlace until a crystalline net work extends over the entire surface before occupied by the liquid, of rare and surpassing beauty, actually dazzling the eye with their rich and radiant configurations.

EPSOM SALTS.

The crystals of this salt are exceedingly beautiful, and as they grow, appear lavishly ornamented with exquisite figures. They shoot out parallel to each other in broad arrow-headed shafts, serrated on each side, and from these lateral crystals grow, until they interlock with each other and form a magnificent crystalline structure, resembling the promiscuous grouping of an immense number of fern leaves, placed one upon the other without the least regard to regularity, each shining with a soft exquisite pearly whiteness like the subdued radiance of the moon.

GLAUBER SALTS.

While crystallizing exhibits a singularly great diversity of combinations, it begins in a spicular cluster, and then spreads in needle-shaped crystals, which intersect others, and thus form a perfect lattice work. Sometimes solid crystals radiate from a center, like the spokes of a wagon wheel; then again they form themselves in rows similar to the teeth of a comb.

Alum is a substance artificially produced, though it is sometimes found in a native state. The form of its crystals are octahedron—that is to say, they have eight equal sides, replete with elegance and beauty, and as they advance in parallel lines, throw out spires laterally at right angles with the parent crystal; and from these others start forth and interlace with each other until they form a glittering sheet of graceful gothic arches of inconceivable beauty.

Common salt in solution, as it crystallizes never spreads out into numerous beautiful ramifications, but as the liquid evaporates, forms on the surface of the glass small sparkling diamonds of eight and twelve-sided figures, by the union of primitive cubical crystals, which sometimes attach to each other, and by degrees build up a hollow structure in the form of a pyramid, and what is very strange, is invariably capped by a single perfect cube.

Verdigris does not crystallize with the same rapidity that other salts do, because the solution evaporates very slowly, and forms small and large crystals, which cross each other in every direction, in many instances representing a perfect fleur-de-lis, of a fine greenish-blue color. The primitive form of the crystals is that of a rhomboid, as well defined and perfect as if cut by the lapidary, and are symmetrical, elegant and beautiful.

I have examined many minute aquatic creatures with the microscope, and among others the polype, which is found abundantly in brooks attached to aquatic plants. Its body consists of many cells, formed of green matter, possessing to a wonderful degree the power of contraction and expansion. Attached to the mouth there are sixteen arms, which the creature employs for the purpose of seizing its food. They appear to the naked eye as thin threads, but through the microscope slender tretles, consisting of numerous cells like the body, usually filled with a fluid. It feeds upon small crustaceous creatures, the structure of which has been so perfectly preserved for ages, that the microscopist readily detects the different species, and assigns them without difficulty to their appropriate place in the vegetable kingdom.

In the Isle of Portland immense forests of pine trees have been transformed into hard stone on the spot where they grew and once flourished. In the Lybian deserts numerous groves of trees have been petrified, crossing each other in every imaginable form as they were swept down by the tornado. And in the guano even, which we import from Ichaboe, have been found the beautiful shell of the coscinodiscus, which has resisted decomposition, after having passed through fish, then birds, and finally the action of the elements for many centuries, to gladden the eye of the naturalist in its unchanged, original, delicate form, sharp and clear as it left the Creator's hands. These secrets of nature would have been covered with impenetrable darkness forever had it not been for the microscope.

I found upon examining Ichaboe guano, that it contained brown earthy particles, mixed with sundry crystalline matters of different sizes. Some of them were evidently sand ; others crystals of saline matters. The Peruvian may be known from the Ichaboe from the fact that it contains very little crystalline matter in comparison. The value of either, however, does not depend upon the crystallization, but upon this organized particles of animalculi of numerous kinds, dried flesh of fish or birds, small shells, sponges, and half digested excrementitious matter. I discovered in Ichaboe guano a most remarkable egg, presenting the appearance of an Indian bow, with a cover attached, through which the insect had made its escape. The substance was hard, like that of isinglass, and profusely ornamented, though it could scarcely be discerned with the naked eye. Birds' eggs generally resemble each other in form, but not those of insects, which are of inconceivable variety and shape, and almost invariably beautifully wrought, representing carved work of the richest description. Butterflies' eggs, that have come under my observation, were of all shapes and sizes, round, cylindrical, elliptical, hemispherical, square, conical, apple-shaped, pear-shaped, and plum-shaped, with surfaces most splendidly ornamented, multiplies by shoots and buds, and possesses the power of reproducing any organs of which it may be accidentally deprived, and the parts so lost soon become complete polypes.

The water flea, is abundant in fresh water brooks, and ponds—its body is covered with plates of shell, overlapping each other ; its eyes are dark crimson. Attached to the lower extremities of the flea, there are sacks containing the eggs, and outside of these a forked tail adorned with a fringe of hair ; the body is often embellished with beautiful tints of a bluish green.

The boat fly, is abundant in my ponds—they swim on their backs, and use their hind legs as propellers, which are fashioned somewhat like oars ; when disturbed they drop to the bottom ; they obtain perfection at six months old, and deposit their eggs, which are small, and look like jelly ; they shed their skins several times during the summer ; it has three pair of feet fringed with hair ; at maturity it has wings, which are delicate and fragile, but protected from injury by hard cases.

The glutton is an aquatic animal, that nearly resembles the caterpillar, and is to a certain extent transparent ; under the microscope, in a good light, its internal structure may be clearly discerned. During fine weather they are generally to be found on the surface of the water, in cloudy weather at the bottom ; you may keep them alive indefinitely in vessels of water, where they will increase rapidly in size. It preys upon live insects, which you may often see attempting to get out of one of its stomachs, of which it has a number, divided from each other by a transparent elastic ring. Its digestive powers are extraordinary, as it often fills itself with the hard shelled monoculi, and remains torpid while digestion is advancing. This creature is found in the Croton, as well as the satyr, monoculi, vorticella, trichoda lyncens, common rotifier, guadricornus, water beetle, closterium sunula, bell shaped, and numerous other animalcules.

I have given much attention to microscopic examinations of woody fibre, and have been particularly delighted with the study. The microscope declares that all trees and plants consist of a woody portion, and pithy portion. The woody portion is composed of an enormous number of small tubes, commencing at the root and extending through numerous ramifications to every branch of the tree, numbering over seven millions to the square inch, and are not arranged as I always supposed they were, throughout the trunks, but are collected into bundles, numbering from thirty to many hundreds of tubes, arranged in regularly disposed concentric circles. I imagined, until the microscope taught me differently, that there were two kinds of tubes in a tree—one to carry air, and the other sap, and that is the reason why we have generally heard them called air vessels, and sap vessels. I am now convinced that they are all sap vessels, and that there are no air vessels in either trees or plants. These tubes are bound together by a tissue, filled with cells, which is usually called cellular tissue. The cells present to the microscope various forms, according to the plant in which they are examined. Some are angular, some square, others globular, triangular, but the greatest proportion are hexagonal. Some of them are so exceedingly minute as to be observed with difficulty by the most powerful microscope. The pith of a plant, or tree, consists almost entirely of cells of different sizes. That in the Canada thistle, appears about the size of honey comb cells ; that in the sumach, cherry, and pear, are much smaller ; and in the oak, so minute that it would require 100 to equal the pith of the thistle in size.

Were it not for this admirable instrument, the microscope, the botanist would be unable to reveal the beautiful structures of plants, and their extraordinary interior organization, thegeologist would fail to read the vegetable history of our world, which is plainly to be discerned in its fossil plants and trees, with exquisite carved work, arranged with longitudinal lines, symmetrically wrought; others are covered with scales, like those of a fish, and provided with lids, which open like a hinge. The butterfly produced by this egg, has wings perfectly resplendent with the most brilliant colors, and when the dust, which attaches to your fingers, on handling them, is examined with a microscope, presents the most beautiful feathers, painted with the hues of the rainbow. Another egg in the shape of a boot, produces one of the shortest lived, yet most perfect insects known in the world—it lives twenty-four hours—and yet God has endowed it with all the powers and organs necessary to discharge the same functions, in the round of existence, as those whose lives are of longer duration. Nothing can exceed the elegance and delicacy of its wing, which is constructed of a membrane thinner than the finest imaginable gauze, and is tinged with green, and otherwise beautifully ornamented.

Immense clouded areas have been noticed from time immemorial by navigators, in all oceans and seas, and in many instances at a great distance from land, and they were unable to account for it, until the microscope revealed that minute marine infusoria imparted their color to the surrounding water in which they existed. An area of twenty-two thousand square miles in the Greenland sea, presents to the eye of the mariner, a very deep olive green color, caused by an infinite number of living animalcules, individually imperceptible to the naked eye. Countless numbers of the huge monsters of the deep, resort to this prolific feeding ground, where they find an exhaustless supply of sustenance. On the east coast of the same sea, a yellow color is imparted to the water, which on examination by the microscope, proved to be lemon-colored animalcules, the largest of which was not more than the two thousand five hundredth of an inch in length—a single drop of water would contain twenty-five thousand of these little creatures.

On the coast of Chili a ship passed through large tracts of water presenting to the eye a deep red color, which, on being submitted to a microscope, proved to be animalcules a thousand one hundredth of an inch in length, oval in form, and encircled by a ring. When caught and placed in a vessel of water, they moved with such celerity against each other as to burst and change the fluid to a muddy chocolate color.

Human blood, when viewed under the microscope, exhibits very small red globules, floating in a colorless liquid. It is of two colors in the venous and arterial systems, dark crimson in the former, and scarlet in the latter. I have examined the blood of the horse, ox, hog, sheep, goose, turkey, eel, perch, frog, and could distinguish a difference between them all, the corpuscles were much larger in the fish and frog than they were in the man, ox and turkey.

The ears of all the grasses and cereal grains are subject to diseases, caused by the attacks of parasitic fungi, animalculæ and insects, because they have a large quantity of nitrogenous matter in them. Smut in grain is generated by a fungus which will entirely destroy it. Rust is formed by a distinct species of fungi. Mildew is probably an animal production.

I have made many interesting microscopical investigations of blight in fruit trees, which was invariably attributed by agriculturists to some mysterious atmospheric influence, an east wind, or thunder, because the discoloration of their leaves, branches, and death, occurred almost simultaneously. The microscope in all such cases has indicated to me innumerable insects as the cause.

The injury to wheat is generally attributed to the wheat midge; whereas my microscope has proved incontestibly that it is owing to the yellow maggot, derived from the egg of the midge deposited in the blossoms of the wheat in June. They are the cause of the abortion of the ovary, so that the grain can never advance beyond the state at which it had arrived at the time the flower first expanded. Wheat is subject also to mildew, smut and rust. The former, when examined under the microscope, indicates the presence of exceedingly minute plants of the mushroom tribe, known as fungi, which grow upon the stem and leaves, and rapidly exhaust the juices of the plant. Finding one field of wheat on my farm abounding more in mildew than another, I was induced, microscope in hand, to search out the cause, and found several barberry bushes in the vicinity covered with mildew. They were removed, and the prevalence of disease with them. When wheat is infected by smut, the integuments of the farina of the grain are converted into black powder, which, if wet with water and examined through the microscope, will present to view an enormous number of transparent globules of viscous fluid, covered with a membrane. And I have proved it infectious, by placing it upon healthy stems at a distance, which were not only attacked by the disease, but conveyed it to the seed, which, when sowed the following year, produced smutty plants.

Rust is another disease that prevails much in some districts. It is a brown dust, produced by a parasitical plant. The poisonous substance known as ergot in rye, is produced by a fungus plant. The smut in barley, when examined by the microscope, is shown to be an entirely different species from that in wheat, and though I could readily prevent it in the former by salt brine and lime, I could not remedy the evil in the latter by any application.

My microscope hints to me that all the grasses are subject to unmistakable diseases, all resulting from attacks of parasitic fungi, animalcules, and insects; and I can only explain it on the ground that they contain a very large amount of nitrogenised matter. At all events they offer to the agriculturist a fertile theme for reflection and observation. Grasses are chiefly injured at the roots from the larvæ of the cockchaffer, which always carry on their work of destruction below the surface of the ground. The lady bird (Cocconella impunctata,) and the moth (Liparis,) do great damage above ground. Insects obtain their food from the most extensive pasture grounds; from the majestic maple to the insignificant moss—all the plants in the universe are brought into requisition to feed and maintain them; every part of every plant, however nauseating, poisonous, or pleasant it may be, yields them provender. Some attack the roots, others the branches and stems, others the leaves and flowers, others still the fruit; no plant, or part of a plant escapes them, so declares the microscope. The potato disease is caused by an insect. And in my opinion it will yet be discovered that the cholera, yellow fever, small pox, and other epidemics, are caused by insects, which attack at the same period and in the same district, all those whose constitutions at the time are ripe for their inception, after which they gradually diminish, and finally disappear.

Suppose a man arrives here from Havana, infected at the time with the cholera insect, and brings only one corpuscle on his body, or in his clothes, and spends four days in a fœtid atmosphere, congenial to disease, this perfectly imperceptible corpuscle, can create by its amazing fertility, one hundred and eighty billions of microscopic life, within that time. Corpuscles increase in various ways, and among others by voluntary division; and this characteristic separates plants from animals. It is a fact that gemmation in plant cells, is similar to the division in animals; plant cells divide by exterior warts, without any internal change. The animal doubles first the inner organs, and decreases externally in size; self division in them proceeds from the centre to the periphery.

Microscopic animalculæ are always the cause of putrefaction. If you would prove this, place a piece of beef in a dish in any position that will favor putrescence, and you will soon observe under the microscope, an immense number of animalcules in it, sometime before smell indicates any change. This may be called the first period of putridity. Twelve hours after, the liquor will turn litmus paper red, when the animalcules will be found quadrupled in number, and from pellicles or eggs, will be discovered floating on the surface of the liquor, and still no unpleasant odour will emit from the mass when meat is in this state. I imagine mankind daily consume in a single meal, billions of monades, as the cook has no way of discovering any thing wrong. At a later period, the microscope indicates detached pieces of animal matters floating in the liquid of the meat, which are nothing more or less than millions of agglomerated animalcules. At this period the odor is slightly unpleasant, but not sufficiently so to be discarded by the cook. Shortly after this, the liquid becomes fœtid, and animalcules are discovered congregated together in masses containing billions.

Microscopic investigations have revealed to us, that the orange, brown, blood red, and rose colors, observed in our beautiful agates, are agglomerated animalcules, distributed through these siliceous compounds, according to circumstances.

I believe that the hair on human heads, is inhabited by microscopic animals, so minute, as to remain unscathed by the comb. I have observed on two occasions, with the naked eye, an elongated white excrescence, near the root of a hair, on two different heads, and on obtaining them from the individuals, submitted them severally to the microscope, and to my amazement, found them to be most beautifully constructed nests, filled to repletion with eggs.

Last summer I saw a small fly alight upon the back of a spider, and after remaining for a few seconds it departed. I caught the spider, but could only perceive a minute wound where the fly had rested; it was placed in a bottle, and in a short time became the residence of a larva, which ultimately assumed the pupa form, at which period the spider died, and a worm proceeded from its carcass, to the side of the bottle, and there inclosed itself in a transparent silk covering, which reflected a metallic lustre ; at the end of three weeks a perfect fly issued from it, and took no notice of a spider that was placed in the bottle, until three days had elapsed, when it deposited an egg in the creature's body, precisely as its parent had done before ; this egg did not come to maturity.   There is a parasite animalcule, having a long body, abdomen, with two arms and four legs, thorax and head, existing in the sebaceous follicles or cutecular cells of every human being ; they are very numerous in the depressions on each side of the nose, and on the breast and back.   During sickness they increase rapidly, and after death abound.

Nearly all microscopic animalcules are complicated in their organization. They form two classes entirely different from each other.   Their distribution, geographically speaking, is governed by the same laws that govern other animals.   They color water, and emit phosphorescent light in the sea they inhabit.   Fifty millions of them may be counted in a square inch of liquid.   They possess wonderful generative powers, as a single individual has been known to produce several millions like itself in a few hours. They constitute rocks, stones, earth, whiting, ochre, &c., by their silicious outer coverings.   They cause water to become impure, kill fish, induce miasma, cholera, yellow fever, and all contagious diseases.   They are always in motion, and never sleep.   Men and animals are full of them, and they again are tormented with parasites.   They abound in the atmosphere, and we breathe them at every breath.   The deposits in all the rivers and harbors of the earth, generally attributed to the accumulation of solid earth, is no doubt mainly the produce of animal organisms.   The red-colored snow of the Alps is caused by them ; in it they deposit their eggs, which develop and reproduce abundantly.   Four millions may be included in a grain of wheat.   They are single-celled organisms.   Last year an immense cloud passed over Shanghai, from which an impalpable powder fell upon the city, which, on being submitted to the microscope, proved to be spores of a confervoid plant, which vegetated in the Chinese sea, and imparted to it a peculiar color.   A shower of dust alighted on a ship's deck near the Cape de Verde Islands, which proved to be minute organisms known as dialomaceæ.   A sample of dust from a similar cloud collected on a ship's deck, five hundred miles from the coast of Africa, exhibited, under the microscope, many species of fresh water and marine diatoms filled with life, and there is no doubt resting in my mind but that they were developed in the air.   Last summer I was standing on my piazza at sunrise, looking towards the Hudson river, but saw nothing in the atmosphere to elicit attention, but moving a few feet, a column obstructed my view of the sun, when to my amazement I found the air, as far as I my eye could reach, filled with minute insect life, which could not be seen in any other position.   On wetting a shingle and passing it quickly through the air, a great number adhered, and though amazingly small, each individual had a parasite attached to it.   Being an unbiased observer, I was stimulated to make sun. dry examinations of atmospheric organisms and their progressive self-development, which at a proper time will be revealed.

The principal characteristic of this immense assemblage of existences, is the entire absence of an internal bony structure. Their hard parts are always outside, and form the necessary covering. Their bodies are invariably divided into transverse joints, and consequently they are called by naturalists annulose or ringed creatures,

I would recommend you, if an opportunity occurs, to examine with a microscope the respiration of the silk worm, which is not possessed of lungs, therefore does not breathe through the mouth, but through spiracles connected with the respiratory tubes, that extend to all parts of the body. All the animals that are not higher than the order of the silk worm, breathe in the same manner. Still life, with all its admirable endowments, belongs to them as well as to us, and each individual of this vast insect world, is as perfectly organized as we are, and not one of them shall "fall to the ground without our Father." And it matters not how powerful our microscopes become, as the omniscient God, through His creative energy, will still reveal to our wondering sight developments so inconceivably small that hundreds of millions may be contained within the diameter of a mite's eye.

There is no subject that I have given more attention to than the honey bee. I had a house constructed and filled with glass hives, so arranged that all their movements were exposed to me at all times, and a single discovery paid me amply for all the trouble I had taken. I placed about thirty thousand working bees in an empty glass hive, and with them a young queen fresh from the royal cell. The workers immediately constructed two combs, containing 400 cells, across the hive, in which the queen at once deposited unimpregnated eggs, some of which I examined from time to time with the microscope, and waited with intense anxiety to discover what they would produce. To my astonishment they were all drones, proving conclusively that the queen possesses the power within herself of impregnating an egg, but that egg only capable of producing a drone or male bee. The drones when born were full size. The queen then passed out of the hive, rose immediately into the atmosphere, was followed by a single drone, and returned after ten minutes absence, when she immediately commenced depositing fecundated eggs, which in due time produced the working bee. It is a remarkable fact that when a working bee leaves the hive to collect the materials for making honey, it invariably alights on flowers of the same species.

THE MICROSCOPE.

(ORIGINAL.)

Nature hides half her wondrous works
   From unassisted eyes;
For in her least developments
   A world of wonder lies.

With teeming life the rock abounds,
   The mist, the ether blue,
And every grain of matter lives
   To microscopic view.

And so the common mind is dull,
  And sees not while it sees,
Till science, like a glass reveals,
  In manifest degrees

The wonders of the hidden powers,
  The powers of sense and sight,
Showing a world where all was void,
  And making darkness light.

Mr. Seeley.—As to theory—telescope and microscope alike. The eye glass magnifies the object transmitted by the object glass; the microscope is much the most interesting and useful—ten dollars will buy the one and thousands of dollars the other.

Mr. Griscom.—The globules of blood, as man's, recently an evidence of the utility of microscope.

Mr. Seeley.—Blood of animals, different from human blood.

Prof. Cyrus Mason.—It is somewhat mortifying that the useful labor of this club is without a report, while at another place the rich are devising an expenditure of $200,000 for an observatory, not at all wanted, for astronomy has made no important advance for a long time. My able and excellent friend Mitchell, is entertaining the crowd well—all the guesses as to the planetary population, do not maintain the Lock Moon Hoax, and we are acquiring nothing at all new. Far more do I hope from the universally useful knowledge opened up to us by the power of the microscope. If I had millions of dollars I would set thousands of proper observers at work with its marvellous power of displaying the great secrets of animal and vegetable existence—the detection of those tremendous but invisible poisons in miasm, in cholera, in all diseases, in certain localities, now shrouded in utter darkness, and the true nature of remedies. I want to have the alkaloids investigated. I found cholera on places apparently as pure as others, under which miasma was covered; from places, the undrained underground gave cholera. If we could see the elements of the disease, we could at least fly from it if we could not cure it. Homœopathy is quackery; we talk of atoms infinitessimal like parrots; we know nothing about it. I read Moses! and believe in him, so does my friend Mitchell!

I have seen hundreds die of cholera; they died easily and without pain. With a view to more knowledge of disease, we should sustain a system of examination by all the means in our power; by analysis long and rigid, looking alone to facts, not so much to theory. In the microscope as we *have it*, or as by improvement we *may have it*, great developments, of the highst import to men may be expected. The doctors, *allo* or *homœopathic*, wish as we do, that they knew enough to meet disease face to face and to conquer it, instead of *dodging* it or flying away from it. We ought to have here, and well read too (which we do not, in matters of science,) the modern work, "Yearbook of Science;" it has superior merit.

Prof. Hedrick.—It is published in German and translated into English; it deserves all that Prof. Mason has said of it. If we had time, I would speak of Hassall's chemical analyses of foods and drugs lately; they have high interest.   The microscope now co-operates in analytical chemistry with great power.   There is great room for its application.   Chemistry wants all the aid that mathematicians can give it.

Prof. Mason.—My want is a grand concentrated system of examination.

Mr. Veeder desired a continuance of this subject, in reference to its great value in discovering the truth in articles of commerce, and hoped that the Institute would place on the table the best microscopes for use, and instruction how to use them—for knowing soils, plants parasitic evils, grain, colors on straw, &c., due to causes, which, when developed by the microscopic power, would also lead us to the preventives and remedies.

Prof. Mason.—I thank the gentleman.   To enlighten our fellow men was the object of our friend Tallmadge, whose portrait looks at us from the wall.   Let us go on !   In the progress of my democracy, I have been compelled, *seriatim*, to drop my hopes of teaching much to the negro or to the masses—some become exceptions—but there are no hopes for the many.   No sir; not even for a bit of our immense dominion on which to concentrate learning in the culture of vegetation !   Our national concentrated political wisdom at Washington, will not, *can not* do that *wise act !*

Prof. Hedrick.—If our learned friend Prof. Mason is right as to the lack of popular wisdom, he must allow me to add "and that of the class Doctor."

Thomas Godwin offered a resolution for a special committee, to confer with the Institute as to the organization, offices, &c., of this club.

On motion, laid on the table.

Prof. Mason.—Arch Bishop Hughes would like a proper examination of the material to be used in his new Cathedral ; so would the Commissioner for building our new City Hall.   Even in England, for lack of proper examination, their buildings in general do not last five hundred years !   Scientific men, there, have taken up this scrutiny of material to be used.

Mr. Stetson.—And in all mechanism, a like examination is very much wanted, especially and *peremptorily* in metals—as boilers, shafts, &c., so that their power to sustain their work safely may be *exactly known*, and so save millions of money and numerous precious lives.

Alanson Nash.—Wished such examination could be made here.   Look well to the structure of our marbles, formed probably by atomic animals ; look through vegetable structure, to the *dead horse* which fed the plants ; look to animal and vegetable, as the origin of existing matter.

Questions, by the committee of science, &c. : " The microscope as related to the nature and quality of materials, in chemistry and mechanic arts," and " The best materials for public buildings in cities."

The club then adjourned.

H. MEIGS, *Secretary.*

March 2d, 1859.

Present.—Messrs. R. L. Pell, Leonard, Nowlan, Prof. Mason, Prof. Hedrick, Everitt, Bruce, Cohen, Seeley, Witt, John Johnson, Haskell,

Davidson, D. Holton, Veeder, Pierson, of Toronto, Canada, Judge Scoville, John W. Chambers, Alanson Nash, John Campbell, Finell, Breisach, Henry Fitz, Dr. Deck, Lawton, Engineer Stetson, and others—58 members in all.

Robert L. Pell in the chair. Henry Meigs, Secretary.

The Secretary read the following extracts from Lindley's Vegetable Kingdom, viz. :

DIATOMACEÆ—(*Divisions.*)

Crystalline, angular, fragmentary bodies, brittle, multiplying by spontaneous separation. They are generally bounded by right lines—rarely by curved lines—flat, stiff, brittle, usually nestling in slime, uniting into various forms, and then parting again. Rocks moistened, hot-house glasses, walls in shade, hard paths in gardens, in damp places after rain, show a green mucous slime, which contains algals in their simplest state of organization. Bory de St. Vincent called them chaodineæ—*a chaos*—*a provisional creation*—assuming afterwards various forms, according to the nature of the corpuscles which penetrate it or are developed in it. It may be said to originate animal and vegetable existence. This mucus sometimes agglomerates and floats over water ; becomes green by forming inside of each corpuscle, vegetable corpuscles. They often have a milky or a ferruginous appearance, when, by the microscope, we find it filled with animalcules, the naviculareæ, lunulinæ, and stylariæ, in such close crowds as to be unable to swim. Agardh calls them plants ; Kützing says that they are as much animal as vegetable. That at all events the achnanth (down flowers,) gomphonema, (like pegs,) exilaria, (thin,) fragiluria, meloseira, schizonema, micromega, and berkleya, are at least plants if frustulia, cymbella, navicula, surirella, &c., are animalcules. He has recently ascertained that the frustules of micromega are metamorphosed into green globular spores. Dr. Dickie, of Aberdeen, has observed something of the same kind. Mr. Ralfs, who has devoted great attention to these doubtful creatures, observes that one division of them, the cymbelleæ, rapidly becomes putrid, have a silicous covering ; consequently their forms do not alter in drying, and are not destroyed by fire. When perfect, their color is brownish, but not unfrequently becomes greenish on drying. Their figures are usually either quadrilateral or prism, with streaks and dots. The desmideæ putrify very slowly ; have no silicious coat. When perfect they have generally a herbaceous green color. Ralfs recognizes the universal diffusion of starch among the desmideæ. He thinks they are undoubtedly vegetable. The genera noted are 45, and the species enumerated some ten years ago, 457. Some of these supposed chaonidæ turned out on examination by Berkley, to be *eggs of insects*

Next in order, confervacea, fucaceæ, ceremaniaceæ, or *rose tangles ;* genera 88, species 682, according to Endlicher. Characeæ water plants, fungus genera, 598, species, 4,000 ; lichen genera 58, species, 2,400.

SUBMARINE TELEGRAPH CABLE.

The *London Artizan* of Feb. 1, 1859, says, that by experiment it is found that fifty miles of the Atlantic cable, recovered from a depth of not more than 140 fathoms, was become unserviceable for the electric use.

[London Mechanic's Magazine, Jan. 28, 1859.]

EXPLORATION OF AUSTRALIA BY BALLOONS.

To take with them an improved gigantic fire balloon, to be carried collapsed, but to be inflated without gas if it should be wanted. Photographic apparatus to be taken for securing accurate bird's eye views.

Mr. Veeder moved to dispense with further miscellaneous business, and take up the regular subjects. Carried.

Mr. Seeley.—Will microscopic observation add important knowledge, or will it, like the science of astronomy, prove to be very limited in its value to the welfare of man ? Will some one tell us how it is relative to human diseases ?

Dr. Holton said he felt modestly inclined in reference to the latter, although great attention is devoted to it. As, for instance, Dr. Virachoux, at Berlin, has 300 students, whose opportunities for microscopic observation are probably equal, if not superior, to others. I saw that school at work with the microscopes. A kind of zig-zag miniature railroad of metal carried the microscope to every student, while the learned Professor lectured on the object under view. The tissues of flesh, &c., in a state of disease underwent full examination through the highest magnifying power. As to infusoriæ, Ehrenberg devoted his life to their study, and, you all know, with deeply interesting developments of microscopic existence. The supposed (vulgarly) rain of blood proved to be animalculæ. In this way some prejudices are removed, which is always positive good. Professor Mitchell's nebulæ appears to have power of concentration, so that the unformed mass may in due time be concentrated into a globe. What can one say of our knowledge ? God alone concentrates them. Mystery, utterly beyond our penetration, conceals His work from us. We find, by great magnifying power, that matter apparently amorphous, yet is organic. We find, as we suppose, the primitive cell; it seems to be homogeneous ; yet on its development this little cell contains the organization of all animal and vegetable life. We have examined with anxious desire to learn the true cause of that terrible disease, cancer. The cells do not yet teach us. Our able physicians are closely studying the cause pathologically, and by every mode of access to the truth, thinking, perhaps very reasonably, that when we find what it really is, they can prevent or heal it. They earnestly try every means of diagnosis.

Prof. Mason was pleased so far, but it reminded him of our lawyer, who lost our cause for us, but claimed the merit of settling a *point of law!* Our inquiry is, by what means we may render life more happy and of greater duration. Therefore we seek for the causes of disease. It is the grand question of the age, for there is a manifest degeneracy among us, very much as in former ages destroyed whole nations. Let us take a grand view of this matter, and try to alter our plan and develop strong bodies with strong minds for our successors here. If it is a vanity, it is at least a glorious one. I feel almost a stranger here. Yet but a short time ago, when I had the honor to deliver an address for the American Institute, I knew almost all its members ; now I see here but one (pointing to Secretary Meigs). Soon shall we all leave. Let us leave good behind us. I have always found my family best in health, most free of the doctors, during the fruit season, when I supply it fresh and ripe.

Mr. Garbanati.—The doctors are often compelled to change their course. We long chased the potato disease, and found its cause, an insect.

Dr. Holton.—Let us reflect the immense *external influences* always bearing upon us.

Engineer Stetson.—Our business here is entirely for practical purposes. Mechanism implies exactness to a given extent. Let us act accordingly, examine, and then report facts. Microscope tell us the true nature of fibre. in all our clothing. We decide with it that the mummy cloth of Egypt was chiefly linen, and not cotton as generally supposed. We test animal fibre cell, &c. I am not aware of its useful test of woody fibre, as yet. It has served well in examining metals. Fuchs has done much in iron. It may lead us to precision in choosing iron, both for strength and for durability ; for in fact we find great difference in iron in these most important particulars—need I mention, in steam boilers !—and the boiler makers, as yet, do not understand it. Good mechanics do much by feeling as well as by fracture, &c., but we want a test good for all ! that we may know positively what our boilers really can bear, and so with other forms of iron. Sugar refiners, by the microscope, discover the best sugar by the crystal, and the grape juice, or molasses, and by a sample, will buy *or not* a whole cargo !

Alanson Nash.—Wool staplers buy wool by microscopic examination ; leather also, as to its fibre and tanning ; so too of drugs, in which the cheating is beyond conception ; so too of counterfeit signatures on bank notes, &c. The very real tremulous signature of the old president or cashier, is detected, although it could not be copied in the counterfeit. I know that I am a very imperfect philosopher, but I love facts.

Mr. Veeder.—The remarks of the gentleman are very pertinent, notwithstanding his disclaimer of being a philosopher.

Dr. Deck had in Egypt examined carefully the mummy cloth. Herodotus says they used some cotton. The main mass, which is very great, is linen, made from some plant more like the *phormium tenax*, of New Zealand, than our flax. They had also, chiefly for garments of their priests, a cloth of a kind of wool not now known. The cotton resembles our Sea Island.

Prof. Mason.—Why may not study of culture and manures for cotton, give us Sea Island fibre, where now we grow only short staple, at one-fourth less value ?

Mr. Seeley.—Nitrate of silver is found in Egyptian work. Did they understand the photograph?

Dr. Deck.—One thousand seven hundred years before our Saviour, they used an amalgam of mercury and copper, with which, while soft, the most perfect and sharp moulds can be made from inscriptions, &c., and which afterwards becomes very hard.

Mr. Davison.—The eye piece is the magnifier. This Ross, of London, instrument, cost $350. It magnifies three thousand diameters. There is no one over 8,500. This uses polarized light, and is therefore superior for showing differences in minute objects. Spencer makes excellent ones.

Mr. Nash adverted to the presence of iron in marbles, and to the observation that marble increases in purity and value in proportion to the distance of its quarry from the equator, so that we may look for the very best in the Arctic circle, where Sir John Franklin lies.

Dr. Deck supposed the quarries on low latitudes were injured by volcanic action, while those of the high latitudes are sedimentary marbles.

Prof. Mason.—Our city hall is of good marble. Fifty years finds it untouched. The rear of it, of red sand stone, is failing. We have marble of good quality at Lenox. Here is a piece from the bottom, near the creek, almost equal to the best statuary marble.

Mr. Stetson.—Have the crystals of it been tried as to strength?

Mr. Nash.—We have discovered to-night, that all the mud of our harbor abounds in shell. We need no longer go to Peru for guano! No need of a quarrel with Peru about that.

Mr. Everitt.—As to vulcanized india rubber. The microscope shows the sulphur perfectly, and chemical analysis could not do that.

Mr. Deck.—As to flour, I find chemistry beat, at least in one case, that of adulteration with beans, for the microscope cannot detect the bean flour, which chemistry can.

Mr. Pierson, of Toronto, Canada, described an extensive quarry of free stone, white limestone, &c., of his, thirty-three miles from Toronto. He wants capital to work it. A specimen of the stone was before the club.

Prof. Mason hoped we might prove our material, then build cathedrals, city halls, &c., to stand for future ages so many monuments of our science, showing that we gloried in the future, as men should do, and not die down like the savage, or the wild animal, leaving no vestige on the earth which we were created to enjoy, to till, to civilize, and be remembered as long as material can survive. I always speak well of Jews! What an immortal race! Beginners of great things! Leaders now in many kingdoms! Never poor, never idle—more durable than monuments.

The Chairman.—And never known to beg!

Prof. Mason moved that the Secretary ask Prof. Henry, of the Smithsonian Institution, for such information as he may please to give us relative to materials for building.

Subjects for next meeting. The committee gave: "The building materials of New York," and "Electrotyping."

Mr. Haskell called for Mr. Pell's article on the microscope.

Mr. Pell.—I will finish at the next meeting.

Mr. Nowlan to have ten minutes for his bridge.

Adjourned at 10 o'clock P. M.

H. MEIGS, *Secretary.*

The title "MECHANICS' CLUB," changed to POLYTECHNIC ASSOCIATION.

A meeting of the committee on manufactures, sciences and arts, of the American Institute, was held at their rooms, on the 3d day of March.

Present—John D. Ward, (Chairman,) Samuel D. Tillman, Alexander H. Everett, Mendes Cohen, (Secretary.)

The following resolution was offered by Mr. Tillman:

Resolved, That the name of "The Mechanics' Club," which is under the supervision of this committee, be and is hereby changed to the *Polytechnic Association.*

Mr. Tillman briefly explained the reasons which should influence the committee in making this change. It was well known that the club contained several prominent chemists, and that chemical subjects were often discussed, yet many persons still believe they are excluded from this club, on account of its title. If the general application of science to the arts furnish proper themes at all times, in this society, it should have a title which will fully define its object—the term "Polytechnic," already made famous in France, is certainly broad enough to embrace all branches of arts, and he hoped the change proposed would be approved.

Mr. Everett seconded the resolution, and it was unanimously adopted.

A copy of the resolution was ordered to be transmitted to the Institute at its next meeting.

March 9, 1859.

Present—Messrs. Robert L. Pell, Prof. Mason, Prof. Hedrick, Civil Engineers, Tillman, Everitt, Stetson; Messrs. Griscom, Garbanati, Seeley, John Johnson, Engineer Haskell, Breisach, Bruce, Veeder, William B. Leonard, John W. Chambers, Judge Scoville, Finell, Hoover, Dwight, of New Haven, and others—forty-five in all.

Robert L. Pell in the chair. Henry Meigs, Secretary.

The Secretary read the following articles extracted by him from the Journal of the London Society of Arts:

[Journal of the Society of Arts, and of the Institutions in Union—London, April, 1858.]

PLATINUM.

It is estimated that the Island of Borneo, can supply about 1,000 lbs. of it, annually. Scales of it being found among the gold sands in the valleys of the Ratoe mountains, in the Laset district. That the yield is about one-tenth of the gold. Where diamonds are plenty, gold and platinum are scarce. Some of the ore of platinum contains grains of cinnabar.

The platinum ore of Banjarmassin, separated by hydrochloric acid gives,

Iron oxide and iron,	1.13
Copper,	0.50
Gold,	3.97
Platinum,	70.21
Osmium,	1.15
Iridium,	6.13
Palladium,	1.44
Rhodium,	0.50
Iron,	5.80
Copper,	0.34
Insoluble in aqua regia, osmiridium and minerals,	8.83

The platinum appears in small circular or oval laminæ, like drops laminated, as if struck with a hammer——seldom has any facettes. The gold in it is like pepitas in miniature, microscopic nuggets. South American platinum resembles it. Last year, Mons. Chapins, of Paris, stated that rhodium alloyed with platinum could be hammered and laminated readily. Aqua regia cannot attack it, rendering it therefore very valuable to the practical chemist.

Batchelder's American patent, takes iridium, alloyed with copper for etching. Rhodium is worth, according to its degrees of purity, from $7, to $250 an ounce. The residue of platinum ore is now worth $100 a pound, and a few years ago it sold for $20 a pound.

April 29th, 1858.

The first conversazione of the present session was held on Saturday evening last, at the Society's house. The whole of the rooms were thrown open, and in the great room was displayed a series of upwards of sixty drawings of curious modes of marine propulsion, prepared and kindly lent by Mr. J. MacGregor. Models, also, patented from 1794 to 1850. Mr. Tompkins kindly attended with his Ross' finest microscope and infusorial animals. Also an historical series of telegraphs, including Wheatstone's first six-line wire needle telegraph, and the needle instruments at present in general use. Wheatstone's magnetic electric dial and capstan instruments; Baines' chemical telegraph; Highton's single needle; Henley's needle telegraph; Siemen's and Halskel's indication relay and magnetic dial, and their recording instrument for sub-marine lines; Varley's. These instruments were in operation during the evening. Specimens of all the cables were exhibited; locomotives, engines, new life boat, &c., &c.

The Society holds two conversazione in April and May.

IRON BUILDING.

Her Majesty's commissioners in 1848 tried experiments on the strength of iron, relative to violent concussions, vibrations, &c. Loaded cars, run down inclined planes. and along iron bars placed horizontally at the bottom; the cars acquired certain velocities in descent. First, a load of 1,120 pounds was placed at rest on a pair of iron bars nine feet long, four inches wide, and one and one-half inches deep, occasioning a deflection of six-tenths of an inch. It was then passed over by the car at the rate of ten miles per hour, whereby the deflection was increased to eight-tenths. Finally, at thirty miles per hour, when the deflection was one and a half inches. It follows that a much less load will break the bars in passing over them than when it is placed on the bars in a state of rest.

In the above example, a weight of 4,150 pounds is required to break the bars when placed on the centers; but a weight of 1,778 pounds is sufficient to produce fracture at the velocity of thirty miles an hour. The bars, when broken, were always broken at points beyond their centers, and often into four or five pieces, thus indicating the great and unusual strain they had been subjected to.

The Britannic Tubular Bridge was tried by a train of twenty-eight wagons and two locomotives, with 280 tons of coal, was drawn into all four tubes and caused a deflection of only three-fourths of an inch. They were then sent through after a start of a mile at the greatest velocity, and the deflection *was less!*

VALUE OF DIAMONDS.

I was informed by a jeweller the other day that diamonds are weighed and valued by the carat, containing four grains. Tennant read a paper recently before the London Society of Arts, in which he says a diamond containing one carat is worth.............................. $40 00
Eight carats, ... 1,000 00
Ten carats, ... 1,500 00
Thirty carats,... 36,000 00
Fifty carats, ... 100.000 00
One hundred carats, ... 400,000 00

The diamond may be known from other precious stones from the fact that it has only single refraction, whereas all others have double, except the garnet; that is to say, they give a two-fold image of a taper or minute light when looking through their facets.

My test, which I suppose is known to every one, to discover artificial from real diamonds, is to immerse them in strong alcohol, when not only artificial diamonds but all real and artificial stones will lose their lustre, except the true diamond alone.

The diamond, when applied to glass, does not cut it as is supposed, but merely forces the particles of glass apart without destroying them, the same as a wedge forces wood. It is not necessary that the diamond should penetrate the glass even to the three hundredth part of an inch to produce the required effect. As it passes over the glass, the crack confines itself to a mathematical point at the bottom of the line, and little or no effect is afterwards required to produce the desired result.

VALUE OF IRON.

The following calculation has been made to show that mechanical labor expended on iron completely exceeds the cost of the material.

Iron that may be purchased for five dollars, can be worked into watch springs worth $45,000 00
Blades for pocket knives, ... 850 00
Finished buttons, ... 4,500 00
Common knives, ... 190 00
Sewing needles, ... 355 00
Shoes for horses, ... 15 00
Cast iron of the same value in shirt buttons would be worth . $29,000 00
Fancy chains, ... 7,000 00
Piston of a steamer, ... 18 00
Buckles for stocks, ... 2,900 00
Rustic work, ... 250 00
Wire two hundred miles in length.

VALUE OF GOLD.

All the gold in the universe, if melted into bars, might be packed in a room twenty-three feet square and seventeen feet high. The gold obtained from Australia and California up to the last arrivals reported in this country and Europe, could be placed with ease in a box eight feet high and ten feet square.

King David received from the people for the sanctuary about three yards and a half of gold, worth thirty-five millions of dollars, besides which he expended four thousand four hundred and fifty-four millions of dollars,— millions more than the whole national debt of Great Britain, which was, March 31st, 1855, $3,873,986,095.

Solomon overlaid a room thirty feet square with gold, at a cost of one hundred and ninety millions of dollars.

One grain of gold may be beat so as to extend over many square feet, and still remain sufficiently compact to prevent a ray of light from being transmitted through it. A cube of gold the size of a thousandth part of an inch, will contain two million five hundred thousand parts visible to the eye through a microscope. A cylinder of gold twenty-one inches long and half an inch in diameter, may be stretched into a wire thread three hundred miles long.

When gold is refined from all alloys it is considered pure gold, or twenty four carats fine. This is the standard at the mint. No gold, however, comes up to this standard in reality. If gold is called twenty-two carats fine, it is alloyed with one part silver and one copper, or two parts of silver.

It is a singular fact that miners can determine with great accuracy the character of metalliferous deposits by their position. Copper veins, for instance, have a westerly and easterly direction in the mine. Lead veins run from north to south. And what is more strange still, if any position of a vein is changed a few degrees by an earthquake or upheaval of the earth's crust, which often happens, the character of the mineral changes immediately; so that one variety prevails when the formation is in one direction, and a different one when it deviates from that line, plainly showing that there is some law of polarity working not generally understood, and I have no doubt but that electricity has much to do with it.

Mr. Tillman opened the discussion of the regular subject of the sitting, "Building materials of this State," by adverting to the known excellence of some of our marble quarries, conveniently situated for us, and asking some member to say why they are not used? I see a gentleman who can tell us.

Professor Cyrus Mason.—Meaning me, sir? I profess to know but little; but I do notwithstanding know that we lose enormous sums of money by means of want of knowledge of the materials proper for building. Boston began with the granite, from her hills, which, however imposing to unstudied observers, is with its mechanical structure of feldspar, mica and quartz, not durable. Buildings of it scarcely fifty years old, show decay. Bricks are very superior to any sand stones, which are also mechanical in structure. Sands cemented with a little iron, failing rapidly, wherever shady and moist, forming a soil for mosses, which aid the power of weather to scale it, and soon disintegrate it—even the very best of it, as in Trinity church, at the head of Wall street, or the rear of our city hall. I call on members for all their strength, to give such a course to the builders, at least of all public edifices, as may leave monuments for ages to come. I desire that a committee may be appointed to examine and report on this subject. Some of our marble buildings are made of a marble containing so much iron as soon stains its surface—as in Barnum's museum, the University, and others.

The history of brick will necessarily be embraced in this examination. In the new country west of Milwaukee, necessity produced an artificial material, that is sand and lime very intimately mixed, pressed into moulds of required forms, of which firm, tight and dry walls have been made. Like material has been made in Connecticut, and in New Hampshire, where they condense it by pressure. The combination consists of nine parts of sand to one of lime, and the pressure stated to be five thousand pounds weight. Partitions are well made of it. It is very valuable to those districts where timber, and clay for bricks are scarce. England first burned her bricks in the 14th century. Buildings of stone and these bricks were decayed, that is the stone, a hundred years ago! while of course the bricks were just as good as when they were taken from the kiln. Great error exists in reference to machines for making brick. Great pressure used on the clay, leaves the edges of the brick brittle, they readily lose the proper sharp edges, and their faces soon begin to show the small pox, being pitted by the dropping out of small granules. Mortar wants our study. Stewart's front structure has nearly every stretcher broken! He employed Brigaldi, an artist of great merit in drawing and painting—superintending a school of design. Mr. Stewart saw some of his work, was highly pleased with him, and trusted his great building to him.   The facade on Chambers street is good.

We must so open the eyes of our people that they will be compelled to employ none but thoroughly educated architects.   Our rich men seem to dream that God foreordained that they must build a house, if it does not stand long enough for his child's home.   This question is vital to the reputation of our great city.   I think that there is no material equal to pure marble.   None of our granites bear the polish of some of the European !

The Year Book of Facts, is very instructive on this as well as many other questions—let it be studied.   And we have a teacher at home, entitled to our fullest respect—Professor Dana, whose knowledge is mature. I quote him a moment on the solidification of materials by crystallization. He gives minutely the forms of the constituent particles, from the angular to the globular.   All sand stones are agglomerations, not crystallizations ; there is not a building in England that can last one thousand years !   Pure lime stone, entirely free from iron ! all carbon !   Unorganized crystal has nothing to wear away ; a building of pure quartz would endure beyond all time.   We manure our land with lime, which unites with carbon and really becomes marble in minute particles !   You know that ancient statues of pure marble, made 2000 or 3000 years ago, whether covered up by the ruins of the cities they adorn, or exposed to air and light during that series of ages, maintain the very polish first received by them from the statuaries. This is also true of the buildings of pure marble, exposed to the weather as long.   Such material is glorious for our transitory corporeal race—it perpetuates the powers of his mind when endless generations of their bodies have become dust.

Within ten years, the lower part of our city has become marble.   When I saw the first marble store, I asked the merchant owner about it   He replied " I built it for a sign."   Every one sees it, contrasted with the dusky looking houses about it.   A better taste than the old one has commenced growing among us.   The brown stone quarry, with its moss growing decaying character, is not so "potential" as it was.   I will willingly work on a committee ; we will call on science for help.

I tried a hard burned brick in water—it gained hardly any weight—it would make a perfectly tight house.   The bricks of the late Presbyterian church, on Beekman street, broke, mortar and all alike—one solid body. We must read Professor Dana's excellent essays on molecular structure of bodies.

Mr. Leonard nominated Prof. Mason as chairman of the committee.

Mr. Veeder.—Let the Chairman name his associates.

The Chairman appointed Messrs. Tillman and Dwight, and added Dr. Deck.

Mr. Dwight.—Nineveh contained no burned bricks.

Mr. Tillman.—The position of our city is admirably adapted to noble edifices, and I join in the enthusiasm of Prof. Mason in relation to monumental building—showing that we did not live in vain.   It is recently proposed to wash the surface of marbles with a silicate of lime, impenetrable to moisture. Silicon and boron belong to the oldest formations.

Prof. Mason.—Michael Angelo, the glorious architect of St. Peter's, of Rome, selected good marble! Time continues to praise his work!

Mr. Stetson was inclined to doubt many, so said improvements. The proposed wash has failed in England, and here, in a government building; nor do I like the crystal shine of some of our new marble buildings—they dazzle more than they please the eye. Silicate of potash is a glass.

Mr. Everitt.—It has been tried on wood. It is a failure on marble. England uses the silicate of soda—it will not do.

Prof. Mason disliked doughfaces in such questions, as much as in politics! Does the gentleman dislike a fair lady because she sparkles with brilliants? Our city hall, in spite of dust, when cleaned, sparkles after half a century of weather beating!

Mr. Everitt.—The Herald wag, sometime ago set an honest black white washer to improve the city hall with his brush! He had spoiled some of the marble face before he was stopped.

Dr. Deck.—Soft marble may be saturated with the sulphate of alumina and rendered as hard as granite, and leaves the marble white.

Prof. Mason.—A neutral tint is desirable. The climate of Italy is more favorable than ours for the preservation of buildings. Michael Angelo understood the art, as we learn from his great works.

Mr. Dwight, of New Haven.—The trap rock of the east and west mountains of that city, are good; two churches have been built of it, and they will endure.

Mr. Tillman illustrated on the black-board the chemical combinations of some materials, the oxygen and carbon, silicon. &c.

Mr. Hoover.—Cast iron surpasses all other materials.

Prof. Hedrick.—We must have something more durable; the mountains contain iron, and will last longer.

Prof. Mason.—Two cast iron stores, in Boston, were failures. Unless kept protected from the weather by paint, constantly renewed, it cannot endure. Tenants complained of them much. Contraction and expansion, by cold and by heat, will constantly keep joints more or less open.

Mr. Garbanati.—Our common contract system is very bad for buildings. The materials are good enough. Look at Dover castle, built by Julius Cæsar! We have lost the mortar, and must learn to make it again; we require change in our houses. I would not build one that would last 1000 years. The abbies, &c., of old, only remind us of the tyranny they represent—gloomy, chilly, damp monuments, that were never warm—very dangerous to health—comfortless! They record all that which had better never existed! No, sir; not such for us! None of that for an enlightened age like this! We are now bound to use all our knowledge of the past and of the present, to make the masses of mankind comfortable! Already men are clothed, fed and housed in a style of comfort never before known. Look back to the hovels of the world, where letters never entered! and where dry pure air, warmth, proper clothing, and food better than that of the ancient Princes, are enjoyed by all! (Applause.)

Mr. Tillman.—We all know the necessity of good mortar, and our chemical science, properly applied, will furnish it again. We must do it.

Mr. Meigs.—Many years ago, a learned gentleman of this city, represented in Congress, and when the question of a monument to Washington, was considered, he said that letters had already consecrated his memory, so that pyramids would moulder away and yet his name be still fresh in glory. You recollect Horace: " Exegi monumentum perennius ære !" His letters have lost none of their force and beauty in 1900 years !

Prof. Mason.—The capital, at Washington, is made of bad material. I still insist on the construction of public edifices to remain for ages. The city of Paris, which is so much distinguished in the civilized world, is rendered so, much by her monumental buildings. How much is due to the period from Louis XIV to Louis Napoleon ! And have not such architects made the way for the improved private dwellings of the world ? Their examples are perpetual instructions, and the people are now housed infinitely better than they ever were before those monuments were built. Our country best housed of all !

Mr. Seeley.—Some edifices should be permanent ; and such edifices require durable materials—such as our aqueducts, bridges, canal locks, &c. The Lockport stone has been found very good. All combustible material to be rejected. No wood unless kyanized—so solidified as to be incombustible. Cities so built would require no fire companies, or heaps of gold to rebuild the burnt districts.

Mr. Garbanati.—Any scientific test which we can apply to material, will only tell us what age has not done to it. The facts of substance and duration, are all before us, like the pyramids of Egypt !—they testify !

Mr. Stetson.—We have not reached our point yet. New York building material is not decided by the testimony of the pyramids—for climate is to be taken into the examination very carefully ! We have been troubled with many theoretical bubbles on this as well as other important matters. The compound of whiting, sand and ox blood, said by Prof. Mapes to last *forever*, wants testing ! The Cayenne stone, now in use here, is justly berated by Prof. Mason.

The committee of arts and sciences, has altered the name of this club to that of " Polytechnic Association."

Mr. Tillman, from the committee, stated that the present subject will be continued.

The Chairman named Dr. Deck, to be added to the committee on building materials. Carried.

Prof. Mason.—Government finds a hornblende, at our Tarrytown, so excellent for buildings that it monopolizes it. It has the peculiar property of burying a cannon ball without fracture.

The committee on "Building materials of the State of New York," is Professor Cyrus Mason, Tillman, Dwight and Dr. Deck.

The Club then adjourned.

H. MEIGS, *Secretary.*

March 16th, 1859.

Present—Messrs. Robert L. Pell, late President of the Institute, Prof. Mason, Prof. Hedrick, civil engineers Tillman, Everitt, Stetson, Haskell, Arts; Messrs. John Johnson, Seeley, Garbanati, Veeder, Wilmarth, Finell, Bresiach, Prof. Bowden, Dwight, Leonard, Chambers, Judge Harris, Scoville, Bushnell, Witt, Hon. R. S. Livingston, Alanson Nash, Boyle, Sykes, and others. Fifty-one members.

Mr. Pell in the chair. Henry Meigs, Secretary.

The secretary read the following papers prepared by him, viz:

MORTAR.

Sand from rivers, where it has been well washed, is far superior to that of land.

The best mortar of the Greeks and Romans was made *two years* before it was used. Their reasoning was just. We make it, if we please, as well as they did, but we use it immediately, and the small quantity between joints loses its virtue; or if not ruined by absorption in the porous material, becomes ultimately pretty strong; but with the ancients, mortar never used until it was *ripe*: the materials and mortar became almost one solid mass. The use of *metal coags*, (as ship builders call them,) to secure the adjustment of walls and of columns, was good, giving much greater strength as it grows older. The gradual hardening of it is owing to slow conversion of the *hydrate* of lime (slacked lime) into *carbonate* of lime, (a marble) by absorption of carbonic acid gas from the atmosphere. If mortar dries too soon, the carbonate formed will remain much divided, and never can afterwards become adhesive. If mortar be kept long moist and exposed to the air, the carbonic acid gas acts slowly but incessantly on the lime, and finally converts it into an almost crystalline carbonate. The proportions of sand and lime in mortar should be one bushel of lime to a bushel and an half of sand. The lime should be thoroughly burned.

Lime stone, which contains considerable silica and alumina, form what we term hydraulic lime. The mortar made with it sets quick either *in or out of water. Parker cement* is such, and sets in fifteen minutes.

The Chairman mentioned experiments tried by him on mortar. The sand and lime intimately mixed dry and left undisturbed in heap for two years, forms an excellent mortar. The same constituents buried in mass in the earth for two years also produced good mortar, far superior to that recently made. This must be due to chemical action, which continues after its use in the building, until ultimately the union of the lime and sand becomes as hard as the stones or bricks which it binds together.

Charles B. Boyle exhibited photographs on wood, of human face, and of still life, such as stoves, machinery, &c. They were admired, and are new. He described his process rather reluctantly, (although his patent is secured) in consequence of the great simplicity of one part, which could be so easily *stolen.* To prevent any penetration of the nitrate to dissolve the wood, he forms over the surface of the piece of wood *a film of albumen or gelatine.* The photograph can be regulated so as to impress mere outlines of objects, so that, by hand, the artist can finish the drawing better than it is done by the photograph, on account of shades, &c. This first drawing being exact, renders the draughtsman almost unnecessary. There is a great saving of time and money, and perfect accuracy.

Mr. Seeley was charmed with this discovery. It is entirely new. The draughtsman is superseded. The thick coat heretofore on the wood, embarrassing the engraver, is done with. It is of very high importance to the arts of design.

Prof. Mason.—Edinburgh photographs failed of effect if taken from the face with the eyes open; they are never good. Some twenty years ago we sent some of Morse's first, taken with eyes open, which were better than those of Edinburgh.

Mr. Tillman.—I regard Boyle's invention as important. By his method the drawing is made on a white ground, which enables the engraver to work more correctly and rapidly. Photography on wood dispenses with the draughtsman, and, therefore, brings us nearer to nature. Could the light engrave as well as paint, we could dispose of these middlemen altogether, and receive our impressions direct from the object. Under the old method we were obliged to trust to the painter's eye, and then to the engraver's eye, before we could have the engraving. But no man can see for another, because no two men can see alike, or receive precisely the same impressions of external objects. No two astronomers observe a transit at the same instant. This Prof. Mitchell has proved, and it has given rise to what he calls "the personal equation." It is evident, then, that no artist can paint nature with precision; he only reports his own impressions. The photograph does better, and yet it does not give us a precisely correct perspective, because the camera can only truly put on a plain surface what it receives from a plain surface; what it reflects from objects not in the same plane is slightly distorted. The artist can easily remedy the defective perspective.

Mr. Meigs exhibited the mechanical dots and lines from the Boston telescope, given by Mr. Batchelder. These, of course, could not be as accurately jotted down by any human hand.

John Johnson.—It is believed that Boyle's method may be extended to etching plates.

Mr. Stetson.—Art does correct nature in most of the daguerreotypes. The angular spectrum shows hands or noses, &c., in advance of face, bad. I agree that Mr. Boyle has made a very valuable improvement.

Mr. Boyle.—We take from nature true outlines and proportions, which a good artist can work on and improve. Many members showed their strong approbation of the new process.

The Chairman now called up the regular subject: "Building Materials of the State of New York."

Prof. Mason.—Inquiry in this matter has proven to me how little I knew about it, and the very extensive field opening before us for research. We want full knowledge. Let us not rest contented in our ignorance of so important a subject! Nature has placed us on the *crust of earth*, and we find it composed of many forms of matter, very various, and not yet well understood—matter *once* disintegrated and then *reformed*, rendered solid, not homogeneous, even in granites, still less in composite rocks. The Plutonic rocks, (the unstratified crystalline rocks, formed deep in the earth, subjected to high heat, and then upheaved through the stratified system of the surface,) and the volcanic rocks, (heated by fire and cooled near the surface.) All these demand strict examination. Art can chemically combine matter so as to form homogeneous matter entirely different from natural bodies—forming new substances. Some *naughty boys* are finding fault with Moses! If we do not understand his cosmogony, and don't learn how it was made his way, we must try to find it out by our learning! *Naughty boys*, as we surely are!

We read the great writers on building, and must now laugh at some of great name. We read Vitruvius on mortar, and laugh heartily at his ignorance! A building on the corner of John and Pearl streets had been first made with much iron; then changed to granite! then back again to iron, and has cost much more than the land it stands on is worth! It seems to require three things to make a man: *wife, child, and build a house!*

Mr. Meigs.—The learned professor forgets that Vitruvius is comparatively one of us! living some centuries after the great Grecian architects—at a period when an approach to the dark ages, when all manner of fantastic edifices were built—(*pretty much as we do now*,) and with that the loss of letters, so that many Kings could not write their own names—and where a criminal that could write, was acquitted because he could, by the plea of benefit of Clergy (Clerkship.)

The unburned bricks of the East would not stand our climate. Claudius James Rich, the learned Consul of England, at Bagdad, 40 years ago, examined that subject in the reputed town of Babel. Iawk Kezra, of Selucia, and the mounds of Nineveh, which he first made known, as buildings reduced on the surface to common earth—and, as he supposed, containing great treasures of art.

Mr. Stetson remarked that Adams, of England, was one of our best tutors in this matter. That all building material demands study; that no two blocks, even of granite, were exactly alike. A common workman on buildings, being questioned closely as to his materials, returns very little and indistinct information. He says not much more than " *It is because it is so.*" An engineer must study to utilize every thing. The chemist must have the rationale. Conflicting judgments must be decided by *science*, not *opinion*. The engineer must act on such judgment. The committee will have to explore a very wide field. The information as to the stone of the locks at Lockport is useful. Facts alone must be made to constitute, as it were, *a pavement* to stand on. I suggest the thorough study of the nature and action of cements as of very great importance, for, figuratively speaking, it has become a mere *rope of sand!* In research, facts come before us ramifying like a tree from branchute twigs. Professor Mapes undertook to define the cohesion of cement and its blocks, bricks, &c., to be a sort of minute dove-tailing of the particles of sand with the building material. This I do not comprehend. In all glues and cements, what is the law of their cohesion?

Engineer Everitt.—I entertain a holy horror of the symbols in modern use for the science of the constituents of bodies. I am not ready to-night to give such facts as I wish to submit.

Prof. Hedrick.—What is cohesion in a diamond? Mortar well made becomes gradually harder than stone. I have made some things, but I have not made a book yet! I have built a house of Thomastown lime and the loose stones on my fields mixed, pressed into moulds, and then made walls of it. The cement being kept several weeks, set the better for it. I used one part of lime to sixteen parts of sand. My neighbors laughed at me for putting in some round stones, and wanted to know why I did not break them! I kept my mortar three or four weeks before putting up wall, and it set well. Climate has much to do with it. A Roman house would not stand in New York.

Mr. Garbanati.—The mortar question is all-important, but the construction of our walls vastly more so. Look at the inner part of them filled with comparative rubbish, with a thin *epidermis* skin of marble or brown stone, or even good brick. It has no strength or durability. The fine looking city hall of Brooklyn is only a skin of marble, and is already decaying. On the plan of Prof. Hedrick we can make strong walls better than disjointed stones. The great acqueduct of Brooklyn, which should not decay for centuries, has in some parts room enough for the passage of rats through it!

Mr. Bruce.—Sand from the sea shore has been improperly used in mortar. The salt in it! The first shot tower built by Mr. Youle here, used it, and soon after crushed all down; and walls made with such mortar are always wet.

Mr. Wilmarth, of Brooklyn.—Notoriously wet. I use one part coal ashes, one sand, and one lime, for mortar. I mix by iron rollers revolving in a pan, having scrapers attached to scrape up the mortar before the rollers constantly. The mortar becomes smooth and soon sets firm.

Mr. Garbanati thought that our sea sand would be more useful spread on our roads.

Mr. Everitt.—Chloride of calcium, with salt, will retain moisture for years.

Prof. Mason.—A man in New Haven makes mortar of good quality.

Burn this piece of white marble, and one part of it with ten parts of the lime makes good mortar.

Prof. Hedrick.—The finer the particles of sand are, the more surface do they afford for contact with the lime, and thus a greater cohesion.

Some conversation on chemistry ensued touching this subject.

Mr. Meigs.—The Italian plaster figure maker, in this building, has just completed a *model partition wall* of plaster, the interior composed of many strong iron wires interlaced and enveloped in the plaster.

Prof. Mason.—The chemist deals with equivalents.

Prof. Hedrick.—But it will be a nice question in the process of the silicate and sand in the time of induration. Analysis might determine the equivalent for that lime " *pro hac vice.*"

Prof. Mason.—The pulverization of the sand, to make good mortar, seems a point gained. It ought to be investigated.

Mr. Wilmarth.—Grind the sand fine, make the mortar, press that into models, blocks, lintels, columns, capitals, &c., &c. A building can be made thus that would grow harder the longer it stands.

Mr. Meigs.—As the shell rock buildings of the island of Bermuda do. Every additional century only gradually converts them into pure hard limestone, so that from what I observed of one-tenth of an inch skin of hard limestone formed on the outside of a house about 100 years old, in city of St. Georges, Bermuda, a wall two feet thick may be converted wholly into the same hard limestone in *twenty-four thousand years !* or at any rate, if that house had been built by our great forefather, Adam, it would now have a hard skin of six inches thick on it.

Mr. Veeder.—As in some buildings or parts of buildings we require hydraulic lime, and wherever moisture is to be prevented access. I tried experiments as follows : Requiring in my business large tight vessels to hold oils, I constructed one cistern of *six thousand gallons*, out of Amsterdam (N. Y.) lime, and Roman cement as a lining to it. I made one of loose field stones and cement, lined same way. They hold oils perfectly. The last cistern holds fifteen hundred gallons, and the construction of it cost me only *thirty dollars*. I had an iron band around the upper rim. English authors recommend *hard burned clay* pulverized as a component of mortar for strength. I built an outer wall, and to the plaster for outside added some soft soap, which, when intimately worked into the mortar, formed a very smooth cement and a hard surface. My workmen told me it would crack off. Never mind, said I, put it on ; let it crack off. That coat is now as hard as stone, and no crack whatever. Hard burned brick pulverized is excellent in mortar. I filled cavities in some of my old fruit and other trees full of it, with the field stones imbedded in it. The trees like it, and are fast growing over the entrance. We observe the condition of flint with its bed of chalk, showing the slow conversion of the flint into chalk. Some English builders require a year or two to build a house, believing that this slow mode serves to add strength and duration.

Mr. Wilmarth.—I am a builder, and late from England ; I did not discover that the slow method was due to any cause but *stoppage or slowness of the cash!* I saw an opera house of great cost, run up in four months, and a hall of music in fifteen weeks.

Mr. Garbanati.—Why, then they did not give it time enough to tumble down in.

John Johnson.—Some singular, hard, durable conglomerates are formed in the sea sand. I found some at the edge of low water on sea shore; they enveloped pebbles, and were as hard as granite. Do these teach us a lesson?

Mr. Veeder.—Workmen tried lately, to save bricks of an old brick house pulled down in Albany, but they could make no profit of it, as the bricks adhered, so that *brick and mortar broke alike.*

Mr. Seeley.—A very great array of facts would be necessary either to sustain or impeach scientific theory! We want, therefore, a multitude of facts. Berzelius, trying chemical experiments on a mere *teaspoon full of matter*, determined more truth than all the masons. I mean *builders*, not *professors.* All precious stones as well as mortars, are silicates.

Mr. Meigs.—Except the diamond, which is pure carbon.

Mr. Seeley.—Certainly; the proximate idea of cement would be bullets in viscid matter—like thick molasses and a certain amount of cohesion.

Mr. Sykes.—Frost is a severe enemy of buildings. I would glaze the outsides of all walls, so as to render them impenetrable to moisture, rendering the walls dry, and leaving nothing for that enemy.

Mr. Meigs said that Alfred Hall, of Perth Amboy, in New Jersey, submitted to the Institute, ten years ago, bricks which he had glazed with that object, and proposed, also, to have such color added to the glazing as taste might select—such as white, blue, green, yellow, brown, &c.; since that the matter sleeps; all the past, all controversy, the *theory* of dry and durable walls is carried out in *facts.*

Mr. Veeder.—Furnace builders find blisters in some fire bricks, on account of their clay having been frosted before burning.

Prof. Hedrick.—As common bricks consist of silicate and alumini, it vitrifies in strong heat, first on its surface, and ultimately almost wholly.

Prof. Mason.—A perfect edifice requires that every stone or brick shall be exactly alike, so that it may be said of it, it is homogeneous; not like that ancient image, so typical of some of our edifices—legs of brass, with feet of clay.

Prof. Hedrick.—We have many popular errors to contend with—like that of my friend the country builder, who wanted me to break the round stones for my cement walls.

Chairman—How did you form the walls?

Prof. Hedrick.—I plastered right on them without furring; I used Hydraulic lime mortar on the bottom of my walls, in order to shut off the capillary rising of moisture from the ground.

Prof. Mason.—Bricks are made with holes through them so arranged, as to anastomose, fit together, so making pipes from top to bottom of the walls. Such are believed to render walls much drier.

Mr. Wilmarth.—And stronger too. Some bricks are now made hollow, and are stronger than the solid bricks, *three to one!*

Mr. Tillman, from the committee on arts and sciences, stated the question for next meeting to be " Electrotyping."

The Club then adjourned.

H. MEIGS, *Secretary.*

March 23, 1859.

Present—Messrs. Robert L. Pell, John A. Bunting, Hon. Robert Swift Livingston, Finell Witt. Civil Engineers, Stetson, Haskell, Everitt, Tillman, Messrs. Wilmarth, Garbanati, John Johnson, Seeley, Godwin, Gove, Judge Scoville, Dr. Deck, Alanson Nash, Veeder, and Prof. Hedrick, with others—forty-seven members.

Robert L. Pell in the Chair. Henry Meigs, Secretary.

The Secretary observed that the scientific articles received by us from Europe, are the results of the labor and talent of *several hundred societies*, there, for instance, the London Society of Arts, and the institutions in union with it, publishes weekly a pamphlet containing the new matters gathered up by them, and they are 350 *to* 400 *societies in one.* From Paris we receive the gatherings every fortnight, from several hundred societies of all Europe ! We have, also, the Year Book of Facts, of 1859, from London. From the latter we extract for this evening, the following viz. :

PLANE STOCKS MADE BY MACHINERY.

Plane Irons are largely made in Sheffield, but it has been necessary to send them to London, Birmingham, &c., to be fitted with stocks.

Messrs. Brooks and Sons of the Howard Works, Sheffield, have commenced extensive operations by machinery, to make them, and do make them better, as well as far more rapidly. There are eight machines in one large room. The *first* one cuts the block out of plank ; the *second*, by two circular cutters, planes their sides ; the *third* takes off the ends of the blocks. Then comes a curious machine for sinking the mortise. Two chisels, from opposite directions, work to and from a point in succession. The bed on which the block rests, gradually rises, bringing it within the reach of the chisels, which, by successive strokes, cuts out the mortise to the required depth. The fifth is the mouth cutting machine. Another circular cutter of still smaller diameter, cuts a groove with two semicircular ends for the *toat.* Then comes the abutment machine. The *wedge* is cut by a separate machine. The next is the *Bedding Machine*, which makes also the breast cut and the cut for the *ware.*

HYDROBORONATED PLASTER.

A patent contains common plaster of Paris, or any plaster having sulphate of lime for its base, indurated by a solution of boron (the base of boracic acid—from borax, the salt found native in the lakes in Thibet and Persia, and is imported from India, by the name of *Fincal*, which is refined and forms our borax.)

This boron can be so varied in quantity in the plaster, that the plaster may be made to set in a *few moments*, or in some hours, as may be required. It makes the plaster very hard, resembling marble or stone. It has considerable strength—is believed to be for columns as strong as freestone. Its surface is fit for paint almost immediately.

NEW METHOD OF ROAD MAKING.

France has it on a part of the Place du Palais Royal, a concrete about *five* inches thick, is first spread out. On that a layer of bitumen powdered and boiling hot, is poured on about *five* inches thick. A quantity of river sand is sifted over that, and rolled in by a cast iron roller of about two tons weight. In a few hours this road may be passed over by the heaviest wagons, without the slightest impression being left by the wheels. It has been applied to the Rue St. Honore, between the Palais Royal and the Rue de Richelieu, and as far as the end of the Theatre Francais.

OAK PAPER.

John Stather, of Hull, prints paper from the oak itself, surpassing any painting. By taking off shaving after shaving, he obtains continual varieties of the shades and grain of the oak.

XYLOPLASTY.

Paris does it. The wood is softened by steam, then imbued with certain ingredients, giving it sufficient ductility to receive impressions from four to five millimetres deep (about three eighths of an inch.)

WATER PROOF PAPER.

Professor Muschamp, of Wurtemberg, uses twenty-four ounces of alum and four ounces of white soap; he dissolves these in two pounds of water. In another vessel, he dissolves two ounces of gum arabic and six ounces of glue in two pounds of water. Add the solutions together; keep warm. Dip paper into it and then pass it between rollers and dry it—or without the rollers—hang it up to dry. The alum, soap, glue and gum, form an artificial leather, and it is somewhat *fire-proof*.

Paper dipped in diluted oil of vitriol and immediately well washed in pure water, render paper strong and somewhat water-proof.

Alanson Nash remarked, in relation to the last subject before the Polytechnic—the building materials of the State of New York—that we possessed masses of Basaltic green stone on Long Island, and in Westchester. It is exceedingly hard, splits into plates, forms elegant walls, is siliceous, with coloring from copper, is a sort of lava, hove up at the time when that great crack through our State, now occupied by the Hudson river. The Palisade rocks, of which on the right bank show it partially columnae and chrystallic. Above the Highlands of the Hudson river, the great basin, once a vast cauldron of burning melted lava, now crystalized in the form of Basaltic green stone slate. This stone is difficult to work, no doubt of that, but a monument made of it will stand the very longest. Brooklyn Heights have this rock. Enormous boulders of it are found there imbedded in earth. I observed one where a cellar was dug for a house; it weighed two hundred tons. Portions of this rock are ferruginous, porous, and will decay; so does some of our granite; that of the monument on Bunker's Hill shows it already! It has metallics in it with the feldspar and mica and silex; it is partially itself an oxide; any granite thus formed is not durable. Marble, also, has its difficulties, its base, calcium; is acted on by sulphuric acid; it is a carbonate of lime; it is not a good material for costly edifices in cities, whose eternal fires diffuse in the air perpetual supplies of acid which gradually attacks the marble nitric, muriatic and carbonic acids; all take a share in the mischief, which slowly sloughs off the exposed surfaces. These acids are plenty; we drink some at Saratoga; we find like waters in Texas, in the Rocky Mountains, and as well as springs of Soda, injurious, without the muriatic, to men and animals; bad for us, as salæratus of our bread is condemned by our Dentists, as hurtful to our teeth. I do not profess to be deep in chemical science, I have said what I know and believe to be useful for us to know.

Electrotyping, the subject of the meeting, was called up.

But before that, by request of members, Mr. Breisach read his paper on Ehrenberg, viz:

The great German Naturalist, CHRISTIAN GODFRERD EHRENBERG, *the Creator of a new Science.*

THE MICROSCOPICAL WORLD.

The researches in one of this most difficult branches of science, commenced already 150 years ago, and were continued on larger scale on the beginning of this century, but the whole that has been performed, is overshadowed by the extraordinary labors, the unperishable zeal, and untiring activity of the Naturalish, Ehrenbert.

Born in April, 1795, in the little town *Dehbisch*, in Saxonia, he received his preparatory education at Pforta, and entered the University of Leipzig, in the year 1815. At an early age, he manifested a strong bias for the study of natural sciences—he thus became a student of medicine, and received his Diploma as Physician, in the year 1819. His thesis was " A New System of Moulds," which on publication, created a sensation in the scientific world. He described in this pamphlet 240 different forms of microscopical plants, which, before his researches became public, were taken as Infusoria. It attracted the attention of the Prussian Academy of Science, and in consequence, he was recommended for similar investigations, which were intended to be made in Egypt. The Prussian Government sent him, at its expense, to that country and extended its period after two years of his stay there—to six years. The result of his labors were published on his return, in his " Symbolae Physica," " On the Corals of the Red Sea," and its Akoliphia.

Although these Coral Banks were known already to Pliny and Strabo, nothing definite could be said of them; they were believed to be plants, which petrify by reaching the surface of the water.   Travelers in this region were amazed on observing the wonderful variety of colors which these banks presented to them.

Ehrenberg enriched natural history by classifying and describing one hundred and fifty different species of these animalculæ, of which the lives of centuries are required to increase in a small degree the height of these banks. Many of the prejudices of the sailors and other travelers on these coral banks, were dispersed by the light of science which Ehrenberg was holding out in his works on the subject.

The Prussian government conferred upon him the Professorship of the University of Berlin, as soon as he returned from Egypt, and invited him, after few years of his appointment, to accompany Humboldt and Rose to Asia, which he accepted, the object being investigations of nature in this part of the world.   They returned in the year 1839, and since that time to this day Ehrenberg's whole activity was devoted to the most difficult investigations and explanations of the wonders of microscopical life.

Two great works are the fruits of his labor; first, "The Infusoria as Perfect Organism," and second, "Microgeology," (1853.)   To these works are attached the best drawings of the subject treated, and which were made by Ehrenberg himself.   The high prices of these works make them inaccessible to private individuals, except rich ones, but for libraries, they belong to the treasures of their collection.

The microscopical life in a small space *of the whole world*, is the great and wonderful subject which Ehrenberg undertook to investigate.   He himself traveled for this purpose in Europe, Asia and Africa, and he opened connections with all parts of America and Australia, from where friendly offers of such assistance were made to him, and thus he was supplied with specimens taken from every part of the world—from the arctic regions as well as from the tropics; from the highest mountains to a depth of 12,000 feet below the surface; from the mud of rivers, as well as from the coasts of lakes; in short, from everywhere on this globe Ehrenberg examined the microscopic beings, and he showed their forms to be as infinite as it is in the world of macrocosme.

He possesses such a wonderful certainty of defination, that by the most minute piece of silica he determines the family and genera of the infusoria, and resembles in this respect, Cuvier, who could do it by a single bone of an animal presented to him.

Not only the forms of infusoria which exist at present are found by him, but also those of thousands of years past.   If we take into consideration that not less than forty microscopic analyses of each specimen sent are made by him, we must be astonished at the activity and perseverance of this learned man to work as he has with the most minute matters.

It is no need stating that his observations are the most accurate and reliable, and it is a prover of the admiration of the scientific world, that there is no scientific society of Europe which has not made him an honorary member.

Cuvier entertained already on the appearance of the first treatise, a very high opinion of Ehrenberg, saying that this naturalist's discoveries will entirely change our ideas in natural history, and he declared Ehrenberg's performance an immortal one.

Ehrenberg improved considerably the microscope, which was very imperfect when he commenced his first labors; and his merits in this line of optics stand as high as of any other inventor. It must be also stated that there is no branch of natural science in which he does not excel.

In personal intercourse he is amiable, humble, unpretending, like most of the great men, listening apparently with great attention to what strangers have to tell him, and answering with great politeness any question in science made to him.

Mr. Meigs stated that a reporter from the office of the Sun newspaper, had presented the following note, at the last meeting :

That is a specimen of bituminous clay, found fifty miles from Bahia, Brazil, two hundred miles from Rio Janeiro. It burns better than the finest Cannel coal, and experiments instituted by an English engineer, show that it yields one-fifth more gas than the very best Liverpool coal. Mr. Leonard can tell you how it burns.

Wm. Filmer, of 17 Dutch street, New York, electrotypist, exhibited plates for the Ledger newspaper, made at his laboratory—plates from which four hundred and fifty thousand copies are now printed every week. The application of our plan is new, and the greatest in this country, and has been so for six or eight years past. This country demands a much greater number of impressions than Europe does, and this demand called forth our invention. The type in page by powerful press is forced into cold wax, which is then finely coated by means of fine badger brush, &c., with black lead, which being the best conductor of electricity which we have been able, after extensive experiments, to successfully apply. The plate is then immersed in a solution of sulphate of copper—is deposited thick or thin as required; perhaps three to four ounces on a page. We call this primary sheet or card, *a shell*. This must afterwards be consolidated for suitable strength by pouring into the type spaces on its back, sufficient lead and antimony. Tin, common stereotype metal answers the purpose. This mode supersedes all the old stereotype processes. Plates from wood cuts impressed in wax are used, but we print better from electrotypes.

Mr. Meigs.—How thick deposits can you have with sharp well defined edges ?

Mr. Filmer.—As thick as you please; but the general surface will be *nubbly*, (uneven.) It will print millions of copies. Outlines, especially of delicacy, are best on the wood cut. Shade best on our plate.

Mr. Stetson.—Impressions from wood cuts are the best.

Mr. Filmer.—The impressions from our plates are better after 50,000 copies have been taken off !

Mr. Everitt.—As to cost, comparatively, this new mode is 300 times cheaper than the old separate type, or the stereotype. The origin of electrotype is due to Spencer, of England, and Jacobi, of Russia. There are numerous claimants for the honor—we owe much to Filmer, here.

Mr. Filmer.—Box-wood gives more impressions than type metal.

Mr. Tillman.—We electrotype iron on copper.

Mr. Stetson.—The wear of copper plate engraving is severe, from the necessary cleaning of it after every copy, by whiting, cloth finished by human palm, the best finisher.

Mr. Filmer.—Our engravers are now using steel in place of copper plates; they are very superior. The impressions from copper plates often imperfect from the under cuttings, made *on an error burnished down*, causing *depressions*. Steel will not supersede electrotype for some purposes. Elkington, of England, first gave us electrotype busts, &c. Our far west already deals largely in electrotyping. Large editions are wanted, and we get off four or five millions of copies of some things, and they look well still. Spencer, of England, first used lead, and deposited the copper on that. Adams, of New York, made the electrotype for Harpers' great bible, in 1841. Wilcox did it in 1847 and '48. I did it in 1849, on types.

John Johnson.—Prof. Mapes, of New York, in 1840, gave electrotype plates in his Repertory—these were the first I knew.

Mr. Filmer.—Our Bruce learned the art from Lord Stanhope, of England.

Mr. Tillman.—Americans go by high steam. The patent office proves that almost every great recent invention has originated here. The Chinese originated stereotyping; but in this country, both the electrotype and stereotype, have been most extensively used.

Mr. Stetson.—We roll wheels over forms and multiply copies immensely. Some have eight or ten presses acting at once. Attempts have been made to electrotype *turtle backs*, (convex plates,) as they are called.

Mr. Fillmer.—We can electrotype a newspaper in fifteen minutes now! The London Times, stereotypes in about twenty minutes. It is done with paper. Sheets of paper with starch between them—the stamp made—metal poured on sets immediately.

Mr. Butler.—castings are not so dense as rolled metal.

Mr. Filmer.—They are harder. The deposit iron is nearly as hard as steel.

Mr. Butler described the difficulties in casting very thin plates for stoves, three-sixteenths of an inch. Can such plates be made by electro deposit? If they can, they must be better than ours, for we can sometimes see through the holes left in our stove plates.

Mr. Tillman.—So thick a plate of copper will cost too much.

Mr. Butler.—A pattern costs me sometimes $300; they are of wood, and wear out. I want one of Iron. Our castings are hard to finish up—the edges are defective on account of the fluid iron deranging the sand mould at the edges, and the sand is often carried into the iron.

Mr. Tillman.—The common table knife is now electrotyped silver, to keep it bright!

Mr. Wilmarth.—All that is done under the Elkington patent.

Mr. Goodwin.—In 1851, our books explain and teach some of these processes.

Mr. Butler.—We cannot consent to step backward to 1851; progress since has overshadowed it.

Mr. Stetson.—How is it as to electro deposits of other materials than our pure metals?

Mr. Filmer.—The study here is endless! I have been through much experiment. Iron is hard to deposit; cannot be relied on. I cannot deposit nickel, nor aluminium! Antimony is easiest.

Dr. Isaiah Deck.—Can specular metal be deposited? It is believed so! I think it can, and be of very great importance in such telescopes as that of Lord Rosse. Brass, which is a compound as well as specular metal, can be deposited, so can bronze.

Mr. Seeley.—Spencer and Jacobi, were first in the electrotype. We Americans claim much. I perhaps the forty-ninth man out of the fifty claimants here! But it was quite perfect in England before we had it. Spencer first used wax, not Jacobi; and Murray used the black lead! We had Elkington's works at our Crystal palace! It is more extensively used in the manufactures of England, than any other country.

Mr. Haskell.—It was used ten years ago in Napier's best work.

Mr. Seeley.—Can silver leaf be used over the wax?

Mr. Filmer.—It was patented, but was a perfect failure! The type broke it to pieces, spoiling the process. Electrotyping plate for printing is an American invention.

Mr. Stetson.—Say art.

Mr. Garbanati alluded to the large circulation of the London illustrated papers, on electro plates.

Prof. Hederick.—Are compounds of iron used?

Mr. Filmer.—After some manipulations.

Mr. Everitt.—Great power being required—the hydraulic press is employed to stamp the cold wax. The warping of the plates by the heat is difficult to avoid. Filmer is modest!

John Johnson.—My partner, Wolcott, attempted this electrotyping in 1837.

Mr. R. L. Pell, made the following remarks on electrotyping, as applied to the industrial arts:

The electrotype process, appears to me to be of some value to those persons engaged in the pursuit of organic analysis.

When high temperatures are desired to effect difficult combinations with chromate of lead, or oxide of copper, as in the determination of carbon in some samples of cast iron, the glass tube is very apt to soften, though made of the best quality of glass, but may be strengthened by covering it with a spiral strip of copper; even then it sometimes breaks during the combustion. A better plan would be to cover the tube with a coat of turpentine, and sprinkle powdered plumbago over it, then connect one end of the combustion tube with a copper wire, and plunge the whole into a sulphate of copper cell, in the ordinary electrotype arrangement. In four hours the tube will be found covered with a jacket of copper, and may be used without the fear of accident, as it would matter little even if the glass broke, as the tube would remain perfectly air tight; the covering of copper is so exceedingly thin that the increased weight to a tube twenty inches long would only be the one-tenth of a grain.

A battery for electro-gilding and metallurgical purposes, may be so constructed that the nitric acid can be replaced by the peroxide of lead, and become capable, when charged with salt water, of decomposing water most rapidly, and at the same time give off the gases separately. The great practical advantage of substituting a peroxide for the nitric acid is, that the battery may be charged with one liquid only.

To decompose water with platinum electrodes, there must exist two chemical actions in the pan of batteries, which will originate two currents, and combine the effects, to wit: the reduction of the peroxide and the oxidation of the zinc.

I think the battery might be simplified by placing nitric acid in a plumbago vessel, this would bring the elements into an exceedingly close contact, and probably be equal to a battery platinized containing the same surface.

A beautiful lace may be made by stretching a net of any material over a copper wire frame, and cover it until perfectly black with plumbago. Then connect it with the negative pole of a galvanic battery, and bring voltaic action to bear, between two copper plates electrified positively, which will, in a short space of time, cover each thread with a tube of copper, which may be silvered or gilded, and used for ladies' fancy work.

Electro deposition occurs when copper and zinc are bathed in a solution of sulphuric acid. In the construction of the batteries for electro plating, it is absolutely necessary to have a correct balance of power, or else, whatever may be exposed to the action of the metallic solution will present a rough, instead of a smooth surface. When these matters are attended to, articles may be immersed, and when withdrawn, will be found covered with a thin coating of the metal used, before being dipped; the article might be considered worth five dollars, and after the process, to the eye, fifty, provided it was most thoroughly freed from grease and other impurities, by boiling in caustic alkali, and rubbing with sand. Without this attention the electro plating process would inevitably fail.

By the old method, copper was the only available metal to plate upon, but by the galvanic process, all metals are equally applicable.

Nickel is white, and nearly the same density as silver. When this substance is plated with great care, and the union of the plating at the bottom scientifically secured, it is almost impossible for any silversmith to indicate any difference between such articles and the best English sterling silver. When nickel is to be silver plated, make a solution by dissolving silver in nitric acid and water. Then attach a copper wire to it, and bring it in connection with the negative pole of the battery. At the same time place a piece of silver in the liquids in connection with the positive pole of the battery. If you desire to plate with gold, place the article in a solution of that metal, prepared in the same manner.

Plating can now be applied to many useful purposes, much cheaper than formerly, when if a peculiar model was required, moulds of plaster, wax, &c., were necessarily prepared; they can now be superseded by a composition made of molasses and glue, which is perfectly flexible, and may be moulded and used in a solid piece, or several pieces.

If our saucepans and other culinary vessels were coated with silver by this process of plating, we might save much coal and wood, as silver is a far better conductor of heat, than tin or iron. Beer barrel faucits should be always plated to prevent the formation of verdigris. Our iron railings around parks and public buildings, should invariably be coated with zinc, by electro plating, which, at a small cost, would protect them indefinitely from destruction, by exposure to atmospheric influences.

I have used a zinc boat for years, and it does not show the least sign of change, as zinc is perfectly insoluble in water, and should therefore always be used on the parts of mill and steamboat wheels exposed to the lasting influence of that element.

Gold and silver gilding, that has consigned thousands of splendid workmen to early graves, in consequence of the use of mercury, ought at once to give way to electro plating, which may be most advantageously applied instead. Magnetoplating possesses advantages over electro plating, because it is effected without galvanism, salts or acids, at a moderate cost, and is capable of plating articles of any size.

Relief letters, ornaments for inscriptions, figures, panels for brooches, designs for mats, centres for books, ornaments for covers, and all similar beautiful work, are now formed by electro depositing in England, at so low a price, as to compete with the most inferior stamped work.

There are three admirable electrotype processes. The first consists in the use of platina wires in the place of copper, and of preparing a skeleton figure so as to resemble the outline of the cast desired to be obtained, by means of which process, statues, busts and groups can, by a single operation, be produced in full relief. The second is a process for galvanizing or coppering iron to any thickness without the cyanide bath, which is not only dangerous but expensive.

The third is a process for strengthening electrotypes, the principle of which is, to leave an opening in the back of the thin electrotype obtained by precipitating, and to place in it various pieces of brass, which, on being melted with an oxyhydrogen blast, becomes diffused over the interior surface of the copper, without injuring it, and thereby imparting to it the strength of cast-iron.

By the extraordinary power of the electrotype, an intaglio printing plate can be readily produced from any photograph, and thousands of copies multiplied, as in letter press. It has fully developed the art of nature printing, which would never have been known but for it. Ordnance maps, which are now so remarkable for their excellence, without its intervention could not have been prepared.

It is only by the agency of the wonderful electrotype that the charming art of the historical engraver can be reproduced with fidelity from the steel. And to the electrotype photography owes its multiplying power, through the medium of a fixed plate.

The most beautiful devices may be obtained for door plates, knobs, etchings, from engravings, ornaments for spoons, forks, dinner plates, &c., by electro-metallurgy, at a small cost. By its use copper may be thrown down on an engraved plate very successfully, and when taken apart, the plate, galvanized, will be a perfect copy in relief of the engraved one, which will serve as a matrix for an infinity of impressions, fully equal to engravings. Wood cuts, steel engravings, casts made of plaster, seals, &c., may be admirably copied.

By the galvano-plastic process, in two hours a coat of copper may be made to cover, with the greatest imaginable accuracy, a colossal plaster statue, giving it the solid appearance of the finest bronze. Copper may thrown down upon moulds representing kettles, pans, urns, &., by the action of galvanic electricity, in such a manner as to complete the article without the aid of other artifice.

If the agriculturist desires to illustrate the size or peculiarities of his apples, pears, plums, potatoes, carrots, or pumpkins, he may coat them with the thinnest imaginable covering of copper by electro-metallurgy. To accomplish the object, cover the desired article with black lead, and thrust a pin in the stalk or stem; to this attach a wire, connect it with the zinc of the battery, and place it in the solution, and complete the arrangement by a piece of copper, which must be connected with the silver of the battery. The form, after the process, is perfectly characteristic, marking distinctly the individual characters of each. After having accomplished the desired object, withdraw the pin, which leaves a hole sufficiently large for the evaporating juices to pass out. Embossed surfaces may be copied with the utmost facility, even if they consist of paper. It is necessary to render them non-absorbent, by varnish, oil or wax. For paper, linseed oil is probably the best. When ordinary type is to be electrotyped, each letter is cast separately in a particular alloy, and, when combined together, form words, and if they are intended to be kept for books having a large circulation, a stereotype copy may be made of them. To accomplish which, a plaster mould of the type is first obtained, which is baked in an oven that it may be perfectly dry, and from this a metallic cast in stereotype metal is made, which is a copy of the original. It is presumed that a new material, made of gum shellac and other substances, will be introduced to take the place of plaster. A useful process has been added to printing, called the anastatic, which has the effect of starting the ink.

The finest execution, most elaborate design, and brilliant conception, can be copied with the same fidelity as the plate without any delicate workmanship upon it, for the reason that the deposit of metal forms an exact cast in both cases. Some electrotype operators possess the secret of forming a pretty fair matrix with gutta percha, but they will not inform me how they accomplish it. When they do, I can give them a much better recipe. This glorious invention will enable the present race of men to hand down to posterity all the prominent works of art known to us, and to perpetuate the portraits of all the great and good among us. We may embellish our common dinner services at the cheapest imaginable rate, with copies of our finest works and most magnificent pictures of nature, when I make known a plan through the medium of which a steel plate can be formed from one single impression, at the cost of a dollar.

Next to electrotyping, there is no art that deserves more praise, in my opinion, than wood cut engraving, which has been brought to the greatest imaginable perfection, so much so, that in minuteness of design and sharpness of cutting, steel engraving cannot surpass it. I have seen specimens lately from which you might take a million of impressions without wearing them out; and they may then be multiplied by electro-metallurgy indefinitely. The title page of the humorous English Punch is electrotyped, and from it nearly six millions of impressions have been taken. The vignette of the London News illustrated is engraved on copper, to represent as near as possible a wood engraving, because it will last longer than wood. The use of electro-metallurgy in the multiplication of the daguerreotype is very great.

The value of electrotyping and electro-metallurgy can scarcely be comprehended even in the present state of the science, and it is utterly impossible to conjecture to what extent it may ultimately be carried. It owes its very existence to electricity, the gigantic power of which everybody recognizes in the thunder storm and devastating lightning. Human intellect is too weak to fathom the amazing and sublime effects that it is, during every instant of our lives, silently producing around us, and God will yet make one brighter than now exists, to cause it to supersede steam, and enable those coming after us to traverse the seas and land borne by the power of lightning.

Mr. Tillman, from the committee on questions, stated the next subject, "Iron best adapted for steam boilers."

Mr. Veeder moved that at next meeting we have Mr. Pell's paper on electrotype. Carried.

Adjourned. H. MEIGS, *Secretary.*

————

March, 30, 1859.

Present—Messrs. Robert L. Pell, Bruce, Witt, Alanson Nash, Veeder, Sykes, Finell, Breisach, Stetson, John Johnson, John W. Cham'ers, Godwin, Garbanati, Haskell, Tillman, Seeley, Robert Simpson, Prof. Hedrick, and others. Forty-two members in all.

Robert L. Pell in the Chair ; Henry Meigs, Secretary.

Mr. Meigs read the following papers prepared by him, viz :

[Year Book of Facts, 1859—London.]

COAL FORMATION.

Stigmaria and Sigillaria.—Stigmaria, is the "roots" of the plant called Sigillaria, and are found in coal *floors*, running thirty feet and striking into the floor of the coal bed. The *rootlets* are six to 10 feet long. The sigillaria must have been plants of rapid growth.

GOLD FIELDS OF AUSTRALIA.

" Mr. Selwyn, the Geologist of Victoria, recognizes gold bearing drifts of three different ages. The deepest contains large quantities of wood, seed vessels, &c., have various depths down to 280 feet, associated with various clays, sands and pebbles, overlaid by sheets of lava. A more recent drift contains bones of living and of extinct marsupial, (such as have pouches.) At Warnamboul, the marine or estuary (bay or arm of the sea,) beds of probably the same age, are overlaid by volcanic ashes. A third drift of gold near the surface. The largest amount of gold is found near the Silurian Schists.

John Phillips, Government Surveyor, finds the gullies with gold all have a fall ; the ancient ones of 16 in a 1,000, while the more recent gullies fall only 8 per 1,000. Silver nuggets are found near Ballarat.

NEW OIL FOR PURE WHITE LIGHT.

Price's Patent Candle Company have prepared " Belmontine Oil." At the late meeting of the British Association, at Leeds, Mr. Warren De la Rue exhibited in an improved reflecting stereoscope, by means of it, his splendid eight inch lunar photographs. These candles are made out of the semi-fluid naphtha, drawn up from the wells in the neighborhood of the river Irawaddy, in the Burmese Empire. The natives use it for lamps, to preserve timber, to destroy insects, and as a medicine. It is partly volatile ; is imported in metal vessels, hermetically sealed. A similar article, in some points, has been obtained from heat and other organic materials, by Reichenback, Gregory, Reese, Young, Wiseman, of Bonn, and others. De la Rue's patent, is, from first to last, a simple separation without chemical changes.

Mr. Henley remarks, that " Earth currents of electricity must always disturb sub-marine and subterranean lines, as atmospheric currents do the overground wires. That these currents have a daily variation, being generally from Southwest to Northeast at one period of the day, and from Northeast to Southwest the rest of the twenty-four hours. These facts were confirmed and elucidated, when the Atlantic telegraph wire parted about 350 miles from Ireland. The phenomena of the earth currents were observed ; they deflected the needle of the galvanometer rapidly, just as if signals were being sent. The greatest vibration was at 10 o'clock A. M., and 10 o'clock P. M., and were always least felt one hour later.

IRON.

The trial of cannon has been made in the United States, as follows : The gun, 32 lbs., cast vertically, and about 18 inches longer than necessary, so that the lighter impurities may rise to the top as so much scum, then sawed off, then bored of an exact calibre and perfectly polished, so that the shot has no point of unequal pressure ; then ascertain by thermometer the temperature of the gun, put in a small charge of powder, one wad and one ball, discharge it, clean it, let it cool to its first temperature. (Before the first loading try its tone with a hammer !) Then try the tone again, and so on to full proof. If the tone has not materially changed, the gun may be fired one thousand times, after which percussion rapidly disintegrates the metal.

Commodore Rodgers ordered an experiment on percussion before a committee of Congress, of which I was one. A man struck the trunnion of a thirty-two pounder with a sledge hammer, while Com. R. counted the blows. At a certain number, he remarked to us, a few more will break it off. We examined the trunnion, and saw no signs of fracture, any more than before the first blow, but it broke as predicted.

There is no better test than the tone or ring of the metal ; it is precise as the tuning fork of a piano tuner.

It is very valuable to railway work, and should be applied to every working part before a start for any considerable run.

Some similar test may be applied to boiler plates. Let each plate be subjected to a scientific assay, for it is of infinitely greater importance than our assay of gold and silver, for the latter can *only touch our pockets*, while the want of the *former destroys thousands of precious lives!*

Each plate, when duly proved, should receive the stamp of the assay office, and to counterfeit that should be punished by hanging !

Nature forms timber of given strength ; man finds it very difficult to imitate her works ; but I do believe that each plate can *be proved*.

H. MEIGS.

ELEMENTARY BODIES.

Faraday simplified chemistry—found but few original elements. Sir John Herschell, the other day, in the chair of the British Association, remarked, "that the formulæ of chemical notation, for chemists are not algebraists, and are becoming more and more repulsive. As the atomic formulæ indicates numerical relations, the aggregate weights of the several atoms in each group, and the groups in each compound, it is distressing to the algebraist to find that he cannot interpret a chemical formulæ—according to the rules of arithmetic. I am slow to believe in similar generalizations," &c.

Note by Meigs.—I object to the admission of the term "atom" in scientific language. We cannot form a conception of an atom. The *infinite divisibility of matter* multiplies every attempt to conceive of an original component.　What common understanding imagines to be unit, is divisible to infinity !

Sir John Herschell—If the phenomena of chemistry are ever destined to be reduced under the dominion of mathematical analysis, it will be, no doubt, by a very circuitous and intricate route, in which at present we see *no glimpse of light !*

Mr. Pell.—The mysterious agency of electricity is little understood, and the establishment of facts is what we require, to gain an insight into the wonderful workings of the subtle fluid.　It is distributed through all substances, and lies entombed beneath their surfaces in a condition of rest ; numerous causes at different periods may break up this state, producing an excitement highly electrical, particularly when the fluid accumulates to excess in some substances which are then positively electrified, while in others it is deficient, and they are negatively electrified.　All metals permit electricity to pass through them very freely, and are called good conductors.　Some substances refuse it a ready passage, and are called non conductors, as for example : silk, glass, air, &c.　If you rob any of the metals of their electricity, by presenting a good conductor to them, it flows off very quietly.　If a bad conductor is presented, it dashes impetuously through it, producing light, fire, and not unfrequently a loud discharge. The atmosphere is positively electrified in fine weather, but during rain or snow falls, or in fact all storms, or fogs, it is negatively electrified.　The electricity of the air has an ebb and flow daily, corresponding with the tides of the ocean, every twenty-four hours ; when it is clear, men are elastic, gay and cheerful ; when in the opposite state, dull, cheerless and heavy. We have all observed when it lightenings, the chain form is assumed, and it traverses the sky in a zig zag direction ; this is because the temperature of the atmosphere is different at the different points it meets in its course ; if the temperature was equable, it would traverse the heavens in a straight line.　There is invariably an overplus of positive electricity in the air, and an excess of negative electricity in the earth, which gives rise to storms, tornadoes, and other well known phenomena.　All plants, in their contact with the earth, are completely filled with negative electricity, and are probably in metallic communication with the ground.　I believe electricity is indispensable to the well being of all living vegetables and trees, and that they constantly, when the weather is dry, draw it from the atmosphere, and that without it their functions would be incomplete.　I have examined many apparently smooth leaves of plants with the microscope, and have always found them covered with minute lightning rods, ever ready to attract electricity.　If you make water slightly alkaline, it will become negatively electrified, and acid positively.　When water evaporates, from the earth, or from a stream, it carries into the atmosphere with it any excess of electricity that there may happen to be, which immediately becomes diffused in the air, and is invariably positive electricity.　As the decomposition of organic substances and evaporation of water, are always at their maximum in the hot season of the year, so at that period we have violent rain and thunder storms, accompanied by lightning ; these are undoubtedly very important questions in terrestrial physics. The atmosphere will be negative when the shower approaches, positive while the same is pouring down, and negative as it passes around us. The aurora borealis is no doubt composed of positive electricity, which floats constantly in the atmosphere with unchecked liberty, and is attracted towards the pole, where floating through the particles of frozen ether, falls to the ice bound earth gradually, exerting all the time partial discharges, which form the magnificent aurora ; and notwithstanding it is a permanent phenomena, is only visible to us when the atmosphere is in a peculiar state of transparency at night. Occasionally in winter, after a few warm days, a strong cold west wind springs up, attended by showers, lightning and thunder, which causes the thermometer to fall, after which electricity abounds in all bodies on the surface, and is noticeable on the hair of the human head, which stands on end, and obstinately refuses to lay smooth, and as you pass your fingers through, follows them, sometimes emitting electric sparks. Our coats and under clothing are charged with electricity, and emit a crackling sound as we throw them off ; if you take a pair of woolen drawers and hold them suspended with one hand, and draw the fingers of the other hand over them, they will appear bathed in a blaze of light, and flashes of light will sparkle for a long time. If you draw your hand over a dog's back, you will hear the crackings of electricity.

The ends of the ears of all animals, exposed to atmospheric influences, under circumstances as above mentioned, are tipped with an electrical light. I have seen a ball of electricity on the mast head of a ship in the gulf stream. The ancients made use of an electric eel as a remedial agent for the cure of paralytic and neuralgic diseases. The head of electric fish, such as the eel, silure, torpedo, gymnotus, &c., is negative, and the tail positive. If you rub a glass rod with a silk handkerchief, you disturb the equilibrium of the electric fluid ; it is imparted to the glass by the silk, consequently the former loses its electricity, and becomes negative, and the latter acquiring it, becomes positive—electrical excitation is the cause of either being in excess or free. Water is found to be a good conductor of electricity, and may be called an electrolyte ; ice is a non conductor, and consequently unsusceptible of electrolysis. All substances susceptible of electrolytic action are probably compounds of single atoms. Protoiodide and protochloride of tin are readily decomposed, but the biniodide and bichloride are not. All metals when positive electrodes may be caused to develop an odoriferous principle, and no metal more readily than iron and nickel.

There exists in man, and in all warm blooded animals, an electro vital current of electricity, which passes continually from one extremity to the other, and when it is weakened, disease sets in ; when stopped at any particular point, rheumatic pains exist ; when increased beyond our strength, we are thrown into convulsions ; and if the currents are reversed we die. I once had three friends, all of whom suffered from colds, fevers, rheumatism, and sundry other ills, if they were so unfortunate as to get their feet wet. On one occasion we all met together, during a rainy day, when this fact was made known, and they dreaded to go out for fear of the consequences which they knew would inevitably follow. I explained to them the fact that there were currents of electricity coursing through them, and that when their feet became wet, water having an affinity for electricity, rapidly drew off an undue quantity from their systems, and they laid them open to numerous attacks, and advised india rubber overshoes, which were forthwith obtained ; and they have repeatedly informed me that they have never suffered since. I believe that volcanoes, tornadoes, thunder storms, and water spouts, are all brought about by electricity, and that it is through God, the prime mover of all things that exist in the universe.

On many occasions I have met complaining men, who never were well, still never sick, and have enquired whether they slept with their heads towards the east or north ? and the reply was east or west ; I suggested that they change them towards the north, as the electric current flows in that direction, and that it would then pass through them, instead of across them. Complaint since with these individuals has ceased. I give it for what it is worth ; try it.

I have prevented the attacks of all sorts of insects to fruit trees, except those having wings, by encircling them with a strip of copper and zinc. The moment the creature, after passing over the zinc, comes in contact with the copper, he receives a galvanic shock, which shakes his nerves to such an extent, that he falls to the earth immediately, and feels disinclined ever after to approach any tree. I was one of the first to be amazed at the facility with which Mr. Morse's manipulator sent a message for me from the Express office in Broadway to the Lyceum of Natural History, near Prince street, over the first wire ever erected for that purpose. And the question asked Mr. Morse was, whether the principle could not be applied to agriculture ? and the reply was, he did not know—obtain a battery and try. I did so, and the result was perfect, causing a tomato to bear three crops of fruit in a single month, a Madeira vine to grow thirty inches in three days, and numerous other plants in like proportion ; a full account of which is in print, and may be seen by any of you.

Much has been said, and many theories advanced, respecting the manner a current passes through a telegraphic wire. My idea is that all metals are filled to repletion with electricity, and consequently, if you force in by a battery a spark at one end of a continuous wire, though it encircled the globe, a corresponding spark, must pass from the other end ; and I do not believe that a battery containing five hundred cells, would expedite the spark more than one thousand miles per second, which feat is accomplished by one of thirty-one cells. And this only leads me to suppose that amazing as the points are which have been reached in this wonderful science, others will be constantly developing, until those unknown, will far exceed those now familiar. And as small beginnings of necessity invariably precede all great things in scientific knowledge, I would respectfully recommend this club not to despise them. Notwithstanding the inconceivable power of electricity takes us unawares, in the most unexpected and mysterious manner, almost upsetting our intellect, still it is governed by a fixed law, the principles of which we must endeavor to comprehend, taking it for granted, that the Creator has placed our comprehension above, and not under it.

Mr. Tillman.—How is that in cotton—for wheat grows in wet cotton as well as in straw?

Mr. Veeder.—The oil of petrolium is very similar to the Belmontine article described. At Hamilton, in Canada West, it is found; at Pittsburgh, also, 45,000 gallons of it were there for sale recently. It preserves timber; the oil of it yields white light. By its light in a steamer's cabin, a stereoscopic view was seen almost as bright as by day light.

Thomas Godwin.—In relation to more safe covering of submarine wires, Bright, of England, recommends a substance which, in the event of fracture in the covering can ooze out sufficiently to protect the wire from water, and thus maintain its insulation. I am a plumber, and in the course of my experiments in some work at Saltus & Co.'s stores, made some discoveries as to electricity applied to vegetation. Iron filings may be employed about plants to aid the operation. I find the Boston Year Book of Facts, very useful.

Mr. Tillman sketched on the black board, a convenient and cheap electrotyping apparatus. It consists of a jar of suitable size, with the acid in it, and two pieces—one zinc and the other copper, suspended in the acid— a curve wire attached to the plates at opposite sides of the jar, meeting the ends of the subject of the process immersed in the metallic solution contained in a suitable vessel below the jar.

The Chairman called up the regular subject, "Boiler Iron."

Engineer Stetson.—Some of us here are old stagers, and I shall be pleased if some one, who now sits here silent, will rise and speak to this question, of which we find difficulty in saying any thing new. After much experiment of copper and iron for boilers, we have resorted to the iron, because of its superior strength, although old copper boilers are still valuable for the metal, while old iron boilers are worthless. We want some means to prevent the corrosion of the iron. The mere question of tensile strength has been determined often, and is easy to decide. The mechanism of a boiler demands great attention, for in warming plates, bending, flanging, &c., it receives injurious strains. Charcoal made iron is deemed best for boilers. That of Pennsylvania—the Juniata.

Mr. Bruce.—And the Tennessee!

Mr. Stetsen.—And the Salisbury! When I utter an opinion here which does not suit any member, let him knock it (*not me*) down! You know that heat up to a certain point, not over 500 degrees of Fahrenheit, adds strength to iron! and that our boilers very rarely have strain over 350°! Government test of iron shows that our best iron has in *square inch rods* a tensile strength of *fifty thousand pounds!*

Mr. Syke.—The effect of the sulphur of our coal on the boiler iron should be determined.

Alanson Nash stated the geological history of iron. That the primitive and secondary formations contain iron ; that the first is strong and durable ; that the iron in mica slate and calco, and hornblende slate rocks, is most pure, sustained by the electricity it contains ; while that of the secondary rock is oxidyzed, is bad and not as good when deoxodyzed. That the true secret of the superiority of American iron consists in this primitive origin, while that of England is all in the secondary. The Staffordshire masses are but vast heaps of *iron rust !* Our Jordan Mott, the worker in iron, finds iron in our city rocks of the primitive formation ; the mica slate rocks, of excellent quality. Salisbury iron lies in primitive formation, and is the strongest known, and so of iron of New Jersey.

Mr. Sykes.—Can boilers be made, as some gun barrels are, of wire, to obtain toughness, strength ? Might the inside be tinned ?

Mr. Veeder desired to know the philosophy of the fact that charcoal makes best iron. An ounce of sound philosophy is worth tons of loose conjecture. I saw the iron boiler of Edson, exploded at Albany—new and apparently strong, was well tested.

Mr. Haskell.—That boiler was tubular, and was not well braced.

Mr. Tillman.—Perfectly chemically pure iron is not used in any of our operations. It seems to me that the problem to be solved is corrosion of iron. The whole subject of boilers is exceedingly important, for we have them at work under our feet, on our sides, by sea and by land, liable to being blown up at any moment. Let us encourage enquiry here !

Mr. Veeder.—Can alkalies be used in boilers, against corrosion ? potassium or sodium ?

Mr. Stetson.—Who will tell us which is the best iron ?

Mr. Seeley believed that the faults of boilers were far more due to mechanism than to metal ! Any is strong enough per se if uniform throughout, for the steam could then be made of uniform force ! If we could coat the inside of them so as to prevent the corrosion of boilers, great would be the advantage.

Mr. Meigs.—Can a boiler be constructed that cannot be burst by steam ?

Mr. Stetson.—Yes !

Mr. Seeley.—The more pure the iron the more difficulty from oxidation ! Can a suitable boiler be made out of cast iron ? or can a boiler be made by electrotype ?—for that must necessarily be perfectly homogeneous, uniform !

Mr. Robert Simpson, railroad engineer.—A boiler twenty-five feet by thirty-two inch diameter, well tested to 120 lbs. per square inch, after much use, was condemned and turned out of house, when it sustained according to the indicator thirty pounds pressure per square inch. I took a small hammer, struck the boiler, and the hammer broke easily through it ! We got a new one, and could not start the engine, a ninety horse power—it had plenty of water in——it exploded! I think that the heat drove off the water below, the iron became red hot, formed gas, and so exploded it.

Mr. Garbanati.——We require a uniform strength——a test that does not *overstrain* the boiler, for that over exertion often spoils a man!

Mr. Stetson.——To sustain Mr. Simson's case, I have known plasters of thick brown paper over a weak spot in a boiler, bear the pressure of (said) 30 lbs. per square inch! while other boilers, perfectly new and strong, explode! So some buildings, soon after having sustained great crowds of people, have tumbled down when empty! I say, dogmatically, that a boiler can be made which will not burst! Cast iron won't do! Electrotype cannot answer, because when deposited thick it is uneven!

Mr. Garbanati.——The *weak spots*, such as shoulders, &c., may be fortified.

The committee on questions, give the following for next meeting, viz: " Materials for boilers," and " Dentistry."

Adjourned.

H. MEIGS, *Secretary.*

———

April 6, 1859.

Present—Messrs. Pell, Tillman, Pierce, Butler, Scoville, Judge Livingston, Prof. Hedrick, John Johnson, Bruce, Garbanati, Haskell, Nash, Breisach, Stetson, Finell, Cohen, Everitt, Seeley, Griffith, Bradford, and others—38 in all.

Robert L. Pell in the chair. H. Meigs, Secretary.

Memoires De La Societe Imperiale Des Sciences Naturelles De Cherbourg. Tome IV, 1856.

Presented by the Society to the American Institute, March, 1859.

Extracts translated by H Meigs, for the Polytechnic Association.

CHARACTER OF DIVISIBILITY IN WHOLE NUMBERS.

The celebrated calculating Pastor of Touraine, Henry Mondeux, when he was last in Cherbourg, in February, 1856, sold a pamphlet in which he exhibited the character of the divisibility of whole numbers by the values comprised between 1 and 50. His formulæ are extensively ingenious, but unaccompanied by any theory, and attest at the same time the marvellous aptitude with which the author is endowed by nature. In fact the former professor of Mondeux, M. Jacobi, in the preface of this pamphlet says: " That his scholar had no knowledge of the principles on which those formulæ depend, and admits it with all humility."

We found it interesting to find them out. We shall find how the four first rules of arithmetic prove this divisibility.

The committee on arts and sciences reported that Professor Cyrus Mason, of Poughkeepsie, had been elected as Chairman, and Henry Meigs Secretary, of the Polytechnic Association for the ensuing year. The Society by a unanimous vote approved of the appointments.

Mr. S. D. Tillman remarked that the extract read by the Secretary, re. lating to mathematics, reminded him of a curious relation of numbers he had discovered. It was doubtless known already to many mathematicians, although he had not met it in print, yet he inferred that Babbage made use of it in his calculating machine. As it may be of service in expediting numerical calculations, he would explain it at the blackboard and give the formula for its use.

The law is, that the sum of a regular series of odd numbers, commencing with one, is always equal to the square of the number of terms used. So the odd numbers may be written with the arithmetical series underneath them thus :

$$1 \quad 3 \quad 5 \quad 7 \quad 9 \quad 11 \quad 13 \quad 15 \quad 17 \quad 19$$
$$1 \quad 2 \quad 3 \quad 4 \quad 5 \quad 6 \quad 7 \quad 8 \quad 9 \quad 10$$

and the square of any number in the lower series is equal to the odd number above it added to all those preceding, thus : $1+3+5+7+9=5 \times 5$. By the following formula, in which n is the last number, we may find the sum of a series of odd numbers : $\left(\frac{n+1}{2}\right)^2$; for example, if the sum of 13 and the odd numbers below it is required, we have $(13+1\div2)^2$, or 49. In this case the process of adding seven terms is expedited by simply multiplying 7 by 7. I have also discovered that the sum of the even numbers, below any odd numbers, is always equal to the square of the number of terms minus the same number. So the formula for the sum of all the numbers below a given odd number is

$$\left(\frac{n+1}{2}\right)^2 + \left(\frac{n+1}{2}\right)^2 - \frac{n+1}{2}, \quad \text{or} \quad \frac{n+1}{2} + \left(\frac{n+1}{2} \times \frac{n-1}{2}\right).$$

For example, the number 17 added to *all* the numbers below it is equal to $9 \times 9 + 9 \times 8$, or 153. By this rule, adding any great number of terms is reduced to the simple process of two multiplications and a single addition.

Mr. Pierce remarked that the waters of the rivers of Hazleton, Luzerne Co., Penn., possessed a peculiar property of corroding iron, so much so, that when a shoal had been left on Saturday night under a dropping of it, a hole would be eaten through it by Monday morning.

Mr. Griffith exhibited a vial of it and iron destroyed by it. He described the effect produced by the surface water also as destructive of iron, causing boilers of some iron to produce very red color in the water. He produced a white material, one of its effects.

Mr. Meigs asked if it was not copperas.

Mr. Seeley.—Yes.

Conversation followed between Messrs. Griffith, Pierce, Seeley, Stetson, Tillman, Cohen, Butler, Garbanati and Pell, relative to preventives by tallow, potato, bran, &c., and the want of homogenity in iron, especially boiler and other plates.

Alanson Nash said that copper was found comby sometimes, owing to impurities in it. A law suit in England grew out of it, against the maker of the copper, and heavy damages awarded. He said that an assay of iron was required as much or more than of gold and silver. The British government assays copper sheets. Old iron of primitive rock, after ages of exposure, made into steel, form excellent razors ; it had not lost its electricity on an old bridge of 1,000 years.   The iron used in that old London bridge was brought from the primitive rock of Saxony.

Mr. Stetson.—This subject is great.   Who shall fully tell us what we want to know, without waiting a thousand years ?

Mr. Bradford.—American iron is better than English.

Mr. Meigs.—Plates spotted with rust showing their unequal qualities.

Mr. Seeley.—That may test plates.

Mr. Butler.—Iron bars and rods stacked show ruin at their ends from rust and very unequal corrosion.

Mr. Everitt.—The cannon balls in the Hussar, sunk in 1776 at Hellgate, lost all the iron.

Chairman.—Paper on iron.

Mr. Cohen.—Percussion on a boiler when steam is up, seems to lead to explosion.   It has happened in Manchester, when a sound locomotive boiler seam was *being caulked !*

John Johnson adverted to the peculiar vibration of boilers when steam is up.

The Chairman saw splendid boilers of *fifty years' service* at Manchester, turned out into the yard.

Mr. Butler.—Safes of plaster of Paris are injured by the corrosion inside.   In a short time holes are eaten through some of them from the inside.   We find alum better.

Mr. Pell made the following remarks on iron :

The discovery of this most important of all metals, has without doubt effected far more than any other substance to facilitate man's advances in the onward career of improvement.   We are amazed to find that it is serviceable to all our desires, caprices and requirements.   It is equally useful in times of peace or war, furnishing us in the former case with the plow, the needle, the watch spring and the chisel ; in the latter, with the bombshell and cannon ; and is actually the only metal that can be used advantageously as a medicine.   It is found in the greatest profusion throughout the world, and though so common, is rarely discovered in a state prepared for use, and really was not worked until after silver, gold, and copper had been a long time in use.   Iron works were established by the Romans in Great Britain, and wood was used for smelting the ore.   In the year 1619 Lord Dudley substituted pit coal for that purpose, and in 1740 his invention was universally adopted, at which period the quantity produced in Wales and England amounted to about sixteen thousand tons ; in 1858, to nearly four millions of tons.

In the United States,	1,300,000
France,	700,000
Russia,	350,000
Prussia,	650,000
Belgium,	300,000

In all the countries in the world the total production may be eight millions of tons.   There are two kinds o iron known, commercially speaking, wrought and cast, and there are two varieties of cast iron, gray and white. The gray is soft, not very brittle, and may be readily turned in a lathe. The white is brittle, exceedingly hard, and when broken, presents to the eye a radiated texture. There are several varieties of cast iron, all differing in their chemical composition, often containing silicum, manganese, phosphorus, sulphur, calcium, carbon, &c. Carburets of iron may be considered the purest. Iron undergoes slow combustion when heated red hot in the air, by combining with the oxygen. Silesian iron is very pure in quality, and has been worked to so great a degree of tenuity, that the leaves can be used as paper, if some Yankee could invent white ink. An album has been made of iron sheets, the pages of which turn with the same flexibility that those made of the finest fabric of rags do. All that is now required to form books that will defy the destructive power of insects in the tropics, is the ink. Nearly eight thousand square feet of this iron paper may be made from one hundred weight of metal. It has been generally allowed that hot blast iron is much better than cold blast. From experiments that I have tried, I am convinced that the hot blast is by far the strongest.

The materials required for iron making are—

1. Mines, or ores, natural or artificial.
2. Fuel, charcoal, peat, coke or coal.
3. Fluxes, limestone generally, occasionally saline matter.
4. Atmospheric air, in quantity equal to eleven tons for a ton of iron.

Iron ores are various in their natures, and are compounds of iron, oxygen, silex, alumine, lime, magnesia, sulphur, carbon, and water. In the conversion of cast iron into wrought iron, two processes are made use of, 1st. puddling ; 2d. boiling in a bath of fluid iron cinders. Which has been practiced as long as iron has been known. The production of iron has been increased ten fold since the invention of puddling-furnaces, and the hot blast.

Two thousand four hundred and eighty pounds of the best metal will yield two thousand two hundred and forty pounds of puddled bars. The principal cause of the loss is the presence of sulphur. If the carbon be removed entirely, and nearly all the sulphur, the bar will be both a red short, and cold short quality, and consequently imperfect. But if the carbon, the metalloids, and the sulphur are altogether removed, then the bar will be ductile, tough, and possess a proper nature, nearly pure, but would still have the red short property, as thirty-four parts of sulphur in one hundred thousand parts of iron, are sufficient to produce a red short metal; but if a larger quantity of sulphur be present the iron will be both red short and cold short. Hot blast iron generally contains more sulphur than cold. Rich ores invariably yield red short iron, which is a quality of purity.

The term red short is applied to a certain arrangement of the particles of the metal when passing into the liquid state. The same ore in the same furnace, with the same kind of fuel, will produce red short, and cold short

iron, by varying the nature of the fluxes used, red short is derived from too small a quantity of carbon to neutralise the sulphur. Iron will be cold short if the metalloids and carbon contained in it be reduced to a minimum, but red short if entirely removed. The cold short property, if not desired, may be corrected by suitable doses of carbon to protect the iron from oxidation, while the metalloids are being removed in the form of oxides. Wrought iron, both hot and cold short, is a worthless result, when the carbon, sulphur and metalloid are equal in the pig or bar. The manufacture of wrought iron involves two fundamental operations, to wit: the removal of impurities from the ore, and from the crude metal, and the oxidation of the metal sufficient to form fibres. A specific variety of iron is required for nails, which to cut smooth and not split, requires an iron of very close grain; cold short answers the purpose better than fibrous. For wire iron, gray pig, containing a large amount of carbon, fluxed by caustic soda and clay is good; but if expense is no object, borax is far better. Fibrous iron is not adapted to wire making. The making of sheet iron is a branch full of difficulties and intricacies, but once well understood, like everything else, becomes simple and agreeable; the main difficulty to be encountered is the quality of the iron. It has always been supposed that the Russians, who are so famous for their sheet iron, possessed some secret respecting its manufacture, which they guarded with incessant care. This is not so; the secret consists in the quality of the iron, which is superior. Iron for the manufacture of coarse bar, railroad, boiler plate, &c., must possess a different texture from wire iron; cold short if rolled into boiler plate is apt to split, and would be dangerous in a boiler. There is nothing so well calculated to impress observing men with the wonderful material progress of our country as the amazing consumption of iron, and its rapid increase. In 1851, or '52, we imported four hundred and fifty thousand tons of iron; in 1850, our consumption amounted to one million of tons, and now probably to one million six hundred thousand. We are second to Great Britain only, in our metallic resources. For example, the value of metals produced in the United States, now is, ... 79,830,000 tons.
In Great Britain, ... 96,170,000 "
In Australia, ... 39,500,000 "

All other countries produce individually less than Australia. Thus the Anglo Saxon race stand before all others in the metallic production. Cast steel plates will supersede wrought iron for ship building, yacht and steamer, besides their machinery, boilers, &c.; or in other words, entire vessels will be built of this material, because a steel plate half as thick as iron will possess far more strength; consequently the vessels will be one-half lighter. Puddled steel may be made as cheap as puddled iron; that is to say, the saving in weight will pay the difference in expense. Puddled steel bars have been tested, and proved that their tensible strength was nearly one hundred and sixty-one thousand to the square inch, while English iron was 56,500; Russian iron, 62,600; American, hammered,

54,000; of cast steel, 150,000. The weight of iron in the tubes of the greatest bridge in the world, the Victoria, in Canada, is 10,000 tons. It might have been built with 3,000 tons of steel, and been equally strong, if not stronger. Locomotive engines might be constructed of steel half the weight of iron, with return tubes in the boiler, so that the heat might traverse twice its length, thus much increasing the evaporative power, adding to the speed, with half the wear and tear upon the rails. This improvement, together with the use of coal instead of wood, would save one hundred and forty thousand dollars per annum upon every seventy-five locomotive engines running in the United States. And if the cars were made of steel strips, instead of wood, they would strike each other, in case of collision, and spring back, instead of rushing into each other and breaking up as they do now, to the imminent danger of life and limb. If high tensile strength is desired in iron, you may continue almost indefinitely to increase it by remelting the pig. For example, if kept twenty minutes in fusion, it will bear a strain of twenty thousand pounds to the square inch; if two and a half hours, twenty-five thousand pounds; five hours, thirty thousand pounds; seven hours, thirty-seven thousand pounds, &c. The tensile strength would be further increased by very slow cooling in each instance. The American government deserves great credit for the able experiments they have caused to be made on the tensile strength and specific gravity of metal in cast iron ordnance. Whenever the strength fell below 20,000 pounds to the square inch, the quality was pronounced bad. We took these important steps before all other governments, and the consequence is, they have been compelled to award us the initiative, and copy our example. The American government was the first also to investigate the quality of coal for a steam navy, and the results were everywhere published before the English made a similar inquiry. The Americans were the first to produce refined steel directly from the ore in the bloomery forges. The Abbe Pauvert has invented a plan of producing steel of a very fine quality from puddled iron and scraps in any state, at a wonderful reduction of price, without the slightest change in the arrangements of the melting furnace, it being effected by chemical ingredients and elastic agency. Steel fabricated by the old process from Swedish iron, costs eighty dollars per ton; whereas, by the Abbe's process it may be procured for twenty-five dollars from refuse iron, without loss of material, as one ton of iron yields one ton of steel. Electricity assists him.

Pig iron, during its conversion into wrought iron, undergoes chemical changes. Carbon is increased during the earlier stages of the process, while silicon diminishes, and carbon again decreases when agglomeration takes place. The following composition will prevent the oxydation of steel or iron, by entering the pores, without in the least injuring the outward appearance: Silver filings, four parts; yellow tincal, 12; bismuth purified, 12; zinc purified, 12; Malacca tin, pure, 120; regulus of antimony, 11; nitre, 11; salt of persecaria, 1.

There is a company in this city who produce steel of every quality and description, at prices much below those current in Europe and America, and their steel is invariably uniform. You are all aware that twenty days were required by the old process to convert iron into steel. By the new New York process the iron is thoroughly refined into cast steel by a single operation, which far surpasses the expensive and tedious process by cementation, and the quality of the steel can be foretold to a certainty before the crucible is placed in the furnace; whereas, by the old plan the end of the ingot was broken off and the quality guessed at. Cyanogen and sal ammoniac are the chief materials used in the new mode, and if all is attained that has been promised, a revolution in the steel trade is near at hand.

Messrs. Bessemer & Co., of Sheffield, have been successful in converting pig iron into steel in a few minutes, without additional fuel, by the infusion of an air blast, and hundreds of large ingots of cast steel are made in quick succession, without a failure, either soft, medium or hard, at pleasure. Steel thus quickly and cheaply made has been manufactured into first quality cutlery and boiler plates of very large dimensions. In Sweden, Bessemer's invention has been carried out to the fullest extent, and ingots of cast steel of admirable quality have been produced from molten crude iron in ten minutes after leaving the blast furnace, without manipulation. By this process one thousand tons of cast steel can be produced with the same quantity of fuel now consumed in the production of five hundred tons of bar iron.

With these facts before me, I prophecy, without hesitation, that in less than ten years steel will supersede iron in the construction of boilers, steam engines, and the hulls of vessels, because equal strength is obtained with less than half the weight.

Subject for next meeting, "Dentistry."
Adjourned.

H. MEIGS, *Secretary.*

April 13, 1859.

Present—Messrs. Robert L. Pell, Prof. Cyrus Mason, Stetson, Prof. Hederick, Tillman, Seeley, Garbanati, Veeder, Godwin, A. Nash, Haskell, Dr. Levi Reuben, Butler, Breisach, John Johnson, Bruce, John W. Chambers, &c.—30 members.

Prof. Mason in the chair. Henry Meigs, Secretary.

The Secretary stated the donation by the Hon. Charles F. Loosey, Consul General of Austria, of additional numbers of the "Zeitschrift Des Œsterreichischen Ingenieur-Vereines X Jahrgang," containing notices of American patents, &c., and the last Transactions of the Société Imperiale et Centrale D'Horticulture, Napoleon III, Protecteur. The Society composed of eminent persons, nobles and others, with 112 corresponding societies, of which two are in the Americas, viz: "The American Institute," and the "Smithsonian Institution."

Mr. Lawrenson exhibited his patent for broadcasting seeds, by ans blowing the seeds some thirty feet in all directions.

On motion of Mr. Tillman, a committee to examine it was ordered, and Mr. Veeder appointed.

Prof. Mason.—I often wanted such a machine to sow my grass seed.

Mr. Veeder.—To avoid the difficulty of sowing grass seed, which is difficult on account of its lightness, in windy weather, I mix the grass seed and grain, moisten them, roll all in plaster, which gives them some more weight, and are then well sown broadcast.

Mr. Tillman asked Mr. Seeley to exhibit his tests of the mine water from Pennsylvania coal mines, laid on the table by Mr. Pierce.

Mr. Seeley.—Showed by its effect on litmus paper, on sesqui oxide of iron, on alumina, its peculiar acid, producing with iron, in a moment, an ink which the Secretary used in taking notes during the remainder of the session.

Prof. Hederick.—It is a sesqui salt of iron.

Prof. Mason.—A like mineral acid may be found perhaps operating very quietly and imperceptibly in ruining the rails, &c., leading to some of those disasters which painfully afflict us! Scrutiny should be used in time by all the intelligent officers of our great railway system!

John Johnson.—Cast iron does not suffer like our wrought iron!

Mr. Seeley.—Pipes of iron suffer occasionally greatly. Lead pipes do not. Percussion, to which we attribute injury to iron, does not affect *lead.*

Mr. Garbanati.—The percussion mentioned at a late meeting, by Mr. Meigs, tried on the trunnion of cannon, is successful at a certain number of blows. Suppose that 100 blows would break off the the trunnion, but we stop at the 97th blow—will not the iron thus almost separated, recover its cohesion? and may we not attribute the destruction of steam boilers in a measure to the repeated percussions, vibrations or strainings it suffers from the steam?

Mr., Meigs said that philosophy had many interesting amusements. Such were part of the Aristotelian plan of instruction, chiefly enjoyed in their peripatetics in the famed groves of Academus, under whose shades they walked for due exercise of body, and put forth the most profound ideas. That school knew no *atoms.* It recognized the infinite divisibility of matter!—that God could compact all the matter of his universe into one grain, and re-expand it!—that a single drop of wine poured into the ocean, would diffuse through all the water and atmosphere of the world! We now say that matter is so far from being solid, is in fact *infinitely divided*, that the component parts of a bar of iron, are *comparatively* as distant from each other as our heavenly bodies! That the body of a man, magnified to the size of the sun, a million miles in diameter! would show its components in action—its electrics, &c., as in the heavens! Nor have we succeeded in the least possible manner in explaining away this theory! Our *sciolists* should do what not one in a thousand does—*read the old philosophers!* and they would learn as Faraday, and the greatest of moderns know, that our supposed very astute chemical science, so far as relates to atoms, and to elements, is quackery, fully a match for Hahnmann's *infinitessimal doses!* Faraday already teaches, instead of the terrible multiplication chemical table of modern chemists; French, more especially, we have but about a dozen constitutional elements to deal with. Some years ago, the Institute of France, translated a very small botanical work of Theophrastus, who lived about 100 years, and taught botany much more perfectly, as regarded a tree, than any other man, ancient or modern. I translated that for our Transactions, some years ago. Your will find it there.

Mr. Tillman.—The ancients knew but little of chemistry and natural philosophy. The blow pipe, the galvanic battery, the thermometer, barometer, telescope, and microscope, have revealed to *moderns only*, the mysteries of nature.

Mr. Meigs.—We do not know how to make such steel as was made by them, or by East Indians; nor can we cut the hardest bodies in nature better than they; nor have we formed cutting instruments as hard as steel out of copper?

Mr. Tillman.—We can harden copper with tin; but there is no proof that the ancients did it in any other way.

Mr. Butler.—I deal largely in iron, for safes, and find trouble in the want of homogeniety in it; suppose we could test it by acids, which would show us the bad spots. I saw a steam boiler, some time ago, lifted from its bed, and at one end left a piece behind—so corroded was it by a trifling action just at that point!

Dr. Levi Reuben.—Iron bars in bundles, in a damp place, found fairly rotted at the ends, and variously so; not one continuous rot as in wood, but in particular places—thus plainly indicating the want of uniform quality in a piece of iron. I have noticed that invisible fractures of iron are rendered visible by means of the corrosion of some fluid in it. There is also molecular play—there is, too, *galvanic action!* Much agitation granulates iron also!

The Chairman.—We used iron pipes through meadow land to conduct water! We lost our outlay, and tried block tin and failed. We are in our infancy as to knowledge of iron.

Mr. Stetson.—We must collect samples of iron corroded every way, and examine them. We must bend all our philosophy to that valuable work.

REMARKS MADE BY R. L. PELL ON BUTTER-MAKING.

I was invited by your committee to visit Mr. Johnson, and examine his churn and mode of making butter; but was unavoidably prevented. However, with your permission, will present the circumstances which affect the quality of butter.

It is well understood by those who have given any attention to this important matter, that butter made in one district of country, differs often in quality from that produced in another, though precisely the same plan of manufacture is pursued in both. In different seasons the same farm even will afford entirely different qualities of butter. Cows depastured in May, yield the most delicious, and the finest flavored is given by cows fed upon clover, but that is universally the hardest from those fed upon dry food, and that made in the fall of the year will keep the longest. The constitution of animals likewise affects the butter seriously, since there are some which with the choicest food give very inferior butter. In all cases the quality is dependent upon the milk with which it is made, and the mode of manufacture ; churn the same cream, and it will make different qualities by different modes of procedure. The manner of extracting it, therefore, is worthy of particular attention. The milk in the udder of the cow is not of the same uniform quality ; that which is first drawn off is thin and capable of giving but little cream, whereas that which is last drawn, is very rich, and yields a large percentage of fine quality ; compared with the first drawn, the same measure of the last, will give eighteen times as much cream, and the milk is far better after the cream is taken off. I have noticed too that the globules in the first drawn milk are small and single, and that they augment in size until those in the last drawn milk form twice the bulk, and are double, having a smaller globule within each, covered with a shell of casein of the thinnest imaginable texture, by which they are prevented from running one into the other, and thus forming drops of oil. When Mr. Johnson heats his cream, these globules immediately rise to the top, press against each other in such quantities as to break their casein coverings, and unite into a mass of melted fat, which ultimately collects in small grains, and forms what we call butter, by the agitation it receives from the rollers.

In Russia cream is heated to one hundred and ninety degrees, and as it cools, butter rises to the surface in the form of oil, and becomes solid, but it has neither the proper flavor or consistence, and is chiefly used, instead of oil, for culinary purposes. I do not know whether the scientific men of this club have noticed the great difference that exists between young children often seen in our streets, in nurses' arms—I have, particularly when the nurses have appeared to enjoy equal health, and I could not account for it, until recently, having two cows equal in size, giving the same quantity of milk, both calving at the same time, both calves at birth very fine—still at five weeks old, the one weighed twice as much as the other. Here arose a philosophical question that puzzled me ; but on examining the milk of the two animals, microscopically, the mystery was explained. The globules of one were more than twice the size of the other. If, therefore, you will take the trouble, when next you see two similar nurses, with two similar children, to examine their milk when the children are five weeks old, you will discover the globules in one small, and the other large, accounting for the difference in growth, health, size and strength of the two infants. I throw this out as a hint for medical men, who generally select wet nurses for their patients.*

* Milk from a woman twenty years old, contains constituents far more solid than from a woman thirty-five years old. Women possessing dark hair give much richer milk than light haired women.

While on this subject of globules, though not strictly pertinent to the question, I must mention a fact, that has come to my knowledge accidentally, which leads me to believe that the globules of milk are a vegetable, and not an animal material. Having a cow with a diseased udder, from which she appeared to suffer great pain, I concluded to examine the matter pressed from it with a microscope, and to my surprise found it full of roots, fibres and actual stems of plants ; examining further, I discovered globules in all stages of advancement towards that end.

For the production of the finest butter, the cream should be partially sour before it is placed in the churn. Butter made from perfectly sweet cream is neither of fine quality nor large quantity. The more rapidly cream or milk is churned, the softer, paler, and less rich will the butter be. Milk cannot be churned advantageously in less than three hours, and cream in less than one and a quarter hours. The churning should be slow in warm weather, and quick in cold, so that the temperature may be kept up, and must on no account be continued after the separation of the butter ; if it is, the yellowish color and waxy appearance will both be lost, and a soft light colored material left behind. Cream when placed in a churn should never be warmer than fifty-five degrees, and when it comes out, sixty-five degrees.

I think the chances of obtaining good butter at all seasons of the year are greater when the whole milk is churned, which is the usual practice in the mountain districts in Switzerland, where they find it necessary to raise the temperature with hot water to 65° before churning, which they think does not injure it, if the water is put in while the dasher is in motion.

The advantages of churning the entire milk, instead of the cream, is :

1st. That a proper temperature can be obtained summer and winter.

2d. That two hundred gallons of milk will yield six per cent more butter than the cream would if taken off and churned separately.

3d. Butter of the same quality may be obtained with proper attention to the food of the animals all the year round.

4th. No particular attention to change of method is necessary at any time—the churning is alike simple the whole year.

It is scarcely necessary for me to state, that without strict attention to cleanliness it is utterly impossible to manufacture good butter, as milk is remarkable for its rapid absorption of tainted odors.

Milk, on being fermented and constantly agitated, yields a species of spirit in consequence of the casein converting a part of the milk sugar into lactic acid, and another portion into grape sugar, which ultimately becomes transformed into alcohol.

Fresh milk is in a small degree alkaline, but it rapidly becomes acid from the formation of lactic acid. The alkaline property is undoubtedly due to soda, which retains the casein in solution, in which form it absorbs a quantity of phosphate of lime. Pasturing cows in the open field is very favorable to the formation of caseine, while yard feeding favors the formation of butter. Potatoes, as food, are exceedingly beneficial to the flow of milk and increase of butter, on account of the large percentage of starch contained in them. I do not agree with the general opinion that butter in milk arises chiefly from the fat contained in the food of the cow; because the refuse from malt is perhaps more favorable to butter than perhaps any other food, and it does not contain even a trace of fat.

Mr. Tillman, from the committee of arts and sciences.—The next meeting will be at our new Repository, in the Cooper Union building, corner of 8th street and 3d Avenue, on the first Thursday of May next.

Subjects, "Dentistry," and "Fire-proof buildings."

At 10½ o'clock adjourned.

H. MEIGS, *Secretary.*

INDEX.

A.

	Page.
Address on the burning of the Crystal Palace	21
at the opening of the 30th fair..	48
Ægilops, fertilization of	207
transformation of	206
Africa, Southern	136
African sugar cane	189
Agricultural education	113
Agriculture, progress of English	90
Aluminium	394
American Guano	313
Institute, finances, 1859	10
17th annual report	7
trustees and Committees,	3
library	44
Ants, to protect fruit trees from	355
Apple trees, how to winter young	134
Aquarium, plants suited to an	125
Arabian horse	158
Art and Architecture	404
Artificial manures	343
Artists, Greek	370
Atlantic cable	381
Australia	185
gold fields of	486
potatoes of	124

B.

Baker apple, the	247
Baking without scorching	342
Bannanas, dwarf	144
Barley	306
Bearded grapes	298
Bee hive, new	351
Belmontine oil	436
Birds useful to agriculture.. 89, 91, 343,	349
song at certain hours	105
Biscuit fodder for stock	181
Black sweet corn	298
Blackberries, Lawton 142,	349
pruning	153
Blackberry wine	314
Blight in corn	151
Boilers, explosions of 386,	392
iron for steam	491
Bones	217
Breisach on Ehrenberg	477
Brick fence posts	281
Buckwheat	310
Building for the American Institute,	407
materials for cities	460
of New York 465, 471,	476
Bullock's mowing machine	259

	Page.
Burning of the Crystal Palace	21
Butter, Illinois	312
making 153,	501
machine 421,	426

C.

Calceolarias	208
Canada thistles 275,	285
Canal steam navigation	395
Carrots	218
Cattle, management and breeding	199
Cerealia, observations on	304
Chemical results	218
Cherries	121
Cherry currants on sandy soil	135
Chess	150
Chinese sugar cane	189
Chinese yam 124, 125,	205
Churn, new 421,	426
Chrysanthemum, by H. Meigs	199
Clay lands, fall plowing of	182
Clover as a manure	75
Coal oil 424, 426,	430
tar, coloring matter from	374
Cochineal	142
Coffee imitations	133
Coloring matter	374
Committees and officers of the Institute	3
Comparison of the season,	57
Converting straw into manure	164
Corn, black sweet	298
blight in	151
fodder, &c. 100,	119
Rocky Mountain	298
(See Indian corn.)	
Cost of premiums from 1835 to 1857	26
a Wisconsin wheat crop	100
Cotton in Algeria	141
long-staple sea-island	124
Cows, how to make them give down	102
Cranberries 78, 172,	238
on dry soil	172
Crystal Palace, burning of the	21
Cultivating pine trees	170
flowers 165, 300, 314,	344
Curculio	105
Currants 128,	257
cherry 128,	135

D.

Dahlias, seedling	156
Decaisne potatoes	360
Deep plowing and weak straw	164

	Page.
Delaware grape	282
Diamond, value of the	463
Diatomaceæ,—divisions	457
Diseases of wheat	275
Divisibility of matter	500
Dogs, nuisance of	91
Drainage	277, 289, 328

E.

Economy of steam	374
Education, Agricultural	113
Effect of change of climate on vegetables	81
Egg examiners	352
plant	95
Ehrenberg, Christian G.	477
Electricity	382, 486, 488
Electro-magnetic engines	374
Electro-magnetism as a motor	389, 391
Electrotyping	479
England, good news from	197
English Agriculture, progress of	90
Engraving, photoglyphic	394
Ergot	177, 201
Exfoliation of paint from brick walls	377
Explosions of boilers	386, 392

F.

Fair, report of managers of the 30th	14
Fairs	197
Fall plowing of clay lands	182
Farmers' Club, proceedings of	55, 368
Subjects:	
Best time to cut grass	109
Drainage	277
Flowers	81
Flower culture	300, 314 344
Fruit for farms	148
Indian corn	64
Lime	362
Liquid manure	318
Mud and peat of salt and fresh water as manure	144
National value of Chinese sugar cane,	192
New varieties of potatoes	339
Pruning the grape vine	315
Renovating old orchards	347, 353
worn out lands 60, 102,	120
Root feeding	210
Small farms	214
Small fruits	78, 92, 94, 110
Spring flowers	338
seeds, plants and trees	250
Strawberries	346
Summer flowers	165
Winter treatment of manure	144
Fawkes' steam plow	171
Fertilizing seeds	338
Financial condition of the Institute	10
Fire engines, steam	405, 412
Fires, extinguishing by steam and gas	402
Fish, production, habits, &c., of	75
raising	124
Flour, keeping wheat	355
Flowers 81, 84, 144, 165, 260, 300, 301, 314 338, 344,	354
Fly catcher	352
Food, manufactured for stock	175
value of the grain of India	80
Fowls	176

	Page.
Fruit boxes, Hallock's	340
for the farm	148
inquiries	148
in winter, keeping	96
small	78, 92, 107, 260
trees, lime for	355
protect from ants	355

G.

Garden, a fifty acre	97
Garden soil, improving	99
Gardens, old	96
Geissenhainer on propulsion of vessels prior to 1810	396
Germination of seeds	261
Gold fields of Australia	486
grinding quartz for	373
value of	464
Grafting	94
Grape, a new	314
native of New Jersey	172
culture	286
the Delaware	282
growing in Connecticut	340
vine, the	315
vine, Hungarian	72
Grapes	256
bearded	298
of Algeria	74
Grass, best time to cut	109
coloring matter from	374
plats, weedy	311
quack	276
lands, manuring	176
Green tea	149
land marl	313
Ground nuts	350
Growing radishes	312
Guano	343, 374
Guano, American	313
United States	342
Gutta percha and submarine cables	393

H.

Hallock's patent fruit boxes	340
Hay, best time to cut grass for	109
quantity per acre	276
Hedges, live	170
Hive, new bee	351
Hog cholera, a curious case	118
disease	131
Hooker's seedling strawberry	147
Horse, Arabian	158
Horse hoe	350
Hot bed glasses	170
How to cultivate peas without the weevil	130
grow seedling plants	107
kill worms	72
make cows give down	102
renovate old trees	284
treat an old orchard	284
winter young apple trees	134
Hughes' telegraph, printing	393
Hungarian grape vines	72
Hydroboronated plaster	475

I.

Icthyology of Japan	317
Illinois butter	312

Page.
Improving rich garden soil............ 99
India, relative food value of the grain
  of.................................. 80
Indian corn.............. 64, 77, 309, 349
Insects, value of.................... 56
Institution of civil engineers.......... 374
Iron....................... 487, 495
  best for steam boilers............ 491
  American and English........... 425
  building 462
  manufacture of 384
  ship building.................. 373
  value of 464

J.

Jacquard or multifarious perforating ma-
  chine 374
Japan rice, ten varieties 124
Jardin des Plantes.................... 180
Jars for plants....................... 301
Jenkins' cast iron fence posts 303

K.

Kaffer Reed........................... 189
Keeping fruit in winter................ 96
Kerosene oil 424, 426, 430

L.

Lamas, South American................ 168
Land, new, brought into cultivation be-
  tween New York and Philadelphia.... 177
Langdon's (Mrs.) farm................ 246
Lawns 344
Laws for flowers and fruit............ 57
Lawton blackberries 142, 349
Leather scraps for manure 119
Library of the Institute............... 44
Lime for trees................. 86, 355
Liquid manure............... 218, 299
List of choice flowers................ 84
  premiums 30th fair......... 28
Lice on plants........................ 301
Live hedges.......................... 170
Locomotive, the first................. 387
Locomotives, Yankee, in Egypt........ 426
Lunar influence................. 87, 362

M.

Magnolia grandiflora.................. 81
Management and breeding of cattle 199
Manure, converting straw into........ 164
  liquid.............. 218, 313, 318
Manures, application of sewer water, &c.,
  to agricultural productions..... 222
  artificial 343, 356
Manuring grass lands................ 176
Manufactured foods for stock 175
Market garden, planting a............ 163
  gardens, vegetables for.... 152
Marl, green land.................... 313
Measurement of the foot............ 378
Mechanics' club, (see Polytechnic asso-
  ciation.)
Meigs, Hon. H., opening address. 48
  (see Translations.)
Melons, raising.................... 260
Metallurgy 384
Microscope, the............... 439, 458

Page.
Milk-weed............................. 164
Miller's safety steam boiler alarm. 35
Millet 311
Mineral phosphates 356
Mistletoe of Great Britain............ 206
Molecular impressions by light and elec-
  tricity............................ 372
Moles 165
Mortar 469
Motive power, electro-magnetism as a .. 389
Mowing machine, Bullock's............ 259

N.

Navigation, canal steam.............. 395
New bee hive......................... 351
  varieties of potatoes......... 339
Numbers 493
Nuts, ground........................ 350

O.

Oak, silk worm....................... 125
Oats 307
  rusty............................ 151
Observations on the cerealia.......... 304
Officers and committees of the Institute.. 3
Opening address at the 30th fair........ 48
Opium, value of..................... 56
Orchards, renovating old.......... 347, 353
Ornamental shrubs................... 255
  trees.......................... 256
Ostrich............................. 203
Oysters of Virginia................. 281

P.

Painted statuary.................... 404
Painters and paintings, great........... 370
Paper, water-proof.................. 476
Paraffine candles.................. 435
Paulownia imperialis................. 185
Pavements, fall of horses............ 383
Paying out machinery on the Niagara.. 35
Peach blight....................... 164
  trees....,....................... 317
  trees, renovation of........... 342
  wood for fuel................ 248
Peas, how to cultivate without the weevil 130
Pell, R. L., application of sewer water,
  &c., to agricultural productions...... 222
  butter making 501
  coal oil.................... 430
  drainage........... 289, 328
  electricity................ 488
  electrotyping 481
  germination of seeds..... 262
  iron 495
  liquid manures........... 318
  observations on cerealia, barley, oats, rye, Indian corn,
  rice, buckwheat, and millet
  304, 311
  on the microscope...... 439
  on the telescope......... 412
  production, habits &c., of fish. 75
Pelham seedling potato............ 340
Perpetual raspberries............. 150
Pests of the farm............. 112, 117
Phosphates of lime................ 357
  mineral &c............ 356
Photographs on wood............. 470

Page.

Photoglyphic engraving................ 394
Physical properties of soil as affecting their fertility........................ 169
Physionometer........................ 405
Pine trees, cultivating................ 170
Pisciculture........................ 304
Plane stocks, made by machinery...... 475
Planting a market garden............ 163
    wheat in drills.............. 160
Plants suited to an aquarium.......... 125
    too many in one frame......... 207
Plaster, hydroboronated.............. 475
Platinum............................ 461
Plums.............................. 185
    on peach stocks.................. 281
Poem by Miss Fanny W. Bruce.......... 111
Polytechnic Association, proceedings of 369–504
    Subjects:
      Building materials of the State of New York.............. 465, 471
      Coral oil................... 426, 434
      Edifice for the Institute.......... 407
      Electrotyping............. 479, 488
      Iron for steam boilers............ 491
      Making butter.................... 421
      Microscope 439
      Microscope applied to nature and the arts, ... 458
      Setting of steam boilers.......... 371
      Steam fire engines............ 405
      Steam or caloric for canal navigation..................... 391, 395
      Telescopes................. 412, 422
      Warming and ventilation.... 375, 378
Pomological Congress at Lyons........ 317
Potatoes, 58, 76, 101, 122, 124, 198, 311, 316, 339, 343, 350, 352, 360
Potato disease........................ 134
Potato, Rainville................ 316, 339
Potato rot, sulphur to prevent.......... 122
Poultry business.................... 285
Premiums awarded at the 30th fair 28
    from 1835 to 1857............ 26
Preparation of flower beds.......... 302
Progress of English agriculture........ 90
Propeller, Sherry's.................. 411
Propulsion of vessels................ 396
Pruning blackberries................ 153
Puddled steel...................... 391

Q.

Quack grass........................ 276
Quantity of hay per acre.............. 276
Quartz, grinding, for gold............ 373

R.

Radishes, growing.................... 312
Railways, speed on 373
Rainville potato................ 316, 339
Raising melons...................... 260
Raspberries 99, 144, 150
Reaping machines, improved........ 92, 259
Receipts and expenditures from '39 to '57 24
    30th annual fair 19
Red cattle of New England............ 282
Relative food value of the grain of India. 86
Renovating old orchards.......... 347, 353
    peach trees.................. 342
    worn out soils....... 60, 102, 120

Page.

Renwick's remarks on lime............ 363
Report, 17th annual, of the Institute.... 7
    committee on manufactures, science and arts, on Millers' safety steam boiler alarm............ 35
    committee on the library 44
    managers of the 30th fair 14
    select committees on the paying out machinery of the Niagara. 35
    of the trustees.................. 7
Rhododendrons, hybrid.............. 174
Rhubarb wine...................... 288
Rice............................ 309
    Japan, 10 varieties............ 124
Road making........................ 476
Rocky Mountain corn................ 298
Royal Agricultural Society.......... 343
Rust on wheat, a preventive.......... 119
Rusty oats........................ 151
Rye.............................. 308

S.

Safety valves........................ 386
Salmon 304
Salt, uses of, in agriculture.......... 217
Sea Island cotton, long staple........ 124
Seed assorting machine.............. 74
Seedling dahlias.................... 166
    plants, how to grow........ 107
    potato 343
    strawberry, Hooker's........ 147
Seeds, fertilizing.................... 338
    germination of............ 261
    steeping.................. 274
    vitality of................ 338
Self-propagation of turnips.......... 150
Setting out peach and pear trees...... 174
    of steam boilers.......... 371
Sewer water........................ 222
Sewerage of Paris.................. 182
Sherry s new propeller.............. 411
Shrubs, ornamental................ 255
    and plant , list of........ 85, 95
Silk of Algeria.................... 142
    from New Zealand............ 180
    worm, oak................ 125
    worms 168
Society of arts, London.............. 383
Soil, physical properties of.......... 169
    for strawberries.......... 346
Sorghum 122, 186, 190
Speed on railways.................. 373
Spinach, New Zealand.............. 237
Statuary, painted.................. 404
Steam, economy of.................. 374
    boilers, iron for.......... 491
    boilers, setting of........ 371
    for extinguishing fires...... 402
    fire engines.......... 405, 412
    on canals................ 395
    plow of Mr. Fawkes........ 171
Steel, puddled...................... 391
Steeping seeds.................... 274
Strawberries 62, 75, 99, 106, 113, 121, 147, 346
    Douglas.................. 106
Straw for manure.................. 164
Stumps of trees.................... 275
Submarine cable........ 381, 393, 394, 395
Sulphur to prevent potato rot........ 122
Sweet corn (black) 298
    Williams'.................. 301

T.

	Page.
Talbot, photoglyphic engraving,	394
Tanner's waste for manure,	298
Tea, green	149
Telegram, world's	393
Telegraph, Atlantic	381
Telescopes	412, 422
Telfer's farm near Ayr	233
Thistles, Canada	275, 285
Tobacco grown in France	126
value of	52
Tomato	95
Traction engine	370
Transformation of Ægilops into wheat..	206
Translations by Hon. H. Meigs:	
Arabian horse	158
Bearded grapes	298
Begoniaceæ, Begonias	104
Cabinet maker's wood of Algeria..	141
Chinese yam	205
Cochineal	142
Cotton in Algeria	141
Crystal Palace and the gardeners.	131
Cuscute or dodder	212
Duration of vitality of seeds	280
Eggs	212
Garden competitors at Versailles.	149
Green tea	149
Haltica, turnip flea	280
Hot bed glasses	170
Hybrid Rhododendrons	174
Lenormand cauliflower	210
Means of anticipating changes of weather	216
Mineral wealth of the old regency of Algiers	142
New trout	167
Nymphæa Gigantea	74
Opening address of vice-president, M. Drouyn de l'Huys	73
Ostrich	202
Paulownia Imperialis	186
Palma Christi	210
Plums	185
Phosphate of lime	357
Preserving useful birds	89
Rainville potato	316, 339
Setting out young peach and pear trees	174
Silk of Algeria	142
worms	168
Societe d'Acclimatation	176
d'Horticulture	348
South American Lamas	168
Spinach, New Zealand	237
Stables	213
Trees from seed	174
of Paris	88
Weather	280
Wine and alcohol of Algeria	142
Wool	247
Wormy fruit	258
Transplanting pine and other trees	261

	Page.
Trees	260
ornamental	256
Trout, new	167
Truffles	90
Trustees, annual report	7
Turnip, the	132, 150
seed	130, 147

U.

Underdraining	153
United States guano	342
Ups and downs of wheat	259
Use of lime for trees	86

V.

Value of diamonds	463
gold	464
iron	464
Valves, safety	386
Vegetables, effect of change of climate on	81
for market gardens	152
Ventilation	375, 378, 388
Velocity and force of the wind	377
Vessels, propulsion of	396
Vitality of seeds	338

W.

Washingtonia gigantea	174
Warming and ventilation	375, 378, 387
Water, red hot	392
Waterproof paper	476
Watering trees, &c	74
Weedy grass plats	311
Wheat crop, cost of a Wisconsin	100
diseases of	275
flour, keeping	355
from Waterloo	361
midge	160
planting in drills	160
rust on, a preventive	119
with weak straw	147
ups and downs of	259
Whortleberries	285
Wind, velocity and force of	377
Wine, blackberry	314
rhubarb	288
and alcohol of Algeria	141
Wines, native	288
Wood, cabinet maker's of Algeria	141
Wood's potato	352
Worms, do they rain down	134
how to kill	72
Wormy fruit	258

Y.

Yam, Chinese (Dioscorea)	124, 125, 205
Yankee locomotives in Egypt	426
Yellow lupin for manure	123
Yellows in peach leaves	341

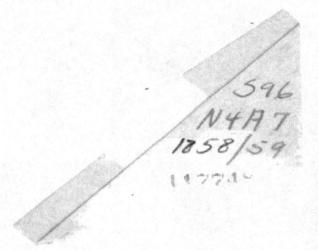

CPSIA information can be obtained
at www.ICGtesting.com
Printed in the USA
BVHW081603120819
555665BV00013B/1001/P